·evergreen·our mountain community·

Gene and Barbara Sternberg

1

Image Credits
Front cover photograph is by Ron Ruhoff.
Gene Sternberg created the sketch on the back cover.
Photograph on back cover is by Jeffrey Schneider.

Dedication

We dedicate this book to all the people of Evergreen. To the pioneers — the miners, loggers, ranchers — who gave our community its historical depth. To the generations of "summer people" who added a particular flair and breadth of outlook. To the thousands who have lived here for a time, added their unique contributions, and moved on. To the many talented artists who enrich us all with their gifts.

We dedicate our book especially to those who live here now. We hope it will give some new insights and information about our community; a few stories to tell; a renewed appreciation for the beauty of the environment we are priveleged to live in and an awareness of the many ways in which, with our help, it can be preserved and enhanced.

For visitors to Evergreen, we hope you will find in these pages a sketch of our community's past, some ideas about what is going on at present and a few thoughts about its future.

The authors are delighted to donate to the Evergreen Kiwanis Foundation the right to reprint this edition. We know that all proceeds will be used to benefit the Evergreen Community.

Acknowledgements— for the original edition

We want to thank all those who helped us, whether with interviews, personal materials, old and new photographs or clippings form various publications. Some opened up for us their entire family records. We listened, we took, we copied, and we thank you all for your indispensable contributions.

We could not have written about Evergreen without the help of the Canyon Courier, especially Editor Debbie Marshall. We appreciate the Courier's generous coverage of our community's life and issues, its dedicated staff and permission to use freely the information in its articles and its photographs.

The Western History Department of the Denver Public Library is a mine of information on local history themes: its staff, especially Elinor Gehres and Bonnie Hardwick, were helpful and friendly. We have benefited greatly from the files of the Hiwan Homestead Museum, especially transcripts of oral history interviews, and we appreciate permission to use a number of photographs from their final collection. Invaluable also has been the personal knowledge of Museum Directors Connie Fahnestock and Sandy Crain about the Evergreen community. Gail Alden and the staff of the Evergreen library made their materials and help freely available to us.

We thank the following for being willing to share their time and memories through personal interviews:

Alderfer, Arleta. 2 August 1981.

Antweiler, Irving and Gertie. 6 Septmeber 1981.

Bradley, Pat and Leo. 21 March 1982.

Christy, Dave (Denver Mountain Parks.) 1979.

Clark, A.R. (Rozzi) and Leona. 3 August 1981.

Colburn, Rus (Forest Heights Lodge.) 1981.

Conway, Pete. 10 and 26 September 1981.

Davidson, Hal. 8 September 1981.

Davis, Margaret Evans (Mrs. Roblin), Peg Hayden and Freddie Lincoln. 15 September 1981.

deDisse, Susie. 1979.

Evans, John III. 23 March 1984.

Grimes, Ross. 15 and 23 June 1982.

Hammond, Paul and Elma. 2 September 1981.

Hayden, Peg. 19 September 1981.

Kircher, Robert. 15 September 1981.

Landy, Joan. 7 September 1981.

Lincoln, Freddie. 12 October 1978.

Livonius, Bruce and Myrt. 4 August 1981.

Marsh, Father "Bud" (Lewis). 7 November 1981.

Marshall, William (Bill) and Miriam. 7 February 1984.

Marquand, Mary. 22 June 1984.

Moore, Mike and Anne. 20 November 1981.

Newkirk, John and Carole. 5 February 1981.

Rouse, Jack and Colleen, with Bill and Betty Bennett. 20 March 1986.

Schneider, John and Rosabel. 3 September 1981.

Schulte, Gerry. 1986.

Smith, Maude. 29 June 1984.

Strand, Harriet and Owen. 8 August 1981.

Underwood, Charlotte. 24 July 1985.

Wallover, Herbert. 7 August 1981.

Ware, Tom and Munk. 18 March 1981.

Zeller, Marty (Colorado Open Lands: telephone interview. 4 January 1984.

Other materials and information was generously supplied to us by:

Anderson, Jodey.

Bennett, Bill: (information about the Hiwan developments and Golf Club.)

County Commissioners, Jefferson County.

Eckhardt, Bob: Jefferson County R–1 School District.

Jackson, Sondra: Principal, Bergen Elementary School.

Jackson, James: Principal, Mount Evans Outdoor Education Laboratory School.

Langberg, Arnie: Principal, Jefferson County Open High School.

Leonard, Sharron: Executive Director, Evergreen Chamber of Commerce.

MacNamara, Chuck and Alice: (especially the many fine articles in their "Mountain Commuter" news paper.)

Planning Department, Jefferson County.

Printz, Ray: Director, Jefferson County Open Space.

Rodriquez, Ruth: Manager of Parks and Recreation, City and County of Denver.

Ruhoff, Ron: (Ron shared his fine photographs with us: unfornately, in being limited to black and white, we have lost much of their impact.)

Short, Bob, and his landscape architect. (materials about the Genesee development.)

Sjoden, Ted: Mountain Bell.

Acknowledgements — for the 2004 Update

The Canyon Courier, for its indispensable weekly coverage of people and events in Evergreen

Serenity Magazine, The Mountain Connection, Evergreen Living Magazine, Carole Lomond's city and mountain Views. From each of these we have taken information and insights.

The Evergreen Library, with special thanks to Reference Librarian Janice Tang

The Evergreen Branch of the Jefferson County Sheriff's Department

and the following individuals:

Eggers, Peter: the EPRD Board, Leadership Evergreen, and Art for the Mountain Community

Foelske, Ken: Jefferson County Open Space

Gutherless, Heather: the Evergreen Plan Update

Hadley, Barbara: Evergreen Scholarship/Bootstraps Inc.

Johnson, Kent and Shirley: the Dos Chappell Nature Center

Jones, Tandy: MALT and the Beaver Brook Watershed

Joos, Lorene: the Evergreen Art Center and the Evergreen Arts Council

Kaussner, Marilyn: Evergreen Garden Club, Community Weed Awareness Campaign

Kiefer, Rita: for composing an Evergreen Poem at our request

Mounsey, Louise: Evergreen Garden Club

Nuchols, Melanie: the Evergreen Area Chamber of Commerce

Pramuk, Laura: U.S.Forest Service

Shanley, Phil: EVFD, EFPD and Art for the Mountain Community

Shaw, Peggy: Humphrey Museum

Schulte, Gerry: Evergreen Metro District

Stoll, Jill: Congregation Beth Evergreen

Tripp, A J.: Denver Mountain Parks

Ware, Tom: Evergreen Metro District

Williams, Linda: MALT and Beaver Brook

Wulf, Dick: Evergreen Park and Recreation District

Zebauers, Valdis (Zeke): Jefferson County Highways and Transportation Department

Appreciation to Greg Walz, our enthusiastic link to Johnson Publishing, and to Erika Echols for her conscientious, speedy, and accurate work on the details of the manuscript

ABOUT THE BOOK (1987)

This book is frankly a personal tribute. It bears the marks of our experience of Evergreen and our interests: for Gene, the relationship of man's creations to the beauty of the natural setting, as well as to each other; for Barbara, the "gifts of nature" and the relationships between human beings.

Originally we planned to have all the illustrations, except for the historical photos, in color. Evergreen scenery deserves better than black and white reproductions of Gene's amateur color photography. In the end, we reluctantly decided to sacrifice color so that the book could be sold at a price that anyone who is interested in Evergreen can afford.

Like anything written about a local community, this account is incomplete. We wish we could have told the story of everyone who has made a contribution to Evergreen life. But there came a point at which we had to stop! It got so we hardly dared to have breakfast at the Wolf House — or shop at Safeway — for fear of hearing another familiar voice asking, "How's the book coming? *When* will it be out?"

Any real community is a seamless whole. To write about it, we have had to chop it up into manageable pieces. Many of the same events, people and institutions are described, from different angles, in two or more sections.

In the interest of readablility, there are few cross-references and no scholarly footnotes. There is, however, a fairly comprehensive index.

The book has been for us a labor of caring and sharing. Although is has been copyrighted, we give permission to anyone to use its contents freely and to quote from it.

Everything written about local history contains inaccuracies. It is the nature of the material, which deals with people's memories, individual interpretations of events and other inexact sources. To say nothing of the deficiencies of the authors!

We believe it is important that any inaccuracies found in this book by you, as readers, should be on record. This is the way local history gets refined and deepened.

The Evergreen Library, to which we are donating much of the material we have gathered has agreed to be the repository of written corrections or amplifications of the text, so that future researchers and writers — as well as interested browsers — may have access to the most complete information possible.

ABOUT THIS 2004 UPDATE

There is no way to do what we have tried to do in this update chapter without leaving out far more — more wonderful people, more organizations doing remarkable things, more incidents and events — than can be included. We know that, compared to the reality of a lively community like Evergreen, what can be sketched in fifty pages is only an impression. We haven't dwelled much on Evergreen's dark side, though as in every human society, there is one: embezzlements, bodies discovered in a back yard or a mountain park, the occasional tragic or bizarre event that hits the national headlines. We hope that what has been included is worthwhile as a snapshot of what has happened in Evergreen between 1993 and the summer of 2004.

CONTENTS

THE BEGINNING

"What are your earliest memories of Evergreen?" we asked people who were born here. To those who came here from somewhere else, our question was, "What was Evergreen like when you first visited it? What was there about the place that made you decide to call it home?"

Sometimes people turned the tables on us, wanting to know how long we had been involved in Evergreen and why we were writing a book celebrating this particular place in the Colorado mountains.

In 1947 we flew from Cornell University in New York to Denver. Gene was to teach architecture at Denver University, Barbara hoped to complete her Master's in urban sociology. We had a six-week old baby and absolutely no money—but a strong desire to pioneer in that unique American tradition we had so admired from Europe.

We lived in a Butler hut on the Denver University campus and wondered how we were ever going to afford to buy a home of our own. Of course, we had no car.

Good friends on the faculty and in the architectural profession drove us out on weekends into the mountains. Many showed us sites they had been looking at for years. One day, they said, they would build themselves a cabin.

Summer, 1949, at the Truesdell cabin

1

The summer of 1948 found us packing diapers, clothes and groceries for a month's stay on the Truesdell Ranch, which is now part of the State Wildlife area at the end of Upper Bear Creek Road. For many years, Mrs. Truesdell ran a summer art school there with faculty drawn mainly from the Denver University Art Department. Her husband's health was failing and the school was discontinued, but for a few years she gladly rented cabins to Denver University faculty. The summer colony that year was made up of Vance Kirkland, head of the Art Department, and his wife Anne, Prof. Bill Sanderson, another capable artist, with his wife Ruth and small daughter, the Truesdells and the three of us.

Our cabin, built by a miner or homesteader, was primitive. We learned to pack food away in containers, and turn plates upside down on the old hutch, because field mice ran freely around at night. There were kerosene lamps and candles. An ingenious overground system, characteristic of much of Evergreen at that time, piped water from springs.

Vance Kirkland did the driving. Psychologically it was a long journey from the city to that remote and idyllic mountain valley. Our cabin stood on a hillside covered with pine trees. It looked out over a huge meadow, filled with wildflowers, and a little stream that ran through it. This is still called the Truesdell Meadow. It is well worth the 3-1/2 mile hike from Groundhog Flat to see it in it's summer glory.

There was a brief shower every afternoon. Mornings were clear and beautiful, nights cold and starlit.

All that remains of the Truesdell home

The Truesdell meadow

Mount Meridian from our cabin

Mrs. Truesdell brought us snapping fresh peas, turnips and beets from the vegetable garden she had planted in late spring. Once a week, Gene drove into "town" with Vance to shop for groceries. "Town" was Evergreen, and Evergreen was Main Street: the grocery store, the Taffy Shop, two or three restaurants, the lumber yard by the bridge, the Drug Store and Round-Up where the Little Bear is today.

The following summer, with another small baby in the family, we rented a better cabin. The routine was much the same as the previous year. Vance Kirkland, a totally disciplined artist, painted his "dead wood" subjects for eight hours a day. Gene studied for something he had hoped he would never have to take again, an examination for his architectural license in Colorado.

When the children were asleep in the evening, we all gathered in the Truesdell's main house to play Canasta, which was the rage in America at the time: the first and last time we ever played cards intensely and regularly.

By 1949, Gene was tired of riding headache-inducing tramcars from the Denver University campus, where we lived, to downtown, where the School of Architecture was located. We also began to savor the prospect of getting up to the mountains under our own steam. Neighbors took us car-shopping, and we put a down payment on a stripped-down, no-frills 1949 Ford. The salesman couldn't believe we wanted it delivered, and looked at us with mixed amusement and disbelief when we told him neither of us could drive.

3

One Saturday in the fall of 1949 we drove ourselves to Evergreen. Stopping at Hugh Taylor's real estate office downtown, we asked if he had a half-acre of mountain land that we could afford to buy—somewhere we could bring the children and a picnic, and eventually put up a simple cabin.

Taylor told us that half acres weren't worth bothering with in the mountains but he could show us some 5-acre parcels. The first was on beautiful Blue Creek Road. It had some meadow, a spruce forest facing the road, and a pine- forested area behind with a fine, fairly level spot for a future cabin. The realtor suggested we go on to look at additional sites. With the naive enthusiasm of people who had never owned land, we said that this piece was perfect.

The land belonged to Ernest and Fredda King. He was the long-time superintendent of the Mountain Parks Protective Association: she a warm, down-to-earth woman who agreed to sell us the 5+ acres for $125 down and $100 a year—with no interest—until the total price of $1250 was paid.

So we became "summer people." We had our little stake in the mountains before we could afford a house of our own.

Our cabin was built in fits and starts. We met our hospitable pioneer neighbors, "Heinie" Livonius and his wife, Mary, who had a little art studio. We bought rough lumber from John Schneider's saw mill up the road. The R.E.A. brought in power. Rozzi Clark had recently started his Evergreen Service Company (ESCO) on Brook Forest Road. For $10.00 a year he kept our cabin key. After we could afford the luxury of drilling a well, he turned our water off in the fall and back on in the spring.

Bill Sanderson

Vance Kirkland

4

Mary Livonius

Evan E. ("Heinie") Livonius

Our cabin on Blue Creek Road

We joined the Mountain Parks Protective Association and were proud to post on our gate their distinctive wooden sign with our name stencilled on it. Winter and summer, the Association's patrol officers drove to our cabin, checked it for security, and left one of their business cards tucked in the screen at each visit. They also checked trees for infestation and arranged for an unwelcome bear to be trapped and carried off by the Division of Game and Fish to a more remote location.

It became a ritual for our children to pay a visit to Nellie Barnetson's little Marshdale store and buy ten cents' worth of penny candy each.

In those years, Evergreen for us was a retreat. We wanted no phone and not much contact with people. We were here to enjoy the peace and beauty of the mountains: the rapid parade of wildflowers from April pasqueflowers to the last purple asters of fall; the black tufty-eared squirrels who greeted our coming; the curious, demanding blue jays and the humming birds.

5

Marshdale Store (recently remodeled)

Livonius home on Blue Creek Road

Looking back, we could easily regret that we did not seek out the many second generation members of pioneer families who were still living in Evergreen—we could have learned so much about the early days here—or that we were not more aware of developments and changes as they occurred. Marshdale Lodge was still a dude ranch when we first visited Evergreen. When did it close down? Hagan's Clock Museum, set back from the road in Bergen Park, was conspicious for its clock tower and floral clock freshly-planted each year. We didn't notice just when it appeared or disappeared. The building now is subdivided for offices and the garden gone wild.

But regrets serve no purpose— we had busy lives in Denver, with a growing family and architectural practice, and many community involvements. Evergreen gave us what we needed then, the refreshment of solitude.

Some twenty years later, our lives were changing. With our household reduced from eight to three and retirement pending, we felt we could consider for the first time living full-time in the mountains. We searched for the ideal place. Aspen was too expensive and too precious for us, though superb in its offerings of natural beauty and music. Steamboat Springs—another of our long-time favorite mountain towns—was far from connections to anywhere else. It was also in a process of transition from the town we had known to a big-time ski resort. And we do not ski.

We took stock: our closest friends were in the Denver area and so were many activities we wanted to continue. We knew we would travel and host many visitors, so accessibility to the airport was important. But we did want mountains and trees around us and, if possible, a stream. It became clear that Evergreen was **the** place.

We looked seriously for a home through the winter, spring, and early summer of 1972. We regretfully eliminated beautiful Blue Creek Road because we wanted a year-round stream. The transformation of Evergreen to a bedroom suburb of Denver was in full swing. Along Upper Bear Creek most of the summer homes were up for sale: most needed extensive work to convert them for year-round living. We were glad we looked first in winter, to learn from experience how many of them— built for summer shade—turned into frozen, sunless ice-chests in the cold months. Finally, we settled happily into a log house on the edge of an open meadow, with Bear Creek curling round it.

6

Log home by the stream

Bird's eye view of our Upper Bear Creek home

IDYLL

We live an idyll
Brown old log house
Sturdily set
On mountain meadow,
Stream curling round it
Aspen, spruce protecting it
Sun washing over it
From a clean firmament
of absolute blue.

Children raised, each seeking
Individuation.
Old tensions loosed
Now we were two again,
New growth pushing
Out of sudden ease.
Young, we denied
What aging cells remind
Idylls are brief
Eroded by time and the world.

Next year the wandering beaver that incised
Our sturdiest aspen down in half an hour
May have a mate and take out twenty.
The stream, which loses every year
Some of its elegant primeval clarity
Could start to smell, and breed
Disasters out of sewage and neglect.

Ten homes may fill the meadow, blot
Out wildflowers with driveways and mowed lawns.
Loved children may exert their lifelong
Hostage hold over our happiness.
Next year, next year the world may end
Or I could die, my love, or even you.

We breathe each day
Extravagantly aware,
Storing poignant images
In retina and soul
Against the idyll's end.

Barbara Edwards Sternberg

(id'yll n. Short description in verse or prose
of picturesque scene or incident, esp. in rustic
life; episode suitable for such treatment.
Oxford Dictionary.)

7

We came to Evergreen when growth, which had previously been accepted and even welcomed, was provoking opposition. We were familiar with life in unincorporated places—our previous home was in unincorporated Arapahoe County—but Evergreen was different. Though there was no city structure there was a feeling of identity. This supported the efforts of "indispensable individuals" to protect and expand community assets.

Without a community that cared, dedicated individuals like Mike Moore—who was a prime mover in securing the half- cent sales tax for buying open space—could not have succeeded. No amount of uproar created by concerned citizens like Sheila Clarke and Pat Sayward could have preserved the beautiful Means Meadow from subdivision. Nor could that small pioneering band led by Connie Fahnestock have salvaged the Hiwan Homestead in the nick of time, creating a physical focus for Evergreen's efforts to preserve some of its historical heritage.

To the casual visitor, Evergreen is the Lake, Main Street and an intermittent commercial strip along both sides of Highway 74. It is the Hiwan Open, a summer Colorado Philharmonic concert, a weekend drive into the mountains for brunch at one of the town's fine restaurants.

To the resident, Evergreen's physical pattern is more intricate. Even 15 years of living here finds us exploring a new valley or another meadow or climbing a different peak each time we are invited to someone's home. Every area has its particular rock formations, it's own views, vegetation and historical character.

As we drove around, we noticed an old mine here, a derelict, once-fine hotel there. We saw castles, cabins and wonderful weathered barns. We met long-settled families, mellow "hippies", and purposeful executives—here for perhaps two to three years before the inevitable move.

Our admiration developed for the sheer amount of time and energy volunteered to keep community and cultural services going: from the Fire Department and Ambulance Service to the Evergreen Chorale and Players. We found a natural sense of service in institutions like the Evergreen Library, the Canyon Courier and local businesses. We learned to "read" the Evergreen year in nature, aided by the unique weekly columns of naturalist Sylvia Brockner.

We ourselves entered into Evergreen life: we helped fight the pine beetle; took sides in issues about schools, about planning and design, and the creation of a permanent home for the arts; attended plays and musicals and haunting Christmas concerts. The fascinating variety of life here intrigued us. The internationally-known live side by side with pioneer descendants. People smugly congratulate themselves on living out of the Denver brown cloud—but most commute alone, contributing their share to the pollution. They genuinely enjoy the solitary time in the car, the magnificent changes of scenery from mountains to foothills to the expanse of the plains, and the reverse transformation in the evening.

We read everything we could get our hands on about Evergreen, especially appreciating Mary Helen Crain's writings on historical buildings and her interviews with settlers and children of pioneers. But we found nothing currently in print about Evergreen that includes its explosive growth of the last 25 years. So we decided to create our personal tribute, hoping that others who love it too will enjoy sharing our experiences of this unique mountain community.

Stable remodeled into a Studio

AS OTHERS SEE US

Whether poking fun at pretentiousness, criticizing defects, or summarizing its qualities at a certain moment in time, the published observations of journalists, residents and visitors over the years are unique snapshots of Evergreen. In some ways, they are the most accurate and lively pictures we have of this community.

SOPHISTICATED, LIVELY, IMAGINATIVE EVERGREEN
Status Symbol in the Pines
4/2/66 — *Main Street, Evergreen, looks like Main Street of many sleepy little towns in Colorado.*

But the little mountain community 27 miles southwest of Denver is different than its alpine sisters. More sophisticated. More "in."

It has become a status symbol in the pines for the New Denverite junior executive.

The setting (with Evergreen Lake mirroring rugged peaks and Bear Creek winding through a myriad of pines) . . . the climate (cooler-than-Denver in summer, warmer-than-Denver in winter and smog free all year round) . . . the accent on informality . . . give the aura of Utopia, mountain-style, for the individual who wants to have his title on his office door and a rural route mailbox too.

Originally on the map as a round-up of dude ranches interspersed with rustic mansions of old Denver's 400, Evergreen startd to get its new image in the beginning of the '60s when a combination of things happened to make living in the mountains and working in town more feasible . . .

The population leaped from 1961 to 1964 and as the handsome homes started to peep through the pines, shopping centers and new businesses sprang up to serve them.

The area developed its own distinctive style of architecture—Affluent Evergreen—batten board, shake shingles, enormous expanses of thermopane and acres of deck. A spectacular view for every window became as important as a coq au vin for every pot . . . Pat Hanna in the **Rocky Mountain News.**

WANT TO LIVE IN THE OLD WEST?

The Evergreen Syndrome: Pioneers End up with Long Island West.

5/29/77 — *"Go West, young man, go West." Horace Greeley said that in 1859, and Colorado has not recovered from it yet . . .*

When all those Easterners with tender feet reached the Rockies and realized they would have to climb over them to go all the way West, most of them decided Colorado was West enough.

Horace counted on this. He founded a city within sight of the mountains, modestly named it Greeley, and sold lots to lots for lots.

This phenomenon of believing the West is along the Front Range is called the Greeley syndrome . . . Easterners arriving today still believe they have come to the Wild West. Once the snow-capped Rockies stop dazzling their eyes, they realize Greeley (or Littleton or Denver) is just Long Island West . . .

Horace was fiendishly clever. In Greeley and the other Front Range settlements he left behind his second call — 'Head for the hills, men!'

Disillusioned people with the Greeley syundrome are not cured. They get, instead, what is known as the Evergreen syndrome: thinking the West is **in** *the mountains, not in front of them . . . People with the Evergreen syndrome go to the mountains seeking the rustic life of the real Old West. They want a spread with a few horses on it so they can wear a sheepskin jacket and smoke Marlboros without feeling foolish.*

It must be pointed out that in order to live poor in Evergreen, you have to rich. Poor people cannot afford to live rustic lives close to nature because everything costs twice as much in places more vertical than horizontal.

Eventually these rich flatlanders find a few pine-beetle-blighted acres full of rabid squirrels and infected ticks at the end of a picturesque dirt road. . . .

They build an expensive rustic house. They get rid of their gas-guzzling Belchfire-8 and buy a gas-guzzling four-wheel drive with a snowplow attachment.

Thye get some dogs and horses.

They install a septic syustem. They drill a well for pure Rocky Mountain Spring water . . .

Evergreen is wonderful. Until, of course, winter comes and the potholes and boulders make their annual migration to the middle of the dirt roads.

Living in the West becomes dust, mud, holed mufflers and front-end needing realignment.

The pioneers get paved roads.

A few kids get hit by cars speeding on the paved roads.

They get street lights and traffic signals.

Burglars can now see their houses and make quick getaways.

The wonderful, born-free doggies munch on some children and a horsey or two.

They get police protection.

Septic tanks run over and pollute the wells .

They get chlorinated water and sewage treatment.

In short, they get a city—just like Greeley. They also get to complain how Evergreen . . . has gone to hell, how it used to be the real West . . . Rob Pudim in the **Rocky Mountain News.**

Real Evergreenites were born in Chicago.

Real Evergreen men are commercial airline pilots and they have wives who sell real estate . . .

Real Evergreenites have two children and they send them to Colorado Academy. . .

Real Evergreenites talk about the Brown Cloud and drive alone to Denver to work. Real Evergreenites don't ride RTD.

Real Evergreenites hang banners over the Stanbro Real Estate office on Main Street and put "Go Cougars" signs on telephone poles on Colorado Highway 784 during the football season.

Real Evergreenites don't want a by-pass around Evergreen Lake and they hate traffic at the stoplight in town. They remember the T-Bar-S and they don't put "Native" bumper stickers on their cars because Real Evergreenites were born in Chicago . . .

Real Evergreenites never plant flowers before June 1 . . .

Real Evergreenites have a Cuisinart in the kitchen and a chain saw iln the garage.

Real Evergreenites take natural vitamin C and run in the Town Race. They also wear cowboy boots in the Rodeo Parade.

Real Evergreen women wear tartan plaid shirts at Christmas and make cheese balls for their neighbors. Real Evergreen women have a photo of their high school kid leaning against a tree. . .

Real Evergreenites keep their hot tubs covered when not in use.

Real Evergreenites still wish they were the last to move here. — John Fellows column in the **Canyon Courier.**

EVERGREEN AREA NO LONGER GREEN

8/1/84 — *For a prime example of seeing something you love destroyed, drive up to Evergreen.*

That's the vaunted mountain living of which we all dream: rolling hillsides mantled in dark pines, dipping to great verdant meadows serenely curving over the earth, majestic snow-capped mountains defining the horizon . . .

But drive up now, for its disappearing. Next year there may be little to admire—unless you have a love of industrial parks and sardine-tins of housing. Including that valley just across from El Rancho, almost every meadow and many of the hillsides have been rezond for development. This cherished open space and sense of country is being given away acre by acre to developers who think big is better, who have no concern that they are eradicating the very thing that makes this mountain community special . . .

. . . some of the most densely populated developments are being planned around the Denver mountain parks . . . Private developers are reaping the economic value of these open spaces . . .

It's a pity to say that beautiful Evergreen is a perfect example of destroying what is good by too much development. . .

Denver Post, *Joanne Ditmer column.*

WHO'S IN CHARGE IN A CITY
THAT ISN'T A CITY?

Evergreen doesn't exist, legally. Its occasional efforts to decide whether it should become a city seem to show that people don't much care for the idea. Its not clear whether this is from mountain orneriness, lack of civic responsibility, or distaste for more taxes and another whole layer of government.

Perhaps Evergreen's Don Stanbro was expressing the gut-level feelings of a lot of people round here, when he explained why he was stepping down after only one 4-year term as Jefferson County Commissioner. "Its been a lot of fun and I've thoroughly enjoyed my time in government," he said, "but for now, I've had just about all the fun I can stand."

The irony is that, as an unincorporated community in Jefferson County, Evergreen has had to develop all kinds of special districts to supplement basic county services. And no type of special district has yet been devised to give the community control over its major concern for the last twenty years—the character and pace of growth.

In its capacity as Evergreen's "local" government, the three-person Jefferson County Board of Commissioners alone has the legal power to rule on proposals for development, and to approve plans for the area.

Through its Sheriff's Department, the county takes care of law and order in our community. County roads are maintained by the county's Road and Bridge department. (On the many private roads in Evergreen, repair and maintenance are the responsibility of landowners.) Both the Sheriff's and the County Road Department maintain local offices in Evergreen. Public health, social services and certain cultural services such as the library are also county responsibilities.

The county acts as tax collector for its own services as well as for the school district and special districts. In Evergreen, these take care of fire protection, water and sanitation service (though many Evergreenites are still on wells and septic systems), and recreation.

Evergreen's Golden Age?
Perhaps part of Evergreen's soul still longs back to the days when it was part of the Unorganized Territory, blessed with absolutely no government whatsoever.

In 1803, land in the Evergreen area was worth four cents an acre. It was sold by Napoleon in that grand historical bargain known as the Louisiana Purchase, along with all the territory owned by France west of the Mississippi River.

For the next 40 years, the change in national status had little effect on this part of the mountains. It was part of a vast area called the Unorganized Territory. In reality it was Indian country, part of the spacious hunting grounds of the mountain Ute tribes, and accessible enough from the plains to be used by Cheyenne and Arapahoe for summer hunting and as a source of the lodgepole pine supports needed for their teepees.

Mountain Men
When Mexico won its independence from Spain in 1821, the old Spanish ban on trading with the United States was repealed. This resulted in the opening up of the Santa Fe Trail which, for the next 20 years, brought hundreds of fur trappers and traders to Colorado. It was the brief, romantic era of the "mountain men", whose memory and way of life is celebrated annually at the Hiwan Homestead's Mountain Rendezvous. These men learned wilderness survival techniques from the Indians. As long as beaver hats were in fashion and the fur boom lasted, the mountain men explored every Indian trail in the Colorado Rockies.

Mountain men left no monuments. It is only from contemporary writings that we can say they were the first white men to know the natural beauties and seasonal treacheries of life in this part of the mountains.

The decline of the fur trade that began in the late 30's might have signalled a return to the timeless symbiosis of Indians and environment, but an altogether different fate was in the making.

The era of the Mountain Men, celebrated annually at the Mountain Rendezvous.

11

The Movement West Begins

Missouri Senator Thomas Hart Benton dispatched his brilliant son-in-law, Lieutenant John Charles Fremont, on a reconnaissance mission through the Rockies. This was to support Benton's stirring call for America to achieve its Manifest Destiny of becoming a continental power—which meant displacing the Mexicans in California and the British in Oregon. Fremont's mission had two functions: military intelligence—to search out routes to accomplish these ends— and a public relations aspect—to make the wilderness more alluring to Americans.

The report of Fremont's exploits through the Colorado high country to Oregon, written in ringing prose by his wife Jessie Benton Fremont, fired the national imagination when it was published in 1845. It helped to establish a mood of enthusiastic expansionism, fueling a flood tide of American migrants to the northwest. Great Britain renounced her claims to Oregon. President Polk had the necessary public support to take on the militarily ineffective Mexican government and bring New Mexico and California into the United States through the 1848 Treaty of Guadalupe Hidalgo.

The 1849 gold strikes in California together with the decision of the persecuted Mormons to seek a new homeland in present-day Utah, vastly increased the numbers of individuals and caravans passing through the northern part of Colorado— along the Oregon Trail. Mountainous areas like Evergreen, inhabited by six loosely affiliated bands of Utes, were little affected. But the Plains Indians reacted with violence to the disturbance of their grazing and hunting grounds, and to the spread of alcoholism and sickness resulting from contact with whites.

In an 1851 treaty with nine Plains tribes, boundaries were set for each Indian nation and the U.S. received rights to build roads and army forts within these boundaries. The Cheyenne and Arapahoe were given the lands lying between the Arkansas and North Platte rivers, with the western boundary "along the main range of the Rocky Mountains"—i.e. the Continental Divide.

New Territories

The Unorganized Territory of the Louisiana Purchase was first broken up into smaller areas in 1850. In that year California won statehood, the Mormons achieved Territorial status for Utah (which at that time stretched west all the way to the Continental Divide), and the Territory of New Mexico was formed with its northern boundary along the Arkansas.

What all this reorganization did for the Evergreen area was to put it into the new Territory of Kansas, formed in 1854. The north boundary was set at the fortieth parallel, which placed Evergreen, Golden and Denver inside Kansas Territory but put Boulder, Greeley and most of the South Platte valley into the new Territory of Nebraska.

In 1855, Kansas Territory was divided into counties. Evergreen was included in Arapahoe County. This started at the 103rd meridian, barely in sight of Pike's Peak, and ran west to the Utah Territory border on the Continental Divide and north to the Nebraska Territory boundary. Since it was a vast wilderness, belonging by treaty to the Cheyenne and Arapahoe and almost devoid of white settlers, the officials appointed for its administration apparently never formally took up their offices.

But it was not in the cards for Arapahoe County to be left to the Indians. The conditions under which Kansas Territory was set up led to fratricidal conflict—the explosive slavery question was left to be decided by the settlers. Some who wanted to escape this conflict pushed on into Arapahoe County's wilderness, joined by disappointed gold seekers returning from California and still others desperate to escape creditors after the business crash of 1857.

Gold Strikes Populate the Rockies

In 1858, small amounts of gold were found near the confluence of Cherry Creek and the South Platte. News of this new strike reached the east attached to the name of Pike's Peak: though 80 miles to the south, this was the best known landmark to locate it by. A gold rush to this new, get-rich-quick paradise was soon underway.

Prospectors lost no time pushing deeper and deeper into the mountains in their search for gold. Soon settlements in the foothills and along Clear Creek were added to the infant communities of St. Charles—later renamed Denver—and Auraria.

Voluntary efforts substituted for the lack of effective government from Kansas Territory. Mining districts were set up, with officers to record land claims. Squatters registered their lands with claim clubs. Vigilant committees and people's courts meted out rough but fair justice.

The pioneers, as a whole, gave hearty support to these pseudo-legal organizations: early-day newspapers were extravagant in their praise of the vigilant committees. The Western Mountaineer for July 26, 1860, carried this story:

VIGILANCE COMMITTEE ORGANIZES IN GOLDEN

A vigilance committee has been organized with almost universal concurrence of the public, to promptly secure, examine and punish offenders. The names of sixty members are already enrolled upon its lists. Its first public session was held. on Tuesday morning. A. L. Drum was tried for stealing. He was found guilty; and on the account of his confession.and physical weakness, was sentenced to receive only twenty-five lashes on his bare back and leave town within twenty-four hours.

Many mining districts and claim clubs, according to Betty Moynihan in her chapter on early government in Colorado (in "From Scratch", the Jefferson County Historical Commission's delightful book on the county's early history) developed often into full-blown, if rough and ready, municipal governments.

However, the need for some coherent, organized government—closer at hand than Kansas—became daily more apparent.

Jefferson—Territory and County

Representations sent to the Kansas Legislature and to Congress yielded no results. The Civil War was in the making, Kansas was already a battlefield, and politicians were disinclined to pay attention to faraway problems. A movement snowballed to separate the new gold region from Kansas Territory and get recognition for a new state, or at least a separate territory.

A resolution to create the Territory of Jefferson was put to a vote of the people in October, 1859, and passed. In November, an elected legislature authorized the formation of counties, including Jefferson County. Its boundaries were substantially the same as today and Golden was the "temporary" county seat. A man called Eli Carter, elected Clerk and Recorder, opened a county record book on January 6, 1860. This book is open to the public and is a fascinating window on early land, timber and mining claims.

Not all of the settlers accepted the new Territorial Government's jurisdiction, in part because of a hated $1.00-a-head poll tax it attempted to levy.

Thomas Cunningham Bergen of Bergen Park

Because of this dissatisfaction there was, for a brief period, a county of Niwot. This seems to have been the brainchild of the founding father of our community, Thomas Cunningham Bergen.

A successful farmer in Illinois, the 39-year-old Bergen was apparently seized by the passion of the times— to go west and seek wider opportunities for himself and his growing family. From letters written by his daughter Martha, we know that he set out in 1859, bringing "10 strong young men about his age (in) Gold Rush time to the Rocky Mountains." Bergen happened onto a broad grassy valley, surrounded by spruce and pine, which he thought was the most beautiful place he had ever seen. Home only to wandering Indians and wild game, it had been named Elk Park by government scouts and surveyors. Bergen got his 10 strong young men to help him build a log cabin there, renamed it Bergen Park, and returned to Illinois. He proceeded to sell his farm, stock up on supplies and bring his family the following summer on the long trek back.

Bergen's influence was felt in many areas of early life in this mountain area, but here we describe his role as a pioneer of local government. According to Moynihan, Bergen and his neighbors met together on July 20, 1860 to set up the Bergen District. Though it was ostensibly a mining district, it had as part of its conscious purpose the creation of some structure of law and order for the area. The organization papers

Thomas Cunningham Bergen.

have so intrigued legal minds that the original documents are on file at the Harvard Law School and have been studied in detail.

A February 20, 1861, story in the Rocky Mountain News reported that the County of Niwot was formed at a Convention of citizens of the Districts of Bergen, Junction (the Conifer area) and Mount Vernon (no longer in existence, though its name is perpetuated in Mount Vernon Canyon and the historic townsite is part of the Jefferson County Open Space Matthews/Winters Park). The citizens agreed to secede from the Provisional Government, forming a Constitution and laws for their own government and protection, and declaring their independence of all government except the United States.

Gunfight at the Niwot Corral

A personal account of this episode came from T. C. Bergen's son, William, who was 15 years old when the family left Illinois. He remembered that his father and some neighbors organized Niwot County and established the county seat at Bergen's Park. (The place was called at different times Bergen Park, Bergen's Park and Bergen's Ranche).

The Bergen home, expanded and serving as a lodging place, was "about all there was of the town, but it was a nucleus, and there was more of it than to any other settlement. . . Father was elected Justice of the Peace and was generally looked to to maintain order and to see that the proprieties were observed."

According to William, a neighbor named R. A. Strain— perhaps feeling slighted because he did not get some office in the county administration—organized a rival county and named it Spruce Park. It lay to the south of Niwot toward Bear Creek, where Evergreen is today, and some of its boundaries overlapped Niwot's. Conflict arose almost immediately. The story, in William's own words, reads like the script for a western movie:

A man named Mallett, a Frenchman, built a sawmill on Bear Creek. Among his employees were two men of his own nationality whom, for some reason, he failed to pay for their labor. They brought suit in Niwot County and attached the mill and other property belonging to Mallett. This property was seized and such of it as was capable of being moved readily was brought to Bergen Park and stored in our warehouse.

Naturally, this proceeding did not please Mr. Mallett, and he undertook to recover his former possessions. Whether he made appeal to the Spruce Park authorities I do not know, but I do know that he made an effort to accomplish his purpose by force of arms. He organized a party of about a dozen men. . .

A friend coming up the road had seen them. "Bergen," he said to my Father, "do you know that you are about to be wiped off of the face of the earth?

Naturally Father replied that he had no such knowledge.

Well, you are, because I have just seen a bunch of twelve men a mile and a half down the road who told me they were coming here for that purpose and to take Mallett's tools away from you and your jurisdiction. They are armed to the teeth with guns, revolvers and knives . . . .
(Father) knew that the purpose was not more for the capture of the attached property than for the destruction of the Niwot County machinery, and he was quite determined that neither end should be achieved.

There were three men on the place, Father, John White the Constable, and a hired man named Joe Early. Not only were they inferior in numbers but they were deficient in equipment, but they made up their

13

minds to fight if necessary. Father owned a Sharp's Rifle, one of the first made. White had a muzzle-loading rifle, and Early carried a six shooter revolver. White was known far and wide as a sure shot and a man devoid of fear, but neither my father nor Early had established an especial reputation in either direction.

When the men came up they stopped at the fence, Father called from the house asking what they wanted.

We have come to get Mallett's mill machinery." Bergen told them that they could not take the property away unless they posted a bond. "We did not come to give bond, but to get the machinery," was the curt response.

By this time White had shown himself. "Gentlemen," he said, "you outnumber us four to one and of course you may be able to overcome us, but I want to tell you the machinery is in the warehouse under lock, and if any one among you wants to die all he has to do is to undertake to break the seal; I'll guarantee he never breaks another."

This seemed to have the effect of bringing the party to their senses. They rode away without further demonstration. Ultimately Mallett paid the debt and recovered the property.

According to William, this was not the last clash between Niwot and Spruce Park counties. Resolution came only when both were eliminated.

William Bergen is the only source we found for the existence of Spruce Park County, but the name of the short-lived Niwot County appears for a few months in the early record books of Jefferson County.

Jefferson Territory Disappears, the County Survives

Jefferson Territory was superceded by the creation of Colorado Territory, proclaimed into existence by President Lincoln on February 28, 1861.

Early in the first session of the new Legislature, a bill to define county boundaries and locate county seats was introduced. The organization of Jefferson County, with substantially the same boundaries as before and with Golden City again the "temporary" county seat, was

approved November 1, 1861. At the election for county officials held in December, T.C. Bergen became one of the original three County Commissioners.

The Commissioners met for the first time on January 6, 1862 and lost no time in getting to grips with the problems of governing the county. By the end of the year, they had rented a place for county offices, established county and school taxes, provided for the erection of a jail, and approved wagon toll roads. The county was divided into nine election precincts. No. 6 was Bergen's Ranche with Bergen's House as the polling place. His old challenger, Mr. Strain, became one of the three precinct judges.

Government services provided by Jefferson County supplemented the extensive mutual help that was a necessary ingredient of early farming, ranching and logging communities in the mountain area.

Only a few towns in this county were incorporated from the outset, with townsites surveyed and platted and city-style lots sold. Some of these, like Mount Vernon and Golden Gate, failed to survive. Morrison and Golden had a better fate.

Most places in the mountains were named after a lodging house, a stage stop or a general store with a post office. When government surveyor F. V. Hayden published his elegant Geographic and Geologic Atlas of Colorado in 1877, only Bergen's P.O. and Junction Ho.—present-day Conifer—were listed as existing places in this part of the mountains.

Enter Evergreen

Evergreen's emergence as a community separate from Bergen Park was helped in 1877 when Amos Post—one of the 'ten strong young men' who came out west with Thomas Bergen— opened a trading post on what is now Evergreen Main Street.

Amos was a tall, heavy-set man with a dark, full beard. He married Bergen's oldest daughter Sarah Ellen in 1862. Shortly thereafter he built a general store near the Bergen's lodging house. He was an energetic and competent man and an excellent carpenter. Like his father-in-law, he was alert to the rapidly changing opportunities of the times. When the strategic importance of Bergen Park as a

transportation crossroads faded with the coming of railroads., Post saw better trade opportunities in the nearby logging settlement growing up on the banks of Bear Creek.

For a number of years, the place was known simply as The Post. Gradually a name used by the influential early settler, D. P. Wilmot, caught on. He acquired a large acreage in the Buffalo Park area around 1875. The Evergreen High School and Wilmot Elementary School, named after him, are on a section of the former Wilmot Ranch. Wilmot was so impressed with the huge and plentiful pines, spruces and firs on the land that he began calling the whole area "Evergreen." (In the 1890's, Wilmot became one of the very few Evergreen residents to be elected a County Commissioner.)

By 1880, the first year in which Evergreen makes its appearance in the Colorado State Business Directory, Evergreen is listed as a small settlement on Bear Creek with a population of 100, but Bergen Park is not listed at all.

By this time, early hopes of finding mineral wealth in the Evergreen-Bergen Park area were fading. The future lay in other enterprises. Logging was one of these. An 1873 item in the Colorado Transcript described the land around Bergen Park as "one of the best timbered sections of Colorado." Farming and ranching, hard though the conditions were, soon became well-established in the meadows and valleys.

Almost from the beginning, the area also began to serve as a summer refuge from the heat of the plains for those that could afford to get away to the mountains. The nucleus of the Evans Ranch was bought in 1868. Mary Neosho Williams acquired her land for "Camp Neosho"—today's Hiwan Homestead Museum—in the 1880's. Some of the early stage stops and lodging houses, like Troutdale-in-the-Pines, made an easy transition from providing overnight facilities for travelers to and from the mines, to offering more extended summer boarding opportunities.

With improvments in transportation, the steady increase in numbers of "summer people" gave rise to a human and social parallel to the contrast between summer and winter in the

Dwight P. Wilmot.

Many of the lands for these parks were purchased for nominal sums from the federal government. Some were bought from private citizens and others were donated.

One of the few acquired by condemnation was the initial Evergreen park. The acquisition of the 420-acre deDisse Ranch, and the associated gift of nearly 18 acres from the Troutdale Hotel and Realty Company (on condition that Denver construct on it, and maintain in perpetuity, an 18-hole golf course) was a milestone in the development of Evergreen. It enabled Denver to build the Evergreen Dam in 1928-9, and so create the lake which has become the central self-image of the community.

The introduction of the City and County of Denver into the life of Evergreen brought a new governmental entity and influence here, to supplement basic Jefferson County services. Denver cooperated with the State and the county to improve the roads, acquired more and more property for parks, thus protecting strategic lands from development, policed the parks and had charge of all activities at the lake and golf course. These naturally were operated primarily for the pleasure and convenience of Denver residents and tourists. Of course, the entire of population of Jefferson County at the time was very small.

The Evergreen Chamber of Commerce welcomed the opportunities for tourism, trade and growth that came in the wake of Denver's investment in the community. This is clear from a delightful little pamphlet published by the Chamber around 1927.

In the wake of the Mountain Park activity came a new rash of subdivisions, most of them ill-conceived and totally unrelated to the land contours. They provided inexpensive lots for middle-income citizens of Denver and other hot plains'cities, where simple cabins could be built either by the owners themselves or by local contractors. Sales of large acreages to wealthier individuals, who could afford to build more substantial homes, also accelerated.

Mountain Parks Protective Association

Proliferation of summer homes and cabins generated a need for a new kind of "law and order". Protective surveillance of buildings that were unoccupied for long stretches of time was provided by the Mountain Parks Protective Association. MPPA was formed in 1925 as a non- profit organization offering patrol service for home-owners in Jefferson, Clear Creek and Park Counties. Their services supplemented those of the County Sheriffs' Departments: the MPPA supervisor and patrolmen had Deputy Sheriff Commissions. For 49 years this hard-working organization, manned by never more than a handful of officers, policed the homes of those who chose to become members. A high proportion of the "summer people" joined, as did as many year-round residents.

The distinctive triangular wooden MPPA membership signs are still visible on many properties around Evergreen. Dues were modest and bought not only regular patrolling of members' properties but also inspection and treatment of trees suffering from the recurrent infestations characteristic of forest life in this region. Officers of MPPA came and went, but the heart and soul of the organization from its beginning—until his death in 1949—was Ernest King.

During the 60's Evergreen moved into a new phase of its development: it became a commuter town of mostly year-round residents. With the establishment of urban fire and sanitation services and increased protection through the Sheriff's Department, the Mountain Parks Protective Association realized that its time of service was coming to an end. With a grace and timing uncharacteristic of entrenched organizations, it voted itself out of existence in 1974. Its directors donated the balance of $75,000 in its treasury for a perpetual scholarship fund to send one or two high school graduates—from Jefferson, Clear Creek or Park Counties—to college.

mountains. The late May explosion—from a long grey-brown dormancy into the vibrant colors of aspen and wildflowers— was mirrored in a vivacious invasion of summer visitors and a round of social activities. The first killer frost, around Labor Day, caused an exodus. After this, the small year-round community—with a certain sense of relief but also of apprehension about the economically difficult months ahead— shrank back to something around one-tenth of its summer size.

Denver Takes Center Stage

Nothing did more to accelerate the trend towards becoming a summer colony than the establishment of the Denver Mountain Parks in 1911. This imaginative venture of a brash young city affected Evergreen life on every level.

The Denver Mountain Parks were a series of acquisitions of mountain lands—most of them in Jefferson County—aimed at giving Denver citizens and tourists free and perpetual access to mountain playgrounds. They were envisioned as places of particular beauty along a loop from Golden to Morrison, easily accessible by the new motorized transportation—buses, limousines and private automobiles. Evergreen was designated as the "hub," "apex" or "crown jewel" of the system, depending on the imagination of the writer describing it.

MAP

OF

TROUTDALE ESTATES

TROUTDALE IN THE PINES

OWNERS
THE DENVER MOUNTAIN PARKS SECURITIES CO
922-24 GAS & ELECTRIC BLDG
DENVER COLO.   Scale 1" 200'

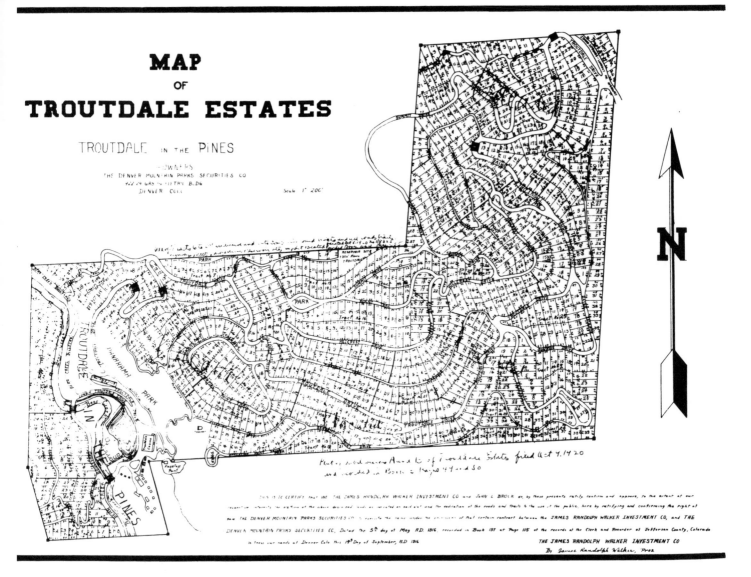

THE JAMES RANDOLPH WALKER INVESTMENT CO
By James Randolph Walker, Pres.

The Fire of '26

Most early western communities, because they were built largely of wood, suffered from disastrous fires. Evergreen's came in early November of 1926.

The November 10th Rocky Mountain News told the story: "Damage in excess of $50,000 resulted from fire of unknown origin, which swept through seven business structures at Evergreen at 3:45 o'clock yesterday morning. The fire raged until 7 o'clock before it was finally put under control by the residents of the resort, augmented by a company of firefighters from Denver."

"The fire was discovered first in the E. R. Riel Mercantile store. Mr. and Mrs. Joseph Minter, in charge of the local telephone office, were notified, and they called every resident of Evergreen to combat the flames."

Ernest King of the Mountain Parks Protective Association organized a bucket brigade, with water passed from creek to the fire by hand. A stiff breeze fanned the flames from one building to another. Two vacant buildings, owned by John Ross of Morrison, were torn down to prevent the fire from spreading to still other buildings. The Minters had called for a pumper truck from Denver. It was late in arriving as it missed a curve coming up Bear Creek canyon, throwing the captain twenty-five feet. Although he was injured, he continued on to Evergreen where he directed his men in pumping streams of water over piles of lumber and a wooden filling station threatened by the fire.

After the fire, Ernest King of the MPPA acquired a truck and some minimal firefighting equipment, which served for many years as Evergreen's only fire protection agency.

The town recovered rapidly. As early as March of 1927, under the headline, "Who Said the Fire Hurt Evergreen?" the Rocky Mountain News reported, "Evergreen has made a rapid recovery from the disastrous fire which destroyed a number of the best business buildings last fall. While all have not yet been replaced, most of the burned area is better than ever and more substantial buildings take the place of those destroyed."

In 1949, a house on Upper Bear Creek—where the "Wilcox on the Rocks" home is now—caught fire. The only part that remained, despite the best efforts of King's truck, was the stone chimney. A number of Evergreen's responsible citizens decided that the time had come to create a fire department.

Evergreen Forms a Fire Department

We heard the story from one of those "founding fathers," A. R. (Rozzi) Clark. "We met at the schoolhouse, and we all chipped in to buy some fire equipment. We finally got enough money to buy a four-wheel Dodge power wagon. Then we went over to the State Forestry Department and under the Clark- McNeary Act, they bought the pump and the hose for us. We started out with a pump and a hose and a Dodge power wagon."

The volunteers immediately went into training for their new responsibilities. Land for a firehouse on Main Street was contributed rent-free by Mrs. Mary Quaintance of the Ross- Lewis Trust and the building was constructed mostly by the firemen themselves.

The original Fire District contained 114 square miles and was later expanded to its present 126. It includes properties with very different kinds of fire hazards—commercial stores and offices, private homes, and many hundreds of acres of ranches and forested land. A variety of specialized equipment had to be bought over the years to serve these needs, and the demands on the increasing numbers of volunteers to train and equip themselves to deal with all emergencies were—and continue to be—very great.

As equipment and personnel increased, a new firehouse was needed. Funds for purchasing land on Highway 73 and building the attractive $90,000 stone and timber building, designed by architect Alan Fredericksen, were raised by bond issue. The Department moved into its new quarters in 1966.

Fires are dangerous, grimy and exciting. We asked some long-time volunteer firemen about their experiences. Rozzi Clark served for twenty years. He remembered as "quite a fire" the blaze that gutted the main building at Bendemeer which today is just a residential section of Upper Bear Creek but was once a well-known resort. Then there was a forest fire up on Rooster Mountain above the Evans Ranch, which was "pretty bad." His wife, Leona, remembered "they were gone several days on that one." She also told us of the time she refused to let Rozzi back in the house until he took his clothes off, after a fire in which he got covered with burnt feathers from a mattress.

Ross Grimes.

Jack Rouse.

Our Signs are a Safeguard!

Since the Association's inception, the distinctive large triangular signs have become a symbol which commands the respect of all who visit the mountain areas. Displayed in conspicuous places of members properties, they are highly effective in the prevention of lawlessness. Each member is also provided a name plate sign and directional signs are provided where required to locate members homes in more heavily populated areas.

EVERGREEN HEADQUARTERS

The Association owns its own modern headquarters building 1½ miles north of downtown Evergreen on State Highway No. 74. This functional as well as attractive headquarters building adequately houses the administrative office, well equipped shop, garage and storage facilities of this energetic and growing organization.

WHAT THE ASSOCIATION MEANS

Three hundred and sixty-five days of the year, and twenty-four hours a day our patrolmen are ready to respond to members calls on a few minutes notice, no matter what or where they are.

Burglaries and vandalism in the patrolled areas have been held to a minimum. A substantial percentage of all goods stolen has been returned to the owners.

We know the mountain area.
We answer calls--day and night.
We check suspicious cars or persons
We spot the prowler.
We direct the tourist and the stranger.
We inspect and spray beetle infested trees
We are as close as your telephone for any emergency.
A membership application is attached for your convenience.

COOPERATING ORGANIZATIONS

United States Forest Service
Colorado State Forest Service
Sheriff's Offices of Park, Clear Creek and Jefferson Counties.
Denver Mountain Parks System
Colorado State Game and Fish Department Commissions

AREA SERVED

The area served by the Mountain Protective Association extends from the foothills on the east to the Continental Divide on the west and from Clear Creek on the north to the North Fork of the South Platte River on the South.

Excerpt from MPPA pamphlet.

Evergreen Volunteer Fire Department, 1952. First row (l. to r.): John Schneider, Walt Anderson, Frank Waggoner, Charles Osborne, Art Lindgren, Alton Tucker, Carol Teske, (background), Everett Gass, Ken Tatum (background), Elmer Bedford, Chuck Feehan (background), Rozzi Clark Sr., Charles Beall, Rozzie Clark Jr., unknown. Second row (l. to r.): John Myers, Hal Davidson, Lew Armbrust, Don Bruce, E. J. Alderfer (background), Bob Hammond, Dale Slater, Mel Crosson, Jerry Olde, Frank Anderson, Jim Davis, unknown, Bill Marshall. Back row (l. to r. on trucks): Herb Snowbarger, Gus Martin, Jack Thomas and Jack Rouse.

Jack Rouse, who served for many years as head of Evergreen's Public Service Company operation, was brief and irreverent about his many years as a volunteer fireman. "The Fire Department was fun: we burned a lot of houses and we froze a lot of pumps."

Dan Scherer, and Evergreen native and Fire Chief in the '70's when the community was growing so rapidly, remembered best the 1968 fire on Mount Evans. He and one other Evergreen fireman were the first sent into the Lincoln Lake area after smoke was reported. No sooner had they arrived when the fire began to crown with 800-foot flames. They were trapped until the blaze miraculously shifted to the east—and they escaped west. "That was one time when I just knew I was going to die."

ROSS GRIMES

One of Evergreen's "movers and shakers," Ross is both an entrepreneur and a community volunteer. He is outspoken, hardworking and not afraid to take on the responsibilities of leadership and the confrontations this involves. After the war, he came west to attend Colorado University where he met his wife, Nancy. Her parents, Willard and Mary Helen Crain—who contributed so much to the Evergreen community—had recently moved here. In the summer of '49 Ross worked for the Woodpeckers, a unique construction firm whose story is told elsewhere in this book. Ross and Nancy were married in 1950. After graduation, he tried working for corporations, but found himself more intrigued helping the Crains with a little candy Christmas wreath business they had started in a small store on Main Street. The Grimes bought the business in 1951. Among his many community activities, Ross has made major contributions to the Volunteer Fire Department the Evergreen Metropolitan Water and Sanitation District.

Ross Grimes has served for many years on the fire department and was one of its most effective Fire Chiefs, from 1963-70. He recalled the fire at Brook Forest Inn as his most difficult and dangerous. "It had snowed 18 inches on top of earlier snows. At the time, we had three trucks: one was very old, one was being repaired, and that left us one decent truck. The fire was blowing out of the roof 50 feet into

the air. It had started in the kitchen, and spread through the whole building." To complicate matters further, the Brook Forest Water District had used different guaged-threads on their fire hydrants. So there they were—with one and a half trucks, very few men and snow up to the door handles. Grimes had to crawl up to the third floor, with gas mask on, to check if anyone was trapped in the rooms. In spite of the frustrations they finally got the fire out.

Grimes also recalled a house fire on Bear Creek, when the temperature was 40 degrees below zero and the pump froze. Ironically, they had to start a fire to unfreeze it.

To increase the efficiency of the Department and cut down on time in reaching a fire, every property in the fire protection district is assigned a fire number. Periodically, the District produces an updated map of the district which is one of the best sources for detailed information about the Evergreen area.

From the beginning the Evergreen Volunteer Fire Department has been fortunate to attract dedicated, intelligent and capable people. For many years, being on the Volunteer Fire Department meant membership in the best club in town—the camaraderie, mutual respect and community appreciation was immense. Dan Scherer was interviewed by the Canyon Courier in 1978. He said that he joined as soon as he was old enough, at the age of 21: "Everyone I respected was in it. It was the thing to do."

As Evergreen has grown, organizations have proliferated. No single group, however dedicated, can draw quite that same spotlight. But Evergreen is aware that it has one of the most alert, best-trained and vigilant fire departments in the state. Volunteers are trained in dealing with potential disasters on a community scale, as well as with the many types of personal and medical emergencies they may encounter in the course of their work. Their skill in fighting fires— along with protecting property as far as is technically feasible—has earned them the lasting respect of Evergreen's citizens.

As the commuter era got into its full stride in the 1970's and the Hiwan Country Club and Soda Creek subdivisions were developed,

there was a need for a second fire station to serve the northern end of the district. With additional money from a bond issue the building facing Highway 74, in front of Bergen Elementary School, was completed in 1976.

There are two entities involved in the fire-fighting program. The tax-supported Evergreen Fire Protection District is governed by an elected board and is responsible for the budget, the buildings and equipment, and for overall policies of the Department as well as for appointment of an increasing number of paid staff. The Evergreen Volunteer Fire Department is the organization of the volunteers who still constitute the bulk of the firefighting force, and who raise supplementary funds for desirable but not essential services such as community and school fire prevention education and food for firemen fighting long-lasting blazes.

The days that realtor Hal Davidson reminisced about for us—when "the fire siren would go off and we felt free to lock up our businesses and go fight a fire"—inevitably passed as the community grew: it became necessary to have some paid staff—dispatchers, Fire Chief, Fire Marshal, etc. The process was a gradual one, starting with out-of-pocket compensation or part-time pay.

Volunteer firemen—and women since 1978—must be willing to undergo a rigorous 6-month training and respond to at least 20% of annual calls in order to remain on the Department's roster. In 1986, there were approximately 50 firefighters in the Department responding to around 400 calls a year.

Until that year, the Fire Department had its own Rescue Squad which responded to medical emergencies and was specially trained for such situations as extricating people trapped in cars in accidents. The process of merging this unit with the personnel of the Evergreen Ambulance Service began in 1985.

Evergreen Ambulance Service

A little girl was hit by a car on Main Street and seriously injured. She had to lay there for one and a half hours before an emergency vehicle arrived from Denver. This was in the early '50,s, and it crystallized in the minds of Evergreen's leading citizens the conviction that it was time for this town to have its own ambulance.

They rounded up some funds, bought a station wagon, outfitted it with the necessary equipment and were in business. The Evergreen Ambulance Service (EAS) was set up as a separate non-profit organization but the first drivers were mostly volunteer firemen. There was always a close working relationship between the fire and ambulance services.

For over 30 years, the EAS was staffed totally by volunteers, and funds to run it came from only two sources: fees for ambulance runs and voluntary contributions.

In 1982, the Service was in very unsatisfactory accomodations—an old garage right on Highway 73, which housed the three ambulances, a few old couches, a TV, a coffeepot and a ragged dart board. Responding to more than 500 calls a year were 16 fully-fledged members of the service, all trained emergency medical technicians, and 7 more in training. Members had to pay for their own training as well as the red lights and sirens to put on their cars. There was no way the entire service could have a meeting or a satisfactory class in their own quarters.

The following spring, the EAS announced an ambitious drive to raise $150,000 to put the Evergreen Ambulance Service into adequate premises for the first time in its existence.

There followed one of those major campaigns that both demonstrate the extent of community involvement in its vital services, and help to solidify it. In February of 1984, a 1-1/2 acre site was found on Highway 73—across from what was known for many years as the "Old Mine" and is now a mini- storage facility—and intensive efforts to raise both cash and donations of labor and materials for a new building got underway.

The Evergreen Design Task Force contributed the design and simple builder's plans for the structure, many contractors donated supplies and services One October weekend, a well-planned "ambulance barn-raising" effort took place.

With the aid of loans from the three local banks, the building was completed in the next few months. A final round of money-raising events officially closed the fund drive on March 31, leaving a debt of around $35,000 on a building and site worth $190,000.

The need to have trained paramedics available at all times, which could not be filled by volunteers, dictated the first hiring

of paid staff for the ambulance service. This financial pressure, together with the continuing need for funds for equipment, operating expenses and servicing the debt on the new building, meant that the Evergreen Ambulance Service had to have some tax revenue to supplement donations. They either had to form a separate new Ambulance District or come under the umbrella of the Fire Department.

At the beginning of 1986, the Ambulance Service entered into a contract with the Fire Department. In return for a substantial monthy payment, the EAS staff and the Fire Department's Rescue Service were merged into the Evergreen Emergency Medical Services (EEMS), and the EAS agreed to provide paid paramedics and volunteer emergency medical technicians for the District's needs.

A special election in October of 1986 regularized the combination of the EEMS and the Fire Department: the voters approved both a mill levy increase to fund emergency medical staff, and a $850,000 bond issue to pay off the $35,000 debt on the ambulance building,buy new fire and ambulance equipment and expand the second fire station building to accomodate the new 911 emergency telephone communications system. Early in 1987, EEMS officially became part of the Evergreen Fire Protection District.

A Delco Battery and Bear Creek Water: Utilities Development

Evergreen's original utility company was a modest affair. It was started around 1904 by the Douglas family to provide water and electricity to the Episcopal Church properties on Lower Bear Creek and to a few existing buildings on Main Street. The equipment consisted of a gas-powered 24-volt Delco Battery and water pumped out of Bear Creek. Around 1903, the water supply was improved by the building of a storage tank on the north side of Forest Hill.

The "plant" was housed in a small building on the stream on Main Street, with the pumping equipment in the basement. Not until the 1980's was the building, which by then housed the Rockin' I Western Store, pulled down to make room for the new brick structure on the same site.

An enterprising young electrical engineer named Clarence Smith came to Evergreen in 1917 from Lincoln, Nebraska. He was doing the electrical work for his fellow-Nebraskan, Harry Sidles, on the new Troutdale Hotel. Finding that he enjoyed living in the mountains, Smith in 1921 purchased the electrical power supply rights from the Douglas family, with its approximately 30 customers, and formed the Evergreen Utilities Co.

In the 1921 State Business Directory, Smith was listed as Manager of this company but Rev. T. B. Rennell, Vicar of the Mission of the Transfiguration, was still Manager of the Water Works. By 1923, Clarence Smith had added the water works to his holdings: he spent the rest of his life running and expanding the utilities service, which he renamed the Evergreen Public Service Co.

Soon after the acquisition, Smith contracted to buy electrical power from Colorado Central Power in Golden and a service line was built over Lookout Mountain to Evergreen. Smith also installed a filtration system for the water supply. Each year additional lines were added to serve customers with electricity. At first most water customers were served through overground pipes in the summer only, but gradually more and more underground pipes were installed to serve the slowly growing year-round population.

Clarence Smith soon acquired a loyal secretary and book-keeper. Maude Cooper came from Michigan to Evergreen in 1922: her husband was a partner in the Bear Creek Transfer Company, located where the Evergreen National Bank is today. Maude went to work in the Evergreen Public Service Company office, taking care of billing and correspondence and whatever else was to be done. She contined her work there for 30 years, while raising a family and becoming a full participant in community affairs. Maude and Clarence married in the 1940's, after both of their first marriages had ended.

We talked with Maude Smith in the pleasant, sunny home on Highway 73 that Clarence built in 1926. It has a three-bay garage which used to be large enough to house all the vehicles needed by the Evergreen Public Service Co. Across the road is the site of the second pumping

station and filtration plant, which was added by Clarence Smith in 1926— a site still owned by Public Service of Colorado.

When Denver created the Evergreen Lake in 1927-9, Smith negotiated to have a new filtration plant built below the dam with new pumping equipment. It was quite a day when the transfer had to be made from the old connecting lines to the new.

Smith also drilled a well to provide the Kittredge area with water.

Colette, one of Maude Smith's daughters, started dating a young man in the military while she was at Colorado College in 1940. His name was Jack Rouse. The two married, and after he got out of the service—and his plans to work for an uncle on Captiva Island in Florida were blown away by a hurricane—the young couple returned to Evergreen where Jack got a job with Clarence Smith. Eventually, Jack Rouse succeeded Clarence as "Mr. Public Service" and became a leader in the community, which valued him almost as much for his humor as for his dedication to Evergreen.

Colorado Central Power Takes Over

In 1953, Clarence Smith died unexpectedly. For the next year, Maude Smith and Jack Rouse continued to run the company. By that time, according to Maude, it was one of only two family-owned utility companies left in Colorado. It was serving a 100-square-mile area with electricity—and a smaller area with water—and had in all about 500 customers. In 1954, the company was sold to Colorado Central Power, with Rouse becoming manager of the Evergreen office.

In order to secure the power franchise, Colorado Central Power had to take over the responsibility for Evergreen's water supply.

The area west of Evergreen was at this time served by R.E.A. for electricity. Between the two service areas was a sort of boundary zone where residents could negotiate for service by either company.

World War II brought many fundamental changes in the character of Evergreen. Beginning in 1949, the first major subdivision planned for year-round residence— Hiwan Hills— was developed in

Maude Smith.

stages. The only utility provided for in the original plans was electricity. Water was to be supplied from individually-drilled wells. Waste water and sewage disposal—like everywhere else in Evergreen at the time—was to be through individual septic tanks and leeching fields.

When many buyers could not get an adequate water supply from wells, the Hiwan Hills developers put in a couple of reservoirs and offered year-round water supply to residents. A tap fee was charged, which was refunded when Colorado Central Power bought out the water system from Hiwan Development Co. in 1957.

Bill Ackerman.

Sewage Problems Prompt Founding of Sanitation District

By the 1940's, Evergreen was in desperate need of the third major utility—sewage disposal. According to Ross Grimes, who has been a consistent supporter of utility development for the community since the early 1950's, raw sewage from septic tanks and leech fields in Douglas Park and Bear Heights was surfacing in fissures and gutters. The two Evergreen schools of the day (the red brick building next to the library and the white concrete building next to that) had a "pretty difficult septic situation", and Main Street businesses, with their "indoor-outdoor" toilets and overworked septic systems, were hardly models of public health.

Under new federal legislation, which permitted unincorporated areas to form special districts, a Sanitation District was voted into existence in 1949. The initial Board members were Jack Rouse, drugstore owner Ed Corbin, Jane Williams and Ward Brown of the Evergreen Hotel on Main Street. It took a couple of elections to get a bond issue passed. The first time around, opponents took it upon themselves to call summer home-owners within the district. Many of these voted against a tax-raising measure from which they could see no personal benefit.

Land for the waste water treatment plant was purchased from Darst Buchanan, owner of the Hiwan Ranch. The first main line ran from the schools, down Main Street and up to Bear Heights. The Ross-Lewis Trust, which owns a large part of Main Street real estate, helped greatly by putting up front-end cash for taps for every lot they owned, including vacant ones.

By 1959, when Hiwan Village—the second Hiwan subdivision—was planned, it was able to advertise itself to a new commuter market as offering *City Living in the Mountains*. Translated, this meant it could offer all three major utilities—water, electric power and sewage disposal. However, the cheapest fuel for year-round heating at that time was natural gas, and this was not yet available in Evergreen. Most homes used propane or butane: owners of bottled gas distribution franchises did a flourishing business.

Enter Public Service Company and Natural Gas

Natural gas came to Evergreen in 1962. In that year, Public Service Company of Colorado finalized its acquisition of Colorado Central Power by merger, and went ahead with plans to bring natural gas to the mountain areas of Idaho Springs and Evergreen. The continuing growth of Evergreen as a commuter community helped to justify the costs of this project.

Proliferation of Sanitation Districts

The nature of the mountain terrain meant that residential growth occurred along separated valleys and stream courses, creating distinct communities with a feeling of separation from other areas. Given the lack of an overall municipal organization, and legal limitations on expansion of existing districts, the rise of many additional sanitation districts (Kittredge, Wah Keeney Park, Bergen Park, North Evergreen, El Pinal, Upper Bear Creek, etc.) was inevitable.

An imaginative Evergreen Sanitation District, under the leadership of Ross Grimes, negotiated for these districts to contract with Evergreen for processing of sewage. This had a two-way advantage: the smaller districts did not have to raise bond money for separate plants of their own, and Evergreen had a more cost-effective operation for its expensive new plant.

This was needed because the treatment plant built in the early 1950's, which used an aerating process according to the best technology of the day, did not work satisfactorily. It is now known that this technology does not operate well above 6,000 feet. Luckily the early 70's was a time of generous federal investment in community "infrastructure," so federal dollars paid for about 80% of the cost of the new plant.

Tennis Games on a Sewer Plant?

The new treatment plant, built on the same site as the old one, was completed in 1974. Unless you look carefully as you drive through the lower end of Evergreen, you will not see it. You will only see two tennis courts. Whoever heard of tennis courts on top of a sewage plant? Nobody, until it was tried in Evergreen.

The notion developed out of an intense dislike for the conventional "dome" roof treatment and a shortage of money. Just as plans for the construction were being finalized, the OPEC-induced energy crisis arose and prices started going up. The project foreman came up with the idea of a flat roof as a money-saver. Ross Grimes and Bill Ackerman, another Board member at the time, measured the potential space. They concluded that if they extended the roof out a bit and made it square, they would have enough room for two tennis courts.

Private money was raised to equip the courts. A private corporation, the SEW-R RACQUET CLUB, pays $1,350 annually to the Evergreen Metro District for a surface lease. Members, of which there were around 40 in 1986, pay an initial $300 and dues of $65.00 per year.

There was some anxious questioning from federal authorities about combining a sewer plant with recreational facilities. When the project was completed, the same authorities started pointing to the courts as an exemplary way to combine different uses in a federally-funded project.

Tennis court on a sewer plant.

The steps at new Post Office.

Fu Hua Chen.

FU HUA CHEN, who designed the structural improvements for strengthening the Evergreen Dam, is the most respected soil engineer in Colorado and internationally known for his expertise in expansive soils. He was born and educated in China, and achieved national recognition there for his work as chief engineer of the famous Burma Road. After the war, Chen taught at universities in Shanghai and in Hongkong while also practicing as an engineer. In 1957, he moved with his wife Edna and their three children to the United States. Chen worked for four years for a Denver consulting firm before opening his own firm of consulting geotechnical engineers in 1961. The Chens live in a striking solar home in Soda Creek.

"Dam" Hysteria

When Public Service Company acquired Colorado Central Power in 1962, it also had to take over Evergreen's water supply. This was the only place where Public Service operated a water system and from the beginning the Company wanted to divest itself of the responsibility. But the Evergreen Sanitation District was reluctant to take on this additional—and major—load.

Catalyst for the change in ownership was an awesome "Act of God"—the Big Thompson flood of 1976—in which 131 people lost their lives. The disaster spotlighted both unpreparedness for disastrous floods in the Colorado mountain areas, and the lack of effective inspection of dams.

In 1976, following recommendations by the Dam Safety Branch of the State Engineer's office, a noted consulting engineering firm performed a safety evaluation of Evergreen Dam for the City & County of Denver. Chen and Associates found that, in spite of three visible cracks in the exposed concrete dam and abutments and some deterioration of the concrete surface, the basic structure was in good condition. However, in the event of water flows of more than 61,000 cubic feet of water per second—established by the State Engineer as those which the dam should be capable of withstanding—the consultants found that water would overtop the spillway by more than 17 feet. Under these conditions, they believed that the backfill behind the abutments would be washed out and the dam would topple.

Initial estimate for the engineering work needed to remedy this situation was around $200,000. The City and County of Denver could be liable, in the event of dam failure, for enormous sums in damages. With the unprecedented inflation of the late 1970's all levels of government were in a financial crunch. Denver did not have a spare $200,000 to repair the dam, and was determined to rid itself of the potential liabilities associated with it. Unless some way could be found for the repair to be financed, Denver announced that it would be forced to drain the lake.

A long and complex series of negotiations ensued. Involved, besides the City and County of Denver, were the Evergreen Sanitation District, the Public Service Co., the Evergreen Recreation District, the Jefferson County Commissioners and Jefferson County Open Space.

When negotiations were concluded, the expanded and renamed Evergreen Metropolitan Water and Sanitation District had acquired the water plant and supply from Public Service Company—and from Denver the responsibility for the Dam and for operation of the Lake and its recreation facilities, as well as its water rights; Jefferson County Open Space (the only one of the many parties that had money already in its coffers) ingeniously bought a 75-year "visual and recreational easement" from the Evergreen Metro Sanitation District for $450,000, which included the

right to manage recreation and other uses for ten acres around the Lake, to operate recreational activities on the Lake, to develop public use trails and to preserve the beauty and functions of the Lake. Open Space in effect turned this contract over to the Evergreen Metropolitan Parks and Recreation District. Denver agreed to contribute up to $50,000 towards the repair of the dam.

Remedy for the potential failure of the dam was to tie it soundly to its foundations with grouted anchors. Eighteen holes were drilled through the abutments and spillway from 28 to 42 feet into the bedrock. Multi-strand tendons were placed in them, which were then grouted and post-tensioned to withstand the required loads. The cost of repair was almost $600,000.

The considerable controversy arising from this expensive repair project was not over the engineering proposals themselves, but about the assumptions for potential flooding that gave rise to them. There was universal agreement that the dam was well-constructed and safe for the flood conditions for which it was designed.

Many people believe that under the "maximum possible flood" conditions imposed by the Corps of Engineers (which from geological evidence have never apparently happened in the Upper Bear Creek basin)—or even half that amount, which was the flood level designated by the State Engineer— disastrous floods would sweep through downtown Evergreen and the areas downstream, even if the dam held. This would partly be due to the sheer volume of water coming over the dam, and partly because of the flooding of Cub Creek and its tributaries. Cub Creek enters Bear Creek just below the dam.

Be that as it may, the dam was strengthened and the control of Evergreen's water supply passed into the hands of a locally-controlled body. Concern and conflict over the possible depletion of underground water table levels, and maintenance of adequate water supplies through the cycles of relative wetness and drought which are characteristic of the mountain areas, entered the local arena. The Evergreen Metropolitan Water and Sanitation District became, in Ross Grimes's words, a "water hog," aggressively buying up water rights as they became available.

The District saw a fundamental difference between the sale of water and the sale of sewage service. The water distribution facilities and water rights have been bought through the sale of revenue bonds. The District is in the business of selling water, and believes from its technical studies that it has ample water to increase its numbers of taps greatly. Furthermore, its present number of water customers is too small for efficient operation. The District does not feel it has an obligation to reserve taps for those inside the District who do not want to hook up at present, since these people are paying nothing towards the cost of water service.

But for sewer service, which is financed by general obligation bonds, the District believes it has a duty to reserve taps to serve all the actual present taxpayers in the District before extending the use of its facilities to those outside.

The District's stand on water taps puts it into conflict with local citizen groups concerned about runaway growth in the Evergreen-Bergen Park area. These groups firmly believe that, whatever figures the District produces, there is a finite number of homes, businesses and industries that can be supported by the limited water supply of a fragile mountain ecological system.

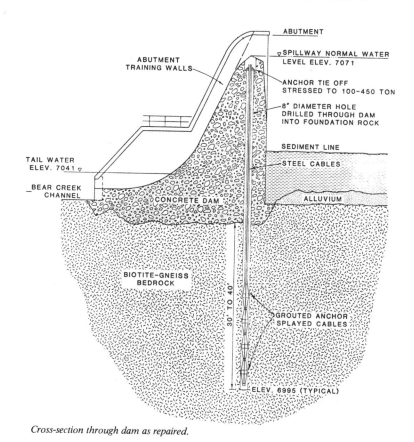

Cross-section through dam as repaired.

Dredging the Lake

The Lake has filled with silt over the years and much of its storage capacity has been lost. But in proposing to dredge it, the District ran into strong opposition from environmentalists, especially the Evergreen Naturalists Audubon Society (TENAS) who were concerned about destruction of existing wetlands around the Lake.

Their anxiety was first aroused in 1980 when the District began dumping fill—including a lot of old asphalt paving material—at the west end of the Lake. By its own admission, the District did not know that this sometimes-muddy, sometimes-dry, apparently "useless" land, did constitute something valuable known as a wetland.

A national policy determination concerning wetlands, which serve as nesting sites for birds and also play a role in flood protection by acting as a kind of sponge to absorb excess water, was included in the federal Clean Water Act. Agencies planning any action which might disturb or displace wetlands were

required to secure a permit from the U.S. Corps of Engineers. The process of applying for the permit involved preparing plans for the future development of the lake, with an exact inventory of existing wetlands and provisions to restore or replace them. The intent to dredge the Lake was announced in 1980. The bright green Mud Cat dredger finally arrived on the scene in April of 1986.

The lake created in 1927 contained 900 acre feet of water: silt had filled in almost 400 of these by the time the Evergreen Metro District took over. Their plans for dredging aimed at removing most of the accumulated 640,000 cubic feet of sediment to provide 880 acre feet of storage.

To prevent further silting of the lake, the plan called for the place where Bear Creek enters the Lake to be widened, deepened, and lined with rocks to catch most of the sediment before water enters the lake. This area could be dredged as frequently as necessary in the future.

The EMD chose the particular method of dredging—by use of a Mud Cat—because it disturbs the water as little as possible. It sucks up sediment from the bottom of the Lake, propels it through floating pipes on the surface and transports it to two successive settling areas at the west end of the Lake. After drying, plans were for the sediment to be separated into topsoil and material suitable for road sanding. Arrangements were made with Denver for a temporary road through Dedisse Park to Highway 74 to truck the dried material away from the Lake. However, the first years's experience was that dredging was slower than expected and trucking away by private concerns was more extensive than expected, so the road might be unnecessary. The operation was expected to take 3 or 4 years.

The dredger itself cost around $110,000: to minimize the impact on boating and fishing, it was decided to operate it only on weekdays (leaving evenings and weekends free) from April to October. Total cost of the operation was estimated at around $900,000, which was included in the Evergreen Metro District's 1983 revenue bond issue.

Besides a great increase in water storage capacity, other dividends from the dredging operation are expected—a better breeding and feeding environment for trout and the return of a clear, blue mountain lake in place of the familiar muddy one.

Gerry Schulte.

GERALD C. SCHULTE, General manager of the Evergreen Metro District. He came to Evergreen in 1977 from Boulder, where he had been in charge of the Waste Water Department for 3 years. In 1977, The Evergreen District was responsible for sewer service only— to around 900 customers. By 1986, the new Metropolitan District was serving approximately 2,000 sanitation customers and 3,200 customers with water. Schulte is also responsible for the operation of the lake dredging program, which will increase storage capacity from 500 to around 900 acre-feet. He supervises a staff of 20, who operate the water and sewer system and maintain the approximately 90 miles each of water and sewer mains. The Evergreen Metro District has a total value of over 11 million dollars, and an operating budget of $1.4 million annually.

Lake Plans

Since Evergreen is not a city, responsibility for decisions about its future fragmented among many different agencies. Perhaps nothing illustrates this as clearly as the almost comical rash of 'Plans for the Lake' that appeared between 1980 and 1985. At least six different plans were offered for public evaluation—by the naturalists group (TENAS), the Evergreen Metropolitan Recreation and Park District (EMRPD), Jefferson County Open Space (JCOS), some private citizens, and landscape architecture students from the University of Colorado at Denver.

Finally, some sensible cooperation between the Evergreen Metro (Water and Sewer) District, the EMRPD, and JCOS produced the most widely accepted plan— developed by the professional planning firm of Denton Harper Marshall. This provides for a trail around the lake, a new warming house and activity center, an amphitheater, boat dock and picnic areas, and new wetlands to replace some of those taken up by recreation facilities.

Existing warming house.

Mudcat dredger on Lake.

Silt dredged from Lake.

Denver's new metal building overlooking lake.

EMD office below dam.

24

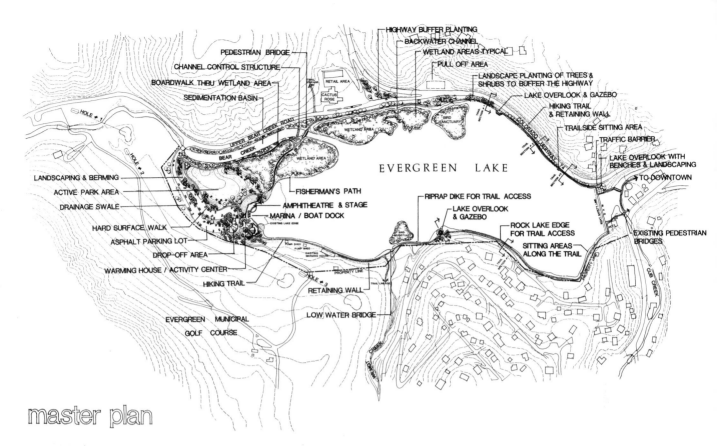

master plan

EVERGREEN LAKE

EVERGREEN METROPOLITAN RECREATION AND PARKS DISTRICT
JEFFERSON COUNTY OPEN SPACE
EVERGREEN METROPOLITIAN DISTRICT

DentonHarperMarshall

SCALE 1":100'-0"

JANUARY 4, 1985

Master Plan for Lake prepared for EMRPD, JCOS and EMD.

The plan was only an overall concept and assumed that there would be detailed, sensitive planning of the individual elements. Before the dredging was even started, however, three unrelated developments emphasized how easily the overall quality of environment around the lake can be spoiled in the absence of effective overall coordination.

- Without consulting any of the agencies involved in direct planning for the lake, the State Highway Department suddenly installed a series of standard street lights—the kind used on busy four-lane highways—along the lake on highway 74.

- Denver, having brought up the quality of the golf course by a large infusion of funds, planted a large metal building on the lovely hill overlooking the lake, and painted it a bilious beige.

- The Recreation District purchased $100,000 worth of metal posts to ram into the lake bed and support a trail alongside the busy, dusty highway. They initially gave little thought to the possibility of creating a cool and pleasant trail at lake level, an arrangement that would not require the residents across the lake to gaze at a rusting metal wall.

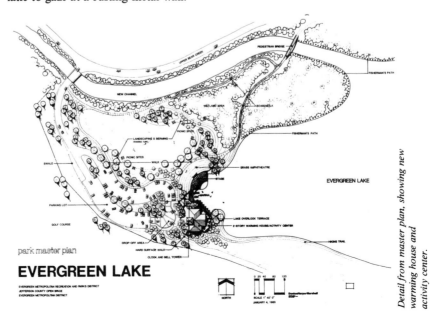

park master plan

EVERGREEN LAKE

EVERGREEN METROPOLITAN RECREATION AND PARKS DISTRICT
JEFFERSON COUNTY OPEN SPACE
EVERGREEN METROPOLITIAN DISTRICT

Detail from master plan, showing new warming house and activity center.

25

Amid Dissension, Evergreen Gets a "Rec" District

You want to learn sailing or kayaking? Scuba dive? Read Tarot cards? Set the body in motion through a Jazzercise, aikido, or aerobics class? Teach your baby to swim, take your kids ice-skating, start them off early on a gymnastics career? Play volleyball, tennis, racquetball, softball, soccer? You can do it all, and much more, through the "Rec. District".

Yet the Evergreen Metropolitan Recreation and Parks District was not born without controversy. The people who worked to create it in the late '60's, including Tom Sjoden, Harriet Strand and Linden Wood, were concerned about the lack of healthy activities for children in Evergreen. Although the population was growing rapidly, there were no recreation facilities except those connected with the schools. No playgrounds or playing fields No indoor spaces in which to exercise, meet or play. Nowhere in the community where kids could learn to swim.

The two old schools on Cub Creek—now the red brick County Building and the Open High School—were soon to be emptied by the opening of the new Junior High School in Bergen Park. It seemed a happy coincidence of need and opportunity.

Two arguments were used against forming a Recreation District: the predictable resistance to any raise in property taxes, and the feeling of many Evergreen residents that 'living in the mountains was recreation enough.'

Among the opponents were many of the town's leaders and Main Street businessmen. Disagreements became bitter at times. The first attempt to get a tax-supported district failed. This was an agreement worked out with the R-1 School District—which was cooperative throughout—for the proposed Recreation District to take over the old school buildings, with the 6-1/2 acres on which they are located, for a recreational center. The emphasis was on young people but programs for adults were also planned, and it was promised that a first priority would be exploring ways to finance the building of a swimming pool.

The proposal needed the approval of the County Commissioners since it involved the creation of a new taxing authority. The opposition managed to convince the Commissioners that the Evergreen community was split on this use of the surplus schools—so the plan was denied.

A totally new program was then worked out with the School District—to build a new recreation center on Evergreen High School grounds, with cooperative funding and joint use of a swimming pool. As the proceedings moved towards a community vote on January 13, 1969, there was intense canvassing of residents by a determined corps of supporters—especially mothers.

Suddenly, a drive to incorporate Evergreen as a municipality was launched. This was seen by recreation district proponents as a deliberate effort to confuse the issue and draw attention away from the forthcoming election.

But the people spoke and the district was formed. Its Board of Directors immediately launched a recreational program in whatever facilities it could obtain. In July of 1970 a $400,000 bond issue was passed to build the center. Denver architect Roland Johnson designed the facility. Rising costs forced a drastic reduction from the original plans: handball courts, saunas, a rifle range and space for the Alpine Rescue Team were eliminated, leaving only the swimming pool, locker rooms, meeting rooms and office space.

By the time the center opened in February of 1973, the bitterness was forgotten: the children of the District's severest opponents lined up, alongside all the others, to jump into the pool.

The facility was used to capacity. In 1976, an addition provided a gymnasium, weight room and racquetball courts. But the population continued to grow, as did a national concern with fitness and exercise.

In 1982 a "Tot Lot"—a well-equipped playground for young children—was carved out of the hillside west of the Center, through the labor and fund-raising efforts of the Blue Spruce Kiwanis.

From the beginning, the District was short of funds. Although its income had always come from a combination of user fees, special grants, donations and taxes, its major revenue source was a property tax levy limited to 4 mills. Since Evergreen has little business and industry, the largely residential tax base provides a rather meager income.

By 1983—the Rec Center's 10th anniversary—there were a few improvements in the financial picture. Jefferson County Open Space was able to make some of its generous funding available to recreation districts. JCOS supplied $453,000 for the second major addition to the Center. Designed by Boulder architects Everett Zeigel Tumpes and Hand, this provided an auxiliary gymnasium, new locker rooms and renovation of some existing space. A small but important share of Colorado's new lottery money was coming to the District. And the District's Board of Directors took to the stump and persuaded voters to raise the mill levy to the new ceiling of 5 mills, authorized by the Legislature.

But the District had also acquired, rather reluctantly, a major new responsibility: operation of the recreation facilities at Evergreen Lake. While adding greatly to the range of activities that could be offered, including boating, fishing and ice-skating, this increased expenses and required additional staff with different skills. It also involved the District heavily in planning for the Lake's future, with the possibility that it might need to build a second recreational center on the shores of the Lake when the dredging process was completed.

The lack of level land for playing fields has plagued the District from the start. Evergreen is an avid softball-playing community, and there has been steadily increasing interest in league soccer playing, especially for younger boys. Fields were used through cooperative agreements at Bergen and Marshdale schools but the need for additional playing areas was still acute. Every possible new site was scrutinized for lease or purchase. Part of the rationale for Open Space acquiring the Alderfer Ranch and surrounding acreage in 1986, was to enable the Recreation District to develop playing fields on a flat portion of the ground.

In 1986, the District made a firm decision to create two fields on the Alderfer property and one on land between the Evergreen High School and Wilmot School.

From the second half of the 1980's the 'Rec District' could look back with satisfaction on more than 15 years of providing a steadily richer program of activities for Evergreen. It looked forward to even more diversified—and more dispersed—opportunities.

Law and Order: Jefferson County Sheriff's Department

It is fortunate for history buffs in Jefferson County that the Sheriff's Department has on its staff a young lieutenant whose avocation is to collect and preserve the history of law and order in this part of the wild west. Lt. Dennis Potter has gathered together personal anecdotes, newspaper reports, official documents and artifacts for what he hopes will one day be both a book and a museum.

Anecdotes of early crimes in the Evergreen area include a particularly gruesome murder in Bergen Park in 1878. Two men asked rancher Reuben Hayward for a ride to Denver. He hitched his horses to his wagon and was seen riding out of town with the two passengers. He was never seen alive again.

Sheriff Harold Bray in Evergreen Rodeo Parade.

New Jefferson County Jail in Golden.

A month later, a culvert near present-day Heritage Square overflowed. Hayward's body was found stuffed into it. After his horses and wagon were sighted in Iowa, the two murderers were brought back to Golden for trial. But incensed citizens formed a midnight necktie party. They seized the prisoners at gunpoint, dragged them down a ravine in back of the jail building and hanged them from a railroad trestle that spanned a deep gulley.

But this was an exception: there was little major crime in the mountain area until the coming of Prohibition in 1919. Moonshiners found here a wealth of inaccessible hideouts where they could manufacture liquor in illegal stills. Some were set up in caves and equipped with elaborate alarm systems. Sheriff's deputies confiscated thousands of gallons of the forbidden stuff. But in Jefferson County, as in the rest of the country, it was a losing battle and the officers were probably relieved when the repeal of Probibition in 1933 allowed them to spend their energies tackling the permanent police problems of communities: burglaries, domestic violence, damage to life and to property.

There is a story to be unearthed about Prohibition days in Evergreen but we only managed to find a few clues from old-timers— about stills in the woods, sales behind today's Little Bear and illicit fortunes stashed away and never recovered.

From the founding of the Sheriff's Department in 1860 until 1986, there were a total of 33 sheriffs. Most served competently and quietly. This was not the case with Evergreen rancher Art Wermuth, who was appointed in 1957 to fill the term of Carl Enlow.

Enlow's own tenure had ended badly and his fate is still a matter of controversy. Dennis Potter credits him with bringing the department into the twentieth century during his 8-year term, by such measures as introducing marked police cars and requiring proper law enforcement training for recruits. In 1956 Enlow and the District Attorney were charged with income tax evasion—for a total of $1,271. Enlow was sentenced to three years at Fort Leavenworth and forced to resign.

Don Stanbro.

Wermuth blazed a five-year trail of colorful publicity stunts before his career too ended in disgrace. A World War II hero who called himself the "One Man Army of Bataan", Wermuth was constantly in the headlines. The well-publicized kidnap-slaying of Golden Brewery owner Adolph Coors III occurred during his tenure: Wermuth created a circus atmosphere during the arrest of the murderer in Canada. After Wermuth's downfall, investigation revealed that he had allowed notorious murderers Arthur Watson and Albert Kostal to escape from prison so that he could make a sensational recapture. Wermuth was finally indicted by a grand jury for embezzlement of county funds and disappeared into anonymity.

Harold Bray, who followed Wermuth in 1962, has the longest tenure of any sheriff since the county was formed. He has presided over a period of enormous growth in the county's population and, consequently, in its number of crimes. During his tenure, the Evergreen substation of the Sheriff's Department was opened: it is now housed in the County Building next to the Library on Highway 73.

"Sheriff's Calls" is a regular and popular feature in the weekly Canyon Courier newspaper. No names are used and only general locations. The pot pourri of incidents—funny, sad, outrageous, crazy—is a pretty fair indicator of the range of "routine" calls received by deputies assigned to the mountain area.

The Evergreen Chamber of Commerce

Evergreen has apparently had a Chamber of Commerce in and out of existence a number of times over the years. It has often served a number of the functions that a municipal government would normally fulfil, as well as being a vehicle to encourage patronage of local business.

The present Chamber came into being in September 1970, when it was incorporated as a private, non-profit association of local businesses. We are grateful to its dedicated Executive Secretary Sharron Leonard for information about its activities.

Current membership is 230 area firms and professionals. Primary goal of the Chamber is the achievement of the community's potential.

Each year, the Chamber selects and honors an Evergreen Person of the Year, a man or woman contributing to the improvement of the town's quality of life. The organization co-sponsored the Evergreen Design Task Force, which offered, without charge, ideas on improving local projects from an aesthetic, economic or overall planning point of view. Over the years, Chamber members have planned numerous community service events such as town meetings, legislative breakfasts and blood drives.

Every summer, the Chamber donates funds for a gala July 4th celebration at Evergreen Lake and assists with promoting other annual events: the Evergreen Rodeo and Parade, Summerfest Faire, the Town Race, Mountain Rendezvous and the Fine Arts Fair. During the Christmas holidays, the Chamber organizes the Evergreen Christmas Tree Lighting Ceremony and a store front decorating contest to encourage community pride. In addition it produces a "Christmas in Evergreen" note card and sponsors such events as Santa's Workshop and the International Gourmet Dinner.

The Chamber funds a visitor's center. Its staff answers inquiries about visiting the area or relocating families to Evergreen. The office also serves as an information and referral point for those seeking local services or planning to locate a business in the area.

To Be Or Not To Be—A City?

From time to time people in Evergreen talk about incorporation. Occasionally, someone gets a bit more serious and calls a meeting, or gets a study going to find out what such a step would involve and how much it would cost. It seems a fair to say that, to date, no-one has taken the idea seriously for any length of time.

As far as we have discovered, there have been only two genuine incorporation attempts. Perhaps only one, for the 1969 effort may have been largely a red herring—as many of those working to create a recreation district believed at the time.

The second flurry of activity arose after a town meeting called in 1977. The real issue at that time was clearly local control of growth; a Local Control Task Force was formed. It found that most necessary services are satisfactorily provided through special districts (fire, ambulance, recreation, water, sanitation) or through the county (roads, police protection, libraries, public health).

The gaping hole was that all power to affect the size, density and visual character of the rapidly growing community was concentrated in the hands of the three elected County Commissioners at the courthouse in Golden, with the advice of a county-wide 7-member Planning Commission, appointed by the County Commissioners. Those same three overworked County Commissioners were responsible for everything else that happened in a large, growing county—most of which was still unincorporated.

All available methods of controlling growth without becoming incorporated were examined, including the possibility of becoming a local planning district, but none offered real power—only advisory status.

What happened next was like a satire on bureaucracy. The Task Force asked the County Planning Department for help in conducting a study to determine the advantages and disadvantages of incorporation. With County sponsorsip, they applied for a federal grant under the Comprehensive Employment and Training Act (CETA) to hire planners for an eight-month study.

The study was begun in the County Planning Department, using CETA

funds, in January of 1978. There were articles on three possible scenarios—dubbed Papa Bear, Mama Bear and Baby Bear—for incorporated areas of different sizes. September arrived, the CETA grant ran out, the study languished. Thanks largely to the dedication of one member of the planning staff, Peter Murphy, the study struggled along for a couple of years. Then a firm of outside consultants was hired to complete it and prepare a report.

This presented four alternatives— Baby Bear disappeared, there were two Mamas and two Papas—each with different areas and potential costs to citizens. The report was finally available in the fall of 1982.

"Who Cares?" was the headline in the Canyon Courier for October 29, 1982. Peter Murphy told a reporter that she had "gotten zippo calls" since news about the finished study had been released. As it turned out, nobody did care. Four and a half years was too long to sustain Evergreen's interest and this effort to incorporate was dead.

The Canyon Courier has been a consistent supporter of incorporation for Evergreen, as the only means of asserting local control. Editorially, it urged early in 1987 that renewed consideration of incorporation be the main focus of a new organization called the Coalition for the Evergreen Mountain Area.

This grew out of a committee organized in 1986 by the Evergreen Center for the Arts, which had come to a dead end in attempting to find a site and funding for a performing arts center. Part of the group expanded its horizons to look into major problems facing Evergreen. Under the chairmanship of Flodie Anderson, the organization selected three areas for study (in addition to the ongoing search for bring an arts facility into being): plans for Evergreen Lake, use and management of public lands, and a continued search for a solution to problems of moving traffic through Evergreen.

One factor in the reluctance of Evergreen citizens to vote themselves into the hard work and expense of sustaining a city government has undoubtedly been that, on the whole, the Jefferson County Commissioners have been a pretty acceptable "local government."

By the very numbers of population, direct representation from the mountains—on any level of government—is rare. Indeed, 1986 was a most unusual year in which the Evergreen area had a County Commissioner (Don Stanbro), a state legislator (House member Tony Grampsas), and even a national candidate for President (Gary Hart) in part-time residence on Troublesome Gulch.

The numbers of Jefferson County Commissioners elected from Evergreen have been few (from 1861 to 1987, as far as we could tell, there were altogether five: Bergen and Wilmot in the last century, Maurice Bauer in the late 50's, Jim Martin elected in 1978 and Stanbro in 1982.) But "flatland" Commissioners—like Bunny Clement and Rich Ferdinandsen in recent years—have valued the distinctive quality of the mountain areas of the county. They have made real efforts to get to know the Evergreen community and to act in its best interests.

Bunny Clement.

Rich Ferdinandsen.

John Stone, elected County Commissioner in 1987, to replace Don Stanbro.

Jim Martin.

JAMES E. MARTIN *moved to Evergreen in 1971. He lives on Upper Bear Creek, where you can often see him in summer manicuring a spacious lawn through which the stream runs. An independent soul, Jim was elected County Commissioner in 1978 and served one four-year term. He had a genuine desire to make government serve and facilitate rather than dictate and control. Warm, friendly and outspoken, Jim does not take himself too seriously. While Commissioner he generated lots of support and also vehement opposition for some of his stands, but he was always accessible.*

Rep. Tony Grampsas.

Maurice Bauer.

A 1927 Plan for Evergreen
The first known plan for Evergreen was an outgrowth of Denver's involvement with the community. Denver Mayor Robert Speer's choice for City Planner and Landcape Architect was a slight, soft-spoken Dutchman named Saco Rienk DeBoer. The planning and planting of the city's major parkways and boulevards—including Speer Boulevard—and of ambitious parks like City Park, were only part of DeBoer's responsibilities. He was also heavily involved in the creation of the mountain park system—in which, surprisingly, Denver did quite a bit of landscaping, especially tree-planting.

DeBoer became concerned that the building of an extensive network of roads into the mountain parks would stimulate increased development, and that the resulting influx of people would destroy the mountain character of communities like Evergreen.

In 1927, he made some sketches and studies of how he thought Evergreen should develop—including a Main Street of chalet-like wooden buildings with open plazas and landscaped squares. He saw Bear Creek opened up to public enjoyment through a pleasant walkway along banks walled with native stone.

29

Like so many of the cast of early characters in our Evergreen drama, DeBoer came west looking for a cure from tuberculosis. Born in Friesland in 1883, he went to university to study engineering. But his studies were continually interrupted by outbreaks of lung disease. While convalescing at home, he studied landscape architecture and opened his own landscaping office. Finally, a severe bout of sickness, with profuse bleeding from the lungs, spurred his loving family to ship him off to a distant relative in New Mexico.

DeBoer came to Denver in 1910 and worked for a while in the city nurseries before Speer singled him out. Together ("planner and planter", as one writer characterized them) they "changed the city from a treeless plain spotted with clumps of broadleaf cottonwood, fringes of willows along the creeks, a few box elders and lanceleaf cottonwoods, into a great green city." DeBoer was always experimenting with the introduction of new species of trees to Denver: by 1933, there were 103 sucessfully growing there.

After Speer's death, DeBoer opened a private firm offering services in planning and landscape architecture, in partnership with another young Dutchman, Walter Pesman. He continued to be the City's landscape and parks consultant until 1958.

One charming mountain legacy of the DeBoer-Pesman firm is the layout of the Gates estate on Bear Creek, below Kittredge. This project for "Chateau Gates" was commissioned by Charles Gates in 1920.

DeBoer was active in city planning and landscape projects until his death, at the age of 90, in 1974.

The Evergreen Area Community Plan: 1984-6
In the early 80's, the Jefferson County Commissioners adopted a new strategy to deal with conflicts over growth in unincorporated areas. In selected communities, they invited applications from all interested citizens who wished to serve on a local community advisory committee, and then appointed what they considered a representative sample of these. The group's assignment was to come up with a community plan, consistent with the overall general land use plan being developed for the county.

Evergreen was the second community to be involved in such a planning affort, and Conifer the third.

The Committee had the technical resources of the County Planning Department at their disposal and were expected to get the input of all interested groups and individuals in the community. The Commissioners made a commitment to be guided in future decisions by the local policy plan.

About 100 individuals were nominated by various interest groups and organizations for the Evergreen planning group. Of these, 18 were selected: Hank Alderfer, John Bohling, Jay Bright, Paul Cockrel, Jane Dahlstrom-Quinn, Keith Dunbar, Sharon Faircloth, Robert Gottsman, Jean Jacobus, Bill Marshall, William Matthews, Marc Musyl, Marilyn Sandifer, Pat Sayward, Rick Vancil and Anne Willhardt.

The group started work in the fall of 1984. Meetings were open to the public: thanks to the inclusion of community wits like Marilyn Sandifer and Willy Matthews, these were serious but not solemn. The group tackled controversial issues of water supply, wildlife habitat, restrictions on new commercial enterprise, guidelines for housing density and preservation of valued open lands.

The committee members dedicated a tremendous amount of time to the process—finding out what the situation was at the time, what would happen if all that was zoned for various types of development actually got built, what powers existed to guide, control or probibit growth. They explored what policies might satisfy competing community interests— naturalists versus developers, design-oriented citizens versus struggling local business owners, rugged individualists ("I came to the mountains so I could get away from government red tape and do exactly what I wanted to on my own piece of land") pitted against those who believed that people who are priveleged to live in the mountains should be required to put the natural environment first (if they cannot accept inconvenience as the price of living with nature they should go live in the suburbs, where they can demand that all services be right next door).

The resulting Evergreen Area Community Plan, modified by community feedback and hearings before the Planning Commission and the County Commissioners, was finally adopted on July 2, 1986. The Plan's main features were:

1. That it came with an accompanying set of Design Guidelines, the first plan in the county to incorporate considerations of design of site layouts and of buildings, as a legitimate matter for decision-making about new developments. The guidelines were couched in terms of encouragement of good design—by giving bonuses of higher density to well-designed projects rather than penalties for poor performance.

2. Six "activity centers" were delineated: El Rancho, Bergen Park, North Evergreen—on both sides of Highway 74 north of Dedisse Park—the Main Street area, Kittredge, Marshdale.

In general, permitted developments in these areas were to create a "village-like atmosphere" and to "encourage site orientation which respects the topography and the environment rather than only responding to highway or frontage road exposure." New projects were to be designed to relate to neighboring ones and to encourage common approaches to traffic, pedestrian circulation and landscaping.

This was an attempt to prevent any more development like the chopped-up and uncoordinated existing strip along Highway 74— from the Public Service Company area to the Senior Citizens apartments—with its visual ugliness and dangerous traffic patterns. The most intense land use should be in the center of the activity areas, with density decreasing towards the edges, which should blend in with the much lower densities of surrounding areas.

3. Outside the activity centers development was to be largely restricted to housing, with density specified on the basis of availablility of water and sewer, need for preserving wildlife habitats, and difficult soil and slope conditions.

S. R. De Boer's 1927 plan for downtown Evergreen.

2. A formal design review process. But design review can only be as creative as the people doing the reviewing. Like most city and county governments, Jefferson County has not been in the habit of hiring people with creative talent and years of experience in physical design for its zoning, planning or building departments.

3. Enhanced coordination between citizens, developers and the County. There are deep divisions between some citizens and some developers: these are matters of values. No mere talking will make them go away. If there were local responsibility, as in a city, citizens would have a forum for battling these out. Opponents of development would have to face the issues of maintaining and strengthening the tax base: proponents would have to consider how to enhance the values that make people want to visit and to live in Evergreen. But Commissioners are elected on county-wide issues and mountain area voters are only a small minority.

4. Down zoning and lot mergers. To change the zoning of a piece of land, for a less intensive use than is already permitted, requires compensation—unless it can be a matter of voluntary agreement. The County has no funds for compensation. It seems unlikely that the planning staff will have the time, energy or knowledge of the community to undertake successful negotiations. If a panel of community- minded and capable local residents, with no axe to grind, were given some support and power to negotiate on behalf of the County, there might be some interesting outcomes.

4. The Plan recommended more cooperation between the owners of existing open space in the Evergreen area—Denver Mountain Parks, Jefferson County Open Space, Arapahoe National Forest, Bureau of Land Management, State of Colorado which owns the Wildlife Management Area, etc.—and the connecting of existing open space, subject to conservation of wildlife habitat, through a trails system. Trails should also link different areas of the community together and take full advantage of the views along the way.

Acquisition of 10 additional specific parcels of land by Jefferson County Open Space was recommended. One of these was the Alderfer Ranch, which was acquired in 1986. It was also recommended that many strategic ranches in the community —such as the Schneider and Fleming ones on Blue Creek Road and the Broce Pony Ranch— should be preserved, with their owners being encouraged to continue agricultural use through a variety of tax and legal incentives.

5. The Plan identified specific historic structures, scenic vistas, ridges, waterways and areas of unique vegetation and made recommendations on how to enhance and preserve them.

The biggest hurdle between the good intentions of the Plan and its being put into effect was exactly the same one that prompted the 1978 move towards incorporation: the issue of how to get some real decision-making power at the local community level.

The authors of the Plan recommended four methods of carrying out their recommendations. There were difficulties with all of these.

1. Creation of a local Evergreen-area planning commission. Under the structure of County government, which places the power to make final decisions in the hands of the elected County Commissioners, the commission could only be advisory—to the County Planning Commission—which in turn is advisory to the County Commissioners. Neither the Planning Commission nor the County Commissioners favored the additional commission. They recommended instead a voluntary organization similar to the Evergreen Design Task Force, which for about 8 years reviewed projects proposed for the Evergreen area, worked with developers on areas of disagreement, and made recommendations to the Planning Commission.

Jefferson County Planning Commission, 1987. Front row (l. to r.): Vickie Agler, Sherry Weinstein, Bunny Malm. Back row: Sandy Peddycoart (Exec. Sec.), Dave Peterson, Dave Krapes, Rick Nelson, Mike M'Gillycuddy, Gene Sternberg.

Evergreen Area Community Plan
Summary Land Use

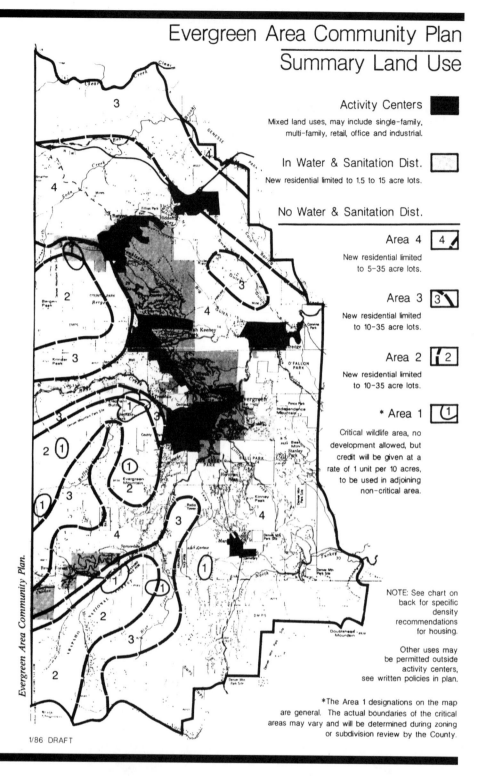

Activity Centers ▮

Mixed land uses, may include single-family, multi-family, retail, office and industrial.

In Water & Sanitation Dist. ▢

New residential limited to 1.5 to 15 acre lots.

No Water & Sanitation Dist.

Area 4 [4/]

New residential limited to 5-35 acre lots.

Area 3 [3\]

New residential limited to 10-35 acre lots.

Area 2 [/2]

New residential limited to 10-35 acre lots.

* Area 1 [(1]

Critical wildlife area, no development allowed, but credit will be given at a rate of 1 unit per 10 acres, to be used in adjoining non-critical area.

NOTE: See chart on back for specific density recommendations for housing.

Other uses may be permitted outside activity centers, see written policies in plan.

*The Area 1 designations on the map are general. The actual boundaries of the critical areas may vary and will be determined during zoning or subdivision review by the County.

1/86 DRAFT

Evergreen Area Community Plan.

Evergreen, several years ago, was a charming little mountain village producing native lumber and timbers and serving the farms and ranches that are tucked away in the beautiful valleys and canyons surrounding it **as a market** *for their produce and the needs of daily life.*

Surrounded by every gift and **blessing which** *nature could bestow; a summer climate almost unparalled in all the world; mountains, meadows and valleys through* **which coursed the clear water of streams** *from the everlasting snows of the Eternal Rockies just beyond; the big Pines on every hand rising toward the skies from hillsides carpeted with fragrant grasses and myriads of native flowers of a thousand tints and colors; with Mount Evans and the high range of the Rockies well inside the horizon, Evergreen awaited only the touch of elementary development to become the Paradise of the Eastern Slope of the Rockies and to face a nearby future as the Playground of Denver's Mountain Park System.'*

Far-seeing men of Denver and of the state at large visioned this need and with faith and energy, built the magnificent "loop" auto boulevard through the Bear Creek canyon, returning to Denver over Mount Lookout; **some 63 miles of the finest mountain road,** *through a scenic paradise, ever constructed in the world; and created the system of some ten mountain parks — open, free and without cost to all comers — which will remain for all time a monument of the civic worth of those who conceived the thought and carried it to a magnificent realization, with Evergreen as the hub. The main highways (25 feet wide) leading from Denver* **to Morrison or Golden, are built of** *concrete. From Morrison or Golden to Evergeeen they are surfaced with crushed granite, thus assuring perfect road conditions at all times.*

From a pamphlet in the Western History Collection of the Denver Public Library, apparrently published by the Evergreen Chamber of Commerce around 1927.

The irony of this whole investment of time and energy in a planning process was that it got started in an atmosphere of fear—and expectation—of continued rapid growth. By the time it was completed, half the houses in Evergreen had "For Sale" signs on them and many of the proposed commercial developments— for which zoning had been won in the face of bitter community opposition—were still open meadows and pine trees.

The Evergreen Library invested in a supply of books on job-hunting, career-changing and writing successful resumes.

Like most of Colorado in 1986, Evergreen was over-built and under-employed. Two-rapid growth was no longer its major problem. Possibly, though, the breathing space would be used for digesting the lessons of the twenty years of boom.

THE GIFTS OF NATURE: EVERGREEN'S YEAR OF MANY BEAUTIES

Why We are Here

Like many others in Evergreen, we lived first on 'the flatlands.' We came to appreciate the beauty of treeless plains and magnificent sunsets. Twice we planted trees, flowers and grass on prickly, inhospitable sites and nurtured them into gardens for a growing family. We appreciated that spring came earlier than in Evergreen, autumn much later, and that summers were long enough to ripen corn and tomatoes.

But we always knew that, for us, there was no comparison between living on the plains and living in the mountains. As soon as changing circumstances allowed, we chose the mountains with their gifts— abundant trees and streams; surprises of view round every corner; the four distinct seasons. A wonderful variety of natural sights, sounds and smells surrounds us here.

Before highlighting the beauties of each season, we say a word or two about the basic conditions of the place we live in.

The Rocks in 'Them Thar Hills': Evergreen Geology

Evergreen is ancient. Not the town—the rocks. Mount Evans is even older, its age estimated at 1700 million years.

This entire area was, millions of years ago, covered by shallow seas. Layers of sediment, thousands of feet deep, were laid down. Along the Front Range these layers— which still lie undisturbed in the Denver basin—were uplifted. Mount Evans was created earlier through a gradual, localized uplift. Its surface, once at sea level, was raised even higher than the present 14,000 feet; originally it had several thousand feet of sedimentary rocks on top.

The rocks we see in Evergreen today are pre-Cambrian 'basement' rocks that were broken and pushed up from below, with the more flexible sedimentary rocks arched over them. Most of the sedimentary layers have been stripped away by erosion leaving only the roots of the mountain range—the gneisses, granites and schists of the core. The broken, banded, faulted, tortured rocks that we see in the road cuts along Bear Creek are vivid testimony to the transforming effects of time, pressure and temperature.

Even as they were rising, the mountains were being torn down by the forces of erosion. Each year, spring rains and melting winter snows washed away accumulated soil and loose rocks, some newly shattered by winter frosts. When mountains were newer and higher the streams had greater speed and cutting power. Ridges and hills are areas of harder, less broken, rocks.

High on Mt. Evans are the marks of ancient glaciers, 'cirques' plucked and gouged out of the rock. Today they form the sites of lakes like Summit Lake, the source of Bear Creek. In the Evergreen area, lower on the mountain, the flowing of streams has carved out vee-shaped valleys.

The Weather

Evergreen is part of the Front Range weather system which means it has a climate of plentiful sunshine, crisp air and low humidity. From its first "discovery" by mountain men and miners in the middle of the last century this climate has drawn ever-increasing numbers of residents—and literally millions of tourists—to our part of Colorado. Along with generally pleasant and sunny conditions, there is enough rain in the summer and snow in the winter to soften the overall dryness. Annual precipitation here averages around 20 inches and annual snowfall around 90.

Evergreen's hours of daylight vary from around 15 in midsummer to 9 in midwinter. The weather is dramatic and changeable from day to day—sometimes from hour to hour.

The Front Range climate is largely governed by the movement of air— the 'jet stream'—at high altitudes over Colorado. In winter the region is at the mercy of westerly winds, which usher wave after wave of Pacific cold fronts through the state. These bring with them the snow, for which ski areas give thanks. In summer, the westerly winds usually move far to the north, leaving a more equable climate.

The mountains create local daily wind patterns. On a summer day the air over the peaks heats up and rises; a pleasant breeze is felt as air to replace it is drawn up the valleys. In the evening the process is reversed. Air on mountain tops cools first, becomes denser, and is pulled down the valleys by the force of gravity. The coldest air falls to the lowest altitudes. This explains why we who live on the banks of Bear Creek can have a frost that kills our African marigolds, while gardens a few hundred feet higher up may go on blooming for days or even weeks longer.

There are two particular winter weather conditions that can make Evergreen more pleasant than the plains. The first is a type of temperature inversion that traps a layer of increasingly polluted air over Denver, while Evergreen may be basking in clear air and smiling sunshine.

Then sometimes, in the dead of winter, the Denver area will be enveloped by a shallow mass of arctic air that spreads southwards across the entire plains. It can just sit there for days on end, miring the plains in damp, bone- chilling below zero temperatures. Mountain areas—only a couple of thousand feet higher up—can be temperate and pleasant.

Getting to Know "Our Evergreen World": The Brockner Contribution.

Part of the privilege of living in Evergreen is Sylvia Brockner's Canyon Courier column, with its weekly interpretation of what is going on in the natural world around us. Though she is not an Evergreen native, her lifelong curiosity about the natural environment and her delightful writing style make her a unique community asset.

If you notice an unusual flower in the woods or spot a new bird at your feeder, chances are you will find a description of it in her column that week. She answers your questions almost before you ask. When did the first bluebirds arrive in Evergreen this year? How to deal with a red-shafted flicker's single-minded determination to carve her nest out of your home?

What is that curious maze of raised tunnels that used to be a lawn? How do you tell a lodgepole from a ponderosa or a spruce from a fir? What is the right formula to feed humming birds, and when should you stop the free lunch? Where can you go to hear the awesome sounds of bugling elk? Sylvia can find a living universe on a single rock in Bell Park, or distil the wonders of the vast tundra on Mount Evans into a half-page of memorable words.

Sylvia Brockner.

Bill Brockner.

If there are "indispensable people" in the life of a community, this couple belongs in that category for Evergreen. They are Mr. and Mrs. Naturalist here. They not only enjoy and know about the natural environment, but consistently put their own energies into preserving it and helping others to know it better. Together they founded the Evergreen Naturalists in 1968, later the Evergreen Naturalists Audubon Society, which has become a respected voice for conservation. Natives of New York State, the Brockners were active naturalists there before coming to Evergreen in 1965. Sylvia Brockner was instrumental in acquiring two nature preserves in western New York State. She worked for 25 years at the Buffalo Museum of Science and served one year as Education Director for the Nashville Children's Museum. She is a licensed bird bander, an activity that helps map bird migrations and gather other valuable information. She writes an award-winning weekly nature column for the Canyon Courier, selected articles from which have been published as "Birds in Our Evergreen World". Bill Brockner is now retired from General Motors and free to indulge his hobby of "chasing birds". By this description, he belies the seriousness of his dedication to ornithology: he is one of only 17 people in the country (and only 2 in Colorado) to identify and record 700 bird species on the North American continent. Bill was a founder of the New York State Federation of Bird Clubs and is a life member of the American Ornithologists Union. As his civic outlet in Evergreen he is active in, and Past President of, the Evergreen Kiwanis.

The Year in Nature: Experiencing Evergreen Month by Month. **January** and February are the months when least is going on in the outdoors, the time of dormancy. Normally they are our coldest months. But since Colorado weather is so fickle, January sometimes has a spell of warm, spring-like days, the gift of a chinook wind. The chinook—an Indian word for 'snow-eater'—is a dry warm wind that blows down the Eastern slope of the Rockies and can produce a dramatic rise in temperature in a few hours. A good time to take an invigorating walk in Means Meadow or round Evergreen Lake, enjoying the delicate winter landscape of browns, silvers and greys and noticing the intricate seedheads of grasses and flowers—the skeletal finery of shrubs and deciduous trees against their background of rocks and evergreens.

If you have not yet joined the ranks of those who feed birds, January is a good month to start. It is the time of greatest need, especially in those years when the weather cycle brings heavy snowstorms and blizzards. There is an unwritten rule that if you start, you must continue the feeding until the cold weather is over. It is cruel to build up a dependency and then withdraw the nourishment. Your reward is to become familiar with the winter birds of Evergreen—a limited number of species.

Most numerous will be the cheerful flocks of juncos. Three of the types to be seen most often at feeders and in bird books—the Oregon, slate-colored and white-winged—all interbreed, so are now known collectively as northern juncos. The indomitable little chickadees— black-capped and mountain —will be regular patrons, as will nuthatches; at our feeder we see mostly the pygmy and white-breasted varieties. You will also have sturdy-beaked, crimson and brown finches, and when you can distinguish the Cassins' variety from the house finch, you're making progress in your birding skills. Depending on location, you may be lucky enough to have splendid evening grosbeaks patronize your lunch station and there will almost certainly be increasing numbers of hungry little pine siskins.

To us, the stars of the winter parade are the raucous, greedy, beautiful Steller's Jays with their brilliant blue plumage, crested heads, and black bandit eye masks. When they loudly announce their arrival most smaller birds move out of the way. If your menu includes suet, cheese and meat scraps, you will probably also attract magpies.

Many people are prejudiced against these strikingly handsome black, white and blue birds because they are carrion eaters, often seen tearing at the carcasses of chipmunks or squirrels killed on the roads. So it's good to remember that magpies also eat many insect pests in the summer, especially the grasshoppers that in some years become a real plague in the mountains.

One year we made the mistake of hanging our suet feeder on the branch of a young aspen tree. The wounds carved in the bark by clawing feet of magpies, jays, flickers and woodpeckers caused the poor tree to bleed sap all the next summer and die the following year. Better to hang the suet from a pole, or the branches of an indestructible ponderosa.

Above 8,000 feet, or even below in hard winters, you may have the mixed blessing of Clark's Nutcrackers at your feeder—those aggressive grey, black and white birds that many people come to define as pests, because they seem to have insatiable appetites and keep quieter species from feeding.

Each family that feeds birds has to decide how generously to provide for the other customers that will come to share the free lunch. Over the years, we have had raccoons, a beautiful grayish red fox, chipmunks, what seemed like hundreds of ground squirrels, black tufty-eared Abert's squirrels, an occasional fat "Denver" squirrel and ravens and crows. There are ingenious bird feeders for sale that keep most of these at bay.

February: If you live, as we do, in a part of Evergreen where elk look for winter food, you will find their fresh droppings in the yard—and perhaps catch a glimpse of them at dusk or dawn. Some of the best places to see part of the 1000-head Mount Evans elk herd at this time of year are in Elk (Means) and Noble Meadows and the open lands along Stage Coach Boulevard.

The number and intensity of snowstorms in an Evergreen winter depend on the frequency of 'upslope' conditions. Sometimes as a cold front passes through the region, an area of low pressure

develops near the Colorado-New Mexico border. The resulting counterclockwise flow of air picks up moisture from the Gulf of Mexico and pulls it in a giant sweep towards the eastern slope of the Front Range. As the moisture-filled air reaches higher elevations, it condenses into clouds— which can produce impressive amounts of snow. If this low pressure area moves very slowly, the heavy snow may last for several days.

When we first came to Colorado we declared that 'Springtime in the Rockies' was a fraud. Until June, we said, it's summer for a day or two, then back to winter for a week. Nothing in between. True, an Evergreen spring is not like England or the eastern United States. But life does return in stages to the mountains. As you learn where to look and what to watch for, your spirits lift even if the snowstorms keep coming. That wonderful annual miracle of renewal starts at the end of February.

Depending on the weather, the first white Townsendia, or Easter, daisies may appear on south-facing slopes around the third or fourth week of February. These bright circles of stemless daisies grow close to the earth and seem to come through successive snowstorms unscathed.

But the truest herald of spring, particularly for those who were brought up on the magic of Maeterlinck's fairy tale, is the mountain bluebird. The first arrival of these favorite, and diminishing, migrants is usually reported around February 21st. In the 1950's, when we used to visit our Blue Creek cabin in late February or March, we sometimes would be lucky enough to see large flocks of these wonderful, gentle birds. The males are a total, unbelievably vivid, blue; the females a softer blue and beige-gray.

We haven't seen a flock for many years, but a pair nests in the meadow near our home each spring and we catch an occasional wonderful flash of blue flying from fencepost to fencepost as we drive along Stage Coach Boulevard.

Some years ago, the Evergreen Naturalists Audubon Society (TENAS) became concerned that nesting sites for bluebirds were rapidly disappearing. The birds do not have strong beaks and cannot excavate nests for themselves. They

used to make homes in old wooden fence posts, dead trees, and naturally-occurring cavities in barns and farm buildings. With the popularity of metal fences, the cutting down of most dead timber and the disappearance of ranches, the bluebird housing shortage became acute. Add to this the increasing numbers of English sparrows and starlings on the Evergreen scene—agressive competitors for nesting cavities— and you will understand why TENAS determined to take action. Each year they build and sell bluebird nest boxes to the public. They also have installed, and maintain, a chain of nest boxes in Elk (Means) Meadow because, as Sylvia Brockner noted in one of her columns, "We might be able to live in a world without bluebirds, but I, for one, would not want to."

Near the end of February in most years, the first robins return to claim their nesting territories, and the welcome 'dawn chorus' of birdsong begins. Each day the sun's rays become a little warmer, and on a mild February day your resident hibernating chipmunk or golden-mantled ground squirrel may put in an appearance.

Though it is many weeks before leaves, or even catkins, will appear, there is a visible brightening of the yellow willow branches along streams. You don't have to go far to see them. The trees along Cub Creek, on Highway 73 from Main Street to the Brook Forest Road, are a glory at this time. As sap rises in aspens and willows, the buds begin to swell and the trees look noticeably thicker.

March: Coloradoans enjoy telling newcomers about their state's mercurial temperament: "You don't like the weather? Wait a few minutes and it will change!" March is the most paradoxical of all months. It is snowy and sunny, windy and balmy, cold and summery. Usually, it is the wettest month of the year. March is the month when spring officially arrives, and it is the time when the visible evidence multiplies almost daily for those who have eyes to see, ears to hear and noses to smell.

Delicate white candytuft and spring beauty come into bloom. Even the vivid yellow of an early dandelion is a welcome sight, especially if it is not on your own lawn. In warmer years, delicate purple pasque flowers, with their sunny yellow

Evergreen Lake. Ron Ruhoff.

centers, bloom in mountain meadows towards the end of the month.

New species of migrant birds join the growing numbers of bluebirds and robins. For us, there is one magical morning in March when we wake to the repeated low liquid trills that announce the return of the redwing blackbirds to their nests in the willows along Bear Creek. They are, too soon, joined by the noisy, gregarious black grackles that have grown steadily in numbers since we moved here in 1972. The melodies of mourning doves and song sparrows join the dawn chorus, along with the trilling, warbling and twittering of finches, pine siskins and juncos.

Except for unusually cold years, March is also the month those wonderful smells—of damp earth, of last year's winey aspen leaves and of aromatic evergreens—return to the outdoors. The ice starts melting on Evergreen Lake as well as on streams and in the earth itself. As watery spaces appear on the lake's surface, the first migrant water birds make stopovers to feed, while others return to their nesting territories there.

By **April** not even the most unobservant can fail to notice that spring has sprung in Evergreen. This is the month when those combative, jewel-like 'hummers' return. People with good hearing know from the distinctive high-pitched whirring of tiny wings that the green and ruby broad-tailed hummingbirds are back in town. Despite continued intermittent snowstorms, it is likely that the first rain will fall before April is through, and you may even hear the unmistakably summery sound of thunder.

From April 15 to June 1 comes the fullest flood-tide of migrating birds. Evergreen is not Capistrano, but there is a happy day when we wake up and see the graceful, swooping flight pattern of swallows outside our bedroom window. Two species, the tree swallow and the barn swallow, make their summer homes along our stream. Williamson's sapsuckers return to the willows. Turkey vultures appear in the skies over Bear Mountain and other rocky slopes where they nest.

But perhaps the most visible sign of a world coming back to life is catkins. Aspen, willow, alder, birch and oak all bear catkins. Probably most people have a favorite spot where they can count on seeing their first silvery aspen catkins: ours is a triangle of land on the turn from Witter Gulch to Greystone Boulevard. The catkins there bloom a full two weeks ahead of the ones in our own yard. The familiar pussy-willow-like catkins are on males trees: they open to shower golden pollen, then shrivel and drop from the trees. Trees with greenish catkins are female. If pollinated, they remain on the trees while seeds mature.

The mountain alder, which grows in damp places and along streams, bears male and female catkins on the same tree: the female looks like a small, hard cone, while the male has a more familiar drooping appearance. Another water-loving tree, the western red river birch with its colorful purplish-red shiny bark, also has beautiful catkins. But the most-loved of all are the 'ordinary' pussy-willows.

If spring seems too long delayed, we have the advantage of being able to enjoy it down on the plains—just 30

Fishing at Evergreen Lake. Ron Ruhoff.

minutes away. When we have savored Denver's spring flowers and lilacs, followed by our own 'show' three weeks later, we can always take a 20-minute drive—in another couple of weeks— to enjoy the display yet again in Idaho Springs or Georgetown.

The Pro's and Con's of **May:** In Evergreen as in Camelot, May is a magic month. One year Barbara and good neighbor Elaine Carlson decided to identify each flower as it came out on Upper Bear Creek. The area provides the four most common Evergreen environments for flowers—along a stream; on rocky, dry, south-facing hillsides; in open meadows; among secretive, shady evergreen forests on north-facing slopes. The two managed to get through April in pretty good shape, but halfway through May, the project defeated them. The flowers were just too many. Listing and labelling was abandoned in favor of appreciation and enjoyment.

Remnants of winter often persist into May in the form of wet, heavy snows. But the sounds of summer— lightning and thunder—are also heard more frequently, harbingers of warmer days to come.

The tide of migrating birds swells. Feeders are rapidly emptied by a large and varied throng. If your garden seems suddenly filled with cascading showers of tuneful song, it is probably a pair of house wrens setting up housekeeping. They seem to thrive on nesting dangerously. For two successive years, a pair chose a two-inch ledge above our kitchen window as the best of all possible places to rear their family.

While the early morning chorus of bird song gets more and more volume, there is another 'chorus' coming from ponds and swampy places. For years in May we would walk across the couple of acres that separated us from an intriguing, definitely frog-like, sound. As we came near, the sounds stopped. If we sat down quietly they started again, but we were never able to see the source of these exuberant noises that seemed to come from everywhere and nowhere. The explanation came in one of Brockner's columns: the sound is not coming from any 'normal-sized' frogs, but from boreal chorus frogs, "tiny midgets, no larger than my thumb."

Sprinkled over rocky south-facing hillsides, the white of sandlilies complements the bright magenta of the mountain ball cactus flowers. Among the profusion of May flowers, most noticeable are the small, narrow-leaved chiming bells (mertensia), yellow cinquefoil, golden banner, whisk broom parsley and masses of snowball saxifrage.

May has its dark side. First, May and June are 'tick' months in this part of the mountains. Although there is in fact a very small rate of infection from wood ticks, it is best to take precautions when walking in the woods, by wearing clothing that protects the skin and by examining yourself and your children for ticks when you get home. Luckily the insects usually take some time before burrowing into the skin.

May is also run-off time. For those who live by streams, it is the month to keep a weather-eye on the rising water level. Most years, this just means enjoying the returning music of running water. But depending on the snowpack, amount of additional snow or rain, and the temperature—which determines the rate of melt—this joy can become anxiety.

Lower Bear Creek, from the point where Cub Creek enters below the dam down to Morrison, has historically suffered from time to time from flooding. John Schneider of Blue Creek Road told us of a time in the late 1800's when a huge flood came down Blue Creek, originating from the Brook Forest area: "I remember my Dad telling me about it, showing me stuff that had washed up on the hills and the banks along the creek. I don't think there was a bridge between here and Morrison left. Took them all out." The most devastating flood in living memory was in 1938 when a large part of Morrison was washed out, nine lives lost, and an estimated half-million dollars worth of property destroyed. There was serious flooding again in 1969 and 1973.

Upper Bear Creek, with its smaller catchment area, seems to have been flood-free. But there have been three times since we have lived beside Bear Creek (May of 1974 and 1979 and August of 1984, because of the sustained heavy rainfall) when we watched the water rise over the stream banks, flood across the adjacent meadow, turn most of our lawn into a spongy

swamp and reach its peak **just** in time to prevent our getting seriously worried.

In years of heavy snow, the May melt-off reveals just how much damage has been done to lawn, trees and shrubs by voles and mice. These little rodents tunnel under the deepest snow drifts and dine all winter long on a diet of grass roots and the bark of aspen and evergreen trees. As the snow recedes, the lawn has scores of holes and tunnels in it and the dead grass comes away in your hands, leaving large bald areas. The first time this happened we panicked, thinking we would have to reseed whole sections of the lawn. We worried too much. Grass roots are many and tenacious: the damage repaired itself as the lawn greened up.

Colorado's springtime is equivocal. Budding lilac branches break with sudden snow; spring beauties bloom in the lace of ice; torrents of water from melting snows unlock their hundred gulleys and break down the doors of silted creeks, pouring in flood down and away, and two days later choke black in a freeze. The wind beats like winter and ravages the leaves of trees not made for mountain country. Flowers the flatlanders planted in last autumn's homesickness heave in the freeze and die before the bone-dry summer has its time with them.

Joanne Greenberg. The Far Side of Victory. New York, Holt, Rinehart and Winston, 1983.

Field of wild iris. Ron Ruhoff.

More vexatious are the miles of what look like above- ground 'tunnels', created by dirt which pocket gophers have excavated all winter from their underground diggings. In summer, their activities produce huge and equally annoying mounds of dirt.

In the spring of 1984, a red shafted flicker took a fancy to a nest site on the north wall of Gene's new studio. She drilled a large hole through the siding in a remarkably short time. Next the pink fiberglass insulation from the wall cavity began to festoon the ground and a spruce tree nearby. Gene blocked up the hole; the flicker started furiously drilling a second one. He stuck a long wooden pole into that hole, far too heavy for her to remove. She flew around in distress and made a half-hearted third attempt before finally giving up. Woodpeckers, flickers and pygmy nuthatches all seem to take a fancy to houses in May: they may be drilling for insects or nests, or simply because the noise on a hollow area has some magical attraction for a mate.

With all its delights and annoyances, May is full of life and promise for the brief and wonderful summer to come.

June begins the summer cycle of bright, clear mornings and evenings, separated by refreshing, though sometimes violent, thunderstorms.

As the sun warms up the mountain slopes the air begins to rise. If it contains enough moisture, small puffy white clouds begin to form. As the ground heats up further, the air rises higher and the clouds grow larger. With enough moisture and heat, they can bloom into enormous thunderheads reaching tens of thousands of feet into the atmosphere. The resulting cloudbursts can create violent winds along with lightning, thunder, rain and hail. One memorable day in June of 1983, we were lunching on Main Street when a summer hailstorm turned mid-day literally as dark as night.

June is penstemon month, especially when there has been a wet spring. The hillsides and open clearings in ponderosa forests are suddenly covered with the blue haze of this lovely mountain flower. (In its effect, it is the nearest thing we have to the bluebells which carpeted the spring woods in Yorkshire where Barbara grew up—even though those were wild hyacinths and very different in scent and

succulence from the penstemons.) There are many varieties of this handsome flower in the Evergreen area, blooming at different times through the summer. They range in color from pink to deep purple and in size from a few inches to well over a foot.

The spring migration of birds slows. Woods, stream borders, meadows and gardens are full of the purposive activity of nest building, egg-laying and hatching, and the noisy, touching care of adult birds feeding their young.

Baby chipmunks dart around on rocks and hillsides. They sit cheekily on our lawn and eat dandelion flowers.

Periodically (ever since we became mountain landowners in 1949 and no doubt for eons before that) some natural or man-made cycle of imbalance generates a plague of insect pests, causing disease or death in first one type of tree and then another. In the early 1950's it was a beetle that decimated the marvellous stands of Englemann Spruce. In the 1970's came the ponderosa pine beetle that struck during a long period of drought. In the late 70's and early 80's, it was the turn of the spruces and Douglas firs to deal with an explosion of spruce budworm. All of these insects are natural to the mountain area.

The long-term effect of the periodic 'plagues'—from an objective point of view—is to thin the forests and create new clearings in which flowers, shrubs and aspen can flourish, as well as many kinds of rotting environments for birds, small animals and insects to live in.

But on a personal level, we value the particular trees we have planted, and we all cherish the vistas of healthy, green evergreens seen from deck and picture window. The threat of disease—the prospect of huge stands of dead or sick trees—is a calamity.

June is the month of decision as to what, if anything, to do on your own land about the ravages of spruce budworm. Some time between the middle and the end of the month, the budworm emerge from winter hibernation to settle in the new buds of firs and spruces and chew on the new growth. If the infestation is heavy, they can turn thse normally luxuriantly-leaved trees into thin, straggly, brownish

Mt. Evans Highway and the Continental
Divide

shadows of their former selves. Trees that are sprayed at just the right moment are rid of most of their unwelcome guests and new growth has a chance to develop, whereas trees heavily infested year after year can die.

Most of us come to accept the naturalists' contention that these periodic disasters are part of a beneficial natural cycle. This doesn't prevent our mourning the deaths of trees, nor making an effort—by spraying—to safeguard treasured specimens around our homes. We can then turn a gloomy attitude around by taking Sylvia Brockner's advice, "the change (from forest to cleared spaces) is fascinating. It is far better to relax and enjoy nature at work than to worry yourself into a stroke."

The frog chorus ceases in June and the ponds fill with tadpoles.

July is the heart of summer, time to feast all the senses on the brief riot of flowers and grasses. Magenta locoweed, alpine penstemon, brilliant prime yellow sulphur flower, salsify with its wonderful silky-golden 'clocks' (the model for Bertoioa's elegant metal sculptures), huge white stemless evening primrose, scarlet paintbrush, sweet-scented wild pink roses, so lovely in the wild, so pesky in the garden. Blue lupines, white prickly poppy, scarlet and white gilia, those 'fairy trumpets' that children love. Above all, the magnificent blue and white columbine, that inspired choice for the Colorado State Flower. Unusually beautiful also are the clusters of large, long-lived daisies that grow along the stream, our favorite 'cut flowers' for July and August.

We live in climatic cycles. Dry years produce fewer and smaller wild flowers in exchange for long days of sunshine and warm air filled with pine fragrance. Wet years compensate for the shortage of "lazy, hazy days of summer" with lush growth of such beauties as the delicate creamy-white Mariposa lilies which are quite scarce in dry years. The deep orange-red wood lily—vivid, rare and perfect enough that we used to think it had seeded itself from someone's garden—also blooms profusely in its preferred places

in moist years. One of these is on the Seger's Acres hillside above our home. 1984 and 1985 were banner years for rainfall and wood lilies.

July is the premier month to visit the high country and enjoy the brief, beautiful burst of life above timberline. One of the great luxuries of living in Evergreen is having the Mount Evans range just outside our back door. In less than an hour we can be in an alpine world, enjoying both the vast panorama spread before us and the microscopic beauty of alpine flowers.

The Mount Evans highway above Echo Lake usually opens some time in June, depending on the depth of snow to be cleared, but the full flowering of this high tundra region is best seen in the last three weeks of July. On our way up, we like to stop off to enjoy the different levels of life and vegetation, and are always on the lookout for the hardy wildlife—bighorn sheep, mountain goat, pika and marmot—that manage to live among the inhospitable rocks.

We also pay our tribute of admiration to those timberline limber pines and bristlecones that are metaphors for survival, pondering the irony that these tortured bristlecone trees—so battered by impossible winds and extremes of weather—should be among the oldest living things on earth.

Sometime in early July the air around humming bird feeders begins to crackle and zing. This signals the return of the rufous hummingbirds and the onset of the annual hummingbird wars. We soon see the feisty little newcomer, his burnished coppery color a clear contrast to the green of the broad-tailed variety, challenging the residents for control of the feeder. Sylvia Brockner has christened him Rufus the Red Baron and tells us that he is not a late spring migrant but an early fall one. He has already nested and mated further north. To his dutiful wife is left the task of rearing the young, while he "departs on a pleasant and leisurely journey, sipping his way southward along the flowery mountain meadows."

One memorable July 4th we were driven with some friends to Summit Lake early on a cloudless, sunny morning. We took a picnic and cameras and followed the course of our beloved Bear Creek from its source in the lake all the way down to the Wildlife Area, where our kindly chauffeur was to pick us up. It was a magical journey. In the beginning, with snow still plentiful, the spongy surface was covered with small willows, patches of white marsh marigolds and masses of king's crown and queen's crown sedum.

Elk (Means) Meadow. Ron Ruhoff.

As we travelled further down, the profusion of flowers left us speechless. The beautiful crimson Parry's primroses, growing beside the stream, remain in our minds as well as microscopic blue alpine forget-me-nots and the innumerable cheery orange-yellow faces of the alpine sunflowers turned towards the sun. There was something of the joy of pioneering as we hiked down from the treeless tundra, through twisted timberline trees and forests of spruce, fir and aspen, to meadows vivid with the little red elephant flowers and dotted with beaver dams.

August: After the wet summers of the early 1980s and the record August rains of 1984, when the hillsides were as green as in June, it is hard to remember that an equally "normal" mountain August is likely to be hot and dry. Wild grasses seed and turn brown. Late-blooming flowers need the hardiness of desert plants to complete their blooming and seeding cycle before the first frost signals the end of summer.

The crimson-lavender-purples and yellow-orange segments of the color spectrum dominate the August flower show. Most prolific are tansy asters, showy daisies, gunweeds, coneflowers, goldenrod sunflowers, gaillardia and sunspots. Yellow sweet clover grows tall along the roadsides, perfuming them with the scent of honey mead. Wild snapdragons, the familiar yellow and orange toadflax or 'butter and eggs,' spring up especially brightly in recently disturbed soil. Blue-purple harebells, those shapely and fragile-looking late bloomers that seem to grow almost everywhere on earth, are much in evidence as are green gentians, or monument plants.

A startlingly beautiful wildflower is one of August's prime attractions, even though it has the bland title of "showy milkweed". Its aromatic scent and elegant pink flowers liven up the roadsides and attract a variety of insects, including the showy monarch butterfly.

One August day the air is full of silky floating seeds as thick as snow—if, like us, you have a stand of fireweed (willowherb) nearby. Earlier, it has colored July days with vivid magenta flowers. The leaves turn vermilion and gold, an early preview of fall.

Stately Russian thistles and the less showy common thistle arouse mixed emotions. In themselves, they are striking and beautiful plants, creating spectacular patches of crimson and lavender-pink color. But they are not natives and they are crowding out less hardy and prolific mountain flowers. Unlike the pine beetle and spruce budworm, thistles are elements introduced by man: perhaps we are obligated to keep them in check.

The first light, night frosts will likely nip at tender plants by August's end, particularly in low-lying areas by streams.

If you have not already noticed the quiet in your garden and in the surrounding woods and meadows by late July, you will certainly be struck by it in August. The birds have raised their families and enter a period of almost furtive quiet. They are molting. August begins the long weeks of southern migration. Shedding their worn plumage, the birds start their journeys with glowing new feather coats.

If, one morning in late August, your lawn or vegetable garden starts to erupt with unsightly mounds of dirt, it is probably a young pocket gopher who has been turned out of his home burrow by an ill-tempered mother, and is trying to set up housekeeping. August is a time to keep doors closed—to forestall the annual invasion of mice, seeking a warm home for the long, long winter.

September: Frosty nights are an inexorable part of September. Garden flowers or vegetables will get a day or a week longer, depending on their hardiness and the vagaries of temperature. But by the end of the second week, you can usually clear out the frost-blackened remnants then relax and enjoy what many think is the best time of year in the mountains—the wonderful sparkling time of Indian Summer. Most years, with occasional brief snow flurries, it lasts well into November.

In the early days of our summer cabin on Blue Creek Road, Rozzi Clark of ESCO would do for us what he did for countless other summer cabin owners—turn off the water supply for the winter, draining all the pipes so they would not freeze, and then reverse the process in the spring. He had two "rule-of-thumb" dates, May 17 to turn the water on and September

41

17 to turn it off. This is still a pretty good fall target date to drain hoses, pumps and sprinklers.

If the year is cool and moist, mushrooms are plentiful. There are many edible varieties in our vicinity, and a few deadly ones. Sources for safe identification abound in Evergreen and the Denver metro area. They include the wonderful Denver Botanical Gardens, knowledgeable individuals, pamphlets, articles, books and groups that specialize in mushroom lore.

Bird migrations swell to a steady stream: chipping sparrows, gray-headed juncos, flocks of audubon warblers. Grasshoppers are at their peak. To us the clickety-clakety noise made by the flying variety is unextricably associated with an Evergreen fall.

Grasshoppers are an old periodic scourge of the mountains. A vivid image of naturally-ocurring hordes in the high country comes from journalist Samuel Bowls' account of a camping trip through the Colorado mountains, as long ago as August of 1868.

"The only life was grasshoppers,— here they were still by thousands, by millions, sporting in the air and frisking over the snow, but the latter's chill seemed soon to overcome their life, for they lay dead in countless numbers upon its white surface. In some places the dead grasshoppers could have been shoveled up by the bushels"

PARABLE

Once I saw an aspen wood
Like a cloud of flaming gold,
Holding in a light embrace
All the leaves that it could hold,
When a sudden gust of wind,
Scarcely stronger than a breeze,
Swept across the valley's floor,
Rustled through the yellow trees;
and the branches, letting go
Loveliness they held so lightly,
Gave their treasures to the air,
Where they whirled and glittered
   bright
Hung above the mountain's
   breast—
Lifted—fluttered— came to rest.
Calm and white the aspens stood;
Brave and lovely aspen wood!
Long I stood and watched the trees,
Wishing I were wise as these—
For the hardest thing to know
Is the grace of letting go.

Jamie Sexton Holme in " I have Been a Pilgrim." New York, Henry Harrison, 1935.

The afternoon showers that are typical of so many Evergreen summers become less frequent, and usually cease around the middle of September. The westerly winds have not yet migrated all the way south from Canada so there are only occasional storms. Fall, perhaps the most beautiful season in the Front Range region, begins. The lack of moisture in the air deepens the blue of the sky. The air is crisp and winy.

September is a blend of opposites: sharp sunlight and deep shadow, warm sunny days and still, cold, starry nights.

The climax of a spectacular wildlife cycle comes in late September. It is the rutting season of the elk, accompanied by the powerful, extraordinary night sounds of bugling bulls.

The Mount Evans elk herd is culled by means of limited hunting permits to around 1200 head. Its summer range is pretty well protected by the existence of the State Mount Evans Wildlife Area and the Arapahoe National Forest and Wilderness Area. But there is a fear that the winter feeding range may be jeopardized by development. Part of this range is now public land— including Elk Meadow, adjoining Denver Mountain Park land on Bergen Peak, and the Alderfer-Three Sisters area. But other critical areas, like the Noble Meadow, have pitted elk-lovers and developers on opposite sides of a controversy.

Mapping of the migration patterns of the elk show that in winter the herd moves down from Mount Evans, either along Squaw Pass or down the Witter Gulch-Stage Coach area, then along Bergen Peak to Means Meadow or to ranges located along Highway 73. The Wildlife Area itself, some 4,000 acres at the end of Upper Bear Creek Road west of Evergreen, is closed from January 1 to June 15 each year to provide a safe area for winter grazing.

". . . .from the hill came the deep throated trumpet call of the bull elk. Rising from the depth of his body it ascended the scale in a tremendously powerful three-noted squeal, followed by several short deep coughing grunts. Like the wail of a bagpipe, the magnificent sound filled the night. It is a sound like no other. It is a sound of pride and glory, of dominance and power. A sound of splendor. It is a sound never to be forgotten." (Brockner's column for October 14, 1981.)

The rutting season starts around the end of August and lasts until mid-November. For most of the year the cows stay together in groups, along with their calves and the young sexually uninitiated males called 'spikes'. The adult males run in herds. As the days grow shorter, the amount of sunlight absorbed through the elks' eyes triggers the animals into rut, a season of sexual frenzy. The males undergo a physical change: necks thicken and antlers shed their velvet. They seek out females in heat, rounding up as many as they can into temporary harems. A bachelor bull approaching another male with a harem encounters a violent show of strength in defense of his females, which starts with bugling.
"The bull with cows will paw the ground and shake his antlers and warn the approaching male he does not want to give up any females. Rarely do they fight, though. The strongest male usually just takes the cows he can service and leaves. Sometimes, however, they do lock antlers in fierce combat, occasionally resulting in death." (Ralph Matzner, Manager, Mount Evans Wildlife Management Area. Quoted in "Mount Evans Elk Herd: A Last Stronghold" by Jacque Scott. Evergreen Magazine. Spring/Summer 1979.)

After rut, males and females again separate into segregated herds. The calves are born in the spring, as the females move up again toward summer feeding grounds. Bergen Peak—above Means Meadow— and part of the Evans Ranch are two favored calving grounds.

Elk are by no means the only wildlife protected by the Management Area. There are bighorn sheep and mountain goats, deer, bear, mountain lion and bobcats, raccoon and coyote, as well as many birds—eagle, hawk, wild turkey and grouse.

October: The full glory of a mountain fall—where aspen groves and forests turn into patches of liquid gold—begins in late September here and is usually at its peak in early October. Most of us in Evergreen develop our own special place to experience this most spectacular show. Two of our favorites are the road in our back yard—up Witter Gulch, through Evergreen West and along the Squaw Pass road to Echo Lake— and the Guanella Pass road above Georgetown. Black Mountain too is glorious in a good year.

The riot of color produces a poignant and exhilarating mood: exhilarating because of the sheer flamboyance and intensity of color, poignant because we know the show is a brief and spirited farewell to summer—to growth, warmth and easy living. The tougher days are ahead, battling snow, frost and cold. Soon hillsides, trees and meadows will set into dormant browns and greys.

Many wildflowers linger in sunny and sheltered spots. But more noticeable now are the glowing reds, golds and oranges of both leaves and fruits of native plants and shrubs: scarlet rose hips, dark, rich fruits of chokecherries and their vivid reddish-pink leaves, the yellow leaves and striking purple-black berries of the bearberry shrubs. On old fences, like many along Upper Bear Creek Road, the sturdy Virginia creeper vines, planted long ago, turn a firery, spectacular red.

There are usually one or two mornings in October when a particular coincidence of warm, moist air meeting a cold mountain night produces an enchanted landscape of hoar frost. It seems to come on cloudless blue mornings. The magic lasts only until the sun's warmth melts the delicate, lacy etching around every seedhead, leaf and evergreen tree.

A heavy snowfall in early October happens every few years, taking everyone by surprise and inevitably being labelled 'out-of-season'. The Canyon Courier of October 8, 1959 reported a snowstorm that caused problems with telephone service, isolating Bailey and Evergreen from Denver. For October 9, 1969 the first fall brought three feet of snow that fell steadily from Friday morning through Saturday night. The morning of October 16, 1984 greeted us with about 27".

November: The fall bird migration ends. The winter regulars settle in at bird feeders, a faithful core of juncos, nuthatches, finches, chickadees and Steller's jays.

At some unspecified date—usually before Thanksgiving— Indian summer ends. On November 15, 1984 Barbara was hanging out washing on a glorious fall day. The next day, snow and biting cold arrived and there was no chance to dry washing outdoors again until late April. But that was a winter of the coldest kind. In other years, sunny days and cold blustery ones alternate with intervals of snow.

"The autumns in Colorado are long and golden mellow. The snows come early and suddenly with snapping cold and black frosts, cold so sharp it tears at the lungs. But just as suddenly the cold is gone and the frost-nipped trees dry in their yellow dress; the days are warm again, not like spring, not like summer, not like any season the East has. Mellow days, cold nights, star-cold, cracking dry. No frost rises because no dew falls. The sun next day forgives everything.

On the high peaks the snows begin to move. Another storm, locking the passes, marooning a thousand towns, and forgiveness again, a forgiveness of singular excitement and energy. The air turns winy as new apples, or smells like the sea; the mornings shine like pearls, the mountains echo, and light pours between them radiant from its slide down the powder snow of the mountains.

Joanne Greenberg. The Far Side of Victory. New York, Holt, Rinehart and Winston, 1983.

Echo Lake. Ron Ruhoff.

43

Evergreen winter snow.

A November walk in one of Evergreen's many parks highlights the bright red rose hips and kinnikinnik berries against a subtle tapestry of bronze, beige and brown. The now leafless aspen trees have a special beauty, as do the willow and alder along the streams.

Some years Thanksgiving is an indoor celebration with snow, and everyone glad of the warmth of a wood fire. Or it may be warm enough to eat turkey and cranberry sauce outside on a sheltered deck in the sunshine. Either way, there is much to be thankful for in Evergreen. We enjoy the best of two worlds: the man-made one—which provides us with warm homes and well-stocked stores, and spares us from the harsh living conditions of the pioneers—and the world of nature, beautiful in all its seasons.

December: There's no pleasing all tastes in December. Plentiful snow delights the skiers and those who care about adequate snowpack for water supplies. But it discourages the reluctant commuter, who looks forward to four more months of the same—and wonders if he can really survive until summer. In some Decembers, like that of 1979, Evergreen can have such sunny and mild days that people begin to talk smugly of living in the mountain banana belt. Or December can be so harsh, cold and snow-filled that you are grateful if your car even starts in the morning.

The band of westerly winds has settled in over the Southern Rockies for the winter. Television weather maps show storm systems tracking through our region pretty regularly from December to June.

Christmas in Evergreen has many connections with the world of nature: gathering local 'greens'— kinnikinnik, spruce or fir boughs— for decoration, and trimming with pine and spruce cones or the lovely winter grasses and wildflower seedheads. At the Evergreen Library, the Audubon Society (TENAS) and the Evergreen Chorale join forces to lead the community in singing carols and decorating a tree with natural goodies for wild birds.

The winter solstice falls around December 23, providing the seed of spring in the very heart of winter: from that moment on, each day is a little longer.

By the end of December the grass is usually truly dormant. Except for our plentiful evergreen trees, everything has turned brown, beige or gray. We look at the photographs we took in the lushness of summer and ask ourselves, "Will it **ever** be green again?"

Birdwatchers look forward to December as the time of participation in the national Christmas Bird Count. This was started in 1900 as a way of drawing attention to the conservation instead of the destruction of birds, since a Christmas bird hunt was at that time a widespread custom. The first count had 27 observers in 25 different areas. By 1986, there were 1,504 Bird Counts in the United States and Canada: 32,956 observers idenitfied 5,390 species.

The Evergreen Naturalists Audubon Society started its Christmas Bird Count in 1969. It is conducted within dates set each year by the National Audubon Society and inside the same 15-mile circle. The territory is divided into sections, with as many groups as possible in the field. The 17th annual Evergreen count in 1986 was 48 different species and almost 3,788 individual birds. Highest numbers were of mountain chickadees, Steller's jays, crows, starlings, pine siskins. In all, since the local count started, 70 species have been sighted.

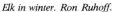

Elk in winter. Ron Ruhoff.

Timberline trees.

Preserving Nature's Gifts

The 1860's did not agonize over ethical conflicts about the use of land and its resources. Wild game was for meat. Timber was for cutting—to burn, to prop up mine shafts, to build houses and barns. Minerals beneath the ground were for digging out and selling. Meadows were for pasturing cattle or for plowing up to raise crops. Life for the original settlers was hard, the farming marginal. If resources ran out it was time to move on.

The patterns of 'moving on' still loom large in our culture: houses in Evergreen turn over frequently, even when there is no drastic change in the economics of airlines or the oil and gas industry. But new attitudes, born from the sight of Planet Earth from space—as one closed and fragile ecosystem—are altering the politics of land use in this mountain area as in the rest of the country.

Realization of the need to keep some wilderness—not just so we can experience it as a natural wonder but for our own survival— has given us the Mount Evans Wilderness Area, so wonderfully accessible from Evergreen

The runaway growth and development of the 1960's and early 1970's showed us how easily our unique mountain environment could be reduced to dusty roads and endless suburban plots. This fueled the demand for less destructive ways of subdividing land, and the desire to protect areas of open space from development. In turn, this produced the Jefferson County Open Space Program which has already generated great benefits for this community.

Evergreen's unique heritage of forests, parks and wilderness is our guarantee of perpetual access to the gifts of nature.

Native Americans saw the world as a unity in which unseen spirits move to keep everything in harmony and balance; the wolf, the buffalo, the earth itself all have a sacred purpose none more vital than the next. So too man had a place in the fabric of life. Respecting all creation, he is meant to spend his days in worship, with love and play.

Nothing must be wasted in such a world. No creature can "own" another. The land lies open to nourish all equally. Every act is sacred and holds the promise of a creative response. A song while grinding corn shows thanks for a good harvest. Ornament added to a basket tells of the joy of the work. "Art" is a part of the harmony of the world, a natural outgrowth of everyday life. Like everything else, art fulfills a purpose in the established order.

From Denver Art Museum Exhibition, "A Persistent Vision: Art of the Reservation Days".

There is a little memorial in Evergreen that marks the site of a significant even in the exploration of nature in the West. It was on the banks of Bear Creek that naturalist Charles Christopher Parry admired and named the Colorado Blue Spruce.

Parry was born in Gloucestershire, England, in 1823. His family moved to New York State when he was nine. Although he developed a very early interest in plants, he studied medicine and graduated with an M.D. from Columbia University, where he studied botany under John Torrey.

After opening a medical practice in Davenport, Iowa, Parry found himself more and more drawn to botanical exploration. In 1849, he was appointed botanist to the United States and Mexican border survey.

For the next forty years, he spent his summers in botanical exploration of the Pacific and Intermountain states and territories.

In Colorado, Parry named Gray and Torrey peaks after admired mentors. Many plants were named in Parry's honor.

The Blue Spruce Memorial is on Highway 74, just below the Church of the Transfiguration. The bronze placque has this inscription: "In honor of Dr. C. C. Parry, discoverer of the Colorado Blue Spruce, 1862. Dedicated by the American Association of Nurserymen, 1928."

Evergreen is enriched by the contributions of these two ladies, Mrs. Helen Crain and daughter-in-law Sandy Crain (preservation of its heritage).

County Commissioner Bob Clement who helpd greatly to secure the Hiwan Homestead as a permanent community asset. Clement died unexpectedly in 1981 at age 64.

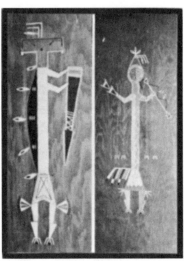

Indian motives painted on wall of Hiwan Homestead by Eric Douglas.

Maine Street, (with wooden bridge long before the dam)

THE WILLIAMS-DOUGLAS LEGACY

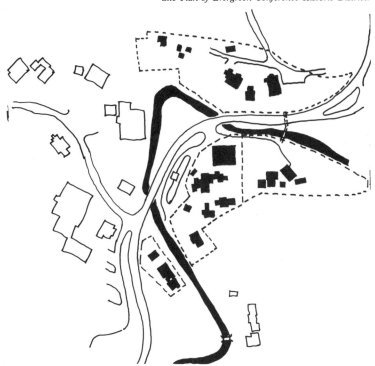

Site Plan of Evergreen Conference Historic District.

A number of signs around Evergreen point the curious visitor in the direction of the Evergreen Conference Center National Historic District. This is a weathered and interesting group of buildings lying on both sides of Highway 74 as it winds through the lower end of town.

The Center includes properties held in three different Episcopalian ownerships, but linked together by history and function. The Colorado Diocese, through its Camps and Conference Board, owns the Evergreen Conference properties. These include the land and 7 buildings on the north side of Highway 74, and the land and 5 buildings south of an agreed property line on the other side of the highway.

Between this line and Bear Creek, the Church of the Transfiguration owns the land, 6 buildings, some miscellaneous structures and the historic Bell Tower.

To the Sisters of St. Mary belongs St. Raphael's, the secluded little property across the creek: three delightful old buildings and a stone-faced root cellar built into the hillside.

Except for the stone structure on top of the hill, which housed Evergreen's public library for fifty years, the main use of the Conference buildings since their construction has been church-related. But many of them have also served community and cultural needs. Part of the first structure, Stewart's Hotel, is now the Little Log Theater of the Evergreen Players. Other past or present uses for buildings include offices for the Colorado Philharmonic Orchestra, the Evergreen Center for the Arts and the University of the Wilderness, premises for a Montessori School, and a pottery studio.

The Conference Center Complex was placed on the National Register of Historic Places in 1977. The application was prepared by a committee chaired by Sandy Crain (at the time, she was Curator of the Hiwan Homestead Museum) for the Jefferson County Historical Society.

Evergreen Churches—Then and Now

Every week, the Canyon Courier publishes a Church Directory. In 1986, for the Evergreen-Bergen Park-Indian Hills-Kittredge area, there were 16 congregations listed as having their own church buildings, with an additional 6 using other premises.

But there was a time when the only resident minister in the entire mountain area was an Episcopalian priest. Because so much of the early history and character of our community is bound up with Episcopalian people and institutions, we think it important to turn the spotlight on them.

The Missionary Church

The popular image of pioneer religion in Colorado is the circuit-riding Methodist preacher. But the Episcopal Church was also deeply committed to the missionary enterprise. Itinerant priests and even bishops visited the smallest population centers in their huge territories, holding services and helping to form permanent congregations.

The first Missionary Bishop whose territory included Colorado was John C. Talbot. He christened himself "Bishop of All Outdoors" because his bailiwick covered Nebraska, Colorado, Wyoming, Montana, Dakota, Nevada and Utah. Talbot served from 1865 to 1873, leaving active congregations in Denver, Central City and the mining camps around Idaho Springs.

His successor, known as the "saintly" Bishop George Maxwell Randall, was the first to have a direct connection with Evergreen. Already 59 when he took up his

Stewart's Hotel, now used by the Evergreen Players.

appointment as Bishop of Colorado, Wyoming and New Mexico, he set himself a gruelling pace. He not only travelled continually through this rugged territory, but also went back East to raise money, recruit missionaries and request prayers for his efforts in western mission fields. These (according to Allen Breck, historian of the Episcopalian Church in Colorado) "seemed as remote to his hearers as the Celestial Empire of China, or Central Africa, which were missionary districts on an equal footing"

One church for which Randall successfully begged funds was in Bergen Park. Many mission congregations in the front range area were served from Jarvis Hall in Golden, an Episcopalian institution which eventually became the nucleus of the Colorado School of Mines. In 1871 the newly-appointed Chaplain of the Hall was a missionary priest, Father Francis Byrne, who held the first Episcopalian services in the Evergreen community.

The setting was the dining room of Stewart's Hotel, a structure that is still standing and still in use.

Father Byrne, who came to Colorado from Ireland after service in the West Indies, was described as "one of the humblest and holiest of missionaries." Just before Colorado became a separate Diocese in 1887, Byrne himself wrote, "It has been my privilege to labour at 39 different points in Colorado, holding services in log cabins, billiard halls, school houses, ranches, wherever and whenever a few could meet to hear the blessed Gospel of Christ." He lived to be 99 years old.

St. Mark's-in-the-Wilderness
In 1871, this entire part of the mountain area was still called Bergen Park. The congregation decided to become formally organized and build a church. Several acres of land now comprising the Evergreen Cemetery—adjacent to Christ The King Catholic Church on Highway 74—were donated by E. J. Mallet. Bishop Randall interested the New York congregation of St. Mark's in the Bouwerie in providing funds for a building, to be called St. Mark's Church at Bergen Park. He laid the cornerstone on May 7, 1872.

By the time the first services were held in the new building in January of 1874, Bishop Randall had succumbed to pneumonia. The Golden Transcript for February 4, 1874, headlined "Church at Bergen Park," ran this news item under the byline of "F. Byrne, Missionary."

"St. Mark's Parish was visited on January 24, when a meeting was held to elect officers to serve for the current year. The church is centrally located in the midst of an extensive farming community, who, for some time, have felt the need of a regular house of prayer for public worship of God, there being no church for many miles near them, though occasional services have been held in school houses by our Methodist brethren. St. Mark's was opened for the first time on Sunday, January 25th, for divine service, when a large congregation was present."

"The building is of Gothic Architecture, with a foundation of stone, 50 by 24 feet, with a modest tower and parapets, stained glass windows, a triple window in the east end The Church will seat 150 or more and is free from debt, though not quite completed, but will soon be ready for consecration by our new Bishop. Services for the present will be held twice a month."

The new Bishop was John Francis Spalding, who found that the hard times caused by the financial panic he had left in the East came westward with him, and lasted for the next five years. Perhaps this was why the new church in Bergen Park faltered so soon after its completion. Breck records that the congregation of St. Mark's was organized in 1871 and disbanded in 1874, very soon after the building was completed. An interesting paper on early settlement in Evergreen, written by Paula Moore, suggests that early settlers here cooperated only when they had compelling mutual interests: "When they did organize a church in 1874," she says, "they abandoned it because they could not agree on how to run it."

An official history of the Evergreen Episcopal Church, written in 1948 for its Golden Jubilee Year, notes that from 1874 to 1878, services were held bi-monthly. "From 1878 to 1883 a few baptisms and burials are recorded; there the Parish

Register abruptly ends." Some have suggested that the congregation dwindled because, with the local economy depressed, people moved away from the Evergreen area.

In 1886, an exchange of property took place between the Methodists and the Episcopalians: St. Mark's was traded for what is now St. Philip's Church in Sedalia. The Methodists in Evergreen subsequently moved the building from the cemetery to a site on Main Street, where the Little Bear stands today. The altar was taken out of the church and left to lie untended for several years. It was rescued by Mrs. F. J. Bancroft, who had it moved for safekeeping to the porch of the Bancroft summer home.

The Remarkable Bancrofts
The Bancrofts were one of the earliest families to summer in Evergreen. Soon after his marriage in 1871, Dr. Frederick J. Bancroft bought some 2400 acres of land stretching from Evergreen to Kittredge for a summer home and ranch.

A good friend of fellow-physician Governor John Evans, Bancroft had a life and accomplishments that were similar to the Governor's in energy and diversity. Bancroft was born in Connecticut in 1834 and came to Denver after the Civil War. He quickly involved himself in his newly-adopted community.

One of his first acts was to import dandelions into Colorado! ("People have been hung for less," said a guest at a dinner party where we shared this piece of news.) In a well-intentioned effort to brighten up the barren landscape of the plains, Bancroft had dandelion seeds shipped out from the east.

Bancroft was an early member of the Denver Medical Society and its President in 1868. Later he was President of the Colorado Society and of the first State Board of Health. For 7 years he was City Physician of Denver and also served as official 'Surgeon' to both the Kansas Pacific and the Denver and Rio Grande Railroads.

Deeply concerned about the welfare of children, Bancroft not only believed that all should be educated (he headed up the Denver Board of Education from 1874-6) but that they should be in "commodious, cheerful, well-ventilated and heated school buildings."

One year, Bancroft became alarmed because too many young children were dying from unknown causes. Suspecting the culprit might be impure milk, Bancroft bought a 640-acre farm west of Denver to pasture a dairy herd and sell uncontaminated milk. The surrounding community became known as Bancroft: a small house on part of the property was turned into a school—the Bancroft District No. 41 of Jefferson County—and the identity still survives in the Bancroft Fire Department.

How Bancroft met his future wife is a story lifted from a Victorian novel. A wealthy Brooklynite, George A. Jarvis, was the largest donor to Bishop Randall's missionary ventures in the West (and the benefactor that made possible the building of Jarvis Hall in Golden). The Jarvis's last surviving child, daughter Mary Caroline, had contracted tuberculosis. Jarvis read an article by Dr. Bancroft asserting that the Colorado climate was an effective cure for this terrible disease. When the Jarvis's decided to send their daughter to Colorado to try the cure, it was only natural that the Randalls should offer her hospitality.

When they went to meet her stage from Cheyenne, the Bishop and his wife invited their friend Dr. Bancroft to accompany them. After the introduction, Miss Mary Caroline— according to an article by her granddaughter and namesake— "swayed into his arms and hemorrhaged."

The climate worked its magic for Mary Caroline as it had for so many others. The Bancrofts had three children. Mary McClean lived as an adult in Pueblo. George Jarvis became a well-known mining and water engineer. Frederick followed his father's calling, and moved back east.

Dr. Bancroft died in 1903. His wife and daughter continued to spend their summers in Evergreen and were deeply involved in Episcopalian activities here. George

married in 1899, opened a consulting office in Denver, and had two daughters—Peggy and Caroline—who also spent their childhood vacations at the family summer home.

Our information about George's work—especially a remarkable water storage project he engineered in the vicinity of James and Bancroft Peaks (the latter named for his father)—comes largely from the writings of daughter Caroline. She idolized him. George himself was a prolific writer in mining and scientific magazines.

In 1925, the main Bancroft summer home and surrounding guest buildings were given to the Evergreen Conference, together with the meadow land surrounding them. They are still there, still used, and the main building is still called Bancroft House.

It seems likely that the remaining land was divided among the three children. George Bancroft, who was divorced from his wife, apparently took title to some 800 acres at the Kittredge end of the property and built himself a home there. In 1938, towards the end of his life, he sold the property to Martin O'Fallon— with the proviso that he was to have the use of the house and five surrounding acres as long as he lived— knowing that O'Fallon intended to make a donation of it to the City of Denver for a mountain park. George Bancroft died in 1945.

To those of us who met her, the name of George's daughter Caroline Bancroft conjures up the image of a feisty, proud and unique personality. She graduated from Smith College, taught in private schools in the east for a number of years and travelled each summer in Europe. Then she returned to Denver to persuade Denver Post mogul Frederick Bonfils that the paper really needed a literary column—a feature she wrote for 5 years.

In the meantime, she took some history courses at Denver University and became intrigued with Colorado's short but lively history. She started writing popular historical booklets, initially publishing and distributing them herself. She wrote 24 in all. They are still to be found at every bookshop, souvenir store and airport news stand in the state.

Caroline Bancroft.

In her memory of childhood summers in Evergreen—of life at Camp Neosho and the main players in the Episcopalian story here— Caroline was opinionated and biassed, as a reading of the interview that Museum Director Connie Fahnestock did for the Hiwan Homestead archives will attest. But she was intensely alive and often dared to say what others only thought.

Caroline Bancroft was born with the new century and died in 1985. The most honest obituary of her was by western historian Sandra Dallas in the Denver Post. "To whitewash this historian would rob us of one of our colorful characters," wrote Dallas, asserting that Caroline is not to be remembered primarily for her writing or her history, "It was Caroline herself that made her a monumental figure .She was not a historian who sat on the sidelines to observe life. She lived it!"

Bancroft House.

The Williams-Douglas Family

To set the stage for the evolution of St. Mark's into the Mission, later the Church, of the Transfiguration, we must make the acquaintance of the Williams-Douglas family— one of Evergreen's founding dynasties and a mainstay of the Episcopal presence in the town for nearly a century.

Mary Neosho Williams was the second of the eighteen children of Dr. Howard Joseph Bailey and his wife, Mary. Only eight lived to maturity. Mary Neosho was born in 1835 at Fort Gibson in what was then Indian Territory, part of the Cherokee Nation. Little is known of her childhood, but in 1853 she married Brigadier General Thomas Williams. They had four children before he was killed in the 1862 Civil War battle of Baton Rouge. The youngest son, Thomas, was just a week old and died the following year.

The oldest child, a son, became an army general; the middle one, Gershom Mott Williams, a Bishop of the Episcopalian Church; the youngest child, daughter Mary Josepha, a physician.

The widowed Mrs. Williams moved to Denver some time in the 1870's. An ardent Episcopalian, she took an active role in the development of St. John's Cathedral. According to the researches of Connie Fahnestock, Director of the Hiwan Homestead Museum and author of the excellent little book about the history of the house, Mary Williams was probably introduced to the Evergreen area by her brother: Dr. Thomas Bailey had a cabin here. In the mid-1880's, she found around 1200 acres of beautiful land that was for sale. It included all of what is now the Evergreen Conference grounds and Meadow Drive as well as most of the land on both sides of Main Street and Evergreen Hill. Where the Hiwan Homestead is today, there was a small log building.

Mary Williams was fortunate to find an able master carpenter to remodel and add to the existing structure, creating a unique summer home and camp for herself and her many relatives, proteges and guests.

"Jock" Spence

Born John Spence in 1860 on the Orkney Islands northeast of Scotland, Jock left his mark on Evergreen. He apparently acquired his unique skills in carpentry and stone masonry from his father before emigrating to Canada. New research being done on Spence's life by Josie and Don Hoover, members of the Jefferson County Historical Society, shows that he crossed into the United States at Port Huron, Michigan, in 1887.

Since both the Bailey and the Williams family came from Detroit, where at least one side was extremely wealthy, it is not impossible that Spence may have made some connection with Mrs. Williams before coming to Denver by train in August of 1888. Be that as it may, Spence somehow found his way to Evergreen, liked the community and always had plenty of work here. He made it his home.

In addition to construction for the Williams-Douglas family at their summer home and the Evergreen Conference, Spence participated in the construction of many fine early Evergreen buildings, either as contractor, carpenter or stonemason and often as all three.

Examples of Spence's meticulous craftsmanship are the Clarence Phelps Dodge home on the Dodge Ranch west of Evergreen (now the Mount Evans Outdoor Education Laboratory School belonging to the Jefferson County R-1 School District), the Margaret Evans Davis home and other buildings on the Evans Ranch and Greystone.

Spence apparently lived for a number of years on the Evans Ranch while he was working there. He married and had two sons and a daughter, moving back into Evergreen when they needed to attend Evergreen School. Spence's name was included in the Evergreen listings of the Colorado State Business Directory for many years. The last listing is in 1934. Spence died in Evergreen in 1935.

Mary Williams named her handsome peeled log home and its surroundings Camp Neosho. It forms the nucleus of today's Hiwan Homestead Museum.

The Mission of the Transfiguration

In the summer of 1893, in one of the tents that surrounded the house, Mrs. Williams started to hold lay services and occasional Holy Communion celebrations when a visiting priest was available. The old St. Mark's altar was installed in the tent.

"Jock" Spence.

Across the stream was Stewart's hotel. After Stewart's death, Mrs. Williams bought the place and had Jock Spence remodel it to provide more permanent quarters for a church and social meeting place. Spence added rough-cut slab lumber siding to the exterior, creating the form of a cross. The altar was moved again, to the former dining room where the first Episcopalian congregation had been formed some 26 years earlier. The first services in St. Mark's new home were joyfully held on Christmas Eve of 1897.

The following year, the church was enlarged by eliminating the wall between the former kitchen and dining area. In 1899 Bishop Spalding dedicated the church under a new name, at the request of Mrs. Bancroft. It became the Mission of the Transfiguration. The old name was retained in the part of the building used for living quarters and a little chapel.

Mary Neosho Williams.

Josepha attended private boarding school in New York state together with a cousin, Madeline Marquette. After graduation in 1887, the two came to Denver together to enroll in the private Gross Medical College, graduating in 1889. Dr. Jo's Colorado medical license—No. 1156—was granted On July 2 of that year.

In 1891, Mrs. Mary Williams and Madeline Marquette founded the Marquette-Williams Sanitarium on Pearl Street in Denver. This was a patient-care facility and one of the first nurses' training schools in Colorado. Dr. Jo was a staff physician, a member of the Board of Directors and one of the teachers in the nursing school.

It was at the Sanitarium that Dr. Jo first met her future husband, Canon Winfred Douglas. One story has it that he was sent to make a sick-call on her by the Dean of St. John's. Less than enchanted, she told the Dean not to send "that awkward young man" around again. Another version is that Canon Douglas spent some time as a patient in the Sanitarium.

What is certain is that Winfred Douglas was one of the many guests invited to enjoy the mountain climate and plentiful sunshine of Camp Neosho, which helped him to regain his health. He and Dr. Jo were married in June of 1896. A year later, Dr. Jo gave birth to their only son, Frederic Huntington Douglas, known to everyone as Eric.

Canon Winfred Douglas.

Canon Douglas
Charles Winfred Douglas was born in 1867 in Oswego, New York, where his father was Superintendent of Schools. His mother, Douglas's second wife, had three children: Mary Louise, who as Mary Seamens spent some of her later years in Evergreen, a son who died in infancy, and Charles Winfred.

There was also a beloved older half-sister from the first marriage, Julia Brewster, who came to Evergreen in 1917 to retire and recover her health. She founded Evergreen's public library and devoted herself to it tirelessly until her death at the age of 83.

Winfred's mother died of tuberculosis when he was six. In 1875 Virgil Douglas married for a third time and a third daughter was born.

Both of Winfred's parents had a deep love of music and books, and he had piano lessons as a youngster. These were stopped for lack of money, but he continued to teach himself music theory and practice. In exchange for copying music for a local choir master, he received a few organ lessons and some practice time on the church organ.

Dr. Jo
Mary Williams' daughter Josepha—or "Dr. Jo" as she was known in Evergreen—seems to have been an interesting but elusive personality. Born in Fort Monroe, Virginia, in 1860, she was one of the first women physicians licensed in Colorado even though she had suffered from ill-health, reportedly tuberculosis, from childhood.

There seem to be no records as to what inspired her to take such a pioneering path. She was named after her physician-grandfather, Dr. Joseph Bailey. Could it be that she heard the family doggerel,

Dr. Bailey had four sons,
John, Will, Tom and Matt,
He made doctors of them all,
What do you think of that?

and thought that there was no reason he couldn't have done the same for some of his daughters?

51

52

Hart House, detail.

During Winfred's last year of high school his father died. Mrs. Douglas had to resume teaching. Winfred put aside his plans for college and worked at a number of jobs— substituting for the Presbyterian Church organist at short notice, moving heavy stock in a hardware store, and working in a thermometer factory. There he contracted mercury poisoning from sucking up liquid mercury into glass tubes, which permanently weakened his general constitution as well as depriving him of all of his teeth before he went to college.

Considering that he was also kicked down a flight of stairs by a jealous school classmate—causing a spinal injury that troubled him throughout his life—and that he had a family heritage of tuberculosis, the miracle is not that Winfred Douglas suffered from periods of ill health during his long life, but that he had the energy to accomplish so much in the rest of it.

Eric and Frieda Douglas.

In 1886 he entered Syracuse University for a degree in music. He earned his way by work which included singing in the choir of St. Paul's Cathedral (his first contact with the Episcopal Church), later becoming assistant choirmaster and organist. He came to know the Bishop of Central New York, Frederic Dan Huntington, who so greatly influenced the future course of Winfred's life that he named his only son after the Bishop, and dedicated his book of collected poems to Huntington's memory. He devoted much time to mission work, was ordained as a lay reader in the church and accepted as a candidate for Holy Orders.

Before completing studies for the ministry, he left to become organist and choirmaster at the Church of Zion and St. Timothy in New York. From this post, reportedly "due to the ill-will of a vestryman", he was abruptly dismissed.

Though he wrote bravely in his diary, "My ostensible failure as a church musician has depressed me no whit, but rather has filled me with a new and indomitable ambition to serve God supremely in just that capacity," he noted later that he had not slept for almost a month. Returning to Syracuse, he enrolled in St. Andrew's Divinity School and was ordained deacon by Huntington in 1893.

He took a second post in New York as curate at the Church of the Redeemer, responsible both for the church music and for teaching in the parochial school. Evergreen has a memento of this period of Douglas's life: when the old Redeemer Church was razed, the congregation sent its metal cross to Douglas. It was placed in its present position on top of the Bell Tower.

It was not long before Winfred's physical reserves were used up. One evening after choir rehearsal, when he had stayed on to practice the organ, he was found lying unconscious. Hospitalized for nine weeks with double pneumonia, he survived the puncturing of several abcesses. But one was too deep to reach. His rector's brother, Irving Peake Johnson, was summoned to administer the last rites. The nurse burst into tears. To cheer her up, Winfred managed a "feeble joke" which sent all three into hysterics. The laughter broke the abcess.

Bell Tower
Meeting House.

Johnson became a lifelong friend of Douglas's and later, as Diocesan Bishop of Colorado from 1918 to 1938, an enthusiastic participant in the summer Evergreen Conference activities sponsored by Douglas and his wife.

To help Winfred regain his health, his rector arranged for an invitation from Henry Martyn Hart, Dean of Denver's St. John's Cathedral, for Douglas to take up a post as minor canon. "Frail and impoverished"— Douglas's own words—he arrived in the fall of 1894.

The Douglas's in Evergreen
Winfred's marriage to Dr. Josepha, and the introduction to Evergreen, was a turning point in his life. He came to love the mountain country passionately, becoming an expert mountaineer and member of the exclusive Explorer's Club.

When they were first married, the young couple spent much of their time in Evergreen. Winfred was elected to the Evergreen School Board in 1898. Dr. Jo held Evergreen's first Sunday school classes at Camp Neosho. They both were quick to offer their support to talented or worthwhile local residents. Later the Douglas's lived in many places—New York, Wisconsin, Europe, and Denver— but they returned to Camp Neosho almost every summer.

Mary Williams and the Douglas's presided over a busy summer household of relatives, children, Episcopalian friends and interesting guests from many walks of life.

Caroline Bancroft, who spent a lot of time around Camp Neosho as a child, remembered that Mary Williams was "small and had white hair and a very sweet face, and was very quiet." She also recalled that the semi-invalid Dr. Josepha occupied the only bedroom in the log house, while Mrs. Williams used one of the tents. "Of course," she said, "these were de luxe tents, with wood floors, wood stoves and double tent flaps."

Mary Neosho Williams, one of our town's "founding mothers," died in 1914.

Dr. Jo's liberal inheritance enabled Canon Douglas to finance much of his later study of church music, as well as to enter enthusiastically with her into the creation of church-related programs and buildings in Evergreen.

An Unconventional Childhood
The Douglas's son, Eric, spent most of his childhood summers in Evergreen.

Such records as exist about Eric's childhood paint a picture in some ways admirable, in some ways sad. Much loved by both his parents, he was the focus of an almost obsessive concern on the part of his mother. Though Dr. Jo apparently indulged Eric's every whim, she could also impose her wishes on him without considering the impact on a proud and sensitive personality.

In an her Hiwan Homestead interview, historian Caroline Bancroft recalled a dress-up party at Camp Neosho when she was 4 and Eric 7. "Josepha had him dressed up as a little girl.in these fancy laces.and he was simply furious because people would come up to Josepha and say, 'Oh, what a pretty girl you have!' Eric would stamp his foot and say, 'I'm not a girl. I'm a boy!'"

Evergreen Conference Cabins.

In her teens, Caroline remembered having terrible fights with Eric. There was a time, when she was around 14, that she didn't speak to him for over a year because he was so rude "to a boyfriend calling on me." Later in his life, she said, after he had graduated from college and traveled in Europe, he developed some attractive qualities to augment the "native charm he had acquired from people like his father." But as a boy, she declared, he was "the most rotten, spoiled individual that you could possibly meet. He had no manners of any kind, he was gosh arrogant."

From a gift made to the Hiwan Museum by Caroline Bancroft not long before she died, it is obvious that there strong feelings between these two at one time. Eric was an accomplished poet, and inscribed volumes of his poetry to Caroline—volumes that Caroline wished to return to the house where she and Eric had played and fought together some 60 years before.

Another teenage member of Evergreen's summer colony was Helen Bromfield, daughter of Genevieve Chandler Phipps who built Greystone on Upper Bear Creek. In another taped interview, Helen Bromfield remembered that her sister and Eric used to ride horses together—which was a terrific thing for him "because he was supposed to be so sickly." But to Helen, he was just a healthy, amiable kid with holes in his blue jeans ("nobody ever mended them for him") and no manners ("they never told him how to behave.")

Eric would ride his horse right up to Greystone, come into the elegant living room with his spurs still on, and stretch out on one of the velvet couches "completely oblivious. Manure all over the place!"

The Douglas's had Jock Spence build a "Baby House" for Eric behind the main building. There Mary Seamens, Canon Douglas's sister, would often look after the child when he was not with his parents.

Helen Bromfield felt Eric had a strange childhood, raised much of the time by a housekeeper. In the summer, she said, church people would just move into Camp Neosho for indefinite stays—a sort of continual open house. When she and her sister were invited to dinner, they would never know who else would be there and there were no introductions. "You were just supposed to talk with whoever was there."

But Helen Bromfield also knew and appreciated the other aspects of Eric Douglas: his abilities as a pianist, poet, artist, art collector, and later as the dedicated Curator of Indian Art Museum.

Part of Douglas Indian Collection, Hiwan Homestead Museum.

Camp Neosho around 1920.

53

Father "Bud" and Helene Marsh.

Early Years of the Evergreen Mission

After additional theological studies under Bishop Spalding and Rev. Percival Hickman, examining chaplain to successive bishops of Colorado, Douglas was ordained priest in the little Evergreen Mission of the Transfiguration in 1899.

For the first four years of its existence, the same Rev. Hickman was Vicar of the Mission. A scholarly, austere Englishman, who like so many others had come to Colorado to regain his health, Hickman's background and personality were probably more suited to academic than to missionary duties among hard-working farmers and rough-and-ready miners.

A number of stories have been handed down about the Hickman family, including one about his daughter. Maggie had ambitions as a singer but her talents were not appreciated by the church choir. She sought singing engagements at weddings and funerals. After agreeing to perform at the funeral of a member of the notorious Jesse James family, she didn't show up. When Canon Douglas later asked her why, she said that her Mama didn't think it proper for her to sing at the funeral of a gentleman she had never met!

The Evergreen Conferences

The Evergreen Conferences were a natural outgrowth of the convictions, interests and energies of the Williams- Douglas family. From the earliest days of Mary Williams' summer gatherings at Camp Neosho, her wish that "Jesus Christ might be preached by the waterside" brought laymen and clergy together to vacation, plan and pray on the banks of Bear Creek.

Canon Douglas's passionate interests in church music, pageantry and liturgy, and his nation-wide contacts among Episcopalian clergy and church musicians, combined with the religious commitment and generous gifts of land and money from Mary Williams and Dr. Jo, to establish the physical plant and many-faceted programs of the Evergreen Conference.

First came a summer series of lectures for candidates for Holy Orders, from 1898 to 1900, by Rev. Hickman.

In 1907, a six-week Summer School of Liturgical Music was held, first of the Evergreen Church Music Schools that were to become nationally famous. To this day, these summer programs for church musicians are regarded as the finest offerings of their kind, drawing

especially from cathedrals and major churches which have the advantage of large choirs and fine pipe organs. However, music directors from quite small churches seem to find the offerings of value for their own work.

A 1985 map on the wall of Hart House dining room showed that participants in the Music Schools' two sessions came from almost every state in the union and from two foreign countries.

In 1909 the Rev. Thornton B. Rennell, who was married to a cousin of Dr. Jo's, came to be Vicar of the Mission. He contributed a great deal of enthusiasm, energy and talent to the building of both the Conference and the Mission. Together with Dr. Jo he was responsible for the design of the Bell Tower, built by Jock Spence in 1911. Two rather extensive repair jobs have kept it standing to this day.

From 1917 to 1920, Bishop Johnson organized five-day Summer Schools for Clergy at the Evergreen Mission. Participants were housed in tented accommodations in the Camp Neosho Meadow. In 1920 a large one-day Conference for Church School Teachers was held.

The need for more permanent accommodations for summer conference groups was apparent. Dr. Jo donated land and money to build what is today Hart House, named after the beloved Dean of St. John's Cathedral. This, like the other two major buildings on the Conference's "Upper Campus," was built by Jock Spence and contained sleeping quarters, common rooms, dining room and kitchen. The other buildings were Williams House—a faculty dormitory with six sleeping rooms, parlor and fireplace completed in 1923—and Meeting House. Finished in 1924, this was a large assembly building with stage and dressing rooms. It originally seated 400 but under later fire codes, this capacity was reduced to between 150 and 200.

Architecturally the most interesting building of the Conference Center, Meeting House has become familiar to Evergreenites as the rustic home of the musical comdey performances of the Evergreen Chorale.

An engineer before his ordination, Father Rennell supervised the construction of many of the simpler Conference buildings at times when Canon and Mrs. Douglas were travelling in Europe. Garven Dalglish, who wrote a history of the Church of the Transfiguration in 1971, noted that "Some of his (Rennell's) economies in construction necessitated replacements that would not have had to be made had he seen how long his groundwork was to last."

Rennell devised an ingenious central heating system serving the old hotel building—which housed the Mission and Rectory—and several other buildings which had come into church ownership at that time, including the stone library and cottage where Canon Douglas's two sisters, Miss Julia and Mary Douglas Seamans lived. Unfortunately, heating oil became too expensive after a few years and the system was ripped out.

Rennell's plumbing efforts were longer-lived however, and became the nucleus of Evergreen's Public Service Company.

The building which served as Evergreen's public library until 1971 was constructed in 1920-21 by Jock Spence, with funds provided by Dr. Josepha. In 1925, she set up a trust fund yielding $1,000 per year for the maintenance of the Conference buildings and the library.

Throughout the twenties and thirties, the Mission Church was most alive and active during the summer months, when a large influx of visitors swelled its congregation, and when its agenda was expanded to cooperate with the programs of the adjacent Evergreen Summer Conferences.

Historian Allen Breck notes that "bold developments in religious thought were continually in the making in Evergreen" and that the conferences held here "made the Evergreen Conference Center an institution of national importance."

From 1907-1934, Canon Douglas was transferred to the Diocese of Fond du Lac in Wisconsin. He had developed a lifelong involvement with plainsong, the medieval form of chanted music used by monastic orders in their daily liturgical worship. Long out of fashion, plainsong had been beautifully preserved by the French Benedictine Order of Solesmes, which in the

early twentieth century was living in exile on the Isle of Wight. Douglas studied with the monks, having first visited them in 1904, and was largely responsible for the reintroduction of plainsong into Episcopal Church services.

The Music Conferences were always the heart and backbone of the Evergreen summer offerings; there were also annual programs for clergy (named for many years the "School of the Prophets"), for Church Workers, and for youth.

Brochures for successive years informed participants about the Conference. In 1926 they were advised to "Come to the Conference in your car, if possible. Fine motor roads radiate in every direction from Evergreen through noble scenery. You may return to Denver through the spectacular beauties of Turkey Creek or Deer Creek; or over the Lookout Mountain road, with a world of plains and two cities spreading far below."

For public transportation there was a choice between Thomas Transfer Company on Wazee Street in Denver or the Evergreen Stage, starting from the Kenmark Hotel. The following year, transportation from the Evergreen Bus Station at 1707 California was advised. Later, and for many years, "buses leave from Bus Terminal on Glenarm Place daily."

There was a brief time in the 70's when the Conference itself, in addition to offering transportation from the airport (which it still does) also had to provide it from downtown Denver. But by 1981, RTD buses were available.

The special flavor of the Conference in 1926 is described:

"The wooded country adjoining the Conference on both sides, although privately owned, is open to all Conference members. Dense forest, picturesque piles of rock, field of wild flowers (to be seen, not picked)—even a mountain above the mission—may be reached without setting foot on a public road. Nearby is Camp Neosho, a home built of logs, where you may see the Douglas collection of Indian handicrafts; and the beautiful St. Joseph's Chapel, open at all times to Conference members."

After the death of Mary Williams in 1914, Dr. Jo and Canon Douglas had Jock Spence add 13 rooms to the original Camp Neosho. This west wing and tower were completed in 1918, and included the little octagonal chapel which has been painstakingly restored and can be enjoyed today by visitors to the Hiwan Museum. From her bedroom, Dr. Jo could hear services in the chapel even when she was, as happened frequently, too ill to leave her bed.

The new quarters included space for servants, and the Douglas's offered employment each summer to a number of local residents for they needed a chauffeur, ranch manager, a maid to clean, a cook and a "companion".

Douglas's Indian Connections
The Douglas collection of Indian handicrafts ended up as part of the founding collection of the Denver Art Museum's Native Arts division. Canon Douglas's interest in American Indians—their beliefs, culture and crafts—was probably sparked by a visit he made as a student to the Onondago Reservation.

In 1902, he suffered another serious physical and nervous breakdown. Attempts to rebuild his strength in the East were unsuccessful, so he spent six months living in the Southwest where, as his strength returned, he explored the Navajo and Hopi back country. The Hopi made him a tribal blood brother, naming him Tall Pine Tree. Sincerely admiring their craft work, he did considerable trading and collecting.

His intense interest in preserving Indian culture was shared by New York musician Kurt Schindler and writer Natalie Curtis. In 1912, these two joined Douglas in accompanying President Theodore Roosevelt on an extensive trip through New Mexico. Douglas's diary particularly notes meetings with Indian potter Nampeyo— listening to her songs and buying her beautiful pottery—and attending a Hopi Flute Ceremony. Through later trips, in 1916 and 1921, Douglas developed close ties with the Santa Clara and Zuni Indians. He brought many Indian friends to enjoy the hospitality of Camp Neosho.

55

Church Music Contributions

Appointment in 1923 to two important Episcopalian Commissions—one on Church Drama and Pageantry and the other on Church Music—brought Douglas into a fertile association with Wallace Goodrich of the New England Conservatory of Music, with whom he published three books of church music. Douglas's own book, *St. Dunstan Kyriale,* was published in 1933 and his magnum opus—*Church Music in History and Practice: Studies in the Praise of God*—in 1937.

Douglas's involvement with Church Pageantry has left Evergreen with a vivid little legacy—the banners which hang in Meeting House on the Conference grounds. Douglas designed these during another bout of severe illness, when he was flat on his back for several weeks in Evergreen. Made from scraps of donated material by women members of the Mission, the banners travelled all over the country on loan to meetings and conventions.

The Last Years of Dr. Jo and Canon Douglas

Transferred back to the Colorado Diocese in 1934, where he became Honorary Canon of St. John's Cathedral, Douglas was spending most of his time on a labor of love that had occupied him intermittently for 30 years—the translation from Latin into English of the Benedictine Day Offices used in many religious orders of the Church. He was delighted to be appointed, for what he looked forward to as semi- retirement years, as Vicar of the Evergreen Mission of the Transfiguration.

By this time, Dr. Jo was coming to the end of her illness-plagued but productive life. A Denver Post article in March of 1938 was titled, "Josepha Douglas, Pioneer Woman Physician, Dies." The Rocky Mountain News, noting that Mrs. Douglas was 78 at the time she succumbed to a heart attack, described her as "A bedfast invalid, sponsoring many philanthropic and charitable enterprises, and active in Episcopalian affairs."

In 1939, still full of enthusiasm for the Evergreen Conference at the age of 72, Douglas sent a letter to potential participants:

"Spring is just around the corner up here in the mountains; Bear Creek is rambling along as usual; and we're beginning to look forward to the time when you and others will be coming back. Your old friends and new ones, the same glorious scenes, the same old hills to climb, all will be here awaiting you."

In 1940, Douglas was asked to participate in the final grand task of his life—the complete revision, in both text and music, of the Church Hymnal.

He worked closely on this task with Anne Woodward, who had been associated with the Colorado Diocese since 1926 and with the Evergreen Conference since 1927. The two were married in 1940. Together they travelled extensively to complete the demanding task. Of the new hymnal, published in 1943, one author wrote, "The final work bears clearly the mark of his (Douglas's) genius, his musical taste and grandeur of spirit."

On January 19, 1944 in Santa Rosa, California—where Douglas was collaborating with two Episcopal scholars on the preparation of a handbook to accompany the new hymnal—he died suddenly of a massive heart attack. The Denver Post obituary noted that "his compositions and arrangements of hymns are known and sung throughout the world."

Canon Douglas's large personal collection of papers, books and music is assembled as the Douglas Collection at the National Cathedral in Washington, D.C.

Behind all this accomplishment, what sort of a person was Winfred Douglas? A picture of his engaging personality, seen through the eyes of the child that Caroline Bancroft was when she first knew him, is given in her Hiwan Homestead interview: "a very vital, very outgoing sort of person . . . he'd take Eric and me and whatever other kids were around, and we'd climb . . . . (As a preacher) he was excellent, quite, quite forceful, had a deep, resonant voice that carried well and a good singing voice."

Douglas was sufficiently creative and confident to work with personalities like Serge Rachmaninoff, Walter Damrosch and Mischa Elman. He had immense and infectious enthusiasm for projects he undertook, including the one most dear to him—the building of the Evergreen summer conferences. He described these as a "powerhouse for the renewal of the spirit" in which he sought to inspire "pure musical worship where the prayer will sing and the music will play."

Enter Father Marsh

To serve the congregation in Evergreen while he was engaged in his work in the Church Hymnal, Douglas brought in a newly-ordained young deacon who became a beloved and well-remembered part of the Evergreen community for the next 24 years.

This was Father Lewis ("Bud") Marsh, whom we had the privilege of interviewing in Wheatridge at the end of 1981. He shared with us his albums of memories and his fund of stories that covered the years of Evergreen's evolution from a pre-war mountain summer resort into a commuter community.

When Father Marsh arrived he was the only resident clergyman in the town. He was ordained to the priesthood in the little Mission church in November of 1941. In summers, he lived in quarters connected with the Mission—part of the original Stewart's Hotel accommodations. In winter he took up residence in the old Liston Lodge below the dam—now incorporated into the Bear Creek Mall.

Father Marsh remembered Evergreen during the Second World War. "When casualty messages came through, they would call me and I would go out to the families . . . . Places around the world like Anzio and Iwo Jima where "my" boys were lost—I called them all "my" boys—still have a very sentimental attachment for me."

After Canon Douglas's death in 1944, Father Marsh became Vicar of the Mission and also Secretary of the Evergreen Conference. In 1946, he married Helene Abbott, who worked for the Conference. The couple lived a rather uncomfortable rotation of summers in the two or three rooms above the Mission and winters in St. Raphael's, after the Sisters had left, until Mrs. Anne Douglas took pity on them. Continuing the Douglas tradition of generosity, she donated land adjacent to the Mission for a Vicarage.

What became an Evergreen Christmas tradition for many years started from a misfortune: the PTA President came running up to Father Marsh one year in great distress. Her planned Christmas program had fallen apart. Father Marsh suggested a living Christmas pageant. He staged it, using many of the town's prominent citizens in the cast. It was a resounding success. As late as 1970, the Canyon Courier noted that "300 people attended the 30th performance of the Evergreen Christmas Pageant at Evergreen High School. Larry Olde, one of the three kings, was the third generation of his family to participate. His father, Gerry, played Joseph, a part Herman Olde played until his death."

As the year-round community grew in numbers and resources, the small church in a pioneer sawmill-turned-hotel was clearly inadequate. Through the efforts of a Building Committee chaired by Don Shephard, Denver architect Richard Headstrom was commissioned to design a new church. It was opened for services in February of 1963. The formidable task of paying for it was eased by an initial $36,000 gift from Mrs. Helen Abbott, mother of Helene Marsh.

Some cherished art from the old Mission was incorporated into the new church, including the work of a farm boy from Bear Mountain named Henry Herzman. His talent had been discovered by Canon Douglas, who nurtured it by commissioning him to do wood carvings of the Stations of the Cross, a manger scene for the Tabernacle Door, and figures for the Rood Beam. Canon Douglas saw to it that Herzman's artistic education was enriched by involvement with the young Denver Art Museum, where Herzman served for many years as an assistant to Douglas's son, Eric. The stone work behind the altar is the work of Brooks Morris, a master mason, woodcarver and musician.

Father Marsh developed health problems and could no longer live at a high altitude. In 1964, he resigned from all his official clerical duties and moved down to Wheatridge. Because of his lifelong interest in church architecture, he kept his hand in Diocesan affairs by taking on the Secretaryship of the Diocesan Architectural Commission.

Hiwan Homestead Museum, detail.

In the centennial year commemorating the first congregational gathering of 1871, Bud Marsh was honored by the parish and the wider community of Evergreen at a festive banquet. This was organized by a large committee under the chairmanship of Jack Rouse. Marsh died in Lutheran Medical Center in 1983 at the age of 70.

On the Feast of the Transfiguration in 1964, Father Charles Blakeslee conducted his first service as the new Vicar of the Evergreen Church. A veteran of the European infantry campaigns of the Second World War, he served in parishes in Chicago and Kansas before coming to Evergreen. He presided over the Church's destiny during a period of great change and growth, serving for more than 20 years before retiring in 1985.

Anne Woodward Douglas
Douglas's second wife, Anne Woodward, lived on until 1985. For most of these years, her home was the little cottage next to the old Library on the Conference grounds in Evergreen.

Her childhood was spent in Leadville. After graduating from Wellesley College, she went to work in 1926 for the Episcopal Diocese in Colorado. She served as Secretary to Bishops Irving Johnson and Fred Ingley and worked with the Evergreen Conference. In 1931 she became executive secretary of its governing committee, a position she held until the conference was incorporated in 1942. In this capacity she came to know Canon Douglas well and to collaborate with him on many of his ongoing projects.

After Douglas's death, Anne became President of the Evergreen Conference Board of Trustees (from 1946 until 1968), was a leader in state and national activities of the Episcopalian Churchwoman, and active in Denver's musical organizations.

To the founders of the Hiwan Homestead Museum, Anne Douglas was a great resource. She had been a frequent guest there in the 1920's and 30's and had lived in the house for a year with Canon Douglas in the early 1940's, when it was still known as Camp Neosho. She served as chief consultant for the restoration of the chapel in the museum, and often gave talks to tour guides about the Homestead buildings and history.

In collaboration with Leonard Ellingood, Anne Douglas wrote a biography of her husband which was published in 1958. Anne Woodward Douglas died in Denver at the age of 90.

The Evergreen Conference Today
Accounts of the early years of the Evergreen Conference say that the conference buildings were transferred to the Diocese in 1925 by Dr. Jo, along with a trust fund for their maintenance, but the matter of clear legal title to land and buildings was not straightened out until 1982—with great effort and patience. Properties belonging to the Church of the Transfiguration, the Colorado Diocese (Evergreen Conference) and St. Raphael's were differentiated.

Church of the Transfiguration built in 1963.

57

Charlotte and Wayne Underwood.

The Evergreen Conference as a private program still exists, providing the annual church music schools. It has exclusive right to first use of the Conference facilities during the month of July. The facilities themselves are under the management of "Episcopal Camps and Conferences, Inc.," a subcommittee within the Episcopal Diocese of Colorado.

Much credit for a patient disentangling of the threads of ownership and negotiation of the property lines goes to Charlotte Underwood, Executive Secretary of the Evergreen Conference. A native of Bavaria, Charlotee had a varied career in interior design and hotel management before coming west with her husband—whose business was in international agricultural marketing. She promised to confine herself to volunteer work. The Underwoods arrived in Evergreen in 1980, and the volunteer work didn't last long. The challenge of her Evergreen Conference job incorporates both her interior design experience and the management of what is essentially a large summer hotel.

Charlotte Underwood described the Conference properties as an "exquisite diamond in the rough." They desperately needed upgrading, winterizing and modernizing. Their purpose needed a clear sense of definition. So did their functional relationship to the Church of the Transfiguration, to St. Raphael's and its possible future, and to the Evergreen community.

Studies were done, estimates of upgrading costs for the different buildings were made, possible resources for funding were surveyed. It was determined that a need did exist for residential conference facilities for from 35 to 125 people, with a mountain atmosphere, comfortable, warm sleeping quarters and adequate cooking and eating facilities. A master plan for stages of modernization and some new construction was prepared by Evergreen architect Charles Younkman and submitted for approval to Jefferson County authorities.

In the mid-1980's, the almost 80 year-old Evergreen Conference was reorganizing itself. It seems likely that it will continue to be an institution of state and national importance in the Episcopalian community, as well as an integral part of the past, present and future of Evergreen.

St. Raphael's

This quiet and lovely little complex is in Evergreen because of Canon Douglas's interest in plainsong. He was invited to give a series of lessons on the Chant to the Convent of the Community of St. Mary in Kenosha, Wisconsin, in 1906. Thus began an association with this Episcopalian order which was to last for the rest of Douglas's life.

The first Anglican religious community in America, the Order was founded in 1865 in Peeksill, New York. Growing rapidly, it was invited to run hospitals, schools and orphanages in New York, Tennessee and Wisconsin. The Order was organized into three Provinces—the Eastern, Western and Southern—with the Mother house remaining in Peekskill.

The founding "Mother," Harriett Starr Canon, had visited religious communities in England and heard the Divine Offices sung in plainsong which the Sisters adapted, using English words, for their community offices.

Canon Douglas was invited to teach them the Solesmes method, which he did with great skill and patience. He became the Community's choirmaster and embarked on a labor of love, adapting the offices in English to plainsong, and writing the accompanying musical notation.

The choirs of the Community tried out his works in manuscript before they were published.

Douglas's plainsong lifework, the *Monastic Diurnal Noted*, was still unfinished when he died in 1944. Appropriately, it was finally published in 1954 by the Community of St. Mary.

Around 1907, the Douglas's gave to the Western Province of the Community of St. Mary a building which had formerly been a tavern (it had been bought up by Mary Williams in order to close it down) for a retreat house for the Sisters. Later, a second house was moved to join the tavern, and an addition built on to allow for expanded sleeping space and the creation of a little chapel. This building is still in use as St. Raphael's House—the original tavern a sitting room, the chapel a dining room and the sleeping rooms neat and orderly, accommodating up to 13 people for residential retreats.

In the late 50's, negotiations were underway for building the Evergreen sewer plant in its present location. This necessitated the moving of both the creek and the road. By this time, the Community of St. Mary owned a house which had belonged to Evergreen's master carpenter, Jock Spence. It sat on solid foundations on top of the hill which had to be blasted through to make room for the new road.

Compensation for their condemned land paid for the removal of the house, and its placement next to St. Raphael's House. It was remodelled into a delightful little chapel which was dedicated by Bishop Minnis on the Feast of the Transfiguration, August 6, 1961.

At the entrance to the chapel is a carved wooden statue of Joseph the Traveler which Canon Douglas brought home to Camp Neosho, after a visit to Oberammergau. Inside, the marble altar with its vivid red painted cross carved in relief into the front, came from the octagonal chapel at Camp Neosho. So did the little carved monks and abbotts on the ends of the pews. The tall wooden candelabras were made as a gift by Father Marsh. A bedroom adjoining the chapel was remodelled for the Sacristy.

On the other side of St. Raphael's House is a delightful memento of pioneer Evergreen—a simple wooden cabin that was the second site of Evergreen's Library. It was used for many years to accommodate people on retreats and is now rented.

The only other "building" in this little complex is a stone-faced root cellar built into the hillside behind the original tavern. Finished in concrete inside, this is used as storage, especially for items like paint which must not freeze. This survival from simpler times teaches us why root cellars were indispensable in days before central heating: they never froze, no matter how cold the winter.

In addition to its use as a retreat house for the members of the Community, St. Raphael's has been a place of quiet prayer and renewal for a great variety of church-affiliated groups during its more than 70 years of existence. For many years St. Raphael's retreats for women were a special part of the Evergreen summer Conference summer programs.

For this Community, as for many other monastic orders, the number of new members has declined sharply. St. Raphael's in the summer of 1985 was staffed by one gentle, grey-haired Sister, 65 years young. Sister Mary Paula came first to St. Raphael's as a novice in the 50's. As a "city girl" she did not enjoy looking out on a landscape where the only sign of life was Hereford cattle!

She did not return until 1975 when she became responsible for the summer program. From the early 1980's she has lived year-round in Evergreen. In 1983, the Sister had surgery for a brain tumor, which left her with some facial paralysis and total loss of hearing in one ear. Nevertheless, when Barbara arrived to interview her, she was busy washing loads of snow-white cotton sheets after the departure of one retreat group, in preparation for the next. She felt that her life was spared in order that she could use her remaining years in this place.

The Western Province of the Community gave up its beautiful old Convent building in Milwaukee because the Sisters were aging and needed to a place with nursing home care available. In 1985, the

Chapel of St. Joseph and St. Mary.

Sisters' cabin, St. Raphael's House, Root Cellar.

Order relinquished another large building in Racine. When Sister Mary Paula is no longer able to maintain the offerings at St. Raphael's— retreats for groups of not more than 13 (vestries, women's groups, clergy, church singles or couples groups, deacon candidates), weekly prayer services in the chapel and various classes and study groups in the winter months—this facility too will have to be given up.

There are many possibilities for its future. Sister Mary Paula told of her dream that it might become a center for members of the Episcopal clergy in crisis. Convinced that St. Raphael's is indeed a place that restores health, the Sister said: "After all, is not St. Raphael the Archangel of healing?"

THE EVANS-EVERGREEN CONNECTION

On April 15, 1984, an innovative organization called Colorado Open Lands closed on a contract to purchase the 3,245-acre Evans Ranch west of Evergreen for $4,050,000. The objective was to preserve the land for its long-time uses—including summer pasturing of cattle, year-round refuge for many varieties of wildlife, and limited hunting—without the expenditure of tax dollars.

The Evans Ranch has been a significant part of the economy and history of the Evergreen area since 1868.

If you drive to the end of Upper Bear Creek Road and take the right fork to the Mount Evans State Wildflife Area, you enter the expansive, beautiful area historically associated with the Evans Ranch.

The pattern of ranching in the mountain area developed along two distinct lines; there were year-round settlers and there were wealthy purchasers of mountain acreages, who hoped to combine some income-producing activities with the joys of a summer family retreat. Though such income rarely justified the ownership, the beauty and peace of the surroundings did. Such was the case with the Evans Ranch.

Margaret Gray Evans

Governor John Evans.

The Evans-Elbert Purchase

Edgar McMechen, pioneer Colorado historian and friend and admirer of Governor John Evans, wrote a book about him in 1924. In it McMechen describes a camping trip made in the summer of 1868 by Evans and some of his family.

Meadow on the Evans Ranch.

The party drove in spring wagons to the mouth of Mount Vernon Canyon, and followed this to Bergen's Ranch. From there they turned southwest towards Bear Creek, reaching the stream at a place now known as Bendemeer where they camped for several weeks.

During this camping trip, Governor Evans and Governor Elbert rode four miles up a branch of Bear Creek to Vance's Park, where the charming vista convinced them that this was the spot they sought for a permanent summer home. Luxuriant grass in the wide creek bottom stood as high as timothy hay, and this feature, together with the width of the valley impressed both as excellent cattle range.

The two men became engrossed in a discussion as to the possibilities of a stock ranch, while the other members in the party were content to lie idly in the grass, exclaiming at the sweep of spruce-clad hills, the rapidly-rushing stream and the billowy clouds in the sky.

Evans and Elbert negotiated with homesteader Vance to purchase 320 acres of land, the nucleus of the Evans-Elbert Ranch. McMechen tells about an abortive attempt to pasture 700 longhorns through a particularly bitter Upper Bear Creek winter. Like so many of the best stories, this one is probably not true. But some unsuccessful attempts at year-round cattle raising did help determine that the Governor "engaged in the cattle business no more."

The early history of the ranch, and of the homes grouped around it, involved the intertwined branches of four family trees: Evans, Gray, Lunt and Elbert.

Governor John Evans

John Evans was born in 1814 to Quaker parents in Waynesville, Ohio. McMechen characterized him as "physician, educator, financier, railroad builder, philanthropist, founder of hospitals, churches and universities, executive and idealist."

Evans practiced medicine first in Indiana, where in 1845 he helped to establish the state mental hospital and became its first superintendent. He is also credited with pushing through Congress the first Quarantine Act for infectious diseases.

Appointment as professor of obstetrics at Rush Medical School took him to Chicago where he met Orrington Lunt, probably through their shared enthusiasm for Methodism and the remarkable oratory of Bishop Matthew Simpson. Evans' first wife died in 1850 leaving him with a small daughter, Josephine. At the home of Orrington and Cornelia Lunt he met his second wife, Margaret Gray, Cornelia's sister.

Orrington was an aggressive businessman. A charter member of the Chicago Board of Trade and director of one of its first railroads, he also, like Evans, of an idealistic and philanthropic disposition. The two men were involved in the founding of Northwestern University in Evanston, Illinois, a town named after John Evans.

The heady world of real estate and finance was beginning to look more exciting to Evans than medicine. He was also drawn into politics. In the Lincoln-Douglas battle for the presidency, he was a wholehearted supporter of Lincoln.

In 1862, Lincoln appointed Evans as the second Governor of the Colorado Territory. The new appointee traveled alone to Denver, arranging for his wife and three children—William and Margaret had joined Josephine by this time—to come when he had found suitable housing.

Five-year-old Margaret came down with scarlet fever. Evans sent his medical recommendations by letter but the girl died before the long journey by covered wagon to Denver began. Perhaps some anger that her doctor-husband was in Denver at this crucial time played a part in Margaret Evans' inability to accept Colorado as her permanent home for many years. But also she had enjoyed life in Evanston, while Denver was a small, raw, and uncultured town when she came to it.

Evans' tenure as governor was cut short by accusations of complicity in the infamous Sand Creek Massacre. While a military commission was in Denver investigating that "engagement" between Col. Chivington and the Indians, President Lincoln—Evans' most powerful friend in Washington —was assassinated. The Secretary of War asked for Evans' resignation.

It is difficult for us to realize the atmosphere of fear in which the Sand Creek affair was possible, but we got a hint of it in a story told us by Margaret Evans Davis. This last surviving granddaughter of Governor Evans was 91 when we were priveleged to talk with her at her summer home near the Evans Ranch in September of 1981. She remembered staying with her grandparents in their large home on Arapahoe Street in Denver; her grandmother would pay her a nickel to close every curtain in the house at dusk. Margaret Evans was terrified of the Indians who would stop and peer into the lighted windows. On one of her early journey west by wagon, she brought a young relative with her for a visit in Denver. Sunie Lowell had glorious red hair—a novelty to a group of Indians who wanted to buy her: they were angry and hostile when their offer was refused. Mrs. Evans made the rest of the journey in mortal fear that they would attack and steal the girl away.

Except for one year as senator-elect, when he worked in Washington for Colorado's statehood, Evans never again held public office or engaged in politics.

The same year Evans became Governor, Samuel Elbert, a young attorney from Nebraska, was appointed by Lincoln to be the Attorney General of the Colorado Territory. He and Evans became lifelong friends.

In 1865, Elbert married Josephine Evans. As a result, he was included in the 1868 Bear Creek family camping trip. It is not recorded whether Josephine went along. If so, it must have been one of her last excursions as she died in October that year from tuberculosis.

Elbert did not remarry. He went on to become Territorial Governor in his own right in the early '70's, and one of the new State of Colorado's first supreme court justices in 1876.

Governor Sam Elbert.

Corrals and barns.

One of many spectacular views.

Kuhlborne Ranch

After the failure of attempts to use the Evans-Elbert Ranch for cattle-raising, there was talk of selling it. However, it was decided to retain it for no other reason than that "Mrs. Evans delighted in the place". The name was changed to Kuhlborne Ranch and its acreage steadily increased by purchases from surrounding homesteaders.

Every summer the ranch was used for family holidays by Mrs. Evans, her children—William, Evan Elbert and Anne—and various combinations of visiting relatives of the Evans, Lunt, Gray and Elbert families.

Evans himself does not seem to have been cut out for leisure. McMechen reports that it took him only one day to find out that he would never be a fisherman:

He once tried trout fishing on the ranch, attacking the sport with his always indomitable patience and persistence. With an old gray shawl draped around his shoulders, to prevent a drenching from the wet willows, he cast hour after hour 'from morn to noon, from noon to dewy eve,' and at sundown he had as many fish as at the break of day.

He decided that he had exhausted all the possibilities of the art, and thereafter confined his interest to trout that appeared, brown and crisp, upon his plate.

Evans was by this time into railroad building. He was well aware of the insatiable demand for lumber both for railroad ties and for mine props. From 1860 to the end of the century, timber was undoubtedly the most profitable harvest in the Evergreen area. From the Evans Ranch it was hauled to Idaho Springs via a steep and perilous road over Squaw Pass—a grueling task, requiring a team of four horses.

Margaret Evans Davis reminisced about those long-ago days when the dirt road to Idaho Springs was crossed, every 100 feet or so, by hand-dug drainage ditches. They were called "thank you, ma'ams" because the driver could sink the back wheels of his wagon into the ditches and so give the team a welcome rest.

Evans was the prime mover in building the Denver, South Platte and Pacific Railroad, whose first phase brought the railroad to Morrison. He also organized the building of the first wagon road down Bear Creek to Morrison, primarily for the transport of lumber.

At first this was a dirt road down by the creek, with simple wooden bridges crossing the stream when necessary. The plan was to make it a toll road, but after a cloudburst destroyed all the bridges (some 50 in number, according to recollections later recorded in an interview with his daughter Anne Evans), Evans decided to give stock in the road to some men in Morrison in exchange for their rebuilding the road when necessary.

Crops Verus Elk

Barley and oats were grown, harvested, and threshed on the ranch. The grain, as well as hay, was then taken to Idaho Springs for sale. Evans' granddaughter told us that a large field of potatoes was also cultivated on the ranch for many years.

The planting of crops virtually stopped in 1917, soon after the fledgling Colorado State Game and Fish Department decided to introduce elk into the Mount Evans basin. The original settlers found a variety of wildlife in the basin including deer, bear, mountain lion, bighorn sheep and mountain goats. But not elk.

Elk were originally plentiful at lower elevations of the Front Range—Bergen Park's first name was Elk Park—but they were wiped out in the wholesale slaughter of easily accessible game that took place in the last half of the nineteenth century. In other areas, elk apparently survived by learning to live at higher altitudes.

A public subscription paid for the transportation of some 26 head of elk by railcar from Wyoming to Idaho Springs. From this original few comes the entire herd of today which must be culled annually to keep it down to around 1,000 head. Ralph Metzner, Manager of the Mount Evans State Wildlife Area, reports with pride that all of the original animals are also keeping a foothold in the Mount Evans basin.

For every benefit, a cost. Free-ranging elk and early greening crops like oats cannot coexist.

The Evans Family and Summers on the Ranch

Allen Breck, a University of Denver historian who has written extensively about the Evans family, notes that "Relations between John Evans and his wife and three children were those of a loving, kindly paternal despot towards those whom he protected and for whom he worked unceasingly." Evans spent little time at the ranch; his life was filled with daring, sometimes risky, financial ventures in which idealistic plans for the future of Denver and Colorado were intermingled with the possibility of large personal gains—or losses.

Evans' religious and philanthropic interests also multiplied. Though an 1864 attempt to found a classically-oriented prep school called the Colorado Seminary temporarily foundered for lack of support, it later blossomed into the University of Denver. Evans also helped to found new Methodist churches as the city grew.

63

Margaret Evans made no secret of her dislike for Denver. She much preferred living and traveling in the cultured capitals of Europe. Governor Evans accompanied her on two trips in the early 70's—their daughter Anne was born in London in 1871—and she took young William on the Grand Tour and settled him into an English School for a term. She spent almost two years, from 1875-77, living in London, Antwerp, Brussels and Italy, according to an interesting paper written by one of her great-great-granddaughters, and then seems to have made her peace with fate and accepted Denver as her permanent home.

Thereafter, she took a leading part in many social causes in Denver, being especially active in promoting educational opportunities for women, and was a vigorous patron of the arts. She came to share her husband's faith in the future of her adopted city. But summers were spent on the Evans Ranch, in which she continued to take great pleasure.

For both William and Anne, the Ranch was a vital part of childhood, but it affected them differently. William was already 13 when the nucleus of the ranch was bought. It was there he learned the art of fishing, that skill so uncongenial to his father. For William, it became a passionate avocation but he graduated from trout streams to the sea. As an adult, he preferred to take his vacations in Florida or other deep sea fishing meccas.

During his university days, William had a brief period of longing to be just a simple, hard-working mountain rancher at 'Kuhlborne'. Perhaps he foresaw the stress and gravity of the responsibilities he would take on as his father's heir in a rapidly changing world. William was a student at Northwestern University in Illinois when his father visited him and heard of his unwelcome ambition. Mrs.

Evans was traveling again, and her husband wrote to her in London in 1875:

Willie seems large and strong and manly. He has got that foolish cattle raising idea so badly that he is already contemplating leaving college before his course is finished . . . I guess you had better try and get him cooled of his 'Kuhlborne' fever. He would not like it long when the play and fishing and hunting were turned into hard work."

For Anne Evans the beautiful land above Evergreen was part of every summer of her life, except when she was traveling abroad. Horace Fletcher Lunt, a cousin and contemporary of Anne Evans, wrote a sketchy but vivid picture of early summers on the Evans Ranch.

Horace was 5 in 1880 when he was brought by train for his first visit by the Orrington Lunts, his grandparents. His own family moved to Colorado Springs in 1887, and for the next 11 years he was up at the ranch for extended visits every summer. At first, the quickest route was a two-hour train ride from Denver to Idaho Springs followed by a three hour ride over Squaw Pass. "That was some road", he wrote, "up 2,300 feet from Idaho Springs, then down 1,700 feet to the ranch, all in 8 miles."

Later, it was better to take advantage of the new train service to Morrison and then the stage to Evergreen, which Lunt described as "a three-seated spring wagon with two horses, driven by an old man with a long beard, at a rather slow pace." Occasionally the road in lower Bear Creek would wash out, then the route would be via Turkey Creek and what is now Indian Hills. "Naturally," wrote Lunt, "when we went up, we stayed for a considerable time."

Margaret Evans Davis' earliest memories went back to 1891, when Evergreen was "three or four houses and three or four stores - and that was it!" There,

Margaret Evans Davis in 1981.

she said, a buckboard from the ranch would meet them, to complete a long day's journey.

The original log house, built in 1869 as a summer residence for the Evans family, was just west of Metz Creek.

According to Lunt, "It had a good many rooms without being very large, and was entirely without 'modern conveniences.'" Running water was ingeniously provided by a little ditch from the creek, running through a wooden trough just outside the house. A laundry shack had a wood stove on which to heat water, and all the children had to take a bath on Sunday mornings. The house was destroyed by fire in 1910.

Homesteader Vance's log cabin was used for many years as a home for the ranch foreman who looked after the stock, did the milking, and hauled in firewood. A few milk cows were the only cattle at this time, but there were, by Lunt's account, "scrub riding ponies as well as a few teams of driving and work horses. They used to pasture a lot of the big draft horses that were used on the ore wagons around Idaho Springs, when they needed a rest." When a new ranch house was built in 1912 the Vance cabin, with additions made over the years, was retained for storage.

Time passed quickly with haying, harvesting and threshing of oats, and occasional rides to round up escaped horses. There were other diversions—trout fishing, picnics, and long horseback rides. These might be along trails—to the top of Mount Evans, Echo Lake, Camp Rock or Groundhog Flats—or to other parts of the vast Mount Evans region where there were no trails at all.

Mount Rosalie, Mount Evans

In the early days, Mount Evans had another name. When the gold seekers first hit the Idaho Springs area, the entire range was named the Chicago Peaks. Then in the early 1860's, William Byers, founder of the Rocky Mountain News, took a visiting artist named Albert Bierstadt to sketch the splendor of the Rocky Mountains.

Bierstadt named the highest peak Mount Rosalie, after his future wife. The next-highest peak, according to Hayden's 1977 Geological and Geographical Atlas of Colorado, was named Mount Evans. However, a story told by Kay Klepetko in her "Tales of the Bar PD" indicates that, at least within the family, the highest peak had been known as Mount Evans for many years. Orrington Lunt's son, Judge Lunt, climbed the mountain with a friend in 1872 and left a note in a tin can buried on the summit. Unearthed 38 years later, it read, "Saturday, September 14, 1872, summit of Mt. Evans, by barometer 14,525 feet above sea level. Seven (7) guns fired at 10:00 a.m. as a salute to Governor Evans of Denver and his mountain. Signed H. G. Lunt and C. Moody."

In the twilight of his life, Gov. Evans was memorialized by the Colorado Legislature. Senate Joint Resolution No. 15, approved on March 15, 1895 and titled "Naming a Mountain," officially recognized the highest peak as Mount Evans. Bierstadt and his wife are still commemorated by two subsidiary peaks.

The Evans Ranch

In the early 1890's, a series of economic misfortunes befell the Evans family. To raise capital, Gov. Evans mortgaged his half of the ranch to Samuel Elbert, his son-in-law and the owner of the other half, for $4,926.

In 1897, the patriarch died without making a will. His sons William and Evan were left with the unenviable task of sorting out the complex of financial assets and debts to arrive at what Allen Breck describes as "the platform from which the family estate was to be rebuilt."

When Elbert died in 1899, he left both his half of the Ranch and the mortgage note to different members of the Evans family. To get the family finances in order, Evans Realty Company was created and what was now officially named the Evans Ranch was put into it.

The Summer Colony Grows

Gov. Evans' widow, Margaret, and William's wife, Cornelia, gave 20-acre parcels of ranch land to William and Cornelia's four children for summer homes. At the same time, the process of adding to the total size of the ranch, by purchases from surrounding owners, continued. A number of relatives also bought land of their own on which to build homes and join this unique summer colony.

The third generation of Evans' to spend summers on the ranch began to arrive in 1884, when John Evans II was born to Evans' oldest son, William, and his wife—who was also his first cousin—Cornelia Gray. The son was followed by daughters Josephine, Margaret and Katherine. For these children, long summers on the ranch west of Evergreen were a treasured part of every year.

Original Evans home on Evans and Elbert Ranch.

Samuel Elbert's niece, Louise, married Leonard Everett. They hired brothers Charlie and Will Devlan to build a summer home on land inherited from Elbert. These brothers were already settled on the land, cutting and hauling timber to Idaho Springs, when Evans and Elbert bought the Vance homestead. The Everetts hired Jock Spence, the Evergreen craftsman who built so many of Evergreen's best early structures, to do the stone work.

The Everett house.

Regina Lunt—daughter of Judge Lunt and a cousin of Anne, William and Evan Evans—married Clarence Phelps Dodge. In 1903, the couple bought the 160-acre homestead of John Newman, and some adjacent land from the Evans-Elbert Ranch. Clarence Dodge had settled in Colorado Springs after graduation from Yale. His father was a Presbyterian minister and founder of the University of Beirut. Clarence was for 18 years the owner and publisher of the Colorado Springs Gazette and a member of the Colorado House of Representatives. He and Regina had two children, a boy and a girl named after them. Regina Lunt Dodge was a talented artist, and her creativity can be seen in the home she designed for them, which was built by Jock Spence.

Newman's homestead cabin was moved and remodelled into an office for Clarence and a skylighted studio for Regina. The ranch complex eventually included guest quarters, a bunkhouse for extra hands hired at harvest time, servants quarters and laundry, ice house (used until 1945) and barn.

Clarence Dodge died of pneumonia in 1939. The ranch was inherited by Clarence Phelps Jr. and his wife Eileen. After the war, they converted many of the auxiliary buildings for guest cabins and ran the ranch as a combination of working cattle ranch and resort. But it was a struggle, and eventually they were happy to sell the property to the Jefferson County R-1 School District for an outdoor education facility—a sale that guaranteed its remaining intact.

The Extraordinary Anne Evans

Gov. Evans' daughter, Anne, developed into one of the most dynamic and influential women in the history of Colorado. Educated in London, Paris, and Berlin, she never married but poured her immense zest for life into establishing cultural institutions.

Anne was a prime mover in the establishment of both the Denver Art Museum and the Denver Public Library, in the restoration of the Central City Opera House and in the development of the summer opera festival there.

One of Anne's most original contributions was an early appreciation of native Indian art as authentic and valuable, at a time when most Americans regarded it either as anthropological artifact or as colorful stuff with which to furnish a den. She found kindred spirits in fellow Evergreen summer residents Canon Winfred Douglas and his son, Eric.

Anne spent much time in New Mexico. When the Denver Art Museum was launched, she talked the board of directors into acquiring a native arts collection and brought Eric in as curator. When she died, she left her own priceless collection to the museum.

Anne commissioned one of Denver's best-known architects, Burnham Hoyt—designer of Red Rocks Theater in Morrison—to create a home for her on the Evans Ranch. She wanted a building that expressed her love of the Mount Evans area and of Indian motifs. Her friend, artist Josephine Hurlburt, designed the Indian-inspired motifs for the gable ends, fire screen and windows.

The new summer home, completed in 1911, was furnished with priceless Navajo rugs and the finest Indian basketry and pottery. Here, according to a Denver Post article, she "presided like a matriarch over an estate which included the homes of all those nearest and dearest to her."

Margaret Evans Davis home, built by Jock Spence.

Peg Hayden, daughter of Margaret Evans Davis, shows her mother's home to Barbara Sternberg.

Anne Evans house: motifs designed by artist Josephine Hurlburt

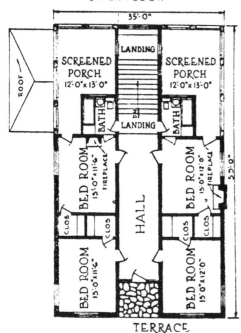

UPPER FLOOR

35'-0"

SCREENED PORCH 12'-0"x13'-0"

LANDING

SCREENED PORCH 12'-0"x13'-0"

ROOF

BATH

LANDING

BATH

BED ROOM 15'-0"x11'-6" FIREPLACE

HALL

BED ROOM 15'-0"x12'-0" FIREPLACE

55'-0"

CLOS

CLOS

CLOS

CLOS

BED ROOM 15'-0"x11'-6"

BED ROOM 15'-0"x12'-0"

TERRACE

Floor plans of Anne Evans home designed by Burnham Hoyt.

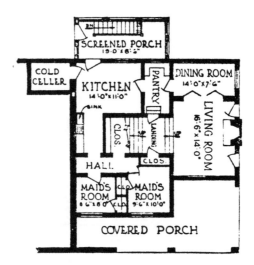

LOWER FLOOR

SCREENED PORCH 19'-0"x16'-2"

COLD CELLER

KITCHEN 14'-0"x11'-0" SINK

PANTRY

DINING ROOM 14'-0"x7'-6"

LANDING

LIVING ROOM 16'-6"x14'-0"

CLOS

CLOS

HALL

CLOS

MAID'S ROOM 8'-6"x8'-0"

CLO

CLO

MAID'S ROOM 9'-6"x10'-0"

COVERED PORCH

The Margaret Evans Davis Home

The Devlan brothers were longtime holdouts from buy-out by the Evans. In 1918 they sold to an Eastern engineer named Metcalf. John Evans III told us how Metcalf came to visit the Evans Ranch. His father, John Evans II, had started the Denver Union Water Co. with a partner. They had literally staked their personal fortunes on building the Cheesman Dam to secure Denver's future water supply.

When they finally realized that "no one had enough private money to finance an adequate municipal water system and so negotiated with Denver city to buy it, they were thoroughly vilified in the press for their efforts. Dad brought Metcalf in from the east: he was one of the finest and most respected appraisers of water values in the entire country. Metcalf fell in love with the Evans Ranch land and negotiated with the Devlan Brothers to sell him their land, and build a house on it for him. They brought Jock Spence in to do the stone work."

Metcalf's idea was to use the house himself in the fall as a hunting lodge, and let his two sisters from Boston use it in the summers. According to John, the sisters "hated the whole idea and only spent one summer here." Metcalf died around 1924, not long after the home was completed.

John Evans bought the home and used it for guests. Later he sold it to his sister Margaret and her husband Roblin Davis. The home still is substantially as the Devlan brothers and Jock Spence built it: sturdy, carefully crafted of local materials, and now beautifully weathered.

It was there, in 1981, that we talked with Margaret Evans Davis, over 40 years after she first moved in. Here was where pioneer Pearl Anderson cooked and cleaned every summer for 25 years. Margaret Evans Davis and her four children spent most of their family summers there. Though she died a couple of years later, we have a vivid image of her energetic and engaging personality as she reminisced about her earliest memories of the Ranch when she was about 2 and the nineteenth century was just ending, and looked ahead to her 100th birthday.

Peg Hayden.

Peg Hayden, one of her daughters, built her own contemporary home nearby and has lived there year-round since 1979. One of Peg's daughters, Meg Hayden, lives in the home built in 1920 for her grandmother. Peg's son, Tom, also lives nearby: he operates the sawmill near the entrance to the Mount Evans State Wildlife Area.

68

Peg Hayden's new home.

Cheesman Realty Takes Title

The ranch grew from the original 320 acres to 800 in the late 1800's and to around 6,000 in the 1920's. The legal title again changed. In 1908 John Evans II married Gladys Cheesman, daughter of Walter Cheesman, who was one of Denver's early movers and shakers in real estate, railroading, and finance. There was a consolidation of the holdings of the two families and the ranch was placed in a trust with title vested in the Cheesman Realty Co.

Evans Ranch Foremen

From the earliest days, the Evans family retained a year-round, resident foreman. They seem to have had the knack of selecting loyal, capable and likable people for the job: three in particular stayed for many years and were well-known and respected in the mountain community.

One of the first was Dan Witter after whom Witter Gulch is named. Another was Bryan Schwartz, who was born and raised in the Idaho Springs area and lived most of his life in Evergreen. Jack Brasel, who succeeded Schwartz in 1945, has retired with his wife Marge to a home they built on land given to them by the Evans family—in recognition of their many years of devoted service.

While Bryan Schwartz was foreman, after the first world war and the end of crop raising on the ranch, cattle-raising was reintroduced as a year-round operation. When Jack Brasel took over, it was decided to run cattle only in summer, and that was still the practice in 1986.

Another Generation

John Evans II built his own large home on the ranch. This house, together with 100 acres separated from the ranch, went to Alice, the oldest of the three children born to Evans and Gladys Cheesman. Alice was married to Hudson Moore, Jr. John Evans III inherited Anne Evans's home, and the youngest daughter, Anne, who married Frank Freyer, built a home for her family on the ranch. A parcel of land around it was deeded to them. John Evans III sometimes lives on the ranch year-round, but the others are summer residents.

As long as Anne Evans, Louise Everett and Regina Dodge were alive, there were memorable and creative summer family get-togethers: plays were written, costumed and acted, and there were horse shows, parades, bonfires and picnics.

Initially, the roads from Denver to the ranch were so bad, and the automobiles so prone to breakdown, that car travel was more of an adventure than an advantage. But the roads gradually improved, along with the vehicles, and what used to be a daylong trek became less than an hour's journey. More and more, the individual families came and went according to their own schedules and all-family activities became rarer.

69

Cabin built by the Devlan Brothers and enlarged by Tom Hayden, great-great-grandson of Gov. John Evans.

The 1950's saw the first major reduction in the size of the Evans Ranch. The neighboring Truesdell property, some 1,874 acres—on which we spent our first happy mountain vacation—was sold to the Colorado Game and Fish Commission for use as a wildlife preserve.

Since there was no public access to it, an agreement was negotiated with Cheesman Realty, owner of the Evans Ranch trust, for the state to put a road through to Camp Rock. But bringing large numbers of people right into the middle of the ranch created many problems. The Evans Ranch owners therefore agreed to sell all of the land on the same side of the road as the Truesdell property to the State, on condition that the State fence all of the remaining parts of the Evans Ranch bordering the Game and Fish property.

In 1958, 1,126 acres of the Evans Ranch was deeded by Cheesman Realty to the State of Colorado. The Truesdell and Evans properties, together with three minor additional purchases, form today's almost 4,000-acre Wildlife Management Area.

Barn built by Evans Ranch foreman Bryan Schwartz.

Jack Brasel, Evans Ranch foreman.

70

A Sale that Preserves

Between them, the three children of John Evans II and Gladys Cheesman had 12 children. As they married and had children of their own, the number of trust beneficiaries kept increasing. Many moved away from Colorado and had no direct benefit from summer visits to the ranch. As we noted earlier, the Evans Ranch never was an economically profitable operation.

One of the heirs demanded that he receive some tangible benefit from his share in a supposedly valuable piece of property. Not getting a response he considered satisfactory from the trustees, he sued and forced the issue of putting the property up for sale.

In the meantime, the organization called Colorado Open Lands (COL) had come into being as a direct outgrowth of Gov. Dick Lamm's 1979 Front Range Planning Project. It had become clear that many interesting and beautiful tracts of land, with important environmental values, were going to be transformed from existing agricultural or open space uses into development areas.

John Evans III.

Neither the State of Colorado nor the counties along the Front Range had the funds to protect even the most vital areas. In response to this need, the Colorado Forum—an association of chief executive officers from major Colorado corporations—created COL in 1981 as a privately supported, non-profit corporation. COL works with private landowners and public bodies to find ways to preserve the most desirable tracts of land as open space without the expenditure of tax dollars.

Because it was already in the courts, the Evans Ranch was identified as the first priority for the new organization. An innovative plan was developed that met COL's multiple objectives. It was economically feasible, preserved the existing ranch headquarters and gave them a function, retained the open space character of the land, conserved the wildlife habitat—especially the calving and foraging grounds of the elk—and allowed for limited public access to parts of the ranch.

The core of the plan provided for 5 separate ranches of from 530 to 580 acres each. For each ranch, a 40-acre homesite was designated for building of a home and related structures. These were carefully selected for view, ease of access, privacy and visual separation from each other.

The five buyers were to subscribe to a philosophy of being stewards of historic and valuable land and buildings. Together they would agree to form an association to own and operate the 129-acre ranch headquarters area. This includes the historic and well-maintained ranch structures and forms an amenity owned by, and benefiting, all ranch owners. The ranch headquarters provides security—all ranch owners enter their own properties through it—and the owners will use the headquarters and its hired staff to board and care for animals, plow and maintain roads and perform contract services on individual properties. In the future, they may choose to develop guest or recreational facilities in the headquarters area.

Three small separate parcels of land totalling 267 acres were retained by COL for a cultural/environmental/educational program developed—in close consultation with ranch owners— to be self-supporting, and with access only to invited participants.

The Gates Foundation provided a loan of $4,500,000 to purchase the land and to develop the plans. By the beginning of 1986, enough property had been sold to repay the loan. It was hoped that sale of the remaining ranches would provide COL with seed money for future projects.

Colorado Open Lands was gratified at the success of its pioneer project. For Evergreen, this solution means that a historic and important element of its life pattern will be preserved.

Marge Brasel.

71

72

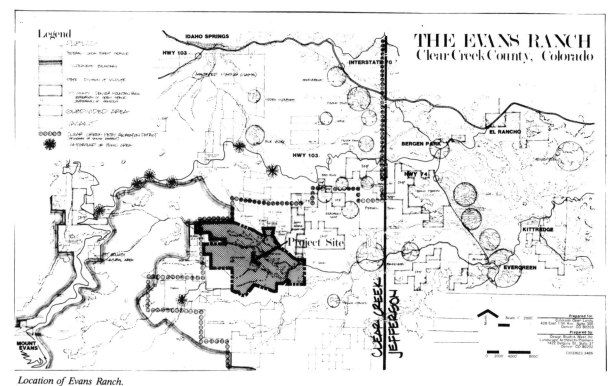

Location of Evans Ranch.

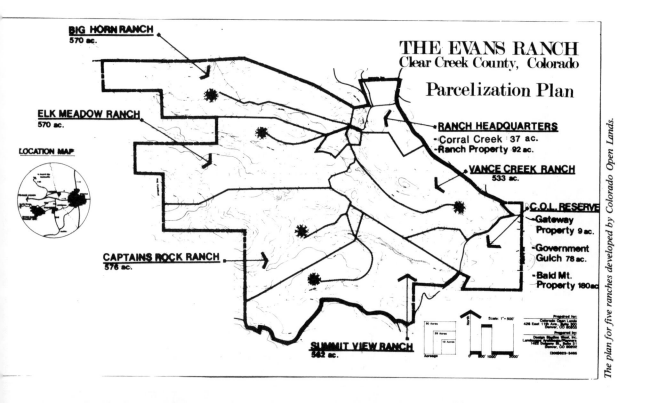

MINING, LOGGING, RANCHING

To make a living in Evergreen has always required versalitilty, ingenuity and a lot of hard work. Although we describe the early activities of settlers under categories such as mining, logging and ranching, these do not say very much about the real lives of people. To survive, everyone had to do a bit of everything.

Take the example of Thomas and Judith Bergen, the first white settlers in this area. They provided shelter and food for travelers, pastured and traded oxen and horses, cut and sold lumber, raised vegetables. Their son-in-law, Amos Post, was a skilled carpenter, founded the first trading post in Bergen Park and later in Evergreen, filed and worked timber and mining claims and served for a time as the Evergreen Postmaster. In an 1882 Rocky Mountain News ad, he is the Proprietor of the Bear Creek Stage Line, and in the 1887 Colorado State Business Directory his activities are listed as "Billiards and Mineral Baths".

Mining

Because the land and hills of the Evergreen area are not scarred by unhealed mine tailings as they are around Georgetown and Central City, newcomers may assume there was no prospecting here. Nothing could be further from the truth. A reading of the earliest land books in the Jefferson County Courthouse reveals that claims were filed on every acre that had any conceivable mineral potential.

This included most of the land along Bear Creek and its tributaries. Our neighbor Freddie Lincoln told us that she has found deep tunnels dug into hillsides on her Upper Bear Creek property, the nucleus of which was acquired by her grandfather in 1920. She also remembers that a cabin on the neighboring property was always known as "the miner's cabin."

Establishing a mining claim in the early days was a simple matter, according to an account left by Bergen's daughter Martha. You just measured off as many feet as you thought you needed for a mine, stuck up your shingle, and went and paid two or three dollars at the land office.

Early hopes of finding gold were soon dashed but for a while there seemed to be promising prospects in silver. A news item in the Colorado Transcript for March 1, 1871 was headlined, THE SILVER MINES NEAR BERGENS RANCH:

"During the past week we have been shown some very fine specimens of silver ore that have been taken out from Mr. Post's discovery west of Bergen's. This lode which is being opened out under the most encouraging prospects, shows a well-defined body of ore, carrying sulphuret of silver, argentiferous galena, and a small amount of pyrites. It is carrying a percentage of from $69 to $150 per ton of silver."

But silver, too, petered out. Next, promising copper deposits were found. 1883 saw the naming of a new mining district as the Evergreen District. A Rocky Mountain News article on April 11 reported that a Dr. E. D. Smith was elated by initial assay results, which showed "59-3/10 per cent copper, a very flattering return." The lodes of the new district, on Cub Creek, had been traced to "within a quarter mile of Troutdale." Noting that "there are quite a number of prospectors in the district, among whom are eight miners from Leadville," the article concluded with the fervent hope that "Jefferson County will yet be the producer of something besides coal and clay."

A 1908 Bulletin of the United States Geological Survey described three developed copper prospects, two of which had actual production to their credit.

The shaft of the Despatch property, "2 miles below Evergreen", was reported to be 140 feet deep, at which depth two veins containing copper were encountered. The F.M.D. property, lying "on a tributary to Bear Creek about 5 miles northwest of Evergreen, at an elevation of 6,800 feet" had a vertical shaft 350 feet deep, where three copper-bearing ore veins had been cut. But by 1908 work had been suspended and the shaft was partly filled with water.

The only mine site that we have been able to locate is the Augusta Lode, "half a mile above Evergreen". This is at the entrance to Skyline Drive on Highway 73. The shabby old building was still standing until early in 1985, when it was torn down to make way for construction of a mini-storage facility. The 1908 Bulletin reported that "ore containing copper and silver was shipped from it several years ago and work has been resumed at intervals."

Logging, Milling and the Sale of Lumber

It was not minerals but trees that first put real money into the hands of Evergreen pioneers. Timber was in great demand in the years from 1860 to the end of the century. At first the need was for building sluices and shoring up mine shafts, siding cabins and providing construction lumber down on the treeless plains. Soon the insatiable demand for railroad ties was added.

The first settlers lost no time in cutting the fine stands of virgin timber, establishing saw mills and moving the lumber to its most profitable markets—no matter what transportation difficulties were involved.

C. H. Deane, a government deputy surveyor working on the Evergreen Township survey in 1867—only eight years after the first settlers arrived—found ". . . a considerable portion of the best timber has been cut and made into lumber." He noted that "dissatisfaction is expressed by one Bergen now living in the township, who heretofore has held several thousand acres of land under the territorial law. His interest is to enable him to cut the balance of the pine timber, large quantities of which he has already cut and sold." Bergen's "dissatisfaction" apparently was with the rapid progress of the government survey, for as soon as it was completed the land was available for homesteading in 160-acre parcels and could no longer be provisionally held in large acreages without payment. In the end, Bergen only formally filed on 80 acres.

The unsightly effect of indiscriminate tree cutting was reported by the redoubtable Isabella Bird, an Edinburgh spinster who travelled throughout Colorado in the summer and fall of 1873. She published her letters home to her sister in a book , "A Lady's Life in the Rocky Mountains." Describing Clear Creek Canyon, "which many people think the grandest scenery in the mountains, as it twists and turns marvellously," she says, "Unfortunately,its sides have been almost entirely denuded of timber its utter desolation occasionally revealed by a beam of intense sunshine. A few stunted pines and cedars, spared because of their inaccessibility, hung here and there out of the rifts."

(Isabella never visited the Evergreen area. A careful study of her travel route has established that the disappointing "Bergens Park" where she stayed a night must have been much nearer to Colorado Springs.)

E. L. Berthoud, who surveyed the interior township lines in the Evergreen area in 1967-9 noted, "The best part of the most available and valuable of the Pine which grows in this township has been used up in Sawmills, which are located upon Bear and Cub Creeks: there are now 4 mills in this township engaged in the manufacture of lumber."

Lumber trade on early Main Street.

Evergreen's lumber on way to Denver market.

74

In the heyday of lumbering in Evergreen there were far more than 4 sawmills. Mary Helen Crain reports that there were six on Upper Bear Creek alone. Most, she notes, were operated by a water wheel in the creek but some were steam- run, with boilers heated by wood scraps. Among 23 businesses in Evergreen listed in the 1887 Colorado State Business Directory, five were saw mills, and by 1895 there were seven.

Early photographs of Main Street show a few scattered buildings, a dirt road and piles of lumber stacked and ready for sale or transport. Lumber was also used for bartering for food staples and other items.

There was also quite a charcoal-burning industry in this area. This was a product in great demand and easier than lumber to haul over the difficult wagon roads of the time. Bruce Livonius, who has lived all his life on Blue Creek Road and whose father was also born there, told us about a number of old farms between Blue Creek Road and the old Shadow Mountain Road, "places that my Dad and my Uncle knew of as working farms when they were children, but they were all entirely deserted—just vacant land—when I was a little boy. The old Miller farm, the old Charlie Welch place. They did a little farming, but the biggest thing they did was to make charcoal to sell in Denver."

Lumbering did not completely die out in the Evergreen area after the turn of the century, but it declined drastically. The reasons were many. The reckless pace of logging had pretty much exhausted the timber supply. As we now know, evergreen forests take a long time to replenish themselves in this climate. Mining in the camps around Evergreen— Idaho Springs, Central City, Blackhawk, Georgetown, Silver Plume—was already on the wane by the 1890's, and a near-fatal blow to silver mining was struck by congressional action in 1893: this put the country on to a single gold standard, devastating the silver market by "demonetizing" it.

Demand for lumber as a building material also declined. The first settlements were built largely of wood. Here is Isabella Bird's not very flattering description of early Golden,

"Golden City by daylight showed its meanness and belied its name. It is ungraded, with here and there a piece of wooden sidewalk, supported on posts, up to which you ascend by planks. Brick, pine and log houses are huddled together, every other house is a saloon and hardly a woman to be seen."

Wooden towns were subject to devastating fires— Evergreen's in 1926 was later than most—and so the practice of building with brick or stone became more widespread.

There were always a few people making a living from lumber. Bruce Livonius remembers that Ray Berrian, one of the descendants of the extensive pioneer Berrian family, lived on the place that was later the Valley-Hi Ranch on Highway 73. He did quite a bit of logging, without a mill; just cut railroad ties and mining props with hand tools and hauled them to Idaho Springs. This was in the early 1930's.

The number of sawmills declined to one or two in operation at any one time. Throughout the 1930's another Berrian—George—had a sawmill on a part of what is now Evergreen Meadows. Old-timer George Walpole has spoken in local interviews about working there.

John Schneider started a sawmill on Blue Creek Road around 1943. He bought the milling machinery in Denver. The motor, salvaged from an old fire engine, came from a wrecking yard on Federal Boulevard. The mill, producing dimension lumber for building, was in operation until 1959.

Beetle Revives Logging
A small bug was responsible for the most recent round of logging and milling in the Evergreen area. For approximately ten years, the mountain pine beetle—always present in the ponderosa forests— went on a rampage, wreaking havoc with mature stands of ponderosa in the entire Front Range area. Trees attacked by beetles in late July or early August were usually dead by the following spring, due to a combination of beetle larvae eating away at the tree's inner bark and the clogging action of a blue-stain fungus which the beetles carried from tree to tree.

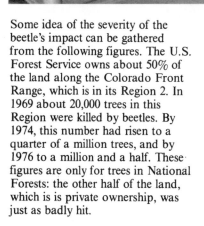

Some idea of the severity of the beetle's impact can be gathered from the following figures. The U.S. Forest Service owns about 50% of the land along the Colorado Front Range, which is in its Region 2. In 1969 about 20,000 trees in this Region were killed by beetles. By 1974, this number had risen to a quarter of a million trees, and by 1976 to a million and a half. These figures are only for trees in National Forests: the other half of the land, which is is private ownership, was just as badly hit.

By 1978, the total went below half a million, and has been declining since then. Of course, this was about the time when the spruce budworm began its equally deadly attack on spruce and fir stands along the Front Range.

Evergreen tree-lovers actively suffered throughout the pine beetle epidemic, viewing with horror and disbelief the spreading stands of dead and dying trees. Individual citizens and entire neighborhoods threw themselves into efforts to minimize the damage. The direct, immediate action involved felling and limbing infested trees, cutting and stacking the trunk wood into piles to be sprayed with insecticide through cooperative efforts with the State Forest Service, then covering the piles with thick plastic to kill the maturing beetles and prevent their flying to attack new host trees.

The second defensive action, in the long run the more important one, was a drastic thinning operation. The aim was to substitute a multi-age, well-spaced forest for the dense stands of under-nourished trees that all grew up together after the logging efforts of the first settlers. The hope was that the remaining trees would get enough moisture to withstand attacks of insects and disease.

The pine beetle problem was especially severe in the Denver Mountain Parks, which are found throughout the Evergreen area like

Tree thinning in Dedisse Park.

Tom Hayden's Forest Products and Firewood Sawmill.

Tom Hayden.

pieces of a patchwork quilt. The Denver city budget was under heavy pressure as a result of inflation and they simply did not have the money to take care of the problem. Private owners of lands bordering the Parks watched in helpless fury as their own efforts to deal with the beetles were rendered ineffective by Denver's inaction. The problem was largely solved by Denver's contracting with the Colorado State Forest Service: the Foresters marked both infested trees and those to be cut down for thinning purposes. Once more logging roads appeared in the forests around Evergreen, in Pence, Dedisse and Bell Parks. The summer air was filled with the buzzing of chain saws, and the sight of trucks, heavily loaded with ponderosa logs, became a familiar one.

Most of this timber was taken elsewhere for processing but the period did see the opening of one new sawmill on Upper Bear Creek by Tom Hayden, a great-great-grandson of Governor John Evans and Bob Hammond, whose parents owned the Hardware on Main Street for many years.

There was quite a vogue for using the distinctive blue- stained wood of beetle-killed ponderosa trees for decorative panelling, as in the interior of the former Post House— now the Wolf House—on Main Street. Some Evergreen residents, including native son Hank Alderfer, were heavily involved in the effort to create an industry from nature's harsh remedy for excessive tree growth.

The beetle epidemic coincided with the drastic increase in energy costs fuelled by the 1972 OPEC oil price raise and the subsequent inflation. Initially, beetle kill produced cheap wood supplies, and this contributed to an explosion in the use of woodburning stoves and fuel-efficient fireplace inserts in the Evergreen area. Suddenly, the Evergreen newspapers were packed with ads for for wood stoves and firewood.

Inevitably, the laws of economics drove up wood prices. By the early 1980's, the preferential edge over other fuels for home heating was disappearing. Only those who had access to wood free for the cutting found it to be a cheap fuel.

Hank Alderfer.

76

Logging News

3/17/1900 - Jack Kirby has shut down his mill and assumed charge of the Barker Mathews mill taking his crew with him. By the way it is a picnic to hear Kirby and Hobbs trading horses and etc. - **The Jefferson County Graphic.**

* * *

5/28/1900 - Sawmills and freighters are commencing to do a little work, but the conditions are such that it is at very small profit. - **The Jefferson County Graphic.**

* * *

9/13/1902 - Elmer Reed was killed almost instantly on Tuesday by a log rolling on him while logging for the Pearson Bros. Efforts were made to locate his relatives and finally a brother was found at Grand Junction. His body was interred in the Evergreen cemetery. - **The Jefferson County Graphic.**

* * *

4/27/1903 - The heavy snows have made lumber hauling somewhat difficult. - **The Jefferson County Graphic.**

1/14/1880 - The old Mount Vernon road, known as the Genesee wagon road has been purchased by the Jefferson county commissioners for $700.00 and declared a public highway. - **The Colorado Transcript.**

* * *

3/5/1914 - J. M. Armbrust has purchased the heavy team of horses, harness and wagon from County Commissioner R.L. Downes. Jack says he could pull anything now, that is loose at one end if only he had a road to pull it over. - **The Morrison Monitor.**

9/10/1914 - Sixty-eight votes were polled at the primary election, mostly Democratic. - **The Morrison Monitor.**

Logging news from Colorado Prospector.

Ranching

Almost from the beginning, ranching in this area developed along two distinct lines. Year-round settlers worked against heavy odds to wrest a living from the high ground during its brief growing season. Affluent summer residents, coming from Denver and other sweltering cities on the plains, bought acreages in the hopes of combining income- producing ranching with a summer family retreat. Such hopes were rarely realized. The two best-known examples of this ranch/summer residence combination were the Evans Ranch, the nucleus of which was acquired in 1868, and the Hiwan Ranch, assembled after World War II. These two stories form separate segments of this book. Here, we concentrate on the year-round ranchers.

The first settlers found the land in the Evergreen township as suitable for farming as any in the Front Range. In addition to the valuable stands of timber, there were natural, lush meadows already in existence. Some naturalists believe that mountain meadows are found where areas of fairly flat land, covered with fine-grained soil and with plenty of moisture, produce such a luxuriant growth of grasses

that tree seedlings cannot establish themselves. Supporting this theory is the fact that, when the grass cover is disturbed by overgrazing or construction, tree seedlings establish themselves in a few years.

We have mentioned that, when the early settlers arrived in the Evergreen-Bergen Park area, it had not yet been surveyed by the United States government. The pioneers had open access to the land and could "squat" on it until the survey was done. Then their holdings could be filed on with a proper legal description.

In fact many did register land claims before the survey was finished—using simple objects like rocks and peculiarly- shaped trees for boundary markers—as well as timber and mining claims. They might file at the Land Office in "Central", as Central City was then known, or with the locally-formed Bergen Mining District or, after 1861, with Jefferson County.

The early land books of Jefferson County, marked simply Book A and Book B, contain many claims like the following: "Beginning at a dead stump" on the east bank of a

creek "and about 280 yards from my cabin at the point of a table mountain, said stump marked 'Ranch Claim for Ranching Purposes, 160 acres.'" Another reads in part, "Beginning at a Spruce Tree about twenty inches in diameter, from which a small spruce tree partially dead bears north about five feet."

In addition to land they legally claimed, most settlers made whatever use they could of the abundant acres of available and unoccupied land. Evergreen resident Paula Moore, in an interesting paper on the first twenty years of land settlement in the Evergreen township, speculates that:

"Very probably, hay was cut for sale in Denver or Idaho from any convenient open meadow, logging teams moved onto any nearby hillside and cattle and oxen were turned out into any ravine or draw that would hold them . . . A man could simply step outside his door and shoot an elk or deer in his meadow, and his headquarters were located on a permanent stream surrounded by hills full of timber, game, bears and lions."

So pasturing cattle and horses was a natural first activity for pioneer ranchers here. According to William Bergen, his father Thomas was already pasturing almost 600 head during the summer of 1859, when he came from Illinois to scout out the possibilities of moving his family west. The cattle were "from emigrants who left them to be cared for, while they went prospecting."

Moore's study shows clearly that the first lands occupied included the natural meadows and open valleys along the streams.

When the government survey was done, between 1867 and 1869, Surveyor E. L. Berthoud described the Evergreen township as follows:

"For a mountain township, the amount and quality of the Land in it is much above the average, and its bottom lands on Bear Creek and Cub Creek are fertile and afford very fair return for those farming upon them. For grass all the valleys and upland meadows can nowhere rend (sic) it in adundance, quality and luxurience (sic): Wheat, Oats, Barley, Rye and Potatoes are raised easily and of excellent quality, altho' the average altitude of the Township exceeds 7100 feet above the sea, while some of its higher peaks soar to 8500."

In the early days, most settler families would have enough milk cows for household needs, a few chickens, and horses to travel and do the farm work. The next thing was to raise enough vegetables for family needs. Potatoes were a successful and prized crop in the mountains. The Bergen family saved their potato peelings on the journey west, and grew a crop from them the first year. The short summer growing season—with cool nights and bright sunny days—also produced excellent lettuce, peas, turnips, carrots and other root vegetables.

Berthoud was right in saying that oats and barley grew well. Some farmers also managed to grow rye, but wheat was much more difficult.

As the years went by, some farmers specialized: they had a dairy herd, like the Earl Hicks family when they were first married, or acquired enough meadow land to profitably sell hay, like Bob Downs on Upper Bear Creek and some of the Schneider family on Blue Creek Road. Later, some ranchers like the Alderfers, the Wallowers and the Buchanans of Hiwan Ranch raised beef cattle, especially Angus and Herefords.

To get a feel for what the ranching life was like, and to understand why it died out as standards of living rose and technology brought Evergreen closer to Denver, we take a look at the family stories of some of Evergreen's pioneers.

The Quiet German Settlers of Blue Creek Road

Long-time Evergreen residents cherish Blue Creek Road because it still looks the same as it did fifty years ago: a few houses visible from the road, weathered barns, expanses of meadow and woodlands, and, in the summer, a fine vegetable garden or two flourishing in places where there is rich black soil.

Three intermarried families, the Schneiders, the Antweilers and the Livonius's, settled much of the land along Blue Creek Road. The pioneer was 16-year old John Schneider who arrived in Evergreen from Germany around 1883. He came alone. At first, he hired out on various ranches on North Turkey Creek as a farm laborer and sawmill operator until, from his wages of around 50 cents a day, he had accumulated a little money. He started to buy land, first on North Turkey Creek, and later along Blue Creek.

He was followed to Colorado by his parents, a sister Margaretha Anna (Maggie), and brothers Pete and Jake. In those days in Germany, every boy learned a trade. John was a blacksmith, Pete, who was crippled, was a shoemaker and Jake a pharmacist. Pete and Jake followed their trades and settled in Morrison. Jake started Schneider's Drug Store, a Morrison fixture for many years.

Probably one of the motivations for young Germans to emigrate at this time was to escape conscription into the Prussian Army. Writing about Denver's prominent Boettcher family, Geraline Bean described the first young Boettcher's emigration to Colorado.

"The decision to leave family and homeland had not been easy, but service in the army of the Hohenzollern kings meant three years with the line, four years in the reserve, and five years in the militia. The length of service, coupled with the saber-rattling determination of Prussia to dominate the German states, made emigration an attractive alternative to thousands of young men of military age."

John Schneider was hard-working and ambitious. He plowed about 45 acres and raised oats, barley, sometimes a little wheat which, his son John told us, "didn't mature too well." From 4 acres the family harvested 20 tons of potatoes. They also cut hay from the meadow.

In addition to farming, John Schneider Sr. had a little blacksmith's shop on his place where he shoed horses for neighbors. He ran a sawmill and sold lumber, was a Road Overseer for the County for a while and did carpentry. One of the buildings he worked on was Brook Forest Inn.

He married Yanna Christensen, daughter of a pioneer Danish family whose ranch included the land where the Safeway is today as well as part of the old Troutdale property.

Two of the four Schneider children from this marriage, sons John Jr. and Jim, stayed on Blue Creek Road, marrying and raising their own families there.

Jacob Schneider, who followed his son to Evergreen, was born in Freilingen, Germany, just south of Bonn. He was a Catholic and a miller by trade but lived as a farmer in Evergreen. He bought land on Blue Creek from a Jacob Roellinger: 104.78 acres for $100. His great-grandson, Irving Antweiler, showed us the treasured patent issued to Roellinger by the United States, and the warranty deed from Roellinger to Schneider.

Anton Antweiler, a baker by trade, knew John Schneider in the old country. He almost settled in Denver, but then decided in favor of Evergreen. He married John's sister, Margaretha Anna, who had been born in Freilingen in 1863. They had two sons, John and Peter. Anton died around 1890 while the sons were still very young, and therefore the grandfather, Jacob, left his land in trust for the Antweiler boys when he died.

Jacob and Anne Marie Schneider.

Rosabel and John Schneider

Maggie had more than her share of grief and hardship. Her son, Peter, died young and was buried in the Evergreen Cemetery. She was married again, to Ernst Livonius—another young German "single" who came to work in Evergreen. Together they had two sons, Evan—known affectionately all his life as "Heinie"—and August, and a daughter, Marie.

Ernst had moved in with Maggie, but later also homesteaded two pieces of land of about 80 acres each.

At the age of 4, August died of diphtheria.

Then came another family tragedy, still a mystery: Ernst Livonius went back for a visit to Germany around 1905, and was never heard from again. Did he meet with an accident, get sick, or simply desert his family? No-one ever found out. But Maggie was left alone again.

Her daughter Marie recalled that, to make ends meet, Maggie took in laundry, did domestic work for different families, made her own butter and sold it for 20 cents a pound, sold eggs, milked cows and sold the milk for 5 cents "in a five pound lard bucket", worked in a hotel in 1911 and 1912, and still managed somehow to knit socks, mittens, capes and shawls for the family. With her oldest son, Johnny, who was 17 when Livonius disappeared, she continued to raise a vegetable garden and 10 tons of potatoes, which they went to "peddle" in Denver once a year.

When John Antweiler needed to get on with making a home and a life for himself, a big load of responsibility was landed on the shoulders of young Evan. At the age of 12 or 13, he left the Conifer School for good to work on the farm.

The land we bought for our cabin, from Ernest and Fredda King in 1950, was part of the original Ernst Livonius homestead. An entry in the abstract puzzled us: in 1906, for a consideration of $250, the land came into the possession of one George Fitch, but was returned to Maggie Livonius and her two children for just $1.00.

Bruce Livonius told us the story. After Ernst left, Maggie borrowed money from Fitch, who took the land as security and then foreclosed on it. When another pioneer German settler and good family friend, Herman Blakeslee— whose land was about two miles north of Blue Creek Road— heard about this, he took it upon himself to pay Fitch a visit. "This woman is a widow trying to raise two children, and she's hard up. You'll get your money, but—deed the place back to her right now, or you just won't be around much longer!"

Of the seven first generation Schneider descendants born in the United States, five stayed on Blue Creek Road. Of 13 children of these five, six stayed. Of the third generation, most went away to college and now live where their jobs require.

Ironically, the one who wanted to be a small-scale farmer, living a self-sufficient life, could not afford to buy land on Blue Creek Road. This was Bruce Livonius's son, David. Except for four 5-acre parcels retained by Bruce, his brother and two sisters, the Livonius land had all been sold by the time David decided he wanted to farm. He had to go to Maine to find 30 affordable acres.

Talking with these Blue Creek families, it is clear that small-scale farming was never able to provide an adequate living here. Irving Antweiler estimated that, at the height of its agricultural use, there were around 200 acres of cleared, cultivable land on Blue Creek Road. In fact, when he brought his bride Gertie—who was used to tractor- efficient farming in fertile Iowa—back to the family "farm" on Blue Creek Road, she took one look at it and said, "This is no ground for farming: it's grounds for divorce!"

Nevertheless, the first generation did farm, and they worked hard at it. Heinie Livonius, after living for a few years in Conifer and working for J.K. Mullen, came back to the family homestead on Blue Creek Road. With his wife Mary, he hand-cleared the field with axe and saw. He removed the stumps with a hand-operated stump puller which is still in his son's possession. "It's terrifically powerful," says Bruce, "It's also terrifically slow. You can pull out a stump of any diameter after about an hour of pumping on that handle, you'll eventually see the ground start heaving up around the stump!" On the newly-cleared land, Livonius grew potatoes, peas and sometimes lettuce. It was a race to see who could harvest the lettuce first—the family or the deer.

Schneider Ranch on Blue Creek Road.

"We'd get a crop of head lettuce going and get three to five deer in that field at night. They'd go right down the row and take a bite out of each head. Just enough to ruin it.they could go through an acre of lettuce in one night."

Heinie and his older half-brother, John Antweiler—who also did some truck farming—used to get a stall in the old farmers' market in Denver. In the evening they drove an old Model T pickup, loaded with fresh vegetables, downtown and sat in the truck all night. About 4 in the morning all the storekeepers would start up and down the stalls, buying what pleased them.

The brothers built themselves good root cellars and stored their potatoes until well into the winter, when they would get a better price. "I recall many a time when, along in December or January, Dad would haul a load of potatoes down and get enough money to buy staples like flour and clothing."

Irving Antweiler also remembered that his family used to sell vegetables to Troutdale Hotel, "onions, lettuce, carrots, radishes, cauliflower, cabbage, peas. How they loved those mountain peas!" To make ends meet, the families supplemented their farm produce with an amazing variety of paid work. Heinie Livonius, for example, learned how to be a carpenter while working for J.K. Mullen. He helped to build the landmark yellow barn at Conifer. Livonius went on to help with many other buildings, and eventually went into contracting with his son, Bruce. Some years Heinie also cut Christmas trees and sold them. In

Irving and Gertrude Antweiler.

the early days of the automobile he fixed cars and trucks—he had a natural mechanical gift—and cut firewood. Even when he stopped cultivating big crops, he still raised enough vegetables for family needs and kept a few chickens.

John Schneider and his wife Rosabel both worked to keep their family supplied with necessities. Rosabel remembered the day in 1933 when she first really noticed John. There had been a five-foot snowfall and he was digging out from his father's house to Blue Creek Road. It took several days. They started going out together when she was 14. They were married in 1936, and celebrated their golden wedding anniversary in 1986, still living on the Blue Creek Road ranch.

Rosabel was a member of the extensive Fleming family and lived as a child above Main Street. She worked first for the telephone company and then for 22 years as cook at Wilmot School.

John never completed high school because he was needed to work on his father's farm. In addition to farming he did many different jobs: built fences for Paul Mayo at the Rosedale Castle on Upper Bear Creek and did lawn work and odd jobs for "the Baroness" at T-Bar-S. In 1934 he went to work for the Duvall Davidson Lumber Company at $16.00 a week. The main lumber yard was in Golden, but there was an Evergreen branch on part of what is now the Bear Creek Mall, right on the creek.

After serving in World War II, John started his own sawmill and ran it until 1959.

The next generation had no illusions about the possibility of making a living from farming. Bruce Livonius has been a building contractor all his working life, doing mainly individual homes. His wife Myrt worked as chief telephone operator until she had a baby. After staying home for a number of years, she then had jobs as manager of the kitchen at the old red brick Evergreen School, when it was a junior high, and as mail carrier.

Irving Antweiler also went into the service, then worked for a few years for Heinie and Bruce Livonius in construction. 1946 saw him with a new baby and a new job— working for Clarence Smith at the Evergreen Public Service Company. Irving did everything from meter reading and laying new lines to repairing existing lines in fair weather and foul. He started at 85 cents an hour and stayed with the Company through several changes in ownership, finally retiring 32 years later from the Public Service Company of Colorado.

The Antweilers' chickens.

Livonius' vegetable garden.

Bruce and Myrt Livonius.

Mary Livonius' art studio, moved and rebuilt by her son, Bruce.

Heine Livonius' stump-puller.

Indomitable Women: Links with Evergreen's Pioneer Past. Mrs. Earl Hicks.

Lillian Ralph Hicks celebrated her 90th birthday in Evergreen on July 28, 1985. She was born in the Indian Hills area in 1895 and married Earl Hicks in 1915. (Earl was a nephew of the early settler family that had a large ranch on Upper Bear Creek, after whom Hicks Mountain is named.) The newly-weds spent their first eight years ranching. They first leased the Davis place on top of Bear Mountain, then for five years leased the Simmons place lower down. This 360-acre farm had been taken up as a homestead by Earl Hicks's grandfather.

There the Hicks had about 20 cows. They sold milk, butter and cream on a route that included Mountain Park Homes and Forest Hill. They tried to have good milk cows, no matter what the breed: Jersey and Holstein were the best. They would have around 20 calves each year, keeping those that had the makings of good milk cows and selling the rest. Though the milk was delivered from a pick-up truck, they also had four good working horses and a couple of saddle horses. They raised a pig every year for their own use.

The milk separator, run by a gasoline engine, was in a separate milk room which was cooled in summer by ice, cut from Turkey Creek and packed in sawdust. Since their land included two large meadows, the Hicks had enough hay for the entire year. They also raised a little alfalfa and planted oats. These were harvested with the aid of travelling threshers.

On their first place, the Hicks raised potatoes so big and of such high quality that they used to call them "gold nuggets." More than 50 years later, Mrs. Hicks remembered with such gratitude the day her husband brought home a wringer paid for with some of that potato money. "Before that, my wrists would be so tired when I got through washing, with all the overalls and things, that I could hardly wring. He noticed and never said a word."

The Hicks' raised their own vegetables—onions, radishes, lettuce, turnips, beans. Mrs. Hicks kept a few laying hens for their own use, and raised little chickens for "fries", which she sold. She had to dress them herself.

A typical ranch day would start at 5 a.m. The couple fed and milked the cattle before a breakfast of bacon, eggs, fruit and—always—pancakes. Next, Mrs. Hicks heated up about 5 gallons of hot water and carried it to the milk house to wash and rinse the separator and all the "milk things". Chores that had to be worked into the day included separating the milk, making butter, washing all the milk bottles as her husband brought them home, washing and ironing clothes, and preparing a large midday dinner and supper.

Dinner included meat—"When people work that hard, they always need meat"—potatoes, at least two vegetables, salad and pie or cake for dessert. Lillian Hicks did all her own baking on a wood stove, using something like a sourdough "starter" for yeast.

Along with the ranch chores went the care of three young sons Chester, Ernest and Ralph.

The items which they had to buy included food staples— canned goods, flour, coffee, sugar—and some clothing. Lillian Hicks had a treadle sewing machine and made her own clothes as well as those for her boys when they were small.

81

Lillian Ralph Hicks.

Frank Anderson on Indian Creek Road around 1900. He is shown with the stage coach in which he used to take people on to the Squaw Pass Road and into Indian Creek Ranch.

Doris Anderson, Pearl Anderson, Jody Anderson.

In 1924 Earl's Uncle, from whom they had rented the farm, wanted to move back onto it. They decided to change occupations. The family moved down to a home on Little Cub Creek Road. They sold their cattle. Earl worked as County Road Overseer for several years then decided to go into business for himself. By this time his boys were old enough to help. The firm, still in business as Hicks Brothers, became well known throughout the mountain area for its work in road building and excavating. Lillian Hicks did the bookkeeping.

When the war came, all three sons went into the service. All were wounded, but returned safely. They continued working together with their father until his health failed in 1956, after which they had to carry on without him.

Earl Hicks had three strokes, the last of which left him totally helpless. Lillian nursed him devotedly, "he lived nine years," she said, "I loved him so much that I took care of him at home." On November 13, 1865, he died in his sleep.

One son, Ernest, found the dust of excavating work affecting his health so he moved with his family to Aurora. The other two carry on with Hicks Brothers firm, and live near to their mother still. All three sons married and had children, which gave her enormous pleasure.

Catherine Dittman, who did the 1977 interview for the Jefferson County Historical Society from which much of the information here is taken, described Lillian Hicks at the conclusion of the tape,

Cathy Dittman, Ralph Mayo and Helen Brush sort historical photographs.

Pearl Anderson in the home of Mrs. Roblin (Margaret Evans) Dvais, where she worked for 25 years.

"Seeing her, you would take her for a woman in her sixties, straight, tall, always well-groomed, with a lovely smile and warm sense of humor."

Cathy Dittman is a long-time resident of Indian Hills. She and her husband Vance had a summer home there for many years, and took up year-round residence when he retired from teaching at Denver University. They were leaders in the fight to save the mountain area from the encroachments of the 1976 Olympic proposals. For her work in gathering county oral histories and other research and writing, Catherine Dittman was named to the Jefferson County Historical Hall of Fame in 1981.

Pearl Anderson

Her father was probably a gambler, but since she knew him only from stories her mother told, Pearl Spencer made up her own legend. At the age of 85, pointing to an animal skin hanging on the wall of her living room, she said, "I'm a cross between a barbed wire fence and a coyote, and that's my father hanging on the wall."

She was born in 1895 in Denver and spent most of her time until she was 11 in foster homes, seeing her mother only occasionally. After her mother died in California, Pearl and her sister were placed in a Catholic orphanage. She spent a year *"asking God over and over to let me live elsewhere . . .I prayed awful hard. Finally, I prayed hard enoguh and I got out."*

"Out" was to an Indian Hills ranch, where she was taken in by the Stasny family in 1907. She was driven there by a neighbor in a horse-driven buggy, and found it was *"just what I wanted. The people were middle age(d) the Mrs. was Swedish and the Mister was Hungarian. Very hard-working people, everything was in order, the little house was so clean with white curtains in front of the cupboards which held the dishes."*

Pearl went to the little one-room Parmalee Gulch School (along with Lillian Ralph Hicks), but spent the rest of her time with farm and household chores. She "worked like a dog and never had any new clothes, only throw-aways". But she loved the mountains and the animals, learning to milk cows, feed chickens, churn butter and become an excellent cook.

Arleta Alderfer.

Advertising for Evergreen area fur farms. (In "Our Memories of Bergen Park" by C.M. Hamilton.)

Within six years, however, Mrs. Stasny became ill. *"Since his wife was dying of cancer, Mr. Stasny decided he was in love with me"*—so Pearl decided it was time for her to get out. *"I had to have a home. I had to have my own family."*

About this time she was getting to know a 28-year old neighbor, Frank Anderson, who lived on a ranch owned by his parents. *"So I asked him to marry me."* He decided she would make a good wife for him even though she was only 18. They married in 1913, and when Pearl moved into Frank's three-room house, she thought it quite wonderful to have a place of her own.

Anna Erickson at 80.

Old mink and fox cages.

83

There wasn't much money but they boarded the Parmalee Gulch schoolteacher, kept chickens, raised a few head of cattle and a vegetable garden from which Pearl canned enough to make it through the winter.

In February the following year, Pearl went by train from Morrison to Denver where she had their first baby in hospital, staying "with Frank's folks" for a few weeks before returning to the farm.

In 1917, Frank's Gustav father died, leaving his mother alone on their Upper Bear Creek ranch. Frank and Pearl, now with two boys, moved in with her and she sold the Parmalee Gulch ranch of approximately 350 acres for $3,000. Pearl lived under the same roof as her Swedish mother-in-law for 16 years and she and her husband stayed on there for the rest of their lives.

For many years they continued to farm, but also did a variety of paid work to make a living for themselves and their three sons, Frank Jr.(Buster), Walter and Harold.

Frank did road construction, which involved a lot of traveling. For 25 summers, Pearl cooked and cleaned for Margaret Evans Davis on the Evans Ranch, and also cooked for boarders, including often the Brookvale shoolteacher. Pearl and Frank delivered the mail between Brookvale and Troutdale for 35 years, first in a horse and carriage and then in a Model T Ford.

Their first car was bought in 1918. Pearl remembered that, "when we went to Denver we never got home without walking part way up these steep hills, or Frank would go home and get the team to pull us up!"

Learning to drive took a bit of courage for Pearl: she remembered feeling panicky during her first attempt on a narrow road: "I didn't know whether to run into a telephone pole or the people coming up the road." She decided on the pole, after which, "we waddled into Evergreen and got the damage repaired." All the while, "Frank's head was on the dashboard and the kids were on the floor at the back."

Pearl's last car, which she drove until 1983, was a '57 Chevrolet.

Interviewed at the age of 85, Pearl Anderson looked back over her life. When she was young, hard work was the norm and not a curse. "Poor old Dad," she said of her husband, "he worked so hard. But he was 93 when he died, so I guess work never hurt him. People don't work now: everything is mechanized."

She remembered when Evergreen was just a general store and a post office and when baby sitters had never been heard of: couples just took their kids along to dances and parties. Everything had changed since her early days on a ranch. "I guess it's progress", said Pearl.

Of her three sons, two have stayed and worked in the Evergreen area. Walt has the Walt Anderson Oil Co. and the Anderson Market on Highway 73. Buster worked for the Clear Creek County Highway Department until his retirement. The other son, Harold, worked in the Denver area.

Pearl celebrated her 90th birthday in February 1985, surrounded by her large family—nine grandchildren and ten great-grandchildren. She died in August of the same year.

Anna Erickson

Fertile Valley Farm on North Turkey Creek is perhaps the only pioneer ranch still in operation in the Evergreen area. In 1986, 80-year old Anna Erickson lives alone in the ranch house built in 1877 and still prefers to cook her Swedish breads and cookies on the Home Comfort woodstove bought for her mother in 1904.

A Swedish immigrant, August Herzman, bought the 320-acre ranch in 1896. He met his future wife, Hilda Pearson, when she was paying a visit from Sweden to some relatives in Morrison. They were married in 1902 and had a son, Oscar, in 1904 and Anna in 1906.

Oscar grew up to be a skilful farmer, experimenting with different cereal grains on the 100 tillable acres of the ranch. In its heyday, the land grew oats, rye, potatoes and a great variety of vegetables. There was always a large hay meadow for cattle.

Anna was pretty enough to be a movie star and, as was traditional, did not do hard "outside work". She married another Swede, Frank Erickson, in the little Church of the Transfiguration, but somehow the marriage did not work out and she moved back home.

In 1943, Oscar married and decided to live on the flatlands: he opened his own nursery and greenhouse. His father was heartbroken. "Anna", he said, "my help is gone. What am I going to do?" Anna decided she could learn to do ranch work as well as a man. She helped her father until his death in 1946, then carried on by herself.

The last year she raised crops was 1970, when she was struck by lightning. She spent 5 weeks in hospital recovering from that near-fatal experience. But she still raises beef cattle, has a few chickens and grows her own herbs and vegetables.

Her most fervent hope is that she can somehow assure that Fertile Valley Farm will never be developed for housing but will remain in perpetuity a mountain ranch.

Of course, we have left out far more pioneer stories than we have included. Families like the Wilmots, Berrians, Blakeslees, Crossons, Snowbargers, Elmgrens, Armbrusts, deDisses, and Johnsons formed the sturdy tapestry of Evergreen life until the commuter explosion of the 60's.

Their children mostly married each other. One descendant told us that you could never say anything against anyone in Evergreen—at school, church or on a picnic: it would be sure to get back to them, since everyone was related to everyone else.

Fox and Mink Raising

For a few years there was a lively fur-raising industry in the mountain area of Jefferson County. If you keep your eyes open you can still see the remnants of mink and fox cages. According to an unpublished 1939 thesis on the history of Jefferson County, the fox fur business on a commercial scale was started in Colorado around 1920. Though temporarily set back by get-rich-quick stock promotion schemes, it settled down after 1930 into a relatively stable industry. One of the largest fox fur farms was operated for the Rocky Mountain National Fox Breeders Association on Genesee Mountain by E. S. Cherry.

Arleta Alderfer, who was raised in Denver but moved up to the mountains with her husband in 1936, remembers that at that time "Evergreen was really a tourist place, with some fox farms and a few big places that had cattle".

The Alderfers first bought a place on Floyd Hill, near Beaverbrook. "Right before World War II," she said, "and right after for a few years, everyone that wanted to move to the mountains . . . bought 10 acres and raised silver foxes, and that's what we did."

We asked her whether fox-farming ever paid. Right at first, it paid well, she told us, because, otherwise, furs had to be shipped in at great expense from countries like Norway. You could get $1,000 for a first-quality pelt, and $3,000-$4,000 for a breeding pair of foxes. Movie stars created the image of silver fox as the glamor fur. After the war, the popularity of fox declined: "you can't sit in a silver fox coat. The hairs break off." So the sturdier short-haired mink became the desirable fur, and mink-raising largely replaced fox raising.

Then Russia began shipping in pelts in great quantity at prices the Evergreen breeders couldn't match. "The market dropped down so you couldn't sell a pelt for $7.00. And it cost $25.00 to feed one. So of course, that's when we got rid of them."

Part of the industry did survive until quite late in the sixties as is indicated by a story in the January 4, 1968 issue of the Canyon Courier. This reported that the Jefferson County Sheriff's Department was investigating a theft of 1,000 mink pelts valued at $20,000. The burglary took place at the Kirkpatrick Mink Ranch on Highway 74, near El Rancho, and the pelts had been readied for shipment to New York.

Raising More Exotic "Live" Stock
As we explored the history of Evergreen, read old newspapers, talked with old-timers, clipped current news for the past eight years and interviewed relative newcomers, we were struck by the variety of "live" stock that people have tried to raise here, for fun or profit or a bit of both.

Cattle and horses we expected—chickens also and maybe trout. But a huge flock of turkeys? Lions and tigers? Peacocks? Elephants? Llamas?
The short-lived **turkey-trial** was one

of a number of semi-serious efforts made by the Buchanan family to get a return on their investment in Evergreen land. The story of the one-year experiment in raising 5,000 turkeys, on the land next to what is now the Hiwan Homestead, was told to us by Joan Landy, one of the Buchanan daughters.

A pheasant **fiasco** was described to us by John and Carol Newkirk. They bought their land on North Turkey Creek around 1968 from a Dane who had emigrated to the U.S. after World War II. He was absolutely determined to make a commercial success of raising pheasants on his ranch, investing all his resources and energy into the project for 14 years. The venture failed.

The **apiary attempt**, on the other hand, is a successful side-venture of the Newkirks. At the time we interviewed them in 1984, they were keeping a dozen hives and producing around 700 pounds of honey a year: they were also collecting bee pollen to help in the treatment of allergies.

The **llama legend** has been a lively part of the Evergreen story for 20 years. In the open meadow about 4 miles from the Lake on Upper Bear Creek Road, the startled visitor sees a bit of the Andes: the haughty figures of llamas watching him from the grounds of "Johnhill". These animals, as well as donkeys, geese and several other contented specimens, were brought to the mountains by Arthur and Helen Johnson, lifetime animal lovers and significant benefactors of the Denver Zoo. The animals are fed and lovingly cared for by long-time caretakers, Everett and Pearle Ault.

More recently, Wes and Mary Mauz bought 20 llamas to their land in Rainbow Hills and founded Timberline Llamas, offering llama pack trips in National Forest areas. In a Canyon Courier interview in 1985, the Mauz's explained that llamas have been bred for 6,000 years for gentleness, that they learn quickly and can carry packs of between 80 to 100 pounds, depending on their body weight. Ardent backpackers with 20 years experience, the Mauzs' said, "It sure is a lot nicer walking without a pack."

Trout-raising efforts have been made from time to time in the Evergreen area. An early enthusiast was the many-talented Denver

Manager of Parks, George Cranmer. When he built the home that grew into today's Singin' River Ranch, he ingeniously devised a system of self-sustaining trout ponds fed from Bear Creek. In the early 1970's, Reed and Elaine Carlson were raising trout from fingerlings on their Upper Bear Creek property, which included a lake and a considerable stretch of the creek. Pollution of Bear Creek water, largely from soil washing down from unpaved roads and driveways, made the project increasingly difficult. It was finally abandoned in the early 80's.

For a **parade of peacocks**, we had to visit Mike and Anne Moore at their Kerr Gulch home. These magnificent, raucous-voiced birds do well in forests at this altitude. When we visited on a November day with the Moores, they had three peacocks, two peahens and two growing chicks. To see the males in their full glory, they said, we would have to return on a day in spring, when the mating urge was at its height.

As to **lions and tigers and elephants:** this was a rather sad effort to raise wild animals on land off Brook Forest Road for use in television commercials and movies. Rocky Mountain Studio Animals was closed down, after due legal process, on grounds of poor care and inadequate shelter conditions.

Through the late 60's and the 70's, there was a new flurry of small farming in the Evergreen area. Many small cabins, not yet winterized, were available for rent cheaply. Some of that multitude of "hippies", soured on the course their country was taking and determined to create a self-sufficient way of life that at least harmed no-one, found their way to Evergreen.

They planted vegetables, experimented with solar greenhouses, bought a few chickens. But the obdurate facts of nature were against them: the growing season was as short for them as it was for the pioneers. Lovely as the mountains are, there are many other places in Colorado more suited to small-farming life.

The long-term trend is clear. In today's money economy, with so much specialization of labor, marginal farming does not make economic sense. So the memories of old-timers and the photographs of once-extensive ranching activities are precious. It does not seem likely those days will ever return.

RESORTS AND DUDE RANCHES

From its earliest days, the Bergen Park-Evergreen area provided accomodations for travelers. Catering at first for those on their way to and from the mines, the early lodging houses and hotels rapidly developed a summer resort trade. Until around 1890, ranching and logging vied with providing services for summer visitors as major sources of income. In his 1885 "Grip-Sack Guide of Colorado" George Crofutt said of Evergreen, "Timber is abundant, as well as game and trout. It is quite a resort for campers."

From 1900 on, the State Business Directory routinely described Evergreen as a "summer resort in Jefferson County." A Denver University student named Ethel Dark wrote her 1939 Master's Thesis on the history of Jefferson County. "As a summer resort," she said, "Evergreen has enjoyed a national reputation for many years. Cabins, cottages, and summer homes ranging from such pretentious structures as the Gates home to the lowly furnished one-room building, dot the hillsides. In summer, the business section, composed of restaurants, curio shops, grocery stores and filling stations, is the scene of much activity. Several large hotels serve the people who desire a more luxurious type of living." To survey the rise and fall of our town as a mountain pleasure resort is the purpose of this section.

Bergen's Ranche

The first building here was Bergen's cabin, finished on July 4, 1859. According to his son William, who recorded some of his memories in 1921, this was a story-and-a-half structure, 18 by 22 feet, made partly of boards which Bergen "had riven from the timber himself. For the time, it was considered pretty comfortable."

Bergen then returned to Illinois to settle up his affairs, outfitted his family in St. Joseph, Missouri and started the long trek west. They left on the last day of April, 1960. Passing through Denver on June 5th, they camped in the foothills and arrived in Bergen Park the following day.

The Bergens immediately started to take in travelers as night boarders, building additional structures as the business increased. First came a 25-

Thomas C. Bergen.

Judith Bergen.

square foot warehouse, then a 30' by 30' log house to serve as dining room. Later, corrals were built and a barn. According to William, they sometimes had as many as 50 boarders a night and rarely less than 20.

Accommodations were minimal: the men slept in one large upstairs room, rolled up on the floor in their own blankets and using coats as pillows. But the food was good. Bergen's wife Judith was up at 3 every morning, according to accounts left by her daughter Martha. Mrs. Bergen milked cows, baked biscuits and fried meat and potatoes for an early breakfast for her family and lodgers.

Judith's meals were "spread for fifty cents, never more or never less", according to William, who was proud that his parents did not try to profiteer from the needs of travelers. He said he could not understand how the family made the business pay, at a time when flour was from $12 to $30 a hundred pounds and had to be brought up from the plains. "However, the meat used was supplied by game hunters, and we had our own vegetables, poultry, milk and butter."

In spite of the common belief that no-one could make a living in the hotel business in those days without having a saloon attached, "none of the receipts came from the sale of whiskey. Father would not allow intoxicants to be sold on the place." Nevertheless, business flourished for a few years while Bergen Park was a busy crossroads and the mines were booming.

Around 1864, Bergen's mother in Missouri became very ill and wrote to Thomas asking that he bring his children back to see her. He felt he could not leave, but sent his indomitable wife Judith, with four children—one less than a year old—two horses and a covered wagon to make the trek back alone. She nursed old Mrs. Bergen all winter back to health, then in spring started back to Bergen Park. Her daughter remembered the journey as full of strange people and misadventures—the last one being that when they got to Denver, the bridge over the Platte River was washed out. They had to leave their wagon behind, just took a few possessions and the horses and got across safely. They were 25 miles from home. Judith and the older children walked, the younger ones rode.

By the time they got back, not suprisingly, "Father was tired of running the boarding house, so he gave it up and built us another house down by the spring."

In 1874, the coming of the railroad had changed the significance of Bergen Park as a crossroads. Thomas Bergen saw more opportunities in the up-and-coming Morrison area, and moved his family to land on the Hogback. There he continued his entrepreneurial ventures—making lakes and ditches for irrigation (they are still used today), raising trout in the lakes and cutting ice for sale in summer.

The original home in Bergen Park is gone, but a stone column with a metal plate marks the place where it stood. "Thomas C. Bergen took up the first squatter's cabin claim here June 1859. On this spot he completed his first log cabin July 4, 1859. "Bergen's Ranch" became a famous way station on the stage coach and wagon road to the mines. This ground acquired for the Denver Mountain Parks System, October 13, 1915."

It is commonly thought that the old house next to the octagonal barn on Highway 74 was the second Bergen house. For many years it was the ranch house for the Johnson farm. When the Johnsons sold to Darst Buchanan after the war, it became home for Hiwan Ranch foreman, Al Parker.

In 1971 the Colorado Historical Society investigated the house for inclusion in the National Register of Historic Places, on the assumption that it was the second Bergen house. They found that it was not eligible—not because it was not built by Bergen, but because it had been so radically altered that it no longer had any historical integrity. However, Catherine Dittman, a meticulous local historian who has made a special study of the original Bergen family, is convinced that this is not the house that Bergen built.

In 1986, the house was acquired by landscape architect Dick Phelps and remodelled for small offices. The overgrown spring next to it was cleaned out and lined with rocks as part of the entryway landscaping for the new Ridge housing development.

The Bergens left, but others entered the business of providing accomodations for visitors. Increasingly, these were either refugees from hot city summers or sick people, many from far places, who came to Colorado seeking renewal of health, and to the mountains for two or three months of the "camp cure."

Isabella Bird, writing about her 1873 experiences in Colorado, paints a vivid picture of summer on the plains. Travelling to Fort Collins from Greeley in an open wagon she felt "the fierce, ungoverned, blazing heat of the sun

on the whitish earth.was terrible.the eyes have never anything green to rest on, except in the river bottoms where there is hay grass." She thought Fort Collins typical of new towns on the flatlands, saying it *"consists of a few frame houses put down recently on the bare and burning plain. The lower floor of this inn swarms with locusts in addition to thousands of black flies. The later cover the ground and rise buzzing from it as you walk."*

Bergen Park historical marker.

Remodeled Bergen home, 1986.

Even in the foothills area Isabella found a plague of hostile reptiles and bugs. *"My life is embittered by the abundance of these reptiles—rattlesnakes and moccasin snakes, both deadly, carpet snakes and 'green racers,' reputed dangerous, water snakes, tree snakes, and mouse snakes, harmless but abominable and besides snakes, the earth and air are alive and noisy with forms of insect life, large and small, stinging, humming, buzzing, striking, rasping, devouring."*

Nevertheless, Isabella saw much evidence of the health benefits of the territory. She wrote, *"The climate of Colorado is considered the finest in North America, and consumptives, asthmatics, dyspeptics, and sufferers from nervous diseases are here in hundreds and thousands, either trying the 'camp cure' for three or four months, or settling here permanently."*

Stewart's Hotel

One of the few buildings still standing from Evergreen's earliest days is now used as the Little Log Theater of the Evergreen Players. The core of the building was a bunkhouse constructed by the Denver and Pacific Railroad for loggers cutting wood, and fashioning it into railroad ties at the nearby sawmill on Bear Creek. The building was a one-and-a- half-story rectangle.

Some time before 1871—when the first meeting of the Episcopalian congregation was held in the dining room of Stewart's Hotel—Robert H. Stewart acquired the bunkhouse. He added dormer windows and two wings and operated it as a summer hotel and way station until his death in 1895. Stewart was apparently a popular figure in Evergreen, known affectionately as "Grandpa" Stewart. He also served as a Justice of the Peace.

Sisty's Brookvale Resort

For quite a few years, Brookvale was listed in the State Business Directory as a separate place from Evergreen, with its own post office and a population of 35. It was described as a "Pleasure Resort in Clear Creek County, 35 miles southwest of Denver." In 1882, there were "tri-weekly stages to Morrison and to Idaho Springs." The hotel's proprietor was W. E. Sisty, so the place was known locally simply as Sisty's. Brookvale had a superb location at the junction of Bear and Yankee Creeks.

The Post office existed on and off from 1876 to 1942 but, after 1900, the Brookvale summer resort was included under Evergreen in the State Business Directory.

Today Brookvale has been broken up and the site is occupied by a number of private homes. The name survives in the little white schoolhouse up on the Yankee Creek fork of Upper Bear Creek Road. No longer in use as a school, the building serves as a community meeting place for Clear Creek County residents of Upper Bear Creek.

In addition to Stewart's Hotel and Brookvale, there were at least four other well-known summer resorts and hotels operating before 1900.

Troutdale-in-the-Pines

It's an arresting sight, that gaunt shell of an old hotel on Upper Bear Creek Road: it seems to provoke questions in those who pass by. Both the Evergreen Library and the Hiwan Historical Museum say they get more enquiries about Troutdale than about any other building in Evergreen.

Shell of Troutdale, waiting for renewal.

Part of Troutdale complex.

Troutdale began as a group of log cabins clustered informally in a dramatic setting of pine, spruce and rocks in Bear Creek canyon. The resort had a one-story hotel containing the dining room, kitchens and a comfortable parlor.

Refugees from summers on the plains came from Colorado, Nebraska, Kansas and beyond. At Troutdale they found comfortably furnished cabins that were fragrant with fresh-cut boughs of pine and spruce, and warmed in the cool mountain evenings by woodburning stoves or fireplaces. For recreation there was boating on Troutdale's own little lake, fishing in Bear Creek, horseback riding, hiking in the surrounding forests and trips to nearby resorts or natural beauty spots.

For many years, Troutdale was operated by Mr. and Mrs. J. D. Babcock, who had previously run a restaurant at the Beaver Brook railroad station. Hospitable hosts, the Babcocks brought their four children to summer with them and act as playmates for small visitors at the resort.

By 1916, the heady dream of a series of Denver Mountain Parks was becoming a reality. Evergreen was the farthest point of a circle from Golden to Morrison, served by new "first-class" roads. Plans to acquire the Dedisse Ranch in Evergreen, and to create a large lake on part of it, had been announced.

In that year the Troutdale resort, with its surrounding acres adjacent to the Dedisse property, was bought for $100,000 by a group incorporated as the Denver Mountain Parks Securities Co. The company promptly started to plat the property into 500 home sites and to market to city folks in eight states the notion of owning a summer cabin in Evergreen. They stocked the little lake with 2,000 trout and planned to construct a casino with dining and dancing facilities and additional cabins.

But, as was to happen more than once in Troutdale's hundred-year history, the plans did not materialize. The property was sold in 1919 to the Troutdale Hotel and Realty Company organized by pioneer Nebraska businessman Harry E. Sidles. Starting at 17 as a bike racer and bicycle shop owner, Sidles went on to acquire a dealership in automobiles and automobile parts that eventually grew to serve all of Nebraska and parts of S. Dakota and Iowa. From there, he moved into the new growth industries of radio and aviation.

With a number of associates, Sidles formed the Troutdale Hotel and Realty Company. On November 7, 1919, construction was begun on a new four-story hotel. It was built with 6,000 wagonloads of local rock which all came from within five miles of the site. The main floor had a large lounge, dining room for 250 and the distinctive Rainbow Ballroom—a 40' by 80' dancing pavilion which extended 75 feet over the expanded lake, and was enclosed by glass and screen. On the 2nd and 3rd floors were 100 guest rooms: in the basement were private dining rooms, billiard room, bar, barber shop, drug store, kitchens and bakery. Above the hotel garage, with space for 10 automobiles, were apartments for guests' maids and chauffeurs, and a dormitory for hotel employes.

The 35 existing cabins were modernized, a swimming pool was added and the grounds were embellished with landscaping and walkways. By the June 1, 1920, grand opening of the new hotel, more that half a million dollars had been spent on construction and improvements.

For Sidles and his associates, Troutdale seems to have been always more of a delight than a business venture. They were continually upgrading and adding to the facilities. By 1927, another story had been added to increase the capacity to 300 guests. Tennis courts, croquet facilities and a children's playground further diversified the resort's offerings.

The 17 acres of the Evergreen Golf Course belonged to the Troutdale Hotel and Realty Co. and were conveyed by them to Denver by waranty deed dated May 28, 1926—with the interesting condition that Denver must always maintain a golf course on the tract, and use the tract as a golf course. If this condition should be broken, the deed would be void and the land revert to Troutdale Hotel and Realty Co. or its successors.

The first nine-hole stage of the golf course (advertised in a 1925 hotel brochure as the "Troutdale Golf Course") appears to have been constructed by Denver prior to the deed of transfer. The delightful little golf clubhouse, probably designed by prominent Denver architect "Jake" Benedict and now the Key's on the Green Restaurant, was commissioned by Denver and completed in 1925.

Throughout the 1920's and 30's, Troutdale was one of the most popular and fashionable resorts in the west and the focus of social life for the upper crust of Evergreen's summer people. The resort was frequently and favorably compared with the Broadmoor. Many influential people in Evergreen's development, such as the Rozzi and Leona Clark and the Darst Buchanans—founders of the Hiwan Ranch—were introduced to this area through a visit to Troutdale.

Elegant dining and moonlight dancing, to Troutdale's own orchestra or to such name bands as Dusty Rhodes, Ted Weems, Paul Whiteman and Tommy Dorsey, were consistent attractions, as were trail rides to Mount Evans and trips in the hotel's touring cars to nearby scenic attractions.

The colorful 1925 brochure gives advice on "How to get to Troutdale": the nearest railroad station is Morrison on the Colorado and Southern Railroad, where " there will be autos to convey you from Morrison to Troutdale." Or you might prefer to take a regularly scheduled Troutdale bus, operated by Thomas Transfer Line of Wazee Street in Denver, which "will meet parties upon arrival of any train at Union Station upon request." Hotel rates were "$5 and up, American Plan."

The hotel also developed quite a lunch and dinner trade in connection with tours from Denver of the Mountain Parks. Mr. and Mrs. Sidles were gracious hosts. At first they lived in a suite of rooms at the hotel and later built a summer home. "Rippling Waters" is now winterized and has considerably taller trees than are seen in original photos of the home. It is one of the many historic homes on Upper Bear Creek.

Troutdale's guest register, which sadly appears to have been lost during many changes of ownership, is said to have been signed by such notables as Greta Garbo, Douglas Fairbanks Sr., Theodore Roosevelt, the Marx Brothers and Mary Pickford, as well as hundreds of others in all walks of life from every state and from many foreign countries.

Subdivision of part of the land as Troutdale Estates, providing 200 summer home sites, went forward. A number of homes on the hill above the hotel were built, with arrangements that their occupants could use all the hotel facilities on the same terms as guests.

Harry Sidles died in 1934. His son Fred took over Troutdale's management. World War II and its austerities marked the beginning of a long, slow decline for the glamorous resort. Because of fuel shortages and consequent transportation difficulties, the hotel was closed for the summers of 1943 and 1944. In 1949, it was sold to a group of Texas businessmen and sold again the following year to H.B. Raskin and James O'Keefe of Chicago.

Two different approaches to building up the hotel's clientele were attempted. The first was to develop Troutdale as both a winter and summer resort, which involved winterizing all the cabins and improving the hotel building. Access to winter sports was stressed.

In 1958 a strong Western accent was introduced. The hotel's lounge and dining room were redecorated with Indian motifs, and the "dude ranch" concept in activities and decor was stressed. But constant remodelling was expensive and maintenance costs became prohibitive. In 1963 the hotel sold again.

A complicated morass of legal entanglements and lawsuits developed over this sale. While they were being resolved, the hotel stood empty for many years. Lack of maintenance, harsh winter weather and vandalism reduced the hotel building to little more than a structural shell before new owners and another dream took shape.

In 1978, plans were announced to convert the old hotel into luxury condominiums at a price tag of

around $250,000 each, with custom features such as private elevators, gold- plated bathroom accessories and individual hot tubs. A model kitchen and bathroom were installed in one of the buildings on the grounds of the hotel. The lake was restored, part of the grounds were newly landscaped and the gutting of the building prior to reconstruction was begun.

A high-powered sales program was planned. We visited the grounds and heard about the plans at a presentation to Upper Bear Creek residents. While the design was not especially to our contemporary-minded liking, we sincerely hoped that the project would succeed so that the derelict ghost of elegant times past could live again.

But this was not to be. Interest rates escalated wildly, resulting in a general economic slowdown—especially in residential real estate. Down payments on the units sold were refunded and construction ceased.

Prime movers in the condominium effort were Evergreen developer Bill Womacks and the Winegards, an Iowa-based family enterprise that manufactures a number of products including television antennas and satellite dishes, and has a small electronics plant on Bryant Drive in Evergreen.

The next effort was to study the feasibility of using the Troutdale site again for a hotel—this time a small luxury establishment of around 55 rooms, designed especially for an executive retreat, with heavy reliance on small corporate conventions and seminars. Ironically, the feasibility study endorsed the concept but recommended razing the existing hotel building.

In the early 1980's an ad in the Denver Metropolitan area real estate multi-list offered "Historical Troutdale-in- the-Pines complex, existing P.U.D. for luxury condos, county may be receptive to conf/center or hotel." The asking price was $2,150,000. There were no takers.

Ownership of the hotel complex, with 24 surrounding acres, was detached from the remaining Troutdale lands. These were the unsold sites from the Troutdale Estates subdivision, approached from Troutdale Scenic Drive off Highway 74.

Until the mid-70's, perhaps because Troutdale already existed as a resort when the Evergreen area was logged, this beautiful land had one of the largest remaining stands of virgin ponderosa pines in this area. Unfortunately, no prevention efforts were undertaken so pine beetles infested the majority of the older trees. A logging company was hired to cut and remove them.

The land was newly subdivided for individual home sites in the 1980's and successfully marketed as "Troutdale: the Tradition Lives On."

The fate of the hotel itself is still in limbo. A new development plan presented to the County Planning Commission in 1986 by Bill Womacks, proposed totally gutting the building, converting it into 45 condominium units with some common use areas, and adding garages to be covered by grassed terraces. The new project was called Troutdale Club and Condominiums.

The Evergreen area was a favorite summer holiday place for "flatlanders" until the outbreak of World War II, though the Depression affected business at summer resorts as it did virtually every other aspect of American life. The 1941 book "Colorado: A Guide to the Highest State", prepared with federal support through the W.P.A., described Evergreen as "the center of a region of hotels, resorts, and summer residences. The town is built along the narrow tree-fringed canyon, and the highway constitutes its only street."

On Upper Bear Creek alone, in the years from 1900 to 1941, at least six summer resorts in addition to Troutdale flourished at different times.

Bendemeer

The name still lives on in a section of Upper Bear Creek road, just inside the Clear Creek County boundary. The canyon suddenly opens up to a beautiful valley through which Bear Creek meanders against the magnificent backdrop of the Mount Evans Range.

The Bendemeer resort consisted of a central lodge and surrounding summer cabins, built in the 1890's. A 1929 brochure, preserved in the Western History Division of the Denver Public Library, speaks of "2,000 acres of jagged mountains, primeval forests of pine, shadowy parks and cool meadows, where guests may wander at will." The air of Bendemeer "is wine and selzer to the senses. Blown from regions of perpetual snow, clean, perfumed by evergreen forests, it carries health, vigor and regeneration to every fibre of the human body."

The water "that is piped from Bendemeer Mountain springs, fed by underground streams of melting snow" is "soft and cold, and it sparkles in absolute purity. No better water exists."

Among the attractions offered were two miles of private fishing on Bear Creek, "a famous trout stream", music, card parties, hiking, horseback riding, beefsteak fries, croquet, horseshoes, a dining room for 100 guests and a store carrying "fresh meats, milk, cream, butter, eggs, ice cream, fountain beverages, fishing tackle, camera supplies, cigars, cigaretts and tobacco."

Gone, however, were the days of enticing the sick to **this** mountain resort. The pamphlet says firmly, "Bendemeer Lodge has no accomodation for helpless invalids. Persons suffering from tuberculosis are rigidly excluded."

After the second world war, the Bendemeer property was sold in two separate transactions to a consortium that included Harold Rolley—a Kansas banker who had been spending his summers in Evergreen with his family since the late 1930's—Jo Hare, a well-known and well-liked Evergreen realtor who combined this largely summer activity with his work as Librarian at the University of Denver, and the three partners of a Nebraska Engineering firm. In 1945, the group paid $15,000 for the 1500 acres south of the stream. The land was dotted with many cabins, though Mrs. Rolley felt that "shacks" was a more accurate description. The remaining acreage north of the stream, which had the Lodge on it, was bought in 1946.

The property was subdivided and advertised in 1949 as the opportunity to have "A Bit of the Rockies for your Home Site." For "$250 and up" you could have a site on a sunny south slope, with roads laid out "by expert engineering so there are no steep grades." Electricity was available, as well as water piped through a 4-inch water line from large springs three miles back on the mountain.

As part of the arrangement that he should take care of land sales and rental of the remaining cabins, Jo Hare received a lot on which he built a house for himself and his wife. He lived there until the tuberculosis, which had brought him to Evergreen, flared up again and he ended his life in National Jewish Hospital in Denver.

Quite a number of lots were sold but the joint venture came to an end because of disagreements among the partners. The land north of the road was sold to a man named Kaiser, who built on it the house that was eventually bought by singer Willie Nelson. Bendemeer Lodge itself had a spectacular finale: it went up in flames in August of 1960. The loss was estimated at $20,000. The Evergreen Fire Department worked gamely but in vain to save it.

TROUTDALE IN THE PINES

Troutdale in the Pines

Truly, one of the outstanding mountain resorts of Colorado. Here, surrounded by indescribable beauty, may be found complete relaxation and freedom from the humdrum of everyday life. Accommodations are fitted to the requirement of each guest, whether it be luxurious or modest. Rates are moderate, including meals, dancing and all recreational facilities with the exception of horseback riding and golf. The rates for these are very moderate. Troutdale is thoroughly modern in every respect. About the 140-room hotel are clustered 35 rustic cabins. A playground equipped with every facility to appeal to childish fancy is only one of the attractions which can be found. Stables where the horse of your particular choice may be had and a big outdoor swimming pool are on the grounds. It has been said that if you remain at Troutdale long enough, you will see every important person in the country.

BROOK FOREST

The stage from Denver rounded the bend and thundered into Evergreen's one street of log houses and false fronted, frame buildings. Dust covered the sweating horses and passengers alike. All of Evergreen was on hand to greet the stage coach and watch the mail bags thrown to the waiting postmaster. Sheriff Armbrust leaned against the door of the blacksmith shop scanning each new face and registering it in his mind—he might need to remember it later and once a face became filed in his memory, there it remained.

The crack of a whip—a shout from the crowd and the stage had gone—on to Bailey's—through South Park to Leadville. Dust settled back into the street—the crowd moved to the post office to wait impatiently for letters and mail. Evergreen basked in the afternoon's sun to awaken again with the next arrival of the Denver-Leadville stage.

The spirit of the west still lives in Evergreen, yet, the Evergreen of today provides the convenience and comfort of a metropolitan center—telephone and telegraph service—daily newspapers—bus and taxi service to Denver—an 18-hole golf course, maintained by the Denver Mountain Parks and considered the best 18-hole mountain course in the country—churches of every faith—If you've never fished for Colorado trout, you've never really fished—Trails winding through pine forests invite the hiker—pack trips to Bear Track lakes—Motor trip to the top of Mt. Evans, America's highest highway. Evergreen offers the ideal vacation to those who come to her. Here, at an altitude of 7,200 feet above the sea, the days are delightfully cool and a blanket is mighty handy at night.

Foundation which operates the West Brothers chain of stores in five southern states. His purpose was to develop an environment for interdenominational Christian camps and conferences. In summer there is an adventure and sports oriented camp program for boys and girls. At other times of the year, the remodelled and expanded facilities on 250 acres are used for adult retreats, seminars and conferences, and for family activities.

Evergreen promotes its resorts, around 1940.

Singin' River Ranch, on the banks of Bear Creek just beyond the Yankee Creek fork in the road, was originally built in 1922 by George Cranmer—later Denver's Manager of Parks—and his wife Jean Chappell Cranmer.

An interesting memoir of Cranmer by journalist and poet Thomas Hornsby Ferril describes him as "an early ecologist." Cranmer built his Singin' River home of local stone with a sod roof for insulation. Freddie Lincoln, who was a young girl when it was built and whose family were good friends of the Cranmers, found it dark and unattractive and said it was just a "soddy". Cranmer also experimented with "self-sustaining trout ponds" on the ranch.

Herb Wallower, a long-time resident of Upper Bear Creek, recalls that there were some of the best horse trails in the entire area leading through the Cranmers' beautiful property.

Cranmer sold the ranch in 1943. It became first a well-known restaurant, then for a while a summer resort and dude ranch. In 1971, it was bought by Glen West, president of the West Brandt

HIWAN RANCH   AN EVERGREEN CABIN

Guest Ranches

Here in such ranches as the Hiwan Ranch, the V Bar Z Ranch, the T Bar S Ranch, the old west still prevails in all its glory, losing none of its atmosphere with the passing of time, yet offering the utmost in modern convenience and luxury. Ranch houses, beautiful in their own estate, now transformed through modern means into the chief attractions of the west. Stables filled with horses that like guests and know how to act in polite society, and there's something about being on a good horse that makes a man feel just a bit superior to those that walk. At the end of the day a hot shower and a grand meal leaves you with that feeling of contentment not experienced in the city. As you settle down into a wonderful bed the songs of the cowboys through your open window send you off to a night's sleep, the like of which you've never known before.

COWBOY PARADE

Dine and Dance at Eddie Ott's

Nights need not be dull in Evergreen. Eddie Ott's on the shore of Evergreen Lake is one of the most attractive night clubs in the west. Each night you can dance to the music of "Big Time" bands and the meals and refreshments are excellent. The prices are moderate. Each Thursday night, following the Cowboy Parade, an old time Cowboy Dance is held at Eddie Ott's. Everyone comes in ranch regalia and enters into the spirit that made the west famous. Eddie Ott's caters to the best and gets them.

Cowboy Jamboree

Every Thursday the cowboys of the region stage an old time cowboy parade and on Saturday, a horse show and rodeo is held where cowboys from the hill ranches match their skill against wall-eyed, sunfishing, pitching outlaw horses whose chief joy in life is to keep a man from sittin' comfortable-like in a saddle.

Nothing in Western life quite compares with the ways of the "cow poke" bent on having a bit of fun after lonesome days on the cattle ranges of the high country.

Greystone

She was a stunning, red-haired woman in the prime of life who had always lived in cities and, since her divorce, almost entirely in hotel suites. Around 1914, she was seized with the idea of building a gracious summer home in the depths of the mountains. Although she would call it a "camp" after the fashion of the day, she had in mind not a rustic cabin but an elegant mansion along the lines of those she had seen in the Adirondacks.

It was about 10 years since Genevieve Chandler Phipps had been divorced from Colorado's multi-millionaire Senator, Lawrence Phipps. She was only 25 then, and there had been a rip-roaring, headline-making, trans-continental battle over custody of their two young daughters, Dorothy and Helen. The judge's decision was to have the girls stay for 6 months a year with each parent. "Absolutely asinine", daughter Helen Bromfield termed it, in an interview some 70 years later.

When the girls were around 15 and 17, according to Helen's recollections, their mother decided they needed a more permanent home. She bought over 1,000 acres next to Bendemeer on Upper Bear Creek and commissioned Denver architect Maurice Briscoe, whose house she had once rented at 1460 High Street, to draw up plans. She herself took a detailed hand in the design and also insisted on being on hand to supervise the construction, which she entrusted to the capable hands of Evergreen's pioneer master builder, Jock Spence.

The family, servants, and some construction workers (the rest were hired in Evergreen) moved to the Upper Bear Creek site in the summer of 1916. They set up elaborate canvas tents with wooden floors, one for Mrs. Phipps, one for the daughters, one for the maid, a large one for the men working on the project, and a cook shack. Oriental rugs and furniture in her tent enabled Genevieve Phipps to camp out in elegance.

Mrs. Phipps laid out the road herself, with a chauffeur along to pound in wooden stakes. When it came time to build the main house, she also selected each piece of lichen-covered rock to be used. The final complex consisted of the spacious three-story main house, a 7-bedroom servants' house, guest quarters, a 20' by 20' stone and concrete root cellar, stable, creamery, blacksmith's shop and an ice house big enough to store 50 tons of ice cut on nearby ponds.

A complex of frame buildings testified to the ambitious efforts at self-sufficiency: there was a cow shed, pig pens, chicken house, rabbitry and dog kennels. A large vegetable garden was planted along the creek, but it proved uneconomic to truck the produce down to Denver to sell so it was discontinued after a couple of seasons. Chickens, cows and pigs were purchased.

Because she feared coyotes would kill the chickens, Genevieve Phipps raised German Shepherds for a short time. However, it was wartime and anything German was unpopular so she practically had to give away her valuable puppies. "She wanted to be a gentle-lady farmer," remembered her daughter, "It was too funny. She was absolutely gorgeous and you could never connect her with this sort of life."

Water was furnished by gravity flow from an elevated wooden tank, with water pumped up from Bear Creek. Electric power was generated by a gasoline-powered engine. A swimming pool, extensive landscaping and green lawns completed the magnificent Greystone Camp.

The furnishings were elegant. Mrs. Phipps would bring a seamstress from the needlework department of the old Daniels and Fisher department store to Greystone on weekends to sew the lampshades, each made of two or three layers of pure silk in delicate colors. Chairs were upholstered in velvet. Andirons for the fireplace were carefully selected from a Fifth Avenue store in New York, and a hand-embroidered cashmere throw covered the table.

At first, Mrs. Phipps used the home year-round, and it was the scene of many lively social functions. The journey was tedious, over narrow, twisting, rutted little Bear Creek Road. One Greystone-Denver round trip produced so much wear and tear on the automobile brakes that they had to be relined. So a Dodge truck was acquired with a trailer to carry the groceries bought in Denver.

Later Mrs. Phipps used Greystone as a summer house only. Apparently, she made an effort to sell it towards the end of the 1920's. A delightful illustrated scrap-book/brochure that she prepared for this purpose is now in the collection of the Hiwan Homestead Museum.

Mrs. Phipps died in 1931 at the age of 52. Greystone was left jointly to her two daughters. By this time they were married, Helen to Donald Bromfield and Dorothy to Van Holt Garrett (partners in the Garrett-Bromfield real estate firm) and had young children. They found the expenses of keeping up the estate more than outweighed the pleasures of the few times they used it and so, in 1959, it was sold to a prominent Denver pump manufacturer, Elmer Wilfley.

Peg and Elmer Wilfley had a large family and used the property as a working cattle ranch, run by one of their sons, and as a family home. They entertained extensively: one of the artifacts in the Hiwan Homestead's 1977 exhibit titled "Three Glimpses of Greystone" was a Peg and Elmer invitation, handwritten on brown paper, to a barbecue lasting from 5:00 p.m. until dawn.

In 1946, Greystone was sold again. The purchasers were Lt. Colonel William R. Sandifer and his wife, Hazel ("Sadie"). The Sandifers had a varied and colorful life before entering the Evergreen community. Sandifer was educated as an architect, and married Hazel in 1929. He was one of the architects on New York's Empire State Building, and stayed on after the exterior was completed as chief architect for the building's interior.

In 1939, he was involved with architectural designs for the New York World's Fair. The two Sandifer children, Patricia and William Jr., were born on Long Island. Sandifer later opened his own office in Charlotte, N.C.

With the outbreak of World War II, he joined the Corps of Engineers and served in the Pacific Theater. He was invalided out with an acute attack of arthritis, weighing only 98 lbs. when he came home.

The family headed for the healthful climate of Colorado. They were negotiating to purchase some of the Bendemeer land when they dropped by Greystone to find out something about water rights. Hearing Wilfley say that he was getting ready to sell Greystone, they bought it almost on the spot. According to a Rocky Mountain News article for September 3, 1947, the estate—including all the buildings and 1250 acres—was sold for approximately $100,000. The article reported that the Sandifers planned to operate the estate as a year-round guest ranch, with emphasis on fishing, hunting and winter sports possibilities in the region.

The early guest register included such familiar names as Cornelia Otis Skinner, Groucho Marx, Mae West, rocket scientist Werner Von Braun and some British aristocrats.

Col. Sandifer and Sadie, a cousin of Ladybird Johnson, owned Greystone until 1981. They operated the guest ranch themselves for many years. When their son Bill Jr. grew up and married a lively young Pennsylvania schoolteacher, who was hired to work at the Lodge one summer, the elder Sandifers turned over to him the responsibility for subdividng a large part of the land into Greystone Estates and Greystone Lazy Acres. Bill Jr. and Marilyn also took over the operation of Greystone Guest Ranch for six years, when Col. Sandifer's health began to fail.

The attractions of Greystone Lodge for guests were its magnificent mountain setting, its peaceful atmosphere and the charm of its architecture, described in the Ranch's last brochure as "finely panelled walls, leaded glass windows, deeply beamed ceilings and many incomparable stone fireplaces." Both the elder and the younger Sandifers were able and welcoming hosts. Over the years the Ranch's guest list included both the rich and famous and hundreds of ordinary vacationers who enjoyed the Greystone experience. The main lodge was the gracious setting for many a local wedding, for chamber concerts and private celebrations. But by the late 1970's, the younger Sandifers needed their own home and time for their growing family, and the elder ones were no longer wanting to carry the burden of running a guest ranch.

From around 1977 to 1981, many rumors and preliminary sales negotiations were reported, including the possibility that the Board of the Evergreen Center for the Arts might turn the historic property into a performing arts complex.

In 1981, the complex of buildings and 55 acres surrounding it were sold for $1.8 million to a retired couple living in Princeton, N.J. Their daughter and son-in-law, Warren and Marjorie Smith, became the year-round occupants of what became once more the private estate of Greystone.

It was home for the Smiths and their two children, as well as headquarters for the financial corporation of Warren A. Smith and Associates.

The buildings were updated and improved and several surrounding homes were purchased as residences for officers of the company.

In 1985 Smith moved the company headquarters to an office building in the new Genesee business complex.

Col. William Sandifer died in November of 1986 at the age of 85.

Marilyn Sandifer.

One of the funniest ladies in Evergreen, Marilyn is warm-hearted and gutsy. She is also a good sport, who teaches aerobics largely for fun, and an energetic supporter of causes she believes in. These have included membership on the Master Plan Advisory Committee in 1985, and being a founder and long-term leader of a parent-based organization that seeks to educate young people about the effects of drug and alcohol abuse and to initiate wholesome and enjoyable activities to reduce the attraction of drug-related parties. The organization has the attention-getting name of M.A.F.I.A., Mountain Area Families in Action.

Col. Wm. Roper Sandifer.

Mrs. William (Sadie) Sandifer.

Besides her life-long support of her husband's professional activities and her skills as a hostess, Sadie Sandifer's deepest interest has been in helping neglected, abused and homeless animals. She is a founder, benefactor and active participant in the Evergreen Animal Protective league.

Bill Sandifer.

93

Evergreen Hotel on Main Street, early 1900's.

Highland Haven Resort.

Greystone main building.

Cranmer summer home in 1920's (later Singin' River Ranch.)

Quartz Tower at Brook Forest Inn.

94

New home of Bill and Marilyn Sandifer.

Monroe home.

The Corral at T-Bar-S.

Jim Ronchetti outside T-Bar-S.

T-Bar-S and the "Baroness of Cadillac Canyon"

Only remnants of this once trim and well-run resort can still be seen. At its zenith, it occupied both sides of Upper Bear Creek Road, some 2.5 miles up from the Lake, up to the top of the hills on either side of the road. There was a string of horses and corrals and barns on the meadow, an outdoor swimming pool, a delightful barbecue area and a popular bar and restaurant open to the public.

High up on the wooded north-facing hillside can still be seen the remnants of a western "ghost town" which was built in the late 40's as an added attraction for ranch guests. Picnics and barbecues were staged up there. One year, as resident Freddie Lincoln recalls, a group of "stunt men" gathered in the "town" and, for a fee, would put on a mock gun fight for visitors. The highpoint was when a gunslinger fell out of a second story hotel window, disappearing from view into a concealed, straw-filled pit.

The T-Bar-S was assembled and run for many years by one of the more colorful and strong-minded ladies in our town's history. Adele Trumbull first started coming to Evergreen for summers when she was married to Roscoe Trumbull, a prominent and wealthy Philadelphia merchant. She came with her three daughters—Louise, the oldest, and twins Gloria and Virginia. Trumbull seems to have died around the time she bought the house on Upper Bear Creek that now belongs to Lloyd and Opal Miller. It is recognizable by its immaculate appearance and beautiful garden, and reminds people who knew the T-Bar-S in its heyday of how the whole complex used to be.

Herb Wallower remembered Adele and her three daughters vividly. He and his three brothers and the "Trumbull girls" were friends, dates and confidantes for years, seeing each other not only in the summer setting of Evergreen but also during winters in the east, where they were all at private schools near Philadelphia.

Adele's second husband was Harry Sommers, a wealthy Atlanta automobile dealer.

After the second war, when Troutdale failed to re-open and the canyon had no focus of activity and social life, Adele decided to buy enough property to open a guest ranch. Herb Wallower says this was not from financial need but "because she just wanted activity. She had a good head and quite a bit of business experience, since she had inherited and acquired a lot of property which she managed herself.

Adele bought the Downs land. Robert Downs had lived on it for many years. A former New England farmer, he had his home and outbuildings on the north side of the canyon, and the fine, lush meadow on the south. Freddie Lincoln remembers that he used to have a wonderfully productive vegetable garden every year and a pond from which he cut ice to sell. The Wallower family bought hay from Downs and had their horses shoed by him for many years.

The energetic Adele built a restaurant on the north side of the road, and some chalet-like duplexes along the stream. She also bought up a number of adjacent properties as they became available, having them trimmed and painted to present a unified, alpine-chalet appearance. Her girls helped with the running of the ranch in the summertime. The "T" in T-Bar-S was for the Trumbull part of the family, and the "S" for Sommers.

However, Adele later divorced Sommers and married Fred Brown, her only Colorado husband, who was associated with the Denver Dry Goods Company.
Adele was, in Freddie Lincoln's words, "a gifted hostess". She was in the forefront of the busy summer social season—a leisurely round of garden parties, dinners, luncheons and cocktail parties, which drew many prominent Denverites up to Evergreen. She was one of the founders of the Upper Bear Creek Homes Association, which had its first meeting in her home in September, 1954.

Wanting a more spacious and spectacular house for her entertaining, Adele had the Hacienda Del Sol built at the crest of a rocky hill on the north side of Bear Creek, taking in a sweeping view of the Mount Evans range.

95

Builder of the Hacienda and other T-Bar-S structures was Rozzi Clark, whom we interviewed along with his wife, Leona, in 1981. They both chuckled over their encounters with the Baroness. "She was pretty domineering," in Leona's opinion. "She loved to entertain, she loved people, but.things had to go Adele's way."

Fred Brown died and Adele's last husband was a real, live Baron, Vladimir Von Poushenthal. He was a White Russian, remembered by the Clarks as a very nice and kind person. Because he apparently had real estate interest back east, and also at one point—according to Freddie Lincoln— ran a potato farm in Maine with which he tried to help refugees earn a living, the Baron did not spend much time in Evergreen.

Rozzi recalled one incident in which he had a contest of wills with Adele. "We were building a rock wall around T-Bar-S, and she came out and started to tell my men how to build it. About that time, I drove up and I said to her, 'If you want that wall built, you go back into the house.' She said, 'I'm paying for it!' I said, 'You **just** quit paying for it. Pack up your tools, boys, we're going home.' And we did. About a week later, she called me back and said, 'I'll stay in the house if you'll come back and finish that wall!'"

The Hammonds, who owned and operated the Hardware store for many years, also remembered Adele. After she attained the rarified status of Baroness, "her companion-secretary would come into the store ahead of her employer's visit, and give us all instructions how to pronounce her name—Baroness Von "Poo-shen-tall"—and how to spell it correctly without having to ask!"

We asked another Evergreen old-timer who used to work occasionally at the T-Bar-S, what the Baroness was like as an employer. He exploded, "She was tighter than the paper on a wall!" A former telephone operator told us that everyone on the switchboard knew when the Baroness was calling: "She would scream into that telephone and you could hear her a mile away."

The Hacienda was an expensive house for its time: $40,000 for the original home plus many additions and a guest house.

When we came to Upper Bear Creek in 1972, the T-Bar-S had been sold and was already in decline as a dude ranch. Though a string of horses was still rented for guests for a couple more summers, more and more of the cabins were leased on a long-term basis.

The restaurant seemed to change operators at least once a year. Its most sucessful period was as the Corral restaurant and Bar, immediately before its flamboyant ending in a 1975 night-time fire that demolished the structure. It was the first restaurant venture of Jim and Lynne Ronchetti, who went on to establish Kilgore Trout's restaurant on Highway 74.

The resort was in the hands of Fred Sidles, grandson of the builder of the Troutdale Hotel. When he retired to Arizona the T-Bar-S property was split up in successive sales. The canyon rejoiced when, in 1985, the land on the north side was bought by the Monroe family. They had already built a new home on a site at one end of it, and they swiftly had the deteriorating structures and old swimming pool removed. The meadow is returning to its natural and best use—as a meadow.

When we talked with Herb Wallower in 1981, we told him we understood that the Baroness had died. "She's still alive!", he told us, "and still partying!." She did pass away in Florida, not many years after her husband the Baron, who died in 1978.

Marshdale Lodge
This friendly, family-oriented dude ranch had a kinder fate then most.
From 1968 to 1986, it was the summer headquarters of the Colorado Philharmonic Orchestra. The lodge served as dining and living room for students and staff, and as a rustic setting for the receptions and parties that helped to draw the Philharmonic and the community together. The former cabins were sleeping quarters and rehearsal spaces for the 75-member Orchestra. For a brief but intensive 8 weeks in the summer, the hills around Marshdale were alive with the sound of music.

Marshdale Lodge was built in the 20's by Dr. Marsh, a dentist,and continued to operate for many years after the war. Leona Clark remembered enjoying dinner at Marshdale Lodge—it was less "de luxe" and more down-to-earth than Troutdale.

An undated brochure gives some idea of Marshdale under the proprietorship of David Eads. Probably around 1938, it offered accomodations from May 27 to September 15. Activities available included horse back riding, hiking, fishing, tennis, "interesting side trips", good food in the Lodge restaurant, access to the nearby "fine municipal golf course" and dancing at "Evergreen by the Lake". A couple could stay at the Marshdale Lodge for a week in a "room with private bath", for $48.00, or $96.00 with meals included!

When the C.P.O., newly-christened the National Repertory Orchestra, announced at the end of the 1986 concert season that it was leaving Evergreen, it gave as one of the reasons the inadequacy of the Marshdale accomodations. There had never been enough money to renovate them properly.

Brook Forest Inn
This resort was the realization of a dream by an immigrant couple to create "a little bit of Switzerland in the heart of the Rockies." It was achieved only by a combination of vision, persistence in the face of major obstacles, and years of hard labor.

Edwin and Riggi Welz came to Colorado in 1910, when a boom in the resort and hotel business was in the making. He was born in Vienna and she in Switzerland. They worked in some of Denver's finer establishments, including the Brown Palace.

In 1913, they found out that some land in the mountains west of Denver was still available for homesteading. 33 miles from Denver, at the end of a tortuous, narrow trail, they found a tract of 160 acres. Two previous attempts to homestead failed. What remained was a little cabin with a board nailed onto it that read "Brook Forest." Because the scenery was the nearest thing to the Alps they had seen since they left Europe, they determined to make a go of homesteading it.

For three years they worked on the land: they raised vegetables, improved on the cabin, added another building and blasted a road through the rocky walls of Cub Creek canyon. The original wagon trail was impassable most of the year, too narrow for a horse and buggy to turn around on, and took 13 hours to travel. Edwin Welz had to use it, for he "commuted" for many years to earn money in Denver to put into their mountain project. He also had to haul building materials.

In 1919, the Welz's opened as a hotel with two guests, both schoolteacher friends from Denver. The reputation of Riggi Welz's superb cooking spread.

Edwin had an architect draw up plans for a Swiss chalet, but could not get financing. So they laid the foundations themselves and by the following summer it was finished and occupied. Continuing to build their resort as time and money made possible, they eventually provided accomodation for 100 guests. They could feed 300 indoors and—with a large outdoor barbecue oven—up to 1,000 at large gatherings.

The resort consisted of the main inn, built of rose and white quartz with enormous weathered beams, a steeply-pitched red roof, and wide, overhanging eaves; nine guest chalet- style cottages; the Tower, constructed in 1935 entirely of white quartz and "housing every modern convenience". Much of the resort's attraction was its medieval atmosphere, enhanced by the use of iron railings, fountains, sundials and street lanterns.

The Welz's were remembered by all who knew them as, to use Leona Clark's words, "lovely people. We called them Maw and Paw Welz and everyone enjoyed the fact that they still spoke with quite a brogue."

Brook Forest Inn has been through many ownerships since the time of the Welz's and its future is uncertain. Year- round houses surround it now. It surely can never again be the remote mountain retreat that was, in the words of one of the original brochures, "an artist's dream of an idyllic spot where life is lived at its fullest in Old World loveliness."

From "No Room at the Inn" to "No Inn?"
It is impossible to describe all the hostelries that operated in the Evergreen area during its first 100 years of settlement. There were many lodges with cabins in delightful locations, like Forest Heights Lodge, Beaverbrook, and Sunnybrook Lodge. There were

accomodations for many years right on Main Street, like the Liston Lodge and the Evergreen Hotel, an intriguing old building much in need of renovation, whose ground floor is now used as an antique shop and a used clothing store.

What is remarkable is how relatively rapid was the transition from a resort town, overflowing with accomodations of all types and prices, to a much larger community with almost no accomodations at all.

In the 1986 "Yellow Pages" for the mountain area, we looked for listings about accomodations. There are three Evergreen listings under both "Motels" and "Resorts"— Bauer's Spruce Island Chalets on Brook Forest Road, Davidson Lodge on Lower Bear Creek and Highland Haven on Independence Trail. There are no hotels.

Baur's Spruce Island Chalets was originally built by neighbor Rozzi Clark for Maurice Baur— apparently the only Democratic County Commissioner ever elected from Evergreen.

Davidson Lodge is below the Evergreen Conference property on the banks of Bear Creek.

Highland Haven Resort Motel, perhaps the last remaining institution making a living exclusively from short-term accomodations, is also on Bear Creek. It is nestled into a quiet corner across the stream from St. Raphaels, on a remaining bit of the old road out of Main Street. Highland Haven is owned by a young couple, Gail Riley and Tom Statzell. They have remodelled the one and two bedroom units "nestled amongst stately spruce and gnarled pine": each unit has a living room with large windows, moss rock fireplaces with ample supplies of firewood, fully-furnished kitchenettes and outdoor barbecue grills and picnic tables.

"Guests run the gamut", according to an article about Highland Haven in the Rocky Mountain News, "from couples wanting a break from their children to grandpas and grandmas; from young people who don't want to drive down the mountain after an evening of live entertainment at the Little Bear bar to 'Willie Nelson gawkers.' In summer, there are families from the Midwest and travelers from Europe."

Gail is a vivacious proprietor who enjoys offering her guests a little something more than comfortable rooms—like dress-up parties on holidays and special occasions. And, according to the News Travel Editor, "it's those little touches that make Highland Haven special."

The reasons for Evergreen's decline as a summer resort are not hard to find: the introduction of air-conditioning, which made the plains bearable, the development of superb automobile roads and other services, which made it possible to live in Evergreen year-round and commute to Denver, and the increasing affordability of high-speed air travel, which brought a variety of exotic vacation spots within the reach of many families who, a generation earlier, might have had a cabin in Evergreen.

Yet there is a persistent sense that the time will come when Evergreen will once again have at least one hotel. Ever since the demise of Troutdale, there have been periodic flurries of publicity about new proposals. These have included remodelling the Troutdale building, providing a hotel-conference center as part of Soda Creek development and building a motel-convention complex off Lewis Ridge Road.

All attempts so far have failed, because of financial problems, community opposition or difficulties in getting plans though planning and zoning authorities on account of poor location.

GUIDE FOR THE VISITOR

(Current information about all seasonal events is in the weekly **Canyon Courier.** The free **Spree Magazine,** available in local stores and supermarkets, focusses on the arts scene.)

Year-Round

Hiwan Homstead Museum, Meadow Drive. Historic log home with permanent and changing exhibits and gift shop. (Described in section "An Abundance of Open Space.") For hours, current activities and exhibits, call 674-6262.

International Bell Museum, "Granite Glen," Upper Bear Creek. Collecting the almost 4,000 bells that date from 400 B.C. to the present, has been the life work of curator Winston H. Jones. Outside, among the pines and rocks, are a Spanish campanile, a 1770 Monterey mission bell, old school bells and and 1,800-pound Leadville church bell cast in 1882. Inside you will find cut glass and crystal bells, bronze, iron, clay and silver creations and bells which have belonged to celebrities the world over. The Museum is open Tuesday through Sunday in the summer, the rest of the year by appointment. For information, call Winston Jones at 674-3422.

Evergreen Library, Highway 73 at the traffic light. Open 7 days a week. Pleasant space to gather local information, read the newspapers, consult a helpful staff, browse. For hours call 674-3389.

Evergreen Chamber of Commerce, Stage Coach Boulevard at Highway 74, 674-3412. Has a visitors' center with information about current activities and a good map. (This is based on the personal efforts of the Evergreen Resident Bill Reefe: you can also buy a booklet of his detailed driving maps of the area, "You Usta Couldn't Get There From Here", in Evergreen stores.)

Armed with your map, get a quick idea of Evergreen's history and layout by locating its historic places and landmarks. Starting from Kittredge, find the **Blue Spruce Memorial,** the Evergreen Conference Historic District, the **Hiwan Homestead Museum, Main Street,** and the **Evergreen Cemetery** off Highway 74. Drive past the **Lake** and see the ghost of **Troutdale Hotel** and the many older homes along **Upper Bear Creek.** Stop for a moment in busy **Bergen Park,** by the **historical marker** where the first log house was built in 1859. Take the peaceful old Soda Creek Road out of Bergen Park and drive past the **Humphrey House/Clark Homestead,** made of handhewn, square-cut logs, which was placed on the National Register of Historic Places in 1974. (Its owner, Hazel Humphrey, has helped to preserve a great deal of Evergreen history: she was a co-founder of the Jefferson County Historical Commission and was inducted into is   Hall of Fame in 1984.)

Take in a play at the **Little Log Theater** (674-4934), a musical by the **Evergreen Chorale** (674-4002) or a concert by the **Evergreen Chamber Orchestra** (674-6707). If you're out for the rousing best in rock 'n roll, do like the rest of the Denver area does: get yourself to the **Little Bear** (674-9991) on Main Street on a Friday or Saturday night.

Year-round in good weather, take a walk in one of Evergreen's many parks. For short hikes, try **Dedisse Park** or the trail from Lakepoint Center Across the Golf Course; for longer ones, the trails in **Alderfer/Three Sisters or Elk Meadow Parks.** (more information on parks is in the section on "An Abundance of Open Space.")

Shopping is varied, leisurely, and competitive in quality and price with the "big city." Each small shopping area (Kittredge, Hiwan Village, Evergreen Main Street, Lakepoint Center, North Evergreen/High Country Square, the Mine Shops/Center at Evergreen, and the Marketplace at Bergen Park) has its special offerings. **Restaurants** are plentiful and in a variety to suit all tastes.

Summer

Hike or backpack. In addition to the parks mentioned above, try the **Mount Evans Wildlife Area, Arapaho National Forest** trails, **Maxwell Falls** off Brook Forest Road.

Play golf on the **Evergreen Golf Course** next to the Lake. Information from 674-5597.

Rent a pedal boat, canoe or sailboat on Evergreen Lake. For hours and charges, call 674-2677.

Drive to the top of Mount Evans. Get out and savor the different climate zones along the way.

Rent a mountain bike from Paragon Sports (670-0092) and explore the backroads and park trails.

Come to Evergreen for Summerfest! Organized by the Evergreen Center for the Arts, this is a lively arts, crafts and entertainment fair that takes place over the July 4th weekend in Heritage Grove, next to the Hiwan Homestead. For information, see the Canyon Courer or call the ECA at 674-4625.

Spend the evening of **July 4th by Evergreen Lake.** Bring a picnic and the family for a **concert by the National Repertory Orchestra** and a rousing **fireworks** finale.

Be part of **Rodeo weekend** in a small town (traditionally the first weekend in August by may move to June in 1987.) A **Parade** down Main Street on Saturday morning, **Rodeo performances** Saturday and Sunday afternoons, the unique **Mountain Rendezvous** in Heritage Grove all day Saturday (with good food, entertainment, displays of 'mountain men' skills and teepees, and fun for kids), the **Evergreen Town Race** down Upper Bear Creek on Sunday morning.

Browse, appreciate and buy at the annual juried **Evergreen Artists' Association Fair** in Heritage Grove one Sunday in late August. Details in the Courier or Spree Magazine.

Winter.

Skate on Evergreen Lake. Skate rentals and warming house available. 674-2677 for details.

Cross-county ski on trails in Elk Meadow or Alderfer/Three Sisters Parks. Ski Touring map available from Library, Chamber of Commerce, local sporting goods stores. Snow information update 277-8340.

Be part of **Winterfest** (annual December arts and crafts fair) in Evergreen and other Christmas celebrations, including: Christmas programs by the arts groups; carolling and decorating a **birds' Christmas tree** outside the Library organized by the Evergreen Naturalists; the annual ceremony of **lighting the Town Tree by Evergreen Lake;** lively celebrations in the shopping centers. (Check Canyon Courier for details.)

AN ABUNDANCE OF OPEN SPACE

One of Evergreen's major assets is being just a short and scenic drive away from Denver. Another is its direct access to a magnificent array of parks, forests and wilderness. Fingers of Arapahoe National Forest reach to within a mile or two of Main Street and cover most of the Mount Evans range with protected forest and wilderness status. Denver Mountain Parks punctuate subdivisions with welcome intervals of unspoiled land. The State Mount Evans Wildlife Area provides far more than a habitat for the elk herd. The strategic purchases of the Jefferson County Open Space program are preserving the most beautiful meadows, woods and peaks for people to explore and enjoy.

Denver Mountain Parks

The system of Denver Mountain Parks—unique in the entire nation—sprang into being in the second decade of this century, and is a case study in what can be achieved by idealism and unbounded enthusiasm.
As the system developed through mid-century, it had the ebbs and flows of activity to be expected in any large-scale enterprise. But by the mid-sixties, the mountain parks were in deep financial trouble. From then on development ceased. What has hit the headlines since has been an ingenious variety of suggestions for bailing them out.

Driving around Evergreen, we are frequently overwhelmed with gratitude for the people who valued the beauty of this area in its natural state. They preserved a part of Indian Hills from scattered summer home development in Pence and O'Fallon Parks, created a little oasis in Bergen Park and rescued a primeval part around Little Cub Creek with Bell Park.

If you decide to take the time—and it's worth doing at least once each separate season—to go to Denver by the now little-travelled road down Bear Creek Canyon through Kittredge and Morrison, you will rejoice to see how much of it is still the way it was from time immemorial.

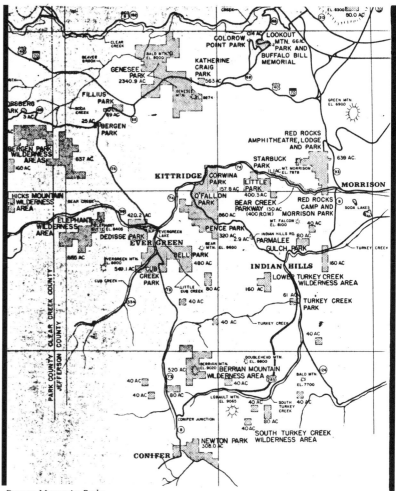

Denver Mountain Parks.

But those of us who have lived here for a while also remember with sadness the times when garbage overflowed from unemptied containers in these same parks, when many of the beautiful stone and timber buildings were a shambles from wear and tear and vandalizing, when ponderosa trees by the thousands were dying because there was no money to combat the pine beetle, and when Denver was ready to drain the Evergreen Lake it had created, for lack of funds to repair the dam.

Unless you have a map in hand on which the Denver Mountain Parks are marked, you will only know where most of them begin and end by the absence of buildings. You will only gather that they are for your use when you spot a shelter or picnic tables. It has been many years since Denver actively promoted their use.

Fathers of the Denver Mountain Parks: John Brisben Walker and Mayor Robert Speer

A remarkable entrepreneur named John Brisben Walker first had the dream: the young, self-confident Denver should encourage the new potential of tourism, made possible by the automobile, by acquiring land in the mountains along scenic motor routes to be laid out and maintained by the city.

Walker first came to Colorado in 1879 when he was 32 with a federal group that was sent to find out if alfalfa could be successfully grown in this state. He had already made his first fortune and lived enough adventures—including a stint as military advisor in China—to last most people a lifetime.

Settling in Denver, Walker made his mark in farming, real estate and the development of imaginative park and pleasure facilities. He left again in 1888 to take up a new challenge, having bought the

John Brisben Walker.

Cosmopolitan, a nearly-extinct little publication. In a few years, he developed it into what is often described as America's first modern, mass- circulation magazine.

Walker had left his first wife and children in Denver. When he returned it was with a beautiful new wife and four young children—as well as a new fortune from the sale of the Cosmpolitan to William Randolph Hearst.

The second time, Walker focussed his entrepreneurial efforts on Morrison, which he believed had great potential as a resort town. Being on the railroad, it was the place from which people took the stage to Troutdale, Bendemeer, Brookvale and Evergreen. (Randolph, Walker's son by his first marriage, spent some time as manager of the Troutdale summer resort.)

Walker bought the Mount Morrison Hotel—the former "Swiss Cottage" built by Governor John Evans—and remodelled it into a family residence while his own mansion was being built on nearby Mount Falcon. He bought up real estate in the town and homesteads around it, until he owned over 4,000 acres.

His holdings included Red Rocks, which he correctly identified as a potential world-class outdoor amphitheater. He christened it the Cave of the Titans, and brought the famous opera singer Mary Garden there to demonstrate its remarkable acoustic properties.

The story of Walker's activities— combining money-making enterprises with idealistic attempts to use his Camp of the Red Rocks as a conference center to promote national and international understanding and peace—has been well-told in local magazine and newspaper articles. For us, the emphasis is upon his vision that Denver ought to encourage both its own residents and a potential flood of tourists to get into the mountains and enjoy their scenic wonders.

Walker believed the natural "gateways", like the Morrison area, should be preserved from unsightly development by making them into park land, and that decent highways should make mountain exploration enjoyable.

Walker had traveled in Switzerland, where he learned that man should not try to improve on what nature has created in the mountains—just preserve it and make it accessible.

Walker's own Colorado hopes collapsed in a series of tragedies: his beautiful young wife died suddenly, his almost-finished mansion on Mount Falcon was struck by lightning and destroyed in the resulting fire, his vision of a summer White House on the mountain faded as national energies were diverted into World War I and its aftermath.

But the mountain parks idea had been taken up by another visionary: this time, a man in a position to turn it into reality.

At the 25th anniversary dinner of the Denver Chamber of Commerce on May 24, 1909, Mayor Robert W. Speer proposed the creation of a mountain parks system, linked by highways to be built by the city. The following year, speaking to the Denver YWCA, Speer elaborated on his suggestion and added a proposal to build a road up to the top of Mount Evans.

The City's business and industrial organizations assumed responsibility for nurturing Speer's plan to full and rapid realization. Committees of the Denver Real Estate Exchange, the Chamber of Commerce and the Denver Motor Club joined to form the Mountain Park Committee of the Commercial Bodies. In 1912 they convinced the people of Denver—then a city of about 215,000—to vote for a charter amendment authorizing the city to develop a mountain parks system and providing a one-half mill levy to finance it.

The Committee persuaded the State Legislature to pass in 1913 a law permitting Denver to acquire land outside its own boundaries. They mobilized their congressional contacts to assure favorable consideration for Denver's request to buy selected mountain lands still owned by the federal government. Many of these had first to be legally withdrawn from the body of land available to homesteaders.

Frederick Law Olmsted, a nationally-known landscape architect and son of the planner of New York's Central Park, was brought to Denver in 1912 to advise on the development of the mountain parks: routes of proposed roads, acquisition of lands and the politics of dealing creatively with county, State and federal authorities. His report recommended that the first acquisitions should be on Lookout and Genesee Mountains and that a circular road be developed, from Morrison to Golden, linking up and improving existing roads and building new ones where needed. Construction was to start from Golden to the top of Lookout Mountain.

The formal opening of the Mountain Parks was on August 27, 1913 when the Denver Park Commission and the Chamber of Commerce joined in taking the members of the American Association of Park

Robert W. Speer.

Superintendents, who were holding their 15th Annual Convention in Denver, on a day-long tour.

In 35 autos the party made its way out of Golden and up the newly-constructed Lariat Trail to the top of Lookout Mountain, where they took a 2-hour break to "stroll among the pines and over the cliffs" and enjoy "a most excellent mountain trout fry". They travelled on to the new Genesee Mountain Park, walking to the 8,284-foot summit "where an unobstructed view of mountain and plain is afforded in every direction."

Leaving around 3.30 p.m., the group drove through Bergen Park and Evergreen and down Bear Creek Canyon to the summer home of Park Commissioner Robinson—where a second meal was served—finishing their return journey to Denver via Bear Creek and the Morrison Road.

In 1914 President Wilson signed a bill giving Denver the right to buy 7,047 acres of federal land at $1.25 an acre. Between 1914 and 1918 road construction and improvement, jointly financed by Denver, the State of Colorado and Jefferson County, proceeded rapidly. Fillius and Bergen Parks were added to the system.

Mayor Speer was in the middle of planning for the most ambitious project of all—the creation of a Denver National Park to embrace the entire Mount Evans Range,

with a highway to the summit—when he died unexpectedly in 1918. The first leg of the proposed highway, the road from Bergen Park to Squaw Pass (now highway 103), was under construction "using 50 men and twelve teams." Negotiations were underway to acquire "patented lands and lakes within the boundaries of the proposed park." These eventually added to the Mountain Park system the Echo Lake area, where Denver built a sturdy lodge, and Summit Lake, with its unique ecological habitat, even though the Denver National Park did not come into being.

Speer appreciated excellence in design and was convinced that only the best was good enough for projects developed by the City of Denver. So Jacques Benedict—the best-known architect of the time and designer of mansions for wealthy Denverites—was asked to draw the plans for most of the lodges and shelter buildings in the new mountain parks.

Robert W. Speer was born in Pennsylvania in 1855 and came to Denver, like many others, seeking a cure for his tuberculosis. Working for 2 years on a cattle ranch gave him back his health. Speer then got a job as a city clerk in Denver. From that position his extraordinary energy, administrative ability and vision propelled him into higher and higher office until he was urged to run for mayor.

He was elected for an unprecedented three terms, during which he not only built up the city's treasury but initiated most of what makes Denver attractive even today—the system of city parks, the walling of Cherry Creek and landscaping along what was later called Speer Boulevard, the building of the Natural History Museum and City Auditorium and the acquisition of lands for the Civic Center.

Speer had retired in 1912 but was soon urged to run again. He died, as one obituary said, "Mayor of Denver and one of the foremost authorities on municipal government in the world."

In 1919, Denver had decided to acquire the 400-acre deDisse Ranch in Evergreen. They wanted to create a multi- purpose park that would be the "apex and crown jewel" of the mountain park system and to build a dam on Bear Creek that

would help control the periodic floods downstream. The resulting lake was also planned as a recreational and scenic element.

Until 1928, work on this and many other mountain park projects proceeded energetically. With the Depression came a period of low activity. But then onto the scene came another of those dynamic, eccentric "characters" who make things happen.

George Cranmer

George Cranmer's summer home (now Singin' River Ranch).

The Cranmer Years
George Cranmer became Mayor Ben Stapleton's Manager of Parks in 1935. A Denver native, he had been educated at Princeton and returned to become a stock broker on 17th Street. He cashed out of the stock market in 1928. This has often been attributed to his economic foresight but his son "Chap" told us it was merely chance. Cranmer had a disagreement with his partner and sold his share of the business to him at just the right moment.

Cranmer was always in hot water with the press because his concern was to get things done rather than to go through the right channels. He firmly believed that money for desirable public projects could always be found, provided the idea was inspiring enough—and his own accomplishments were proof of his theory.

In the Mountain Parks system, Cranmer skilfully used the new Depression-era sources of labor and funds—the P.W.A., the C.C.C., the W.P.A.—as well as existing agencies like the National Park Service, to build roads, bridges, rock walls, shelters and trails in the existing parks; to bring into being Walker's dream of a magnificent outdoor amphitheater at Red Rocks; to acquire land at Winter Park and develop a ski area for Denver citizens.

The post-war period in Denver brought a new administration to city hall. Cranmer left office in 1947. Though he lived a vigorous life, and was involved with matters of public interest until 1975 when he died at the age of 91, he did not hold public office again.

His era at the Parks Commission was summarized in the obituary published by the Rocky Mountain News: "At a time when bureaucratic bungling and red tape seem to characterize government efficiency, or lack thereof, Cranmer stands as a giant. He was a doer, not a procrastinator or an apologist for what couldn't be done. At times he was ornery and arbitrary. Sometimes even irascible. But his interest was the commonweal, and there arose no doubt about his priorities."

Cranmer built his own summer home near Evergreen on Yankee Creek. He sold it during the war, when his children were grown, and it is today the Singin' River Ranch.

Change and the Search for a New Direction
When the Mountain Parks system started, Denver virtually **was** Colorado: it had most of the population, controlled the State Legislature and was generally perceived to represent the best interests of the young state. There were few people in the mountain areas of the Front Range and such small towns as did exist, like Evergreen, welcomed the influx of tourists brought by mountain parks development as well as the sale of lands for summer homes and cabins made possible by improved roads.

But by the early '60's, the situation had changed. The majority of the population no longer lived in Denver. Conflicts between Denver and the rest of the state, including the suburbs, were mounting.

Jefferson County, where the great majority of the mountain parks are located, was experiencing explosive growth.

The initial half-mill levy was reduced to one-third of a mill and then dropped altogether in 1955. Energy for acquiring new parks vanished, and the maintenance of the existing ones was thrown into the general parks budget—with predictable results. As budget crunches came with increasing frequency, the mountain parks suffered in comparison with those located in the city. Denver's capacity to fund cultural and recreational resources for the growing state was reaching its limits.

The most severe cut in the mountain parks budget came in 1982, when it was slashed from $700,000 to $350,000. The maintenance staff was cut from 24 to 9. The budget dropped slightly from then to 1986. In that year, even the small contribution of inmates from the Denver County jail picking up litter in the mountain parks was withdrawn for lack of money.

It was obvious that there was a need to redefine the purposes and funding base of the Denver Mountain Parks to adjust to the fact that many of them were now located among considerable populations. These people benefited from the parks' existence without paying for them and suffered from their neglect without power to demand improvement.

Some of the solutions offered in the years between 1966 and 1986 were:

1. Let the State of Colorado take over. This proposal foundered on the issue of ownership. The parks belong to Denver and whether they could be given to anyone else raised difficult legal issues. The State was unwilling to be financially responsible for them without ownership.

2. In the early 80's, there were serious negotiations between Jefferson County Open Space and Denver for Jeffo to take over maintenance of the parks in Jefferson County—but there were many issues of pride, money and trust that prevented a successful outcome.

3. Closing many of the parks down. This threat was less a possibility than a strategy to force the counties in which the parks are located—Grand, Douglas and Clear Creek, and, chiefly, Jefferson—into some form of cost-sharing, since obviously people would still continue to use and misuse open parks even if they were officially "closed".

4. Making the parks pay. There were studies of charging fees for admission, but main roads run through many of the parks. There were ideas of developing more revenue-producing activities in the parks for which precedents already exist: Chief Hosa Campground operates in a part of Genesee Park on a concession basis (nearby residents sued Denver in 1971 over the campground, but lost), as does the Evergreen Golf Course, Key's on the Green Restaurant and the restaurant at Echo Lake Lodge.

5. In 1986, in a bold bid for an overall solution that would enable Denver to regain a leadership role in recreational park planning, the city hired a nationally-respected firm of California consultants—Royston, Hanamoto, Abel and Abey—to do a master plan for the entire Denver Park System, urban as well as mountain.

Draft proposals were presented to a number of "publics" soliciting input. Of the eight major proposals for the mountain parks, four were rather obvious general goals (increase the benefit and enjoyment Denver residents get from mountain parks; protect the parks' natural beauty; cooperate with other jurisdictions to improve maintenance, reduce costs and increase the return on investment; buy no additional mountain land); two, aimed at increasing use of the parks, would require a considerable investment of money (developing a marketing plan to promote the parks, increasing public access through development of trail connections, public transit and new roads).

It seems clear that the planners had been requested to think in terms of funding any increased expenditures on mountain parks with revenues generated by the parks themselves. The remaining two proposals are for developing a range of mountain programs (outdoor education, fishing, organized hiking and camping excursions) for which fees could be charged, and developing

103

new amenities in some of the parks that could produce income. Suggested are: a conference center and a mountain zoo in Genesee Park; equestrian facilities, snowmobiling, cross-country skiing, snoeshoeing and skating at Echo Lake (with rental equipment available); golf course and restaurant at Lookout Mountain; facilities for group picnics, to be available on a reservation basis for a fee.

Some of these proposals may stimulate opposition from environmentalists or from neighboring residents afraid of increased noise or traffic. Some require a large initial outlay of capital by Denver citizens. There is no immediate prospect in them of funds for better maintenance, increased patrolling, or the trail construction that would make them really accessible to the public.

There is probably no politically possible way to do what history suggests as the only method by which the Denver Mountain Parks could get adequate funding for their operation: to designate a fractional mill levy or sales tax that would be used specifically to build up a trust fund for perpetual mountain park maintenance, and to keep it in force until the fund is adequate in size.

It seems likely that the eventual solution will involve Jefferson County Open Space cooperating in maintenance of many of the Denver Mountain Parks in and around Evergreen.

The Parks
The accompanying map shows two kinds of Denver Mountain Parks: the "named", which are developed and accessible for public use, and the "unnamed". These are undeveloped, many of them accessible only to hikers, some with no legal access. They are tops of mountains—like Hicks, Berrian, Elephant Butte—or other areas acquired by Denver from the Federal government or through donation. The accessible parks of most importance to the Evergreen area are:

Bell Park:
480 acres, acquired in 1915. Accessible from Highway 73. Has picnic areas and hiking trails.

Cub Creek Park:
549 acres, acquired in 1922. Picnic and recreational areas are accessible from Little Cub Creek Road.

Dillion Park:
160 acres, acquired in 1922. One mile south of Evergreen on Highway 78. Has fireplaces, picnic tables and hiking trails.

Bergen Park:
25 acres, donated to Denver in 1915 by Evergreen rancher Oscar Johnson. The park was opened in 1917 and is one of the most heavily-used of all the mountain parks. Has playgrounds, picnic tables, fireplaces and shelter house.

Fillius Park:
105 acres just east of Bergen Park on Highway 74. Acquired in 1914, partly by a rancher's gift and partly by condemnation. Named for an early Denver Park Board member, Jacob Fillius. Has picnic tables, playgrounds, a shelter house and fireplaces.

Fillius Park sign: Denver Mountain Parks.

Genesee Park:
the first mountain park, this started in 1912 with a purchase of 1200 acres including Genesee Mountain itself. Later gifts and purchases expanded the acreage to 2400. In addition to playgrounds, softball field, picnic tables, fireplaces and shelter house, and the 200-acre Chief Hosa campground for fee camping by reservation, this park offers the attraction of a protected elk herd and the unusual view of a buffalo herd—often seen from highway 70. The herd is maintained at around 25 adults, including 3 bulls. New calves delight large audiences of passing motorists each year: most are sold in the fall to zoos or commercial buffalo herds. The buffalo are moved periodically from one side of the highway to the other, through a tunnel under I-70, to take advantage of the best grazing: they are fed hay in the winter.

Forsberg Park:
this 9 acres on Highway 68—between Bergen Park and Echo Lake—was donated to Denver by C. A. Forsberg in 1918, and is one of three named parks in Clear Creek County.

Echo Lake Lodge and Park:
includes one of the most beautiful of mountain lakes. It is reached via Highway 103 from Bergen Park. Has playgrounds, picnic tables, fireplaces, a shelter house and hiking trails as well as the Echo Lake Lodge open for meals in the summer.

Summit Lake:
this 160-acre acquisition of 1924 surrounds and includes Summit Lake, the source of Bear Creek. Above timberline at an altitude of 13,000 feet, the park has both spectacular mountain scenery and unique plants. Access is via the road that Denver initiated, Highway 5, reputedly the highest automobile road in the world. It starts at Echo Lake and ends a few hundred yards from the 14,264 summit of Mount Evans. Besides the fragile botanical area, the park has a shelter house.

Pence Park:
Originally known as Dixie Park, this covers 320 acres and was added to the mountain park system in 1928. It is a couple of miles southeast of Kittredge, on both sides of Parmalee Gulch Road. It was renamed after Kingsley A. Pence, chairman of the 1911 joint committee of the Chamber of Commerce and the Real Estate Exchange that did so much to bring the idea of the mountain parks into being. There are picnic grounds and fireplaces. Pence Park used to be one of the favorite sites for "tubing" in the winter time, but an accident there, which killed a little girl there in 1978, was the impetus for Denver's decision to ban all tubing in the mountain parks.

Corwina Park:
One of the early acquisitions, Corwina Park covers 297 acres. It is accessible from Highway 74 and has playgrounds, picnic tables, shelter house and fireplaces.

O'Fallon Park:
A gift to the city of Denver in 1938—and the last major Mountain Park acquisition—this 860-acre park effectively forms one continuous recreation area with Pence on the south and Corwina on the north. It has hiking trails, fireplaces and picnic grounds with tables, and can be entered from Highway 74. The land was bought from George Bancroft with the express intention of donating it to Denver.

The donor, Martin O'Fallon, was an Irish immigrant who founded a small plumbing supply company in Denver in 1899. He retired in 1936 after building it into the largest such operation between the Mississippi and California. A public-spirited Catholic layman and philanthropist, O'Fallon wanted to make a permanent contribution to benefit the people of the city where he had enjoyed such success.

Little Park:

400 acres in lower Bear Creek Canyon, just west of Idledale, was bought in 1917 from the Bureau of Land Management for $1.50 an acre. It has fireplaces and picnic tables.

Bear Creek Canyon Park is a 400-foot strip extending for 4 miles along Bear Creek canyon between Idledale and Morrison and serves mainly to protect the area from development. It was acquired in 1928. The only facilities are picnic grounds. It was known for many years as Starbuck Park after the original name for Idledale.

The grand finale of the "circle tour" of mountain parks at the Morrison end is, of course, the 640-acre **Red Rocks Park**, purchased from John Ross of Morrison in 1927, with its magnificent red sandstone formations and outdoor amphitheater. At the Golden end there is the 66-acre **Lookout Mountain Park**, with its enduring attractions of Buffalo Bill's grave and museum and unique two-way panoramas of the entire metro area of Denver to the east—especially lovely at night—and the mountain ranges to the west.

The Special Case: Dedisse Park, Evergreen Lake and Dam and the Evergreen Golf Course

Community surveys show that the most common image Evergreen people have of their community is the Evergreen Lake. Surrounded by mountains and not far from Main Street, it is the site of celebrations and a pretty good geographical center of the settled area that calls itself Evergreen. The Lake and its adjacent attractions—Dam, Golf Course and Dedisse Park—symbolize this mountain community.

Yet all of these amenities were created by Denver, primarily for the enjoyment and use of Denverites and tourists. In a 1919 in a proceeding in Jefferson County Court, Denver acquired the 420-

Genesee Park buffalo herd.

acre deDisse Ranch by condemnation for $25,000. Originally homesteaded by a French pioneer, Jerome deDisse, and his wife Mary in the 1860's, the ranch included forested land on the hillsides and meadows on either side of Bear Creek.

In a 1959 article on the building of the dam, local historian Mary Helen Crain wrote that these meadows were among the lushest in the entire area, with a profusion of wildflowers and "hay so tall that the men and horses were out of sight when they were cutting it." Part of the meadow was an improvised town ball field where a hometown baseball team took on visiting players from Idaho Springs, Golden and Troutdale.

Jerome deDisse was dead by 1919 and title to the ranch was divided among his wife, in her nineties by this time, and their children and grandchildren. A small site of little more than 2 acres—where the Lakepoint Center is today—was reserved by the family for its own use. An additional small piece of land on which to build the dam was donated by John S. McBeth.

Denver's desire was to create a lake but the purposes were ambiguous. Much of the publicity of the time was in terms of flood control, yet the testimony of both George Ball engineer and designer of the Dam, and Walter Ailinger, Parks

Department Engineer, stresses other aspects: recreational use, an enlarged water supply for Evergreen and emergency water storage for Denver in case of severe drought. It appears that some flood control gates were built into the dam but were never operated and eventually became inoperable. Whatever flood control effect the project has had is due solely to the absorption capacity of the "wetlands" created by the lake.

One never-used provision was for the addition of small turbines to generate enough electricity "to put a string of ornamental lights around the lake . . . and also light up a portion of the golf links and the club house, for skating in the evening."

Construction of the dam was started in 1926 and completed in 1927, with the lake filling to capacity during the spring run-off of 1928. According to a article in Denver Municipal Facts magazine, "The dam is of the gravity type. It contains 15,000 barrels of cement or 60,000 sacks; eight tons of steel were used in its construction and 11,617 cubic yards of concrete. It is keyed in bed rock 45 feet across the bottom and has a capacity for water pressure to its full height. It will retain 700 acre feet of water before the spillway comes into use." "The new lake," said the same article, "will cover a territory of 55 acres, its greatest depth being 35 feet and its average depth 17 feet." Total construction cost for the dam was $214,374.58.

de Disse Ranch.

Rock needed for the project was quarried from a site on Cub Creek.

In 1926, Troutdale Hotel and Realty Company gave to the City and County of Denver "17.867 acres, more or less— subject to the condition that (Denver) shall always maintain a golf course on said tract and use said tract as a golf course."

The first nine holes of the golf course and the rustic little clubhouse, probably designed by Benedict, were completed in 1925.

The course was expanded to 18 holes the following year. For many years, as the only golf course in the area, it was well-patronized and was usually described as one of the "sportiest" mountain golf courses in the country.

The Lake also was well-used and well-loved from the beginning. In winter, it was a favorite destination for family skating and sledding and the site of many a group outing and organized festivity. In summer, the State Game and Fish Department stocked it generously with trout. Summer houses and cabins sprang up around Evergreen Lake and it became a favorite photographic subject.

Then came the sixties and the financial troubles of Denver. The golf course, with its sand greens and low-budget maintenance, was drawing fewer players. The shores of the Lake were beginning to look tacky.

In 1968, during one of the periodic efforts to get Evergreen incorporated, Mayor Tom Currigan surprisingly agreed to the possibility that Denver Mountain Parks within the proposed boundaries might be bought by the new City of Evergreen. Had the incorporation gone through, it would have saved a whole lot of later negotiations by a multitude of officials.

In the crisis atmosphere following the 1976 Big Thompson flood, negotiations took place between all the parties who had something at stake.

In the resulting agreements, all gained something important.

Denver relieved itself of responsibility for the dam in the event of a flood and restricted its own cost for the dam repair to $50,000. The Evergreen Metropolitan Water and Sanitation District got a lease on the lake and dam for 50 years, with a renewal clause for an additional 25, permission to dredge the lake to create additional water storage capacity, and Denver's storage rights. Jefferson County Open Space leased from Evergreen Metro the rights to operate recreational facilities at the lake for 75 years at $6,000 a year, paying them the total of $450,000 in cash, which they promptly used for the dam repair.

Open Space then leased to the Evergreen Metropolitan Recreation and Parks District, for a nominal sum, the authority to organize recreation programs for the lake area.

Denver retained full control of the Evergreen Golf Course, the agreement providing for the Evergreen Metro District to supply water for irrigation. To the great surprise—and delight—of Evergreen residents, the same City and County of Denver that could not find $200,000 to repair the dam managed to rustle up a reported $1,000,000 for a total upgrading of the golf course in 1983-4.

Dedisse Park sign.

Evergreen Golf Course.

Homesteaders Jerome F. and Mary Jane de Disse.

Jerome de Disse Jr. and his wife, Carmen.

Sand greens were replaced by carefully tended grass. The entire 5,103-yard course was redesigned by Charles Lind, director of Denver's seven golf courses and one of the state's all-time top golfers. A small temporary building was erected to serve as a golf pro shop and a supply of new golf carts added to the amenities of the course. Par for the course—which Lind says "is so easy it's tough"—is 69 for men and 72 for women. The golf course and restaurant are run on a concession basis.

The refurbishing has been a huge success: the course is crowded with players during the summer season.

The Evergreen community was less enthusiastic about the sudden appearance of a large metal building halfway up the golf course hillside which Denver put up for storage of maintenance equipment. New Denver Parks Department Manager Ruth Rodriguez in 1986 volunteered to mitigate the damage through landscaping and the installation of a wooden fence.

There is a price to be paid for agreements that involve a multitude of independent agencies, and that is the difficulty of coordinating separate efforts into one coherent plan. Master planning for the Lake area has run into difficulties on this account.

Jefferson County Open Space

There are some striking parallels between the Jefferson County Open Space Program and the early days of the Denver Mountain Parks: a similar missionary enthusiasm, the "can-do" energy, the spate of accomplishments within a very short period of time. There are also real differences: all of Jeffco's acquisitions are within its own borders and the very way it was set up requires that it be able to cooperate with other agencies.

The impetus to acquiring and preserving open space sprang out of the rapid growth of population, business and industry in Jefferson County following World War II. It became clear that cherished mountain views and approaches could be lost forever through ill-considered development, and that there was less and less public access to unspoiled open areas on the plains and in the foothills.

In 1971, a group of concerned citizens formed an organization called PLAN JEFFCO and formulated a resolution to provide a one-half cent sales tax to be used for acquiring open space lands. The following spring, they launched a successful drive to get the resolution on the ballot by petition then campaigned vigorously for the proposition right up to election day. The vote of the citizens was overwhelmingly positive.

Clubhouse on Evergreen Golf Course.

As interpreted for the next six years, the mandate was to use open space revenues—initially about $4,000,000 per year—for planning, developing access to, acquiring, maintaining and preserving open space lands; developing paths and trails on them; acquiring historic sites for the use and benefit of the public.

The money was apportioned among the 11 cities in the county and the unincorporated areas. A 10-member Open Space Advisory Committee (JCOSAC) was established to advise the County Commissioners on the acquisition of lands, with 3 members representing the cities, 3 county representatives, 3 members at large and 1 representing the parks and recreations districts in the county. Four Evergreen citizens have served as at-large members: Mike Moore, an influential member of the original PLAN JEFFO group, Nan Rickey, Joe Mackey and Bev Snell.

Negotiations for land acquisition started immediately. By the end of 1974, Jeffco Open Space funds had bought six properties totalling 6,344 acres. These included the site of John Brisben Walker's ruined dreams, Mount Falcon, and Evergreen's Hiwan Homestead—a purchase made in a crisis atmosphere since the land all around it was being developed and the future of the unique and historic log house was uncertain.

In 1974, the District hired experienced parks administrator Ray Printz to direct its rapidly growing program. Printz had previously been Executive Director of the South Suburban Recreation and Park District which serves a large area south of Denver, Recreation Manager for the Ken Caryl Ranch Corporation and Assistant Director for the Englewood Parks Department.

Until 1978, acquisitions were of three types:

1. Urban parklands, acquired for development of active recreational opportunities and usually acquired in conjunction with existing cities. In these cases, Open Space money financed the land purchase while city or other revenues developed it.

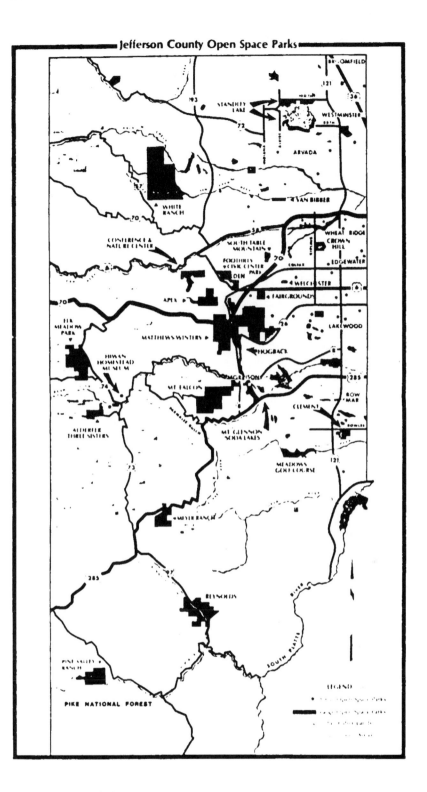

Jefferson County Open Space Parks

2. Open spaces still in their natural state, where the only development was carefully planned hiking and equestrian trails to make the always interesting, often spectacular, beauties available to the public—and to keep people off the rest of the land, preventing damage to the fragile ground cover.

3. Historic buildings with some potentially valuable public use.

In 1978 came the first ballot box attempt to redefine how Open Space monies could be used and how they were apportioned. The three ballot proposals—to allow Open Space to negotiate for water rights along with land purchases and to buy land in adjoining counties, to permit funds to be used for capital development on open space and park land, and to give cities a larger share of the open space funds (though they have 75% of the population, they receive only a third of the funds)—were defeated.

In 1980 came another attempt at modification with three ballot proposals, two similar to the 1978 ones. The third suggestion that the County Commissioners be allowed to divert half of the Open Space funds for the next 15 years to build a jail was soundly defeated. The cities again failed to win support for a larger share of the funds, but the voters did authorize the expenditure of future funds for development as well as acquisition of lands.

1980 also saw the adoption of a master plan relating to Open Space which spelled out the county's goals—to provide neighborhood open space for plains and mountain communities, as well as community-wide parks and regional parks with a ten mile service radius. By this time, more than 11,000 acres of parks and open space had been acquired in the county, 7,300 of them in the mountains. These included Evergreen's Means (later Elk) Meadow Park and the Alderfer/Three Sisters Park.

In 1981 Director Ray Printz, with the agreement of the Open Space Advisory Committee, presented a major new proposal to the County Commissioners. Mindful of the unplanned and unwilled "decline and fall" of the Denver Mountain Parks, and believing that the time when the county would have acquired enough park lands was in sight—though still a number of years away—he proposed setting up a trust fund for maintenance with part of the Open Space funds.

He believed that there would be enough money to buy the open space still needed and to build up the maintenance fund (the sales tax was raising around $8,000,000 annually by this time), so that by 1991 the one-half cent sales tax could be discontinued. Thus he hoped the maintenance of the parks in perpetuity could be assured, long after the inevitable decline in public interest and diversion of money to other purposes.

The proposal hung fire while legalities and differing philosophies were discussed. In the meantime, the acquisition program continued enthusiastically, along with planning for a major investment in development of the largest urban park acquisition—Clement Park—in the rapidly growing southern part of the county.

One of the major accomplishments of the Open Space Program has

been its construction of trails. both pedestrian and equestrian. The objective is to create a network of trails, both within the open space lands and outside, to connect the parks with community activity centers (schools, shopping centers, civic centers, etc.) and with each other.

A full-time trails planner is on the Open Space staff, and a great deal of the actual work is done under a summer Youth Work Program. As of 1985, some 130 miles of trails had been completed that take campers, hikers, skiers and horseback riders into secluded mountain areas and offer walking, jogging and bicycling paths within the more urban places.

In 1985, large and angry crowds filled the Courthouse Hearing Room in Golden with arguments for and against using a parcel of the Means Meadow Park—across Stage Coach Boulevard from the main body of park land—for a performing arts center for Evergreen. Other "hot" issues had also arisen, especially about what proportion of Open Space funds should be used for development as compared with acquisition, and what were the priorities in new acquisitions.

In response to these public controversies, the County Commissioners took two actions: they set up a 12-person special committee to make a one-time study and report, and they widened the scope of the continuing Open Space Advisory Committee's functions, from merely advising about which properties to purchase to making recommendations about about acquisition costs, maintenance and security, and what kind of uses are appropriate on Open Space sites.

In round figures by the end of 1986, Open Space had spent $53 million to buy 150 parcels of land totalling 14,000 acres, with $12 million already earmarked for the purchase of 31 additional parcels.

Open Space Investments in Evergreen
Attractive brochures describing each separate Open Space property, with maps of trails through the parks, are available at trailheads in the parks, in the Evergreen Library, and at the Chamber of Commerce and sporting goods stores.

Ray Printz.

The design of Open Space publications is notable and received well-deserved recognition, when its handsome 1986 calendar was selected for a national award.

Hiwan Homestead Museum and Heritage Grove. An illustrated booklet by the Museum's first Director, Connie Fahnestock—telling the history of this 17-room log house with its twin octagonal towers—is available from the Museum gift shop.

Fahnestock, as president of the small and newly-formed historical society, was the guiding force behind the effort to rescue the Hiwan Homestead from imminent sale and possible destruction in the early 70's. She served as the Museum's tireless and imaginative Director until 1986, ably assisted by Curator Sandy Crain—who was appointed to the Director's post when Connie resigned.

The house and one acre of land were placed on the National Register of Historic Places in 1974, purchased with Open Space funds in the same year as a historic site, and opened to the public as a Museum in August, 1975. The Museum programming, which is managed by the Jefferson County Historical Society, is in three main areas:

1. Exhibition of items related to Jefferson County History.

2. Development of a school program of enrichment in local history in conjunction with R-1 schools: the museum has been especially innovative in its development of "hands-on" exhibits.

3. Teaching and perpetuating of "old crafts".

110

The adjacent parking was bought by Open Space in 1977. At the same time, Open Space supported a community fund-raising effort to buy the 3-1/2 acre Heritage Grove, just in the nick of time to prevent it from becoming the site of a condominium development.

The Grove, which is now owned by the Jefferson County Historical Society, is the site of some of Evergreen's most attractive and successful community events: the July 4th weekend Summerfest organized by the Evergreen Center for the Arts; the annual Mountain Rendezvous in August; the summer Fine Arts Show of the Evergreen Artists Association.

Elk (formely Means) Meadow Park: Purchased in 1977, this 1140 acres was snatched from imminent development by the diligent and persuasive efforts of concerned Evergreen Citizens.

Prime mover in the campaigns to preserve the Grove and Means Meadow was community activist Sheila Clarke. Originally from Los Angeles, Clarke has been described by the Canyon Courier as a "heavyweight in service to the Evergreen community".

As chair of the Committee for the Preservation of Heritage Grove, she helped to raise $158,000 to purchase the 3.2 acres that constitute Evergreen's only community park. In 1986, she led the fight to acquire Means Meadow for Open Space when it was about to be sold for development.

In recognition of her efforts, Sheila Clarke was selected, along with Pat Sayward, as Evergreen's 1981 Person of the Year.

Clarke is active in many other community endeavors, including the Mountain Area Schools Forum and the League of Women Voters. She is a founding member and leader in the Evergreen North Area Balanced Land-Use Effort (ENABLE), an active and thoughtful coalition of homeowners' groups. She also teaches a women's conditioning class for the Jefferson County Adult Education program and sings in the Evergreen Chorale.

The County Commissioners changed the name of Means Meadow in 1986 after a lengthy dispute with the Means family over a payment, missed through an oversight, on the last 128 acres the County had contracted to buy in 1977.

When more money was asked for the land, the County filed suit. They lost, and while an appeal was pending, an out-of-court settlement was reached whereby the County paid $2,500 more per acre than the original price.

The Commissioners' announcement of a change of name to Elk Meadow Park was debated in letters to the Canyon Courier. Some felt the action was petty,

MEANS MEADOW PARK

The outstanding features of this Open Space Park are the wide diversities of ecosystems within the park itself and along the trails leading to adjacent public lands.

The meadow and grassland ecosystems are found on the less steep, lower elevations. This environment is one of grasses, wild flowers, and open, rolling land. One may see the gapping oval hole that is home to the badger, as well as the smaller holes of pocket gophers. These shy animals are rarely seen, but on almost any day from February through August one can see the Richardson ground squirrel. Several colonies of this relative of the prairie dog can be found on the park.

Traveling higher into the park, one crosses the transitional zone of the scattered forest. Here Ponderosa Pine grow at a distance from one another to create a park-like stand. Within this edge of the forest many types of wildlife seek both shelter and food. Here one may see elk or deer, especially in the winter when snowfall drives them from higher altitudes. The tassel-eared Abert Squirrel makes his home year-round in this area of the park.

Still higher in the park, one finds the Foothills Zone. This is characterized by a steeper slope and a more dense forest made up mostly of Douglas Fir and scattered aspen groves. The aspen fill an important role in the evolution of the forest, as they provide the shade which young coniferous trees need to get started.

The highest points within the park itself are part of the Montane Zone. Here the slopes are even steeper, and the predominant plants are the thick stands of Lodgepole Pine. In this area one should be on the lookout for the Blue Grouse and Porcupines common to this environment.

As one continues along the trail out of the park itself and arrives at Bergen Peak, one ends up in a sub-alpine environment. Here there is little plant life, aside from the lichens on the exposed rock outcrops. Though the scene close at hand may be barren, the scenic vistas from the Peak are magnificent. From this vantage point, one can see over the foothills to the plains in the East, and across intervening canyons to the Continental Divide in the West.

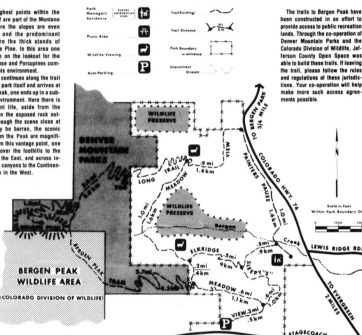

LEGEND

Park Managers Residence (REPORT EMERGENCIES HERE)

Picnic Area

Wildlife Viewing

Auto Parking

Trail (Existing)

Trail Distance

Park Boundary w entrance

Intermittent Stream

The trails to Bergen Peak have been constructed in an effort to provide access to public recreation lands. Through the co-operation of Denver Mountain Parks and the Colorado Division of Wildlife, Jefferson County Open Space was able to build these trails. If leaving the trail, please follow the rules and regulations of these jurisdictions. Your co-operation will help make more such access agreements possible.

pointing out what an astronomical sum could have been extracted for such prime development land at current market prices. Others sided with the Commissioners, believing that representatives of the Means interests should not have tried to profit from the oversight of a County employe.

This park offers many riches to the community. First is the visual beauty of the meadow, with 9708-foot Bergen Peak rising behind it, that is seen from busy Highway 74. Elk Meadow adjoins Denver Mountain Park land on Bergen Peak, which in turn abuts onto a State Wildlife refuge.

The headwaters of both Bergen and Troublesome creeks are on these lands, as are an important part of the habitat of the Mount Evans elk herd. Bergen Peak is one of the herd's calving grounds. In spring it is not unusual to see herds of up to 40 elk wandering on the meadow.

With the cooperation of the other land owners, Open Space has developed a satisfying variety of trails to explore the five different ecosystems represented in the Park: the open, rolling meadows and grasslands—covered in summer with wild flowers; the parklike stands of ponderosa pine in the transition zone, favorite habitat of elk, deer and squirrel; the steeper slopes of the foothills zone, marked by Douglas fir and aspen groves; the thick stands of lodgepole pine in the next higher, montane, zone; finally, on Bergen Peak itself, one enters the subalpine zone where lichens and rock predominate and the lack of trees affords a magnificent 360-degree view—to the plains on the East and the continental divide on the west.

Trailheads for Elk Meadow Park are on Highway 74 and Stage Coach Boulevard.

111

Sandy Crain.

Connie Fahnestock.

Hiwan Homestead Museum.

112

Alderfer/Three Sisters Park and Alderfer Ranch: These properties were acquired at two different times. The 242- acre Park itself consists of land acquired from the Alderfer family—part donated and part bought by Open Space—and from the Spencer Wyant family, who also made a gift of part of the property.

Arleta and E. J. Alderfer moved onto their ranch in 1945, into the ranch house built in 1894 by George Dollason. They remodelled the house and raised silver fox and Angus cattle on the ranch until around 1970, when the pasturing of horses became the main use of the land.

The area that included the Three Sisters Peaks—and a fourth known as the Brother—belonged to the Spencer Wyant family. The formations have long been an Evergreen landmark, dominating the golf course and lake. Trails in the parks explore ponderosa and aspen woods, and one trail leads to the 7,800-foot top of "The Brother", from which there is an interesting view of the Evergreen area and its surroundings. The trailhead is across Buffalo Park Road from Wilmot School, where parking is available when school is not in session.

The remaining 95 acres of the Alderfer Ranch, lying on both sides of Buffalo Park Road and including the ranch house and outbuildings, were bought in May of 1986. One of the reasons for the purchase was to develop some of the flatter southeast part of the property for softball and soccer fields, in cooperation with the Evergreen Metropolitan Recreation and Park District, and possibly a "historic living farm" on the north side of the ranch.

Evergreen Lake Recreation Rights:
In the multi-agency negotiations with Denver over the Dam and Lake, Jefferson County Open Space played a crucial role in leasing recreation rights to the Lake for 75 years. These rights are sublet to the Evergreen Metropolitan Recreation District, which operates a year-round recreation program at the Lake. The purchase also gave the Open Space Program a role in the important and complex problem of long-range planning for the Lake.

Kittredge Community Park was also purchased in May of 1986. It is a 1.5 acre piece of land on Highway 74 with frontage on Bear Creek. The price of $80,000 seemed high, compared with the $6,800 per acre price of the Alderfer Ranch, but the property was commercially zoned. Reason for the purchase was to provide a playground and picnic area for Kittredge: development of the facilities and operation of the park is the responsibility of the Evergreen Metropolitan Recreation and Park District.

Trail System for Evergreen Area:
Planning for a comprehensive trail system to provide safe and scenic routes for cyclists and hikers in the Evergreen area has been underway since the mid-seventies, when the Evergreen Recreation and Parks District initiated a study of potential trail corridors. The first fruit of this endeavor was the DeDisse Trail from Highway 74, across from the Lakeshore Center, through part of the golf course to Buffalo Park Road.

Jefferson County Open Space planner, Ken Foehlske, is aware of both the opportunities and difficulties of trails development here. "Vast acreages of undeveloped wild land, extensive public holdings, mountain ridge lines and stream valleys" seem to offer unlimited possibilities.

But in fact, the same stream beds that would make for good trails were the obvious sites for automobile roads, and many of these are too narrow to allow for safe hiking or biking at the same time. The more exclusive residential developments resist the placing of public trails through their properties, fearing that the introduction of outsiders into their neigborhoods might lead to increased crime. Many of the best trail possibilities involve Denver Mountain Park land, but Denver is at present too pressed financially to be able to develop and maintain them.

A recent example of cooperation with great public benefit is the renovation and ongoing maintenance of the old Beaverbrook Trail, developed by Denver many years ago and offering magnificent views of the Clear Creek drainage basin.

In spite of difficulties, a trail system for the Evergreen area is being planned, coordinated with a county-wide program.

Shiela Clarke and Pat Sayward.

Three Sisters.

Views of Alderfer/Three Sisters Park.

113

Alderfer Ranch.

Alderfer barn on ranch homesite.

For bikers, there are the greatest difficulties: the best solution is seen as on-road treatments such as paved shoulders, where sufficient road width exists. For hikers and horseback riders, it will be a series of naturally- surfaced "spinal" trails skirting Evergreen itself, but linked to it by a network of community and neighborhood trails. The major trails are being designed for limited access and long—overnight or extended backpacking—trips. These will link up with the vast existing network of trails in the Mount Evans Region, created by the National Forest Service and the Mount Evans State Wildlife Area, and with the extensive trail networks within other Open Space parks in the foothills and mountains.

A well-written guide, "Foothills to Mountain Evans: A Trail Guide" by two Evergreen residents, is available in local book stores and the Evergreen Library.

Open Space properties and parks which are easily reached from Evergreen include **Mount Falcon Park**, a 1,408-acre tract of land that includes the ruins of John Brisben Walker's mansion, some remnants of his ambitious project to build a summer home for U.S. presidents, and nine miles of well- marked hiking trails. The park lies between Indian Hills and Morrison, with a trailhead off Parmalee Gulch Road. **Windy Saddle Park**, up on Lookout Mountain, includes part of the old Beaver Brook Trail originally developed jointly by Denver Mountain Parks and the Colorado Mountain Club.

Jefferson County Conference and Nature Center on Lookout Mountain is the former Charles Boettcher summer home, designed by architects Fisher and Fisher. It was donated to Jefferson County by his granddaughter and opened to the public in 1975. It makes a charming setting for weddings and other social occasions, has an intriguing nature museum and is used for seminars and conferences. There is a 1-1/4 mile, self-guided, nature trail on the surrounding 110 acres of forest and meadows. Three foothills parks—**Apex, Matthews/Winters and Hogback**— offer trails through a different type of scenery and vegetation and include sites of some of the area's earliest towns.

In the Conifer area, the most important acquisition is the 397 acres of the **Meyer Ranch** near Aspen Park, which was purchased in August of 1986. The handsome Victorian ranch house, seen from Highway 285, has been a familiar landmark for many years. Under the purchase terms the Meyers will retain the historic home and surrounding 10 acres for a maximum of 15 years, when it will be available for purchase by Open Space. Besides the values of visual and historic preservation, the property was acquired to provide hiking and equestrian trails, picnic areas and informal soccer and softball fields.

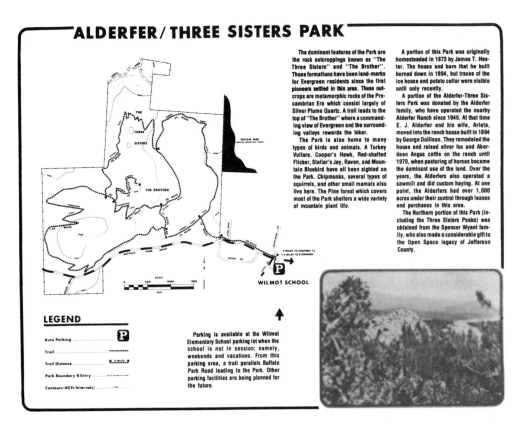

ALDERFER/ THREE SISTERS PARK

The dominant features of the Park are the rock outcroppings known as "The Three Sisters" and "The Brother". These formations have been land-marks for Evergreen residents since the first pioneers settled in this area. These outcrops are metamorphic rocks of the Precambrian Era which consist largely of Silver Plume Quartz. A trail leads to the top of "The Brother" where a commanding view of Evergreen and the surrounding valleys rewards the hiker.

The Park is also home to many types of birds and animals. A Turkey Vulture, Cooper's Hawk, Red-shafted Flicker, Stellar's Jay, Raven, and Mountain Bluebird have all been sighted on the Park. Chipmunks, several types of squirrels, and other small mamals also live here. The Pine forest which covers most of the Park shelters a wide variety of mountain plant life.

A portion of this Park was originally homesteaded in 1873 by James T. Hester. The house and barn that he built burned down in 1894, but traces of the ice house and potato cellar were visible until only recently.

A portion of the Alderfer-Three Sisters Park was donated by the Alderfer family, who have operated the nearby Alderfer Ranch since 1945. At that time E. J. Alderfer and his wife, Arleta, moved into the ranch house built in 1894 by George Dollison. They remodeled the house and raised silver fox and Aberdeen Angus cattle on the ranch until 1970, when pasturing of horses became the dominant use of the land. Over the years, the Alderfers also operated a sawmill and did custom haying. At one point, the Alderfers had over 1,000 acres under their control through leases and purchases in this area.

The Northern portion of this Park (including the Three Sisters Peaks) was obtained from the Spencer Wyant family, who also made a considerable gift to the Open Space legacy of Jefferson County.

WILMOT SCHOOL

Parking is available at the Wilmot Elementary School parking lot when the school is not in session; namely, weekends and vacations. From this parking area, a trail parallels Buffalo Park Road leading to the Park. Other parking facilities are being planned for the future.

LEGEND

Auto Parking	**P**
Trail	
Trail Distance	
Park Boundary & Entry	
Contours (40 ft. Intervals)	

Pine Valley Ranch, an 820-acre mountain property 15 miles south of Evergreen and a mile from Pine, was purchased in March of 1986 from Winegard Realty of Burlington, Iowa—the same family that has been involved in development of the Troutdale properties.

Purchase price of Pine Valley was $2.35 million, including $90,000 worth of water rights. The extensive complex of buildings, including a remodelled three-story lodge with dining room, kitchen, indoor swimming pool and sauna, was donated to the county. There was some public criticism of this acquisition, on the grounds that upkeep of the buildings was a tremendous financial undertaking and no clear use for them had been established before the acquisition. With the buildings as a donation, Open Space has no investment in them, even if a decision should be made to tear them all down.

Reynolds Park, an 1100-acre former dude ranch is 5 miles southeast of Conifer on the Foxton Road. When we asked old-timer Rosabel Schneider of Blue Creek Road what the early families there did for fun, she mentioned parties and picnics on the Reynolds Ranch as one of the annual highlights. The area is a major wintering ground for elk and deer and offers great diversity of terrain to the hiker and horseback rider. **Cross-country skiing** opportunities abound in several Open Space Parks—especially Elk Meadow, Alderfer/Three Sisters and Mount Falcon—when there is sufficient snow. Open Space has mapped out the most likely places for good skiing in each of these parks—color-coded for degree of difficulty—in its brochure "Ski Touring Information" and encourages calls to 277-8340 for up-to-date information on snow conditions.

The Open Space Program has brought a generous and benevolent public presence into the Evergreen community. Through years when public monies seemed to be constantly shrinking and costs rising, the fact that Open Space funds might be available to save treasured lands, views and historic buildings has made a difference.

Preparing a case to present to the Open Space Advisory Committee forces people to weigh up pro's and cons and to move from emotion to a well-reasoned approach. The public in turn is educated about open space issues through the lobbying, petitioning and newspaper coverage involved.

Many acquisition proposals—such as the Bell Museum on Upper Bear Creek and a pond in Aspen Park—are rejected.

Sometimes persistence and good documentation are rewarded, as in the case of a 313-acre tract of land on lower Bear Creek known as the **Lair of the Bear**, which was bought for $1.2 million in 1986. The Evergreen Naturalists worked for several years to secure this acquisition for the protection of wildlife habitat and the enjoyment of nature-lovers. Open Space's initial approval of this purchase, however, was conditional on being able to transfer the valuable water rights that went with the property to the new **Clement Park** on Bowles and S. Wadsworth.

In the end, the Lair of the Bear was bought for half-a-million dollars less than originally proposed, and the county was left to do the "legal footwork" with the water court in Greeley over the water rights.

In fall of 1986, Open Space decided to acquire 114 acres in Foothills Business Park near Golden, adjacent to the new County Jail. This will provide a spacious setting for a new governmental center for Jefferson County Government, for which the Commissioners have bought land, and includes new headquarters for the Open Space Program.

This should give Evergreen—along with all the other unincorporated areas of Jefferson County—a new "Civic Center in a Park", which is important since the prospects of Evergreen having a city government of its own seem remote.

Mount Evans State Wildlife Area
Sometimes referred to as the Elk Management Area, this belongs to the State of Colorado and is one of more than 200 properties throughout the state that are managed by the Colorado Division of Wildlife. Covering some quarter of a million acres, these range from small parcels to large tracts. The 4,500-acre Mount Evans Area is unique in being so close to a large metropolitan area, and in containing such a diversity of wildlife.

Pine Valley Ranch location.

115

Land for this Wildlife Area came from a number of owners but most was purchased from the Truesdells (1,874 acres in 1950), and the Evans Ranch (1126 acres in 1958).

Since this area is where we spent our first Colorado summers in 1948 and 1949, we have a particular fondness for the meadows, forests, streams and vistas of this lovely region.

By the beginning of this century, elk were almost extinct in the entire Front Range area due to many years of uncontrolled hunting. A herd of 23 elk was brought to the Mount Evans basin in 1913 from Yellowstone National Park by the Colorado Game and Fish Commission, forerunner of the present Division of Wildlife. They have multiplied into today's large herd of 1000-1200 head.

The Wildlife Area is reached by driving six miles on Upper Bear

View of living room wing, Pine Valley Lodge.

View of Pine Valley Lodge from deck.

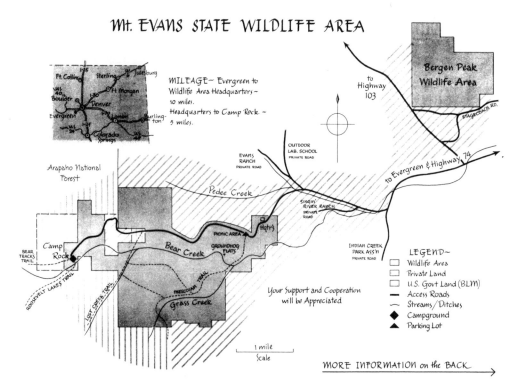

Mt. EVANS STATE WILDLIFE AREA

MILEAGE— Evergreen to Wildlife Area Headquarters ~ 10 miles. Headquarters to Camp Rock ~ 5 miles.

LEGEND~
☐ Wildlife Area
☐ Private Land
☐ U.S. Gov't Land (BLM)
— Access Roads
~ Streams/Ditches
◆ Campground
▲ Parking Lot

Your Support and Cooperation will be Appreciated

1 mile Scale

MORE INFORMATION on the BACK →

Mount Evans State Wildlife Area.

Creek Road, taking the right fork towards Singin' River Ranch and then a left turn at a second intersection two miles further on: adequate signs then point the visitor to the Area Headquarters where the Manager of the Wildlife Area both lives and works.

Half-a-mile further is the first parking area and picnic ground at Groundhog Flats. The old road to the Truesdell Ranch branches off here, closed now to vehicles but open to hikers as the scenic Grass Creek Trail, a pleasant walk of nearly three miles to the Truesdell Meadows. A stone chimney is the only relic of the main house and the cabins have all disappeared. The area, never seriously changed by human habitation, has returned to nature.

There are two other parking areas from which additional trails originate, one 2-1/4 miles beyond the first and the other at the end of the road at Camp Rock Campground. The last time we travelled this road it was rocky and rough but negotiable if taken slowly. There is an extensive network of trails through the Wildlife Area, coordinated with the trails sytem of the adjoining Arapahoe National Forest. A free trail map is usually available from dispensers at the parking areas and the "Foothills to Mount Evans"

trail guide also covers this area well.

The Division of Wildlife is charged by law with managing all wildlife and its environment "for the use, benefit and enjoyment of the people of this state and its visitors". In pursuit of this aim, the Wildlife Area is closed to all human activity from January 1 to June 15 each year. This is to allow elk and deer undisturbed access to winter feeding grounds.

In addition, the road from the headquarters building to Camp Rock is closed to all but pedestrian traffic after Labor Day. Hikers intending to use any but the Grass Creek trailhead should plan their activities for the summer months. Bighorn sheep and mountain goats are prized residents of the Mount Evans basin. Each year, the Department of Wildlife does a count of the animals. Numbers of the native sheep are declining— down from around 250 in 1978 to around 125 in 1985. Environmental stresses, avalanches, falls and lungworm disease are the chief threats to survival of the species here—as well as competition for food with the more prolific goats. A few head of these were introduced from South Dakota and Montana in 1961 and have multiplied to around 170 today.

The road to Camp Rock is reopened briefly in late October and early November for the rifle hunting season, which brings us to an issue that generates a lot of heat from time to time in the Evergreen community.

Letters of protest poured into the Canyon Courier in 1984 when a mountain goat was shot and loaded up in full view of people visiting Summit Lake, and again in 1986 when a young housewife bagged a black bear in the woods near Conifer, after spending six nights in a tree platform watching bait she and her husband had left on the hillside.

As non-hunters and as people who have never owned a gun, we think it worthwhile to share a few facts we ran into while gathering information on the Mount Evans Wildlife Area and the adjacent National Forest.

1. The program of wildlife management is financed mainly from hunting and fishing license fees ($30 million in 1985) and excise taxes on hunting and fishing equipment. The money to buy wildlife preserves, to pay wildlife managers, to finance studies of different species, to stock streams and lakes like the one in Evergreen, and to monitor herds like the Mount Evans elk, deer, goats and bighorn sheep, comes almost entirely from hunters and fishermen. Since 1977, there has been a check-off provision on the state income tax forms for people to contribute a small part of their tax refund to the Colorado Non-Game Wildlife Program, but this raises a minute and diminishing part of total Wildlife Department costs.

2. The Mount Evans elk herd is something over 1200 head. Since there are no longer enough predators to maintain this population at a level the available range can support, the alternatives are to allow "natural" limitation through starvation and disease, or to cull the herd through limited hunting or some other method.

3. The entire state is divided into Big Game Management Units. Evergreen is in Unit 39, which covers the Evergreen, Conifer, and Mount Evans region. Each year in each unit, the winter population of deer and elk is counted and the age and sex structure determined. Together with the ratio of hunter "successes" to licenses issued the previous year, these figures are used to determine how many bull and cow licenses should be issued for the current year.

Approximately 600 elk licenses were issued for Unit 39, mostly to local residents, in 1986. Department of Wildlife Ranger Susan Werner estimates she checked out around 30 elk killed here by hunters. So far, it must be admitted, the system has achieved its objective of "ensuring that future generations will enjoy the presence of elk in the Evergreen area."

4. The biggest threat to wildlife today is not legal hunting but poaching, or "illegal harvesting" as the Department of Wildlife calls it. Penalties for poaching are severe, and a major program was launched in 1984 to secure public cooperation in bringing poachers to justice.

But facts are only a small part of the hunting controversy.

When we came to spend the summer in the mountains in 1948, we had a year-old child and another on the way: we were not very mobile. We read aloud to each other from a new book by one of our favorite authors, urban critic and philosopher Lewis Mumford, whom we had met in England.

"Green Memories" was Mumford's tribute to his son, killed in the recent war. The two had obviously had a difficult relationship and, in almost all the important areas of life, a conflict of values. Mumford described one rare experience that helped him appreciate his son's very different world.

The father loved cities, crowds, civilization. His son valued nature, solitude and land unspoiled by the imprint of man. Mumford despised all blood sports, among which he included hunting. For his son, as for the Indians, hunting was a sacred experience.

Like Mumford, we had never understood the mentality that could enjoy the pursuit and slaughter of a beautiful, rare, wild animal. But

through his eyes we followed the animals through the autumn forest, shared the campfire intimacy and gained a little insight into hunting as a reaffirmation of the primeval bond between animal and man.

Arapaho National Forest

Writing a guide to America's National Forests for Rand McNally, author Len Hilts characterizes the Arapaho National Forest as a "land of big, big mountains, high altitude hiking, fantastic winter sports areas, difficult but gorgeous scenic drives, and cool, crisp air." The sprawling million- acre forest adjoins Pike National Forest on the south and Roosevelt National Forest on the northwest, but the part that concerns us here is the Mount Evans basin—Evergreen's magnificent backdrop and spacious outdoor playground.

If you live in Evergreen for any length of time, you cannot help but feel the presence of this guardian peak, Mount Evans. Most of our weather comes west from the mountains, of which Evans is the symbol. Winter arrives and recedes according to the amount of snow on its rocky, treeless summit. The mountain is a constant surprise, waiting to be glimpsed round a bend in the road, up a stream valley or from a hilltop. Realtors long ago sensed its magic, advertising lots and homes as specially valuable if they have a "Mount Evans view".

The fact that there is a road up to within a few hundred yards of the top of the 14,264-foot mountain helps us to identify with this awesome summit. We have all driven up there. We have experienced the startling differences of climate and vegetation as we climbed. Its a rare trip, even in the middle of summer, that doesn't have a little rain, a little sleet or snow, swirling clouds, sudden winds and intervals of brilliant sunshine. The road is open only in summer: exact dates of opening and closing depend on snowfall.

A glance at the map shows that Arapaho National Forest has fingers, and even isolated patches, of land that are just 3 miles from Evergreen's Main Street. The forest was created after much of the land here had been claimed by homesteaders. It included small pieces of land that either were not taken up, or where the process of acquisition lapsed and the land reverted to federal ownership.

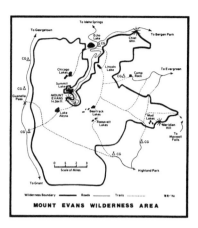

MOUNT EVANS WILDERNESS AREA

In recent years, the National Forest Service has made serious efforts to involve all segments of the public in decisions about the future of the lands they manage. The NFS charge is to administer these lands on a multi-use, multi- service basis—which means that they can let out timber, mineral or cattle-grazing leases on them, create public recreational facilities, lease land out for ski areas, manage existing wildlife, make decisions about introducing new species.

National Forest lands are not, as many of us may think, automatically protected from development or use. If we are fortunate, they are managed in such a way that the natural environment is protected—or restored after use— as a legacy for future generations at least as magnificent as we ourselves received.

Much greater protection of natural habitat is achieved when an area is granted wilderness status. Lovers of the Mount Evans basin were delighted when the 1980 Colorado Wilderness Act was passed. This expanded a number of existing wilderness areas in the state and added two new ones: the 106,000-acre Lost Creek Wilderness Area, 15 miles south of Conifer, and the 73,000-acre **Mount Evans Wilderness Area.**

In wilderness areas, man is a visitor and not a resident. The Forest Service has set itself specific guidelines in managing these areas, which affect the way we are allowed—and priveleged—to experience them. Among these objectives are:

- To perpetuate for present and future generations a long- lasting system of high quality wilderness that represents the natural ecosystems found in the Natural Forest System.

117

- To provide opportunities for public use, enjoyment, and understanding of a wilderness experience.

- To maintain the primitive character of wilderness as a benchmark for comparison with lands that have been developed.

No motorized vehicles are allowed in these areas. There are no roads, no buildings, power lines or developed public recreation facilities. There is no timber harvesting and no tampering with vegetation. Certain exceptions of course are made: e.g. fires may be fought with mechanical equipment if adjacent properties or lives are threatened (this provision is important in the Mount Evans Wilderness Area where a great many homes are near the boundaries), insect and disease epidemics may, if deemed best, be controlled by modern technologies.

What is permitted is the construction of trails and bridges over streams: this allows public access to the area with the maximum distribution of people throughout and the minimum pollution of water and disturbance of vegetation.

Except for a narrow strip of the Arapaho National Forest between the State Wildlife Area and the Mount Evans Wilderness Area, and those parts of the National Forest that surround Brook Forest and penetrate into the built-up area of Evergreen, all of the Arapaho National Forest land that is immediately accessible from Evergreen is in the Wilderness Area. This means that that the only way to experience it is on foot or on horseback, observing the stringent regulations designed to maintain the area's ecosytem intact.

The area not included in the Wilderness category has been designated by the Forest Service as the Evergreen Management Area. Public input into its best use has been invited. There seems to be support for general goal of managing the land primarily for the benefit of the elk herd.

Currently, this means a good deal of forest thinning to encourage greater growth of ground cover for forage. In 1986, the Forest Service issued some 200 wood-cutting permits to clear dozens of small pockets of land totalling around 650 acres, including many sites in the Brook Forest area.

The road to the top of Mount Evans was left out of the Wilderness Area, thus preserving the ability of the infirm, the elderly, the handicapped, the very young—and we physically unambitious!—to experience the dramatic journey from plains to alpine tundra in less than an hour. The road is Highway 5, a 14-mile adventure from Echo Lake to the top. Access from Evergreen is either via Highway 103 from Bergen Park to Echo Lake, or via unpaved but scenic Witter Gulch Road.

A few hundred yards from Echo Lake is the 9-acre compound of Denver University's High Altitude Laboratory founded in 1930. In summers, the facility is used by researchers from DU and other academic institutions—over 150 since it was opened—studying mountain geology, biology, botany and ornithology.

In winter, the only inhabitants of the facility at 10,700 feet are the resident manager and his wife. Since 1983, this has been Ralph Reiner and Australian-born Lorraine Reiner. The couple maintain the U.S. Weather Station on the site—the second-highest manned station in the country. Reiner has recorded temperatures of 52 degrees below zero, annual snowfall of 500 inches and winds of 134 m.p.h.

But at the summit of Mount Evans, where DU has a building sheltering a 24-inch telescope, Reiner has measured temperatures of 68 below (with a windchill reading of 198 below), 700 inches of snowfall and winds of more than 200 m.p.h.

Reiner, who spent many years as a National Park Ranger and published two books about Glacier National Park, has written about the Mount Evans environment in a book titled, "The Magestic 'Front Range' Region of Clear Creek County, Colorado".

Good pauses on the way up on the Mount Evans road, to experience the different climatic levels and stretch the legs, are at either end of the Mount Goliath Trail (the lower end is three miles from Echo Lake) and at Summit Lake.

The Mount Goliath Trail was orignally known as the M. Walter Pesman Trail and was developed jointly by the Denver Botanic Gardens and the Arapaho National Forest in 1958. We remember, as a high point of our experiences on

Justus "Gus" Roehling.

Mount Evans Crest House.

Mount Evans, a tour of the marvels of alpine vegetation along this trail led by retired Denver University Botany Professor Dr. Ernest Brunquist.

The journey used to culminate at the summit with hot chocolate, freshly made donuts—and a chance, for those who wished, to buy tourist souvenirs at the unique Crest house, built by a long-time Kittredge contractor named Justus (Gus) Roehling.

This stone and glass structure, often described in newspapers as "futuristic", was the outward manifestation of an inner dream for the German-born Roehling, something that gave meaning to his life. He called it his "Castle in the Sky".

Born in 1895, Roehling immigrated to the United Stated from a German boat stranded off Boston in the first World War. He came to Colorado to find a cure for tuberculosis, which killed both his parents. He worked at first as a carpenter in Denver. But a great longing to live in the mountains brought him to a caretaker's job in Kittredge. Later he built a number of houses for Charles Kittredge and developed a small contracting business: among other structures he built the original Christ the King Church in Evergreen—pulled down when the present church was built—and the Hiwan Barn, now the Hardware Store.

Roehling's first trip to the summit of Mount Evans was with his Kittredge girl friend, Edith, later his wife. He conceived an intense desire to create a building in this incredible location, so that more people could enjoy in comfort a panorama covering—on a clear day—more land than the entire country of Switzerland.

Eleven years later, his dream came true. Crest House was designed by Denver architect Edwin Francis, with more than a little input from Roehling who was engaged to build it at a cost of $50,000. Conceived as a tourist attraction, the facility was owned by Thayer Tutt of the Colorado Springs Broadmoor Hotel—who was associated with two similar tourist facilities on Pike's Peak—and Quigg Newton, later Mayor of Denver.

Crest House was built during the brief summers of 1940 and 1941 by Roehling and a small crew who lived in tents. They endured fierce extremes of weather, and more than once violent storms demolished their day's efforts. When completed, the structure proved durable and serviceable. It had an upper area for enjoying the view, a souvenir shop, snack bar, toilets and living quarters for employes—who were usually students.

When Crest House was a reality Roehling published an autobiographical booklet about it. "Castle in the Sky" was dedicated to his only son, John, born when Roehling was 53 years old. Roehling lost his wife to cancer in 1967.

In 1956, Crest House was bought by an enterprising woman who, as a little girl, sold flowers and newspapers on the Pike's Peak Cog Railway and later took over the operation of the Summit House for the Broadmoor. She eventually formed a family corporation, the Mount Evans Company, to operate her enterprises. Under an agreement with the U. S. Forest Service, ownership of Crest house was to to be transferred to the Service when net profit from the concession equalled her investment. This happened in 1968. The Mount Evans Company continued to operate the Crest House facility, in addition to the two Pikes Peak facilities, Echo Lake Lodge, the Red Rocks Trading Post and Hidden Inn at the Garden of the Gods.

On September 1, 1979, a relatively inexperienced employe of an Evergreen propane company was refilling the tank outside Crest House. He failed to secure a safety valve. Gas sprayed out of the tank, vaporized and burst into flames. Manager Bill Carle alerted employes and some 15 visitors, who all got out safely. Firefighting efforts were hampered by lack of water and 30-mile winds. The building was totally destroyed before the fire department arrived. The Forest Service had no insurance coverage on the building.

Gus Roehling, 86 years old by this time, was heartbroken. He immediately set to work preparing plans for a new and expanded Crest House.

The settlement of a lawsuit filed by the Forest Service found the gas companies negligent and awarded $450,000 to the Service, on condition that it be spent on a new facility. Roehling and the concessionaires, backed by quite a segment of the public (Barbara Carle Day, manager of the Echo Lake Lodge and a member of the family owning the concessions, gathered over 3,000 signatures on a petition) argued that a facility similar to Crest House should be built.

They said that the summit of Mount Evans, accessible as it is by car, is a major tourist attraction. Tourists expect, and are entitled to, a warm, closed-in facility at the end of the journey. People enjoy a warm drink, a snack and an opportunity to purchase a souvenir of a unique experience, to say nothing of access to a telephone. More tourists will visit the site if they know there is a welcoming lace at the top. The benefits to the state in terms of employment of young people and sales tax revenue are considerable.

Law enforcement authorities and Evergreen's Alpine Rescue Team also expressed interest in replacing Crest House so they could use it as a command post for the frequent occasions when hikers or climbers are lost or injured.

Environmentalists, and the Forest Service itself, argued that even the existence of a road right through the middle of a wilderness area is incongruous. Summits of 14,000-foot mountains, which are dangerous places with rarefied air and unpredictable weather, are not appropriate places for tourists in automobiles. The Forest Service considered trying to get the road closed, but decided this was not feasible.

Granted that the road will stay, and large numbers of people will drive up it, the Forest Service came out in 1986 with a plan to build an unmanned facility to replace Crest House. It had already installed outhouse-type toilet facilities in a separate building. The new structure would be a simple combination of viewing deck and wind shelter, incorporating the Crest House ruins, which they hoped to have placed on the National Register of Historic Places.

Barbara Carle Day filed an appeal with the Forest Service, claiming that the proposed plan was not what the public wanted and did not fulfil the needs formerly met by Crest House. The Denver Post had already gone on record as supporting the rebuilding of the facility along its former lines. The Canyon Courier wanted a dignified facility, free of any taint of "tourist trap", that would meet the needs for warm shelter, educational displays, emergency medical help and availablity as a command post for rescue. They suggested that it might be manned by forestry students.

Whatever the outcome, Gus Roehling did not live to see it. In July of 1984, 89 years old and still fighting for the rebuilding of his sky castle, he was taken up one last time to visit the summit he loved. Three weeks later, he died. His coffin made the trip to the ruins of Crest House, where a memorial service was held in snow and sleet, then was brought down for burial on the quiet hillside of Evergreen Cemetery.

MOUNTAIN SCHOOLING

The Evergreen area has been settled for just over 125 years. Most of it lies in Jefferson County, and for the first 90 years it was divided into individual school districts, each operating a one or two-room school. In the early 30's, Evergreeen developed a basic high school program which was offered to students of surrounding districts, including those in the Upper Bear Creek part of Clear Creek County. This area, geographically and historically, has much in common with Evergreen. There were no private schools.

By the mid-80's, the Jefferson County part of the mountain area was integrated into the county-wide R-1 School District, the largest in Colorado with almost 76,000 students. There were five elementary schools in the Bergen Park-Evergreen-Kittredge-Indian Hills-Conifer area—with a sixth planned for Conifer—two junior high schools and two high schools. Clear Creek had also become a one-county school district, one of the smaller ones in the state with less than 1500 students. A local elementary school served the Evergreen area Clear Creek residents and students were bussed into Idaho Springs for high school.

There were nine privately-operated schools for young children in the same area, a nationally respected residential treatment center for severely disturbed boys, lively pre-school and adult education programs offered by the two public school districts and a changing variety of privately-offered lessons, workshops and classes for children and adults.

Old Bergen School

From 3 R's to R-1
Early schools in the mountain area were of the simplest kind. When a few settlers decided their children needed some education they would get together, designate a room in one of their homes as the classroom and hire a school teacher for a few weeks or months of the year. One of the families would board the teacher, whose salary could be as little as $30.00 a month. If the population remained stable or grew, the landowners would build a simple one-room school house. Later they might apply to the Jefferson County Superintendent of Schools for permission to organize a school district so they could impose a small tax to pay expenses and perhaps get help from the minimal county school levy.

Jefferson County's first school superintendent in 1862 was Golden educator George West. The levy was 2 mills. In 1863, the first district in the county was organized. The number of districts rose to 10 in 1868, 24 in 1873. The First Biennial Report of the Colorado State Superintendent of Public Instruction for 1877-78 noted that there were 39 teachers in Jefferson County in 1878 and that, since the economy was poor, their salaries had declined from previous levels. Average male salaries were $46.13 a month, females earned $41.60. The Superintendent used the occasion to express forcibly his view that, though it might be alright for Germany and other European countries, "education cannot be made compulsory in the United States!"

The equally-opinionated 1884 Report sounded off on another topic ("I am fully convinced that a great portion of the immorality of the day owes its existence to improperly erected or protected outhouses") and showed that Jefferson County had 2,476 pupils instructed by 23 teachers in "graded" (usually more urban) schools and 49 in rural (mostly one-room) schools. The average pay for men in rural schools was $50.55 a month, for women $43.26. There were altogether 48 schoolhouses.

In 1890 there were 43 school districts in the county. Rural schools operated for an average of 125 days a year. The county had a 3 mill levy, with additional levies in individual districts varying from 1 to 10 mills. Golden had the only high school.

Between 1900 and 1940 there was surprisingly little change in district numbers and boundaries and the county mill levy rose very slowly.

A 1939 history of Jefferson County shows a total of 45 school districts, of which 6 were in the Evergreen area: Evergreen, Kittredge, Conifer, Hodgson, Soda Creek and Parmalee Gulch. Evergreen— District C-2—was one of only two consolidated districts in the county, the other being Bear Creek.

Some merging of districts took place between 1940 and the momentous year of 1949, when the State Legislature passed a bill to ensure consolidation of single-school districts into more efficient units. When Jefferson County, through a vote of the people, took the pioneering step of merging **all** its districts into the county- wide R-1 system, there were still 39 separate districts enrolling altogether around 11,000 students. Though the new system was created in 1950, the old independent School Boards carried on until January of 1951.

Evergreen seems to have been rather a progressive district for its rural location. It was the only mountain district offering high school education and operated on a levy of 19.19 mills. Its total assessed valuation was $1,773,345.

There was a deep division in Evergreen over the county-wide consolidation issue, as there was in all the mountain districts. Indeed, the controversy was so lively that Edward R. Murrow brought a CBS television team out to air the views on either side.

In small communities the school was the focus of life. There was a lot of sadness and resentment that control was shifting down to the flatlands, to say nothing of the conviction that taxes were bound to go way up. Which, of course, they did, reaching a level of 61.55 mills by 1986.

But the benefits have been great. No longer are mountain residents at an educational disadvantage compared with Denver or the suburbs. Well-designed schools, as modern as anywhere in Colorado, are built as needs arise. Teaching staff is of the same quality as anywhere in the metro area. Salaries, which used to be so much lower in rural and mountain areas, are equal throughout the county. For good or ill, the quality of schooling contributed substantially to the growth of the mountain area: by 1986, Bergen Park, Evergreen, Conifer, Kittredge and Indian Hills had half as many students enrolled as there were in the entire county in 1950.

The Early Schoolhouses

One of the earliest separate schoolhouses built in the Evergreen area was the **Bergen School**. In the recollections of Martha Greene, pioneer Bergen's daughter, it stood in 1877 on the "Idaho Cut-off"—the intersection of the road to Evergreen and Bradford Junction, as Conifer was then known, and the one to Idaho Springs. The school was first used only two months of the year, slowly expanding to six. The weathered old building was still standing on the Hiwan property near Bergen Park until a few years ago. No-one remembers it being torn down: it was probably carted off board by board for firewood or to adorn someone's den as 'old barn wood'.

Other early school houses had a kinder fate.

The Buffalo Park School, built in 1877 on the Vezina Ranch, served the Evergreen population for many years until the white frame building on Highway 73 at Cub Creek Road went into use. It is now a Baptist Church. The Vezina School was built by early French Canadian homesteaders Selim Vezina, Leon Mallet and Antoine Roy—who used to raise Texas longhorns, according to a 1967 Jefferson County Sentinel story about the little schoolhouse.

The 10' by 15' chink-log building, restored by the Evergreen Woman's Club in 1967, sits today in the middle of a grass circle in front of Wilmot Elementary School on Buffalo Park Road. Walking into the small cabin, it is hard to imagine that it once housed 22 children in all grades, warmed by a crude long-burning stove. Coats

Restored 1877 Buffalo Park School, on grounds of Wilmot School.

and mufflers were hung on wooden pegs stuck in the chinks, and the teacher surveyed the entire school from a small podium at the end of the room.

Selim Vezina's son, Samuel, was one of the first teachers. Since Selim believed that teaching was a woman's job, he persuaded his son to step down in favor of sister Emma after she completed her training at Loretto Heights. Teachers came and went, boarding with local families. They often kept school open well into the summer to make up for time lost during heavy snow storms when it was impossible for children to walk four or five miles through heavy drifts.

The Soda Creek School was another one-room log building located on Highway 103, near Bergen Park. It was moved and incorporated as a wing of the Bergen Park Community Church. In 1936, when E.J. and Arleta Alderfer bought a place on Floyd Hill near Beaverbrook, they found themselves in the Soda Creek District. Arleta says she "nearly had a fit" when she first saw the schoolhouse. She herself had been educated in Denver, graduating from the elegant and spacious new South High School. However, both Alderfers pitched in and served on the School Board until E.J. had to go off into service in World War II.

The **Kittredge District,** Jefferson County No. 3, built a sturdy schoolhouse high up off Highway 74, which passed into the hands of the R-1 Schools at the time of consolidation. In June of 1967, The Kittredge Union Church bought the Kittredge elementary school for $5,750.00.

Kittredge School, now a church, in 1986 before remodeling.

The first **Conifer School,** District No. 9, was located at Bradford Junction—so-called because it used to form the junction between the main road up S. Turkey Creek and the road across from Evergreen—about where the old yellow barn is today. The schoolhouse was a small wooden building, according to long-time mountain area school teacher Phebe Granzella, and mainly served the 11 children of Rev. and Mrs. Kemp. The couple came originally from England and arrived in the mountains in 1879.

The next schoolhouse was the Hutchinson School, which was built in 1885 about one mile south of Bradford Junction.

Conifer School.

121

Bruce Livonius of Blue Creek Road remembered his father, Heine, talking about his schooldays in Conifer. He usually walked the 2-1/2 miles each way but sometimes went on horseback. Most of the boys took a rifle with them, shooting rabbits or other small animals along the way. "It was nothing unusual too, from the way he talked, to have a kid that was 17 or 18 years old in the third or fourth grade. Some of the fifth graders were as old as the teacher. They'd go back to school year after year, never finish that year, and start again the next."

In 1911, school was again moved, to a former Mormon church about half a mile south of the Hutchinson School. This building was known as the Junction School, where classes were held until 1923. According to Bruce, this school had to be pulled down as it was right in the path of the new Highway 285.

In that year, John Mullen had just finished rebuilding Bradford Junction and put up the handsome new yellow barn. He made available one acre for a new school. The little white building, which is still standing up the hill from the barn, was ready for service by January 15, 1923.

It was known first just as Junction, later Conifer Junction School, and was used as a grade school until 1955. Since that time, it has housed a small branch library—closed in 1984 due to a budget crunch—and a kindergarten.

The Parmalee Gulch (Indian Hills) School District was formed in 1889. Its teacher received $45 a month for a four month- school year. Probably a home or rented space was used for a few years because the first separate schoolhouse was built in 1895. It was about 3 miles from the Turkey Creek Road and was in service until 1919, when it was destroyed by fire. Because it was difficult to heat the rudimentary one-room structure adequately, school was often closed for weeks in the coldest part of the winter.

After the fire, rented premises were again used until developer George Olinger donated a piece of land, about one mile from the present Highway 285, on which to build a new schoolhouse. The white frame building was opened in 1925 for classes and served until 1949. By then, not even split sessions could accomodate all the children. The choice was either to consolidate with the Evergreen District or to build a new school: the people chose consolidation and the school was closed.

In 1952 the Indian Hills Improvement Association acquired the building from the Jefferson County R-1 School Board. An addition was put on and the whole structure covered with siding to convert it into the Indian Hills Community Center.

Parmalee Gulch (Indian Hills) School, now a community center.

Hodgson School District No. 26 is another mountain school building that is still serving its community, as home of the Wild Rose Grange. It is located on North Turkey Creek Road, about half way between Highway 285 and County Road 73. The first school was a little frame building, known as the District 26 School, which stood a little to the east of the Grange. Ralph and Alice Hodgson, originally from England, settled the land in 1860. Later they sold 160 acres to pioneers August and Hilda Herzman, who donated one acre for a new school.

Hodgson School, now the Wild Rose Grange.

August Herzman generously contributed his own labor and wagon team to haul the supplies needed to build and equip the school from the railroad depot in Morrison. Mrs. Herzman was the first president of the new School Board and proposed that it be named Hodgson after the original settlers. She spent many hours raising money for the school, travelling to Denver to buy desks and other equipment. The Hodgson School opened in 1915 with 18 students.

The building served the North Turkey Creek area until consolidation, when it was closed. Students travelled to school in Evergreen. The Wild Rose Grange, which had been chartered in 1907, took over the building and has been holding its meetings there ever since.

Brookvale School.

Brookvale, the little white building about a mile up the left fork of Upper Bear Creek Road in Clear Creek County, was closed down as a school around 1946. But it had a unique short renaissance as a kindergarten for seven eager youngsters from 1979 to 1982.

The school was built around 1870. Pioneer Pearl Anderson's memories of the "good old days", when Brookvale was all the schooling there was for settlers' children, were vividly recorded in several Canyon Courier articles.

Old Evergreen School, now Baptist Church.

The building continued to be used for community meetings, as a polling place, and sometimes for church services. With consolidation, ownership passed into the hands of the Clear Creek County District School Board.

The little white building on the west side of Highway 73 opposite the Cub Creek intersection served for many years as the **Evergreen School.** Maude Smith, long-time Evergreen resident who first visited here from Michigan around 1920, remembered vividly the time when it was the only school for Evergreen children.

The Gustav Andersons, parents of Pearl's husband Frank, came from Sweden. Gustav spent some years as overseer for the railroad, living on Floyd Hill, before deciding to try his hand at farming. He bought land on Upper Bear Creek in 1885 and that same year, Frank entered the Brookvale School.

Frank and Pearl were renting a place in Indian Hills when Frank's father died. They moved into the Upper Bear Creek home and there Pearl lived until her own death in 1985 at the age of 90. Their three boys went to Brookvale for the first through eighth grades, then into Evergreen for high school.

The school had no running water, an outside privy, a wood burning stove and kerosene lamps. "We had water and wood carried in," Mrs. Anderson remembered, "everybody drank out of the same cup. They weren't so particular in those days." The Andersons sent their oldest son, Frank Jr., off to school on a donkey. "We'd put a sack of grain on with him, and that donkey would go no farther than the school."

The teachers were young, most had only a high school education. They made $50 a month and paid $20 of it for room and board at Mrs. Anderson's. There was no electricity in the area until 1945. The school's population was never very large, though at one time it would probably have qualified as the only school in the mountain area that was racially integrated! A black family lived up Witter Gulch and a Mexican sheepherder had settled in Indian Creek Park with his family.

By 1946, there were so few students in the school, and such a variety of grade levels to be taught, that it was decided to close the school and send the children into Evergreen.

It's interesting to speculate about just how old this building really is and who originally built it. A member of the large pioneer Fleming family, Dorothy Fleming McKee, told a Canyon Courier reporter that "The little white community church was located where the Little Bear is now. It was moved when Prince McCraken built his drugstore and dancehall."

The red brick **Evergreen School,** still standing next to the library and now the County Building, was constructed in two stages. The core Section was completed in 1922. It was a proud day indeed when classes opened for the first time in the brand new facility, by far the finest and most modern in the mountain area. The School Board is named on the brass dedication plaque: D. P. Wilmot, President; Iva M. Downes, Secretary; Julia B. Douglas, Treasurer.

Evergreen School, now County Building.

123

Most students did not stay in school beyond the 8th or 9th grade in rural areas, but in the late 1920's the Evergreen school started to make a high school curriculum available to those who wanted it. The first "class", consisting of one student, graduated in 1931. But Evergreen High School officially dates its beginning back to 1932: in 1982, all alumni were officially invited to a grand 50-year celebration.

By 1936 the red brick school was too small. A large new addition, placing wings on both sides of the original building, was designed by Denver architects F. W. Frewen and Earl Morris and built with the help of the Federal Emergency Administration of Public Works. This was in the Depression era. The School Board at that time consisted of Clara Wilmot-Herzman, President; Bryan B. Blakeslee, Secretary; Oscar R. Johnson, Treasurer.

There were some high—and low!—jinks at the red brick school. Longtime Evergreen citizen Jack Rouse, a born story teller, remembered a female teacher coming near to panic because a student released a flapping, terrified hen in her classroom. Then there was one day of havoc, when the entire school tried noisily to catch a greased pig that had been let loose inside the building. And another memorable occasion when all students had to go home early: the never-reliable sewer system—an inadequate septic tank and leeching field—stopped up, and a somewhat inebriated "helper" unscrewed the clean-out cover in the basement, producing a cascading fountain of sewage.

Mrs. Mary Marquand came to teach at the Evergreen School in 1936, when the two wings were still brand new. She was one of seven on the staff teaching 120 children in all. Mrs. Marquand had 22 students in both first and second grades. We interviewed her in her Bergen Park home, where she had lived for almost 50 years. She reminisced about her 30 years of teaching in Evergreen and being part of the area's growth, from one all-grade school to a still- growing number of separate elementary, junior high and high schools.

Teacher Mary Marquand.

All grades were housed in the red brick building until 1948 when the **Evergreen High School**—the white concrete building next to the red brick construction, now the Open High School—was built for grades 9 through 12.

Enter R-1

County-wide consolidation in 1950 found the Evergreen District in better shape than many others: the red brick building was adequate for the first eight grades, the new high school was only 2 years old, and a recent consolidation with Indian Hills (Parmalee Gulch) had been arranged. Still, the population was beginning to grow. By 1955, when Jim Mellor moved over from teaching 40 students in all grades at the one-room Buffalo Creek schoolhouse—east of Highway 285—to take on the 4th, 5th, and 6th grades at the Evergreen red brick school, his classroom was a converted lavatory space and his desk was out in the hall.

Evergreen Elementary School was built to take the first through sixth graders out of the red brick school. Its history is curious and one cannot imagine that it ever represented efficient school planning. It forms one part of what is today the Evergreen High School and was used as an elementary school until the building of **Wilmot School** in 1962.

Wilmot cost approximately $426,000. In just two years, enrollment had increased enough to warrant an additional investment of $163,000 in a 12-room addition.

In the meantime the Evergreen elementary school was remodelled and enlarged to convert it into the **Evergreen High School**, which opened its doors to students in grades 10, 11, and 12 in 1962. Its facilities were increased by the addition of a Vocational Technical facility in 1971. Another major remodelling and expansion project was completed in 1979 at a cost of $.6 million, which enabled the school to go from split sessions to a regular schedule.

After the placement of both elementary and high school students in new facilities, the two original Evergreen school buildings were used for grades 7, 8, and 9. But they were outdated and suffered in comparison with many of the R-1 District's handsome new junior high schools. In the fall of 1969, on 20 acres of land bought from the developers of the Hiwan Country Club subdivision, the new **Evergreen Junior High School** greeted 7th, 8th, and 9th graders with a totally contemporary environment designed by Colorado Springs architect, Lamar Kelsey. In tune with the educational philosophy of the late 1960's, this was a school without classroom walls, designed for modular scheduling and team teaching. However, this teaching philosophy was no more successful at EJHS than at the majority of "open space" schools throughout the country. By 1982, when nearly $1,000,000 of improvements and additions to the school were budgeted, the partitioning of all classrooms into a separate walled spaces was virtually completed. Another major addition to EJHS was made in 1986.

Numbers of elementary school students kept increasing and by 1969 Wilmot had more than 1,000 students. **Bergen Elementary School**, built on 15 acres of land bought from the Hiwan developers, was opened in the fall of 1970. This was another building designed with open interior spaces by W. C. Muchow and Associates. With a capacity of 430 students, the building needed supplementary "temporaries" almost immediately. By 1986, a major renovation and addition was budgeted, out of bond funds voted in 1985, to replace all the temporaries and complete the "walling" of all open space classrooms.

The Conifer area's first new school after consolidation was a charming structure, using native stone, known as **West Jefferson (West Jeff) Elementary**. This opened in 1955. Our family used to pass it as we took the turn-off from Highway 285 to our cabin. We would fantasize about living on Blue Creek Road so that some of our kids could attend this little mountain school.

In the 1980-81 school year, our oldest daughter lived for a year on Blue Creek Road and her two sons did indeed attend West Jeff Elementary. By this time, it was a far cry from the original rural schoolhouse. The elementary building had been expanded and there was a forest of temporary buildings around it. Even the old white frame Conifer School had been pressed back into service as a kindergarten, and there our younger grandson enjoyed his introduction to the world of learning. In addition, an entire new **West Jefferson Junior High School** had been built in the same vicinity.

By 1986 the elementary school had almost 900 students and the Junior High over 500. A site was selected for an additional 440- student capacity grade school, expected to be ready by 1989. West Jeff Junior High, originally built for a maximum of 266 students, had also sprouted a proliferation of temporaries and looked forward to the 1987 completion of a substantial additition.

Parmalee School was built in 1962, a grade school typical of much school architecture of that period. Temporaries soon had to be added to house students drawn from Kittredge, Indian Hills, the Ken Caryl Ranch and the Halms subdivision. Smallest of the mountain area elementary schools—it enrolled around 200 students in 1986— Parmalee continues the role played by the early Parmalee Gulch Schools, as a focal point for civic and social activities.

Marshdale Elementary School serves the North Turkey Creek area once served by the Hodgson School as well as many new subdivisions along Highway 73. Designed by the Denver architectural firm of Hoover Berg Desmond, the school was built in 1980 and rapidly reached a near-capacity enrollment of 570 students. As the first community building in Marshdale, it has unusually strong parental support and serves as a meeting place for over 50 different community organizations.

Evergreen Junior High School.

Evergreen Junior High School Addition, 1986.

"Temporary" buildings at Bergen Elementary School.

In 1978 the Clear Creek County School Board voted to end the 'tuitioning' of students in the Upper Bear Creek area of the county into Jefferson County Schools. This meant bussing students into Idaho Springs—until a new elementary school could be built for the growing southeast part of the county—so they looked around for a facility to take care of the kindergarten students.

125

Brookvale by this time had running water and an inside toilet, so it seemed a perfect solution. The young teacher—who had all of her seven students reading and doing the basics of math by the end of their kindergarten year—said that this experience of teaching a small group of children in a rural one-room schoolhouse was one she would treasure all her life. The school closed down again in June of 1982 and the building reverted to its use as a community center.

In September of that year, the new **King-Murphy Elementary School** was dedicated. Finding the right site had been difficult. An original acreage on Stage Coach Boulevard in Jefferson County, owned by the State Board of Land Commissioners, ran into problems of access and citizen opposition. Long-time Evergreen resident Ellece Murphy offered land on Witter Gulch for significantly less than its appraised price. The Clear Creek School Board voted unanimously to name the School after Ellece and her father, Beth King, who had bought the land originally.

Architect Max Saul of Denver revised the plans originally made for the Stage Coach site. Because the school hooked into the Upper Bear Creek Sanitation system but had to draw water from wells, it had to provide a "water augmentation pond". With the unexpected series of problems finally resolved, the school opened its doors to almost 200 children from Floyd Hill, Hyland Hills, Saddleback, Pine Valley, Blue Valley Acres, Echo Hills, Witter Gulch, Upper Bear Creek and some of Brook Forest.

In addition to a full complement of elementary, junior high and high schools, two unique Jefferson County District R-1 schools are located in Evergreen.

The Jefferson County Mount Evans Outdoor Education Laboratory School is located high up on Upper Bear Creek Road. Each week during the school year, a new batch of 6th grade children from an elementary school somewhere in Jefferson County arrives at the former Phelps Dodge Ranch. They are full of noise and energy and, for a couple of days, they see very little wildlife.

By mid-week, a little miracle happens: school principal Jim Jackson and his carefully chosen staff have managed to transmit to the students a way of being that gets them in tune with nature. The elk and deer return to the ranch and sightings of wild animals increase almost hourly.

The outdoor education program, which Jefferson County pioneered in Colorado, began in 1956. At first a camp was rented, but in 1962 the District bought the 554-acre Phelps Dodge Ranch for $125,000. The price included a lodge—originally the family house—foreman's house, homestead house and guest house together with barn, bunkhouse, root cellar and several sheds.

The ranch was the creation of Regina Lunt Dodge and her husband, Clarence Phelps Dodge, of Colorado Springs. At the time of the sale to the R-1 District, the place was the home of the Dodge's son and his wife. Phelps was nearing the end of his life (he died while the sale was being negotiated) and the couple very much wanted the property to remain whole and unsubdivided, and to be appreciated for its special beauty and natural riches.

An appreciative history of the Phelps Dodge Ranch and its buildings, "Tales of the Bar PD", was prepared for the School District by Kay Klepetko.

The Outdoor Lab School has been nationally recognized for the quality of its program. In 1971, the U.S. Department of the Interior and the National Parks Service selected it, from 3,200 similar schools, to be one of 11 National Landmarks in its field.

Every sixth grader in the county has the opportunity of taking part in the 5-day experience of outdoor education. (As school enrollment grew, the R-1 School District acquired a second outdoor education school called Windy Peak.)

The program at the Evergreen school is a mixture of summer camp and seminars. The curriculum includes study of mountain ecosystems, forestry, geology, pioneer life, wildlife, and compass and mapping skills. Students sleep in dorms, eat family-style in a large cafeteria and take part in ceremonies. Each morning and

afternoon they participate in a variety of educational programs created by teachers from their own schools with the help of high school volunteers.

The major aim of the program, according to Jackson, is to raise a generation with a feeling for the outdoors, a sense of the responsibility that goes with inheriting a country as beautiful as America.

We visited this fascinating school in its magnificent environment on a late October afternoon. It was Thursday. The children seemed relaxed and very much at home. Deer wandered through the wide meadow in front of the main lodge. The atmosphere was informal, warm, hospitable. Principal Jim Jackson and school secretary Caroline Collins shared their experiences and files of materials with us generously.

We could understand why, when Jefferson County high school seniors are questioned about the value of their R-1 school experiences, there is always such a high percentage that rate their week at the Outdoor Lab School as the highlight.

Jefferson County Open High School. If you find yourself in a bustling environment where students are on a first-name basis with principal and faculty, running a lunch program called "Munchie Central" and talking about their next "walkabout passage", you have undoubtedly strayed into the Open High School. It is located in Evergreen's first high school building off Highway 73 at the Buffalo Park intersection.

An alternative open to all Jefferson County students of high school age on a first-come, first-served basis, provided they have parental approval, this school has an enrollment of 210 students and a sizeable waiting list. The program has no grades, is geared to the individual learner and is self-paced. A high degree of responsibility and self-discipline is necessary for success.

Each student chooses an advisor from among the staff, with whom he or she plans a personal learning program. There is no prescribed way to pursue this program: it might be through classes—at the school or at other Jefferson County

Marshdale Elementary School. Hoover Berg Desmond, Architects.

schools or colleges— guided independent study, group projects, educational trips, or apprenticeships in the community. With the advisor's help, the student is responsible for documenting all learning experiences and for obtaining supporting statements from people with whom he or she has worked.

The Open High School was started in Evergreen in 1975, the initiative coming from community members and the students, parents and staff of the two kindergarten through 9th grade open living schools then existing in the county, one of which had been operating in Evergreen since 1971. These two schools have since been combined into one larger school, Tanglewood.

The Open High School's primary aim is to support the transformation of kids into adults. "Treat a kid like an adult," said first Principal Arnie Langberg, "and he will behave like an adult." The "walkabout" program—named after the lonely passage undertaken by the Australian aboriginal adolescent to secure tribal acceptance as a man—requires Open High students first to demonstrate mastery of some 50 skills (running the gamut from basic survival to academic competence, from understanding taxation and insurance to driving a car) and then to plan and carry through their personal "Passages" in areas of adventure, career exploration, practical skills, logical enquiry, global awareness and creativity.

Students and parents are involved in school governance, in policy decisions and the selection of staff. There is never a lack of applications for teaching positions at the Open High School, but the intensity of commitment demanded from the staff—as well as the adventurous type of personality attracted to this kind of program— means that faculty tend to give their all for a few years, and then move on to other experiences. Only three of the original faculty hired in the summer of 1975 were still with the school at the close of the school year in 1986: Principal Arnie Langberg, art teacher Susie Irby Bogard, and Jeff Bogard, whose field is science.

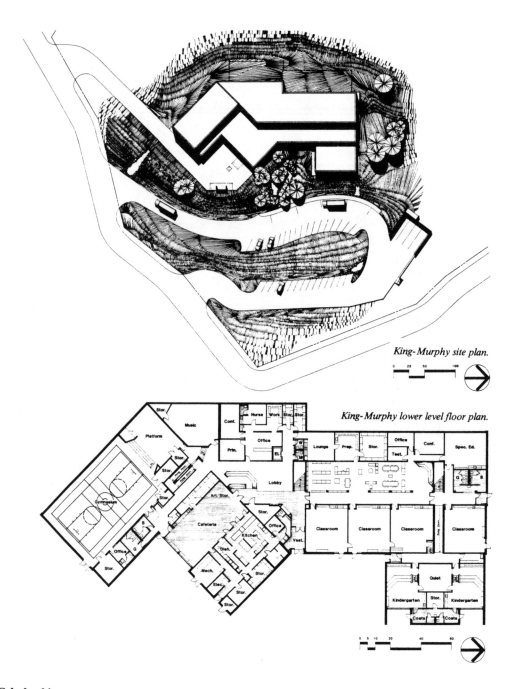

King-Murphy site plan.

King-Murphy lower level floor plan.

Evergreen's Unusual Scholarships

The Mountain Parks Protective Association Scholarship was established with the approximately $75,000 remaining in the treasury when the Mountain Protective Association—that longtime organization geared to Evergreen's era as a summer resort— went out of existence in 1974. Each year scholarships—of $1,500 a year for four years— are offered to one or two students attending a college in Colorado and graduating from one of the four high schools in the area formerly served by MPA: Evergreen High School, Platte Canyon Senior High in Bailey, Clear Creek Secondary in Idaho Springs and the Jefferson County Open High.

Mount Evans Outdoor Education Laboratory School,

King-Murphy Elementary School. Max Saul and Assoc., Architects.

formerly the Phelps Dodge Ranch.

The Evergreen Scholarship Association, one of the oldest civic institutions in the community, is believed to be the only such association in Colorado supported solely through local citizen contributions. It was started in 1944 by the Evergreen Woman's Club and the PTA. Each year, the board administering the fund does a mailing to local citizens and has one fund-raising event—frequently a community breakfast. The first year, a scholarship of $150 was awarded to Violet Gwen Massey. In 1986, six scholarships for one or two years were awarded at Evergreen High School graduation ceremonies—the most ever in one year.

Bootstraps Inc. aims at helping a different type of student— not the highly-motivated achiever but basically good, responsible young people with unfulfilled potential. Many, from one-parent families or for other reasons, have had little consistent adult guidance. Bootstraps operates on the philosophy that the local community can help students to help themselves. It makes available, to each student accepted into the program, the support and experience of local people active in the field in which the student has a career interest. Students also receive, if necessary, interest-free loans to supplement their own earning efforts while in college or vocational training. Funds are raised through an annual fund-raiser, sale of Chirstmas trees, contributions from local service organizations and individual donations.

Adult Education
Beyond high school, in addition to the Adult Education program offered by the R-1 School District, Evergreen residents have access to two interesting and very different institutions. **Red Rocks Community College**, like all the state-sponsored community colleges, offers a wide variety of courses to post-high school students. These include academic studies transferable to degree programs, vocational learning, self-improvement courses, adult learning for its own sake and recreational skills. Located off Sixth Avenue in the foothills west of Denver, is the most accessible community college for Evergreen residents.

The University of the Wilderness has its administrative headquarters in a small, inadequately heated office on the grounds of the Evergreen Conference. Founded in 1973 by Evergreen residents Bill and Louise Mounsey and Boyd Norton, the school's goal is adult education about issues concerning the wilderness—and how, in the end, these issues affect us all. In 1981, the school acquired a 13.5 acre campus 35 miles from Laramie, which used to be a base camp for field work for the University of Wyoming. For the Evergreen-based university, its main use is as a gateway to a vast outdoor classroom of many different wilderness ecosystems. The school sponsors several field trips each year, ranging from week-long backpacking or canoe trips to short seminars in writing, photography and water quality. It also offers classes in wildlife, mountaineering and wilderness politics. Some classes carry college credit, but most of the people attracted to the unique learning experiences of the University of the Wilderness are more interested in experiential learning than in credits.

Forest Heights Lodge: a Special Kind of School

These are the bare bones of the remarkable Forest Heights story. The Lodge was founded in 1954 as a residential treatment center for emotionally disturbed boys. It is fully accredited, and incorporated as a non-profit private facility. A 15-member board of trustees employs the executive director who, in turn, administers the professional staff.

The program is geared especially to boys with severe behavioral or neurotic problems, not for those whose primary problem is retardation. The maximum number of boys in residence is limited to 23 at any one time in order to maintain the close, family-like relationship that is the basis of the Lodge's outstanding 86% success record.

Forest Heights Lodge also operates an outpatient program and does extensive training of professionals all over the United States and in Canada.

To bring these dry words to life requires an understanding of two extraordinary couples, Hank and Claire Swartwood, who founded the Lodge, and Russ Colburn and Dr. Vee Fahlberg Colburn, Executive and Medical Director respectively, who carry on the work with the Swartwoods' distinctive philosophy of treatment—and have extended its outreach.

The Swartwoods were a professional couple with two children, living in the San Francisco Bay area. He was public relations director for Kaiser Industries and she a professional social worker. They became interested in the plight of severely disturbed children. Claire's brother, Tom, had similar concerns. They all left their jobs and moved up the northwest where they founded Secret Harbor Farms, which still exists to serve pre-delinquent adolescent boys.

But Hank and Claire were interested in working with more profoundly disturbed boys—psychotic, autistic or severely neurotic- -for whom little successful treatment was available. When the home in which they were working burned down, they moved to Colorado Springs and rented a large home. They soon had six or seven severely disturbed boys living with them. They lost their lease in the spring of 1954. While figuring out what came next, they loaded the children into a large station wagon and took them on a camping trip in the mountains.

The experience of primitive camping turned out to be profoundly therapeutic and the Swartwoods incorporated it into every Forest Heights year from then on. In Hank Swartwood's own words:

"We as a group had to get along together; each of us had to contribute his share if all of us were to live with any degree of security. Warmth did not come out of furnaces or vents; it came from wood that had to be gathered, cut to size, and used sensibly. Food did not appear magically out of a kitchen oven; instead, it came from fish cooked on the sheepherders' stove. Misuse of any food meant less for everyone. Hunger was often real, and therefore persnickety eating habits quickly disappeared. Since it frequently was cold during the night, it was not always possible to stay warm .

The major rules and controls which grew out of the camping situation were simple, and thus were easily explained. They applied to everybody because they were necessary for our well-being. And because they were so soundly based, the rules produced a feeling of security rather than one of regimentation. In retrospect, we cannot remember a child who did not drastically change during the period.Each child achieved stature from his ability to contribute in some manner to the ongoing life of the group."

Dorothy Stalder, who sold Forest Heights Lodge to the Swartwoods, wrote about the transaction. The Stalders had bought the property in 1942 from the Stransky's, who in turn had purchased it from the Wilfley family when they bought Greystone. It was originally built by a Swede named Oleson.

Since their own family was grown, the Stalders had for several years been trying to get good long-term tenants to lease the main lodge building but, in Mrs. Stalder's words, "We would always get it back, in bad shape. It fell to me to get it cleaned up, ready to try again." It had been on the market from time to time, but there were no buyers.

One day, when Mrs. Stalder was cleaning up yet again, realtor Hal Davidson called her to see if the Lodge was still for sale as he had a couple 'with a large family' who were interested. When Hank and Claire came into the Lodge they stopped, open-mouthed, said that the place was exactly like their previous place that had burned. They told Dorothy Stalder about themselves and their 'family' and why they needed this place.

Dorothy was so moved by their story that she took $10,000 off the sales price. When her husband Walter came up from Denver in the evening, he equally enthusiastic. The Stalders remained interested and supportive of the work of the Lodge. Walter served on the Board until his health failed and then his son served in his place. Hal Davidson also became an enthusiastic and loyal supporter and served on the board for a number of years.

Though the Swartwoods kept a low profile, it was not long before word got around that Forest Heights was a unique residential facility with a phenomenal success rate in working with severely disturbed boys. The numbers remained small because Hank and Claire (with one part-time housekeeper) were "psychologists, teachers, cooks and Mom and Dad to the boys". In the late 50's, the Swartwoods began to take on some extra staff, including students who helped with summer and weekend activities.

One of these was the present Executive Director, Russ Colburn, who was a part-time child-care worker while taking his M.S.W. degree at Denver University. By 1963, the Swartwoods were in their 60's and Hank had had two heart attacks. They decided to retire to write about their experiences, and called upon Russ—who was then working at the Northeast Colorado Mental Health Center in Sterling— to take over.

The Swartwoods moved to a little village in the state of Vera Cruz in Mexico. Three months later, Claire died unexpectedly of a perforated ulcer. Russ Colburn, who used to visit Hank Swartwood there, says that a part of Hank died with Claire. But he lived on in the village, married a local woman, and had two more young children before dying of leukemia.

Russ Colburn looks more like Paul Bunyan than a social worker: he is 6'4" tall, of ruddy complexion, and has bushy eyebrows, sandy-red hair and a beard. Together with his wife, pediatrician Vee Fahlberg—who is Medical Director of the Lodge and head of its training program—he has built up the staff, added to the physical facilities, expanded the outpatient and training program and increased the number of boys at the Lodge to 23.

Individual therapy is used for some children but the major emphasis is on supportive, consistent, loving and intense personal relationships between all the adults involved with the child—child care workers (who live with the children 3.5 days a week and are required to have homes of their own away from child care duties during the other 3.5 days)—teachers, psychologists, secretarial and kitchen staff. The demanding task that these individuals set for themselves is best described in Hank Swartwood's own words:

"Much of what can be gained will be based primarily on our willingness to devote the best, most knowledgeable and understanding part of ourselves to the life that we accept in living with disturbed children. We cannot, as automatons, follow a set of definite, programmed instructions which will accomplish our work. Instead, we offer our intelligence, certainly, but more important, we devote our morality, our personality—both in strength and weakness—and our ability to empathize with another human being who is in travail and toward whom we have the deepest desire to help.

. . .we have an obligation to permit the child to perceive our love for him.with a near certainty that the return of love will for a time be inadequate and interspersed with hatred and anger.we are faced with the responsibility for knowing ourselves perhaps better than we ever have.The aim of such a requirement is to provide a small group of children with a better understanding of a world in which they have had little belief—an opportunity to live without dread inhibiting the inherent potential for joy."

Since his appointment as Executive Director of the Lodge, Russ has served in consultative capacities to mental health centers, Veterans' Hospitals and school systems. He has been President of the Colorado Association of Child Care, Inc., and was elected in 1979 to Fellowship in the American Association of Childrens' Residental Centers.

His wife, pediatrician Vera (Vee) Fahlberg, graduated first in her class of 151 from Indiana University School of Medicin in 1959. She interned at Denver General Hospital and did her residency in pediatrics at the University of Colorado Medical Center, which was when she first came to Forest Heights Lodge.

Russ and Vee have lived at Forest Heights Lodge since their marriage, raising their own two daughters there and serving also as foster parents. In addition to her Forest Heights duties, Vee is consultant to the El Paso County Department of Social Services where she works primarily with older children going into foster care and adoptive homes, and with their new families.

131

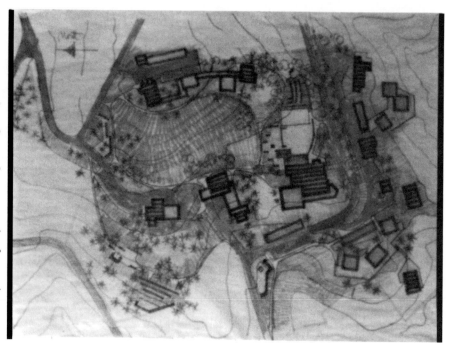

As Ray Curtis, Director of Social Services, puts it, "They take time to teach one kid tennis, to hand out ribbons on field day, to organize ski days or to wrap gifts at Christmas time."

Maryanna Ware, the Lodge's Development Coordinator, explains that Friends also fulfil an important fundraising function for the Lodge with their annual Oktoberfest held at the Elks Club and other fundraising endeavors.

By 1986, many of the buildings at the Lodge were needing major remodelling or replacement. A master plan for the facilities as an integrated campus was developed by Gene Sternberg and, after some modification to meet neighbors' concerns, was approved by the County Commissioners. Since fees paid by the boys cover only operating costs, the capital expenditures needed to implement the plan involved a major fund-raising campaign.

Vee has presented workshops for numerous Departments of Social Services in Colorado and throughout the U.S. and has written extensively on matters relating to protection services, adoption and foster care services.

Children come to Forest Heights with their own consent: most have been through other treatment programs without success. They get one last chance to recover from whatever happened in their lives that destroyed their desire to be with other people and their trust in adults.

Boys are immediately made aware of the two basic assumptions of life at the Lodge: "We will not allow you to be hurt and you will not be allowed to hurt others." "We must know where you are at all times." A treatment plan is worked out for each child and reevaluated regularly. All the experiences of life at Forest Heights—games, birthdays, work chores, school, starting with the Lodge's own school and working into full participation in Evergreen's public schools—are used as ways for the child to experience success, joy, trust. He learns that to risk participating fully in life and rolling with its punches is more fun and more rewarding than withdrawing, having a tantrum or striking out physically.

One measure of the success of Forest Heights is a devoted staff that tends to stay on, instead of burning out quickly, as happens at so many other residential treatment facilities.

Russ Colburn credits much of the successful readjustment of the boys into the mainstream of life, to the cooperation of the Evergreen schools. Here as in many other aspects of Evergreen life, the name of Riley Scott—former Principal of Wilmot School—is mentioned with gratitude. He established a precedent of genuine interest in the Lodge boys. The Lodge also makes extensive use of the Evergreen "Rec" Center.

In 1980, Russ and Vee Colburn were fittingly honored jointly as Evergreen's "Person of the Year".

A 15-member Board drawn mainly from the Evergreen community has overall responsibility for administrative policies and the financial health of the Lodge. This financial role becomes more difficult as expenses rise and governmental units which pay many of the boys'expenses find themselves under increasing financial strain.
The Friends of Forest Heights Lodge give the boys and staff a personal link with the community.

Education for the Youngest

In the mid-80's, parents of pre-school children could choose from nine early learning programs available in the mountain area. Some also provided kindergarten and first grade education, and most supplemented the educational offerings with baby-sitting services for working parents.

Unfortunately, all were privately owned and therefore had to cover expenses out of fees paid by parents. For families with few resources, such as single mothers raising children on their own earnings, there were no subsidized child care programs available: most had to settle for whatever baby-sitting they could arrange.

The Montessori approach to early learning became very popular in the 80's: two Montessori schools were operating in Evergreen, one in Kittredge and one in Conifer. In addition, there were two pre-schools in Evergreeen, Children's Center and Children's World, two in Indian Hills, Geneva Glen and Indian Hills Early Learning Center, and Child Garden in Conifer.

Arnie and Dag Langberg.

Jeff and Susie Bogard.

Arnie Langberg *graduated from the Massachussetts Institute of Technology and taught math at a conventional school on Long Island for 8 years. When an alternative school—the Great Neck Village School—was organized, he taught there for 5 years before being selected to head up the Open High School in Evergreen. Arnie has proved himself a skilled administrator but also teaches and participates in school activities with students and faculty. He and his wife Dag—a language teacher who taught at the Open High School for a number of years and is now with The Littleton School District—are active participants in the community, especially in the arts. Arnie has been a forceful member of the board of the National Repertory Orchestra (Colorado Philharmonic), ran a foreign film festival in Evergreen and gave classes on music appreciation at the Evergreen Library. Dag, a skilful potter, has served for many years on the board—and for a term as president—of the Evergreen Center for the Arts. They have cooperated in developing the Open High School as a community resource, bringing into Evergreen the Cleo Parker Robinson Dance Company and many other attractions. In the fall of 1986, Arnie took on a new job and a new challenge as Director of Alternate Education for the Denver Public Schools.*

Jeff and Susie Bogard
Jeff Bogard says he would classify himself as a Naturalist/Philosopher/Educator. He grew up in Iowa with childhood memories of "smells and feelings associated with marshes, lakes, rivers, grass, earth, barns, baseball gloves, ice-skates and hooded coats." Interests aroused by working for the Iowa Conservation Commission led to a degree in biology and chemistry from Mankato State University in Minnesota. Experience tutoring Native American students led to an interest in education and student teaching in some of the pioneer open schools in Minnesota. Still a sixties "idealist", Jeff is convinced that only the most dedicated and exciting people should be involved in education. Using the world as his educational curriculum, he finds himself faced with "endless possibilities". Susie Irby Bogard is profiled in the segment on Arts in the Mountains. Both Jeff and Susie are ardent outdoor enthusiasts, enjoying skiing, canoeing, hiking and traveling. Together they have taken many groups of Open High students adventuring.

Paul McEncroe, who is profiled in another section as the longtime operator of El Rancho Restaurant, also served on the Jefferson County School Board, to which he was appointed in 1969.

133

Sondra and James Jackson

Sondra and James Jackson are both principals in the Jefferson County R-1 School District—Jim of the Outdoor Lab School and Sondra of Bergen Elementary. Sondra is a third- and Jim a fourth-generation Coloradoan, and they share a profound love of nature and the outdoors. During their 1968 summer teaching break, the couple tent-camped in Alaska for nine weeks and fell in love with that environment. They returned many times. In 1983 they bought some land on the Kenai Peninsula which they use as a camp base, and where they plan eventually to build a home and retire. They have one daughter, who has been camping since she was 6 months old. The Jacksons both attended the same Jefferson County high school.

From there, Sondra went on to Boulder for her B.A. in Elementary Education. She has since added an M.A. from the University of Northern Colorado and an Administrative Principal Certificate from Western State. When you visit Bergen and attend its functions, you sense that this is a happy school. Jackson's goal is to have all children feel that they are worthwhile individuals, which is necessary before they can be confident about setting goals for themselves. A place where the faculty cares about kids and the kids have a positive opinion about teachers is Sondra Jackson's kind of school. Jim went to the University of Denver for a degree in biology and taught at the Evergreen High School for a number of years before coming to live and work at the Outdoor Lab School as its Principal in 1971.

Vee Colburn.

Russ Colburn.

Evergreen Contributions to the R-1 School Board

*Named Evergreen's "Person of the Year" in 1984, **Luanne Hazelrigg** became active in the community from the moment she moved up here from Denver with her husband and three daughters. This was in 1972. She was in the forefront of a movement to organize parent support groups on the junior high and high school levels (at a time when these were not particularly welcomed), which led to involvement as a citizen with school curriculum, students' rights and responsibilities and other educational concerns. Luanne served on special committees and the Mountain Area Schools Forum. She was elected to the county-wide School Board in 1977 and served for 8 years, including a term as President, during which time she put around 40 hours a week into this "totally consuming responsibility." Hazelrigg also was involved with Girl Scouts for 10 years, and does a great deal of work with the Christian Science Church.*

Luanne Hazelrigg.

__Liz Baum's__ election to the School Board in 1985 was also preceded by extraordinary volunteer contributions. Baum had herself taught, in Georgia, for 12 years before coming to Colorado, and deciding to devote more time to her own children. For her work in chairing a committee that undertook a systematic review of the entire R-1 curriculum, as well as her service on the Mountain area Schools Forum, Baum was nominated for the Governor's School Volunteer Award.

Liz Baum.

MAKING A LIVING

Most people who live in Evergreen today do not work here. They commute to all parts of the Denver area. This has a profound effect on the character of our community and on the livelihood of those who do try to make a living here.

Evergreen is now largely residential: some commuters are willing to put lots of energy into keeping it that way, opposing any type of industry, no matter how unpolluting or well-screened. Except for groceries, they can do most of their shopping in Denver and so oppose commercial expansion— not too surprising considering the unlovely character of the commercial strip development along Highway 74. Most commuters see little advantage to them in having the town congested with tourists.

Good schools and recreational facilities for kids, a few choice restaurants, lots of open space and severe limitations on further growth: these are the goals of many commuter-residents, who have paid a lot of money to live in a mountain setting they would like to preserve.

Those who both live and work in Evergreen, on the other hand, need a broader range of enterprises, services and customers. Most are becoming sensitive to the need to select business, industry and building designs that are compatible with the mountain environment.

We start this overview of business in Evergreen with a look at retailing here, as it was and as it is.

Early Days on Main Street
T.C. Bergen's son-in-law, Amos Post, was our area's first known retailer. Soon after his wedding to Sarah Bergen in 1862, he established a trading post, first in Bergen Park and later in the small logging settlement down in Bear Creek Canyon.

Besides Post, there were two other listings in the category of "General Merchandise" in Evergreen's first appearance in the Colorado State Business Directory. The year was 1880 and the merchants were Mrs. Hamer and the Gee Brothers. T. W. Gee was also Postmaster.

The Evergreen Post Office has been in continuous operation since July 7, 1876. Amos Post continued to be listed as a retailer of general merchandise until 1891, also serving as Postmaster for a brief period.

In 1880 the population of Evergreen was estimated at 100: it stayed near this level until 1926, when it rose to 300. In 1930, it was 483, and in 1956, the last year the all-state Business Directory was published, the resident population was still only 596.

Though by no means an exhaustive inventory of all businesses in the community, the State Business Directory is about the only guide we have to the commercial life of Evergreen for its first 70 years— other than the valuable recorded memories of individuals and advertising in occasional publications.

Until the Second War, Evergreen retail stores listed in the Directory were mostly of the general merchandise variety. In 1895, for example, there were 7 saw mills, 1 hotel, 3 summer resorts, 1 general merchandise store, 1 grocery, 1 lumber dealer, 2 carpenters, 1 blacksmith, a photographer, a veterinarian, and the first mention of M. L. Luther, but as a stock raiser and broker rather than a merchant.

Luther then opened his general store, which apparently was located in a two-story frame building in the lower end of town. It was a combination grocery store, meat market and Post Office—in short, "the place to pass the time of day as well as stock up on provisions and collect the mail".

Later, the store passed into the hands of Andy and Nellie Mickey. In the 1940's it was moved to a new quarters under the dam. This building was finally purchased by the Public Service Company, who demolished it in order to build their new water plant on the site.

A. R. Riel's was another Main Street general store. Located about where the Wolf House is today, it was the place where the disastrous 1926 fire broke out. Much of Main Street was demolished. But by the following year, most businesses were in bigger and better quarters.

In March of 1927, the Rocky Mountain News described the new

Strip commercial development on Highway

Riel's Store, "It is a fire-proof building filled with a brand new stock of goods, with up-to-date fixtures—a store that would be a credit to a much larger place than Evergreen. The new store has a 58-foot front and 48 feet of it is in plate glass. It is supplied with a Frigidair plant for the meat and green grocery department, and everything else about the new store speaks of enterprise and progress."

An 1883 photograph of Evergreen's Main Street shows just one building on the south side, along with a large fenced space for lumber and a pasture. On the north side, besides "The Post", there are just a few scattered small structures.

Slowly, the spaces on both sides of the road were filled in by restaurants, specialty stores for tourists, and the curious combination of drug store and dance hall operated for many years by "Prince" McCracken. This later became the Red Ram and today is still entertaining Evergreen and the Denver metro area under the name of the Little Bear.

For many years there was a hotel on Main Street, as well as the distributing plant for utilities (where the Rockin' I Western Store is today), and the headquarters for the Mountain Parks Protective Association. This had a stall for the rather primitive fire-fighting equipment acquired after the 1926 fire, Evergreen's only protection until 1949.

A vivid impression of Main Street in the Twenties and early Thirties was given to us by Rosabel Schneider, who lived right above Main Street with her mother.

135

Amos and Sarah Bergen Post and their children.

"I was the town's child. I knew all of the business people, and I'm a person that loves to eat! I can go up and down the street and tell you about the smells and tastes. There was Mr. Riel's store—he used to have sawdust on his meat market floor and I remember the smells of the different foods. Next, there was a barber's shop, then there was a restaurant Bedfords used to run. I can still remember her pies and cakes. Down the street, there was the Brown Cabin Cafe. My mother used to wait tables in there, and my, their food smelled good! Then there was a curio shop, and another restaurant called the Fireside: they used to have chocolate candy bars with nuts on the outside, and the inside was like whipped cream. Next was the drug store, where Maud McCracken used to let me come in back of the fountain and wash her glasses. I can still smell the stuff they used to squirt on their showcases to clean 'em. I remember the ice house, along on the Creek. I can still smell the sawdust in there. Jack Fleming used to deliver ice."

McCracken's drug store on Main Street (now the Little Bear.)

Rosabel's husband, John, told us the ice was cut from Bob Down's pond on Upper Bear Creek, later the T-Bar-S Resort.

A favorite pre-war restaurant on Main Street was Hamiltons' Rustic Tearoom, located where the Evergreen Crafters is today. Like most of the tourist-oriented businesses, it was open only in the summer.

The Hamiltons came out each year from Kansas, and the reputation of their little cafe drew many visitors up from Denver. Father Lewis Marsh proudly showed us that two recipes from the Tearoom were included in an early edition of the Duncan Hines cookbook.

"It was **the** place to go in Evergreen," said Mrs. Marsh, remembering that during the war Denverites would save up their red stamps for gas, and come to the Tearoom for "a really nice dinner on weekends, and a lovely outing in the mountains."

Main Street, 1925.

The end of the Tearoom, we hear, came with a dispute over a toilet! The Health Department demanded that the restaurant put in a restroom and the Hamilton's landlord, John Ross, refused. This was before Main Street had any sewer system, and the few existing toilets were pretty disgusting. The Hamiltons decided to give up their business here. They auctioned off all the fixtures and furniture and retired.

John Ross and the Ross-Lewis Trust: A Big Stake in Main Street
John Ross was a "character". He owned much of Evergreen's Main Street though he lived in Morrison and was involved in many enterprises there. Before Denver induced him to sell, by initiating a court action, he owned the land that is now Red Rocks Park.

His granddaughter, Pat Bradley of Golden, remembered that Ross was very sharp, had twinkly eyes, a

great sense of humor, and was an inveterate trader. He would trade anything, down to the watch on his wrist, for something he fancied.

A family story tells something about his wit. Approached to donate some money towards fencing in the Morrison cemetery, he asked, "Why, do you know anybody that wants to get in there?" "No!" "Well, do you know anybody that wants out?" "No!" Whether he made the donation is not recorded.

Of Scotch-Irish background, Ross came to America from Ireland after his young wife died in childbirth, leaving his son Robert to be raised by an aunt. (Robert came to Colorado when he was grown.) Ross was in Chicago at the time of the great fire and later came to Colorado, settling first in Alma. Around 1882, he married Mary Snell and the couple had one child, also called Mary. They moved to Morrison in 1889.

Like so many settlers, Ross had his finger in many pies. He ran a mercantile store in Morrison. He bought and traded land and took out timber leases in the Evergreen area. That's how he came to buy Main Street. When he was cutting timber above Evergreen, he would haul the logs down to the open area on what is now Main Street, put them on big wagons, haul them down the narrow road to Morrison and then load them onto railroad cars for the trip to Denver.

He figured it would be convenient to own the place where the lumber was stored and loaded. Though his heirs are not certain, they believe he bought the land—which is labelled on county maps as the John Ross Tract—directly from Mary Neosho Williams.

The tract started at the bridge, went on the north side to Douglas Park Road (across from the Little Bear) directly across the road to the creek and up to the bridge on the south side: 600' long and averaging 250' wide, it was about 4-5 acres in all. During his lifetime, John Ross sold only one piece of the land. That was the corner now occupied by the Baskin-Robbins store: Ross sold it to a buddy who was a landman for Continental Oil Co. Until the late 70's, it was the site of a Conoco service station. Ross sold it for $6,000. It cost his heirs more than 30 times that amount to buy it back in 1980.

John Ross, 1941.

During his liftime, Ross put up a number of structures as Evergreen grew into a tourist town: on the south side, a building between Clarence Smith's Evergreen Public Service Co. and the Conoco station—a rather large restaurant, best known when it was the Ranch House, owned and operated by Gordon Busley. On the north side was a grocery store, some small log buildings, the Evergreen Transfer and Storage, the Hamilton Tearoom and a small restaurant on the corner.

Ross came up to Evergreen at least once a week: in his later years he was driven by a friend. When Father Lewis Marsh first came to Evergreen, he remembered Ross as the major business power in the town. By that time he was lame and on crutches, but would often walk the entire length of Main Street.

Ross died in the early 1940's when he was 90. Before that, however, he had transferred ownership of the Main Street land to the Ross-Lewis Trust. The trust agreement was prepared in 1942 by Arthur Quaintance, the husband of Ross's daughter Mary. They were married in 1919 in the little Mission of the Transfiguration in Evergreen.

A Mrs. Lewis, who owned a farm east of Morrison, had asked John Ross to manage her property. It was decided to pool certain of her's and Ross's properties, and create a steady income for each of the trust beneficiaries. There were five in the original trust—Ross, his wife and daughter, his son Robert and Mrs. Lewis.

After Ross's death, Mary Quaintance managed the Evergreen properties. Ross Grimes of the Crafters store remembers her well: if repairs or remodelling were needed she would suggest adjusting the rent and letting the tenants do the work themselves. Gradually, however, Mrs. Quaintance was happy to hand over responsibility for developments on Main Street to a son-in-law that she liked and trusted.

The Quaintances, who lived out their lives in Arthur Quaintance's hometown of Golden, had two daughters, Pat and Maryanna. In 1949, Pat married Leo Bradley who came to Golden in 1946, after serving in the army, to attend the School of Mines. He worked for a few years in mining, then took a law degree and set up practice in Golden.

Around 1953, Leo Bradley started to make decisions about the development of the Ross-Lewis holdings on Main Street. His first action was to tear down, with his own hands, two outdated little restaurants: one on the corner of Douglas Park Road, another across the street.

In 1955-6, the flagstone and timber building at the upper end of town was put up, originally housing a trading post and three other tenants. In 1957 a new supermarket- style grocery store was built and opened to great acceptance by the community.

The former Evergreen Transfer and Storage premises were remodelled for the community's first Bank, the Evergreen State Bank, which opened in 1960. Next came the small mall next to the bank building, and two or three additions to the bank.

Pat and Leo Bradley.

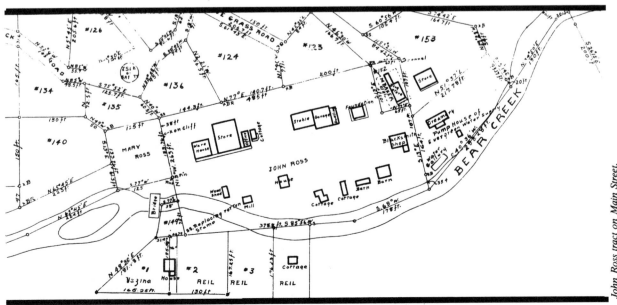

Much of what is now the parking lot was taken up by the Evergreen Fire House, built by the Volunteer Fire Department in 1950. When the new Fire Station was completed on Highway 73, the old building was donated to the Evergreen Conference. They moved it down to the Conference grounds in 1965 and renamed it Douglas House.

In 1967 ground was broken for an addition that tripled the area of the former Thrifty Market Grocery Store: it had a grand reopening as the Evergreen Food King.

December 3, 1970 saw the debut of the Rockin' I Western Wear Store, owned by Clair and Kay Iversen, in the old Public Service building: in 1975, the Trust bought the building from Maude Smith. Later it was torn down and replaced with the present red brick structure.

A large drive-in facility for the Evergreen National Bank, across the street from its main office, was designed with considerable sensitivity to the rock background and the stream.

The once-spacious "supermarket" was not able to survive against the combined competition of King's Soopers and Safeway and went out of business. The premises stood empty until a part was remodelled by Paragon Sports in 1985. Plans were approved in 1986 for the entire building to be developed into additional stores and possibly a restaurant.

We asked Pat and Leo Bradley what they have in mind for Main Street, as far as they can influence its development. They both hope to see a small mountain town atmosphere retained, would like to open up the Creek to public use and enjoyment, and felt that denser occupation of the hillsides— by both commercial enterprises and housing—would make for a more lively and successful downtown.

The Bradley's son, Jeff, has gone into the building field and has worked on all the recent building and remodelling projects of the Trust in Evergreen.

But Main Street is not all contained in the Ross Lewis Trust. Twenty-four different ownerships of commercial property were found in a study that was done in the mid-70's. A large part of the lower end of the town is in the ownership of the Stransky family.

Above the bridge the various properties that have been integrated into the Bear Creek Mall— including the structures formerly housing the Liston Lodge and Duval Lumber—were assembled and developed by Reginald Morland, a native of England.

Business Outgrows Main Street
Parking is limited in the little canyon section that is Evergreen's Main Street, and so is the potential for large areas of retail space. The first expansion of business outside Main Street was the Hiwan Village Center, which originally contained the first Evergreen chain supermarket, Safeway (in what in now the Bear Rug building), a new Evergreen Post Office and several small shops.

Building of the new Post Office, according to the Canyon Courier, was delayed "partly because the local committee to approve the style of construction decided it did not particularly like the architecture. One committee member said the plans looked like an old-time Western jail." The simple building, faced with native stone, did open in 1961.

When Public Service bought out Colorado Central Power in 1962, it developed a second area of business use by building its offices and storage yard off Highway 74 north of Evergreen. These opened in November of 1964. In time, a collection of small stores, restaurant, gas station and car wash were developed by one-time barber, Bill Ackerman, to the south of the Public Service buildings and another area of small offices and stores to the north.

Before the building of Hiwan Village Shopping Center, almost the only areas zoned for commercial use outside Main Street were either restaurants or resorts.

One of these sites was on Evergreen Lake, a 2 plus acre piece of land that the deDisse family had reserved for themselves when the ranch was sold to Denver.

A Denver restaurateur, Eddie Ott, acquired the land— though probably not, as one old timer told us, in a poker game. In 1938, he opened his glamorous summer restaurant, Eddie Ott's by the Lake. Designed by a New York Architect, Frank Dorn, the building was a stucco and stone combination of restaurant and dancing pavilion.

Hiwan Village Center.

Gala Opening Night was on June 11 and people came from all over to dine and dance by the Lake.

Soon Evergreen and Denver adopted Eddie Ott's as a favorite spot for evening entertainment. People came to dance—at a price of ten cents entrance fee and ten cents a dance or a dollar for a couple—to music of the likes of Tommy Dorsey, Lawrence Welk and Eddie Young.

For a time, Ott organized a Cowboy Night once a week, with a parade starting at Troutdale and ending in a barbecue, with everyone dressed in western clothes.

World War II put an end to Eddie Ott's Evergreen enterprise. He was involved in the war effort, and gasoline rationing drastically reduced the numbers of diners and dancers. The restaurant was closed, stood idle for a number of years, and was sold in 1944.

From that date until 1985, when the structure was demolished, the restaurant went through many name changes and ownerships. Just since we came to Upper Bear Creek in 1972, it was the Big Bear, the James Gang, the Waterworks, Lakeshore Inn, Evergreen-by-the-Lake, and the Million Dollar Cactus Rose, which opened with a huge "bash" in Sept, 1983 and closed quietly in August 1984.

In 1977, a small row of stores with offices above was built behind the restaurant. When the last attempt at running the restaurant failed, the entire property was owned by Ed Novak—who started the successful "Broker" restaurant chain in Denver—in partnership with Bob Hammond of Evergreen and a Denver businessman.

After some negotiations and changes to meet concerns of the Evergreen Design Task Force, a redevelopment project upgrading the existing structures and building a new combination of medical center, restaurant and offices, was undertaken in 1986. The landscaping was especially generous, using mature trees and ensuring good maintenance by installation of a sprinkler system. A public contest produced the new name of Lakepoint for both the restaurant and the shopping center.

Lakepoint Center.

Another resort site, that of the abortive Lazy Valley Inn project, saw the next major expansion in retailing. The Lazy Valley resort was started with much enthusiasm but too little capital after the war by Kirby Beckett. It never quite got off the ground, and passed into a succession of ownerships. In 1966, it was the Evergreen Shadows Inn: use of it was donated to the Colorado Philharmonic for their first season in Evergreen.

A new banking group affiliated with Central Bank of Denver bought the ground, which included the former resort lodge last used as Cavalieri's Restaurant (torn down in the 1970's) and the small number of "cabins" that were virtually all that remained of the ambitious project. Today, these are used for small businesses: a shoe repair, real estate office, John's Barber Shop, cosmetics outlet, etc.

Safeway, feeling the need for larger premises, more parking and a better location relative to the growing Hiwan and Soda Creek subdivisions, anchored High County Square, the new shopping center developed north of the bank site, which celebrated its grand opening in 1973.

The Post Office relocated, first to rented premises in the new North Evergreen Shopping and Office center, then further north — along the same uncoordinated strip — to its own building designed by the Denver architectural firm of Seracuse-Lawlor. The new facility opened its doors early in 1982.

Banking

It took a hundred years for the mountain area to get its first bank.

The early history of Evergreen is peppered with stories about how the community managed without one. The Evergreen Woman's Club kept its treasury in a metal box in the safe of the Public Service Company. Evergreen Public Service tried to have enough cash on hand to supply the needs of Main Street merchants for change.

"Doc" Hunt, for many years the only doctor in town, used to pick up cash from businesses like the Telephone Company and make bank deposits when he went down to the flatlands to make his hospital rounds. Local merchants—like Olde's Texaco, the hardware, and the town's grocery stores—used to "carry" many local residents through the winter when times were bad: there was nowhere to get a formal loan.

In 1957, a serious and sustained effort was begun to secure a charter for a local bank. After many disappointments and delays the charter was granted in 1959. In March the next year the Evergreen State Bank opened on Main Street. It was immediately, according to the Canyon Courier, "snowed under with business." The first Directors were Leo Bradley, John Casey, Frank Devitt, Jack Rouse and Charles Glover. Dave Scruby was brought from Chillicothe, Missouri, to be Vice-President and Cashier.

In 1971, Evergreen got its first branch of a Savings and Loan— Golden Savings opened in premises that had previously been occupied by the Trail's End Restaurant, on Highway 74 at Troutdale Scenic Drive.

A group affiliated with Central Bank of Denver decided that rapid growth and the volume of construction in the mountain area justified the creation of another commercial bank. Their application for a charter in 1971 was unsuccessfully challenged by the existing bank, which was now the Evergreen National Bank.

The new Bank of Evergreen opened for business in temporary quarters in 1973, removed when their new building was opened in 1977.

In a somewhat complicated series of transactions, Evergreen National Bank passed out of local hands,

became the Colorado National Bank of Evergreen, and moved out of Main Street—along with the Evergreen office of Van Schaack and Co.—to the development on Highway 74 at Lewis Ridge Road known as the Center at Evergreen.

As a result of a merger, Golden Savings became First Federal Savings. Evergreen got its first branch of an industrial bank, Jefferson Industrial Bank, located on Highway 74 near the traffic light.

Main Street missed its bank: the premises remained empty until Leo Bradley of the Ross-Lewis Trust and a number of local businessmen, interested in maintaining the business viability of Main Street, incorporated the town's third commercial bank, again called the Evergreen National Bank. This occupied the old premises, remodelled and updated. Dave Scruby, who had remained an Evergreen resident but was working with a suburban Denver bank, was brought back to head up the new venture.

First Federal Savings and Loan decided to close its Evergreen office: accounts were transferred to Denver or to the new Evergreen office of Capitol Federal Savings and Loan in the High Country Square (Safeway) shopping Center.

With the opening of a new retail center in Bergen Park came another Savings and Loan branch—World Savings—and a fourth commercial bank, Bergen Park National Bank. This occupied part of the Hiwan lands, behind the octagonal barn off Highway 74, that were zoned commercial but as yet undeveloped.

One hundred years to get one bank in the mountain area. Twenty-five years later, there are five commercial banks (three in Evergreen, one each in Conifer and Bergen Park), two savings and loans and one industrial bank. Whether the area can continue to support all these financial institutions, with a drastically changed economy and banks all over Colorado facing large losses on real estate and business loans, remains to be seen.

139

Dave and Jean Scruby.

Evergreen's Banker, Dave Scruby
By 1986 Dave Scruby and his wife, Jean, had lived in Evergreen for 27 years. They raised their family here, and have been involved with most of the significant developments that have transformed Evergreen from the small town that it was in 1960—when they came here with some misgivings from their native Missouri—to the diversified and extended community that it is today.

Invited to head up the first bank in Evergreen, Dave Scruby found the early days here "rough, from the standpoint of adjusting to the type of community and to more prolonged and severe winters than we had been used to." As the bank and the community began to grow and "there was always something new happening, it was not long until we had our roots down in this lovely mountain community."

Opportunities for career advancement by moving elsewhere came up from time to time but, says Dave, "we were never quite able to separate ourselves from Evergreen."

Bergen Park Rises Again
The fortunes of Bergen Park have risen and fallen according to transportation routes. For a few years from 1860 it was at a strategic crossroads of traffic to and from the mines, using the Mount Vernon toll road. Some travelers went on to the Idaho Springs area, others branched off at Bergen Park to get to what was originally known as Bradford Junction, later Conifer, and to the road that went to the mines at Fairplay and beyond.

When the railroad from Morrison reached up to Fairplay and the South Park area—and road access up the Turkey Creek Canyon, the present 285, also improved—and when the railroad on the other side made a stop at Beaver Brook and continued up to the "Idaho" and "Central" mining camps, Bergen Park became a backwater. Evergreen developed first as a small logging settlement, then as a resort and retail center.

Bergen Park had another flurry of commercial activity— as a center for tourist and camping supplies and the location of inexpensive motel rooms—when it was located directly on the old Highway 40.

We interviewed Mrs. Mary Marquand at her little white frame house on Highway 103 (across from the Whipple Tree) where she had lived since 1936. At one time, it was a grocery store and cafe.

This small-scale activity virtually died out when the rerouting of highway 40 by-passed Bergen Park, leaving a sign-infested, run down commercial strip that could only be described as "tacky".

Twenty-five years later, the development of new subdivisions at Hiwan, Soda Creek and Genesee placed Bergen Park once more in a commercial location.

In the face of intense opposition from many residents, the early 1980's saw a veritable flood of development proposals for Bergen Park. These included plans for a hospital, a hotel and conference center, five or six major shopping malls, senior citizens' housing and office complexes.

Developers typically faced a hostile crowd at hearings before the Jefferson County Planning Commission. Individual citizens, community groups like P.O.M.E. (Protect Our Mountain Environment) and design-oriented interests organized as the Evergreen Design Task Force argued the merits and defects of proposals in public meetings and through the newspapers.

An additional complication was the proposed relocation of Highway 74 around Bergen Park, which stalled development for several years. Developers faced years of hearings, drawing and redrawing of proposals and political manoeuvering. Many projects died. Others appealed negative decisions of the Planning Commission to the County Commissioners, and won their approval. Even after approval, some faltered for lack of financing or changes in circumstances.

Bergen Park commercial area before building of King Soopers store.

Ironically, just at the time mountain residents interested in keeping their community to a human scale were beginning to despair, impersonal economic forces changed the nature of the game. Permission had been won to develop commercial and light industrial projects on both sides of Highway 74 leading into Bergen Park from Evergreen, within the community itself, and at several sites surrounding El Rancho. But the boom in the entire Denver metro area was fuelled by energy development and its collapse had drastic effects on Front Range commuter communities.

The first of three proposed three-story offices, anchored by Moore Realty, was built in Bergen Park in 1981. Individual suites in the building were sold as office-condominiums. Sales did not justify development of the other two buildings.

After acrimonious exchanges with the Planning Commission and the Design Task Force, the Market Place at Bergen Park project—bringing King Soopers to the mountains—was opened in December of 1983. This project was not well-adapted to its mountain environment in materials or design. Its planners missed a golden opportunity to create a community meeting place. The only Task Force recommendation adopted by the owners was the creation of a landscaped berm along the highway: this in itself was a vast improvement over most of the developments in North Evergreen, along Highway 74.

Rents for the small stores at the Market Place were at Denver levels—but the stores did not have Denver-sized clienteles. A number of the original businesses failed. Nevertheless, the presence of this new development altered the face of Bergen Park and the pattern of commercial activity in the mountain area.

A large proposed commercial development across the street from the Market Place did a lot of ground clearing and earth moving but, as of 1986, did not result in any construction.

Most mountain-area realtors deal in all types of real estate. One man, who came here to retire and entered real estate just "to keep active and involved", was involved primarily in commercial real estate. This was Pat Sayward, who came to Evergreen

Pat Sayward.

in 1968 and was associated with Ambrose Investment and Management Inc.

In the following 18 years, Sayward accomplished more, both as a businessman and a civic volunteer, than most people do in a normal working lifetime. He came from Boston, graduated from Brown University in economic geology, and was involved in the oil exploration, air freight and interstate trucking industries.

In World War II he was a Lt. Colonel in the Air Force, in charge of personnel services. His last corporate assignment was to the Denver area, with a national trucking firm.

Sayward was involved in the development of the Evergreen North, Lakeshore and Bergen Park shopping centers and other commercial ventures. He served as a member of the boards of such community organizations as the Evergreen Trails Committee, the Mountain Area Open Space Advisory Committee, Evergreen Road Improvement Task Force, Chamber of Commerce, Jefferson County Historical Society, Colorado Philharmonic Orchestra, the Evergreen Kiwanis Club and was an active member of the Church of the Transfiguration.

For all of his community services, and especially for his role in helping to secure the Means Meadow as permanent open space, he was named "Person of the Year" in 1981 (jointly with Sheila Clarke) by the Evergreen Chamber of Commerce. His philosophy was always to put energy into positive activities that he could support.

After almost 20 years the Saywards left Evergreen in 1986 for California, where their three daughters had settled. Pat was 83 by this time. The couple were honored at a community-wide "roast and toast" celebration, intended to leave them in no doubt that they will be missed.

The Small Store: Hard Work, Sometimes Heartbreak
The chain or franchise store first came to Evergreen many years ago. First, perhaps, when Herman Olde affiliated his gas station with Texaco in 1926 and next in the form of an A & W Root Beer Stand on Highway 74.

Safeway came in 1960, Burger Chef entered with Safeway's relocation to North Evergreen in 1973. Against considerable community protest, the Village Inn Pancake House and Pizza Hut were opened in the commercial development off Lewis Ridge Road, and King Soopers came to Bergen Park in 1983.

However, the great majority of retail stores and restaurants in this mountain community have always been, and still are, individual proprietorships.

Some of these have been long-lived—Luther's general store lasted from 1896 to 1920, Riel's from 1921 to 1935. The Hardware is a survivor, whose story is told a little later, so is Ross Grimes' Crafters—a combination of high quality Indian pieces with tourist souvenirs—and Ed Skaff's Evergreen Drug Store. Prince McCracken's Round-Up, a drug store and dance hall, opened in 1921. It successively became the Red Ram and the Little Bear, and always seems to have had energy and life.

Some shops have come and gone so quickly that people scarcely noticed their presence.

Making a go of a store or restaurant in Evergreen is tough. Denver is accessible: most people go there regularly to work and do much of their shopping in the big city.

People have invested their life savings, dreams and enormous amounts of time and energy into a multitude of enterprises since Amos Post first opened his little trading post in Bergen Park. Of all the enterprises that have contributed to the life of Evergreen, we here profile just a few, knowing that the selection is arbitrary and we must leave out far more than we can include.

Olde's Texaco -the "Olde-est" Family Business in Town?

On February 4, 1921, young Herman Olde went into business for himself in Evergreen. Above the sign of the "Evergreen Filling Station" on Main Street the words "Herman Olde, Prop." were proudly added.

Olde was born in Philadelphia in 1898, and came with his family to live in Denver in 1900. While working as personal secretary to the President of Mountain States Telephone and Telegraph Company, Olde also pursued his avocation—which was playing the violin for dances, weddings and other social affairs in Denver and neighboring communities. He often came up to Evergreen to play at Troutdale and the Round-Up, owned by "Prince" McCracken.

When he was just 21, Herman moved up to Evergreen. He first rented and then bought the small filling station that McCracken had opened across the road from the Round-Up. At first, it was just a little corrugated iron building with the roof extended to form a covered driveway: there was one gas pump and one drum of oil. The following year, 1922, the station became a Texaco outlet.

Business in summer, with the influx of summer people and the new fascination with automobile travel, was brisk. Winters were slow—and often meant hard times for the few year-round residents. Olde was asked to stock a steadily increasing range of items—shoes, work clothes, underwear, etc.— which gave him a little extra income. He put an addition on for the expanded business, and eventually replaced the old structures with a handsome brick building.

Herman Olde was never just a businessman. Many of the old-timers we interviewed talked of his quiet compassion, allowing families in need to "charge" gas and oil supplies until summer's plenty allowed them to pay up. He was also active in the local grange and in community and political affairs. He served as the first secretary of the newly- formed Chamber of Commerce, president of the Fire District and secretary of the Evergreen Sanitation District.

A tribute in the Canyon Courier of February 2, 1961, marking the occasion of the 40th anniversary of Olde's opening for business in Evergreen, said, "To all churches, worthwhile projects and organizations, he has lent his support and assistance."

On December 6, 1962, Herman Olde died. The measure of Evergreen's love and respect for him was that all businesses on Main Street closed their doors so that everyone could attend his funeral. More than 500 people were there to hear Father Lewis Marsh review Olde's life. He said that no list of accomplishments or organizational memberships could give an adequate picture of "the Herman we knew, he was a smile, a bit of humor, and much sage advice" and a man who "gave so freely to so many of his time, his wisdom and his wealth."

Herman's son, Gerald (Gerry), carried on with the building of the business: the brick building on Main Street was expanded, and a second service station established on the frontage road of Highway 74, near the intersection with Bryant Drive. Gerald's two sons, Larry and Rick, went into the business in their turn.

By 1985, the changing conditions of gasoline sales, including the popularity of self-service outlets, and the congested traffic on Main Street spelt diminishing returns for service stations located there. The Conoco Station by the bridge gave way to a Baskin Robbins, and the Olde family made the decision to sell its Main Street property and expand the service station on Highway 74.

More than 60 years after Herman Olde came to Evergreen to serve this mountain community in every way he could, the business he established is still going strong in the capable hands of his grandsons.

Kilgore Trout's: the Ronchetti's Restaurant

Jim and Lynne Ronchetti met in Taiwan, where Jim was involved with a design, graphics and photography enterprise and having fun with amateur theater on the side, and Lynne was playing the role of "pampered overseas housewife" with executive husband and two young children. After a divorce, Lynne came to Denver in 1973, doing some writing for the magazine "Leisure Living". Jim joined her and they married in 1975.

Lynn was assigned to write an article on Evergreen, part of which was to profile guest ranches like Greystone and the T-Bar-S. Jim came along as photographer. They liked the mountains and not only found a house to rent at the T-Bar but also took on the challenge of running the restaurant.

Jim had worked for about three weeks as assistant manager at Greystone: Lynne had waited tables. This was the sum of their working restaurant experience. But both had considerable experience of food preparation and large scale entertaining overseas. They poured their energy, charm and talent for learning into the new venture. At their own expense, they remodeled and spruced up the restaurant's interior.

Though their initial menu was routine, the Ronchetti's soon began to branch out into more adventurous fare. Their wide range of interests and welcoming manner was attracting customers to the low-key bar. It was less than a year after they took over the operation, but they felt confident enough to buy a house and a car.

Then, not for the last time in their eventful lives, disaster struck. The restaurant and their hopes went up in smoke. They had no insurance.

T-Bar-S Restaurant after fire.

After paying off accumulated debts by working at any jobs they could find—driving delivery trucks, cleaning houses, working in restaurants—they signed a lease to open a restaurant in an old building off Highway 74, at the corner of Hilltop Drive. The name Kilgore Trout's, taken from a Kurt Vonnegut novel, was arrived at over a liberal outpouring of wine with a little help from their friends.

For the psychological framework of their new restaurant the Ronchettis took a combination of their newly-acquired enthusiasm for EST and the Hawthorne Stone theory of business success. This produced a mid-70's world-view that included taking the responsibility for one's life, mutual support for personal and institutional (restaurant) goals, and putting loving and caring energies into staff relations and the operation of the restaurant.

The new premises had previously served as a home with a store in front, then successively as the Trail's End and Sena's restaurants. The Ronchetti's gutted the places, redecorated and opened for business in December, 1976.

Only a "new age" outlook would see a series of strange occurrences— glasses moving across tables, doors opening, chandeliers swaying, lights turning themselves on and perfectly good kitchen equipment refusing to work—as the province of spirits, and accept a psychic's diagnosis and prescription for cure.

Lynne was told that a man had died very unhappily on the premises and needed the right kind of encouragement and rituals to move on. Lynne alone, and—of course— at night, conducted the ceremonies for a 10-day period. At the price of some nightmarish experiences, and the entire kitchen equipment burning out one night, the "spirits" moved on.

Kilgore's won favorable reviews from Denver newspapers and became a favorite spot for mountain dining.

We met Lynne and Jim both at their restaurant and in the course of our own Evergreen activities. Lynne helped Eugene to launch the Evergreen Design Task Force, and both she and Jim took a leadership role in it for a period. Barbara met Lynne in several lively groups that explored "new age" experiences and ideas through the 70's and early 80's—a loosely-knit circle of around 100 people—including anti- Viet Nam war activists, "hippie" drop-outs, artists, musicians, back-to-nature enthusiasts and health food advocates: a colorful and warm-hearted segment of Evergreen's life at the time.

After toying for a number of years with the notion of starting a second restaurant, the Ronchettis took the plunge in 1984. They invested all of their credit and cash into an elegant remodelling of an old cleaning plant on E. 17th Avenue in Denver. Their Cafe Ronchetti, with its cool, white decor, rapidly became a new "in" place for lunches, dinners and anytime drinks and gourmet snacks.

In less that a year, it crashed. Taking on too much debt, competition with an inordinately large number of new restaurants in Denver at that time, and some rather nasty adverse publicity probably combined to kill the short-lived venture, into which the Ronchettis had poured their all.

Broke and in debt again, the Ronchettis put their personal energies back into Kilgore's. They set themselves once more to sort out finances and to answer, from their personal framework of "taking responsiblity" for events in their lives, what was it they needed to learn from this latest experience?

Lynne and Jim Ronchetti.

Kilgore Trout's Restaurant.

After a year of bringing up patronage at Kilgore's, the Ronchettis invited all their many Evergreen friends to a party at the restaurant to celebrate its sale. (New owners Kenneth Mueller and Sig Lewison renamed it Margarita Longneckers.)

Jim and Lynne had experienced what they felt as a surge of personal spiritual growth, and planned to spend the energies released from demanding restaurant work in conducting support groups, workshops and "whatever puts us, and others, in touch with their true nature."

143

Hans and his Wolf House

It's still the Post House to people who have lived any length of time in Evergreen. He didn't change the name because he wanted to, but because of some proprietary claims by the Greyhound Bus people. Hans Wolf, a native of Switzerland, bought it in 1978 when it was a small, popular eatery on Main Street. In several stages, he remodelled and expanded the restaurant, renamed it the Wolf House, added a bar, transformed the menu and introduced delicious pastries, baked on the premises.

In 1984, he opened a second restaurant called Jasmine's, in the new Conifer shopping center, but found that splitting energies between two places did not work for him.

Hans Wolf was born and raised on a dairy farm in the small Swiss mountain village of Davos Glaris. Though he was an enthusiastic and accomplished skier, and spent several years instructing and racing, his heart was really in the dream of having his own restaurant.

After working in several European restaurants to gain experience, and getting a degree in Restaurant Management from the University of Zurich, he emigrated with his American wife to the United States. He tried big city living, but realized that life in a small mountain town—with easy access to good skiing—was more to his taste. Which was Evergreen's good fortune.

Hans Wolf.

El Rancho

Its been called a Colorado tradition. Its also been cited as an example of "genuine mountain hokey". While numberless restaurants have come and gone here in the past 35 years, El Rancho has been a consistent success.

Two brothers from Minnesota named Jahnke, together with their father, bought the 35-acre site of the former Front Range Cafe in the late '40's. There they built their restaurant, with living quarters upstairs for the three families. Eleven bedrooms. After the two younger families left, the senior Jahnkes turned the upstairs into a hotel.

The next owners were the Ray Zipprichs. After selling a pie distribution business in Milwaukee, they had fallen in love with Evergreen and bought the Rosedale Ranch on Upper Bear Creek. In 1953, they sold that for $100,000 and bought El Rancho.

By 1958, they had put so much life and energy into the restaurant that they needed their daughter, Donna, and son-in-law Paul McEncroe to come to Colorado and help out. In 1965, the McEncroes took over the operation.

El Rancho's reputation is for plentiful, high quality meals at one all-inclusive price. Beef, fresh seafood and excellent wine constitute the core of the menu, though the restaurant now features lighter fare for those who eat "less hearty". Though El Rancho is a high-volume restaurant, all its soups, sauces and rolls are made on the premises.

The self-service gas station, wine store and deli, located across the street from the restaurant, are what Paul McEncroe calls "anti-depression insurance. People will always drink booze and drive cars."

The McEncroes raised their four children in the mountains: all worked hard at a variety of jobs in the restaurant while they were growing up. Both Donna and Paul have been active in community affairs. Paul served a stint on the R-1 School Board. Currently, he is most active in the promotion of Colorado travel and tourism, having been elected President of the Colorado Tourism Board in 1985.

The McEncroes now make their home in downtown Denver, a location Donna has celebrated with her popular little book "Off the Mall", a guide to interesting places within walking distance of the 16th Street Mall.

The many other good restaurants in the Evergreen area include **Key's on the Green**, a rustic bar and eating house located in the former clubhouse of the Denver Mountain Parks' Evergreen Golf Course; **Mark Singer-A Restaurant** in Kittredge, specially noted for its hearty homemade breakfasts; the **Tivoli Deer**, also in Kittredge, a charming country-inn type of restaurant with a Scandinavian flair, imparted by Danish owner Mogens Sorenson who operates the restaurant with his wife Lynn; the **River Sage** in the Bear Creek Mall, with a summer eating terrace overlooking Bear Creek and healthy, home-cooked food in the vegetarian tradition.

From Evergreen Transfer to the Hardware: A Long-Lived Evergreen Institution

In 1984, the Hardware celebrated its 60th year of continuous business in Evergreen with an old-fashioned Country Fair.

Located in a small building on Main Street, the store was founded in 1924 as the Evergreen Transfer by a man with the interesting name of Alva Bubenzer. He has been described as "a colorful ex-fireman and Wallace Beery look-alike from Missouri."

As its name suggests, the Evergreen Transfer hauled freight. It also sold hardware items, feed, ice, bottled water, lumber and coal. The Bubenzer's home was on Buffalo Park Road, where the Church of the Hills Presbyterian Church now stands.

In 1926, Lonnie Hillyer became a partner in the store. His wife, Chloe, was the Evergreen school teacher in the little white schoolhouse that still stands on Highway 73. The Hillyer's home, off Little Cub Creek above the Silver Spruce Condominiums, is also still standing.

In the same year of 1926, the store hired a man who worked there continuously for more than 40 years, and who is the nearest thing Evergreen has to a community memory.

George Walpole.

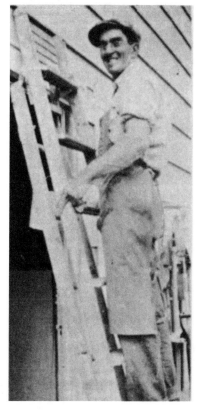

George remembers delivering luggage to Troutdale-in-the- Pines during its heyday as a premier Colorado mountain resort. He used to drive a solid-tire Denby truck on a delivery route from Evergreen to Denver, via the old road along Bear Creek canyon. The journey took four hours round- trip, and involved crossing the more than 14 bridges between Evergreen and Morrison.

The hardware store was always a community gathering place, especially when Evergreen was much smaller and there were few places open year-round.

The successive owners of the store helped many a local builder through hard times, by carrying bills for lumber and other materials for 6 or 8 months until a house he was building was completed. One such builder was our gentle and hardworking former Blue Creek neighbor, Heinie Livonius.

Evergreen Transfer was bought in 1941 by Beth LeRoe King and his son Laird, and renamed Kings' Hardware. King's business in Oklahoma had failed during the depression. The family knew Evergreen because they used to spend the summers here to escape the oppressive heat. When they moved here, both father and son worked for a while for the Mountain Parks Protective Association.

Although they owned the store for only seven years, the Kings made many changes. The feed and freight aspects of the business were wound down and hardware and lumber emphasized. The building was

Ellece King Murphy and Olive King.

expanded down Main Street to between two and three times its original size, which involved considerable blasting of the rock behind the building. (When Bruce Livonius built a home on Witter Gulch for Beth King's daughter, Ellece King Murphy, and her husband Jim, that rock was used to build the fireplace.)

Evergreen was still mainly a resort community, with only a small year-round population, while the Kings owned the hardware store. In the war years, shortage of materials and lack of work for local construction people were real concerns for Beth and Laird King, according to Ellece Murphy. She believes they continued expanding the store mainly to give employment. The Kings also travelled to abandoned army camps to bring to Evergreen inexpensive windows, doors and other building elements.

George Walpole was born in Idaho Springs in 1905, where his father worked for the Arco Mill. The family later moved to a home near what is now the Museum of Historic Bells on Upper Bear Creek, then to Morrison. George graduated from high school in 1923 and worked for some years cutting lumber in Evergreen. He quit when his employer refused him 50 cents stagecoach fare to visit his mother in Morrison, and spent the rest of his working life at The Hardware.

Paul and Elma Hammond.

145

Kise and Ted La Montagne.

The Hardware.

The practice of hanging part of the store inventory from the ceiling, which gave the hardware its rustic and inviting character, was started by the Kings mainly as a way of expanding display space.

The next owners were Paul and Elma Hammond, who are still very much a part of the Evergreen community. Paul had traveled most of the years of their married life. He worked for Skelly Oil Co. in Denver, visiting Skelgas distributors in his sales territory. The Hammonds decided to settle down and look for a business of their own.

In Mrs. Hammond's words, "Paul came up to make his regular call in Evergreen and told Laird that this would probably be his last call, because we were wanting to get into something of our own. Laird said, 'Why don't you buy this?' Paul said, 'I didn't know it was for sale.' Laird said, "It wasn't yesterday, but it is today!"

Paul told his wife that she would need to work in the office for about a year while they got to know the business, and then she could quit. When they had to sell the business 30 years later because of Paul's health, Elma was still working there. It was she who found herself missing the store and all its associations, much more than her husband or her son Bob, who had taken over the major responsibility for management but found it stressful.

The Hammonds kept the lumber part of the business going until the mid-1960's, and the Skelgas franchise for many years. Eventually, both of these were phased out, and the business concentrated on hardware. The new owners retained the invaluable services of George Walpole, who continued his round trips to Denver, hauling most of the materials needed to stock the store.

Life for the Hammonds revolved around the store. We who frequented it in those days, even if only as "summer people", felt the ambience of friendship and welcome. "Our customers were our neighbors and our friends," says Elma Hammond.

Paul and Bob Hammond had always admired the Hiwan Barn, built as a show barn to display the prize Hereford cattle raised on the Hiwan Ranch owned by Darst and Ruth Buchanan. Buchanan's daughter Joan Landy, who was living in the Hiwan Homestead building at the time, knew how much the Hammonds wanted the barn.

When the Buchanan family decided to develop this part of the Hiwan lands, Joan Landy saw to it that Bob Hammond was able to purchase the barn, with one cabin that had been a bunkhouse and 3.75 acres. (The cabin was the building in which the La Montagnes, present owners of the hardware, operated their first business in Evergreen, Shadow Mountain Sound.)

The Hammonds were only in the handsome new premises for a year before they sold the business to Ted and Kise LaMontagne in 1976. The LaMontagne's had lived in Evergreen since 1970. Kise was a geologist and Ted a banker, but they decided they wanted to put down roots in the Evergreen community and operate a business here.

They have been sensitive to the long tradition of community involvement and service that have been part of the store since its foundation. They have been personally active in many community organizations and, through the store, support many others. Each year, for instance, their Christmas tree sales support the Evergreen Bootstraps Scholarship. For a while, the "cabin" sold art supplies and offered art classes.

Later, it was converted into Mountain Home, an elegant little housewares center.

The Evergreen Pastry Shop

For most of Evergreen's history, there was a bakery somewhere in town. But for a number of years after the coming of the large supermarkets, there was a break in this tradition. So when Roger Dougherty opened his Evergreen Pastry Shop in 1980, it was an instant success.

Roger first brought his pastry-making and cake-decorating skills to the Hiwan Country Club, where he worked for six years. Born and raised in Minneapolis, Minnesota, he started working while still in high school under a skilled pastry chef who took an interest in his career. Later, he studied cake decorating and managed two bakeries in Minneapolis before coming to Colorado in 1970. Roger's "best-sellers" are his 24 varieties of bread, Danish pastries and hand-decorated cakes.

Roger Dougherty.

Mountain Industries and Offices

There is little industrial activity in Evergreen and small sentiment for increasing the amount—except in the form of creative "cottage" enterprises, and those offering direct service to the Evergreen area.

A few quiet corporate headquarters are tucked away in the community's office buildings. Perhaps the increasing use of electronic methods of communicating, and of gathering and conveying information, will increase this number in the future since corporate leaders will have more leeway to live and work where they choose.

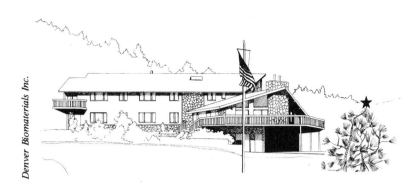

The Newkirks' Denver Biomaterials in Marshdale

"Triumph and Tragedy" could be the theme of the lives John and Carol Newkirk. In 1967, their 3-year old daughter, Vickey, developed hydrocephalus and had a shunting device implanted by surgery to drain the fluid from the brain. Shortly after leaving the hospital, the little girl fell off a bicycle, and was rushed back to hospital with concussion. She was critically ill for five **weeks,** during which time her mother hardly left her bedside.

One day, Vickey developed choking and convulsions. While frantically waiting for help Carol Newkirk prayed. If God would let this one child live, Carol promised she would find a way to help 10,000 people.

Vickey got over the seizure but doctors told the Newkirks **she** would need additional surgery to replace the shunt that had been clogged by bleeding. Wasn't it a pity, one doctor said, that these shunts clogged so easily and there was no way to clear them? It meant so much additional surgery for hydrocephalic kids.

Dr. John Newkirk, Vickey's father, raced against time to perfect a new type of shunt that could be used on Vickey when she needed it. Newkirk was a professor of chemistry at Denver University and affiliated with the Denver University Research Institute where he specialized in physical metallurgy. Before that, he had been a research associate at General Electric and a professor at Cornell. With help from Carol and the neurosurgeon, he perfected a shunt within a year that stood up to all the necessary tests.

Carol and John Newkirk.

Ironically, Vickey's condition cleared up naturally and she never did need the replacement. But the device was tested and patented. Since no commercial manufacturer would produce it, Carol started to make the shunts herself, at first in their Denver home and later in the three-room laboratory which they added to the house they were building off North Turkey Creek.

They gave away the first 200 shunts and soon surgeons began asking by name for the "Denver Hydrocephalus Shunt". Carol reckons that, within three years, she personally made 10,000 shunts. She had fulfilled her promise.

She also had a growing "cottage" industry on her hands which, with more employees, needed more space. The Newkirks bought land in Marshdale, developed architectural plans that they felt fitted into a mountain environment, and Carol confidently began the process of applying for County planning and zoning approval to change the land from agricultural to its new use.

They were obviously producing a product that benefited many. The little company was a rare source of employment in the mountains. Carol was shocked at the vigor and bitteness of public opposition. "I thought they would love me!", she told us. Oppenents were mainly concerned that one piece of light industrial zoning would lead to others, and about the water supply.

It took three years, 9 public hearings involving the hiring of expensive expert witnesses, and a great deal of nervous wear and tear to get the project through. The Newkirks credited the Evergreen Design Task Force with encouragement and an open-minded approach at a crucial time. The building was finally constructed in 1981.

Another personal tragedy during this period almost robbed them of the will to go on. Their oldest son disappeared late in 1979. All efforts to find him failed. His body was discovered in California about a year later. The Newkirks were considering walking away from their business, having reached, in Carol's words, "the absolute bottom of discouragement."

It was the need of an unborn child that drew them back into life. Inside the womb, the baby of a 26-year old mother was developing fluid on the brain. Newkirk was asked if he could develop a shunt tiny enough to be implanted into the fetus's brain. The shunt was ready in three days, and was implanted in pioneering surgery at the University of Colorado's University Hospital in April of 1981.

This fetal shunt brought to six the number of shunts for different purposes that have been patented by John Newkirk to meet specific needs, including a shunt for the relief of intractable glaucoma and an inner ear shunt for treatment of Meniere's disease.

Orders were coming in from all over the nation and from nearly 30 foreign countries. Employment rose to 25. The Newkirks realized it was time to update their "Mom and Pop" image. Though they listened to a presentation from a top Madison Avenue advertising firm, they found the expertise they needed right here in Evergreen. Their new graphics and corporate packaging won a prestigious advertising award.

Vickey Newkirk graduated from Denver University and is a healthy and attractive young woman. The industry produced out of her childhood need is a unique and flourishing part of our Evergreen community.

Anne Moore.

Anne and Mike Moore and the Snugli Story

It was with a real sense of loss that many Evergreenites read this headline in the July 31, 1985 Canyon Courier, "Snugli Sold to Baby Product Competitor."

Snugli, a cloth baby-carrier based on the kind traditionally used by women in West Africa, was a commercially successful expression of the positive "new age" values that came out of the 60's and 70's. Life-enhancing, back-to-nature, promoting a strong bond between mother and child, the Snugli was helped into the national big time by an ad in the Whole Earth Catalog.

Mike and Anne Moore met during a Peace Corps training program. Six weeks later they married, just before leaving for two years of service in West Africa. Mike came from an old Denver family. His grandfather founded the H. W. Moore Equipment Co., and his father Tom was the "Moore" part of the Denver architectural firm of Smith, Hegner and Moore.

In 1947 Tom Moore moved his family to Grand Junction and set up his own practice on the Western Slope. Mike went to school there and in the east, and graduated from Yale— "interrupting" his education for a year and a half of work and travel in Europe and the Middle East.

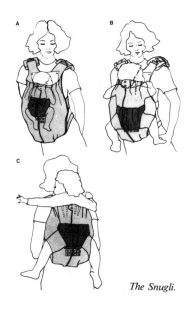

The Snugli.

Anne's home was in Ohio, in a family of Dunkards—a fundamental sect similar to the Amish. Her parents, she explained, were strictly speaking no longer Dunkards. They had been excommunicated for possessing a radio! But they still were accepted as members of the community.

Most Dunkard girls married into a farming life right out of high school. But Anne had trained as a pediatric nurse and was already 27 so everyone had given up hope of her ever getting married. To the 'small family wedding' came 12 of Mike's family and about 450 joyful Dunkard relatives and neighbors.

In pediatric wards in Togoland, Anne noticed that even very sick small children were much more peaceful than in the States. In the busy marketplaces, both Mike and Anne would marvel at the contented children fastened to their mothers, either sleeping peacefully or peering at the world with big, inquisitive eyes.

Mike Moore.

In 1964 the Moores returned to Denver, after a period of activity on the Democratic side of the Presidential campaign. Mike Moore became Director of Denver's anti-poverty agency.

Anne had her first baby. She and her mother, Lucy, fashioned a modified African-style baby-carrier, the first and prototype "Snugli". Everywhere Anne went, carrying her contented baby with her, people would stop and ask where they could buy such a carrier for themselves. Back to Ohio went the orders.

After a year or so, Anne's mother started involving Dunkard women friends and neighbors to help. So Snugli developed as a cottage industry—in Ohio—with marketing and shipping headquarters in Evergreen.

Most of the business's early development was Anne's work, along with having two more babies. At first the office was in the Moore's small home on Kerr Gulch. As the business grew, Mike made it his full-time activity. By the time there were 8 or 9 employees, the office had to be moved first to rented quarters then to a remodelled dog kennel and home adjoining their property on Kerr Gulch.

In addition to the approximately 150 "cottage" workers in Ohio, the Snugli company developed a less expensive machine-made baby-carrier, manufactured in a plant in Lakewood. They also branched out into 5 or 6 additional child-related products.

After 20 years of building the company, raising three children, poring over sales projections, worrying about future trends in the market and downturns in the economy, it was time for the Moores to have less pressure. The idea of selling their "Snugli" baby made sense.

Mike and Anne Moore are many-talented contributors to the Evergreen community. Their names appear again—in the arts section, in education and in developing the Jefferson County Open Space program.

From a Blue Spruce Nursery to ESCO: Clark Family Enterprises

It was hot in Denver in the summer of 1925. An early morning racket of jackhammers made sleep impossible for Leona and Rozzi Clark in their room at the Cosmopolitan Hotel, where they were attending a Rotary Convention. Everyone they met in Denver told them they must visit the Troutdale Hotel in Evergreen. So they drove up, liked it, took a room there and commuted to Denver for the rest of the convention.

Evergreen became their summer resort. As soon as school was out they would pack their three boys into their car and leave the heat of Wichita, Kansas, where Rozzi had a Pierce Arrow dealership. In 1942, after renting cabins for a few years, Rozzi bought "Tranquila", a little house above the Lake—"for my birthday", Leona added.

At the end of the summer of 1943, the Clarks took their boys back to school in Kansas, then returned to Evergreen for some elk hunting. But it was too dry: "the elk could hear you a mile away". So they drove out to the Rocky Mountain Evergreen Nursery on Brook Forest Road to buy a few blue spruces to plant around their cottage.

Rozzi ended up buying the entire place—160 acres and over a million blue spruces—on the spot. The Nursery's founder and owner, a man named Belcher, had bought the land from the Rock Island Railroad Company. He moved to Evergreen in 1927 and planted the nursery which became known all over the world.

"I knew nothing about nurseries, but I operated the business for 7 or 8 years," Rozzi told us. "I never planted a thing, but sold enough off to pay for the place." People came in person to buy and the Clarks shipped young trees all over the world—10,000 seedlings to Philadelphia in one order.

The nursery business naturally led to work in landscaping, then to people asking Clark to put on a porch for them. Pretty soon, with some good hired help, he was building houses. The name was changed to Evergreen Supply Company (ESCO). As they became old enough, his sons joined him. Clark built or remodelled many buildings on Evergreen's Main Street including the bank complex and the Mountain Pharmacy Building, as well as the El Rancho

Rozzi and Leona Clark.

Restaurant, the Rectory at the Christ the King Church, several homes on Upper Bear Creek, homes in Hiwan Hills and more modest houses for middle income families in the Greenwood subdivision and at Alpine Village in Kittredge.

Another early activity was taking care of people's summer cabins: turning water on in spring, off in fall and doing repairs and additions. At one time, Clark had keys to over 400 summer homes and cabins.

Then there was an extensive LP gas business which the Clark's bought for their son, Rozzi Jr., when he returned from service in the Phillipines.

Construction activity led into heavy excavating and pipe-laying. The family developed a western slope branch, based in Aspen. For a while they also had a real estate company, which occupied the premises on Main Street later taken over by Don Stanbro.

After Rozzi had both his ankles broken during an elk-hunting expedition, Leona was "gradually worked to where I was running the office". Duties included taking all phone calls—they had jacks installed everywhere, including the greenhouse and by the washing machine in the basement. "I all but had that phone hanging round my neck". By this time, they had their own radio connecting all the trucks and Leona became the "dispatcher".

Rozzi Clark was devoted to Evergreen. He was a founder and long-time member of the Volunteer Fire Department. He helped to secure the first ambulance for Evergreen and drove it, alternating with other volunteer firemen, until he was 71 years old. In general, as his son Bud Clark put it, "Anytime anyone needed something, they would come and see Dad, and he'd do everything he could to help them with it."

He retired in 1967, splitting the business between his three sons: "The one that ran the business got the business". The youngest son was over in Aspen so he took over the western slope business. Rozzi Jr. took the LP gas (which he later sold and moved with his family to Arizona), and "Bud wanted the home place". Bud now runs ESCO in Evergreen with his own sons, Pat and Mike.

Rozzi and Leona did some well-earned world travelling and settled into a pattern of winters in Arizona and summers in their beloved Evergreen. They died within a few months of each other, Rozzi first in October of 1982 at the age of 80 and Leona a little while later.

Corporate HQ: Robert Benson's Children's World Inc.

Children's World Inc. is an imaginative young corporation serving the growing market for well-designed, well-run child care centers. Most of its centers are in suburban areas where working mothers of young children can afford high-quality, non-subsidized child care.

149

The corporation started operations in the Dallas-Fort Worth area in 1969. Its stock was first publicly traded in 1971 when it had 8 centers. By mergers and the building of new centers, this total had increased to 112 in 1982 and 237 in 1986, when it had more than 25,000 children enrolled. By then the corporation was operating in Illinois, Michigan, Ohio, Southern California as well as Colorado and Texas.

The centers offer a program of "educationally oriented preschool day care" for children from two and a half to six and an after-school and summer program for children 6 through 10. Some provide toddler care. The centers are typically open from Monday through Friday, 6:45 a.m. to 6 p.m.

The majority of Children's World buildings are new and designed specifically for the needs of the children they serve. Increasingly, the Corporation acts as developer and negotiates a sales-leaseback arrangement as construction is completed. The attractive Children's World Center in Evergreen on Highway 73 is unusual in that it is in a remodelled older home.

The President of Children's World is Robert Benson, who runs his corporation from an office in Evergreen. A graduate of Harvard in Economics and a product of the Harvard Business School, Benson worked for various agencies of the federal government before opting for a career as entrepreneur. Benson lives with his wife Cynthia, an attorney, and two children in the home in Glen Eyrie that was built by Ben Sweet. Sweet was an early Evergreen summer resident who developed the subdivision, off Upper Bear Creek Road, for summer home sites.

Benson is an active participant in the life of Evergreen and has particularly lent his energies and leadership to the Colorado Philharmonic Orchestra, having served for many years on its Board of Directors and a term as President.

An Evergreen Original—Abel Manzanares

Born on the Ute Reservation in Ignacio, Colorado, Abel spent his childhood in Denver. His family moved to Evergreen in 1934 and Abel graduated from Evergreen High School in 1937. So did his wife-to-be, Dixie Jane Whitmore.

Abel Manzanares.

Abel then went to work for his father (a carpenter) and uncle (a stonemason) in their construction firm.

In 1942 he joined the navy—and stayed in for 20 years. The Manzanares had five children. After his discharge, Abel worked for NASA in California for five years and also learned a new trade from an Italian family of tile-setters.

In 1967, he returned to Evergreen and took up this craft—and was still working at it in 1986. What Abel will not tell you, but others will, is that he has an abiding interest in young people and in seeing them make the most of their abilities. He has trained many a young man in tile- setting and has used his own resources to help others get a college education. Abel has also volunteered his time and tile-setting talents to non-profit organizations like the Library and the Senior Center.

The Tool Mender

Ron Butler created this one-man service center for power tools and equipment of all kinds. He gained his experience working as a mobile repair man for a major power tool manufacturer. Located in simple quarters in Bergen Park, the Tool Mender was the kind of artisan enterprise that made a valuable contribution to our community.

With the enormous increase in land values in Bergen Park, rent soared out of proportion to any possible earnings from this kind of low-key business. The last we heard, Ron was building custom furniture out of his own home.

Ron Butler.

He Makes House Calls—on your Subaru!

"Buddy" (Charles O.) Richardson is the founder of Mobile Mechanics Inc., a complete Subaru service that comes to your door by appointment. He was born and educated in New York State, but got hooked on Colorado while attending the Denver Automotive and Diesel College.

From 1973 to 1980, Buddy worked for several dealers servicing Subarus and receiving factory training. Then he started his mobile service in the Evergreen area. The location was a natural, for Subaru was the pioneer of the fuel-efficient, small, four-wheel-drive cars that are such a boon to mountain dwellers.

Buddy also services many Evergreen owners' cars at their workplaces in Denver. But he enjoys his mountain rounds, where at any moment he may see a herd of elk or deer, a fox, a coyote or a big horned owl. Considering the impossible angles of many Evergreen driveways—especially when icy, deep in snow or sloshing in mud—it's no surprise that Buddy says, "Each day for a mobile mechanic is a new adventure."

Dave and Annette Saling.

An Independent Carpenter

There is an important segment of Evergreen for whom life's main value is not money-making or achievement in one special area, but rather an overall balance. Such a person is Dave Saling, who values equally friendships, hobbies, outdoor activities and congenial work.

Dave makes his living as a carpenter, working on framing or remodelling projects. He likes to be paid an hour's wage for an hour's work rather than getting into the headaches of bidding. Dave is good-humored, hard-working and responsible.

His Australian wife, Annette, is a qualified nurse and midwife who has a demanding job on the labor and delivery section of St. Joseph's Hospital in Denver. The two have "friends of all ages all over", play recreational softball and volleyball and love to fish and camp.

Dave learned his carpentry on the job when he came to Evergreen in 1967 and helped to build the Newgate Bar, with Rash Hendryx and Jim Musser. He became a minor partner with the two in the Bar and later in Evergreen's first ski shop— also called the Newgate— that opened up in an adjoining building. (The premises are now remodelled into the Evergreen Inn, at the lower end of town.)

The enterprises in the end did not fare too well and the ownership of both passed into other hands. In the meantime Dave had met Annette and the two went together to Australia, where they were married and worked for some time before returning to Evergreen.

Bringing the Office Nearer Home: Consulting Engineer Rich Cassens

The firm of Rea, Cassens and Associates goes back to 1948, when Dale Rea established his practice in Denver. Rich Cassens, a civil engineering graduate of Colorado State University, started working with the firm in 1970, became a partner in 1972, and President in 1976 when Rea retired.

Cassens had a diversified engineering background, having worked for the Colorado Department of Highways and put in four years of service with the U.S. Army Corps of Engineers, in Vietnam and in Europe.

The Rea Cassens firm is involved in the engineering of water distribution and sewer collection systems, water pumps and sewage lift stations and water storage tanks. A great deal of the firm's work is for water and sanitation districts in the Evergreen area, and another large portion is in Aspen.

So Cassens—who has lived in Evergreen with his family for many years—decided to close down the office in the flatlands. The firm now has an office in Evergreen and one in Aspen.

Buddy Richardson.

Rich Cassens.

A "Blossoming" of Realtors

When Gene interviewed Hal Davidson in 1981 in his refurbished log office building at the bridge in downtown Evergreen, Hal was proud of his status as the longest-established realtor in Evergreen.

Davidson came to Denver in 1946, seeking relief from the asthma that had plagued him in Ohio and kept him out of service with a 4F classification. His parents were semi- retired and decided to come west with him. They liked Evergreen and bought a half-completed house on the banks of Bear Creek, near Kittredge. After finishing the house they added some cabins, called it Davidson's Lodge and operated it as a motel.

The realtor for the deal was Hugh Taylor, the same genial agent through whom we purchased our cabin land. According to Hal Davidson, there were then just a few real estate offices in town: Taylor's, which was in a little stone building in the middle of town, Jo Hare's, located where the Telephone Company parking lot is now, and a newcomer, Harry Rockey.

Hal spent four unsuccessful years with a business venture in Denver. Then Hugh Taylor asked him to "come in and sell a little real estate and a little insurance with me." At the time, Taylor was just pouring the foundation for the building that Davidson still occupies.

Six months later, Taylor said he'd like to retire and would Davidson like to buy him out? Hal had no money, but Taylor accepted about $500 in life insurance as a down payment, and a long-term arrangement to buy out the business and the building.

Another long-time Evergreen realtor, Don Shephard, came to work for Davidson. Then, ironically enough, Davidson got drafted in 1953 because he had completely recovered from his asthma! Shephard and Hal's bride of three months operated the business for two years. When Davidson

returned, Shephard made a deal to go into business for himself by buying out Harry Rockey.

This was about the size of the Evergreen real estate business until the early 1960's. Davidson recalls that the year-round population was then around 2,000, increasing to between six and seven thousand in summer. Business was brisk in summer, since most sales were of summer homes and cabins.

After Labor Day "we would go back to very leisured living . . . a little bit of business going, but we could spend time in the coffee shops, chatting. The fire siren would go off and we felt free to lock our business up and go fight a fire, or take an ambulance call."

Davidson himself was involved in only one land subdivision—the Hangen Ranch up on Buffalo Park Road—but saw the effect of accelerated suburban growth on real estate development and sales. There was a great explosion at the end of the 60's, with the coming of Martin Marietta and other large companies to the Denver area, and with increasing ease of commuting to the mountains.

The 1970's saw a frenzy of house-building, home sales and resales that dotted the entire Bergen Park-Evergreen- Kittredge-Conifer area with real estate offices.

In fact, the major business of the fifteen years between 1968 and 1983 in Evergreen was real estate. The Canyon Courier was filled with news about new subdivisions and with ads for sales of lots, homes and land.

In round numbers, there were more than 300 realtors at work in this part of the mountain area by the early 1980's. Branches of most of the major real estate companies in the Denver area were established here, starting with Van Schaack in 1968: their first office was on Main Street, where the B- Bar-K is today. There was also a bewildering kaleidoscope of independent new offices opening, and real estate agents announcing their affiliation with first one firm and then another.

House prices soared. Astronomical amounts were asked— and paid— for homes with unique locations or historic value. New home price tags were as large as any in the Denver metro area.

Cabins on hillsides, with no insulation and no utilities, were bought up for remodelling and resale at handsome profits. Housing for those with modest incomes became extremely scarce.

But by 1983, the situation was changing. There was probably no single cause, but certainly the world oil glut and the bursting of Denver's oil and energy bubble was a major factor. So was airline deregulation and the loss of jobs and income among airline pilots, many of whom lived in the mountains. Each year, homes went onto the market because their owners were transferred or lost jobs and had to move elsewhere for employment.

Few houses sold, and the next year a new wave of "for sale" signs were added. There was a point in 1985 when one third of all the home in the Hiwan Golf Club area were for sale. On Upper Bear Creek the percentage was about the same. Prices were slow in coming down until 1986, when the lapse of time and foreclosures had a sobering effect.

The number of realtors and real estate offices declined drastically. In 1985 and 1986, mergers and reshufflings among real estate companies were reported almost weekly. By 1986, the number of individual realtors in the mountain area had almost halved.

Whatever was next in line as the major productive activity in this always-changing mountain community, it seemed certain that it would be something other than the buying, selling and developing of real estate.

Bear Creek Mall.

SPREADING THE WORD

Tom Sjoden.

Number, Please

An item in the June 2, 1900, issue of the Jefferson County Graphic lets us know that the telephone came to Evergreen along with the new century.

"We are now certain of having a telephone line in Evergreen, which will be built and operated by the Colorado Telephone Co. The matter has been fully arranged so that the line will be in readiness by July 1. It is a much needed commodity for this section, more especially during the summer, and we will hail its advent with great gladness."

The "Number, please" era of operator and switchboard lasted until 1960 in this community. Old-timers enjoyed telling us about those days. Myrt Livonius of Blue Creek Road was chief operator before her marriage. "In the summer, we were busy and had five operators. In the winter we had three. The streets just closed up after Labor Day. We would sit and play cards at the switchboard. . . . I can also remember when different people didn't pay their bills. You just shut off their service and in a day or two, they came down and paid up."

When Rozzi and Leona Clark came to live in Evergreen in 1944, there were 177 phones operated from one switchboard. "If I needed Rozzi," recalled Leona, "I'd call the operator and say, 'Do you know where my husband is?' She'd say, 'No, but I'll find out.' And she'd call down the line until she found him."

The Clarks used to play poker on winter nights with 5 or 6 couples, including one that would leave their three children sleeping at home. They would call the operator and tell her, "We'll be over at the Clarks: If you hear the baby cry, call us." Then they'd leave the phone off the hook.

Realtor Hal Davidson also came right after the war and enjoyed the small-town telephone service. "I'd ring the girls on the switchboard and say, 'Well, I'm going down to the Fireside Cafe for lunch. If I get any calls, reach me there.'"

For more than 20 years, Ma Bell's "Man In Evergreen" was Tom Sjoden. He came in 1959 with his family to the little house on Main Street that was a combination of Telephone Company headquarters and residence.

Sjoden was born and raised in Leadville, and did part-time work for the telephone company there after serving in the Navy. He then went to work fulltime "temporarily" for Mountain Bell, while waiting to get into college. He never did go back to school, but served the phone company in a number of capacities and communities before the move to Evergreen. As Mountain Bell manager here, he initially had 1600 phones in his service area.

In 1960, ground was broken for a new telephone office building on Main Street: a 2,243 square-foot addition in 1967 completed the structure that is there today.

The main purpose of the building was to house the new switching equipment needed to put Evergreen onto a direct dialling system. Until this time, phone calls from Evergreen to the Denver area were toll calls. Owen Strand was probably typical, as one who conducted a lot of his insurance business by telephone from his home, in feeling that it simply was not possible to live in Evergreen until this long-distance charge was eliminated. Along with the installation of utilities here and the improvement of highways, the establishment of the Denver metro single-rate dialling area was a key factor in the growth of Evergreen in the 1965-83 period.

However, the great majority of people in the mountain area were on party lines: 8-party lines were standard, 12-party lines were common in the Bergen Park area.

Sjoden was an active participant in the Evergreen community during its time of transformation from summer resort to year-round community. He was one of the founders of the Evergreen Metropolitan Parks and Recreation District and its president for 10 years, an active member of the Evergreen Kiwanis and a founder of the Blue Spruce Kiwanis (designed to serve younger men who commuted to work in Denver), a volunteer fireman for 13 years and ambulance driver for 8, a devoted member of, and teacher at, Christ the King Catholic Church.

Company reorganization sent Sjoden back to work in Denver in 1979. By then, he had served Evergreen for 20 years. Major changes in phone service had taken place: the number of phones had increased more that 7 times, to a total of 11,486, and Evergreen had become part of the direct long distance dialling network. Sjoden returned to work in Evergreen in 1982.

One of the small delights of living here used to be that when someone in Evergreen asked you for your phone number, you could just reel off the last four digits. Everyone knew you had a "674" prefix. Not so after January of 1982. Because each prefix can handle only a limited group of numbers and "674" was almost there, the phone company introduced "670".

By this time, the massive nation-wide reorganization of the telephone company was underway. Mountain Bell decided to reduce the numbers in management personnel by offering early retirement. In 1983, after 37 years with the phone company, Sjoden accepted this offer. He and his wife stayed, and remained active, in Evergreen.

By this time, the 8-party lines—with which we had become familiar through the service at our cabin—were a thing of the past in the Evergreen area. But 4-party lines, outside denser "base-rate" areas, were still the rule rather than the exception.

No doubt there will be nostalgic stories about the "good old days" of the party line once they are all gone. However, most people who can afford the price of a home in Evergreen have come to think of a private line as something of a right.

Still, not everyone will go to such lengths to get their one-party line as the lady from whom we bought our home. She was a diabetic, subject to falling into a coma with very little warning. Innumerable calls and letters to the phone company brought no results. She took the rug she was hooking and a large bag of yarn, and settled into a chair at the Mountain Bell office on Main Street. When asked if she wanted something, she answered cheerfully, "Yes, I need a private line and I am just going to sit quietly here and work on my rug until you agree to put one in!"

The Customer Service Center in downtown Evergreen closed its doors in mid-1983, farming out its services—bill-paying, phone return, distribution of extra directories—to merchants in the area. The central switching services remained in the downtown building, and the installation and maintenance center in a rather untidy group of buildings on Highway 73,

With the separation of local telephone companies like Mountain Bell from their long-distance parent, A.T.& T.—and the consequent loss of subsidy to local service by long-distance service—a bombshell hit rural Colorado, including large parts of the Evergreen area.

Outside of relatively dense "base rate" areas—like downtown Evergreen, Kittredge, Genesee—Mountain Bell announced early in 1984 that customers wanting a new private line would have to pay $4,100 per airline mile for cable extension and installation. Even if they wanted 4-party line service, they would have to pay the same rate where no space on a cable was available.

The new policy had, in the opinion of area realtors, a visible effect on home sales outside base rate areas. As a result of many protests, Mountain Bell modified its rate policies in 1986 to average upfront costs among all customers in a particular area, thus reducing installation for a customer living 5 miles outside the Evergreen base rate area, for example, to $1,472 instead of $20,500.

There was still much unhappiness and considerable support for a demand that Mountain Bell should provide Colorado with One Party Universal Service (OPUS) as is done in some other mountain states.

In the fall of 1986, Mountain Bell filed a request with the Public Utilities Commission for a rate increase that would provide funds for an overall improvement in rural telephone service.

Miss Julia's Library
The original Evergreen Public Library was opened in 1917 in an old grocery store on Main Street by Miss Julia Brewster Douglas, the sister of Canon Winfred Douglas. Bins along the wall held the handful of books, coal oil lamps furnished the light, and rickety, cast-off chairs and a table were the furniture. Miss Julia had the princely sum of $25.00 in cash as her library budget.

Miss Julia had been forced by ill-health to retire from her work as Children's Librarian in the Newark, New Jersey Public Library. Librarianship was already a second career for her: she had spent most of her life as a teacher. Some accounts say she had severe pneumonia, others tuberculosis. In any case, she came at the age of 62 to Colorado—and especially to Evergreen—to save her life and to retire.

A summer in the mountains with her brother and sister-in-law, Dr. Josepha Douglas, restored her to health. Being an energetic woman, she looked around her new community to see what she could contribute—and found that there was no library.

One brief history of the Evergreen Library, written in 1939, says that the origins of the library go back to 1897, when Canon Winfred Douglas stocked a reading room for the Evergreen Conference and the Mission of the Transfiguration with some 100 books from his personal library. After Miss Julia was fully recovered, "brother and sister decided to convert the reading room into a public library. It was started in an old abandoned grocery store, the shelves of which were used for the books that were checked out to the public over the grocery counter."

Exterior of library.

The head of the Newark Public Library was John Cotton Dana, an important and innovative figure in the history of public libraries in this country. He too had spent time in the west, recovering from poor health, and was the first head of the Denver Public Library. Appointed in 1889 at the age of 33, he served for more than eight lively, expansive years. He advertised the Library's offerings extensively, a radical idea which outraged the country's conservative librarians. But such opposition did nothing to daunt a man who described himself as an agnostic, egoist, pessimist and anarchist. A bit of a Henry George adherent, a free trader and "an unterrifed Jeffersonian Democrat."

Miss Julia interested Dana and other former colleagues in her new project, and they sent her some 400 discarded books to help start her collection.

Miss Julia's enthusiasm for books and for people, and her special gift for developing a love of reading among children, were the ingredients of her success. Soon the library was sufficiently known that she could move it from Main Street into a little house on the Conference grounds— apparently the small log cabin on Highway 74, now part of the St. Raphael's complex.

The next move was into the little combination of library and living quarters, built of field stone and timber, that still stands on the hill above the Church of the Transfiguration. According to a taped interview with Mrs. Jane Kemble—the third of Evergreen's librarians, who knew Miss Julia well—this was not a wholly altruistic gesture on the part of Dr. Josepha, who paid the $16,000 cost of the new facility.

Jane Kemble was an outspoken and lively lady: we quote her views only because they put the easy-to idealize Williams-Douglas family into a more human light. Jane obviously loved and admired Miss Julia. She felt that the Williams were "a very aloof family", who were interested in the Episcopalian community but "never mingled with the hoi polloi." Miss Julia was sincerely interested in the local community and wanted to be part of it. So providing her with a library and her own home got her "out of the Douglas's hair."

Be that as it may, Dr. Jo's provisions were generous. Part of the library was an exact replica of

the small museum in the Newark Library. Miss Julia's library served for 50 years as the Evergreen Public Library—from its opening in 1921 until 1971.

Miss Julia's modest living expenses, and the cost of heating and maintaining the building, were paid for by "a gift" (no doubt also from Dr. Jo.) But it was up to Julia Douglas to raise funds for all the library's other needs. So she not only staffed the library and conducted an extensive correspondence on its behalf to secure any materials that people needed or requested, but she also became an indefatigable fundraiser for her beloved institution.

Summer residents paid 25 cents to get a library card, and there was a small "rental" section where the latest books cost a penny a day. When Miss Julia first came to Evergreen, there were some 250 permanent residents and about 1000 "summer people". She solicited gifts of books and money from the summer visitors, and also items to add to her growing museum collection.

This was an idea she took from John Cotton Dana, her mentor at the Newark Library. He believed that libraries should also be museums. Miss Julia collected "things illustrative of the history of Colorado": minerals, Indian basketry and pottery—and a unique doll collection. These she shared with children, with teachers in the little one- room schoolhouses that dotted this mountain area, and with the public at large.

The doll collection started with a gift of three dolls dressed as Indians, with faces made from apples, that were reportedly sent to her from one of the Indian Mission Schools in New Mexico. She used the dolls at story-telling time with children. Pretty soon every one she knew or met, who was planning some travel, was urged to bring back dolls. By 1932, she wrote in an article titled "A Small Library in Colorado" that she had 131 dolls in her collection from many distant lands, as well as from all over the United States.

When she received a doll from a new country, Julia pleaded with friends for a story book so that she could use the new addition: when she managed to get funds for some new children's books, she asked people to find dolls to help her tell

the stories. She "worked both sides" to get her collection.

An account of Miss Julia's remarkable personality, and of her ability to stimulate interest in books and in learning, is contained in Jane Kemble's long interview. Mrs. Kemble first visited the Library as a college student in 1920. She marvelled that in 1923, when the resident population was only 400 and the summer people numbered around 1200, Miss Julia—with only 4,700 books—managed a circulation of 4,000.

By 1935, the Library had some 12,000 volumes, including some rare and choice books. When the American Library Association met in Denver that year, a trip was organized to visit Miss Julia's Library. It was described as on of the most interesting small libraries in the country.

Miss Julia used to say that she operated the library "on nothing certain", and during the depression years, on "nothing rather than certain". The highlight of the summer season was the library party, where the 'local' and the 'summer' people met and mingled and contributed their dollars to the support of the library.

Julia Douglas wrote an appeal for support to the Carnegie Foundation. She kept hoping that "something will be available from the School Board, especially as the Library furnishes nearly all of the supplementary and required reading for the different grades, as well as much reference materials, books, periodicals, clippings, pictures."

All efforts to secure a regular source sof funding were unsuccessful. Miss Julia continued her labor of love until she died in 1936 at the age of 81.

Canon Douglas tried to arrange for the library to continue. He donated 2,000 volumes to the consolidated Evergreen School, now the red brick County Building, to start their library. He asked the Sisters of St. Mary, who spent summers at St. Raphael's House on the grounds of the Evergreen Conference—and who had already been helping Miss Julia—to staff the library in the summer. One of them, Sister Johanna, was a trained librarian.

By 1943, the Douglas's were selling their Evergreen holdings to the Buchanans, founders of the Hiwan

155

Ranch. The survival of the library was in jeopardy. Father Lewis Marsh, Vicar of the Mission of the Transfiguration and one of the most active community leaders ever to serve Evergreen, organized a Board of three dedicated volunteers who managed to keep the library open during the summer.

Olive King was employed as part-time Librarian: she would take around 50 books home with her when she closed up the library for the winter, and people who managed to make it up the steep pathway to her house could check them out.

In 1947 the Jefferson County Community Chest took over the modest costs of operating the library, but discontinued its support in 1952 when the Jefferson County Library system was established.

Though there were few funds left in the library's coffers, there was opposition to being absorbed by the county system—partly because it was itself very poorly funded in the beginning.

In 1952, Jane Kemble had retired from her career as a social worker in Chicago (where she had worked with Jane Addams, the famed founder of Hull House and Nobel Peace Prize winner of 1931) and had come to live in Evergreen with her sister. She was shocked to find the library closed for nine months of the year. After she was hired as librarian in July of 1953 "for the magnificent sum of twenty-five dollars a month," she encouraged people to let Father Marsh know that they wanted year-round service. A meeting of representatives of all the organizations in Evergreen was called.

A new Library Board was formed. The patrons responded to having the library open some days in the winter, even though heating was far from satisfactory.

There were benefits, talent shows and teas as well as gifts from many community organizations and an energetic membership drive. Families paid a dollar a year. There were card parties at the recently-opened El Rancho restaurant. From 1954 to 1959, these fund-raising efforts continued, but an immense amount of energy was required to raise the minimal $1,000 a year budget.

It became clear to Mrs. Kemble that Evergreen's library was now suffering, in comparison with others in the county system, from having no continuing basis of tax support.

Jefferson County was a county-wide library system, ruled by state statutes. Governance was by a seven-member Library Board appointed by and responsible to the County Commissioners.

After the Evergreen Library Board officially voted to join the Jefferson County system, Mrs. Kemble continued as Librarian in the small building up on the hill until 1965, the year she became 65. The building was now totally inadequate to the needs of a growing Evergreen. To maximize space for books, Father Marsh and Arleta Alderfer (the Librarian at Evergreen High School and a long-time supporter and Board Member of the Evergreen Library) arranged for the doll collection to be given to Wilmot School, as well as many of the reference materials stored up in the attic.

Jane Kemble wrote to the County Library Board, "(The Library's) location above the parking space is not acceptable nor convenient to the present clientele, who object to climbing a mountain to get to it".

But, because it had stayed out of the County system so long, Mrs. Kemble felt that the then County Librarian took her resentment out on the Evergreen Library and on Jane Kemble personally. "We never had an aide up here, though circulating 2,000-3,000 books a

Gail Alden.

1971 building for Evergreen Regional Library.

Miss Julia's Library-Museum built in 1921.

month. We never had a telephone. We never had a book drop." After Pauline Kermeit took over, these things were taken care of. But the citizens apparently felt they needed to become actively involved in order to secure a new library building for the area.

After many lean years of subsisting out of the County's General Fund, the Jefferson County Library was the beneficiary of a new state law that provided for the setting of a separate library fund of up to 1.5 mills, up to 2 mills by a vote of the people. The Jefferson County Commissioners set the levy at 1 mill. This seemed like a princely allowance, and now that libraries had money for books and staff, the Commissioners were willing to use some of their Public Works Fund for the construction of libraries. Friends of Mountain Libraries was formed April 17, 1968. It spoke on behalf of library patrons of Conifer, Evergreen, Kittredge, Morrison (all of which had small libraries) and the bookmobile stations. The group appears to have vanished with the completion of the new library.

On land made available by the School Board, a new building was opened in 1971. It was designed by local architect Alan Fredericksen. The new library was planned to serve Bergen Park, Kittredge, Morrison, Conifer and Indian Hills. The small libraries in Kittredge and Morrison were closed down, and the one in Conifer, housed in a charming old schoolhouse, was kept open for just a few hours each week, serving mainly children.

Though it was intended to meet needs up to 1980, the new building was in many ways inadequate from the start. It was designed on an open-plan philosophy prescribed by the library administration, with no workroom, no staff offices and no public meeting rooms that could have been so well-used in the Evergreen community.

A new librarian, Maryanne Brush, was hired while the building was still under construction. She was responsible for the purchase of a new book collection and all other preparations for the opening of a greatly expanded library and staff. Pauline Kermeit came into the new building as Children's Librarian. She later died of cancer: her contribution to the children of Evergreen is memorialized in the library garden named for her.

The new building was designed for books and magazines, but not to function simultaneously as a museum. There was little wall space and no secure areas where artifacts of value could be displayed. Maryanne Brush boxed up the collection of Indian baskets and other items and took them to Richard Conn at the Denver Art Museum for an appraisal. She was amazed to find just how valuable many of them were and felt that they properly belonged in a museum. They were donated to the Hiwan Homestead Museum, where they are handsomely displayed.

Miss Julia's doll collection was also moved, in 1984, to the Hiwan Homestead. Much loving effort went into restoring the dolls and researching their history.

But Miss Julia's enthusiastic conviction that a library should serve the community, which was totally shared by Jane Kemble, is still flourishing at the Evergreen Library. Under Maryanne Brush and her successor Gail Alden (there were two brief interim Librarians before Gail was appointed) the library has served as a community clearing house, especially for social and cultural organizations and events.

An innovative array of festivals, talks, foreign films, art exhibits, old movies, baroque music recitals, special workshops, children's story hours, plays and rummage sales have been sponsored. Whatever imaginable event it is possible to stage in a library the size of Evergreen's—and with its limitations—probably has been!

One special occasion that resulted in a unique donation to the Evergreen Library, the Martha Bennett King Collection of Folk Music, was a concert by the Ritchie Family Folk Singers in 1977.

For its fine record of creative programming and public relations, the Evergreen Library received the John Cotton Dana Award from the American Library Association. How appropriate—an award honoring the memory of Miss Julia's invaluable mentor!

By 1980, there were 25,000 people living in the service area of a library building designed for 10,000. The massive budget crunch that hit all levels of government in the early 1980's made any thought of

Library staff members Kathy Steele and Robin Liebert.

Phillip the Library Cat. He came to Evergreen in 1983 from Los Angeles, and was placed in the Library through the Evergreen Animal Protective League when his people (a group of 8 middle-aged hippies) had to give him up because their landlord would not allow cats on the premises. Phillip has been featured in the Rocky Mountain News and the Canyon Courier, and is an engaging mascot for the Library. Both children and adults stop in daily to visit Phillip as they browse in the Library.

expanding or replacing the existing library an impossible dream. On the contrary, it was the beginning of a period of cuts in real purchasing power, due to the unprecedented inflation rates,and—in 1985 and 1986—of drastic cuts in existing hours and staff.

This situation stimulated another wave of citizen involvement in the fate of the Evergreen Library.. The Friends of the Evergreen Library was formed in May of 1982, primarily as an advocacy group to "secure, support and promote library resources and programs."

The Friends saw themselves as part of a movement in Colorado—and indeed in the nation—to convert general public goodwill into an active, sustained effort to prevent the imminent starvation of libraries from drastic under-funding.

Other aspects of this changed mood were a transformation in the attitude of the County Commissioners, spearheaded by library-advocate Bunny Clement, and the consequent appointment of two County Library Board members—Elena Grissom and Sue Rickert—with a determined and activist attitude about expanding libraries and library services to meet the needs of a rapidly growing county. This in turn allowed the Library Administration, under Library Director Bill Knott, to become actively involved with forward-looking plans that helped to secure the cooperation of groups like the Evergreen Friends.

In 1984, the State Legislature raised the permitted ceiling for library funding in districts like Jefferson County, provided the people voted to approve the levy, from 2.5 to 4 mills. The Jefferson County Commissioners agreed to put on the 1986 ballot a referendum to raise the levy for Jefferson County Libraries from 1.5 to 3.5 mills.

A vigorous campaign on behalf of the proposal was waged in the mountain area, spearheaded by the Friends' group. The proposal passed comfortably here, as well as in the rest of the county.

For 1987, the new monies meant increased hours (all libraries open 7 days a week), increased staffing, more books. In the longer run, along with the construction of two large libraries in the north and south areas of the "flatlands", the increasing funding meant expansion of library space in the mountain area.

In some important ways, the Evergreen Library is now light years ahead of the limited local collection that Miss Julia made available in her little stone building of 1921. Even before the increases made possible by more generous funding, the Evergreen Library had a stock of some 45,000 volumes and subscribed to 210 newspapers, magazines and reference services. More than 9,000 people in the Evergreen area held current library cards and materials were circulating at a rate of over 150,000 items per year.

The rapid moving from a card catalogue to a mimeographed listing of books throughout the library system, to a microfiche catalogue, and then to a totally automated one is more than a technological change. Every volume in the Jefferson County system is available to every patron: deliveries are made daily of books ordered by one branch from another. Soon the computer will give patrons access to the catalogues of all the library systems in metro Denver, and eventually to the entire state, including the academic libraries. In the wings is access to a wide range of up-to- date information through computerized data bases.

Just what this means in terms of needed library buildings and facilities will have to be worked out in a dialogue between librarians, computer experts and the interested public.

Still, the Evergreen Library remains true to Miss Julia's legacy. The Library is an information center, a human center, a children's center. A spark. A focus. A yeast in our community.

Community volunteers help upgrade Library entrance: Front: Andy Baird, Tom Ware. Back, Gene Sternberg, Robin Liebert, Abel Manzanares, Bob Jacobus.

Read All About It!

Evergreen did not have a newspaper of its own until 1946. This is not to say there were no headlines about our mountain community, nor even that small items of social news or gossip went unreported.

Major Evergreen events—"Blaze Sweeps Town," about the 1926 Main Street fire, or "Bear Creek Flood: Bloomer Camp Party Safe," concerning the 1896 flood—were always reported in the Rocky Mountain News and the Denver Post. Items of more limited local interest found a place in such early Jefferson County newspapers as the Jefferson County Graphic, Jefferson County Republican, Morrison Monitor, Colorado Transcript and Golden Transcript.

The Mountaineer was a simple little mimeographed publication when it began in February 1946 but its masthead was ambitious. It described itself as a "Mid-Weekly for the Evergreen Empire." Later, it became a hybrid—a pre-printed format of national news with local items reproduced in designated spaces. It lasted only until January 28 1948. The most charming article we found in the Mountaineer files was by Mary A. Livonius of Blue Creek Road, about a week in the life of her lovable but unpredictable father.

The Mountain News seems to have been the first bona fide local weekly in Evergreen. It was published out of an office at 57 Main Street from 1950 to 1959. For most of that time, its owners and publishers were Ruth and George Gilfillan. An article in the Colorado Editor Magazine of April 1956 describes how they came west from Detroit, to visit a son stationed at Fort Carson. Exploring the surrounding area, they "stopped in the beautiful mountain and resort center of Evergreen. In the window of the Mountain News was a 'For Sale' sign. They bought it."

Though they were both newspaper people, they knew nothing about printing. In two weeks, they learned from the previous owner everything they could about operating a "12 x 18 Chandler and Price Kluge, an Old Style Gordon, and hand-setting type." After that, they were on their own.

By 1956, they were setting about one-third of the type: the rest was set in Denver where the paper was printed. In addition to getting out a 6-page weekly (10 pages in the week of the annual Evergreen Rodeo) they printed letterheads, business cards and wedding announcements. Ruth was typesetter and pressman, as well as running the town's book shop in the same building as the paper. George was editor and manager, proof-reader and layout man.

We could find out very little about why the Mountain News went out of existence in 1959. According to Arleta Alderfer, the Gilfillans left to take over a newspaper in another mountain community, possibly Leadville.

The Canyon Courier mushroomed from an unlikely beginning as a mimeographed monthly bulletin put out by members of the Indian Hills Volunteer Fire Department. Started in May 1955, it was called "Smoke Signals" and had two main objectives: an energetic public relations campaign on behalf of both the Indian Hills Improvement Association and the newly-formed Fire Department, and the betterment of communications between different communities in the mountain area.

The monthly effort soon grew beyond the capacities of the original volunteers—Dick Perkins, Norman McDonald, Indian Hills Postmistress Fran Wald and Wayne Turner—to sell ads, write editorials, type copy, and stamp and address envelopes. They began sending their typewritten stories to Vern and Helen Manning, Kansas friends of the MacDonalds, who had a small printing business. Two years after the project began, the Mannings moved to Evergreen and took over publication.

At this point, Willard Crain entered the picture. With 20 years experience in the retail and wholesale florist business, Crain was former president of Florists' Telegraph Delivery Association International. As such, he was associated for many years with the publishing of FTD News. For nine years he also edited an in-house organ in Denver, the Park Elitch Parade.

The Crains had lived since 1947 in Evergreen, where they had started the Evergreen Crafters as a little business that was later taken over by their daughter and son-in-law, Ross and Nancy Grimes. Willard became actively involved in many

Willard Crain.

community affairs and was one of the founding members of the Evergreen Volunteer Fire Department, the Evergreen Ambulance Service, the Chamber of Commerce, the Evergreen Players and the Jefferson County Historical Society.

Crain approached the Chamber of Commerce with the idea that Smoke Signals was an ideal beginning for a weekly Evergreen area newspaper. The Chamber agreed—and told him he was just the person to take it on.

With a name change to the Canyon Courier, the expanded paper came out with its first issue on October 23, 1958. Vern Manning was editor and publisher, Willard Crain the Executive editor and Fran Wald Associate editor. It was a gruelling schedule for Crain to get the newspaper out each week, especially as he was also in charge of getting the ads to pay the bills.

He soon roped his wife, Mary Helen Crain, into helping with the writing. Her weekly column, Chit Chat, was immensely popular, as were her articles on local Evergreen history, which resulted in the publication of two books, **Evergreen, Colorado** and **A Circle of Pioneers**. Mary Helen continued to write for the paper until 1975.

Together with Willard and daughter-in-law Sandy Crain, Mary Helen was a founding member of the Jefferson County Historical Society (Sandy became the second Director of the Hiwan Homestead Historical Museum in 1986). In 1978, Mary Helen Crain was fittingly recognized as Evergreen's Historian Emeritus and Person of the Year by the Chamber of Commerce.

Owen and Katherine Ball.

"This has to make a difference in handling stories, and requires a great deal more tact if the essence of the story is to appear. The bull-in-a-china-shop reporter won't last long in the small town: nor will the editor who makes a fetish of attacking advertisers or established institutions to prove he's got guts. He may prove the latter, but he won't have a newspaper very long. At the same time, I see no need to knuckle under, suppress news, kowtow to advertisers, or otherwise do anything that compromises principles."

Ball certainly had to deal with his share of momentous issues facing Evergreen at a time of explosive growth: incorporation, how to pay for school expansion, the best way to provide for recreation, traffic problems, disputes over planning and zoning—and the giant of them all, the proposed 1976 Olympics. Ball's major aim was to provide a forum for all sides to have their say.

Paid circulation when Ball bought the paper was around 1700. When he sold it in January 1975 to William Johnson, it was 5,500. In size, it had grown from 16 pages to between 36 and 40.

Ball's major reason for selling was that, with the continuing growth of Evergreen and it's economy, there was a need for more than a family-type newspaper operation.

The new owner, William Potter Johnson, was a newspaperman of a totally different type. His interest was in the business side of a paper. Far too many weeklies, in his opinion, were owned by former reporters and editors with no background in business. Potter's first newspaper acquisition was in Sebastopol, California.

In 1960, the Canyon Courier was bought by Olen and Mary Bell who had been publishers of the Aurora Advocate since 1949.

In May of 1963 the paper was sold again, to Owen Ball. He was to be the energetic owner, publisher and editor for the next 11 years, years of transition for the Evergreen community.

Ball was managing editor of the Miami News in Florida before coming to Evergreen. He had always wanted to own a small town newspaper, and shopped around for five years for the right one. At first, he was shocked by the pressure involved in getting out a small weekly as compared with a metropolitan daily: "I worked seven days a week, many of those days sixteen hours, missing meals and wondering if it was worth it." He was editor, bookkeeper, phone answerer and "miscellaneous doer".

Every member of his family was roped in. At a pinch, he, his wife and two children could get the newspaper out by themselves. At first the paper was printed on an ancient sheet-fed Webendorfer Press, the whole process taking 30 hours. Printing was partly contracted out from 1966 on, but it wasn't until 1969 that the "Webendorfer was shut down forever."

Another difference Ball found was that in the small town you know every newsmaker personally, while in a big city "you deal mostly with strangers."

Bill Johnson.

As soon as Ball was ready to sell the Courier, Bill Johnson and his wife, Pauley, bought it. Johnson immediately hired as editor someone who would be involved in the community and would "accept all the bouquets and all the brickbats." This liberated Johnson to get on with what really fascinated him—the advertising and marketing of the product.

Johnson subsequently acquired many other Colorado newspapers under the banner of Johnson Newspapers, Inc. He also gave the Conifer/285-Corridor a paper of its own, the High Timber Times. Although allergies to evergreen trees forced the Johnson family to move to Arizona, Bill Johnson himself spent about half of the month at work in Colorado.

John Fellows.

The first editor under Johnson was John Fellows, a University of Colorado graduate who has lived in Evergreen since 1974. Fellows served until he left to work with Coors Brewery in Golden—though continuing to write a regular humorous column for the Courier. Successive editors—including Carole McKelvey, Douglas McCrimmon and Debbie Marshall—aided by a changing corps of young, capable and dedicated reporters, continued to produce a newspaper that strove to cover the major events and issues in the life of this mountain area.

The Courier makes room for profiles of interesting individuals, both old-timers and newcomers, coverage of the natural world and wildlife issues in Sylvia Brockner's column, and information about local sports in great detail. It covers developments in the community's economic life and devotes space to news about clubs and other organizations. The editorial page takes stands on issues affecting the mountain area, and features columns by staffers and ex-staffers. Guest editorial space is generously given to individuals to express their views.

Jacque Scott.

As in most small town newspapers, the classifed section and letters to the editor are widely read—as is the law and order coverage labelled "Sheriff's Calls".

The High Timber Times is edited by Jacque Scott, a fourth-generation Coloradoan whose family has lived for many years on Upper Bear Creek. Jacque spent some years in Hawaii, graduating from University there and gaining quite a reputation as a television newscaster before coming to live in Evergreen. She was a lively and prolific writer for the Canyon Courier and the Evergreen Magazine until taking on the High Timber Times assignment. In November of 1986, the Canyon Courier and the High Timber Times were both sold to a newspaper executive from Charlottesville, North Carolina, named Dennis Scott Rooker.

Bill Johnson, who had owned the Courier from almost 13 years, said of the sale, "It's a bittersweet day. I am sad leaving Evergreen because I . . . loved the area, love the people . . . it's the end of an era." Johnson said that Rooker had the financial resources as well as the hands-on newspaper experience to take on these mountain publications, at a time of continuing growth and change in the Front Range communities. Rooker named Kamal Eways of Chicago, Illinois, as the new publisher and president of Evergreen Newsapapers Inc.

Evergreen Magazine was a high quality magazine published twice a year by Johnson Newspapers. It featured fine color photography and articles on every conceivable aspect of living in this community. Some issues contained poetry, others

fiction, and the magazine also served as a guide to seasonal happenings. The first issue came out in the Spring of 1977. Like many good things, the cost was too great and the support too little. Evergreen Magazine ceased publication with its issue of Summer, 1983.

The Mountain Commuter was a creative and intelligent newspaper that was published from October of 1979 to February of 1983. It was the brainchild of Charles and Alice McNamara, who had grown tired of living in the 'big city' of Denver and moved to Pine Junction in 1976. Chuck is a journalism graduate of Arizona University and has a master's degree from the University of Northern Colorado. His background and experience—after a four-year stint in the Army as a newspaper editor and information officer—was in public relations, advertising and journalism.

Alice McNamara.

Charles McNamara.

For a year after publication began, Alice continued to work in Denver to help pay the bills while Chuck poured all his energies and experience into writing the new publication, selling ads and arranging for distribution. Alice was an economics and accounting major at the University of Arizona and worked on legal newspapers and as office manager of a law firm before becoming Mountain Commuter's manager of production. The publication was a monthly one but advertisers began to pressure for more frequent issues to compete with the weeklies.

The recession in the Denver area economy, in Chuck's words "devastated Evergreen's retailers." Ads were increasingly hard to sell and the McNamaras felt they had to make a choice between cheapening their product or stopping publication of "a thoughtfully-written and designed newsmagazine."

The McNamaras chose to close that chapter of their lives and convert their equipment and staff to a design and advertising and publishing firm.

Chuck became an active and innovative President of the Evergreen Chamber of Commerce in 1983-4. Since the family was happily settled in an area church fellowship and loved the small town atmosphere, they decided to make Evergreen their 'hometown'.

Evergreen Today was a project started by Carol Wilcox and Cary Stiff who founded the Idaho Springs Clear Creek Courant in 1973. The Evergreen newspaper started publication in 1980 but apparently did not find enough subscriber and advertiser support to continue operations. The paper was phased out by merging with the Courant in December of 1982.

From time to time a new magazine or newspaper, free to the public, makes it's appearance on the Evergreen scene. Some last for a few issues, others much longer. Among recent appearances, we might mention **Spree**, an arts magazine that started a separate Evergreen issue, with the primary aim of focussing attention on attainment of one of the community's long-time dreams—the creation of a performing arts center in the community through the organization known as the

161

Evergreen Center for the Arts (ECA). Spree's subtitle is "Evergreen's Newsmagazine of the Arts", and it describes itself as "dedicated to the promotion and furtherance of the arts in Evergreen area and the Rocky Mountain Region."

Spree highlights developments in the on-going ECA saga, describes upcoming arts events—exhibits, concerts, performances of plays, musicals, dance—profiles individuals in the arts who live in the mountain area and introduces some elements from the Denver arts scene. It carries regular advertising and also does "Spotlight on Business" segments, profiling individual enterprises.

Spree is owned by Jon and Peg DeStefano, who are responsible altogether for 24 monthly publications. One of these is the monthly newspaper of the Denver Classroom Teachers' Association, which Jon edited for 15 years.

The DeStefanos came to Colorado in 1963 and have lived in Evergreen since 1979, with their family of four children. Peg's university background is in English literature, Jon's in education. He taught English and journalism for almost 7 years in the Denver Public Schools before becoming a full-time publisher.

Debbie Marshall.

Debbie Marshall *joined the staff of the Courier in 1977 as sports editor, having graduated from the University of Iowa in journalism and psychology. Debbie served in many capacities, won many awards, and eventually became Courier Editor. She took a leave of absence in late 1986 to enjoy the experience of a new baby.*

Carole McKelvey.

Carole McKelvey *had a busy and responsible career with Johnson Newspapers—serving as Editor of the Courier, Editor of the Evergreen magazine and Editor of one of their western slope newspapers—before leaving to join the staff of the Rocky Mountain News. There she rose to the position of Editor of the Sunday Magazine. Carole consistently won awards for her work while with JNI, and continues to do so at the News.*

Doug McCrimmon *served for 23 years in the U.S. Navy, where his career culminated in command of the aircraft carrier Ranger. He then moved to Evergreen and worked with a Denver firm manufacturing commercial greenhouses. He joined the Courier in 1981 and became successively its managing editor, general manager of both the Courier and Johnson Newspapers Inc., and Publisher of the Courier and vice-president of JNI. McCrimmon ran into some conflict-of-interest allegations in 1982, when he announced his candidacy for the office of County Commissioner in the Republican primary while still retaining his leadership role in the publishing of the Courier. Eventually, he dropped out of the political race. Later, he also took on another business assignment in Denver and left the newspaper business in Evergreen, except that he continued his weekly column, "The View from Here."*

Doug McCrimmon.

Jill Jamieson-Nichols *was named Acting Editor of the Courier when Marshall went on maternity leave. She graduated from the University of Southern Colorado in journalism and worked as a reporter in Alamosa before coming to live in Golden. She joined the Courier in 1983 as a part-time reporter and was soon promoted to Associate Editor.*

Jill Jamieson-Nichols.

Sally Bassett.

Sally Bassett *was also a regular award-winner while at the Courier, especially for her feature articles and profiles based on personal interviewing. She also wrote some fascinating articles for the Evergreen magazine. Bassett came to the Denver area from Massachussetts in 1968 to attend the University of Denver—where she studied creative writing and journalism—and never left. Before moving to Evergreen in 1976 and joining the Courier as Associate Editor in 1977, Bassett worked for the Sentinel Newspapers in southeast Denver. She now lives and works in Denver.*

MEETING SOCIAL NEEDS

Clubs and Voluntary Organizations

Miss Julia Douglas, our town's first Librarian, would be astonished by the Evergreen of the 1980's. From the little mountain community of the 1920's that had, as she lamented, *"no clubs or organizations of community support"*, it has developed an overlapping network of between 60 and 125 organizations—the number depending on which kinds of groups are included.

The Evergreen Area Community Advisory Group, in gathering data for its recommendations about a master plan presented to the County Commissioners in 1986, found 61 *"clubs and organizations"* and an additional 32 homeowners associations. Few groups affiliated with churches were included.

Organizations run the gamut from nationally affiliated women's groups (like A.A.U.W., League of Women Voters, National Organization of Women, Daughters of the American Revolution) and men's fraternal and service clubs (Kiwanis, Elks, Rotary) to groups catering for specific ages (Seniors, pre-school mothers, the newly-divorced, Boy Scouts, Camp Fire Girls, 4-H) and specific interests (naturalists, duck-lovers, gardeners, weavers, potters, amateur players and singers, photographers, bridge players, stamp collectors, writers, quilters).

There are support groups for worthy organizations, like the Friends of Forest Heights Lodge, the Friends of the Evergreen Library, the Evergreen Chapter of Children's Hospital Guild.

Some groups are associated with political parties, some with schools, others with local churches. Some have a continuous life from their beginning. Others, like the succession of groups formed to combat unplanned, unattractive or environmentally questionable growth—Mountain Area Planning Council, Protect our Mountain Environment, the Evergreen Design Task Force—may flourish for a while then fade away.

There is a dynamic Newcomers' group that helps incoming residents to know the community and an active Animal Protective Association that sees to the welfare of stray or abandoned pets. A wide variety of volunteer organizations, from the Fire Department to the Alpine Rescue Team and the Jefferson County Sheriff's Mounted Posse, give trained help in emergency situations.

One way of writing the history of Evergreen, from the 1930's on, would be in terms of its growing and changing network of social organizations. But that task will have to be done by others.

The raw data exists—in the club columns of local newspapers, the minutes of individual organizations, the memories of long-time residents, and some of the oral history interviews done by various organizations.

For instance, as part of the Jefferson County Public Library History Project, former Librarian Jane Kemble commented on the social life of Evergreen. She summered here on an off from 1920 and came to settle with her sister in 1952.

"There weren't too many churches," she said, *"but my Lord o'Mercy I don't know how many were built after (we came). My sister and I were always in on these things."* She remembered that the Presbyterians sold donuts from a truck every Saturday to raise funds for their new church, and that she and her sister nearly killed themselves eating enough of *"those Presbyterian donuts"* to help out.

One winter, she remembered, she and her sister baked all the cookies for the PTA. *"I'd never had chick nor child, I'd never had anything to do with PTA, and I was just amazed at the number of things they were trying to do. So I would go to these meetings faithfully."*

There are references to specific organizations throughout this book. Here, in symbolic tribute to the immense contribution made by voluntary groups to the richness and depth of life in the mountain area, is the story of the oldest continuous club in Evergreen.

Blue Spruce Kiwanis annual volunteer clean-up.

We are indebted to Mrs. Maude Smith for most of our information about the **Evergreen Woman's Club**. She came to Evergreen in 1922 and lived here, except for winters in Arizona in her later years, until her death in 1984. She wrote a little history of the club in 1980, and also talked with us about it when we interviewed her.

The club grew out of a small weekly gathering of 5 or 6 women in the Episcopal Church parlor. They would bring their young children and *"visit"* while they did their own knitting and sewing. Then, *"in 1938, several enterprising young women—namely Rosabel Schneider, Dorothy Young, Marge Herzman and Louise Hendryx—decided that Evergreen needed some kind of organization to sew for the needy and provide fellowship for its members, as there was no social club in the area at the time."*

The two groups joined forces and organized the Evergreen Woman's Club in 1938. Qualifications for membership were that you lived in the area, attended three meetings, promised to entertain once a year and worked on craft articles *"according to your ability"*. Meetings were held monthly in members' homes. The hostess served coffee and dessert. Members brought their young children with them, and left at 3 p.m. to be home when older children arrived from school.

Until Evergreen got a bank, Maude Smith—who was treasurer and materials buyer for 17 years—kept the club's money in a metal box in the safe of the Evergreen Public Service Co. Her main purchases were *"yards of pillow tubing, unbleached muslin, gingham, yarn and crochet cotton."*

163

Money was raised mostly from two annual sales, in July and November. The club welcomed summer members who not only made and donated items but also did their Christmas shopping at the sales. In addition to handcraft items, the club sold homemade foods. *"One lady, who baked for her husband's grocery store, brought two dozen cream puffs. Another made delicious pies which we sold for $1.00 apiece. Others excelled in cakes, brownies, cookies, bread, taffy, fudge, divinity, baked beans and potato salad."*

annual Fall Festival and *"made popcorn balls for each student at Christmas time—until the enrolment reached 80 students."*

In 1962, the Club got around to writing by-laws and assessing dues of $3.00 per member. In 1974, under the presidency of Hazel Humphrey, the Club became affiliated with the National and Colorado Federation of Women's Clubs.

Evergreen Woman's Club, 1948. Front row (seated), l. to r., Mrs. Maude McCracken, Mrs. Don Ambler. Second row, Mrs. Lewis Marsh, Mrs. Harry Rockey, Mrs. Kitty Scott. Standing and top row, Mrs. Maude Smith, Miss Clara Sperry, Mrs. Laird King, Mrs. Leonard (guest), Mrs. Willard Crain, Mrs. Beth King and Mrs Ed. Dieter.

Summer meetings were often picnics or luncheons at local hotels: Troutdale, Brook Forest Inn, Beaver Brook, the Singing River Ranch. Thanksgiving was a pot luck at the Reynolds Ranch (now an Open Space Park) with Mrs. Reynolds contributing elk meat balls and spaghetti.

Over the years, this Evergreen Woman's Club quietly financed an incredible variety of community needs and services. They bought cooking equipment and tea towels so the school could have a lunch program; paid for the restoration of the pioneer Buffalo Park School that now sits on the grounds of Wilmot School; sponsored a grand clean-up of the Evergreen Cemetery; bought tools for the Cemetery Association, band instruments and a piano for the High School, a fire siren for the fire department and trash barrels for downtown Evergreen. In addition, they contributed to most ongoing community services, sponsored an

In 1983, the Evergreen Club was recognized by the Colorado Federation for its contributions in conservation, education, public service and the visual arts, and also received the President's Award for maintaining the high ideals and principles of the Federation.

The Evergreen Woman's Club is still a vital element of our community. Though the first image that comes to mind today may be of Cornish Pasties, those delicious hot pies filled with meat and potatoes that the Club sells at the annual Mountain Rendezvous, the charitable side of their work goes quietly on, with annual donations to causes they believe important to Evergreen. In recent years, primary recipients have been the Alpine Rescue Team, Colorado Philharmonic Orchestra, Evergreen Ambulance Service, Evergreen Volunteer Fire Department and the Mount Evans Hospice.

Entertainment, Social Life and Celebrations

The Mountain Rendezvous, which takes place annually in Heritage Grove during Rodeo Weekend, is a showcase for local non-profit organizations and a good place to get acquainted with a sampling of Evergreen's social network.

Evergreen is quite good at celebrations, which punctuate the year and help to bring this physically scattered mountain community together.

Summer starts off with a bang on the Fourth of July. It is Summerfest time in Evergreen, sponsored by the Evergreen Center for the Arts. A three-day event, it involves a fine celebration in Heritage Grove—with continuous entertainment on a specially-constructed stage—an arts and crafts fair, food booths and activities for children. On the Fourth itself, the day starts out with the 5K and 10K Freedom Run, which benefits the Mount Evans Hospice. Later activities focus on the Lake, with a pancake breakfast, Crazy Boat Race, rousing concert by the National Repertory Orchestra (formerly the Colorado Philharmonic) and a high-quality fireworks display at dusk, put on by the Chamber of Commerce. As many as 12,000 people show up for the concert and fireworks. Some of the rest of us sit on strategic rooftops and watch in relative calm as brilliant bursts light up the Lake and the mountains.

Next comes the Rodeo. This has traditionally been the first weekend in August, though a 1986 decision by the Rodeo Association to reaffiliate with the Professional Rodeo Cowboys' Association may push it back to June. Saturday morning sees all those who love a parade jamming Main Street to watch the floats, bands, antique cars, horseback riders (and garbage can drill team, or other humorous inspiration of the Evergreen Disposal Service) pass by the judges' stand. The Parade assembles off Highway 74 by the Public Service Company, and ends at Heritage Grove.

Here, the next phase of the celebration is in full swing from 11 in the morning to five in the evening. The Mountain Rendezvous, which celebrated its tenth year in 1986, is sponsored by the Jefferson County Historical Society. An inspired combination of exhibits and demonstrations of skills of the "mountain man" era of western history, with booths manned by representatives of non-profit organizations in the Evergreen area, the Rendezvous annually attracts over 10,000 visitors. Again, there is continuous live entertainment, mostly from Evergreen's own talented amateur groups and individuals. The booths offer food, drink, hand-crafted items and games. The organizations get a chance to showcase themselves and their objectives and do a little fund-raising.

The Rodeo has performances at its arena in El Pinal on Saturday and Sunday afternoons. On Sunday morning, the Evergreen Town Race is run down Upper Bear Creek. 2,500 entrants make the 5K or 10K effort each year, about half from the Evergreen area.

The third big event of summer is the Fine Arts Fair sponsored by the Evergreen Artists' Association. This was started in 1968 as a sidewalk artists show on Main Street, and later moved to Heritage Grove. It takes place usually on the last weekend in August and is a serious artistic event. All entrants are selected by jury. At the Fair itself, prizes are awarded in eight categories of fine arts and crafts.

Winter celebrations take place almost continuously from Thanksgiving to Christmas. While there are variations from year to year, there are certain staples. The two Evergreen Kiwanis Clubs and other volunteers ring bells for donations to the traditional Salvation Army kettles outside the two major grocery stores and at certain other locations. Many organizations contribute their services to collect money and food for distribution to mountain families down on their luck. Santa puts in an appearance—by helicopter, sleigh or horse-drawn cart—on Main Street, at the Library, in some of the newer shopping centers like Bergen Park and Genesee.

The Winterfest Faire, sponsored by the Evergreen Center for the Arts, is an event of growing popularity that takes place on a Saturday at the beginning of December at the Open High School and the County Building, off Highway 73. As many as 75 artisans and craftsmen bring their wares for display and sale. 60% are from the Denver metro area, but the rest come from as far away as Iowa and Nebraska.

Crowd at Evergreen Lake for Fourth of July fireworks.

Susie Vancil conducts Alpine Choristers in Summerfest performance.

Summerfest: Evergreen Chorale performance from "My Fair Lady."

165

The annual Rodeo Parade down Main Street.

On the same day, TENAS (The Evergreen Naturalists Audubon Society) sponsors a charming event in the Reading Park at the Evergreen Library. Children are invited to bring an edible ornament to decorate an outdoor Christmas Trees for the Birds, followed by carolling and marshmallow-roasting over an open fire.

On another Saturday evening in December is the annual lighting of the Evergreen Christmas tree at Evergreen Lake. Santa and candy may be waiting for the children, and there is hot cider and carolling for all.

One of the most joyful of all Evergreen Christmas events is the winter concert of the Evergreen Chorale, which used to take place in an area church but in recent years has been a sold-out event in the Marshdale School auditorium.

It is easy to assume that in Evergreen's early days, when population was sparse and money limited, social activities for the year-round population would have been limited to extended family gatherings and events sponsored by school, grange of church. But an intriguing news item in the Colorado Transcript of February 18, 1885 made us realize that further research by some future local historian may turn up unexpected festivities.

Headlined *"Minstrel Show",* the article reports that *"on the last day of January the inhabitants of Evergreen and the vicinity were delighted and amused at witnessing a dramatic and musical entertainment given by members of the Evergreen Lyceum."* A *"nigger minstrel show ably rendered by the 'Armstrong troupe'"* was followed by *"declamations, recitations and duets"* and the performance was *"concluded with a little drama titled The California Uncle."*

Besides the Armstrong brothers, the following performers were listed: Douglas Wilmot, J. B. Nelson, F. D. Hines, Will Trumbull, E. Oliver, and A. A. Robinson, *"also the following ladies: Miss Dottie Stuart, Miss Mabel Bennet, Mrs. Nora Fuller and Mrs. Lizzie Armstrong."*

That there was a lively summer social season in Evergreen, there is no doubt. Especially after the establishment of the Denver Mountain Parks there was a great flurry of summer home-building in the Evergreen area. A 1916 Rocky Mountain News article titled, *"Bear Creek Fast Becoming One of Denver's Great Show Places"* notes that, *"Capital is flocking to Bear Creek."* Resorts are *"springing up in a night",* building operations are progressing *"all along the line",* and *"thousands of dollars are being spent in handsome homes."*

A great many of Denver's rich, famous and socially elite families chose to locate their summer homes in Evergreen. Summer time was a virtual round of luncheons, picnics, horseback rides, cocktail and dinner parties. These involved people in summer residence, their relatives and house guests from everywhere, and visitors driving up from Denver.

For a brief 20 years, from 1921 until the outbreak of the second war, the Sidles' Troutdale Hotel was a brilliant focus for summer society, providing an enchanted setting for every kind of social activity from a small luncheon to a moonlight horseback expedition or an elegant costume ball.

We heard about summer social life and Troutdale from many people we interviewed—Herb Wallower, Freddie Lincoln, Joan Landy, the Rozzi Clarks, Arleta Alderfer, Father Marsh. Two individual stories help to bring the picture to life.

The first is a romantic and sad tale. It is about two young lovers whose apparently idyllic marriage was cut short by death after less than five years. She was Margery Reed, daughter of Verner Z. Reed, who was not only one of Denver's wealthiest men but one with a lively mind and a wide range of interests.

166

The Denver Post described Margery as *"one of the most popular and brilliant young women in Denver society, possessing a rare intellect and charming beauty. She traveled extensively thru Europe Later she was an instructor in the Later whe was an instructor in the literary department of the University of Denver and her books have been eagerly sought after in literary circles throughout the nation."*

At Denver University, Margery met Paul Mayo, the son of methodist minister Henry Chilton Mayo—who was active in building the University of Denver in its days as the Colorado Seminary. Paul received his B.A. and M.A. at D.U. before volunteering for service in France in the first world war. He returned to teach in the English Department at Denver University and, in January of 1920, he married Margery Reed.

The marriage was a quiet one for such a high level of Denver society: it was conducted in the shadow of the recent deaths of both the father of the bride and the father of the groom. Even so, there were 100 guests, including the Colorado Governor, the Chancellor of Denver University, H. Tammen, co-owner of the Denver Post, Mrs. Charles Boettcher and an assortment of the most influential professional and business people in town.

The newly-weds commissioned Denver's favorite society architect, Jake Benedict, to design them a town home and a mountain hideaway on a hill above Bear Creek, not far from Mrs. Phipp's recently completed Greystone

Entertainment at Mountain Rendezvous.

Camp. Included in a delightful little leather-bound book of poetry titled simply *"Love Cycle"*, Margery expressed her feelings about the mountains and her new love.

THESE hills at night, like mystic visions
Rising far above the earth
Where souls are freed from sordid man-
  made ways
And cleansed of daily things.

My Soul, uncomprehending seeks in vain
Then stands back in mute acceptance
Aghast before these works of God
Mystery unsolved that shrouds this earth
What soul can touch its depth.
Longing, searching, all have gone
Life is new radiance is mine as I stand
Far above the cities of the plains
In this quiet refuge.

Struggles, sorrows, all have faded
The still breath of night is on these
  mountains
Peace has come to me—
And the perfect love of man.

Mountain Rendezvous in Heritage Grove.

Paul Mayo decided to study for the difficult examinations to enter the diplomatic service, and passed with flying colors. The young couple left for Lima, Peru, in 1923 where he took up his first foreign service post. There in 1925, Margery contracted an incurable disease: though she was brought home by boat in the hope that some cure might be found in the U.S., she died.

167

168

People who knew Paul Mayo say that he never recovered from Margery's death. He married again twice and had two children; continued his diplomatic career in Belgium for a number of years; then returned to teach at Denver University (of which he was a generous benefactor), alternating this with further studies at universities here and abroad.

But he also took to drinking too much and died far too young in 1940. We talked with a number of long-time Evergreen residents who knew Paul Mayo, either socially or through working for him on his estate at what has now become known as the Rosedale Castle. All describe him as a warm, generous and intelligent person. But most of our information comes from our old friends, Peg and Ralph Mayo, who also have a long and varied association with the Evergreen community.

As Margaret Oliver, Peg spent part the happiest part of her childhood—from 1919 to 1925—on a 4800-acre ranch along Deer Creek, in the shadow of Mount Rosalie. She never forgot the satisfaction of home-made food and entertainment nor the joy of living in the beauty of a mountain setting.

She met Ralph Mayo while both were students at Denver University. Ralph was Paul Mayo's nephew and the son of Ralph B. Mayo, who built up the largest independent accounting practice in Denver, which eventually became—by merger—the Denver office of Arthur Young and Co.

Ralph remembers that during their courtship, he sometimes brought Peg up to the elegant tea-dances at the Troutdale Hotel. They were married in 1936. Ralph went into his father's firm and the newly weds started to live the normal social life of a successful young Denver couple, contributing their time and talents to worthwhile community endeavors.

But Peg was yearning for the mountains. When we met them in 1948 (Barbara and Peg were both graduate students in the Sociology Department at D. U.) the Mayos were building a cabin on a steep hill above Highway 73, a family enterprise which also involved their two sons. Some years later, when their sons were grown, they had a brand-new home built on Bear Mountain, looking over a magnificent panorama of the Mount Evans range.

Peg continues with her skilful handweaving, though illness has forced her to scale this down from the rugs and wall-hangings she used to create. Ralph continued to serve on the boards of many civic and cultural organizations—both in Denver and in Evergreen—until a 1986 stroke forced his retirement. They still attend faithfully the winter concerts of the Denver Symphony and the summer offerings of the National Repertory Orchestra.

Another lively source of information about the development of Evergreen's social life was our neighbor, Freddie Lincoln. Forest Lynne, the rustic home where Freddie lives today, was first rented by her grandfather in the summer of 1919. He bought it the following year.

Owen LeFevre had come to Denver with his wife Eva from Ohio. They had only one child, Freddie's mother, who had a beautiful singing voice. Much of their time was spent in Europe so she could have the best of singing lessons. In 1912 she married Harry Bellamy of Denver, and in 1915 Freddie was born.

The original purchase included only 40 acres. The first additional land, bordering Highway 74, was purchased after Paul Mayo presented Freddie with a horse. Her father said that was fine but they had nowhere to pasture it, so Paul would have to sell them some meadow land. Which he did *"at a very small price."*

It was strictly a summer retreat, with no phone and little contact with neighbors: Mr. Bellamy came up only for weekends. Slowly an adult summer social life developed in Evergreen, and young people like Freddie started socializing with friends they knew from Denver. Freddie enjoyed dressing up occasionally to go dancing at the Troutdale pavilion. She admired the *"handsome cowboys"* there, and remembers seeing slot machines on the premises in the later '20's. But she preferred the informality of Bendemeer, which at that time was a delightful lodge and cabins owned by the Hoffschroeders, who also ran had a successful cafeteria in Denver.

Freddie met her handsome young army officer, George Lincoln, when he was a lieutenant stationed at Fort Logan. *"He had a happy assignment building CCC camps all*

Wedding of Margery Reed and Paul T. Mayo. Standing, left to right: Verner Z. Reed, Jr., Ralph Mayo, Paul Mayo, the groom, Joseph Reed. Sitting: Mrs. John Leeming Jr., matron of honor, Mrs. Paul Mayo, the bride, Miss Helen Yeaman, bridesmaid.

169

over the state." They were married in 1936. From then on, Freddie lived the interesting and sometimes demanding life of an Army officer's wife, raising her four children in a number of different environments. Her husband, generally known as Abe, became a Brigadier General: he taught at West Point, served overseas during the second war and also in Washington. One of Freddie's lifelong passions, which she transmitted to all her children and still exercises today, was for horses and for riding.

Freddie has entered into the new life of Evergreen as a year-round community, serving actively in many organizations including P.O.M.E., the Historical Society, the Colorado Philharmonic. Her children have lived in many different places—the Phillipines, Egypt, Iran—but now two of them live near her: son Dan, retired after 20 years in the army and living with his wife Beth in the remodelled second house bought in 1963, and daughter Joyce Conrey, a teacher at King- Murphy School, who lives in

General George ("Abe") Lincoln.

Harry and Freddie Bellamy (parents of Freddie Lincoln) around 1948.

a nearby home with her husband, Keith, and two children. Another daughter, Lorna, who also lived in Evergreen, was tragically killed in an auto accident in 1981. The Lincoln's oldest daughter Fritzi lives near Castle Rock with her Iranian husband, Manucher Riahi.

Harry Bellamy considered selling Forest Lynne, because Freddie rarely seemed to be able to get back to it, but she persuaded him that as long as he and her mother enjoyed it, it should stay in the family. He died in 1956, and her mother in 1963.

Abe loved the Evergreen retreat as much as Freddie, and in 1963 they bought a second adjoining property. After Lincoln's retirement, they decided to make their permanent home at Forest Lynne: a thought, Freddie says, that would never have occurred to her grandfather or her father.

Abe Lincoln enjoyed the peaceful life of a gentleman- rancher: we fondly remember him chopping wood, mending fences and reminiscing about his many adventures and associations during his years in the army. He served a brief and hectic stint as the nation's Energy Czar (Director of the Office of Emergency Preparedness) in 1969, and continued with occasional university teaching. He died suddenly, as perhaps he would have wished, on horseback, while making a visit to the Air Force Academy in Colorado Springs.

The Lincoln family in 1954. Back row, left to right: Frederica Bellamy Lincoln, Daniel lincoln, Lorna Lincoln, Frederica LeFevre Bellamy. Front: Frederica (Fritzi) Lincoln, Joyce Lincoln.

Housing for the Elderly in Evergreen.

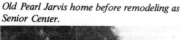

Old Pearl Jarvis home before remodeling as Senior Center.

Carriage House remodeled.

In addition to its more glamorous events, Troutdale also offered *"picture shows"* to the community, but was not the first to do so. A story recorded by Mary Helen Crain notes that a mother and daughter—Mrs. Mary Castell and Mrs. Beth Goodrich—built a small movie theater near their home (on a site now occupied by the Bear Creek Mall) which proved very popular but had a short life: after less than a year, its entire roof collapsed under the weight of snow from a particularly heavy storm.

But by then, Prince McCracken was building the dancehall next to his large drug store (both now in use as the Little Bear). In summers—when there were enough paying customers around—McCracken would cover the dance floor and show movies.

Around 1940 came the Trail Theater, located just off Main Street on Douglas Park Road. This awkward-looking little building served as Evergreen's movie house until the mid-70's, when a brand-new facility was opened in the Showbarn Center next to the old Hiwan barn. Originally affiliated with the Flick, an art cinema in Larimer Square, it was later remodelled into a twin-theater facility.

The Trail Theater went through a succession of uses, including a spell as a home of electronic games for teens: in 1986 it was the Coal Mine Dragon Chinese restaurant.

The Senior Scene
Life must be pretty healthy in the mountains—there are a lot of senior citizens here. The Jefferson County Seniors' Resource Center believes that about 2,500 people over 65 live in the mountain area and expects the number to grow to over 6,000 by the year 2000.

There are two institutions serving the elderly in the Evergreen community. The first is a subsidized senior housing complex, Green Ridge Meadows, located on Highway 74 in North Evergreen. The second is Mountain Services, one of many programs of the county-wide Jefferson County Seniors' Resource Center (SRC).

Plans to build Green Ridge Meadows were first announced in 1978. In May of that year the Jefferson County Planning Commission approved the project: in September, HUD gave its go-

ahead for a 108-unit apartment building, granting a $4 million subsidy over 30 years to aid seniors who could not otherwise afford the full economic rent. Though bids came in high in 1979, and the project had to be scaled down to 79 units, construction went ahead and the facility was opened in 1981. The need for the project is demonstrated by the fact that its units are always in demand.

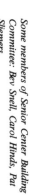

Some members of Senior Center Building Committee: Bev Snell, Carol Hinds, Pat Sliemers.

170

Some of the occupants are Evergreen natives, many are long-time residents here. It seems certain that Green Ridge Meadows has enabled many to stay near family and friends in Evergreen.

The complex has also made it easier to know the needs of the older ranks of the elderly in our community, and to serve them better.

Until 1986, Mountain Services was headquartered in Green Ridge Meadows. This organization provides a variety of services to the elderly here—with the major goal of helping them to maintain their independence. Senior Wheels offers transportation from homes to medical appointments, stores, recreational events. Meals on Wheels supplies hot daily meals. People are helped to survive crises through a well-organized peer counselling program. Emergency food and fuel needs are met through a food and wood bank. Part-time employment is organized for those who need it, and meaningful volunteer work for others through RSVP (Retired Seniors' Volunteer Program).

Because space for Mountain Services activities in Green Ridge Meadows was very limited, an active search was started in 1984 for a site for a separate senior community center. The old Pearl Jarvis home on Highway 73, just beyond the traffic light, was acquired for $220,000 in 1985. The down payment was helped by a loan—later converted into a grant—of $30,000 from the Jefferson County Commissioners.

The home and a separate cottage (called the Carriage House, though Evergreen old-timer George Walpole says he can never remember it housing a carriage) were always painted yellow. The house was built in 1924 for Jim and Bertha Berrian—Walpole's aunt and uncle—who were members of the large pioneer Berrian family which at one time owned much of the land on both sides of Highway 73.

Pearl Jarvis occupied the home for many years, running a resale business which she advertised with the intriguing sign, "Stuff for Sale". She was very active in community organizations, and also for several years wrote a column in the Canyon Courier.

The buildings were in a deteriorated condition when purchased by SRC/Mountain Services and needed a great investment of money, time and energy in remodeling. The first phase, completed in the fall of 1986, fixed up the Carriage House, providing offices for Mountain Services, and creating a small community room.

It was completed with the help of donations of cash, building materials, services, fixtures and furnishings from a great many individuals, organizations and businesses, under the leadership of Mountain Services Coordinator John Sabawa and his successor, Bob MacDonald. The seniors themselves compiled and sold *"The Yellow House Cookbook"* as a fund-raiser. Benefit concerts were held by the Little Bear and the National Repertory Orchestra.

The second phase is the remodelling of the main house. If present plans are followed, the facility will be completed by a building joining the two houses. Total cost of the project is estimated at $475,000.

Mountain Services believes the new center will allow it to offer such a variety of programs and services that it will meet the needs of many more seniors than was possible before. The Center's facilities will be available for other community groups when not in use by seniors.

In Sickness and Health
For its first eighty years Evergreen had virtually no formal health facilities. A paradox. Because, in itself, it **was** a health facility.

Isabella Bird, that remarkable Edinburgh lady who travelled through Colorado alone in 1873, wrote in her letters home that the whole state was renowned for its healthful climate. For serious cases of asthma and consumption, she noted, the summer *"camp cure"* in the mountains was remarkably effective.

Though we knew this as a generality, it has been surprising to find out just how many of the people who figured in Evergreen's history came to Colorado because of tuberculosis or asthma. To name just a few, there was Canon Douglas, founder of the music schools of the Evergreen Conference, his sister, Julia, who started our public library, Senator Lawrence Phipps, whose former

wife built Greystone, realtors Jo Hare and Hal Davidson, Denver Mountain Parks "father". Mayor Robert Speer, and his landscape planner, S. R. De Boer.

From 1861, Evergreen came under the jurisdiction of Jefferson County and of its Health Department. Since very few people here were served by a public water supply until after the second war, and the first public sewage disposal facility came in 1959, the impact of this Department was minimal until the middle of this century.

The first physicians to practice in Evergreen were a husband and wife named Baker. Madeline Marquette was a partner with Mary Williams in the Marquette-Williams Sanitarium on Pearl Street in Denver. One of the board members was Dr. Michael Baker, who subsequently became Madeline's husband. They were part of Evergreen's summer colony, and according to Connie Fahnestock, were "practicing physicians in Evergreen." It seems likely that they practiced in summer only and served mainly the community of summer visitors. Quite a number of these, at any one time, would have been tuberculosis or asthma sufferers invited to take the cure at Camp Neosho (today's Hiwan Homestead Museum.)

What the year-round settlers did, when there was sickness in the family, needs more study. Like all rural populations, they no doubt had their folk remedies. There were probably some special individuals known for their healing skills. The child mortality rate was high, as can be gathered from family histories and from the many small graves in the Evergreen Cemetery.

In cases of severe sickness, patients were no doubt taken to Denver. From the beginning, people from Evergreen made the journey there regularly to buy and to sell. In the early days, when Idaho and Central were booming, there could well have been medical help available there also.

Evergreen's first resident physician was "Doc" John Hunt, who came here during the second world war. Because of some respiratory condition, possibly TB, he was not eligible for service in the armed forces. At first he had an office on Main Street (next to today's

171

Shadow Mountain Interiors), and, later, in what Arleta Alderfer described as a sort of portable time building near the dam. The structure was later torn down to provide parking for what is now the Bear Creek Mall.

Hunt lived near the Hangen Ranch on Buffalo Park Road and rendered almost 20 years of devoted one-man medical service to the mountain area. We heard about Doc Hunt in our interviews with Rozzi and Leona Clark, Bruce and Myrt Livonius and Arleta Alderfer.

Winter and summer, Hunt would drive down to Mercy Hospital in Denver for early morning rounds, frequently staying to operate. He held both afternoon and evening office hours in Evergreen and made house calls as far afield as Bailey.

A divorce separated Hunt from both his wife and Evergreen. After a brief time in Sheridan, Wyoming, he returned to Colorado and set up a practice in Lakewood. When we interviewed the Clarks and the Livonius's in 1981, both families said they still doctored with Hunt. But an attempt in 1986 by Connie Fahnestock and Arleta Alderfer to conduct an interview with him—to get his memories of 20 years of being Evergreen's only doctor—was not successful: his memory was failing.

After Hunt left in the early 60's, Evergreen was again without medical services until the opening of a new medical clinic on Meadow Drive, the nucleus of which was completed in 1969. The founder and enduring center of this medical practice for many years was Holly — Dr. Elbert Hollister. He had a number of partners and associates over the years, either family or general practitioners. The clinic brought two very important services to Evergreen: the Flight-for-Life helicopter from St. Antony's Hospital, and the a licensed emergency room—affiliated with Lutheran Medical Center and staffed with a physician 24 hours a day, 7 days a week.

For Holly too, a divorce resulted in a split from Evergreen. After some time out from medicine, he opened a new practice in Lakewood.

As what became known as the Evergreen Medical Clinic increased its number of full-time family practitioners to four, added nurses and part-time specialists—in nutrition, orthopedics, endocrinology, dermatology and surgery—more space was needed. At the end of 1986, the clinic moved to a new building at the Lakepoint Center under the new name of Lakepoint Medical Center. The core of the new Center was the fulltime staff of four board-certifed family practitioners, with services of many specialists available at Lakepoint Center by appointment. The new premises contained 5,000 square feet, an increase from 3,500 in the former facility.

In 1973, a second medical clinic was built, the Buffalo Park Medical Center on Buffalo Park Road, across from the Church of the Hills. From the beginning, this housed some independent practices—in dentistry, opthalmology, etc.—and a group medical practice. This practice went through a number of different organizational changes and in 1984 reopened as the Evergreen Healthcare Center, offering health care for families, special expertise in sports medicine, diagnostic ultrasound and clinical psychology.

In medical services, as in so many other areas of life in Evergreen, the 70's saw an explosion of offerings: pediatricians, obstetricians, independent family and general practitioners and dentists (pediatric, orthodontic, oral surgeons, general family) opened practices here. In addition, medical clinics, private

medical practices and/or dental practices opened in Conifer, Bailey, Bergen Park, Kittredge and Genesee.

A surprising array of facilities for the mentally ill and emotionally disturbed is available in the Evergreen area. Much of the credit for this belongs to a remarkable dynamo of a psychiatrist named Foster Cline.

Cline is a native of Denver and first remembers coming to Evergreen as a 7-year old, brought by his family to skate on Evergreen Lake. At that time he thought, *"This is where I want to live."* After graduating from the University of Colorado Medical School, doing an interneship in the Panama Canal Zone and a residency at the University of Washington, he did come to Evergreen in 1971.

Many people told him that it would be impossible to make a living as a psychiatrist here, but he rented a small space in the office building adjoining the medical clinic on Meadow Drive and soon had a thriving practice.

This was just the beginning. Cline went on to establish a group of independent practioners—who work together as a team under his direction—called the Evergreen Consultants in Human Behavior. Pretty soon, therapists and graduate students from all over the country were coming for training with the Consultants, especially well-known for its work with children and for its parenting and re-parenting techniques.

Foster Cline worked for many years with the emotionally disturbed boys at Forest Heights Lodge.

In 1972, he set up a unique program to help troubled children learn what a good family is like and how to behave. Under Cline's supervision, the staff of the Youth Behavior Program work closely with carefully screened and specially- trained foster families and with the children themselves. If the child is returning to the birth family the staff works with this family also. But frequently the parents relinquish custody, and the foster parenting may lead to adoption. The Program has a high 70% rate of success.

Cline is in great demand as a provocative, positive and lively speaker. His philosophy about successful parenting is simple. *"I don't think God meant parenting to be a hassle,"* he says, *"Raising kids is basically easy. People make it hard."* He stresses the need for parents to allow kids to make mistakes and learn from them. *"If life and limb are in danger, tell him what to do. If not, let him make a mistake."* Children who are not encouraged to think for themselves are the ones who become rebellious in adolescence, he believes.

Cline has written four books, more than 20 professional papers and numerous articles, teaches classes on child psychology and parenting, and is a well-known speaker and workshop leader in the U.S., Canada, Australia and Europe. With his wife Hermie he finds time to parent four children of his own.

Fifteen years after Dr. Cline came to Evergreen there are more than 20 mental health professionals in private practice in the mountain area, including psychiatrists, social workers, psychologists and psychotherapists.

For those who cannot afford private therapy, there is an office of the Jefferson County Mental Health Center Inc. located on Meadow Drive, which charges fees according to income. This is a private, non-profit agency serving residents of Jefferson, Clear Creek and Gilpin Counties. Outpatient care, 24-hour emergency services and a day treatment program for the chronically mentally ill are among the services provided by the Center.

If Yoga, Tai Chi Chuan, Chanting, Rebirthing, Meditational Stretch and Tone, the Course in Miracles, the Feldenkrais Method of Body Movement, Dream Interpretation or World Healing Meditations are more in your line than X-rays and pharmaceuticals, then your needs may be met at the Evergreen Wellness Center.

Many of the healing and preventive health modalities that are being offered anywhere in the U.S. today—as alternatives to conventional medical practices—are gathered in Evergreen under the umbrella of the Wellness Center.

This non-profit center opened in 1980 and moved in 1986 to offices in the Bear Creek Mall. In addition to the areas listed above, it offers classes in nutrition, herbal remedies,

self-improvement, stress management, trance channeling and astrology.

Those affiliated with the Wellness Center include people certified through regular accreditation channels (R.N., Ph. D. in Clinical Psychology, M.S.W., etc.) and those with qualifications in alternative healing disciplines.

In her childbirth education classes as well as in her own life, Peggy Eggers has a foot in both worlds. She has been teaching her own version of the Lamaze method—incorporating useful pieces of other theories, like the importance of coaching by the father—since 1975.

Peggy was born in Virginia and says she emerged from childhood with two convictions, *"That the only person who can live my life is me, and that I am happier when I operate according to my own inner ethics."* She left Virginia to find *"a place where I could serve others simply by being myself. When I arrived in Evergreen, I felt as if I were a bird who had landed in a strong, solid, expansive tree. The view was inspiring, there was plenty of room, and the other inhabitants were harmonious."*

Here she met her husband, Peter, a fine custom woodworker. They had their own family of four children, while Peggy's life-work began to unfold, *"to support the well-being of families, and to choose childbirth education as my vehicle."* Peggy finds that pregnancy is a *"great motivator of personal growth—a time of openness toward self. Inherent in the condition is self-examination, wonder and promise. It is this fertile mentality that excites me about my clients."*

In 1984, Peggy was certified as a childbirth educator by the International Childbirth Education Association, a worldwide organization of over 11,500 members united in the belief that all childbearing families should have freedom of choice about methods of childbirth and infant feeding, based on knowledge about alternatives available. The ICEA particularly emphasizes adequate preparation for childbearing and breast-feeding, encourages individualized maternity care with a minimum of medical intervention, and encourages the development of safe low-cost alternatives in child birth. In 1986, Peggy Eggers

became the U.S. Western Director of the ICEA, monitoring its activities in 13 Western states and representing their interests to the international board of directors.

The Mount Evans Hospice was founded in 1980. At first it served the needs of the dying and their families. The driving force was Carol Linke, whose awareness of the need for a hospice program arose out of her own experience with her father's death. The agency operated at first out of Carol's basement, moving into rented offices as it gained a better financial base.

The agency soon began getting requests to care for people not terminally ill, but recuperating from an injury or illness at home. In July 1984 it was certified as a home health agency, which enabled it to obtain reimbursement for some part of its services. It expanded its name to Mount Evans Hospice Inc., Mount Evans Home Health Care.

The agency has drawn together a diversified team of paid professionals and trained volunteers. In addition to home nursing care, it offers physical, speech and occupational therapy and sponsors support groups for parents who have lost a child, for widows and widowers, and for others suffering from stress or from grief. It defines its service area as the mountain communities along the Interstate-70 and U.S. Highway 285 corridors.

Mount Evans Hospice/Home Health Care is a non-profit agency and many of its services are not reimbursed by insurance or social programs. A lively fund-raising effort is an ongoing necessity: the July 4th Freedom Run is one of its annual benefit events.

In 1980, Evergreen's growth was at its height. Proposals for new developments were hitting the Canyon Courier headlines weekly. There was a well-publicized joint effort by three Denver hospitals (Presbyterian, St. Luke's and Lutheran) to get 11 acres of Bergen Park land rezoned. This was the land that had orignally been sold to the Evergreen Center for the Arts, across from the old Hiwan barns. The plan was to build a 25,000 square-foot medical office and clinic complex, a 130,000 square-foot, three-story hospital, and a 75,000 square-foot nursing home.

173

Debate ensued. Some argued that Evergreen already had the Flight-for-Life helicopter, a 24-hour emergency room and good ambulance service and didn't need a hospital. Furthermore, they said, a hospital is just one giant laundromat, and Evergreen doesn't have enough water to support it. Proponents countered that helicopters can't fly in bad weather and that immediate access to coronary care required a hospital nearer than Denver.

The rezoning was granted, conditional upon improvements being made on Highway 74. Nothing has happened since.

Another flurry of planning applications came in 1985 for a nursing home facility operated by Life Care Centers of America, to be built on another site in Bergen Park. Statistics were produced showing that the Evergreen-area population of those over 65 would be 2,500 by 1987. Again, permission was secured but nothing had materialized by the time we went to press.

Final Resting Places

Ten acres of peace and local history lie undisturbed just a stone's throw from Highway 74. A simple wrought iron gateway and arch, with Evergreen written on it. mark the entrance to **The Evergreen Cemetery** which adjoinins the grounds of Christ the King Church.

No-one knows exactly how or when the Evergreen Cemetery came into existence. Probably it was originally a graveyard associated with the small Episcopalian mission church known as St. Mark's in the Wilderness, which was built on the site in 1872-4. Later, the church building was moved and only the scanty remains of a rock foundation mark the location.

Land for the church was given by a French-Canadian settler named E. J. Mallett. The earliest marked grave in the cemetery has a small headstone with a dove carved in the top and the words *"Emma, dau(ghter) of J. T. and M. E. Hester. Died Dec. 31, 1871."* In the early days, people used to come by wagon from as far away as Conifer to bury their dead in what was then known as St. Mark's Cemetery.

The congregation of the church dwindled away, so in 1886 an interesting exchange took place: the Episcopalians acquired an

unfinished church in Sedalia, which became St. Phillip's, and the Methodists received St. Mark's.

According to Marian and John Arnold, who compiled a history of the Evergreen Cemetery as part of the the county- wide effort of the Foothills Genealogical Society to document cemeteries in Jefferson County, the Methodists purchased and held in trust the land that belonged to St. Mark's Church. In addition they bought the present site of Christ the King Catholic Church. The cemetery apparently continued to serve its function.

In 1901, according to the Arnolds, a Methodist Church was organized. The St. Mark's building was moved to the site on Main Street now occupied by the Little Bear.

One of Evergreen's leading citizens, rancher D. P. Wilmot, bought the cemetery land in 1907. The following year the Bear Creek Cemetery Association was incorporated for a period of 20 years. Wilmot, Michael Baker and Robert L. Downs served as the Board of Directors until the deaths of Wilmot in 1935 and Downs in 1938. As long as Wilmot was alive, an American flag always flew over the graves of Evergreen soldiers killed in the Civil War.

The cemetery land was then sold for *"one dollar and other good and valuable considerations"* to Walter Berglund, John Antweiler and Earl E. Hicks, who became the Trustees of the re-incorporated Cemetery Association.

The new Trustees realized that the cemetery grounds, with their many scattered graves, needed mapping. The task was undertaken by Earl Hicks. Up to this time, there had been no charge for burial sites, but the increasing costs of even minimal upkeep together with expenses incurred during mapping made it necessary to impose a modest fee. It is reported that Hicks would pay for lots out of his own pocket for families without funds.

The iron gates to the cemetery were erected in 1951 as a memorial to William G. and Florence Ames. The flag pole, with its little surrounding garden area, was built by the American Legion Post No. 80 to memorialize former member H. P. Lamer of Upper Bear Creek. The Evergreen Garden Club faithfully plants flowers around this memorial every year and tends them through the summer months.

Gate to Evergreen Cemetery.

Ernest and Alminda Hicks gravestone.

In 1960, the ten acres of cemetery land were officially deeded to the Bear Creek Cemetery Association and a new Board—consisting of Earl Hicks' son, Ernest, John C. Antweiler and Andrew Anderson of Kittredge—was appointed, with staggered terms of office.

The Board has remained a three-member organization, service is voluntary, and expenses are kept to a minimum. In the 1970's, when recruitment of Board members became difficult, a liaison with the Chamber of Commerce was worked out. The Chamber takes an ongoing interet in the well-being of the organization and approves the appointment of new board members. No telephone listing is maintained. Information about cemetery plots is obtained directly from individual board members or through the Chamber.

As the need for gravesites increased, two new *"subdivisions"* were opened up within the cemetery boundaries, the 1959 Addition and, in 1975, Whispering Pines.

Cemetery records date from 1905, such earlier records as did exist having been destroyed in a fire. (A history of the Mission of the Transfiguration Church, written in 1948, says, *"From 1878 to 1883 a few baptisms and burials are recorded; there the Parish Register abruptly ends."*)

Purchase of lots in the Evergreen Cemetery is restricted to those who live, or have lived, in Evergreen. This seems fair, since the Cemetery is a community possession which has been preserved and kept accessible through more than 100 years of dedicated voluntary service. The current Board members, Susie DeDisse, Ken Knoll and Rhea Craig, carry on this tradition.

Winter funerals have always meant problems for people trying to walk to graveside services in bad weather, and some hearses found it difficult to negotiate the narrow roads in the cemetery in snow and ice. The building of a little wooden chapel near the cemetery entrance solves these problems. When funerals must be held in unpleasant weather, the service is held in the chapel and actual burial is done later by grave laborers.

Each old cemetery has its legacy of legends: there are three commonly told about the Evergreen Cemetery.

Don Sailor, a long-time member of the Cemetery Association Board, told us of finding a number of

"pitch stakes" on the grounds, about 2½" in diameter and arranged in a methodical pattern. He tied these in with a persistent story he had heard from old-timers.

After the notorious Sand Creek Massacre of November 1864, in which some 105 Indian women and children were killed aong with 28 Indian men and 9 or 10 of Col. Chivington's arm, it was said that the bodies of the soldiers were brought to Denver. Because of a sense of shame about the whole episode, burial there was refused and the bodies were finally interred in the Evergreen Cemetery.

Unfortunately, a note in the Rocky Mountain News for December 4, 1864, lists the name of the 10 soldiers killed "on the 20th of November on the Big Sandy", and says they were all buried at Fort Lyon. Which still leaves the mystery of just who—or what— the "pitch stakes" memorialize?

Another legend, told by Mary Helen Crain, is that land was originally donated for the cemetery, provided that a burial take place within one year. *"When the year had nearly expired and no one in the area had passed away, word came of the forthcoming hanging of a horse thief in Cheyenne, Wyoming. There would be no one to claim the body. A group of men are said to have made the trek to Cheyenne, claimed the body, and brought it back to save the burying ground."* Crain concludes that this is probably just a good western yarn.

Finally, there is the story that this cemetery was formerly an Indian burial ground. Liz Burdick, who coordinated the Genealogical Society's historical studies, smiled when we asked her about that one. *"It depended on tribal customs, but most Indians were buried in trees,"* she told us, *"there were not nearly as many Indian burial grounds as there are rumors about them."*

The Evergreen Cemetery is not manicured lawns and perpetual care, but a rough, hilly place. A little spring stream runs through overgrown willows, wild flowers make a brief summer carpet, elk and deer roam around during the long winter months. It is a fine resting place for those who have loved the mountains.

Old headstone in Evergreen Cemetery.

Evergreen Memorial Park is owned and operated by another of those *"characters"* who create so much of the vitality and drama in a community. Ron Lewis is an unordained minister, a controversial land developer, a quiet philanthropist. There are few grey areas in his thinking—and fewer still in people's reactions to him. He's one of those strong-minded individuals that some people love, and others love to hate.

Lewis spend some of his childhood summers on Pearl and Frank Anderson's ranch on Upper Bear Creek, helping Frank grade roads and Pearl deliver the mail. He bought his first piece of land in Coal Creek when he was 15. After putting up an *"oversized outhouse"* on the lot, he sold it in time to help with his first year's college expenses. His father had died when he was young.

While in college—he attended Colorado State University and the University of Colorado, then spent three years at the Conservative Baptist Seminary in Denver—Lewis started two companies, one to haul fertilizer and one to paint roofs.

Once out of college, Lewis's land development and other enterprises proliferated. Though living in Evergreen and having many interests here—he was the developer of Bear Mountain Vista, has been responsible for most of the commercial development in Marshdale and was embroiled in the 1976 Olympics controversy (since it was his land on Doubleheader Mountain that was to be used for some of the events), Lewis also had companies developing land in Larimer, Lake, Boulder, Gilpin, Park, Denver and Weld counties.

Lewis has a religious view of the obligation to develop land: *"I believe God created man to manage his environment to its maximum potential to serve mankind,"* he said in an interview in the Canyon Courier. His commitment is not to local residents but to *"those who haven't had an opportunity to have a part of the good life."*

Convinced that the major opposition to development comes not from the natives—who have long looked forward to the new Evergreen—but from those who moved in recently, Lewis says there were no good old days. Some

things, like serenity, may be lost with growth, *"but most of those things which were lost, the natives were willing to surrender. And the area has gained in educational opportunities, health services, transportation and recreational facilities."*

Lewis's good deeds are not advertised. For example, he has long been a member of the small Salvation Army Committee for Evergreen, an organization that has no physical facilities. It just raises money to take care of the immediate needs of people who fall through the cracks of existing social programs. Lewis and his wife have sheltered many a homeless adult and runaway teenager in their own home, while arranging for a more permanent solution.

Earlier, they operated a cottage program for a while for Forest Heights Lodge. Lewis served as wrestling coach at Evergreen High School, was a youth pastor for a Bergen Park church and has been active in MAFIA, the mountain area family program to combat drug and alcohol abuse among schoolchildren.

As another outlet for his overflowing energy, Lewis has raised buffalo on his North Turkey Creek land since 1975.

Lewis obtained his license to create the Evergreen Memorial Park from the Colorado State Cemetery Board in 1965. The land is adjacent to his own home on North Turkey Creek, not too far from its intersection with Highway 73. It is advertised in the 1986 Yellow Pages as *"Evergreen Cemetery and Funeral Home"* offering *"conventional ground internment, lawn crypts, cremation facilities, historic pioneer garden." "This Park"*, concludes the ad, *"Has A Natural Wildlife Preserve Where Elk, Buffalo, Birds, And Wild Flowers Can Be Seen."*

Lewis is quite a wit: Gene remembers a rather acrimonious public hearing on one of Lewis's development proposals. *"Let them carry on,"* said Lewis, *"I need their help now, but one day they'll need me. I own the cemetery!"*

Compared with the rustic, informal Evergreen Cemetery, the Memorial Park is a rather conventional last resting place. Neat, mostly flat, and well-kept, it lies in a wide valley, surrounded by rocks and hills.

Ron Lewis.

'Nevergreen'

To the business establishment of Denver, Colo., the 1976 Olympics loom as a major financial windfall. Besides the enhancement of its reputation as an international ski center, Denver expects some 250,000 free-spending winter-sports fans to pour into town, and hotels, restaurants and outfitters are gearing up for a land-office business. But some 25 miles to the southwest, the residents of the little Rocky Mountain town of Evergreen are reacting with considerably less enthusiasm. For Evergreen (population: 10,000) is where many of the Olympic competitions are scheduled to be held, and Evergreen's citizens are justifiably fearful that the planned construction of roads, parking lots and ski facilities will desecrate their wilderness retreat, turn Evergreen into an instant city and disrupt a whole way of life.

The tiny town boasts but one stoplight, one main street and two grocery stores—and almost no services to handle the hordes of visitors. Evergreen's sewage system consists merely of septic tanks; its garbage collection is marginal at best, and for police protection the town has only the county sheriff and a handful of widely scattered deputies. What's more, since there are no local zoning laws, residents fear their mountain views will be despoiled by real-estate developers, their easygoing commercial life disrupted by new business enterprises. More damaging would be the games' effect on the city's water supply. Because snowfall is light in February—the month the Olympics are to be held—the ski jump, bobsled and huge runs would have to be artificially coatd by snow-making machines that could well drain the town's whole water supply.

Greed: A similarly dismal prospect to the locals is what the games would do to the natural environment. For along with the paving over of acres of green space for parking lots, some 25 acres of trees would have to be felled for the bobsled run and a 55-mile-long, 8-foot-wide path chopped out of the wilderness for a cross-country ski trail. And after it's over, the town would be stuck with 90- and 70-meter ski jumps and a huge open amphitheater, just ripe for development by greedy outsiders.

For their part, the townspeople are collecting a war chest to battle the project to the end. **"If they get away with this,"** said one local, **"we might as well change the town's name to "Nevergreen."'**
Article in Newsweek Magazine, December 14, 1970

177

Whichever way you come to Evergreen from Denver, you have the opportunity to experience extraordinary examples of the combination of natural beauty with man-made structures. To the south is the Red Rocks Theater, one of the most outstanding outdoor amphitheaters in the world in a brilliant natural setting. Via I-70, you suddenly see that most-photographed panorama of snow-capped peaks, framed by an elegant single-span concrete bridge.

Coming into the Bergen Park-Evergreen area from I-70, you will also pass through some of the most sensitively- planned subdivisions in the mountain area—Genesee, Soda Creek, the Ridge and the Hiwan developments. These have respected the contours of the land, preserved existing trees, insisted on minimum artificial landscaping and avoided garish signs that detract from the natural mountain setting.

The natural assets of the Evergreen area are streams, valleys, meadows, wonderful rock outcroppings. Hills, forests of pine and spruce. Brilliant sunshine year-round. A carpet of colorful wild flowers in summer. A riot of golden aspen in fall. The vivid winter contrast of dark evergreens and white snow. What man has done here is little by comparison with the contributions of nature—and, we must admit, much of our imprint is inharmonious and inappropriate.

Yet we are human. The sense of being part of a community, and links in a historic chain, is important to us. So it is vital that we become conscious of which elements in this mountain area symbolize our sense of being at home here—in this specific place of all places, and at this particular time in its development. We have an obligation to preserve and enhance these elements, and to make our own additions in ways that do not violate the sense of place.

We are a contemporary society: to produce design that is compatible with nature does not mean that our vocabulary is restricted to Victorian architecture or false fronts. Contemporary concepts in architectural and planning design can be beautifully interwoven into an established environment.

Award-winning bridge on Highway I-70.

Main Street

One of our town's vital assets, this is our historical beginning— a place that has grown up slowly over the years. It has been here in good times and in bad. This is where innumerable people have offered their services. Most locations along this short piece of Bear Creek Canyon have had a succession of buildings on them since the 1860's, and have served many uses.

Views of Main Street, 1925.

Red Rocks Theater.

Certain businesses that require large amounts of space have moved away from Main Street and there are questions about its proper role in Evergreen's future.

One day, Main Street's limitations will be seen as its greatest asset: it cannot spread in all directions, it is a small, definite area with obdurate natural features. To develop it to its fullest potential involves making the best possible use of every inch of the land, preserving its rock outcroppings, working with its steep contours, emphasizing one of its great advantages—the lovely little stretch of Bear Creek that runs through it.

Since downtown Evergreen is such a precious area, there is no need to waste even a few square feet of land. Meaningless little spaces between buildings should be eliminated. This is a place for zero setbacks in all directions.

The downtown area could, and should, be built out to five times its present density, both commercially and residentially. It needs to be a lively area of mixed uses, operating on many different levels that are connected by covered walkways. There is nothing wrong with having apartments for singles and young couples over stores and offices.

Wouldn't we all be drawn to stroll around a brick-paved downtown, to eat a lunch under the shade of blue spruces along the stream? The Little Bear and the Wolf House already demonstrate that people like to come to Main Street for a meal and for entertainment.

Some present buildings on Main Street detract from its intimate smalltown character: the Mountain Bell structure and the concrete building across the street are examples. Perhaps skilful remodeling could mitigate their impersonal impact and relate them to other structures, perhaps in a long-term plan they may need to be replaced.

It is second nature for an architect to visualize what could be. New structures and additions to the Main Street area that have a rustic character—using heavy timber, native stone work, with deeply-recessed windows and doors to protect against bad weather and to create those deep shadows that delight the eye. Wrought iron details. Low stone walls to sit on, that create an element of continuity. A minimum of signage allowing the rooftops and the rocks outcroppings to dominate the scene. The dust eliminated.

And what about traffic? Parking? There are many solutions. Space could be provided at both ends of Main Street—well screened, connected by attractive and safe walkways—and also at a number of places above the downtown area. Cars would continue to travel through, but in a slow pattern, winding through attractive spaces. A short stretch of slow travel has been made acceptable in many similar central places.

The long overdue "by-pass" will help greatly in keeping downtown intimate, clean and enjoyable for many years to come. All over the country downtown areas are being revitalized: not only in big cities, like the 16th Street Mall in Denver, but in much smaller ones, like Boulder and Aspen. They are successes, not only from a business point of view but also from a social standpoint. People take pride in them: they are good places to spend time in, to show to visitors.

A long-range commitment to the health and lively future of the downtown area is important for Evergreen, to honor our heritage and enhance our sense of identity.

Improvements on Main Street.

Cross-section of downtown architectural character.

The old Evergreen Hotel today.

Hotel, exterior detail.

Main Street homes converted to stores.

Remnant of the past on Main Street.

181

Celebration in Heritage Grove.

Hiwan Homestead/Heritage Grove

Here is a shining example of what the community can do when a small but dedicated group of citizens focuses on a specific place.

It would have been in keeping with the breakneck speed of land development in the early 70's for the large, old-fashioned, former Hiwan Ranch headquarters to have been torn down to make room for new homes. Or used as a real estate office and allowed to fall into disrepair.

Instead, it came into the hands of a developer who cared about historical heritage. The crisis of its possible fate coincided with the modest beginning of a local historical society, and with the creation of the Open Space Program in Jefferson County.

The acquisition of the adjacent Heritage Grove through citizen fund-raising accomplished something that seems essential to successful preservation: it moved the Hiwan Homestead enterprise beyond an emphasis on the past, into diverse and energetic new programs for the community—the Mountain Rendezvous, arts and craft fairs, community celebrations.

Evergreen Lake, Golf Course, Key's on the Green, Lakepoint Center

Much thought and money has been invested in this area in the last ten years. The remodeled and expanded Lakepoint Center is an unqualified improvement over its predecessor and the renewed Golf Course is a summer magnet.

The Lake itself—a man-made element—has many functions and even greater potential. Symbolically it represents Evergreen to people who live here, and therefore everyone who cares about Evergreen has an investment in its future. The architect in Gene visualizes sturdy rustic pavilions catering for the needs of skaters, hikers, boaters and fishermen, a simple bandstand silhouetted against the water, well-landscaped and well-kept walkways along the lake's edge, stone walls incorporating benches, lighting, litter containers, wooden bridges—all fitting, well-designed, unobtrusive and carefully maintained.

The naturalists emphasize undisturbed wetlands and bird sanctuaries. Recreation-oriented citizens have their own visions.

In the three to four years of the dredging operation, there is time to work out a community consensus on the future of the Lake. The future will judge us severely if we let this opportunity—which comes once in a lifetime—slip away from us.

Since the Lake is the most dramatic landmark in our community, we must be very careful how it is developed and by whom. Translating the consensus into physical terms must be in the hands of sensitive designers, with experience and talent. The manner in which the Preliminary Master Plan was created is a good beginning.

The Old Schools, the Library, the Senior Center

Another opportunity, another question mark. The six-acre site that now contains the Evergreen Regional Library, the red brick County Building and the white concrete Open High School is not an attractive complex. Aside from a little reading park attached to the Library, hardly visible unless you go looking for it, the general appearance is of a rundown, piecemeal assemblage.

The parking lot is crumbling, there is no visible landscaping except for the lovely line of blue spruces that some parents long ago put around the white building. There is an unlovely temporary building next to the school. Metal fences have been planted in odd places, and bits of projects started and abandoned.

Yet this is the site of what used to be Evergreen's pride and joy—its brand-new school of 1922 (the red brick building) and its modern high school of 1948 (the one-story concrete building). Generations of mountain-area kids graduated from these schools.

This is six acres of prime land right on what used to be a willow-lined and beautiful little stream, Cub Creek, that backs up onto a Denver Mountain Park. (A lot of the beauty and vegetation of the stream was destroyed when the highway department enlarged the intersection of Buffalo Park Road and Highway 73, to make it safer for the many school buses that must turn there, and built a new bridge across the stream.)

Instead of treating a live stream as a feature to treasure, it has been ignored—and even, along the part by the Open High School, alienated from the site by a metal fence and made part of a busy highway. Cannot an innovative school incorporate a stream as an element of education, a source from which to learn respect for nature? If one single step could begin to transform this site into a thing of beauty, it would be to bring the stream right through the heart of it. The next step would be to banish chain link fences: they do not belong in a mountain environment.

The red brick building, partially used by the County for offices, has been waiting for a proper function ever since it closed its doors as a school almost 20 years ago. It is a good building, historically valuable, and quite spacious. At various times different uses have been considered: recreation center, community center, senior center, performing arts center. So far, nothing has "jelled". Former County Commissioner Bob Clement, and all subsequent Boards of Commissioners, have said they would be happy to have some worthwhile use made of this building—if they could only receive a feasible proposal with sufficient general community support.

The Jefferson County Open High School serves a county-wide population. From time to time, announcements are made about moving it to a site on the flatlands. The School District has never made any sizeable investment in the updating of this physical plant as it has for every other school in the mountain area.

The Evergreen Library, completed in 1971, has an attractive native stone exterior, is well maintained and—in spite of remodeling efforts initiated by Library Friends that increased the value of existing space—bulging at the seams.

Key's on the Green, originally the Evergreen Golf Course Clubhouse.

For a public education effort initiated by the Evergreen Design Task Force, Gene suggested some possible plans for this important site: re-routing part of the stream through it, screening parking with landscaping and berms, creating an outdoor amphitheater behind the red brick building, and remodelling that structure for multiple community uses.

The acquisition of the old Pearl Jarvis property, a few houses along Highway 73 from the library-schools complex, raises tantalizing possibilities for linking this new Senior Center with a revitalized community-civic center.

Perhaps the prospect of expanding the library, made possible by the passage of the 1986 referendum on increased taxes, may be used as a catalyst for realizing the potential of this unique six acres of Evergreen history.

Idea for redeveloping the 6-acre school-library site.

183

Hiwan Village/Showbarn Complex/Meadow Drive Clinics and Offices

Meadow Drive Office Building.

Here is a cautionary tale for Evergreen. The Village commercial area, the first retail expansion outside Main Street, was a busy location as long as the Post Office and Safeway were there. When those leases expired, and the community had expanded in a different direction, both institutions relocated in North Evergreen. The small Village stores suffered without the traffic generated by their busy neighbors. The former Safeway store was difficult to re-rent.

There is speculation in 1986 that Safeway is preparing to move from its second location in North Evergreen to a new Bergen Park development.

What kind of authority resides anywhere—within the Evergreen community or at the County level—to protect ourselves against this happening every ten years? The process leaves blighted commercial spaces that landlords struggle to lease, while former meadows are covered with asphalt and the buildings to house bigger and better supermarkets—and the inevitable small stores that surround them. If the power to persuade or require does not exist, is there any way in which, if enough of us are interested, we could create a vehicle through which to negotiate?

Do we need in this small mountain community supermarkets that would be at home in Denver or Chicago? Can we not find a way to persuade these chains to design something suitable to our mountain environment— something which, in the end, would also be a source of pride to themselves?

The conversion of the historic Hiwan Barn to a hardware store was imaginative and aesthetically satisfying, though perhaps less than efficient in terms of supervising customers and merchandise. The Showbarn Center development—with its main combined office and retail building, twin theater, and small stores—is attractive, though it seems to have had some struggles commercially.

The Meadow Drive office/clinic complex has readjustments to make since its long-time anchor, the Evergreen Medical Center, has relocated to Lakepoint. As a node of commercial activity, a pleasant "people place", this lower end of Evergreen is somewhat in transition. Perhaps in the future it could be more closely tied in with Main Street, via safe and pleasant trails.

It is ironic that this "strip" should start with some of the most pleasing relationships between the mountain environment and human creation (the entry sign and trails of Dedisse Park, Christ the King Church, the unobtrusive RTD Park 'N Ride and the Evergreen Cemetery) and then turn into Evergreen's version of West Colfax Avenue.

North Evergreen Strip No. 1: Christ the King Church to Bryant Drive

The strip is a prime example of how each enterprise, planning for its own well-being, can produce a totality that is dangerous—from a traffic standpoint—and visually offensive. It could be redeemed—over time and at a cost. The frontage road should be continuous, the entire strip between the highway and the buildings needs landscaping and the chaotic signage needs totally re-thinking.

Those merchants who try to compel our patronage with vulgar signage need to be made aware that most of us live in the mountains because we admire and love the natural beauties. It is possible to succeed in business while respecting this magnificent setting.

As long ago as 1954, the United States Supreme Court decided that "It is within the power of the legislature to determine that the community should be beautiful as well as healthy, spacious as well as clean." Jefferson County has incorporated design guidelines into its new overall master plan for the county as well as into the Evergreen area plan. Plentiful precedents exist for regulating signs so that they "enhance rather than impair the attractiveness and pleasantness of appearance" of the community.

The guidelines are a good beginning. Follow-through is even more important. We need people in charge of administering these guidelines who are qualified and experienced designers—who can persuade and encourage "offenders" to mend their ways by showing them better means to reach their objectives.

Christ the King Catholic Church.

Old Hiwan Barns and Bergen House

This familiar cluster that includes the original Johnson octagonal barn is in process of transformation. It is part of a larger commercial zone for which plans have been delayed by the faltering economy.

It is perhaps unfortunate that this piece of community history is now dispersed into several ownerships. The former Bergen home is owned by landscape arhitect Dick Phelps and has been remodelled for small offices; the little spring beside it is included in the landscaping activity of the Ridge development: the octagonal barn is in the hands of another landowner and remodelled for retail space. Bergen National Park owns a substantial portion of the land and the balance, including two large barns, is in the hands of the Jefferson Land Associates (the Hiwan developers). They are exploring what kinds of development might best fit this area.

North Evergreen Strip No. 2: Chestnut Lane to Lewis Ridge Road

Another area of mixed design— some chaotic, some ordered. At the northern end is the Center at Evergreen, consisting of two chain restaurants, office buildings, the Colorado National Bank and the Evergreen Athletic Club. Although there was a community outcry at the imposition of red brick multi-story buildings which had very little to do with the mountain environment, this Center has tied its elements together with well-maintained landscaping, making skilful use of existing features such as a natural water channel that flows in the springtime.

South of this is the contemporary Mine Shops complex with shed roof elements, designed by architect Chuck Sink, set in a rather poor existing environment.

The Center at Evergreen.

One of the real assets of this area is that it has one continuous frontage road running its entire length. Plans for remodelling and new construction, on land that includes Kilgore Trout's, have been approved and would improve the southernmost part of this strip. In between these projects are individual buildings, unrelated to each other or to their surroundings, that will probably not be replaced or upgraded until a new round of prosperity arrives in Evergreen.

The Mine Shops.

Elk (formerly Means) Meadow Park

When this spacious meadow, seen by every traveler along Highway 74 against the backdrop of the 9,708' Bergen Peak, was in danger of being lost through development, a campaign to save it got into high gear. Its purchase by Jefferson County Open Space saved it for us all.

In the campaign to save it, there were letters to the local paper from people who said they didn't need the right to walk on the land, or to have it owned publicly. They would be satisfied if they could just look at it each day, as long as the weathered barn stayed in the foreground.

About Old Barns

Even more than original houses, old barns are important punctuations in the mountains. They serve as a reminder of the settlers and the ranchers who preceded us. They give a human scale to the vastness and timelessness of nature. And—they are great subjects for artists to sketch and for both visitors and residents to photograph.

The first barns were sometimes combined with living quarters. They were simple log huts and rough post structures. Architects have always admired barns as a forthright expression of functional building. Throughout the country, they are some of our truly distinctive indigeneous forms. Ironically, barns are excellent examples of architecture without architects.

Barns were utilitarian structures for sheltering livestock and storing feed and tools—built with materials locally available and suitable to the climate. Barns have served as the inspiration for some of our most interesting domestic architecture. They are essentially flexible, often expanded by lean-to additions that create interesting compositions—informal, adaptable, asymmetrical.

Ponds at Soda Creek

Nationally, barns are an endangered species. We have some fine barns in the Evergreen area: the Johnsons' octagonal creation, the Hiwan showbarn, the yellow Conifer barn and many little weathered log structures dotted around the mountain meadows. Let us not allow them to decay unnoticed, or be torn down without thought. There is great value in preserving and re-using old barns.

"We used to call it Cadillac Canyon," a descendant of one of the settler families told us. It is a canyon of great scenic beauties, from narrow rock-walled sections to meadows like Bendemeer that open up to a magnificent view of the Mount Evans range. The road begins at the Lake and splits into four endings—Indian Creek Park, Singin' River Ranch, the State Wildlife Management Area and the Evans Ranch. Each of these is rich in both history and magnificent scenery.

Because it was an area of early summer home building by the wealthy, Upper Bear Creek has a disproportionate number of Evergreen's interesting older buildings: the old Troutdale Hotel and two homes (Rippling Waters and Swiss Haven) built by its owner, Harry Sidles; the Rosedale Castle, an exuberant creation by Denver's Beaux Arts architect Jacques Benedict for Paul and Margery Reed Mayo; Greystone, designed by Denver architect Maurice Briscoe—and built by the same contractor and craftsman, Jock Spence, who built the Hiwan Homestead and so many of the older homes on the Evans Ranch. One of these, the former Phelps Dodge Ranch, is now the Outdoor Education Laboratory School belonging to the R-1 School District. Another home on the Evans Ranch was designed for Anne Evans by Burnham Hoyt, architect for the Red Rocks Theater.

One of the delights of Upper Bear Creek is the multitude of walls of native stone, both along the stream and the road. Many of these were built apparently during the depression years by W.P.A. workers. Alas, there are also many not so good-looking metal fences strung along the roads.

Design Elements

Rock walls are a delightful theme of older Evergreen: they line Highway 73, for example, between Main Street and the Library. How pleasant it would be if we could renew this distinctive local feature.

Another material which has been used in an imaginative way throughout this region is wrought iron. Perhaps we could establish a vocational program, through Red Rocks Community College in Evergreen, to train craftsmen in working with native stone and wrought iron. The school could serve both those who want make a living with these satisfying skills and people who would like to develop them as an avocation.

A more recent Evergreen design theme is the hand-carved, hand-painted sign. We are fortunate to have two talented sign artists—Helen Paisley, better known as "H.P.", and Dennie Ibbotson—working enthusiastically in Evergreen.

Upper Bear Creek homes: heavy timber and stone.

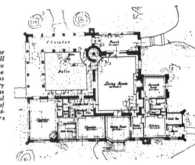

The floor plan is well adapted to life in the mountains for every room has beautiful vistas of the out-of-doors

Creative signage.

189

Subdividing Mountain Land

Evergreen's first subdivisions date from early in this century: there was a flurry of activity after the establishment of the Denver Mountain Parks system. In general, these subdivisions were for middle income people— ordinary citizens. Plats were usually drawn up by a Denver engineers who never visited the land. They created impossible subdivisions with many unbuildable lots.

Developments like Troutdale Estates, Stanley Park and WahKeeney Park were meant for summer cabin sites. If there was any water, it was piped over the surface of the ground and shut off in winter. Otherwise, you brought your own water and roughed it. Cooking was on woodstoves. All cabins had outhouses.

A few refinements on this pattern can be seen from a brochure for Evergreen Hills, a subdivision of part of the Mary N. Williams estate, dating from around 1920. It is before any mention of the creation of Evergreen Lake, but after the mountain parks came into being. Though the sites were rectangular, the sellers promised that "each lot has a good practicable building site." Lots ranged in size from 100' x 150' to several acres, and cost from $50 up. A rustic bungalow 24' x 24' could be built for $280—$350 with a stone fireplace.

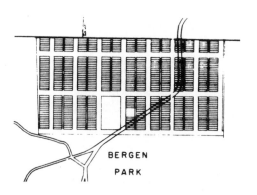
Bergen Park, original subdivision.

Small subdivisions for year-round living were first developed above Main Street: the plat for Douglas Park, on land belonging to Dr. Josepha Douglas, was filed in 1937 just one year before she died.

We devote a later section to the next major development in Evergreen's growth, the Hiwan subdivisions, which pioneered sensitive site planning in the Evergreen area. These started in a modest way in 1949 and continued right through to the 1980's.

In 1968 the 2,400 Centaur Ranch on Highway 73, a landmark for many years, was sold for half a million dollars. By November, the first filing of Evergreen Meadows offered 40 homesites for sale. The entire period from the mid-60's to the collapse of the real estate boom in the early 1980's was punctuated with such announcements.

Great progress in the art of mountain subdivision can be seen by reviewing plats from the earliest days through to those for Soda Creek, Genesee and the Ridge.

Typical suburban subdivisions have no place in the mountains. Each mountain area is unique, and each site has to be studied for slope, orientation, vegetation, drainage, view. There is no room for poor land use—the price is too high. Cuts for roads should follow contours, with minimum disturbance of vegetation. It takes many years for a cut to revegetate naturally.

Contrary to a "flatland" developer's reflexes, the meadows should not be covered with houses. These precious open spaces should be preserved wherever possible. Nor should mountains be bulldozed down for the convenience of engineers. Houses are best sited among trees on hillsides— as long as the designer respects nature. The new structure should defer to the natural assets of the site—rock outcroppings, existing trees,

views. Lots should vary in size with the steepness of the slope, with larger sites on steeper hillsides.

Clustering of homes on a large acreage is often appropriate, so that remaining lands can left in their natural state and used as common areas cared for through homeowners' agreements.

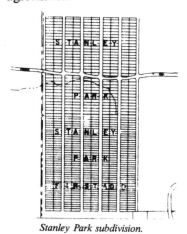
Stanley Park subdivision.

An early principle of American architect Frank Lloyd Wright's is still worth remembering. When it comes to hills, man should be humble: he can build on the hillsides but should leave the ridges to nature. The Greeks also respected this principle.

New subdivisions should always be handled as Planned Unit Developments (PUD's) rather than simply as matters of rezoning. Developers then commit themselves to a finished product: road layout, materials, landscaping, density, siting and character of buildings. They can be required to make good on their promises.

Still unsolved is the problem of how to get sympathetic and skillful review of proposed projects—by people who know and care about this special mountain environment—when the power of approval is located in Golden. We need a process that offers help to developers in the design of both residential and commercial areas. Perhaps some form of local Review Board could function as an advisor to the County Planning Commission.

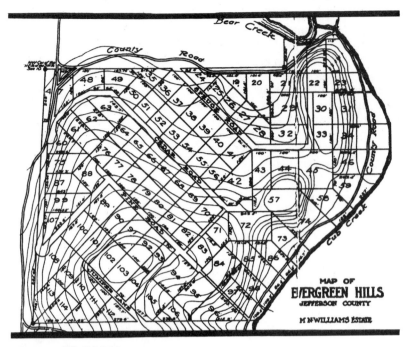

Evergreen Hills Subdivision.

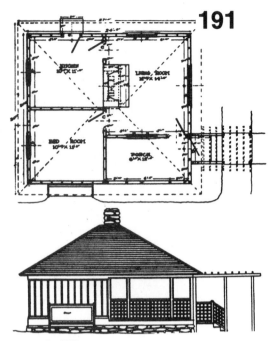

Rustic bungalow for $250.

The Limits of Regulation

There was a time when Gene had straightforward solutions to the problems of designing good communities.
"If no structures could be built without an architect," he said, "then we would create beautiful towns and cities." That was before we both had appointments as Fulbright Professors in Chile in 1959. In Santiago, the law required that every building be designed by an architect. What were most of the buildings like? Conventional, safe, dull.

During the war in England, public hopes for the future focussed on the rebuilding of old cities and the creation of new ones. City planning was infused with idealism, and young designers like Gene were excited about the challenge of integrating all the design elements for a new town—or for redeveloping an existing one—into a harmonious whole.

About fifteen years after we came to America, we had a visit from one of his classmates from student days in Cambridge. This man had become a well-known planner in Britain. While we were exploding about unbridled uburban commercialism and

ssprawl here, he was envying the freedom and the vitality of American city development. "You cannot imagine," he told us, "how the dead hand of the planning bureaucracy is choking creativity."

How to get that necessary balance between individual creativity and community regulation? Between the interests of those who already live here and others who who like to? Between speculative investors and the community that needs their capital, but doesn't want to be left with the physical leftovers of their enterprise?

When we first knew Evergreen, it was easy to buy a small piece of land or a simple cabin: almost anyone could do it. In the early 70's, there were plenty of places that people without much money could rent. We have become a wealthy community. The people who do the work in Evergreen— waitresses, teachers, policemen, carpenters, sales clerks— can no longer afford to live here.

Other mountain communities like Aspen and Vail have the same problem and have found some solutions. We have managed to build some

affordable housing for senior citizens, even though we are not a city. Now its time to do something for other age groups.

Perhaps we also could pioneer a return to the era of individual enterprise. The pioneers built their own houses. As long as personal dwellings are well-screened from public roads, why couldn't we have sections of mountain land where building regulations are minimal and people can obtain help in building for themselves?

One thing we have learned: beauty is not created through legal rules and regulations. We must search for better ways. We have plenty of technical know-how in our do- it-yourself society. Somehow we need to combine this, through education, with sensitivity to beauty and good taste.

Historic home, now information center for Soda Creek Development.

Citizen Role in Assuring Good Environmental Design

There is a history of intense activity by voluntary organizations in Evergreen to combat haphazard growth and preserve those qualities of the mountain environment that make people want to live here.

The earliest efforts, in the 1950's, were modest, directed at community clean-up campaigns and the removal of one or two obnoxious signs. In 1961, the Evergreen Civic Association was organized to provide a community-wide approach to local needs and problems: roads, recreation zoning, utilities, tourist promotion.

The first sustained action was orchestrated by the **Mountain Area Planning Council (MAPC)**, formed in 1967. Composed of representatives of mountain community organizations, MAPC set itself the goal of trying to understand what was happening to mountain communities as they experienced unprecedented growth: how best to cope with the avalanche of new subdivisions, destruction of the environment and loss of community identity.

In 1971, MAPC collected more than 3,000 signatures on a petition to the Jefferson County Commissioners to impose a moratorium on further development in the mountain area, until an effective land use plan was adopted. The request was refused, but MAPC felt that its efforts did have one positive result: the county decision to make an environmental inventory for the entire mountain area of Jefferson County.

Protect Our Mountain Environment (POME) was organized in 1970 by citizens of Evergreen and Indian Hills, to focus opposition to the proposals to hold parts of the 1976 Winter Olympics in this area. POME's efforts were eminently successful, expressing as they did the accumulated frustration of mountain area residents with being at the mercy of developers and other outside forces that were threatening cherished community values.

POME was initially a member of MAPC, but eventually outlasted that organization and became a powerful anti-growth spokesman throughout the 1970's. Eventually, it's negative posture caused a drastic drop in membership and influence.

Next on the scene was the **Evergreen Design Task Force.** This organization lasted for some eight years, meeting regularly. Its aim was to help individuals or groups to develop designs for buildings, remodelling proposals or subdivisions that were appropriate to the mountain environment. The group assisted with design concepts, site layout, subdivision possibilities, and other technical aspects of improving on matters of design—all on a volunteer basis. Sometimes there were as many as 20 involved— architects, landscape architects, designers, builders and people with experience and interest in the man-made environment.

The organization was sponsored and supported by the Evergreen Chamber of Commerce, as well as by individuals who felt there was a need for services of this kind. After the Design Task Force had been in existence for a year or so, the staff of the Planning Office would refer proposed projects for Task Force comments, which were presented in written and oral form to the Planning Commission and the County Commissioners. This established a fruitful relationship between these groups and was, in effect, a design review process in operation.

The Master Plan for Evergreen, adopted by the County Commissioners in 1986, includes design guidelines and hopefully makes some of the duties

Charles E. Younkman has been a practicing architect since 1961 and came to work in Evergreen in 1968. He is a native of Denver and a graduate of the Colorado University School of Architecture. Younkman selected his profession while serving in the Air Force, when he had the opportunity to visit Japan. He was impressed with how contemporary Japan's traditional architecture appeared, and with its simplicity of design. In addition to many individual homes in Evergreen, Younkman has done the master plan for revitalizing the Evergreen Conference, remodelled Hart House and Williams House, designed the new buildings at the Lakepoint Center and remodelled the existing ones. Younkman's avocation is working with theater set dsigns: he has been President of the Evergreen Players and has also served on the Facilities Committee of the Colorado Philharmonic.

Lynne Ronchetti

Michael K. Whitehouse is an architect-contractor who has lived and worked in Evergreen since 1976. His undergraduate and graduate studies in architecture and art history were at Princeton: he worked with a number of distinguished architectural firms in the east, before deciding that his particular interest was in combining the design of new and remodelled homes with construction

Lynne Ronchetti   Chuck Younkman Mike Whitehouse and Gene Sternberg started the Design Task Force.

performed by the Design Task Force unnecessary. To ensure projects of good design in the mountain area, however, we may find that some local design review agency is necessary.

The most recent citizen groups to take on the role of environmental watchdogs are combinations of area homeowners' associations: PLEASE (Planned Living Environment of South Evergreen), The Tri-Gulch Homeowners and neighborhood organizations in the area from Evergreen Lake to I-70. ENABLE was formed in 1985, with monthly meetings and four active co-ordinators: Shiela Clarke, Mary D. Silleck, Jane Dahlstrom Quinn and Tandy M. Jones.

Its stated objectives: to monitor land use issues before the County Commissioners and the Planning Commission; establish positions and testify where appropriate; meet with developers before their plans are finalized and, where appropriate, even before they are submitted to the County.

ENABLE identified a number of specific concerns which it believed must be taken into account if the unique environment of Evergreen is to be respected. These included view preservation, an end to strip commercial development, proper consideration for the impact of development on air and water quality, the assurance of adequate roads, schools and other community services to serve proposed developments, and the protection of any unique elements—whether geological, historical or habitats for plants or wildlife.

Design also has an important role in ENABLE's concerns. "Landscaping, signage and architectural design," according to their guidelines, "should be compatible with adjacent areas and should reflect the unique character of the mountain area."

Genesee commercial buildings.

Housing at Genesee.

193

Burnham Hoyt was born in Denver in 1887 and died there in 1960. His father, a carriage designer who had his own shop on Larimer Street, came from New Brunswick in Canada. While still very young, Burnham sold the Rocky Mountain News and picked berries on nearby farms to earn money. Throughout his schooldays, he sketched and drew whenever possible. He graduated from North High School. An older brother, Merrill, became an architect so Burnham followed in his footsteps, getting his architectural education in New York. After serving in the first war, in which he was wounded, Burnham returned to Denver and practiced for six years with his brother, carrying on the practice alone after Merrill's death. Burnham married Mildred Fuller, sister of Denver's well-known interior designer Thornton Fuller. Among the many buildings Hoyt designed—besides the Red Rocks Theater and Anne Evans' mountain home on the Evans Ranch—were the Boettcher Schools for crippled children, Lake Junior High and Children's Hospital. Known as "Burnie", Hoyt had a ready sense of humor and a capacity to laugh at himself: "Some of my ideas," he said, "seemed good at the time, but increasingly poor as the years pass." He loved music and literature and was a skilful painter, especially in watercolor. When George Cranmer became the Manager of Denver's Parks Department, Hoyt served as his architectural advisor. In his spare time, Burnie Hoyt organized the Denver Atelier where many of Denver's next generation of architects received their education. While the School of Architecture was in existence at Denver University, Hoyt was regularly invited to critique student work. Gene remembers that he was already ill, needing to sit while he made his comments, but students and faculty enjoyed his warmth and intelligence.

Burnham Hoyt.

J. B. Benedict.

J.B. Benedict, who lived from 1879 to 1948, was known as an architect of strong opinions, often overriding his clients' wishes. He hated halls and corridors, for example, as a "waste of space": in houses he designed, one had sometimes to walk through one bedroom to get to another. Benedict lived for many years outside Littleton on his "Wyldmere Farm", where he bred prize livestock and registered bull terriers. "Jake", as he was called (his name was Jacques), was born in Chicago, received his architectural education at the Beaux Arts school in Paris, and practiced in New York and Chicago before coming to Colorado. An intellectual and a person of wide-ranging interests, Benedict became the favorite architect of Denver's social elite. But he also designed many civic buildings— the Littleton Town Hall and Library, for instance, and most of the first shelters and lodges for the Denver Mountain Parks. When commissioned to design the North Denver Branch Library, he was told that it must not cost more than $14,000. His design needed $18,000, so he personally went out and raised the difference. Benedict designed John Brisben Walker's ill-fated mansion on the top of Mount Morrison and prepared the ambitious plans for the Summer White House there. When the time came for Benedict to move from his farm to an apartment in Denver, he had to sell most of a priceless art collection he had built up. Some of his old farm is now a Littleton City Park and his home a convent for the closely-cloistered Carmelite order. In the Evergreen area, besides the Mayo Lodge (Rosedale Castle), Benedict designed the Waring (later Baborka) house on Upper Bear Creek, the original Evergreen Golf Course Clubhouse (now Key's on the Green), the Chief Hosa Lodge and the shelter houses in Fillius and Bergen Parks.

194

Bill Marshall and "The Woodpeckers." Marshall spent the second world war in a pacifist work camp, where he met Paul Lappala and Ed Hendley. In 1947, the two called Bill in California and asked him to come help them with some cabinet work at the Teepees—on what was then Highway 40. Bill came out with his wife Miriam. The three men decided they would like to have a little cabinet shop together, somewhere in the mountains. After looking all over the state, they decided Evergreen "looked pretty good". They needed three-phase power, and ended up buying a small piece on a hill, near where Safeway is today, from D. E. Buchanan of the Hiwan Ranch. "All the local people thought we were out of our tree—we paid $1,000 for that acre." They built a 30' by 60' building, with a little office, and opened up as Rocky Mountain Woodworkers Inc. It was a struggle at first: since there was not enough cabinetry to sustain them in the mountains, they did remodelling and bid on work for tract builders in Denver. But slowly their reputation for excellent and well-designed work spread and they moved into building custom homes. Their very first house was for A. G. Kaiser: it now belongs to Willie Nelson. They also did work for Helen and Arthur Johnson at their "llama farm" in Bendemeer, remodelling the main house ("there wasn't a level floor or a plumb wall in the place") and putting up a new 40' x 60' barn. The principals of the company—popularly known as the Woodpeckers—changed some over the years. Another wartime friend, Ken Tatum, joined the firm. Ed Hendley sold out and returned to Denver. Paul Lappala decided to become a teacher: he taught social studies at Evergreen High School for ten years before going to Hong Kong to run a project for the Friends' Service Committee. In 1967, the Woodpecker building stood right in the path of the new four-lane highway. Negotiations for compensation in effect bought out Rocky Mountain Woodworkers. Marshall elected to carry on the business on his own. He bought back the building at salvage value from the Highway Department, moved it to its present site, and went on designing and building for five more years. In 1972 he figured he could "keep the wolf from the door" by renting the building as offices, and keep himself adequately occupied in maintaining it. The only regret was in letting go the excellent staff he had assembled over the years. But the Marshalls' three sons were raised and it was time for a little golf, a little travelling and time to enjoy the home they had built for themselves on Bear Mountain. Looking back over 25 productive years in Evergreen, Bill Marshall could be proud of a reputation for fine workmanship and of knowing how many Evergreen people value the heritage of a "Woodpecker" house.

Bill Marshall.

Johnson Barn,

Alan Frederickson, described by the Canyon Courier as a "successful Evergreen architect, accomplished musician, world traveler and founder of the Queen City Jazz Band" is certainly one of the most interesting characters on the Evergreen scene. Architect for such Evergreen buildings as the Library, the first Fire Station on Highway 73 and the Winegard electronics plant on Bryant Drive, Frederickson's energies also went for 20 years into playing every weekend with the Queen City Jazz Band—which was declared "a cultural monument of the state" in 1978 by the Colorado Legislature. Frederickson next spent a number of years sailing the oceans of the world. Now semi-retired, he plays his trombone as guest artist at jazz festivals and, with a group called the No Name Jazz Band, for engagements at unexpected times and places.

Alan Frederickson.

195

Evergreen Bridges

New housing in Genesee and Upper Bear Creek

196

I wrote the following in 1976, and include it here for two reasons. The experience of the hike down from Summit Lake is still as vivid in my mind, and as valid, as it was ten years ago. And the paragraphs at the end do prove that, in some ways, we are doing better by our beautiful environment.

Gene Sternberg

THE SOURCE OF EVERGREEN

A few days after we moved to our old log house on the banks of Bear Creek I woke up suddenly, hearing my name on Gene Amole's relentlessly cheerful early KVOD broadcast. "Upper Bear Creek isn't exactly the Moldau," he was saying, "but I'm playing this piece for Gene Sternberg who thinks the two have something in common."

He was right. When Bedrich Smetana was nearing the end of his life and nearly deaf, he was caught up in the surging movement for cultural and political freedom for the Czech people. He composed an immortal cycle of six symphonic poems which he called "Ma Vlast" (My Country). My favorite has always been the one about Bohemia's River Vltava (in German, Moldau), which Smetana describes in the notes for his music:

The sources of the river are two small springs, one warm and swift, suggested by the flute, and the other icy and slow, suggested by the clarinets. They are united into a small stream, and here the strings and oboe join in, giving the rich Vltava theme derived from a folk song. The stream dances and chatters in the sunlight, passes through dark forests, flows through emerald meadows and lowlands. At the Rapids of St. John the stream hews a path for its foaming waters through a rocky chasm and into a broad river bed. In majestic calm it then flows through Prague and finally fades into the distance.

More descriptive than any words or pictures, Smetana's music was singing in my mind one magnificent summer morning when I set out to follow Bear Creek from its source.

To stand by Summit Lake before all the snows have melted—among the bare rocks, strong winds and sheer power and majesty of that environment—is to be back at the beginning of time. In these naked surroundings is the start of Evergreen's creek.

Weather and mood shift constantly and dramatically. The sun shines brilliantly and cleanly, then from nowhere mists and clouds swirl up. It rains, hails, snows, and is sunny again, all in an hour. Under these conditions, the fragile assertions of life are a miracle.

Summit Lake that morning was a deep, cold blue, reflecting a cloudless sky and the remnant snows on the slopes of Mount Evans. A seemingly aimless finger of water pools over to the left of the road, and from this a small crystal-clear rivulet wanders gently out over the edge of the horizon. And that's it— the first few hundred feet of Bear Creek.

So clear it is, and so shallow, that every rock is totally visible and magnified, its colors, shape, texture exposed as if under a microscope. In some places, the new stream does not even have a channel. It widens out into a pool, disappears under a swamp of alpine willows, and you have to listen for the gurgling sound to find where it reappears. The whole broad slope is awash with melting snow so there is no special vegetation along the

197

stream that makes its path clearly visible.

Up there at the treeless top of the world there is a curious irony. This is where man could not survive and his impact is utterly insignificant. Yet, as an individual, you stand very tall in contrast to the tiny vegetation. Further down in the trees and rocky canyons, you are much more at home but also less significant, dwarfed by the surroundings.

Before reaching timberline, the stream suddenly disappears under a bank of frozen snow. Then with each few yards of descent, the vegetation changes, becoming taller, richer. Soon there is a marked difference between the water-loving plants growing along the stream and the plants in drier places.

Like all Coloradoans, I am used to driving through timberline. Its done in a flash and we take it for granted. But hiking down, following each foot of the stream, you pass in stages from open fields of alpine sunflowers into the shade of trees, and it is a spectacular experience.

The slopes become steeper, the volume and speed of the water increase. From time to time there are small waterfalls as the stream rushes headlong over piles of boulders. Because of the dramatic changes—in weather, altitude, vegetation, views—the walk is like an epic, an eternity of time and space compressed into a few hours.
At almost every step, I am tempted to stop, listen, look. Knowing how brief the summer is, and how long it may be before I do this again, I want to imprint on my senses each extraordinary moment of this experience.
Until I reach the Wildlife Area, I see no beer cans, no pop tops, no plastic sandwich bags. I fervently hope that no-one will ever follow Bear Creek down from its source, unless they step very lightly on fragile vegetation and leave no trace of their passage.

As I reach the lush meadows and beaver dams and the hard trails of civilization, my mind wanders forward to the ongoing course of Bear Creek. I see it winding its way through willow-lined banks and mountain meadows, between trim lawns and neatly rocked walls. I see it joined by all its small meandering tributaries that have helped determine Evergreen's road system and patterns of settlement—Buffalo Creek, Cub Creek, Troublesome Creek and so many more.

I see the stream blend into Evergreen Lake and fall over the dam. It strikes me again how badly American settlements have abused rivers and streams, their most precious assets. Even our small town center of Evergreen doesn't know how to appreciate its beautiful little creek: its the back of a parking lot, a nuisance to be bridged over with concrete, a convenient receptacle for trash.

As I project the further course of the creek through the rocky foothills and onto the plains, I come to its bitter ending. After wandering through trailer courts, automobile junk yards, sand and gravel pits, the creek dumps unseen and unmarked into the ugly, ruined Platte. I almost cannot bear to think at the same moment of the spectacularly beautiful source of Bear Creek and the meanness of its final miles.

But then I remember, and am grateful, that man can learn and nature is forgiving. I think of one fine suburban park that has been shaped out of a neglected stretch of the creek, and of the lake that the new Bear Creek Dam will offer to thousands of water-hungry people.

Even above Evergreen, I have noticed in recent years disturbing signs that the creek is degenerating. There is more algy, more foamy scum accumulating in backwaters. There are fewer times we can look down through the water and see the boulders crystal-clear and almost glowing. Some of this pollution is dirt washed down from new roads and driveways, but much is from too many, too-ancient leeching fields, and that's why we need a main sewer line along Upper Bear Creek. Then all who love this sparkling little stream can listen undisturbed to its music and enjoy its beauty.

In Smetana'a tone poem about the Vltava you can hear the activities of people who live along its banks, the wedding dances, festivals, harvest celebrations.

In my mind's eye, I too see festivals along the banks of Bear Creek. Music, dancing and creative art and the endless, fascinating flow of water go together. When Evergreen creates its new center for the practice and enjoyment of all the arts, I hope it will be placed in its most natural and beautiful setting—on the banks of Bear Creek and looking over the reflective blue lake.

There have been some tremendous improvements in the treatment of the Platte. Bear Creek now enters it through a new commercial center, more kindly dealt with than before. Bear Creek Lake is being developed as a fine recreational center. We who live along Upper Bear Creek paid the price— and a high price it was and is—to get the sewage out of the creek and into the Evergreen treatment plant. Some beginnings have been made in the direction of opening up the creek for public enjoyment along Main Street.

The vision of a joyful center for the arts on the banks of the creek, or overlooking Evergreen Lake, is still a vision.

199

Hiwan Golf Course.

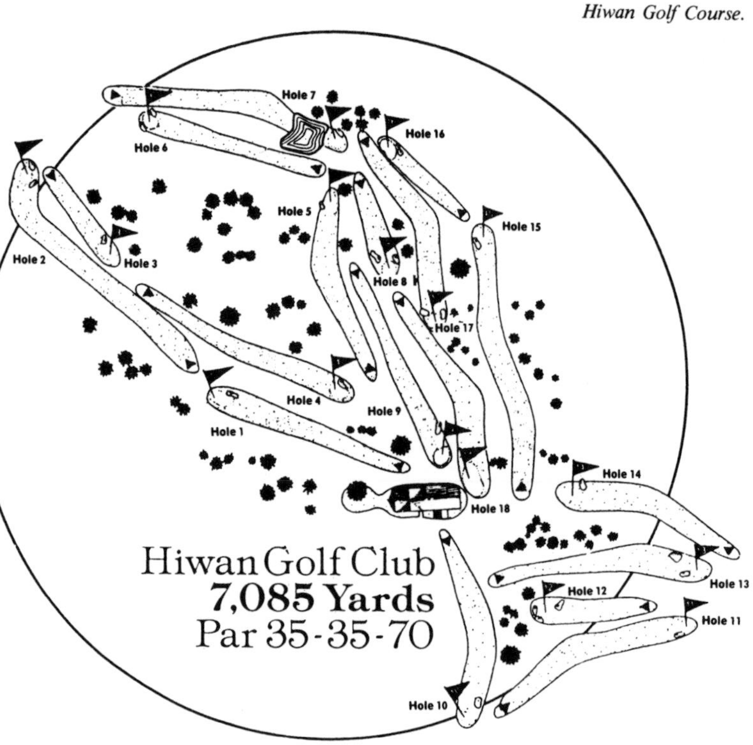

Hiwan Golf Club
7,085 Yards
Par 35·35·70

Gene grew up with soccer in Eastern Europe. Barbara played left wing on a field hockey team at an English girls' school. These long-ago experiences don't exactly qualify us to write about the Evergreen sporting scene. But some attention must be paid to it: people here love the outdoors and enjoy a wide variety of sports as spectators and participants. We know this because:
- the local paper, in tune with community interests, devotes up to a third of its space to sporting events and issues.
- nothing in Evergreen—no lecture, meeting or social engagement—takes precedence over Sunday Bronco games.
- large numbers of people play softball for fun. Some 60 teams, sponsored by local businesses, are in the summer leagues organized by the Evergreen Rec District.
- though Evergreen itself has no skiing facilities—except fine cross-country opportunities when there is enough snow —there are a whole lot of people here passionately devoted to downhill or cross-country skiing.

Here goes, then, with a far from expert or exhaustive rundown of the sports scene in Evergreen.

Colorado Open at the Hiwan Golf Course: this largest of state open tournaments takes place at the end of July and attracts both professionals and top-flight amateurs. According to a Canyon Courier reporter, while the Open does not usually draw the very top current names from the Professional Golfers' Association (PGA) tour, the $100,000 contest has carved a niche as an attractive tournament for up-and-coming pro's, former PGA stars preparing for the Seniors' Tour, and leading amateurs. A quick look at some who have played in the Hiwan Open since its first year in 1964—Al Geiberger, Dave Hill, Tommy Aaron, Australian Bruce Devlin, Don January—certainly looks like a roster of notables.

The event is well-attended by spectators, some 41,000 in a good year. Proceeds benefit Denver's Craig Hospital and its program for the acutely disabled: by 1986 total donations had amounted to almost $1.6 million.

The course at Hiwan comes in for its share of compliments and criticisms from golfers. Laid out in 1963 by Pres Maxwell, the 7,127-yard links cover an undulating—sometimes termed 'roller-coaster'—course, winding through pine trees. One metro-area reporter likened Hiwan to *"a seductive and comely lady, as dangerous as she is beautiful."*

Grasses at Hiwan were carefully selected for the Evergreen climate and are meticulously groomed by the course superintendent, Gary Russell: his main problems come from Mother Nature—in the form of hailstorms, elk (their urine is more deadly than their hooves), mice and gophers.

Notwithstanding difficulties, Hiwan is regarded as one of the finer mountain golf course in the country.

In 1985, there was some talk of moving the Open from Evergreen. Golf club members, who pay dearly for their playing privileges, felt that 8 days for the Open and associated events was too big a slice of the short summer season. Tournament organizers objected to a proposal that they should pay Hiwan to stage the event.

A Courier editorial summarized the way most people here felt about the Open: *"It would be a loss for both if the Colorado Open and Hiwan Golf Club parted company. The annual tournament is the largest state open in the country, but to hold onto that distinction it must retain its unique location among the pines. It needs the aura created by occasional sightings of elk and the whispers that all putts are mysteriously pulled toward Bergen Mountain to lure top-notch pros and amateurs to Colorado. And Evergreen needs the Open. It's a prestigious event that draws large crowds to spend money in our town without damaging the environment or even clogging the roads."* A compromise was worked out, to keep the Open at Hiwan, at least through 1988.

A major $250,000 expansion of the Hiwan Clubhouse facilities greeted the 1986 tournament players and spectators.

Evergreen Ice Carnival, 1948.

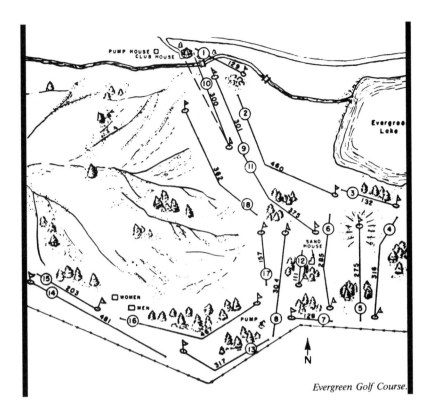

Evergreen Golf Course.

Ice hockey on the Lake.

Evergreen Golf Course. This is our community's public golf course—created, owned and operated by Denver since 1926. The 5,103-yard course adjoins Evergreen Lake and is shorter and narrower than most. But those who play it are convinced that *"what it gives up in distance, it demands back in accuracy."* The 12th hole is notorious: players have to drive over a huge rock.

Competition at the Evergreen course is not as prestigious as the Colorado Open at Hiwan, running more to good-humored affairs like the annual VFW Annual Evergreen Invitational Golf Tournament and the 'Wide Open' of 1985, co-sponsored by Key's on the Green Restaurant and Hiwan Liquors. However, since its major refurbishing in 1983, the course is popular and well-used.

Evergreen Lake. While the current spectator sport is watching the dredge at work, spewing out some 40 years of accumulated sludge to be dried and hauled away, the Lake is the site of many less passive activities.

Summertime is for fishing. In normal years, the Lake is stocked several times during the spring and summer months by the Colorado Division of Wildlife, with a total of around 17,000 catchable rainbow trout. During the two to four years of the current dredging operation, the Division plans to continue stocking as long as their observations show the fish surviving—although they are usually fished out pretty rapidly anyway. Wildlife Division biologists hope that when the dredging is completed, the trout may start moving up the stream for spawning, so that some natural replacement of the fish supply may take place once again.

Summer is also for boating. A variety of vessels- -canoes, sailboats, pedal boats—are available for rent.

Winter brings ice-fishing for the few and ice-skating for the multitude. There is a modest fee for skating. Rental skates and a warming house, with snack bar, are available. One of the loveliest sights in Evergreen, by day or by night, is the lively pattern of skaters of all ages on the Lake, framed by snow-covered hills.

When the Lake opens for skating depends entirely on the weather: the ice must be of a certain thickness to be safe both for skaters and for clearing and maintenance

Skating on Evergreen Lake, 1984. Ron Ruhoff.

202

Evergreen Town Race.

equipment. (The Evergreen Rec District found this out soon after they took over the Lake's recreational programs from Denver, when one of their trucks broke through the ice: although it was pulled out, it was a total loss.) Opening is usually around Christmas time, but can be as late as mid-January.

Recreation activities at the Lake are operated by the Evergreen Metropolitan Parks and Recreation District, which determines fees and hours.

Evergreen "Rec" Center. Also operated by the Recreation District, the story of this facility is told in more detail in the section called "Who's in Charge"? A great diversity of classes ranging from swimming to volleyball, gymnastics, racquetball, dance and fitness are offered for both children and adults. Outdoor programs in skiing, biking and team sports are also offered through the Rec District at various locations.

Town Race course.

The Evergreen Town Race. One of the joyful community events associated with Rodeo Weekend— at the beginning of August— is this run down Upper Bear Creek. The Sunday race begins at 8 a.m., with the 10K starting place at Yankee Point and the 5K at Rosedale. Upper Bear Creek Road is closed to traffic for a couple of hours and runners are ferried by shuttle buses from parking lots around town.

The first Town Race was in 1978, when Governor Richard Lamm joined about 800 other runners. The Evergreen Race has survived the fall-off from the first wave of high enthusiasm for running, and is established as one of the 10 largest races in Colorado. This may be because it is the fastest course in the state (it drops steadily for 800 feet over the 10K course) and the most scenic. Perhaps it is the weather— usually clear, sunny and cool. The organizers think it may also have something to do with the free beer and good brunch they offer after the race, in the Lakepoint parking lot, along with live music and a well-designed T-shirt for all entrants.

The number of runners is limited to 2,500. About half come from Evergreen, keeping the community flavor of the event intact, and half from out of town. The race attracts a fair share of nationally competitive runners. Men's 10K record for the course is 28.51, held by Evergreen's own Pat Porter who, amazingly enough, has clocked exactly the same time in three wins.

Since the 10K runners reach their half-way point practically at our back door, we are usually out to cheer them on and to marvel at the infinite variety of individual running styles.

The race benefits the Alpine Rescue Team. There have been many different sponsors over the years but consistent leadership and support have come from Dick Petersen and his insurance agency, and from Evergreen's Timber Ridge Runners.

Freedom Run. This annual July 4th race, started in 1982, benefits the Mount Evans Hospice/Home Health Care, Inc. The 10K section starts at Bergen elementary School, and the 5K near the Village Inn Restaurant. The course winds through the Hiwan Country Club area to a finish line at the Hiwan Homestead Museum.

Barb Early of Evergreen winning 1985 5K Town Race.

In its first year, organisers expected around 200 entrants and had to cope with 500. 742 took part in 1986, raising $6500 for the Hospice.

Mount Evans Trophy Run. This gruelling race from Echo Lake Lodge to the 14,260 summit of Mount Evans usually attracts enough runners to fill its registration limit of 1200— despite the possibility of snow, sleet, rain, fog and high winds, and the certainty of thin air at the top. Experienced runners classify this 14+ mile run as requiring the same energy and training as a marathon on level ground: the course involves a vertical climb of almost a mile. Best time in the race, which is sponsored by the YMCA and the Rocky Mountain News, is 1 hour 41.85 minutes.

Pat Porter wins 1981 Mt. Evans Trophy Run.

Pat Porter, Evergreen's Olympic Runner, finally won the 14th annual Mount Evans Run in 1981 on his fourth try, battling sub-freezing weather, 30 mph winds and snow flurries. Porter was an outstanding track and field athlete at Evergreen High School, from which he graduated in 1977. At Adams State College in Alamosa he was a five-time All-American in track and cross-country and in 1982 became national cross-country champion, a title he successfully defended in 1983 and 1984.

After graduation, Porter stayed on in Alamosa to continue training with his coach, and was invited to join the highly selective Athletics West running team, sponsored by Nike. This earned him a monthly stipend to support his bid for a berth on the U.S. team in the 1984 Summer Olympics. In that year, Porter placed fourth in the World Cross-Country Championships, the top American finisher. He won his place on the Olympic Team, a signal accomplishment even though he did not manage a medal.

In November Pat Porter came home to Evergreen High School as guest speaker at the cross-country team's annual banquet. He reminded the young athletes that his own high school times were not as good as those run by some of them. *"Never underestimate yourselves,"* he told them, *"if you can dream it, you can become it."*

In 1985, Porter won is fourth straight national title at the U.S. Cross Country Championships, matching the accomplishment of fellow-Coloradoan Frank Shorter. Porter now is a resident of Alamosa though his parents still live in Evergreen. He is planning a bid for the 1988 Summer Games in Korea and even looking at the possibility of 1992 and 1996. In 1986, Porter was named Colorado Athlete of the Year, an award which is supported by proclamations by the Mayor of Denver and the State's Governor and is presented at a Denver Athletic Club dinner.

Lo Hunter. This "diminutive dynamo", as reporters love to call her, was the only daughter in a large family of boys. She credits much of her success to her father, who was able to take pride in her athletic accomplishments rather than demanding that she limit herself to traditional feminine roles. After teaching in Kansas and Texas, she came to Evergreen High

Evergreen High School volleyball coach Lo Hunter.

School in 1966 with experience in playing and coaching a variety of sports. In 1973, she began coaching the EHS girls' volleyball team, in a foothills league with no formal standings. When a state league was formed, Lo Hunter's teams took four out of the first five state championships.

By 1980, when she was named Coach of the Year by the National High School Athletic Coaches Association, she had already garnered many state honors and her string of successes was legendary. Totally dedicated and very demanding, she also took pride in the fact that her girls were good athletes without losing their femininity, active in school affairs, and serious students. From time to time, Hunter coached basketball and tennis in addition to volleyball—and EHS Parents appreciated that she had opened up the opportunity of collegiate athletic scholarships for their daughters, as well as career opportunities in athletics. Her coaching philosophy could have come from the Boy Scouts: *"We never lose by being unprepared." "We go to the best clinics,"* she explained, *"learn new techniques, practice like heck, and know that we can only lose if the other team plays the game of their lives."* In both 1981 and 1982, the EHS Girls' Volleyball team clinched spots in the record books by having the longest winning streaks in the nation: the number was stretched to 182 consecutive wins before being snapped in September, 1985.

1985 brought the 8th straight state championship and also saw Lo Hunter involved in persuading the University of Colorado to adopt volleyball as its 7th women's NCAA sport. In that year, Lo Hunter was inducted into the

Colorado Sports Hall of Fame, not only for her athletic accomplishments but for her great contributions to girls' athletics in Colorado.

By 1986, Coach Hunter's example of dedicated coaching and serious training had been followed by a number of other high schools: the Evergreen girls team was edged out of the title in the final play-offs. But perhaps, in reality, this is the greatest tribute to her achievement.

Tanya Haave was the first of Lo Hunter's proteges to achieve national recognition. Haave was a vital element in the EHS volleyball team's early string of victories. In one of the best high school athletic careers ever recorded in Colorado, Haave shone in volleyball, basketball and track and racked up numerous awards and honors. After graduation in 1980, she won a 4-year athletic scholarship to the University of Tennessee, playing both volleyball and basketball and managing a 3.45 grade point average. As forward, she paced the UT basketball team to a place in the National championship play-offs in 3 out of 4 years. 1984, her final battle, was a heartbreaker. In a nationally-televised game, the Tennessee team was beaten by USC, but Haave shared Player-of-the-Game honors awarded by CBS.

Haave was one of 106 women invited to Colorado Springs to try out for the 12-member U.S. women's basketball team for the Los Angeles Olympics: she survived two rounds but was then cut. Tanya Haave was inducted into the Colorado YWCA Hall of Fame in 1984 and awarded a $2,000 scholarship by the NCAA for graduate studies.

Sherri Danielson, another standout EHS volleyball player, went on to play for Colorado State University, where she was a two-time All-American selection. In January of 1986, this 5'9" college senior was selected as the youngest member of the U.S. Women's Olympic Volleyball Team. She moved to San Diego to start a gruelling regime of practice with the squad.

203

Everest climber John Evans of Conifer, left 1981.

Evergreen, describes the difference between all-terrain bikes and *"those skinny- wheeled, drop handlebar machines"*. Mountain bicycles are sturdy, lightweight and geared to allow steep climbing. They have strong brakes and place the rider in an upright, comfortable position over balloon tires. Downing explains that this *"brings out the kid in many adults and puts something into exercise that every program should have for success— fun."* The Canyon Courier Sports reporter described the bikes as *"two-wheeled fountains of youth."*

Evans, Evergreen and Everest. On July 3, 1981, the Evergreen-based Colorado Philharmonic played a special concert to benefit the American Medical Research Expedition to Mount Everest, led by Conifer resident John Evans. Evans had already made one successful Everest climb in 1971, via a difficult route never before attempted. He had also made many other big climbs in the Antarctic, Russia, India, Europe, Africa and New Zealand, and was serving as associate director of the Colorado Outward Bound School. In 1976, he was asked by Dr. John West to organize a group of climbers to Everest, this time as a research project on the effects of altitude on human physiology and psychology. Besides rounding up funds and equipment and making the necessary arrangements with the Nepal government, his assignment was to find five team-mates "aggressive enough to be accomplished climbers and laid-back enough to put up with the distraction of research." In late July, 1981, the six climbers joined 6 climbing scientists, five non-climbing scientists and some assistants on the first leg of a long and successful expedition. Five climbers reached the summit, including 2 Sherpas and 3 Americans—the 9th, 10th and 11th Americans to conquer Everest. All but one of the demanding roster of medical research experiments were completed and there were no serious injuries.

Cycling has become increasingly popular in Evergreen as in the rest of Colorado. Slender enthusiasts in helmets and skin-tight racing gear are becoming a common sight on our mountain roads. But for many, interest in cycling as a personal activity has been revived by the introduction of mountain or all-terrain bicycles. Cycling conditions on highways in and around

Evergreen range from enjoyable— on wide and little-travelled routes like Squaw Pass and Shadow Mountain Road—to suicidal—like Upper Bear Creek or Highway 74 past Evergreen Lake. A few surfaced off-road trails suitable for conventional bicycles are being developed but the mountain bikes open up to the recreational cyclist a wide array of dirt roads and trails in parks like Alderfer- Three Sisters and Elk (Means) Meadow.

Phil Downing, cycling enthusiast and co-owner of Paragon Mountain Bikes in downtown

Bob Cook Memorial Mount Evans Hill Climb is a gruelling 28- mile amateur race held in July or August each year. Starting at an altitude of 7540 in Idaho Springs, the course gains 6724 vertical feet by the time it ends at the summit. The race started in 1962, when the winning time was 2 hours 28 minutes. It is now named after a remarkable young cyclist from Englewood, Colorado who won the race five times in six attempts between 1975 and 1980. He was a member of the U.S. National and the 1980 U.S. Olympic Cycling Teams and a mathematical engineer.

Bob Cook Memorial Mount Evans Hill Climb.

204

Bob Cook was 23 when he died in 1981 of brain cancer. In his memory, his parents have endowed two scholarship funds and continue to support the modest prize list for the Mount Evans race. Screenwriter Steve Tesich, who lives part of the year in Conifer, embodied his feelings about Cook's life and indomitable spirit in his screenplay for the movie, *"American Flyers"*.

Cook's record 1978 time of 1:54:27 stood until 1983 when Todd Gogulski shaved it to 1:53:43. In spite of the small monetary rewards and the exclusion of big-name professional cyclists, the Mount Evans Hill Climb is highly regarded and attracts over 300 contestants.

Olympic gold medalist Alexi Grewal holds the current Hill Climb record time of 1:47:51 and, as a pro, is now ineligible to compete. He says, *"I grew up with that race and nothing will take its place. It bares you to the bone. It's not so much you against the mountain as you against yourself. You can never beat the mountain."*

Alpine Rescue Team June 9, 1984 was proclaimed Alpine Rescue Day in Colorado by Governor Richard Lamm, in recognition of the team's 25 years of volunteer service in the Rocky Mountain region. In that time, the team had racked up more than a quarter of a million man-hours donated time and service and had saved some 427 lives.

The team was started by members of the Idledale, Indian Hills and Evergreen fire departments, after a rescue of injured climbers on rocks near Highway 285. Originally called IIE, the name was changed to the more explicit Alpine Rescue Team in 1960. In that year, it qualified for membership in the national Mountain Rescue Association, which is dedicated to the rescue of people in mountain hiking and climbing accidents and to mountain safety education. The Team is also affiliated with the Colorado Search and Rescue Board which coordinates the efforts of the state's 49 search and rescue related groups.

ART's members, usually around 50, vary in age from 16 to 50. They are all volunteers, who undertake an arduous initial training and must take regular refresher sessions to keep in good standing. To stick with the time-consuming and physically wearying work, team members must be people who find great satisfaction in helping others and have a taste for high

adventure—even though 90% of the work is described as *"dirty, hot, grimy and fatiguing—not hero business."*

The rescue efforts take a lot of weekends, searching in summer for lost and injured mountain hikers and climbers and in winter for cross-country skiers in trouble. The ART has its own *"Team Shack"* on Independence Mountain and relies heavily on donations and grants for meeting its expenses. Team members take part in rescue missions on their own time and at their own expense.

Historical Notes: The Jefferson County Graphic for July 14, 1900 reported, *"The contest between the Morrison and Evergreen baseball teams resulted in a score of 10 to 19 in favor of Morrison."* Bowling here had a short but enthusiastic run. The Canyon Courier announced in February of 1960 that a new sport had arrived in the mountain area with the opening of the Bergen Park Bowling Lanes (in the building that is now a real estate office). The Hiwan Bowl came a little later. In August of 1969, the Hiwan Bowl closed down permanently; the Elks Club, which had been using the lower level since its formation, purchased the building in 1970.

Evergreen made the national news media in 1970 for its considerable part in killing the Denver bid for the 1976 Olympics, on the grounds that the activities proposed for here involved too much destruction of the environment with very doubtful benefits.

Evergreen Athletic Club. Located in the Colorado National Bank Building off Highway 74, this private club offers racquetball courts, exercise equipment, fitness classes, tennis courts and an outdoor swimming pool.

The Evergreen Rodeo and Other Horse Shows. This mountain area has a love affair with horses. We have not found any reliable census of the equine population. But we know from the many personal acquaintances who keep horses, from the high proportion of real estate ads offering 'great horse properties' and from the number of horse-related news items culminating in the annual Rodeo extravaganza, that the ancient relationship between people and horses is alive and well here.

Alpine Rescue Team member Bill Butler teaching vertical evacuation skills, 1984.

Rider at Evergreen Rodeo.

There has been an Evergreen Rodeo on and off since at least 1947. We have family photographs of our young children watching one, in the early fifties, in a rustic arena where the Safeway is today. But the Rodeo tradition lapsed in the 60's, mainly for lack of a suitable site. A dedicated few formed the Bear Creek Rodeo Association. In 1966, the present site in El Pinal was found and purchased and an arena constructed.

In 1967, nationally recognized cowboys came from everywhere to participate in the 1st Annual Evergreen Rodeo and to welcome the new addition to the circuit of the Professional Rodeo Cowboys Association. The Rodeo was always preceded by such events as the selection of a Rodeo Queen and a lively Rodeo Parade down Main Street.

Over the years, expenses to put on the Rodeo as a professional event mounted and attendance diminished. In 1984, the Bear Creek Rodeo Association elected to cut its expenses by severing its connection with the PRCA and 'going amateur'—affiliating with the Colorado State Rodeo Association.

The rousing 1986 event lacked a Rodeo Queen and had no beer for sale—liability insurance rates had become prohibitive. Still, over 2,000 came to the Saturday and Sunday afternoon Rodeo performances to watch bareback and saddle bronc riding, calf roping, steer wrestling, team roping, mixed team roping and ladies' barrel racing.

Cross-country ski areas, Alderfer/Three Sisters Park.

ALDERFER / THREE SISTERS PARK

Located in the heart of Evergreen, the 300-acre Alderfer/Three Sisters Park offers scenic views, intriguing rock formations, and highly variable terrain for the skier. The park can be reached from downtown Evergreen via Highway 73 and Buffalo Park Road. Parking is available at Wilmot Elementary when school is not in session, and a short trail leads visitors to the park itself.

LEGEND

Auto Parking	P
Trail	
Trail Distance	
Park Boundary & Entry	

BEST SNOW AREAS

SISTERS TRAIL .68mi

THE THREE SISTERS .28mi

THE BROTHER

FAWN TRAIL .64mi

HIDDEN .13mi

.26mi

PONDEROSA TRAIL 1.32mi

BUFFALO PARK ROAD

SYNDT ROAD

.25mi

GREENWOOD DRIVE

.9 miles to Hwy 73
1.5 miles to Evergreen

WOODS DRIVE

HATCH DRIVE

WILMOT SCHOOL

Crowd at Evergreen Rodeo.

Best snow areas, Elk (Means) Meadow park.

SKI TOURING INFORMATION

Because snow cover is quite variable at these elevations, selected areas of each park are shown as the most likely places for good skiing. During mild winters and between storms, there may not be enough snow for safe and enjoyable skiing, so call the Open Space Information number, 277-8340, for snow conditions.

MEANS MEADOW PARK

This 1,100 acre Open Space Park provides many opportunities for the cross-country skier to enjoy winter in the foothills of the Rockies. Situated in the Evergreen area, the park is easily accessible. Picnicking, wildlife viewing, nature study, and photography are some of the activities available to the adventurous skier. Challenging and gently sloping terrain provide skiing opportunities for both the expert and beginning skier.

BERGEN PARK - ¾ mile

Bergen Peak 3.4 miles

TOO LONG TRAIL

MEADOW VIEW .9 mi

1.0 mi

BEST SNOW AREA

ELKRIDGE .5 mi SLEEPY "S"

PAINTERS PAUSE 1.0 mi

COLORADO HIGHWAY 73

Bergen Peak 3.7 miles

BERGEN PEAK TRAIL

MEADOW VIEW .6 mi

.3 mi

LEGEND

Auto Parking	**P**
Trail	- - - -
Trail Distance	● X MILE ●
Park Boundary & Entry	⌐ ⌐

STAGECOACH BLVD 1¼ miles

EVERGREEN 2 miles

Two other annual horse shows are held in the El Pinal Arena: the ***Little Britches Rodeo*** and the 2-day ***Saddle Tramp Gymkhana,*** sponsored by the 4-H Saddle Tramps of Evergreen.

The Ski Scene: Since the small Squaw Pass Ski Area—which was about 10 miles from Bergen Park off Highway 103—closed up around 1970, there has been no downhill ski facility in the Evergreen area, though of course there is easy access to Colorado's major ski areas via I-70.

Squaw Pass Ski Area itself was around 90 acres, surrounded by National Forest. Though high—around 11,000 feet—and therefore cold and often windy, Squaw Pass was a great place for Evergreen's youngsters to learn to ski and to find part-time winter jobs.

In the years when snow is plentiful in Evergreen, there are excellent cross-country skiing opportunities in such Open Space Parks as Alderfer-Three Sisters and Elk (Means) Meadow and these are attractively mapped in a free Open Space publication.

Both cross-country and downhill ski equipment is available for rental at Evergreen's four sporting goods stores (Evergreen Ski Co., Paragon Sports, Snow Leopard and Sports Mine). Ski instruction at different skill levels is available from the Evergreen Recreation Center. Casey Boone of Paragon Sports offers specialty clinics, with field experience, in avalanche awareness (for back-country skiers, climbers and mountaineers) and cross-country and telemark skiing.

With all this said, something is still missing that would capture the real sports story in Evergreen. It has to do with all the activity done for its own sake, not for glory or financial reward. Its the individual joggers out, at risk of life and limb, along the winding roads. The hikers, bikers, and skiers. The fishermen and hunters and horseback riders. Those hardy souls who make it to a 6 a.m. aerobics class in a blizzard, and others who get back from a tiring Denver commute and make a raquetball date at the Rec Center or the Evergreen Athletic Club.

And 650 energetic players of both sexes who make up those 60 softball teams.

Cross-country ski trails, Hiwan Country Club

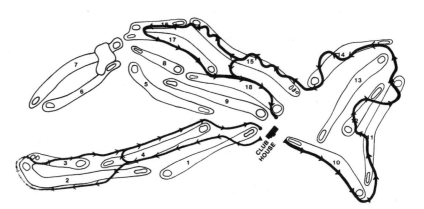

207

THE HIWAN FACTOR IN THE GROWTH OF EVERGREEN

Hiwan. You cannot be in Evergreen very long before the name forces itself into your consciousness. If you come in from Bergen Park, an intriguing little group of buildings that includes an old octagonal barn will draw your attention to a sign advertising 'exclusive Hiwan sites' for sale.

Soon after Highway 74 explodes into a brief one-mile stretch as a four-lane highway, another entrance takes off to the left, bearing the same Hiwan name.

Approaching from Kittredge, you come first to the Hiwan Village Stores and offices. A brown and white sign invites you to visit the Jefferson County Hiwan Homestead.

A sports enthusiast is likely to focus on Evergreen on those days when the Colorado Open is being played out on the pine-bordered greens of the Hiwan Golf Course.

Even if all you know about Evergreen is that a young former resident tried to assassinate President Ronald Reagan, you will have read that his family lived in the Hiwan area whose atmosphere, said the New York Times on April 16, 1982, is "a bit on the order of a country club built in a national park."

A map of the Evergreen area shows a patchwork of subdivisions. They are located along stream beds, on hillsides and in natural mountain meadows. Prominent among these are the Hiwan subdivisions: Hiwan Hills, Hiwan Village and the many filings in the Hiwan Golf and Country Club area.

If you start to ask questions around town, you learn that there was once a vast ranch called Hiwan which bred prize Hereford cattle.

Someone may mention that it used to stretch all the way from Evergreen to Central City, and maybe even to the outskirts of Denver. You ask where the name came from. Nobody seems to know but there's usually someone who guesses it is of Indian origin.

Sooner or later, you'll be advised to go to the Hiwan Homestead Museum 'because that used to be the headquarters of the Hiwan Ranch.'

If you happen to meet some old timers, they'll probably tell you that it was the subdividing of the Hiwan lands that sealed the fate of Evergreen, changing it from a farming community and sleepy summer tourist village to an automobile- congested suburb of Denver.

The Hiwan Homestead Museum is indeed a good place to start digging into the history of the Hiwan Ranch and its people. Former Director Connie Fahnestock and her successor, Sandy Crain, have spent many years assembling materials so that the story of the house, the people who lived in it and the lands that went with it, will not be lost. In 1986 the Jefferson County Historical Society published Fahnestock's fascinating little book telling the building's story.

Buchanans Purchase the Williams-Douglas Lands

The Hiwan part of the Homestead story begins in 1938. In that year, a Tulsa oilman named Darst Buchanan and his wife, Ruth, rented the Douglas's Camp Neosho for the summer. The following year, they bought the nucleus of what was to become the Hiwan Ranch from the Douglas family, for about $50,000.

The purchase included what remained of the Mary Neosho Williams estate. The story of this influential figure in Evergreen's history is told in the segment on the Williams- Douglas Legacy.

The original Williams land stretched from the far side of Independence Mountain, included all of Hiwan Village and most of the business section of Main Street, and continued up over the hills on both sides of Main Street. By the 1920's, there were a number of

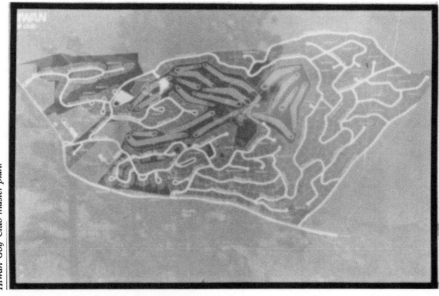

Hiwan Golf Club master plan.

subdivisions in the Evergreen area— summer communities with 'rustic' sanitation (outhouses, cesspools or septic tanks) and water either drawn from wells or brought from springs through surface pipes, which were drained for the winter.

One of the first Evergreen subdivisions planned for year-round homes was developed by Dr. Josepha Douglas. The small but dynamic Evergreen Public Service Company, owned by Clarence Smith, could provide water and electric power to the land above Main Street. The plat for the Douglas Park subdivision, providing for 34 one-acre home sites, was filed in 1937, one year before Dr. Josepha's death.

By this time her husband, Canon Douglas, was deep into his last major task, the complete revision of the Episcopalian Church Hymnal. Eric, their only child, was involved in his own life work as Curator of Native Arts at the Denver Art Museum.

Money was short, for these were depression times, and it was time for the Douglas's to sell their Evergreen holdings.

Darst and Ruth Buchanan came to Denver around 1930 for an oil convention. Like so many people of that era, they first came to Evergreen to attend an affair at the elegant Troutdale Hotel. Their daughter Joan Landy, who still lives in Evergreen, remembers hearing them say that, as they drove up Main Street, *"something just caught."*

"And," she said, *"you probably know that Tulsa's awful hot in the summertime!"*

Mrs. Buchanan and her three daughters, Barbara, Betty and Joan, started to spend their summers in Evergreen, renting a different cabin or home each year. Mr Buchanan was usually too busy with his oil interests to spend much time on vacation.

Joan remembers those summers of the Thirties as 'glorious times'. They would rent horses and have races down the length of Main Street with other *"summer"* teenagers. There were long lazy days, ice cream sodas at the drug store in the old Round-up building (now the Little Bear), and evening dances and movies at Troutdale.

Ruth Buchanan.

Darst Buchanan.

When Darst Buchanan rented the Homestead in 1938, and the family found out that it was for sale, Joan Landy says they all set to work to *"talk Daddy into buying the place."* He did not need much persuading. He and his wife had been spending their spare time since 1935 looking for the ideal ranch to which they could retire one day.

So, the Buchanans bought the Douglas property, consisting of the Homestead, its surrounding buildings and some 1,100 acres of land—including the unsold lots in Douglas Park.

The Hiwan Name
Joan Landy recalls that her mother had a passion for naming things. As soon as the family acquired the Homestead complex, she started to christen the various buildings. One of them she called *"Who's House",* because, as she said, you never knew who was going to be staying there. Canon Douglas had left an old Anglo-Saxon Dictionary in the house, which is understandable since one of his avocations had been translating early English plainsong into modern verse for use in contemporary church services.

In this dictionary, Ruth Buchanan found the name for their Evergreen home: HIWAN. The dictionary has disappeared. It has become a delightful bit of family—and now community—mythology as to just it means. Joan remembers hearing about two definitions: *"a high, secluded place"* and *"the amount of land a man can plow from sunup to sundown with one ox."* An early real estate brochure extolling the attractions of the Hiwan Country Club subdivision said that Hiwan was an ancient Scots word.

A 1962 article in the Denver Daily Journal noted, *"Hiwan Development Co. owns some 30,000 acres of land in the Evergreen-Bergen Park area. It was once the Hiwan Ranch controlled by Buchanan family. The name Hiwan refers to the amount of land a team of oxen can plow around in a year's time. It is, as the names Buchanan and Casey imply, an Irish name."*

As good researchers, we consulted an Anglo-Saxon dictionary and found that indeed the word Hiwan is Anglo-Saxon, but had nothing to do with plowing, or with oxen or with high ground. Hiwan signified simply *"members of a household"* or *"land let to members of a household."* Mr. Buchanan might have enjoyed its third meaning, *"a king's household."*

No matter. Hiwan was a poetic choice of name. Its constantly expanding usage in Evergreen is proof of its appeal.

Darst Buchanan
Darst Buchanan was one of those attractive, driving, self-made men who were perhaps more characteristic of the nineteenth century that the twentieth. A successful, acquisitive businessman, he also had an imaginative and curious mind and absolutely no

inhibitions about launching into completely new ventures. His daughter says he was a 'black Scot', with dark hair and a swarthy complexion that allowed him to pass himself off as Greek, Italian, French or Portuguese as a diversion—and he had the linguistic flair to carry off such charades.

He was born on a farm near Lima, Ohio in 1892, the eldest of three children and the only boy. His education in the one-room country school lasted until he was 13: he enjoyed telling his daughters how he skated down a frozen stream to school in the winter, holding a hot potato in his hands to keep them warm.
He then did a *"man's work on the farm for a year, intending to save enough money to attend high school in Lima the next year. But as it turned out, I never got the time and the money together at the same time."*

The family moved to St. Mary's, Ohio, where he got a job as a foundry time-keeper. Then an uncle *"way out west in Springfield, Missouri"* urged him to come out and take a job as timekeeper on one of the railroad track's maintenance crews. From section crew timekeeper at 15 he became the superintendent's chief clerk by the age of 20.

In 1912 he married Ruth Peake of Springfield, and in 1917 was transferred to the railroad's division office at Sapulpa, Oklahoma.

There, Buchanan was caught up in the oil companies' raids on employees of railroads and other businesses. The lure was higher salaries. He took a job with the Sapulpa Refining Company, later moving to Tulsa and joining Chestnut and Smith who were at that time the world's largest producers of natural gasoline. Within a few months, he was vice-president.

Ten years later, and two days after the great stock market crash, Buchanan and three other Chestnut and Smith associates pooled $250,000 and launched their own natural gas production company, Hanlon-Buchanan Inc., with Buchanan as president. A family story has it that there was a glut of gasoline on the market so Buchanan and his friends bought every tank car they could lay their hands on, betting that the price would make a comeback. The

company not only survived the Depression but proliferated into five companies dealing in pipelines, manufacturing and production.

Another family recollection is that Buchanan sent the first shipload of natural gasoline—so-called because it was a pure, high-gravity product that needed no refining—to England. His company became a major European supplier of airplane fuel, and he spent much of his time on business travels in Europe.

Buchanan a pioneer of the oil and gas business. With his capacity for hard work and natural gift for public relations, he was typical of the early *"go-go-go"* era of oil and gas exploration. Influential in the U.S. petroleum community, he was appointed chairman of the official U.S. delegation to the 1937 Paris World Petroleum Conference.

In 1942, Interior Secretary Harold Ickes named Buchanan director in charge of District 3 of the Petroleum Administration for War—an area that then produced 70 percent of the nations's oil.

After the war, according to a 1952 article in the Denver Post, the assets of Hanlon-Buchanan were sold to the Warren Petroleum Company for $13 million, and Buchanan *"retired"*. He and his wife moved from Tulsa to Cherry Hills Village, southeast of Denver. There they bought the Martin home, just off South Clarkson, which at that time was a charming English-style house on a small stream, surrounded by huge old cottonwoods. The house is still there, though the land around it is now subdivided into a secluded yet accessible residential area.

Retirement did not last long. In addition to the Hiwan operations, Buchanan was soon back in corporate harness. In January, 1950, fellow-rancher Bill Allen of Ken Caryl, near Littleton, persuaded Bucanan to invest some money in Heco — the Heckethorn Manufacturing and Supply Co. Allen was the largest stockholder. When he died suddenly in December of the same year, the stockholders asked Buchanan to take over the presidency. In the first nine months of Buchanan's administration, according to The Denver Post, Heco quadrupled both its business volume and the number of its employees.

Hiwan Ranch herefords.

The Hiwan Ranch
Much of the Buchanans' time was spent in Evergreen. Darst's restless energies turned to exploring uses for his new holdings. He had been intrigued for some time with the idea of raising prize cattle and in this he had a willing ally in one of his three sons-in-law.

At one time or another, all of his daughters' husbands played a part in the Hiwan story: Betty Buchanan married John Casey, Joan was married first to Fred Goodale and later to Nelson Landy, and Barbara's husband was Robert Kirchner.

John Casey came from Texas. He had a law degree from the University of Colorado but his natural preference was for an outdoor life. He became the manager of the Hiwan Hereford Ranch and also the prime mover in the later development of Hiwan lands for commercial and residential use.

The ranch was initially a prize breeding operation. No expense was spared to secure the finest stock. In 1947, Buchanan set a world's record when he paid $61,000 to a Cheyenne, Wyoming, Hereford Ranch for a bull named WHR Helmsman 89th.

At its peak the ranch had around 750 breeding cows. More grazing lands were needed. Buchanan began to buy up farms and ranches as they came onto the market. He acquired the properties of Oscar and George Johnson—which included the areas now covered by the Hiwan Golf and Country Club subdivisions on one side of the road and the Elk (Means) Meadow Park on the other—and the Hamrich place adjoining Wah Keeney Park.

The biggest single purchase was the Blackmer Ranch, which was the portion of the Buchanan lands that stretched from outside Evergreen to the borders of Central City.
Buchanan also bought a large piece of property on Wadsworth Avenue, southwest of Denver.

Buchanan family at wedding of Barbara Buchanan to Robert Kirchner.

Naively, we asked Robert Kirchner if he could help us to draw a map showing the extent of the Hiwan Ranch at its zenith. It didn't take him long to explain why he could not do this, and why it probably never will be possible. Buchanan was constantly both buying and selling land. Not all of the lands acquired were part of the Hiwan Ranch, some being held in other partnership or corporate names. Finally, the lands were in three different counties—Jefferson, Gilpin and Clear Creek. Tracing down of titles and dates would involve long and tedious research in three courthouses.

The Caseys lived in one of the houses that is now part of the Hiwan Museum property. Ranch foreman Al Parker lived in the little house in Bergen Park, next to the octagonal barn.

At first the ranch was a breeding operation for high grade, purebred Herefords. Later, grade or meat cattle were also raised and sold.

Joan Landy remembers when she and her sister used to help move cattle up to summer pastures. Al Parker would drive the herd as far as the Idaho Springs road, probably borrowing a neighbor's pens to keep them overnight. Joan and Barbara joined the operation at 5 the next morning. They moved the cattle up the main highway, and then took off at Rattlesnake Gulch, *"right up the side of the hill."* In the fall, the operation was reversed.

The handsome barn—later The Hardware—was built as a showbarn for the Hiwan prize Herefords, so the name *"Showbarn Plaza"* for the commercial complex next to the barn is an appropriate historical footnote.

We tried to find out if this vast Hiwan Ranch had ever made a go of it financially. From talking with pioneer families still living in the Evergreen area we have learned that farming and ranching was always a tough and marginal activity. Even families living with extreme simplicity, meeting only the barest human needs, had to supplement agricultural earnings with additional paid work.

We discussed the topic with Herb Wallower, whose father established a cattle ranching operation at the same time the Hiwan Ranch was in full swing.

Herb Wallower, Sr. and Darst Buchanan were good friends, who also bought and sold cattle and land to—and from—each other. Herb says that his family's ranch was more of a retirement hobby than a business venture for his father, who felt very good indeed in years when it did not actually lose money. He suspects that the same situation was probably true of the Hiwan, and that seems to be the impression of the Buchanan family members that we talked with.

211

Herbert and Dora Wallower.

Glendora, the Wallower home on Upper Bear Creek.

Herb Wallower Jr.

Other Evergreen Enterprises

The Buchanan family was always willing to try new ventures. One year it was turkeys. Over the hillside near the Hiwan Homestead roamed 5,000 of the noisy birds. The experience was not particularly pleasant or profitable and was not repeated.

Another year, Darst Buchanan thought they should turn the main Homestead building into a guest lodge. Literature was prepared, some mailing done and guests actually did stay in the house for one season. The 1943 Colorado Business Directory has a listing for the Hiwan Ranch Resort, with John Casey as Manager.

But it was not very enjoyable to occupy a small cabin while other people lived in comfort at the main house! So that experiment was not repeated either.

There were also early excursions into building and land development. The family built and sold two or three homes on lots behind the Drug Store and Round-up (a dancehall)—now the Little Bear. The Round-up was bought by Buchanan in 1940 from Prince McCracken, its owner and manager for many years. The 1943 State Business Directory has a listing for D. E. Buchanan, Drugs. The drug store and Round-up operation was managed by Joan's first husband, Fred Goodale, until he went into the Marines in World War II. The property was sold around 1954.

Breaking Down the Summer/Year-Round Barriers: Wallowers and Buchanans

Before World War II, there was a pretty solid social line drawn between permanent Evergreen residents and the 'summer people'. For the softening of this line, a lot of credit goes to two friendly and informal families who mixed easily in both worlds, and who became at home in Evergreen in winter as well as summer.

One of these families was the Wallowers: Herbert and Dora and their four sons. Herb Sr. bought the Field home, one of the earliest summer homes on Upper Bear Creek, in 1927. It was rechristened "Glendora" by a loving husband, in honor of his not-too-enthusiastic wife. The family lived year-round in Evergreen for a while in the mid-thirties, and returned again after the war to acquire a ranch, breed cattle, cut lumber and become an integral part of Evergreen life.

The other family was the Buchanans. Although Darst and Ruth did not live full time in Evergreen they spent a good part of each year between 1946 and 1960 here, and became well-known in the community. All of their daughters and husbands lived year-round in Evergreen for longer or shorter periods.

Robert Kirchner had completed his undergraduate studies at Colorado University before going into the Navy in World War II. When he came out, he told us, *"It was a kind of restless period for everybody: no one knew what was ahead."* So, along with four or five others including Darst Buchanan and John Casey, he bought out the old Evergreen Lumber Company— which was located under the dam where Bear Creek Mall is today— from Duval in Golden. This became quite a large scale operation, with 40 to 50 people on the payroll.

212

Bob and Barbara Kirchner lived in Evergreen, with Bob taking care of the accounting side of the business. After a year or so he accepted an offer to go to work for Boettcher and Co. The family moved to Denver. Later, Bob established his own specialized bond firm, Kirchner, Moore and Co.

The family member with the longest-lasting ties to Evergreen is Joan Landy. She and her family were living in Lakewood when the senior Buchanans died, Darst in 1960 and Ruth in 1962.

"We moved up for the summer and thought we would put the Lakewood house on the market. If it sold, fine! There wasn't anyone living in the Homestead then. If it didn't sell, maybe we would move back to Lakewood in the fall. But the children loved it so in Evergreen, and the house did sell. After that, I bought the house from my two sisters." Joan raised her family in the house. In 1973, when the children were grown, she sold it. But she still lives in Evergreen, as do two of her grown children.

John Casey and his wife Betty settled into the easy- going, friendly and informal small-town life of the Evergreen of the 40s and 50s, and raised their family here.

The First Hiwan Subdivision
It would be historically tidy to be able to name a specific date on which the Buchanan family decided to subdivide the vast Hiwan Ranch holdings into attractive mountain homesites, and so alter the character and destiny of Evergreen. Tidy but inaccurate.

The fact is that the original purchase of the Douglas holdings included one already-platted subdivision (Douglas Park) with most of its sites unsold. John Casey remembers that his intent in developing Hiwan Hills, the first subdivision using the Hiwan name, was to serve a need in the community for additional, in-town homesites for people living year-round in Evergreen.

There was no conscious strategy of attracting commuters. Among the early site buyers were people already living and working in the town, some who wanted to retire here and a hardy few who valued mountain living enough to make the old commute—via Hampden and up Bear Creek Canyon from

Morrison, or by way the old Highways 6 and 40 and through Bergen Park.

The first subdivision map for Hiwan Hills, according to the records of the Jefferson County Planning Department, was approved in December of 1949. It was designated as Block 1, covering an area of some 94 acres: 52 were platted into 50 homesites, the remainder going into roads and open space. In the next ten years four additional blocks were approved, creating an additional 197 homesites and bringing the total subdivided area to 278 acres.

Other than roads, the only utility available to the first site buyers was electric power. Water was to be supplied from individually-drilled wells. As the subdivision developed, many homeowners were not able to get adequate water from wells so the Hiwan developers put in a couple of reservoirs and offered year-round water supply to existing residents and new buyers. A tap fee was charged, then later refunded when Colorado Central Power bought out the water system from Hiwan Development Co. around 1957.

There was no community opposition to these initial Hiwan Hills developments. They were a natural extension of the Douglas Park subdivision, catering to people who were using the existing services of the town. The sales techniques were low-key and no disproportionate numbers of new people were brought into Evergreen.

Commuter Era Begins
But, as has happened many times in the brief 125 years of Evergreen history, a period of relative stability was coming to an end.

On the surface, the Evergreen of the 40s and 50s changed little: its permanent population of hundreds still exploded into thousands in the summer. Dude ranches such as the T- Bar-S and Marshdale Lodge continued to operate. Denverites and visitors from Texas, Oklahoma and Kansas came to their cabins or castles to enjoy the cool mountain air. But each year there were fewer of them.

Increasing affluence and technological advances stimulated by the war effort were at work to change Evergreen. To Father

Robert Kirchner.

Marsh we owe an insight into one of these factors. He remembers sitting on *"Mr. Worsham's porch in Troutdale Estates one hot summer day, speculating about why the number of summer residents was declining."* Mr. Worsham said, *"Well, at the price of air-conditioning in cars and in homes, people don't need to come to places like Evergreen anymore."*

Good roads and cheap automobiles were making Evergreen too accessible to be a desirable summer resort, while commercial air travel was bringing more exotic vacation areas into the realm of the possible. So the summer tourist appeal was declining at the same time as year-round accessibility was improving. If it had not been a Hiwan development that offered to Denverites the option of an easily-reached, high- quality mountain environment to live in, it would have been another one. The time was ripe.

By 1958, the Hiwan Ranch activities were already greatly curtailed. The Buchanan family interests, doing business as Hiwan Development Company with John Casey as President, were becoming more focussed on land subdivision.

213

The plans for the next development—Hiwan Village—involved heavy front-end investment in site development. Water and sewer were now available and a significant commercial section was part of the plan.

The development, approved by Jefferson County in 1958, involved a number of firsts for Evergreen. Its commercial section was the first major expansion of business beyond Main Street. It brought in the first large supermarket—Safeway—to the building now occupied by Bear Rug Co., and contained the first building specifically constructed for a U. S. Post Office—the building which now contains a variety of stores, including a travel agency and office supply. (Unlike the 1983 post office building in North Evergreen, the Hiwan Village one had no steps and was easily accessible). There was also a Phillips 66 service station and a number of smaller stores.

The section set aside for single-family home sites was the first subdivision in Evergreen able to offer all utilities. The apartment building above the Hiwan Village stores, which has a magnificent view, was the first multi-story rental building in Evergreen.

Interestingly enough, this was the only building that drew objections from Evergreen residents. According to the May 17, 1962 Canyon Courier, representatives from the Hiwan Improvement Association and Douglas Park protested that "there is no need for this type of building in the area." Today, many still object to any high-density development in Evergreen, convinced that only single homes on an acre or more of land should be permitted.

In 1962, Block 6 of the Hiwan Hills subdivision was opened up, providing 31 new lots on 44 acres of land. In the planning stage was the ambitious concept of a well-designed mountain residential community built around a top-ranking golf course and club house.

The land was there, and so was the enthusiasm and imagination to make large plans. But there was a problem of generating enough cash to pay the heavy development costs of a golf course—with a price tag of more than $500,000—and an extensive network of roads and utilities.

Hiwan Village apartment building.

Financial arrangements in Evergreen were grossly discriminatory as compared with those available in suburban Denver; in 1961 mortgage companies were charging interest rates of six% in Denver but they were demanding 50% down and 10% interest for mountain property. By negotiation, first with Colorado Federal Savings and later with Capitol Federal, this was changed to a 10% minimum down payment, with the balance paid over 25 years at 6.25%.

Compared with other suburban real estate, prices on existing sites in Hiwan Hills were unrealistically low. Almost overnight, the price tag on a $1,500 site went up to $7,500.

Another problem was that existing firms of home builders in Evergreen were not able to produce the quantity, type, and variety of housing that would appeal to commuting executives. Four homebuilders were brought in from out of town and the entire Hiwan Village residential area was sold out to them. In turn these builders contracted with a new and quite aggressive Hiwan Development Co. marketing team to do sales and promotion.

Sales potential for the Hiwan developments was also enhanced by the timely development of utilities.

Public Service Company of Colorado acquired the Colorado Central Power Company, which serviced Evergreen, by a merger finalized in January 1962. This gave PSC responsibility for both electricity and water in Evergreen, a historical quirk that made this the only area where Public Service operated a community water supply system.

The Evergreen Sanitation District, organized in 1949, had installed a sewage treatment plant on land bought from Buchanan, near the proposed Hiwan Village. Hiwan Development Co. advanced the

money to hook the residential part of the Village into the system.

Finally, there was the matter of natural gas. Until 1962, the only heating fuels available in Evergreen were butane or propane, and electricity. Both were expensive for year-round heating as compared with the (then!) cheap natural gas. With its acquisition of Colorado Central Power, Public Service was making plans to bring natural gas up to the mountain areas. It was undoubtedly encouraged by the rapidly developing Hiwan properties to proceed promptly with the Evergreen installation.

By the spring of 1962 all pieces were in place. The sales team launched a high-powered campaign to sell the builders' sites in Hiwan Village, the remaining sites in Blocks 1 through 5 in Hiwan Hills, and the new Block 6. They were also gearing up to sell the first sites in the brand new Hiwan Golf Club area.

The Denver firm of Harmon, O'Donnell and Henninger did the overall layout for this new "mountain residential community." How great an advance this Hiwan subdivision was over early land planning in Evergreen can be seen by comparison with such geometric layouts as Stanley Park, Wah Keeney Park and the early Troutdale Estates—or with such irrationally chopped-up plats as Mountain Park Homes. In neither type was there any relationship to land contours or to the amenities of view and orientation.

Renowned golf course architect J. Presley (Press) Maxwell was engaged to plan the golf course. The designer of such courses as Kissing Camels near Colorado Springs and suburban Denver's Pinehurst, Maxwell told the Denver Daily Journal that Hiwan was one of the best he had ever done.

It is a 7,155-yard course covering about 170 acres, complete with water obstacles, trees, and greens, and complemented by a large four and one-half acre club house area.

What was new about the promotion campaign? A man who was part of the sales team for some time told us, *"The main thing we did was to get a new image going. This is where you can live, and work down in Denver. We started getting the airline pilots and other similar people up here who were willing to spend the money, not for a cabin, but for a full- fledged, expensive house."*

The sales drive was successful. The Village area was virtually sold out in 1962, and the sales office was moved from its site by the Woodpecker Building to the new entrance to the Golf Club area. There, three successive filings were opened in 1963. In addition to the Golf Course and open space areas, they contained 328 individual home sites and a 35-acre site between fairways for future multi-family or condominium development.

In spite of the volume of land sales, the persistent problems of not enough available capital remained. By 1964 both of the senior Buchanans had died. (Darst Buchanan died in 1960 at the age of 68, after a long illness.) The need for capital was in danger of draining the resources of the Buchanan heirs. New development ground to a halt.

Jefferson Land Associates Takes Over
Bob Kirchner managed to put together a group of about a dozen investors who could bring the needed cash into the Hiwan properties. The group, under the name of Jefferson Land Associates (JLA), bought out the Hiwan assets from the Buchanan heirs, leaving latter with a 15 percent stock in and no liabilities against their other The Kirchners came in on the side. Eventually, all the family sold out their interests in JLA.

The JLA agreement was finalized in May of 1966. There was no break in continuity of goals for the Hiwan properties—to provide a high-quality, well-secluded community which as much as possible of the natural

Covenants, incorporated into the were designed to assure a certain harmony in the architecture, limit the amount of artificial landscaping, and require preservation of existing trees and natural vegetation.

One of the new JLA limited partners was Tony Tyrone, whom Bob Kirchner had met while serving on the Board of Directors of the Denver-based Hamilton Funds. Tyrone, in Denver since 1949, was Chairman of the Board and President of both Hamilton Management Co. and Hamilton Funds, as well as of Alexander Life Insurance Co. He was asked to become both General and Managing Partner for JLA in 1972.

Tony Tyrone.

Tyrone was not a man who enjoyed the publicity limelight, but there is no doubt that he was the moving force behind the last major Hiwan developments. He was also the drive behind the steady building of the Hiwan Colorado Open Golf Tournament—now the Coors Colorado Open—of which he *became chairman in 1976. He* turned the event into one ot the country's top five charity golf tournaments.

Hiwan Homestead becomes a Museum
Before continuing the story of the Hiwan subdivisions, we need to catch up with that other Hiwan namesake—the Homestead, into which Joan Landy moved after the death of her parents.

She lived there for almost ten years—raising her six children, loving the house and expanding it considerably by adding a third floor to the main building. When the children were grown, the house, with its 17 rooms and seven bathrooms, was far too large for her needs. She sold it, together with the surrounding 18 acres, to developer George Hurst. He got county permission for a Planned Unit Development on the site. But George and his wife, both sincerely interested in historical buildings, felt that there was a better use for the Homestead than conversion into a real estate office.

With the initial impetus provided by Hurst, and the persistent and skilful efforts of a small new historical society led by Connie Fahnestock, the Homestead was purchased under the recently-organized Jefferson County Open Space Program. It became The Hiwan Homestead Historical Museum. The adjacent land, now known as Heritage Grove, was acquired through a heroic community fund-raising effort.

By 1977, Evergreen had a permanent piece of its history secured in the Hiwan Homestead Museum as well as a gracious outdoor site for an annual round of historical exhibits, community festivals, art shows, fairs and celebrations.

The Rise of Opposition to Development
The first development activity of JLA was to construct 20 condominiums on sites in the filing already opened. Since condos were a rather novel idea in an exclusive subdivision, they were designed to look like huge private houses, with interior courtyards giving access to individual units.

In 1971 development started again with the Fourth Filing of the Golf Club area, and continued steadily through the seventies in three stages: these included the Fifth Filing and Filing Number Six, totalling 150 sites, whose plat was officially approved in 1979.

During the same period, Block 7 of the Hiwan Hills subdivision was opened in three stages in 1974, 76 and 77.

The first outspoken opposition to these Hiwan developments began to appear in public hearings, letters to newspapers and organized group activity. There was particular hostility to any proposed commercial development. It is worth examining briefly some of the reasons for this rising opposition.

In part it was the understandable selfishness of 'now that we've arrived, let's lock the door so no on else can get in.' More substantially, there was the Evergreen experience of the ill-conceived proposal to secure the 1976 Winter Olympic Games for Colorado. This involved plans to chop up mountains in the Evergreen area, re-route roads, tear down cherished landmarks like the Evergreen Golf Course Clubhouse —now Key's on the Green Restaurant—and put in outsized replacements, for which there would be no known use after the Olympics were over.

Triathalon competitors armed with rifles were scheduled to ski through private back yards, and the parking of thousands of cars was to be supported by the frozen waters of Lake Evergreen!

215

Jack Rouse and Bill Bennett.

A mantle of snow, airbrushed onto the photographs of the Evergreen area, formed part of the presentation to the International Olympic Committee. Angry meetings of Olympic planners and Evergreen residents convinced the *"natives"* that profit-seeking *"flatlanders"* did not know much about the mountain area, and did not care what effects their short-sighted interferences might have.

Of course, the opposition was not unanimous. Bill Bennett, a minority partner in Jefferson Land Associates, took out a one-page ad in the Canyon Courier to counter what he felt were biases in Newsweek's reporting of Evergreen's reactions to the Olympic proposals. Jack Rouse, head of Public Service in Evergreen, chaired a committee to support the Olympics bid. Developer Ron Lewis of North Turkey Creek, on whose land some of the Olympic events were scehduled to be held, characteristically opposed the majority view.

Overall, the Olympics proposals were a major factor in raising this area's consciousness that it must organize to protect its own environment.

There was also a more subtle source of opposition to the later Hiwan developments. The first filings in Hiwan Hills and the Hiwan Village development were conceived as additions to the community of Evergreen, using its services and adding to its range of facilities. With the development of the country club area, the sense of place began to blur. It fell between the two communities of Evergreen and Bergen Park, which until that time had felt themselves to be separate— though their fortunes had been linked from the beginning. In the

Hiwan sales literature, Evergreen became a *"quaint nearby mountain town"* and Bergen Park was scarcely mentioned at all.

Indeed, prospective residents of the country club area were wooed with the offer of an irresistible world of access to everything and responsibility for nothing.

Sales brochures promised an easy journey to work in Denver and a home in the mountains, with clean air and *"space which allows the mind to expand out of the steel and concrete which circumscribe the working hours of most of us."*

Evergreen offered horseback riding, ice skating, hiking and trail biking, summer concerts by the Colorado Philharmonic Orchestra, shopping, library and medical facilities. Jefferson County's contribution was *"its famed school system, paved roads and curbs maintained year round."* Denver, only minutes away via I-70, gave access to the Denver Symphony, a growing theater season, ballet, nightclubs and fine restaurants. And all only 30 minutes from Stapleton International Airport.

Emphasis was also placed on the many facilities provided by Hiwan itself, allowing the prospective resident to live an active and satisfying life within its magical, well-planned acres: the sociability of a country club—with swimming, golf, tennis—or just walking and enjoying the *"views of spectacular mountain ranges, meadows, birds, chipmunks, an occasional deer."*

There was also the appeal of status. With disarming frankness, Hiwan was offered to the successful and wealthy who were looking for a clearly-defined community of people of like income and accomplishments.

". . . the Hiwan community is composed of people who have achieved a level of success far above the ordinary. Hiwan is a true community of successful people who have made an appreciating investment, who have built elegant homes enhancing the environment . . . . The Hiwan experience is not for everyone, but if you can afford it, if you want the best of both worlds, come live with us!"

Indeed, the old-time Evergreen resident who expressed to us the feeling that the Hiwan Country Club area residents don't really *"belong"* to the Evergreen community, had a real point. They tend to be well-educated, well-traveled and highly mobile, belonging to a broader world than Evergreen, in fact, to a number of different 'worlds'. While this may reduce their commitment to the local community, it has the compensation of attracting a wider perspective into the Evergreen scene and providing support for such enterprises as high-quality restaurants, specialty stores, concerts and drama.

In all fairness it must be said that if residents of Evergreen or Bergen Park—or Conifer or Kittredge, or any combination of them—had truly wanted to be responsible for their own future, they could have shouldered the burdens of time and cost involved in incorporating as a city.

Paradoxically, the more subdivisions that were added, stimulating opposition and a desire to contain growth, the less possible a solution by incorporation became, because of the dilution of the sense of community and the sheer size and spread of developed areas.

Two other specific concerns fueled the opposition to continued extension of the subdivision. Concern over the possible limits of the Evergreen water supply, and the inflammatory issue of roads. The Colorado Highway Department started developing plans to improve the traffic flow into and out of Evergreen in 1966. The four-lane stretch of Highway 74, running past the commercial strip, was completed in 1971. It was seen as one part of a four-lane connection between I-70 and Evergreen, possibly continuing all the way to Highway 285 at Conifer.

Since 1971, there have been innumerable task forces, reports and public meetings suggesting a variety of alternate routes. Underlying the division over specific proposals are widely different values about the importance of rapid access compared with retaining the scale and shape of a small town.

The Ridge at Hiwan

In 1979 JLA reorganized, putting its ongoing management responsibilities into the newly-formed Hiwan Service Corporation. It sold off the largest part of its undeveloped land—some 930 acres—to a group incorporated as The Ridge at Hiwan Ltd.

Owners Jerry Agnew, Thomas Sullivan and Hayden Thompson tried unsuccessfully to rezone the land for over 900 dwelling units. In April of 1984, the County Commissioners approved a revised layout with a maximum of 616 units—265 single and 351 multi-family homesites.

In October of the same year a new company, P. T. Land Ltd., bought the land; major owners were Herb Prouty and John Thompson. Prouty, from a respected surveying family in Denver, was associated with the firm of Stearns Rogers for 40 years. Thompson, a self-styled farm boy and 1971 graduate of the Air Force Academy, was a civil engineer and lawyer.

A notable feature of the development team was the high proportion of Evergreen residents; Rich Cassens as engineer, Bud Clark and sons Pat and Mike doing the road, water and sewer work, Kenny Jeronimus as landscape contractor. Other development team members were Bud Simons, site planner and landscape architect, and Chris Lamen and Jeff Zimmerman, experienced architects from San Francisco.

Site development started in 1985, with a first filing of 35 single-family home sites selling at between $53,000 and $78,000. The second filing also contained individual home sites.

From the beginning, the Ridge project generated heated opposition on grounds of increased traffic problems, potential school overcrowding and interference with wildlife habitat. It must, however, be said that this development, with its use of high-quality professional expertise, is a far cry from

unprotested earlier projects where road cuts were left unrestored, orientation was ignored, privacy was not safeguarded and the character of buildings was regarded as unimportant.

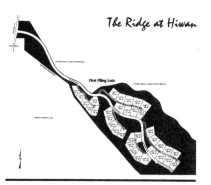

The Greens at Hiwan.

The Ridge at Hiwan.

John Thompson and landscape architect Bud Simons.

217

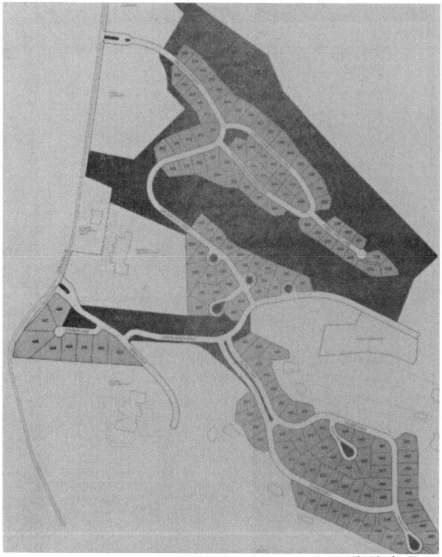

The Island at Hiwan.

Bill Bennett Picks Up the Reins at Hiwan

Tony Tyrone died unexpectedly in December of 1983. The ongoing management of Hiwan affairs devolved upon an unassuming long-time Evergreen resident, Bill Bennett, one of the original minority owners of JLA.

Bill regards himself as fortunate in being the product of the depression and having had the experience of becoming the sole breadwinner, at the age of 17, for his widowed mother and younger brother and sister. After marriage to his wife, Betty, he came to live and work in Denver. One summer, they rented a cottage on Evergreen Lake from Carrie Stransky. *"It was full of holes in the walls and miller moths;"* says Bill, *"we filled it with relatives and fell in love with Evergreen."*

Searching for a home site here, they settled on a piece of land on the Hiwan Ranch. *"We gave John Casey $200 and said we would buy a few acres if we found well water. Elmer Josephson brought in the best well on the hill. We bought the land and built our home. We could see only a few lights at night. Hiwan Hills was later platted around us. We still live there."*

They became involved with the small community: Bill in Scouts, Betty in Campfire Girls. They *"gave up a couple of vacations"* to help build the Church of the Hills, and Bill served on committees dealing with the expansion of schools.

"We found that our valley and mountain had everything that others found hours away in Western Colorado. We camped, fished, rode and hunted in the Bear Creek drainage, climbed to the Bear Track Lakes and dropped down to Abyss and Lincoln Lakes. What a great place to raise three children!"

Bill has given an immense amount of his time and energy to volunteer work for Craig Hospital—the beneficiary of the Colorado Open—and to Forest Heights Lodge, the residential treatment center for severely emotionally disturbed boys, located in Evergreen.

"My corporate life," Bill told us, *"was with a national firm who pioneered in solving environmental water problems. My management responsibilities were for the west— from the Mississippi to the Pacific. In my travels I never found any place to compare with Evergreen. It is unique in its beauty, its people and its way of life. Betty and I will live out our lives here."*

David Fowler, son-in-law of Bowers Holt—who owned the major interest in JLA—joined Bill in the management of the Golf and Country Club and responsibility for the remaining real estate. They shared the task of overseeing the site preparation and sales of the Sixth Filing, responsibility for a number of unsold sites in the first five filings, and sites for some 110 additional condominiums.

The last, and perhaps the choicest, block of Hiwan real estate was a part of the Sixth Filing totally surrounded by the Golf Course, and designated as The Island at Hiwan. Developed for 60 homesites, it was opened for sale in the summer of 1986 with site prices ranging from $50,000 to $100,000 each.

Some 11 acres of land—across Highway 74 from the octagonal barn—was originally offered at a favorable price to the Evergreen Center for the Arts for a performing arts center. When the ECA was unable to meet annual interest payments a trade was arranged for land on Lewis Ridge Road. The original 11 acres was sold to Lutheran Medical Center as a site for a hospital and medical clinic.

There remained also the area already zoned for commercial development, lying on both sides of the entrance to the new Sixth Filing. The octagonal barn, with a half-acre of land, was sold and developed into a ski rental store.

The small green *"Bergen"* house, with one acre, was sold in 1986 to golf course architect Dick Phelps. *"I had been looking for years for a home for a design studio,"* Phelps told a Canyon Courier reporter, *"I loved this house with its view."* He said that he originally thought the house was Bergen's second home, *"but after researching it further I found it was not. It was built sometime between 1900 and 1920."*

Phelps is one of only 85 members of the American Society of Golf Course Architects and is a past president of the group. His profession would allow him to live anywhere, but with his wife Marcia and three children he has chosen Evergreen since 1971. *"I love Evergreen. We moved up from Denver for the clean air. The schools are great and the people for the most part are friendly."*

The Bergen Park National Bank bought three acres and put up a modest temporary building on the site in 1984. Development of the remainder awaited a more propitious economic climate.

Summing up the Hiwan Factor
Overall, the Hiwan subdivisions undoubtedly raised the general standards of land planning and preservation of the natural environment in Evergreen. While no single Hiwan buildings have won prizes for architectural merit, the overall development set standards for restraint and harmony.

Provisions for adult recreation in the Hiwan Golf Club area are extensive and well-designed. In 1986, Bennett's son, David, was responsible for a major remodelling and addition to the clubhouse. Use of the facilities does not come with a bargain price tag. In 1986, a golf club membership at Hiwan cost $12,000 for initiation fees, with monthly dues of $150.

Provisions for integrating other community needs have not been quite so successful. The overall layout for Hiwan set aside two sites for schools which the R-1 School District bought at $3,000 per acre. The junior high, with 20 acres, was

David Fowler.

opened in 1969. Bergen Elementary, with a 15-acre site, was completed in 1970.

The School District is an entity unto itself, not subject to Hiwan's architectural or planning control. Yet as a reflection of community values it is striking that adult golfers are integrated into the core of Hiwan, walking through lovingly-tended greens and pine groves, while the children are spun off to the edges of the community; much of their allotted acreage is covered with gravel. Bergen School and the adjacent Fire Station, built much later, stand out particularly as unlandscaped and unintegrated elements.

What then has been the effect of the *"Hiwan factor"* in Evergreen's growth? The assembling of lands into the ownership of one family made the Hiwan Ranch the largest single operation in Evergreen history. It was a source of community reputation and pride—a last, grand fling for the ranching mode of life which had been a mainstay of the year-round community for some 100 years.

David Bennett.

Hiwan homes.

As an interesting footnote, we learned that the Hiwan cattle brand lives on. The Robert Kirchners acquired the rights to it, and it is being used by their son on a family farm in Weld County.

The the very assemblage that made the huge ranch possible also set the stage for the subdividing of those lands on a large scale, and that development transformed the appearance and the character of Evergreen.

The long occupation of the Hiwan Homestead by the Buchanan family from 1938 to 1973 safeguarded this invaluable bit of Evergreen's historical heritage.

The entire Hiwan saga, now drawing to a close, is arguably the most influential single happening of this community's brief but colorful life story.

1986 addition to Hiwan clubhouse.

219

ARTS IN THE MOUNTAINS

The arts are sturdily rooted in this community despite laments that Evergreen's small-town vitality is leeching away as it becomes a bedroom satellite to Denver. A lively network of individuals and organizations has developed around every conceivable facet of life here. No facet sparkles more engagingly than the one that reflects the arts.

Though the Colorado Philharmonic Orchestra took a new name and a new location in 1986, after a twenty-year affiliation with Evergreen, there is still a year-round chamber orchestra here, a performing musical chorale of near-professional caliber, an energetic, talented amateur theatrical troupe producing plays on a demanding schedule, and an artists' association of long standing that encourages appreciation of the visual arts. At any one time, there is a large and diverse group of artists living in this part of the mountains—painters, writers, musicians, sculptors, weavers, potters, dancers, singers. Some stay for a lifetime, others find something here that nourishes their talents for a while and then move on.

A few are nationally-known: singer Willie Nelson has a secluded home on Upper Bear Creek, screen-writer Steve ("Breaking Away") Tesich lives part-time in Conifer, violinist Eugene Fodor is a native of North Turkey Creek, authors Joanne Greenberg and Clive Cussler live on Lookout Mountain. There are some regional stars, and many more whose gifts are shared mainly with a local audience. In Evergreen's arts endeavors, seasoned professionals mingle with people who make their living in many different arenas— for whom art is an avocation.

After a brief historical overview, we profile here some of the organizations and individuals that enrich the quality of life in Evergreen by their artistic contributions.

The Artists' Role in Westward Expansion

The splendid, romantic vision of the West presented by landscape painters in the nineteenth century was a major factor in the westward expansion of the new nation.

After the opening up of vast new lands through the Louisiana Purchase, the first artists on the scene came with official government expeditions to make a careful, factual, pictorial record of these unknown regions.

But in the 1830's, according to Patricia Trenton and Peter Hassrick in their fascinating book about the artistic vision of the Rocky Mountains in the last century, artist Alfred Jacob Miller dared to make form and mood more important in his paintings than accuracy of topographical detail.

He paved the way for the epic statements of Albert Bierstadt and his followers. People suddenly saw the Rockies in a new way.

Albert Bierstadt in the Evergreen Area

Born in Germany in 1830, Bierstadt came to live in Massachussetts with his family when he was just two. When he grew up, young Albert worked in a frame shop and probably had some local art training. By 1850, he was himself offering painting classes, but soon realized that he could benefit from some European education.

Bierstadt went to Germany for three and a half years, studying drawing and painting in Dusseldorf. He shared a studio with American painter T. Worthington Whittredge and, in the company of fellow students, made a number of industrious sketching tours in Germany, Switzerland and Italy. He returned in 1857, filled with a desire to create landscape paintings "full of character and masterly effect." His first trek to the American West was with the wagon train party of Colonel Lander, which started from St. Joseph, Missouri and reached the southern edge of the Wind River Mountains in June of 1859.

Bierstadt did most of his sketches from the plains. His attempts to synthesize his western studies into large oil paintings culminated in a monumental picture titled simply "The Rocky Mountains." It was exhibited in New York and Chicago, purchased by railroad tycoon James McHenry for the then unheard-of sum of $25,000, and shipped off to Europe for a round of showings and acclaim.

Willie Nelson.

Willie Nelson home on Upper Bear Creek.

Bierstadt's second expedition in the spring of 1863 brought him a direct, personal experience of the mountains. Out of this, he produced his fully-realized epic painting, "A Storm in the Rocky Mountains—Mount Rosalie", in 1866. Bierstadt made the trip with his friend, New York Post critic Fitz Hugh Ludlow, who published his account of the journey in a series of articles in the Atlantic Monthly.

One measure of Bierstadt's fame by this time was that Governor John Evans graciously furnished transportation for the couple's first foray out of Denver—to the Pike's Peak region. The artist's second venture was in the company of William N. Byers—founder, editor and publisher of the Rocky Mountain News—on a trip "to the summit of the snowy cluster directly west of Denver". Along the route, according to Byers' account in the News, Bierstadt was to "take likenesses, true to life, of mountain and canyon views."

On the first day's journey to Idaho Springs, Bierstadt chose to make "two fine drawings". One was of the view cherished by every Evergreen commuter along I-70, that first magnificent panorama of snowy peaks. The other pictured "Pleasant, or Elk Park" (today's Bergen Park).

The second day's trek took the couple up Chicago Creek to lower Chicago Lake. Byers describes how Bierstadt restrained himself, though "in raptures with the scenery", until two or three miles below timberline. When "a vast amphitheater of snowy peaks, lofty cliffs and timbered mountainsides burst suddenly upon the view", the artist, in nervous haste, unpacked his canvas, paint and brushes.

Next morning they made the precipitous climb to upper Chicago Lake and then to a third and separate lake, "the loftiest and largest". Because it sat on a summit of some 12,500 feet they named it Summit Lake, noting that it was formed in the shape of a three-pointed star. Bierstadt sketched the mountain looming above it, christening it Mount Rosalie after, as he told Byers, "an absent friend".

A bit of a love triangle is usually glossed over here, by reporting that Bierstadt named the mountain after his wife. Miss Rosalie seems to have been the object of the affections of both Bierstadt and his friend Ludlow. She married Ludlow first. After his death, she became Mrs. Albert Bierstadt. The highest peak was later renamed Mount Evans to commemorate the many services of Governor John Evans to the State of Colorado: the next highest peak was named Mount Bierstadt and a third one, Mount Rosalie.

Byers and Bierstadt climbed the remaining 2,000 feet to the summit where the artist quickly sketched in pencil "the vast panorama of mountain, valleys and plains spread out before and around them." Three more quick sketches were made the following day, heading back to Idaho Springs. One of these showed a storm brewing over a small crystal lake, part of the inspiration for Bierstadt's Colorado painting.

Ludlow and Bierstadt resumed their journey west: Bierstadt made a fruitful sketching tour of Yosemite Valley. The travelers had been away for 8 months when they finally returned to New York. Bierstadt spent two years working on California themes, but early in 1865 he began his monumental painting of the Rocky Mountains. This was the first of his canvases to "combine heroic landscapes with dramatic sky effects."

"A Storm in the Mountains—Mount Rosalie" created quite a sensation when it made its appearance at a New York gallery's benefit exhibition for a children's hospital. Though some condemned it as "scene-painting" and criticized its size, its hard coloring, and its mechanical 'Dusseldorfian' finish, others pronounced it a work of American genius and praised its powerful impression of overwhelming natural grandeur.

In 1867, the painting was sent for exhibit in the International Exposition in Paris, sold to an English financier, and shown to enormous popular acclaim throughout Britain. Successive sales took the painting out of the public eye. It was considered lost until rediscovered in a London warehouse in 1974. Today it is in the permanent collection of the Brooklyn Art Museum.

None of Bierstadt's sketches from the 1863 trip have survived. A smaller painting titled "Summit Lake, Colorado", which was shown at the National Academy in 1888, has also vanished.

Following the enormous public interest shown in Bierstadt's western pictures, many other artists came to paint and sketch in the Rockies and to contribute their perceptions to the rising 'cult of the wilderness'.

Bergen Park and the Hudson River School

Appreciation of Bergen Park's natural beauty was not limited to first settler Thomas Bergen. Bierstadt's former Dusseldorf roommate, Thomas Worthington Whittredge, made trips to Colorado in 1866, 1870 and 1871. The 1870 visit was in the company of fellow-artists John F. Kensett and Sandford R. Gifford. All were members of what came to be known as the Hudson River School of landscape painting.

One of their many sketching trips was by coach to the top of Loveland Pass. Both Whittredge and Kensett produced a number of paintings of the Bergen Park area. One of Whittredge's, "In the Rockies (Bergen Park, Colorado)", is now in a private Denver collection.

One of Kensett's small oil sketches titled "Landscape (Bergen Park), 1870" is in the Metropolitan Museum of Art. Trenton and Hassrick comment, "The dense rows of evergreens in and around Bergen Park offered picturesque prospects for Kensett's brush. From an elevated position, the artist captured sweeping views of these dense patches of green in the high-meadow country with the snow peaks beyond." A second Bergen Park painting, which is in a private New York gallery, is described as a "small, appealing picture, in which "through painterly effects and contrasts of lights and shadow, Kensett gives pleasing and animated life to this forest landscape."

The combined lure of gold, new land and the wilderness—dramatized by painters, journalists and poets—succeeded in populating the West by the end of the nineteenth century. Then fashions in painting changed, monumental canvases with inspirational themes went out of favor, and the western states developed flourishing art colonies of their own.

"A Storm in the Rocky Mountains: Mount Rosalie", painting by Albert Bierstadt.

"Indian Encampment" by Bierstadt.

Separate Cultures—Settlers and Summer People

As in most settler societies, the early arts of Evergreen were mostly crafts: a finely-built cabin, handmade furniture, flowers grown by women for delight next to the necessary vegetables, hand-sewn clothes and household linens. Ranching life was hard and left little time for "frills". Artistic talents came out most noticeably at celebrations. There were always a few—like John Schneider and his brothers in the early days, and later Herman Olde—who could make merry music for weekend dances, weddings and parties.

"In the Rockies—Bergen Park" painting by Thomas Worthington Wittredge.

Julia Douglas.

Eric (Frederic Huntington) Douglas.

The summer residents, on the other hand, were people with some means and leisure. Among them were individuals of talent as well as sensitive, active patrons of the arts.

Most of these regarded time spent in Evergreen as essentially private. They found renewal of spirit in the mountain setting, then returned to the challenges of their lives in Denver and other cities.

But others, like the Williams-Douglas family, shared their cultural riches with the community. Evergreen Conference music was made available through church services and public concerts, the fine Douglas collection of native Indian artifacts through access to Camp Neosho and the delightful library-museum run by Canon Douglas's sister, Miss Julia. When talent showed itself in an Evergreen native, the Douglas's would likely aid its flowering, as they did in the case of woodcarver Henry Hertzman. Douglas family members served on the Evergreen School Board and donated books to start its first school library. There was one Douglas family member for whom art was at the center of life.

Frederic (Eric) Huntington Douglas: 1897-1956

From birth, this only son of two distinguished older parents, Canon Winfred and Dr. Josepha Douglas, spent his summers in Evergreen. Out of an unconventional upbringing, Eric Douglas developed into a talented, brilliant and idiosyncratic adult. By the time he died of cancer, at the age of 58, he had made a unique contribution to the cultural life of Colorado through his lifelong interest in Indian art and artifacts.

This interest was undoubtedly fueled by his father's longtime involvement with Southwest Indian tribes and exquisite collection of Indian objects. Eric was taken along on many of the elder Douglas's trips to Indian Country. When listing his travels for a biograpical record in the Denver Public Library, Eric noted that he had been in the southwest in 1911, 1913, 1916, 1918, 1921, 1925, 1926, 1928 and 1930. Apparently Dr. Josepha also collected Indian art, an interest which dated back to a girlhood visit to a physician-uncle in Taos.

Another influence came from the remarkable Anne Evans, daughter of Governor Evans, a friend of Douglas's parents both in Evergreen and Denver and one of Colorado's most distinguished patrons of the arts.

After graduating from the University of Colorado in 1921, Douglas studied for four years at the Pennsylvania Academy of Fine Arts. In 1926, he married a beautiful young Philadelphia socialite, Frieda Gillespie, who gave up aspirations to a medical career to come west and live on what one newspaper article described as "Eric's old family homestead in Evergreen".

Rumor has it that Dr. Jo found it so hard to be deprived of her beloved son's company that she insisted on his being with her, and apart from his wife, during the first winters of their married life. The couple adopted twin girls in 1928 and a son in 1933.

At first, the family lived year-round in Evergreen, in quarters expanded from the separate "baby house" built for Eric by Jock Spence at

"In the Heart of the Rockies (Bergen Park) 1870" painting by John F. Kensett.

Eric Douglas and his Indian Style Show.

Eric's parents, Canon Winfred and Dr. Josepha Douglas.

Camp Neosho. The young Douglas's were part of the local community. Eric served as President of the Evergreen School Board from 1929-1932.

At this time, he described himself as a portrait painter and wood carver. He was soon roped in by Anne Evans to help, on a volunteer basis, with the new Indian Arts Collection of the fledgling Denver Art Museum. This was housed in Chappell House, a magnificent old mansion on 13th and Logan (no longer in existence) which had its own Evergreen association. It was donated to the Museum, after the death of their parents, by the Chappell children. One of these was Jean Chappell Cranmer who, with her husband, George Cranmer—the flamboyant Denver Manager of Parks—built what is now the Singin' River Ranch on Yankee Creek.

In 1929, Eric was named Curator of the Native Arts Division of the Denver Art Museum, a post he held until his death, with the exception of 3-1/2 years service in the South Pacific in World War II and a brief stint in 1941-2 as interim Director of the entire Art Museum.

Eric was totally dedicated to, and involved with, the Museum. He built its Native Arts collection to eminence, establishing the far from affluent institution as a world leader in the collection and study of American Indian art.

We get a glimpse of just how he made these acquisitions from an interview taped by the Jeferson County Historical Society with Helen Bromfield. She was one of the two daughters of Genevieve Phipps, who built Greystone, and a longtime friend of Eric Douglas. "He knew that big collectors were few and far between, and were dying off. A small museum like Denver's never would be able to afford the items years down the road . . . So Eric 'pledged his soul' to get these things. He'd sign notes at times to get a loan to buy this or that collection . . . The money just wasn't there in the museum and the trustees weren't too enthusiastic. The bank finally refused to honor just his name, so I'd go along with him."
"Say there was a collection of baskets: 'Out of a hundred', he'd say, 'there are just 3 or 4 of the highest quality. But we can sell the rest off, we have to buy the entire collection to get the worthwhile item.'"

223

Douglas prepared a series of 119 illustrated pamphlets, published by the Denvar Art Museum, about different aspects of the collection. He also developed a unique method of getting part of his fabulous collection out of the Museum and into peoples' lives. His Indian Style Shows, presented to groups throughout the United States, were enormously popular. Group members modeled the priceless authentic costumes while Douglas gave a lively, informative commentary.

Another of his innovations was presented to resounding applause at the 1939 San Francisco World's Fair. Instead of the then-normal "dead" museum-style display, Douglas chose to set his exhibits of native arts and crafts in dramatic natural settings. The Museum of Modern Art invited him to set up a similar show in New York in 1941. For this occasion, he co-authored a pioneering book, "Indian Art of the United States".

Before entering the service, Douglas started a small travelling museum to acquaint soldiers with the native cultures of parts of Africa and the Pacific Islands where they might be serving. These touring exhibits became the nucleus of the expanded Native Arts collection of the Denver Art Museum. During his own Pacific theater service, chiefly in the New Hebrides, Douglas started an extensive collection of the region's native arts.

This material, along with most of his own and his parents' American Indian collections and donations by Anne Evans, formed the backbone of the Museum's fine collection.

Douglas served as consultant to many prestigious museums, including Harvard's Peabody, in classifying and rearranging their Indian art collections.

Eric Douglas was an accomplished pianist and an effective choirmaster. He published five volumes of poetry. He painted; a small example of his work can be seen in the little Indian motifs that decorate the walls of the Hiwan Homestead Museum.

But his major legacy was to the people of Colorado. When he came to the Denver Art Museum in 1929, there was one solitary volume in the Native Arts Library, and around 200 art objects. When he left there were 30,000 books and more than 20,000 carefully selected pieces of native art.

Douglas coped courageously with a difficult illness and death. He had an arm amputated and a kidney removed because of cancer in 1955. Though he returned to work with characteristic optimism and enthusiasm, the cancer spread and he died in 1956. His three children—Pauline Maher, Eve Jolivette and David Douglas—were grown and married by that time and there were already three grandchildren. His wife, Frieda, outlived him by many years.

Vance Kirkland.

Vance Kirkland
One of the most prolific and dedicated painters this region has produced, Vance Kirkland spent many summers on the Truesdell Ranch (now part of the Mount Evans Elk Management Area) teaching at Mrs. Truesdell's summer art school and painting his own canvases.

Born in 1904 in Ohio, Kirkland graduated in 1928 from the Cleveland School of Art. He was hired the following year by Denver University to head up its newly acquired Chappell School of Art. All the years he was teaching Vance continued to paint on a rigorous self-imposed schedule. Each summer, as we observed with admiration the two years we spent with him on the Truesdell Ranch, he painted 7 days a week, 8 hours a day. After he retired in 1969, this was his routine until his death.

In his Evergreen summers of the 30's and 40's Vance was enchanted with "the violent struggle of twisted and gnarled timberline tree forms," being involved in what a mutual friend irreverently dubbed his 'dead wood phase.' Kirkland moved successively into a number of distinct stylistic periods in his long painting career and is perhaps best known for his huge space-related canvases.

Of the early Nebulae series, Vance wrote that "the abstract shapes made by exploding and splashing colors on the background actually appeared to leave the surface of the canvas and become an illusion of outer space, suggesting what happened billions of years ago." The later works done exclusively with dots of color, "related to the billions of stars in space."

A witty, self-confident personality, Kirkland was full of entertaining stories about teaching and the art world. (We pitied the poor student sent off to the art supply store for a box of 'vanishing points' to improve his perspective drawing!)

During his lifetime, Kirkland's paintings were better known in New York than in Colorado. It was a long-overdue tribute when the Denver Art Museum held a 50-year retrospective of his work in 1978. Vance was a working artist to the end: "If I just sat on a beach," he said in an interview, "I'd go nuts. It's a circle, if I keep working, I keep my health. If I keep my health, I keep working." He died in 1981 at the age of 77.

Edith Truesdell
In 1971 at nearly 80, Edith Truesdell drove back to Colorado from Carmel Valley in California to put up a one-woman show of her vibrant acrylic paintings. Still a productive artist, she had completed 20 large and medium-sized paintings in the year since a similar show at the Cannery in San Francisco.

She loved to teach art, and for many years conducted a summer art school on the 2,000-acre ranch her husband Jack had acquired on the slopes of Mount Evans in the early 1920's. Winters were spent teaching in Boston, for Edith was a New England native. Around 1940, Jack developed a terminal illness. To nurse him, Edith gave up the journeys east, the summer teaching and the painting.

Edith Truesdell

The Truesdells bought a house in Englewood and sold their beloved ranch to the State of Colorado for the creation of the Wildlife Management Area—with a provision for lifetime use of the main house.

Jack died in 1953, and Edith had to make up her mind "whether to stay there in the house on Clarkson or go back and join my old sisters at the farm house in New England or turn a new leaf and go somewhere else. I decided to try living alone and concentrating on my painting—that's when I moved to California." She settled in a retirement home, took up acrylics instead of oils and taught art classes to "the old girls there." Last we heard, well into her 90's, she was still painting.

Robert Frost in Evergreen
Colorado poet Thomas Hornsby Ferrill wrote about his recollections of the visit of Robert Frost to our state in July of 1931. ". . .Joe Hare (Evergreen realtor and Denver University's Librarian) and I took him to Denver University where he read poems. That evening Joe Hare and I drove Frost to Evergreen where we slept in Eric Douglas's tents, Frost in one and Joe and I in the other. . . On August 1, 1931, Helen and I drove the three Frosts—Robert, his wife Elinor and his daughter Marjorie—to the ranch of George and Jean Cranmer at the head of Bear Creek."

"Frost, angling in one of the heavily-stocked pools, accidentally caught a trout as he was pulling the line back to cast, not knowing he'd hooked one. . . The following Tuesday. . . Helen, Joe Hare and I drove Robert and Elinor Frost to the Evans ranch where we had dinner with Anne Evans. . . (Later, in Boulder) "We spoke of Joe Hare's problem with tuberculosis and Frost said he himself had once had tuberculosis." From the Childe Herald Ideas and Comments column in the Rocky Mountain Herald, February 2, 1963.

Navajo Chief Blanket (1870)

Black-on-black plate

Samples of Evans and Douglas gifts to Native Arts collection of Denver Art Museum. *(Courtesty of the DAM)*

The National Repertory Orchestra (Colorado Philharmonic)
One of the rewards of living in Evergreen was always the annual delight of attending summer concerts given by this fine young orchestra, unique for the immense zest and joy—as well as the high quality—of its music-making. Long called Evergreen's best-kept secret, the CPO made major strides in 1985 in achieving well-deserved national recognition and getting a more secure funding base.

Founded in 1960 by conductor Walter Charles, the orchestra was based for its first 6 years in Estes Park, where it was known as the Blue Jeans Symphony. It moved to Evergreen in 1966. Its most recent name, officially adopted in 1986, is the National Repertory Orchestra. This spotlights the group's major purpose—to remedy the situation in which young musicians cannot get jobs in professional orchestras because they don't have experience, and cannot get experience because they don't have jobs.

In an intense nine-week period the orchestra plays around 30 concerts, the equivalent of a full season. The music is of great variety, played in many different situations: classical concerts in Evergreen, Genesee, Arvada, Denver, Vail, Colorado Springs, Fort Collins; children's concerts; pop performances outdoors; joint endeavors with groups like the Evergreen Chorale; concerts of contemporary music; chamber music performed by smaller groups. Each year, the Director brings in outstanding guest conductors and soloists.

CPO at home in Evergreen.

225

The 75 members of the orchestra, aged 18 to 26, are selected each year by audition from more than 1,000 of the finest young musicians studying at conservatories and music schools all over the United States and Canada. To date, CPO "alumni" are represented in more than 90 different professional orchestras all over the world.

The NRO also sponsors an annual conductor's competition, through which it selects its own assistant conductors. Carl Topilow, who succeeded Walter Charles as Music Director, was himself CPO's Assistant Conductor from 1972-75. All musicians receive a small stipend and room and board. An energetic, mostly Evergreen, board of directors has overall responsibility for raising funds, hiring professional and management personnel, and establishing general policies. The CPO Guild, established in 1966, undertakes many voluntary contributions to the orchestra's well-being.

In 1984, the CPO was invited to play in Los Angeles as part of the Olympic Arts Festival. The same year, it was selected to receive from the National Endowment for the Arts and Humanities a $75,000 Advancement Grant, aimed at getting the orchestra onto a more secure and permanent financial footing.

Much of the credit for the blossoming of the CPO's fortunes goes to Dick Zellner who became General Manager of the orchestra in 1982, with prime responsibility for carrying out the policies of the Board to develop both funding and audiences.

September of 1985 saw the CPO playing at the Kennedy Center, having been selected as the leading participant in the nation-wide celebration of the 20th Anniversary of the establishment of the National Endowment. The summer's orchestra was "reconstituted" in Washington and played a unique program of American music to an appreciative audience that included government officials, leaders in the arts community and 100 stalwart Colorado supporters of the orchestra.

In 1986, the newly-named National Repertory Orchestra was one of three recipients of the prestigious Governor's Awards for Excellence in the Arts, on the recommendation of the Colorado Council on the Arts and Humanities.

At the end of the 1986 season, the NRO announced a new affiliation with Keystone, which was able to offer better living accomodations and a more energetic promotion program than Evergreen. The NRO will continue to play its vigorous annual July 4th concert at Evergreen Lake and its series at the Genesee amphitheater.

Evergreen Artists' Association

Though the Evergreen Artists' Association's biggest impact on the Evergreen community is in August, when its annual Fine Arts Fair is on display in Heritage Grove, the organization functions actively throughout the year. Begun in 1958 as a small group of artists interested in a support group and a forum for issues related to the arts, the EAA was incorporated as a non-profit organization in 1972 and currently has more than 60 members.

Artists in all forms of the visual arts—oils, watercolor, acrylics, pottery, weaving, woodcarving, photography, graphics, prints, sculpture and crafts—are eligible for membership. Annual events include a Youth Art Show, held each November since 1964; the awarding of an annual scholarship to a graduating senior interested in developing demonstrated talent in the fine arts; two juried shows for EAA members.

The Evergreen Fine Arts Fair—begun in 1966 on the sidewalks of Evergreen Main Street—moved to the cooler confines of Heritage Grove in 1980. Open to all artists and craftsmen in Colorado, it is a one-day display and sale. Judges in each area of fine arts and crafts consider pieces submitted for jurying, and award prizes on the afternoon of the show.

Monthly meetings—with speakers, demonstrations, or workshops—are held throughout the year and are open to anyone interested in the arts.

Evergreen Players

The Players originated in 1950 as a play-reading group in the home of Willard and Mary Helen Crain. Soon it seemed feasible to present a full play to the people of Evergreen. Willard Crain was the logical choice for director since he had experience of amateur and semi-professional theater work in Cincinnatti.

Dick Zellner.

Work on the play "Outward Bound" began at the Crain home. Every member of the small group had to do everything, and the play was successfully presented in the original Evergreen High school Gymnasium/Auditorium.

The Players' activities developed rapidly for 10 years, during which they put on two or three plays a year. Then came a gap. Some members were burned out. The new High School theater was too expensive to rent. The group went into dormancy for 6 years.

In 1965, a few newcomers enlisted the help of some of the old-timers, and a new company of Evergreen Players was organized. In 1966 they signed a lease with the Episcopal Church of the Transfiguration, renting a part of the building, which had formerly been in use as a church, and converting it into the Little Log Theater.

The new group was larger than the original one and better organized. It has a good Board structure that considers suggestions for plays, makes selections, plans budgets and schedules and assigns responsibilities.

Everything is done within the group—no money is solicited from the outside except through ticket sales. Admission prices are kept within reason. No less, and often more, than six productions—ranging from musicals and comedies to mysteries and dramas—are scheduled each year. Audiences are drawn from the entire Denver metro area.

To increase their professional skills, the Players offer classes in acting, stage design, etc., which are open to the public. The Players also offer a drama scholarship to a promising young area resident each year.

The Players have been one of the leading forces working for a performing arts center in Evergreen, since they are very limited in their present quarters by inadequate stage space and small seating capacity. But they are quite firm about needing space that fits their stringent budget limitations.

The Evergreen Chorale
It all started with an ad in the Canyon Courier, inviting those interested in forming a singing group of professional quality to meet at the home of Roy and Ruth Seeber on a night in January, 1972. Seven singers responded, and soon the group was rehearsing.

Since that time, the Evergreen Chorale has never ceased to stretch the abilities of its members and the experience of its audiences. They have "kept these hills alive with music", to borrow a theme from an early Evergreen Magazine article on the Chorale.

The Seebers, musicians of professional training and experience, were forcibly transplanted from a 25-year residence in a small Hudson River Valley town by the decision of Johns-Manville to move its headquarters to Colorado. In Garrison, New York, the Seebers had been the moving force behind the creation of both a choral group and a little theater.

227

In the Evergreen Chorale, Roy was the demanding and creative director—who always asked from people a little more than they thought they could give—and Ruth took care of public relations and was one of the top singers. The Seebers found that Evergreen was blessed with a better-than-average share of fine voices. Membership in the Chorale was (and still is) through a tough audition. From the beginning the group tackled a wide variety of musical performances: classical music—both secular and sacred—musical comedy and light opera.

After Roy Seeber left Evergreen in 1976, the second Musical Director was Duain Wolfe, a Kittredge resident and probably one of the most talented choral directors in Colorado's history. He worked with the Chorale for four successful years of great musical growth then moved on to broader horizons and great critical acclaim.

Michael Weiker.

Dr. William Morse.

Alpine Choristers with Director Susie Vancil.

Michael Weiker, the current Music Director, is Chairman of the Music Department at Bear Creek High School and Director of Choral Music there. Weiker also finds time to direct the Temple Sinai Choir.

Norman Luboff, well-known composer, arranger and choral director, honored the Chorale by accepting an invitation to conduct it in two concerts—one in Evergreen and the other at the Paramount Theater in Denver—in April of 1986. He paid tribute to the high caliber of the singers and their excellent preparation by Weiker.

From time to time, smaller groups of Chorale singers have been formed to undertake specialized assignments; in the early years, a camerata and a children's chorale, more recently the Troupe, started in 1984 under the direction of Susie Vancil. This is a 14-member performing group, chosen by audition, which presents varied programs of fully-costumed production numbers to non-profit organizations and corporate and private audiences throughout the state. The all-volunteer group makes its own costumes and rehearses in individual homes but its lively variety programs are of professional quality.

Evergreen Chamber Orchestra
Formed in 1983, this orchestra "provides an opportunity for area musicians to perform the unique and beautiful musical repertoire available for chamber ensembles." It was born out of a discussion between Rick Vancil, Harlow Kittle and Ann Ludwig about the need for an orchestra that would give Evergreen instrumental musicians the same opportunities for performance that the Chorale gives to singers.

Vancil approached Dr. William Morse about the idea. Morse lives in Evergreen, is a member of the music faculty of Metroplitan State College and conductor of its orchestra. He became the new orchestra's Music Director and Conductor and, with his musical expertise and enthusiasm, the Evergreen Chamber Orchestra quickly made its mark on the local music scene.

With music degrees from Oberlin College and a doctorate in conducting from the University of Arizona, Dr. Morse brings—according to "Spree" Magazine—"a delightful conducting style and impeccable taste" to the Orchestra's four annual public concerts and recitals.

Concerts feature guest soloists. Musicians in the orchestra are drawn both from Evergreen and the wider Denver metro area.

Alpine Choristers
A brainchild of Susie Vancil, who directs it, this is a girls' chorus of 40-50 voices. The Choristers is an independent non-profit organization with the dual purposes of performance and education. It is supported by ticket sales for its public concerts (usually two per year), member tuition, individual and corporate gifts, and foundation grants.

The talented and enthusiastic group is divided into a Junior Choir, aged 8 through 6th grade, and a Senior Choir of girls from 7th through 12th grade. Director Vancil's philosophy is that, "Singing can be, and should be, a great deal of fun. This is the goal of the Alpine Choristers, along with artistic excellence. We work very hard on increasing the musical skills of all of the children."

The Moore Family
Talented, exuberant and an inspiration for their many artistic—as well as civic, educational and economic— contributions to our community, this family performs as a unit and individually.

Mike and Anne, with daughters Mande, Hopi and Nicole turned their family music-making into concerts of international folk and early popular music, accompanied by an assortment of unusual instruments collected during travels in this country and abroad.

Mike Moore came from a music-loving and music-making family, and broadened his skills and repertoire as a member of Yale's Whiffenpoof Chorus. He has starred in many of the Evergreen Chorale's musical productions, particularly shining in the role of Tony Esposito in "Most Happy Fella."

228

The Moore family.

Anne sings regularly in Chorale productions. The couple played recorders for many years in the delightful, renaissance-costumed Baroque Ensemble. The three Moore daughters were all seasoned performers before graduating from high school, with appearances in school productions and singing groups like the selective Colorado Children's Chorale.

Susie and Rick Vancil
For many years, this has been the foremost musical couple performing on the Evergreen scene. Though they sang together professionally in Puerto Rico in their early married days, their many starring roles in Evergreen Chorale's musical productions are strictly for the joy of singing and acting. Founding members of the Chorale in 1972, they have been seen together in such productions as Oklahoma, Guys and Dolls and Carousel.

Susie, with her lively stage presence and extraordinary voice, is a riveting performer. In addition to starring in the majority of Chorale performances—her own favorite role was as Eliza Doolittle in "My Fair Lady"—she serves as Orff Music Director at the Montessori Children's House of Evergreen.

Together with Roy Seeber, Rick started to work for the building of a community center to do justice to the many cultural activities that take place in Evergreen: this evolved into the Evergreen Center for the Arts.

Evergreen Center for the Arts

The primary goal of the ECA has, at least up to the beginning of 1987, remained unfulfilled: to build a facility in Evergreen for the rehearsals and performances of all, or most, of the performing arts groups in Evergreen as well as to provide galleries and studio space for fine arts and crafts.

The ECA's program side, especially its sponsoring of Summerfest and Winterfest, have met with much greater success.

At least a dozen sites for an arts center have been seriously investigated, including two in Dedisse Park and one in part of Means Meadow Park—which caused a great outpouring of protest. Many people felt such a use would violate the purpose of acquiring open space properties in the mountains.

In the mid-70's, the Jefferson Land Associates offered 11 acres, at very favorable terms, off Highway 74 near Bergen Park, but the ECA could not get its funding together in time to meet the terms of the sales contract. The site was then exchanged for a less desirable one off Lewis Ridge Road, on which the ECA did finally complete payment. But there was widespread dissatisfaction with locating the proposed Center there.

It is difficult to pinpoint just why the best efforts of many citizens devoted to the performing arts in the mountain area have not yet had a successful outcome. Perhaps the plans are too ambitious, the financial foundations too shaky. Perhaps, despite genuine efforts in this direction, there has so far been a lack of sustained, broad-based citizen involvement.

Failure to come up with a decent performance facility was certainly one factor in the NRO's decision to move to Keystone. But, though the relocation of the NRO undoubtedly impoverishes Evergreen, it does leave the ECA with a more clearly-defined task—to find appropriate, affordable performing, studio and exhibition spaces for Evergreen's year-round performing and fine arts groups.

Susie Vancil.

229

Rick Vancil.

Walter Charles

This man, using his great musical talents in the service of a lifelong dream, is responsible for bringing to Evergreen what was, for twenty years, one of its greatest cultural assets—the National Repertory Orchestra (Colorado Philharmonic).

Walter Charles.

Charles was a cellist and a conductor, a native of Jersey City. At the age of 16, while at Julliard, he auditioned for the position of first cellist and assistant conductor in Leopold Stokowski's All-American Youth Orchestra. He won the audition—and went on to serve as both conductor and solo cellist in cities throughout the country. But his long-term life course was determined by Stokowski's complaint that the young and talented Walter had no experience. The CPO was Charles' answer to the Catch 22 question: how can a young musician acquire professional experience if no orchestra will hire him without it?

In 1960, when he founded the Blue Jeans Symphony in Estes Park, Charles was still pursuing his own career as cello soloist, as guest conductor of major orchestras and as resident music director or conductor of such orchestras as the Plainfield Symphony in New Jersey and the Abilene and Wichita Falls Orchestras in Texas. But the demands of auditioning young musicians from all over the nation for each summer's orchestra, raising the funds to make the venture possible and developing each season's varied and demanding repertoire, soon took all of his time and energy.

Walter Charles' last season with the CPO was in 1977. From this time until his death in 1980, Charles devoted his energies to "Music Magic", a program introducing schoolchildren to the grandeur of our western musical heritage.

Charles' wife, Virginia, was herself a virtuoso musician with a distinguished career as a flutist, soloing with major orchestras on the east and west coasts. After the founding of the orchestra in 1960, she devoted herself to working with her husband. She died in 1986 after a long illness.

Carl Topilow.

Carl Topilow

The CPO's second Music Director is one of its distinguished alumni. Topilow graduated from the Manhattan School of Music with a performance degree in clarinet and a master's in music education and then held a four-year fellowship for the study of conducting at the National Orchestral Association.

He served as Assistant Conductor of the CPO from 1972-6 and was appointed for a three-year stint as Exxon/Arts Endowment Conductor of the Denver Symphony. He became CPO Music Director in 1978, and has built on and diversified the heritage from Walter Charles. Topilow's contributions have included the establishment of the CPO's Assistant Conductor Competition, Conductors Seminars, the bringing in of outstanding guest soloists and conductors, and development of a fruitful relationship with the Young Concert Artists program in New York City.

Topilow serves as Conductor and Director of the Orchestral Program of the Cleveland Institute of Music and as guest conductor with orchestras in the U.S. and abroad.

Jenise Harper

Jenise is another of those sparkling, multi-talented personalities that will not fit into a pigeonhole. She grew up in a small Nebraska town, where her schoolteacher mother encouraged her natural interest in performing in plays and musicals.

While at the University of Nebraska, majoring in drama, speech and English, she had a "super part-time job at the educational television station". As a high school teacher in Santa Ana, California, she used this experience to advantage: "the videotapes my students produced are still used in the school system today."

After marriage, several moves and two children, Jenise came to live in Aurora. But when she and her husband were taken to dinner one evening at Brook Forest Inn, they "fell in love with this picturesque mountain community", purchased land and built a home here.

Jenise Harper.

All facets of the arts community in Evergreen have benefited from Jenise's efforts. She has performed with the Evergreen Chorale and the Evergreen Players; she has directed several Players' musicals—concentrating on productions involving young people—as well as productions at local schools; she was for several years executive director of the Evergreen Center for the Arts, where she helped to originate both the Summerfest Evergreen and Winterfest fairs; for two years, she was executive director of the Evergreen Area Chamber of Commerce, where some of her efforts were directed to drawing the business and arts communities together for mutual benefit.

The entire Harper family has joined Jenise in her love of performing: some of their most enjoyable family times, she says, "have been when the four of us were involved in such shows as "Annie, Get Your Gun," "The Wizard of Oz, "Annie", and "Bye Bye Birdie".

Duain Wolfe.

Duain Wolfe

One of the shining musical talents now working in Colorado, Wolfe has carved a unique niche for himself through his remarkable work with children and with choral music. He founded the Colorado Children's Chorale in 1974 to give children an opportunity for advanced musical training and significant performing experience.

The originally small but ambitious ensemble has grown to 4 choral groups with over 300 children. The Concert Choir— in addition to its own concert series—has appeared with most of the major orchestras in Colorado and also sings for senior citizens, for church concert series and to honor significant individuals.

The Tour Choir was invited by Mrs. Anwar Sadat to be part of the "Children as Teachers of Peace" Conference in San Francisco in 1982, toured the People's Republic of China in 1980 and Great Britain in 1982 and made its debut at New York's Avery Fisher Hall in 1985. It makes a concert tour in some part of the U.S. annually.

Wolfe's other work with children has included an 8-year stint as Chairmen of Colorado Academy's Fine and Performing Arts Department, and the remarkable feat of convincing kids in metro-

area schools—under the auspices of Young Audiences Inc.—that they really like opera after all.

Wolfe is also a superb choral director for adults. He was Musical Director of the Evergreen Chorale for four years, has been deeply involved with the Central City Opera since 1974, and in 1984 founded the Denver Symphony Chorus. 140 singers, hand-picked through auditions of applicants from the entire front range region, made their debut in the fall of 1984 with a performance of Verdi's "Requiem". In the words of one observer, this "left audiences stunned and was acclaimed with rave reviews."

Bob Hohnstock

Good-humored, talented and creative, Bob Hohnstock has contributed to the cultural life of our community in many ways since he and his family came to live in Evergreen in 1974. As president and creative director of his award-winning Denver advertising agency, R. L. Hohnstock and Associates Inc., he helped to transmit the essence of the CPO—its integrity, its high quality, the vigor and impact of its musical performances—to a wide public through fresh and appealing promotional materials.

Bob is well-known to audiences of the Evergreen Chorale, with which he is a frequent performer, and also made quite an impact with his leading role in the Evergreen Players production of Death Trap. He has also contributed lively articles about the arts in Evergreen to local publications.

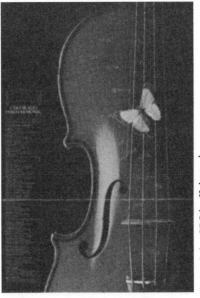

Artwork for CPO by Hohnstock.

231

Eugene Fodor

One of the world's fine young violinists, Fodor is a native Coloradoan and was raised on a ranch on North Turkey Creek. Exuberantly young, immensely talented and undeniably handsome, Fodor lived until 1985 on Upper Bear Creek in Evergreen, with his beautiful young wife Susan—daughter of the U.S. Ambassador to Paraguay—and their three small children.

They bought Eagle's Nest, a large and secluded home built and originally occupied by Rick Vancil, which has a magnificent view over the Mount Evans range. (The house had a brief and unhappy association with publisher Larry Flynt, who was shot in Georgia 6 weeks after the purchase).

Fodor's major teachers were Harold Whippler of the Denver Symphony Orchestra, Ivan Galamian at the Julliard School of Music—to which Fodor won a scholarship—and Jascha Heifetz. Fodor is usually described as having suddenly blazed, like a meteor, across the international musical horizon with his winning of the first prize at the 1972 Paganini Competition in Italy and his sharing of prize honors with two Soviet violinists at the 1974 Tchaikowsky Violin Competition in Moscow.

Fodor plays some 100 concerts a year throughout the world. He was selected in 1984 to join the company of such musical giants as Leonard Bernstein and Beverly Sills as recipient of the Atlantic Performing Arts Award.

Young Eugene Fodor has many other skills and interests besides concert performance: he is an avid horseman, a scuba diver, enjoys teaching and recording and is fascinated by photography. His major reason for moving from Evergreen was the need to be in closer and more frequent relationship with fellow performers and musicians.

Four Artist-Teachers

Evergreen is fortunate to have among its art teachers a number who actively express their own creativity, as well as being catalysts for the development of talent in our young people.

Andrew Baird is a talented artist and dedicated art teacher who has chosen to live in Evergreen since 1973. Its easy-going life style matches Andy's friendly nature and gives him access to his outdoor interests of cross country and water skiing.

Born in Colorado, Andy received his B.A. and M.A. from the University of Northern Colorado, where he developed his skills in drawing, painting and ceramics—as well as his qualifications in art education.

Because his family's roots are in the early days of the southwest, he has a particular interest in Southwestern American culture and especially in American Indian pottery.

Baird was first introduced to Evergreen residents as an unusually gifted art teacher at Evergreen High School. He now teaches art at Kent Denver Country Day School, as well as giving workshops and classes at Arapahoe Community College, U.N.C., and Southern Colorado State College. His award-winning painting and ceramic works have been shown extensively in Colorado and New Mexico.

Andrew Baird.

Susie Irby Bogard came to Evergreen in 1975 to teach art, as a member of the original staff of the new Mountain Open High School. Educated at Arkansas and Colorado Universities, Susie is attractive to adults and kids alike for her energy, spontaneity and talent.

She has struggled to keep her own painting, drawing and ceramics going while serving in several demanding roles simultaneously: teacher and counselor in a school whose intense involvement with kids can lead to rapid burnout; wife of fellow Open High teacher Jeff Bogard; mother of two young and energetic children.

"Artist is a lofty title", Susie says, "I am in the process of becoming one."

Jon Powers, a Conifer resident and art teacher at Wilmot Elementary School, thinks it is important for his students to know he is a working artist. Favorite subjects of his mixed media work, mainly pen and ink and water color, are the landscapes, weathered barns—especially the unique and historic old yellow Conifer barn—and log houses abundant in the Evergreen area.

A former teacher of photography, Powers does most of his work now from his own photographs, rather than directly from outdoors. "I got tired of having sunburned eyes, frozen fingers and of general discomfort."

Jon Powers has been an active member of the Evergreen Artists Association for more than 20 years. He comes originally from Oklahoma, where he earned his undergraduate degree in art education and industrial arts and his Master's in Fine Arts.

His submission, a watercolor of Main Street, was selected as the 1986 Evergreen Christmas card.

Roger Ambrosier came to the attention of Evergreen in 1984, when for the second year his artwork was selected for the official poster for Denver's National Western Stock Show, (although his wife, Jeanne, says that he's best known around Evergreen for his drawings of pigs!)

Ambrosier is an art teacher at West Jeff Junior High School and has lived here with his family since 1970. His art deals mainly with what he describes as "midwestern, rural subject matter." His preferred medium is pencil drawing, but he does two or three water colors a year.

Since 1967, his work has been included in more than 30 exhibits and about a dozen one-man shows in Colorado, Iowa, Ohio, Nebraska—and Missouri, where he was born.

Harriet Strand.

233

Harriet Strand

An accomplished printmaker, Harriet worked out of her own home-based studio on Upper Bear Creek until 1986, when she and her husband Owen migrated for health reasons to southern California. Her work is delicate and individual and has received wide recognition: she has been accepted to more than 30 juried shows in New York, Massachussetts, Ohio, Montana and Colorado, has been included in many group shows, won purchase awards and been Visiting Artist at Colorado Academy.

One of her greatest contributions to the arts in Colorado was as a prime mover in the founding of the Foothills Art Center in Golden.

The Strands' daughter, **Sally Strand**, is a talented and successful painter now married and working in Laguna Niguel, California. Educated at Denver University, the New York Art Students League and the American Academy of Art in Chicago, Sally has developed a personal painting style and has been featured in television and newspaper profiles.

"Wyoming 1981" by Roger Ambrosier.

Sally Ochsner.

Sally Ochsner

A talented folksinger, often accompanying herself on the dulcimer, Sally also sings in the Evergreen Chorale. She is known to people in Evergreen as a quiet but efficient and helpful member of the staff of the Evergreen Library.

Sally Strand.

Joan Landy.

Joan Landy

Joan Landy belongs to the Hiwan part of the Evergreen story, being a daughter of Darst and Ruth Buchanan and having raised her large family in what is today the Hiwan Homestead Museum. But her dimension as an artist, long submerged as she played out her other life-roles, goes back to her student days at Syracuse University and has occupied the center of her life since the early 1980's.

Landy originally focussed on textiles and wallpaper design in her early days as a free-lance artist in New York, but her later-life careeer is as a watercolorist, with subjects that include portraits, flowers, small landscapes and still life. Her works have won awards and been included in juried shows in a number of Colorado communities: she is a hard-working and productive artist showing regularly in Evergreen.

Joan's daughter, **Cathy Goodale**, is also a talented and accomplished artist whose works are seen more regularly in Loveland, Fort Collins and Golden than in Evergreen. Educated at Stephens College in Columbia, at UNC in Greeley and at the University of Denver, Cathy is particularly fond of doing portraits of children.

Nancy J. Hendryx

An artist whose natural talent was obvious as a child, Nancy was born and raised in Chicago. By the age of eight, she was already taking sculpture classes. She had a scholarship by the time she was 12 to study painting at the Chicago Art Institute. After graduating from Southern Illinois University, Nancy spent a year teaching in a Headstart nursery in Hawaii.

She met her husband, "Rash" Hendryx, at a party at his family's Evergreen ranch in 1966. The two were married in 1970 and have lived ever since in their home overlooking Evergreen Lake. Nancy teaches in a Denver middle school—for 10 years it was physical education, "until 1977, when my principal discovered I could teach art."

The Hendryx's vacation with their three children in Alaska and Florida, and Nancy joins a group of teacher-artists every summer in Taos for an art program with graduate credit.

Both Rash and Louise are devoted to Evergreen Lake and involved in working for its best future development. Nancy is so inspired by its continually changing moods, that she sketches and paints it from every angle and in all kinds of weather.

Painting of lower Main Street by Hendryx.

Nancy Hendryx.

Brooks Morris

Brooks came to live in Evergreen in 1951, and left the community much richer for having made it his home for more than 30 years. What he has left behind, besides the memory of a humble, seeking, loving and contributing personality, are tangible evidences of his craftsmanship: beautifully laid native stone walls and fireplaces, handcarved wooden doors and furniture.

We remember him in costume—the ancient handmade blue sweater that was his everyday wear, the colorful renaissance clothes he devised for performances of the Baroque Ensemble and the top hat and formal wear he affected in the 1981 Evergreen Players melodrama.

Brooks dropped out of the Greenwich Village 'beat' scene before it even knew it was a beat scene. He came to Evergreen in 1951 and entered with gusto into its close-knit smalltown life, serving for 8 years on the volunteer fire department and operating a little fix-it business for a year in the Main Street Building that today houses Shadow Mountain Interiors.

Next, Brooks became intrigued with the ancient art of stonemasonry: he learned that trade while working for 8 years for ESCO. A serious back injury put an end to that craft, so Brooks returned to an old avocation—woodworking. He made cabinets and furniture, but his mainstay was the unique Morris brand of hand-carved door, individually devised for each customer. Brooks' wood work can be seen in many private homes: the stone work behind the altar of the Church of the Transfiguration is also his.

Morris came from a musically talented family. His father was founder and first conductor of the Fort Worth Symphony, his mother taught piano and voice, his sister was a violin prodigy. Brooks himself came to music through craft— he tuned pianos, created handmade harpsichords and loved beautifully made wood recorders.

He was part of an Evergreen community of the 60's and 70's that is no more—that loosely-knit "hippie crowd", without which we are wealthier, more law-abiding, probably cleaner, but not quite so alive.

Brooks Morris.

Myron McClellan

Son of a country doctor, Myron was a child musical prodigy: he say he "was born wanting to play the piano." By the age of 7, he had his first set of formal "tails" and performed in concert for the Governor of West Virginia, his native state.

All through his schooling—at Castle Heights Military Academy, Wesleyan University and Princeton, where he had a Danforth Fellowship to study music but made a switch to religion and philosophy—Myron continued to practice, to compose and to concertize.

Teaching at Princeton, Marshall University and Wesleyan, he got caught up in the intense cross-currents of the early 1970's, attracting national attention for his lively 'mixed media' presentations of moral, spiritual and social issues.

He gave it all up to come to Denver and spend a year practicing the piano "in dire poverty." Why? "Burnout. A desire not to live out my life like so many faculty members I saw, talking about a life of love but not living it. Wanting to teach a more varied group of people."

Next he decided to offer piano lessons: some sage advice to start out in a small town brought him to Evergreen in 1973. Myron was introduced to the musical world here by General and Mrs. (Abe and Freddie) Lincoln. Soon he was teaching piano and voice to around 50 students, accompanying the Evergreen Chorale in some of its performances, and conducting its Camerata group.

His other major interest in life received expression through a series of classes in spiritual awareness: subject matter varied from the Seth Material to Zen Buddhism to the Gospel of St. John. As many as 45 people were involved in these classes from time to time, forming a sort of close-knit family that is still a significant dimension in Myron's life.

On the working side, McClellan took on a number of different roles at Kilgore Trout's restaurant—wine steward, maitre d'hotel, manager. Musically, he was involved in two-piano recitals with Kathie Davis, was twice commissioned to compose and perform concertos with the Colorado Philharmonic Orchestra and wrote scores for two movies.

In 1981, Myron married Libby Miller and moved to Denver, where he continues to teach classes, give piano concerts with Davis, and compose.

Kathie Davis

Slight of build, humble and quiet in manner, Kathie Davis lives out what most would consider the schedule of a superwoman who manages to "do it all". She is wife, mother of young children, a gifted piano teacher, consultant for the International Piano Teaching Foundation, a superb performer on the piano and harpsichord (she graduated from the Oberlin Conservatory of Music), and—in her spare time—a frequent contributor to productions of the Evergreen Players and the Evergreen Chorale.

Kathie played the role of Fanny Brice's mother in "Funny Girl", directed productions of "Sleuth" and "The Crucible", was musical director for "Man of La Mancha" and "Money, Money" and has accompanied many Chorale productions. As a concert pianist and harpsichordist, Davis has appeared with the Colorado Philharmonic, Columbine Symphony and Denver Symphony Orchestras and gives two-piano concerts with Myron McClellan.

Myron McClellan and Kathie Davis.

Polar bears by Wells.

Paula Chandler Wells.

Paula Chandler Wells

"Through my work, I want others to live the experience of my journeys, not just to bring back a snapshot." A nationally-known wildlife artist, Paula travels each year with her family to be in touch with the wilds—hiking, wilderness backpacking, and scuba diving to "swim with the whales."

Paula has exhibited nationally, regionally and locally in Audubon Society Shows, has had one-woman exhibits in several regional galleries and has been featured in such juried shows as the 1979 Foothills oil exhibit. She came to live in Evergreen in 1951 when she was 3 months old, graduated from Evergreen High School, took her B.A. in art education at the University of Northern Colorado and has taught students on all levels, including university.

She is a sensitive and talented artist, working in watercolor, colored pencils and oils. More recently, Paula has been using her artistic expertise to create graphic designs in advertising. She was commissioned by the Bank of Evergreen to do a series of paintings of the area's historic ranches that adorned its 1985 calendar. In 1986 she produced a calendar of her own, with sponsorship from several Evergreen businesses, featuring her watercolor of Elk Meadow Park.

235

Tom Ware

Tom occupies a special place in the art scene of Evergreen. His studio, overlooking Evergreen Lake, is full of friends and artists of this area who enjoy an evening of drawing or sculpture with a glass of wine and a well-proportioned model.

Tom and his wife Maryanna ('Munk') have lived in Evergreen since 1960. A geologist by training and occupation, Tom is an artist by choice. He is passionately fond of the mountains and has a partisan bias against flatlands. A sculptor and painter—and one of the most gifted artists in the region—Tom's work has won prizes and is regularly selected in the best juried shows throughout the metro area.

But perhaps Tom's role as a catalyst for artistic development and as a constant advocate for the arts in our community is as important as his own impressive production.

One of Tom's hobbies is wine-making—so far, he says, 1978 was his 'vintage' year. He and Maryanna participate with gusto, hard work and financial support in many projects that contribute to the welfare of the Evergreen community. For 8 years Tom served on the volunteer fire department (he says he was a 'nozzle' man) and is an active board member of the Evergreen Water and Sanitation District.

The Wares' daughter, **Caty**, grew up in Evergreen and has been painting most of her life. After graduating from Evergreen High School, she took her BFA in Arizona and studied at the Art Students' League in Manhattan. Her work at a 1983 one-woman show in Evergreen dealt mainly with floral images done in oils— with some prints, drawings and watercolors. Caty, now married and a mother, lives and paints in Montana.

Tom Ware.

The Cliff Benton Family

You may have noticed them— painted deer, like modern petroglyphs, prancing across the surfaces of the rocks just past the Fire Station on Highway 73. Designed to cover some mindless senior class graffitti, they are the work of one of the most accomplished artists that ever made Evergreen his home.

Cliff Benton "retired" to Evergreen, with his artist-wife Ruth, in 1958. Their combined home and studios, perched on the hill above Highway 73, came to be a center for a group Evergreen artists who drew and painted there together weekly.

Ruth and Cliff were active in the Evergreen Artists Association, serving their turns as officers and exhibiting in the little Art Gallery the EAA maintained for many years on Main Street.

In his Evergreen years, Cliff's work was mainly oil landscapes and portraits—he developed a particular interest in portraying the Indians of the southwest, feeling that their way of life would all too soon be changed for ever.

Throughout his long career, he had always painted in oil—winning awards and exhibiting in many places, including the Chicago Art

Cliff Benton.

236

Institute—but his living was made from commercial art. He worked in a variety of media, doing lurid covers for nickel and dime detective magazines, serving as art editor for a well-known children's magazine, designing posters, calendars, book illustrations and advertisements.

Benton created stirring posters for the World War II war effort and, for 23 years, did the art work and photography— another sphere in which he excelled—for the National Safety Association.

Cliff was born in Denver, raised for many years in the east, and came back to the west to try to make his fortune in farming in Idaho. But two hot dry seasons blew his crops away and with them, the hope of financing himself through medical school. Instead, he accepted an athletic scholarship to Cornell College Iowa, where he discovered both a talent for art and his future wife.

Unlike Ruth, who had known she wanted to paint since she was a child, Cliff sort of backed into the art business, enrolling in the commercial art program because it didn't sound quite as "sissy" as fine arts. The couple continued their art studies at the Chicago Art Institute and the Chicago Academy of Fine Arts.

Ruth's favored medium was watercolor. Though she "allowed her art to take a back seat" while her two children were young, she took up her painting again as they grew. She studied to add another dimension, that of nature subjects, to her artistic vocabulary. Ruth also illustrated children's books and articles, exhibited widely and, like her husband, won many prizes. The Bentons' daughter, **Jan White**—now living in Lakewood—carried on the family tradition. She graduated in fine arts from Denver University and did further studies at the Chicago Academy of Art. She has taught art and worked both as a commercial and a fine artist, exhibiting in many Colorado shows.

Cliff Benton's Evergreen "rock paintings".

A. Thomas Schomberg
Schomberg grew up in the Iowa of the 40's and 50's, a time and place he sums up as "a combination of Grant Wood's gothic paintings and Aaron Copeland's classical western music."

For a number of years now Schomberg and his wife, Cynthia, have made their home in Evergreen, and sculptor Schomberg maintains his studio here.

This artist has made his name with large, sometimes larger than life-size, bronze pieces of athletes. His works are exhibited and collected internationally: in addition to many private collections, they can be found in the permanent collections of the National Art Museum of Sport, Denver Fine Arts Museum, China's Shenyang National Art Gallery and the Phillip's Petroleum Collection.

Life-size memorial statues, produced for the International Amateur Boxing Association in memory of the American Olympic boxing group killed in a 1980 plane crash on the way to Poland, are installed in Warsaw and at the U.S. Olympic Training Center in Colorado Springs. Schomberg's Veteran's Memorial, unveiled on May 26, 1986, stands in front of the Holy Ghost Church in downtown Denver.

Schomberg came to the attention of Evergreen citizens most recently when he presented the working model of his statue "Rocky"— which he created in 1982 for the movie Rocky III—to the boys of Forest Heights Lodge.

Since Forest Heights serves boys with severe emotional problems, Schomberg felt that the Rocky story theme of heroic struggle against heavy odds—and of eventual victory—has a special meaning for them.

Painting of Main Street by Cliff Benton. (Property of Paul and Elma Hammond.)

237

Kitty Brown

The "angle" from which Kitty Brown approaches art is a lofty one—she is an avid and ambitious mountain climber and the first artist to be invited to accompany an American Mount Everest expedition, the effort of 1985. This sadly failed to materialize for lack of funding, mainly due to an unusual number of Everest attempts that particular year.

A self-taught artist, Kitty has been sketching since the age of 8. By the time she reached high school she was painting portraits of her friends.

Both Kitty and her husband find excitement and satisfaction in mountain climbing. Their life together has revolved around mountains; the couple has climbed in Europe, South America and the Himalayas. In addition to her dramatic paintings of high mountain landscapes, Kitty took up sculpture in 1982 and has become intensely involved in the creation of work that expresses the way body muscles flex and strain to conquer various mountaineering obstacles.

Now that her three children are out of the nest, Kitty plans to explore in more depth both the inner and the outer landscape ("Mountaineering has taught me that there are more important things in life that being a well-known artist", she says) and to express her findings in painting and sculpture. Kitty's sculpture had been shown most recently at the Foothills Art Gallery.

In 1986 came one of Kitty Brown's most satisfying moments, when she was able to present her own tribute in person to Mother Theresa: it was a bronze bust which she had created of the Nobel Prize winner, who was visiting Fort Collins.

Willy Matthews

To Evergreen residents, the most familiar of Matthews' paintings are his nostalgic designs for three successive annual Evergreen Christmas posters and cards, commissioned through competition by the Chamber of Commerce. The 1983 design, featuring young skaters at Evergreen Lake, was given the Denver Advertising Federation's coveted "Alfie" award as best poster of 1983.

In 1986, Matthews produced a fine watercolor of Evergreen Lake which was reproduced as a Christmas card to benefit the Evergreen Center for the Arts. A lover of both music and art, California-born Matthews started his artistic career designing record album covers. He moved to Evergreen in 1972 to escape California's urban sprawl. "The arid high desert and dry pine forest drew me in. I learned to live on ice and wrap heat tape."

Willy lived in Europe from 1975 to 1980, spending his time "painting and drawing, working in museums, refinishing furniture, dodging immigration authorities, selling jewelry, playing banjo, testing for the truly great wines, designing record covers, struggling with the Irish pipes, and defending my rather limited view of the world."

Returning to live in Evergreen, Matthews taught watercolor painting and worked as creative director with a Denver advertising agency. Eventually he established his own design graphics firm in downtown Denver and continues, as an avocation, to develop his skills as a watercolor painter.

Ron Ruhoff

A superb landscape photographer, Ron Ruhoff has seen his Colorado photographs widely used used in most of the conventional ways—in books and magazines, on calendars and as postcards. But this Minnesota-born artist has developed a series of unique programs for blending his two great enthusiasms—classical music and photographic images. He calls these "Photomusical Adventures"; they utilize a dual- projection dissolve technique and are enhanced by an appropriate background of descriptive music.

Ruhoff has generously shared these programs with the Evergreen community through the Library at no charge. He has also presented programs to the accompaniment of live symphony music: appearances with the Denver Symphony Orchestra and the Colorado Philharmonic have met with both audience and critical acclaim.

Ruhoff works full-time for A.T.& T. but he is also a professional photographer, and teaches his craft through Red Rocks College and the Jeffco Adult Education program.

238

June Simon

Simon Studios, Ltd. of Evergreen produces stained glass designs and panels used in homes, offices and churches throughout the U.S. June Simon, studio artist and owner, has an extensive background in art history and contemporary design from Ohio State University and Mexico's College of the Americas.

Before coming to Evergreen, Simon was associated with Aspen Studio. Simon has studied privately with Cecil Wilson, the developer of lightweight epoxy. The studio has a reputation for fine craftsmanship and fabricates for other designers as well as for Simon's own designs; it is a full studio member of the Stained Glass Association of America.

Some of its installations can be seen locally at the Conference Baptist Church and El Rancho Restaurant, and in Denver at the Tabor Center Galleria and the Tracy-Locke Agency.

Shane Dimmick

A hard-working, dedicated animal artist, Shane Dimmick has quietly garnered a sheaf of honors and increasing recognition in her chosen field. Shane is an animal-lover who used to manage an animal shelter in Denver and now does volunteer work with the Evergreen Animal Protection League.

She began selling her artwork while still in college. Working mostly from photographs, Dimmick produces finely detailed pen, ink and wash drawings, and paintings. In 1981 she was elected to the Society of Animal Artists in New York.

In 1982, two of her works were selected for the Society's annual show held at the Denver Museum of Natural History. Her painting titled "Migration" won best of show award in fine arts at the 1983 Evergreen Fine Arts Fair in Heritage Grove. In 1984, her works were juried into three prestigious shows, in Wisconsin, Alaska and Cleveland.

Nikolo Balkanski

This talented young Bulgarian artist spent the summers of 1984 and 1985 in Evergreen, producing an impressive body of commissioned portraits and landscape work.

At the age of 22, Balkanski held his first one-man show in Sofia, featuring portraits of well-known Bulgarian poets, artists, writers and actors. In 1980, he moved to Finland where his 1981 exhibition, "Finland in Portraits", drew critical acclaim "for his incisive and perceptive style, as well as for the sense of brotherhood and humanity in his work." Balkanski was honored with a one-man show at the October Gallery in London in 1984 and had a second exhibit in Helsinki in 1985.

In 1986, Nikolo was once again painting in Evergreen— hoping to make his permanent home in America. His painting, "Singing River", won best of show in the oil painting division at the 1896 Evergreen Artists Association summer show.

Dyan Zaslowsky

Having moved frequently with her family while growing up, Dyan has lived longer in Evergreen than anywhere and her goal is to stay here, "partly because it is close to paradise and partly because staying in one place is much more challenging than moving around."

She values the dual opportunity that Evergreen offers: easy access to the city's cultural offerings and the privelege of gazing "out over largely unpeopled forests, toward shining mountains."

Dyan usually describes herself as a conservation writer, contributing to Audubon and Wilderness Magazines, but she also makes fine and varied free-lance contributions to the Canyon Courier, the Denver Post and the New York Times. Her first book, **These American Lands** published by Henry Holt and Co., is a history of federal conservation programs in the public land systems.

Combining history and policy analysis, Dyan found the work on the book was like being back in school, which she says she handled very well "once I learned to read in second grade."

She is a Phi Beta Kappa graduate of Michigan State and would like one day to take a doctorate in American history. But for now she feels blessed in having her husband Michael and growing family as the most important aspects of her life. Part of her commitment to staying in Evergreen is to work through the easy phase of being disgusted with the way things are going—in relation to the preservation of nature's wonders—and "to take on the challenge of being more optimistic about outcomes."

239

Suzie de Disse

If the name rings a bell, it should: Suzie's great-grandparents homesteaded the deDisse Ranch which Denver bought to create the Lake and Dedisse Park.

Suzie is always active in community affairs: an ardent animal-lover, she was a co-founder of the Evergreen Animal Protective League, she has served for many years on the board of the non-profit Bear Creek Cemetery Association, and is active in many capacities in the Evergreen Chamber of Commerce. Suzie richly deserved her award as the Chamber's selection for Evergreen Person of the Year in 1985.

Her 'avocations' are woodcarving and the creation of stained glass windows, an art she learned as a student of June Simon.

Employed by Public Service Company, where some of her carved wood panels can be seen in the community room, Suzie spends much of her spare time pursuing her crafts and sharing them with community groups.

Gail Frasier

A maker of fine, functional stoneware, Gail Frasier says that she enjoys "designing details that will make pieces easier to use. Pots should be a pleasurable part of a daily routine, pleasing the senses of touch and sight. Incorporating the mountain environment in stylized designs is also an important part of my work." Gail achieves this by working from her own original sketches and experimenting with clays, additives, forms and designs.

She was raised in central Florida and received her B.A. from the University of South Florida. In 1974, Gail and her husband, a Colorado native, came to live here. Largely a self-taught craftsman, Gail gives a lot of credit to the Evergreen Artists Association for being a constant source of encouragement in her work— through its stimulating programs, the opportunity to associate with other artists, and member exhibits.

She has served for a number of years on the EAA Board and for a term as president. Gail has also exhibited at Foothills Art Gallery, with the Colorado Artists-Craftsmen in Arvada, and her pottery is carried by several private galleries.

Georgia Sartoris

Her art medium is pottery, and Georgia Sartoris is receiving increasing regional and national recognition for her work. In 1983, she was the first Evergreen artist to be included in the juried Colorado Biennial at the Denver Art Museum.

A native of Arkansas, Sartoris graduated from Colorado State University and moved to Evergreen in 1972. She concentrated on functional pottery for about ten years, then moved into the field of architectural ceramics. Her work has often taken the form of repetitive chevrons, triangles or crosses in wall-mounted sculptures, but Sartoris is clear that change is part of the challenge of being a creative artist.

In an interesting article in the Denver Post—part of a series on Colorado's top artists—Georgia said she sometimes looks at her old pieces and, while she's fond of them, wouldn't want to do them again.

One of her earthenware free-form pieces was selected for the Spring Collectors' Plate series at Foothills Art Gallery, where Georgia's work has appeared in the prestigious "Colorado Clay" exhibit. She received a purchase award in the 1982 Craft Biennial in Colorado Springs, was included in the 1982 and 1984 Biennials of Ceramic Art in Vallauris, France, and was one of the 5 Ceramic Sculptors in the 1986 Denver Art Museum's show of that name.

Joanne Greenberg

She is a member of the Lookout Mountain Volunteer Fire Department and a long-time volunteer teacher, about the meanings of words, to elementary school children. The mother of two grown sons, she freely admits that she loved raising boys. She misses, day-to-day, the special relationship with them that is like no other, because it "cuts to the bone."

Devoted to her husband, Albert, a retired social worker, she is also passionately involved with her family heritage of Judaism and its challenging paradoxes. But Joanne Greenberg has a steady central focus to her days and to her life: she is a writer.

Her first novel, over which she says she "sweated and blazed for years," was **The King's Persons**, about the massacre of the Jewish community in York in 12th century England. In 1964, one year later, her best-known work was published. **I Never Promised You a Rose Garden** was a fictional account of her own adolescent experience of an inner world of suicidal voices. The novel, which sold over half a million copies, appeared under the pen name of Hannah Green.
Since then, writing in the early morning for a committed one-and-a-half hours each day, Greenberg has produced eight other books and many short stories. Her themes are intriguing, serious, highly personal: **In This Sign** is about being deaf in a hearing world, **Founder's Praise** is set in an eastern Colorado farming community and deals with the corruption of an original religious

inspiration, **Monday Voices** takes up the theme of the difficulties of "doing good", through a character who attempts vocational counselling with delinquents and the handicapped. **Rites of Passage, Summering** and **High Crimes and Misdemeanors** are volumes of short stories, each with its unique character.

In 1983 came **Far Side of Victory**, a chilling modern version of a Greek tragedy—a novel, in Greenberg's own words, about "guilt, revenge and skiing." Her 1986 work was **Simple Gifts,** the story of a Colorado family suddenly thrust into the limelight.

Joanne is a vivacious and humorous speaker, especially stimulated by audience questions. At a speech she gave to the Evergreen League of Women Voters some years ago, the exchange went something like this: "Which is your favorite character out of all your books?" "A book is your baby. You nurture it for months—or years—and finally it is born. After that, you put it out for adoption and it doesn't belong to you anymore."

"Do you find it difficult to create male characters?" "I have a secret theory that men are just male women. In so many ways, they are more like us than they care to admit. I've learned that as a member of the Lookout Fire Department."

"How do you find titles for your books?" "I often feel like Snoopy. When he finally got his first book finished, he found that all the good titles had been taken. I thought I had a good title for **Founder's Praise:** my working title was **His Yoke is Easy.** But my husband took the zing out of that by calling it **His Yokes are Over Easy.**"
"How did you feel when someone stole your title, **I Never Promised You a Rose Garden** and turned it into a pop hit?" "The way a shin feels when someone's foot gives it a good, hard kick. It was such a bad song too, but I just didn't want to come in out of the sunshine and sit through a long lawsuit. It was quite a different story with Charles Schulz's book, **I Never Promised You an Apple Orchard.** He is a friend and asked my reaction before using the title."

Boyd Norton

Norton is a man with a fascinating past: former nuclear physicist turned conservationist, author, white water rafter and wilderness photographer, he is a person who lives by, and works for, strongly-held convictions.

At the end of a nine-year stint as research physicist with the Atomic Energy Commission's National Reactor Testing Station in Idaho, Boyd's assignment to blow up a nuclear reactor in a deliberate runaway test left him firmly opposed to further development of nuclear power. He gave up science to become a free-lance photographer and writer specializing in nature, wilderness preservation and matters affecting the environment.

He is the author/photographer of six books **(Snake Wilderness,** published by the Sierra Club; **The Grand Tetons,** Viking; **Rivers of the Rockies,** Rand McNally; **Wilderness Photography and Alaska,** Reader's Digest Press; **Backroads of Colorado,** co-authored by his wife Barbara, Rand McNally), and his articles and photographs have appeared in more than a dozen national magazines including Time, National Geographic and the New York Times.

As an environmental activist, Boyd's most successful campaigns have been to help, with camera and pen, in saving Hell's Canyon as a Wilderness and National Recreation Area, to be a leading part of the battle against holding the 1976 Olympics in Colorado, and to work against time to preserve Alaska'a wild lands.

242

"The Baroque Ensemble"

Sculpture session in Ware's studio.

Norton is a a co-founder and President of Evergreen's University of the Wilderness, a non-profit environmental education organization. He regularly conducts workshops in wilderness and underwater photography: sessions to date have taken him to the wilds of Wyoming and Alaska, to the Caribbean and to Africa. He is much in demand as a speaker on environmental issues—partly because of his articulate, humorous approach and perhaps also because he so perfectly looks the part of combination prophet and mountain man.

Divided Twins: Alaska and Siberia is the intriguing subject of Norton's most recent book, due out in 1988. It is a collaborative effort between photographer Norton and Russian poet Yevgeny Yevtuchenko.

Board of Evergreen Center for the Arts, 1986. Left to right: Dick Scheurer, Doug Cornell, C.C. Andrews, Marvin Knedler, Shirley Ryan, Mike Moore, Kise La Montagne, Karen Osband, Marybeth Coonan, Sharon Faircloth, Matt Loufek, Frank Plaut, Willy Matthews. (Not present: John Berry, Bruce Burrows, Hugh Grove, Carolyn McCants, Theresa Orwig, Jan Roberts, Linda Smith, Laura Snyder, Paul Tillotson.)

A LOT CAN HAPPEN IN SIX YEARS!

EVERGREEN: OUR MOUNTAIN COMMUNITY was published in March of 1987. Until the last moment, we kept gathering information and tucking it into the text. Far more copies were printed than either we or anyone else thought could be sold. We happily donated all our research materials and notes to the Evergreen Library and moved on to other activities. But by the middle of 1992, the book was sold out and we were getting inquiries about when it was going to be reprinted. Someday soon, we said, when we had time to bring the story of this mountain community up-to-date. The power of inertia being what it is, the matter might have rested there indefinitely.

At this point, the Evergreen Kiwanis Foundation came in as a powerful motivator. We agreed to give them the rights to reprint the book, including a new chapter bridging the gap between 1987 and 1993, and they agreed to distribute it in the community. All profits will go to the Foundation, which is well-known in Evergreen for its generous contributions to worthwhile community causes and organizations.

Evergreen Skate/Boat House, winter scene, 1993.

Evergreen Christmas Stamp and official First Day Cover, 1990.

THE SITUATION IN 1987

We left Evergreen in an economic recession, its stock of existing homes for sale piling up and local businesses facing hard times. The only new construction of any volume was of expensive new homes in areas like The Ridge, Soda Creek and a few remaining pockets in the Hiwan Country Club area. We knew additional library space for the Evergreen area was likely, but not when it would appear nor whether it would be a new building or an expansion of the existing one. Controversy over plans for a new and larger warming house on Evergreen Lake seemed likely to delay construction indefinitely. The outlook for acquiring any permanent facilities for either the performing or the visual arts in Evergreen was murky.

A round of school building and remodeling was finishing up. The slowdown in population growth, along with the increasing reluctance of citizens to vote any more money for schools in a dismal economy, seemed to rule out any new school construction in the near future. Plans for a variety of new commercial and social projects appeared from time to time in the Canyon Courier, but few seemed likely to materialize. In short, Evergreen was in a slump. A not-unwelcome state to those of us fortunate enough to have the preservation of the environment as our first concern.

So what can happen, and how much can things change, in the short span of six years? The answer is, "A lot!" Here are the highlights.

In 1990, Evergreen had a special early Christmas celebration. On October 18, the new national Christmas stamp was officially launched from the Evergreen Post Office, which became the busy site of a First Day Issue.

WHO'S IN CHARGE? (p. 11-32)

A Democratic majority on the Board of Commissioners? In Jefferson County? Impossible, we might have said in 1987. But a constellation of factors in the November 1992 election resulted in the replacement of Republicans Bunny Clement and Rich Ferdinansen by Democrats Betty Miller and Gary Laura.

Miller, a Jeffco resident since 1959, has an extensive background in government, both in elective office and administration: she was a member of the Lakewood City Council and the Colorado General Assembly, and directed the Colorado Department of Local Affairs. In 1977 she was the Regional administrator of HUD for an 8-state region and was serving as Sen. Tim Wirth's state director when he was elected to the Senate. She has also long been active as a community volunteer. Gary Laura's background is in planning and marketing, and in public health. He also has a considerable background of community volunteer work.

Among the conditions that brought the electoral shift, besides the national switch to a Democratic administration, were dissatisfaction with the manner in which county government was being managed and resentment at what was perceived as "secret" financing of the new complex of County Government buildings in Golden. Instead of going for a bond issue for capital construction, the Commissioners chose the route of "certificates of participation": the bill for construction still goes to the taxpayers, but they have no vote in the matter. Many people were shocked to see the huge, domed courthouse asserting itself into the foothills landscape. Just who first named it the Taj Mahal we do not know, but the description matched the feelings of a lot of Jeffco residents.

County Commissioner Betty Miller.

County Commissioner Gary Laura.

244

We ourselves support the concept of concentrating most county government functions onto a pleasing, well-ordered campus. The 113-acre property, known as the Foothills Business Center, was acquired by the county in 1986. Perhaps a mistake was made in not going to the voters for building funds so that they would have had a stake in the new facilities. But in fairness to the County Commissioners who made the decisions it must be remembered that voters twice rejected any increase in taxes to fund a new county jail. Under a federal mandate to relieve overcrowding, the Commissioners had little option but to resort to the certificates of participation form of financing which does not need voter approval. The jail was the first new building in the county complex. The Planning Department and Open Space moved into an existing office building on the site.

The Denver firm of Fentress Bradburn and Associates, architects for the Convention Center and the new International Airport, was commissioned to design the 151,000 square-foot Human Services Building, completed in 1989, which consolidates more than 20 social services agency programs previously scattered on 8 different sites. The architects' concern was to create a building that would not intimidate troubled clients but would rather greet them by "inviting them to enter for the services they need." Striving for warmth and human scale, they organized the facility into a welcoming, semi-circular shape and covered it in brick of a coloring that "reiterates the area's golden wheat, burnt sage, and dramatic mineral and soil colorations."

The 531,000 sq. ft. County Government building itself was completed in spring of 1993. It unifies services previously housed in many different facilities and more than triples previous courtroom space. Ironically, in view of the building's Taj Mahal name tag, architect Fentress was striving for a "sunlit, user-friendly building without a single dark corridor to suggest secrecy." He did also succeed in meeting the Commissioners' desire that the new county government building, rather than the jail, should visually dominate the new center. Denver Post columnist J. Sebastian Sinisi noted that the monumental glass dome, topping a 130-foot-high central rotunda and entrance atrium, brings to mind a hotel lobby designed by John Portman. But "the important thing about this complex," he wrote, "is that it promises to work. And to work efficiently at that." He felt that the building has considerable design merit and will serve the public well. However, to us the architectural character of the building is in conflict with the democratic philosophy that local government should be down-to-earth, simple and humble. The Human Services Building meets these criteria.

One of the powerhouses in the Jefferson County Democratic campaign, as well as in a many other innovative community organizations, was Evergreen resident and activist Linda Williams. She came to Evergreen to live in 1982 with her husband, Stewart, and two sons. Her background includes medical research and a stint as schoolteacher. Her first involvement in the larger Evergreen community was as a coordinator, along with Sheila Clarke, Dan Lincoln, and Tandy Jones, for ENABLE (the

Evergreen North Area Balanced Land-use Effort), which she saw as a way of enabling citizens to participate in county government. She sat in hearing rooms, listening to Republican officials make decisions. Williams told the Canyon Courier in 1991, "I saw firsthand that Jefferson County could benefit by the two-party system. When both parties are strong, the citizens win." Linda was elected secretary of the County Democratic Party. Her goal was "to see that every Republican in office has a Democratic challenger who is competent, capable and well-funded." The election of Joan Fitz-Gerald as Jefferson County Clerk In 1990, after the retirement of long-time incumbent Norm Allen, was a shot in the arm for the Democrats. Linda was next active in the Pro-5 campaign to place on the ballot a proposal to increase the number of Jefferson County Commissioners from three, elected at large, to five, elected by district. The proponents did not succeed in gathering enough signatures. In the November 1992 elections, besides the two Commissioners, voters put Democrat Dave Thomas in the District Attorney's office. In February, 1993, Linda was elected Chair of the Jefferson County Democratic Party.

In September 1987 the Jefferson County Planning Commission published the Master Plan for the Conifer-285 Corridor Area. This was the result of a cooperative effort between a citizen's advisory group and the Planning Commission staff. The area includes Aspen Park, Conifer, Pine Junction, Schaffer's Crossing, Buffalo Creek.

Jefferson County Government Center, Golden.

On the **State Government** level,
Evergreen Republican representative
Tony Grampsas ran successfully for three
new two-year terms since 1987 (five
terms in all), while rising through the
House ranks to become Chairman of two
powerful Committees: the Joint Budget
Committee and the Joint Appropriations
Committee. These assignments
guaranteed major headaches in the
1992–3 session, after voters approved the
tax-limitation Amendment 1, severely
limiting the Legislature's power to
increase state spending. Republican State
Senator Sally Hopper of Lookout
Mountain, who represents most of
Evergreen, also ran successfully in 1990
for another 4-year term. The rest of the
Conifer-Evergreen area is represented in
the Senate by Dick Mutzebaugh of
Conifer, formerly Jefferson County
attorney and Republican State
Representative, who
in 1990 won the seat vacated by
Sen. Joe Winkler.

The City of Evergreen? There has been
virtually no momentum since 1987 in the
periodic urge to incorporate. With it's
quite successful network of special
districts serving specific needs
(recreation, water, sewer, fire protection,
ambulance service, etc.) and Jefferson
County apparently doing a good enough
job with police protection and social
services, the only area of real unmet need
is that of control of land development
and preservation of open space. The
County Planning Department has taken
account of the input of responsible
citizen bodies like ENABLE and
PLEASE. But still final decisions are
made, not at the local level, but by the
County Commissioners.

The Evergreen Metropolitan District
(EMD) continued its successful efforts to
stay ahead of demand for its water and
sanitation services, according to its
capable manager, Gerry Schulte (p. 24).
The District supplies water to, and/or
treats the sewage of, a number of
separate districts, in addition to the
Evergreen Central District it directly
serves. These include Wahkeeney Park,
Kittredge, North Evergreen, Upper Bear
Creek, West Jefferson, Bergen Park and
El Rancho. The EMD operates three
wastewater treatment facilities. In order
to limit phosphorus going into the Bear
Creek Reservoir, the District is spending
$1 million for additional treatment for
phosphorus removal. 1993 will also see
the construction of a new 400,000-gallon
treated water reservoir to serve
downtown Evergreen. In 1993, the
District was serving 3900 taps. The
present plan can accommodate 200 new
taps per year, at a cost of $4,500 each,
up to the maximum of 7500 that the
availability of water in Bear Creek
permits.

Jefferson County Human Services Building, Golden.

Linda Williams.

A delightful small park was created in
1989 on the EMD property below the
dam. When veteran Ross Grimes (p. 18)
was defeated In the 1992 EMD Board
elections, the Board voted to dedicate the
park to him in honor of his more than 30
years of service and leadership, and to
commission a plaque and bas-relief of
him to be created by sculptor Tom Ware
and placed in the park. Ware, a long-time
Board member, was elected Chairman of
the Board. Grimes became an authentic
Evergreen hero in the summer of 1989.
The Rocky Mountain News described
the event: " . . . on Evergreen's normally
quiet (Main) street, an out-of-control car
slammed into a pedestrian, trapping him
beneath its wheels. Its driver apparently
wasn't going to stop. Grimes, who was
driving his van in the opposite
direction . . . did a U-turn and gave

chase. He honked and waved, trying to
get the other driver's attention. Finally,
Grimes drove in front of the errant car. It
smashed into Grimes' van and came to a
halt . . . The way Grimes executed his
maneuver avoided injuring other
bystanders in a fast-moving, critical
situation." It turned out that the victim
was a long-time friend of Grimes and a
former member of the Fire Department,
Dick Merkel. The driver was a man with
a long history of mental problems and
was apparently under the influence of
drugs. Merkel made a long, slow
recovery.

Fire Districts. The mountain area
continues to be well-served by its
network of volunteer fire departments,
Elk Creek, Evergreen, Inter-Canyon and
Lookout Mountain.

News from the **Evergreen Volunteer
Fire Department** (EFD) since 1987?
The place of women as full members of
the Department is no longer an issue. A
far cry from 1977, when Reggie Dutka
signed on and about half the existing
members threatened to quit because they
didn't want to work with a woman. An
experiment with a paid fire chief didn't
work well: the department in 1988
decided to return to having a volunteer
chief elected by members and to hire a
paid administrator. The then fire marshal,
Carol Small, was appointed to the job,
which she ably fills today. Carol was
born and raised in Illinois. Before
moving to Colorado, she and her
husband were teachers. Carol says they
chose Evergreen as the home for their
young family "for the best combination
of mountain living and community

benefits." She joined the EFD as a volunteer in 1980 and became a paid fire fighter with the Denver Federal Center for 5 years before being hired as Fire Marshal for the EFD in 1985.

First Mark Davidson and then Mike Clark were elected as Volunteer Fire Chief. Both come from fire-fighting families. Mark's father, Hal Davidson (p. 152) and Mike's father and grandfather (p. 149) were active in the Department for many years. The Department's No. 2 Firehouse on Highway 74, in front of Bergen School, got a welcome facelift and expansion in 1988. Architects were the Hoffman Partnership Inc. with Evergreen resident architect Jim Smith in charge.

Evergreen Metropolitan Parks and Recreation District (EPRD). To the board members of all these special districts, who carry the burden of government in our town-that-is-not-a-town, the community owes an enormous debt. They serve without pay, they meet for endless hours and wrestle with difficult decisions, they rarely hear from the public except when a well-meant decision angers some individuals or groups. Then they are likely to be unkindly lambasted. No Board deserves more gratitude over the last six years than the "Rec Board," especially Chairman Hank Alderfer and his predecessor A. J. Johnson.

Along with the EMD, Rec Board members have wrestled with the single most contentious issue in the community: the proper development for Evergreen Lake and its environs. Part of this issue was whether or not to replace the ancient warming house, unobtrusively nestled into the hillside, and if so, what to replace it with. It was a Herculean task to try to balance the concerns of naturalists and environmentalists with those of recreationists: softball and soccer lovers, music buffs who wanted concerts on the Lake, skaters, boaters and community members who wanted much, much more meeting space for Evergreen's huge variety of interest and service groups.

To complicate matters, two new agencies, the EPA and the U.S. Corps of Engineers (COE) were added to those already involved in anything affecting the Lake, the City and County of Denver, the EMD, Jefferson County Open Space, EPRD. The debate got down, at times, to such issues as one-tenth of an acre of *wetlands.* The EMD argued that the wetlands were not natural but an accidental creation. They tried to persuade the Corps of Engineers (COE) to "unclassify" them. (There was no Evergreen Dam before 1927–9, they

said, and so no natural wetlands. Until 1978, the area in question west of the Lake was a dry grassland used for midget football league practice: a tractor they were using, to create softer soil to practice on, fell into a hole. The hole filled up with water and so began the wetlands.) The appeal was unsuccessful. A 1980 blunder, when a company under contract to EMD illegally dumped fill and old asphalt into the west end of the Lake, alerted not only the EPA and the COE but The Evergreen Naturalists Audubon Association (TENAS) and one of its most active members, Carl Keiser. These groups contended that it was irrelevant how the wetlands were created: they existed and must be protected under the law. Susan Werner, District Wildlife Manager, testified that 155 species of birds used the Lake wetlands.

Carl Keiser is one of those indispensable activists we call the "yeast" of a community. They do not modify their opinions to please people, they sometimes rouse anger because of what others perceive as their intransigence, but they define values and set limits within which negotiating can take place. Keiser retired from 30 years in the army in 1972 and served three years as army attaché to the U.S. Embassy in Vienna, Austria, before deciding to settle in Evergreen with his wife, Mildred. Here he got involved with the Evergreen Players and taught German to students in the Open High School. But then he discovered TENAS "and the wonderful people who make it the truly active and meaningful club that it is." He served a term as President and is currently the Conservation Chairman as well as the State Legislative Chairman for the Audubon Society. The Keisers also love to travel, usually to places where they can pursue their joint interest in wildlife.

The joint decisions of the EMD and the Rec District finally resulted in: one-tenth

Carol E. Small.

Mike Clark.

of an acre more wetlands than existed previously, but contoured in a more functional and pleasing manner and attractively planted, with raised walks traversing some segments; a handsome new Lake Building commissioned by the Rec District, fitting sensitively into the west end of the Lake; parking for a maximum of 220 cars; preservation of the existing warming house, with its restoration and future uses to be financed and determined by the Evergreen Metro District.

The Evergreen Lake Boat and Skate House was designed by the architectural firm of Murata Outland Associates of Denver and built by the Evergreen's Arrowhead Design company, headed by longtime resident Scott MacKenzie. The building's 5,000 square foot size was a compromise between those who argued it should be a large community center and those who wanted it limited strictly to its functions as a skate rental and warming house and boat house. It's cost was approximately $1 million. The handsome simple log and stone structure,

Carl Keiser.

247

Evergreen Skate/Boat House, east elevation.

with ample windows framing views of the Lake and mountains beyond, was dedicated March 13, 1993. When it does not interfere with the building's primary function—handling ice skating and boating activities at the Lake—the building's two main areas are available for rental, with special rates for nonprofit groups. The Great Room can accommodate 170 seated or 364 standing and the Octagon Room 48 seated or 104 standing. From its opening, this facility demonstrated how starved the community had been for pleasant space for private and public gatherings: the Rec District was deluged with reservations for weddings, receptions and programs of nonprofit organizations.

The Rec District was also involved in the brief but intensive attempts to secure the old Open Living High School for a community center, described below in the section on the Evergreen Library. The Board and Director Dick Wulf are well aware that there is still a deficiency of space for community use in the mountain area, and that most people believe the only practical long-term solution is for the Rec District to be the owner and operator of such a facility.

All of this activity was, of course, over and above the normal operations of a busy recreation organization (p. 26–7) under the seasoned management of Dick Wulf. One perennial problem nagged on, as it had from the District's organization in 1973: the lack of playing fields for expanding soccer, baseball and softball programs. This issue also has pitted some environmentalists (real mountain boys don't play soccer: soccer players belong in the suburbs) against parents who think there must surely be a few acres somewhere in the entire Evergreen area for such a healthy use. It has also run afoul of policies developed by the Open Space Advisory Committee (OSAC) about the proper use of Open

Space monies. A plan to use part of the Alderfer Ranch for playing fields was shot down by OSAC. An ad hoc committee chaired by Rec Board member Peter Eggers did an exhaustive survey of existing fields and of potential new acquisitions in the spring of 1993. It recommended focusing on the improvement of existing fields, all of which are owned by the R-1 School District. At its May 19 meeting, the EPRD Board gave subcommittee status to the Citizen's Field Advisory Committee, representing all facets of

the community interested in playing field development, and charged it with recommending improvements to existing fields and developing proposals for future sites.

Other important contributions by the Rec District to the enrichment of the Evergreen community are developments at Alderfer Ranch and the evolution of a trail system. Because these also involve Jefferson County Open Space, they are dealt with in that segment.

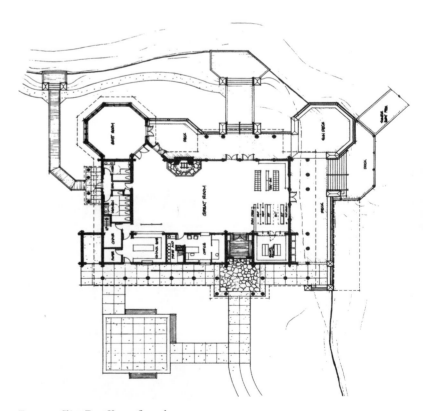

Evergreen Skate/Boat House, floor plan.

Dick Wulf.

From 1987 to 1993, three black bears had to be shot by Division of Wildlife personnel in the Evergreen area. One developed a habit of entering homes here. Another had to be killed at the Camp Chief Hosa Campground. In the Witter Gulch area a 400-pound traveler, known to the DOW as Bear No. 91, was lured into a trap baited with blueberry pie, doughnuts, and anise and reluctantly shot by District Wildlife Manager Susan Werner. No. 91 had already been relocated twice by the DOW to other areas in the state. A young bear "with yuppie taste buds" (according to the *Denver Post*) was tranquilized and relocated in early June, after feasting on the kitchen contents of a Genesee home and raiding Mike and Ann Moore's chicken coop on Kerr Gulch Road.

country. But on that date a jogging teenager, Scott Lancaster, was killed. In October 1991, three out of the four much-loved and photographed llamas of the JohnHill ranch on Upper Bear Creek were killed by a mountain lion. In January 1993 a lion killed, and dragged off to its lair, a 150-pound pet malamute in the Mount Vernon Country Club area. Because the lion had killed a pet when there was plenty of its normal prey (deer) around, the DOW reluctantly decided to authorize its killing.

Werner's advice on living with bear and mountain lion is: don't tempt them with food or pets. Keep a watch on children playing outside after dusk. Make sufficient noise when hiking in their territory to let them get out of your way.

Dedication of Skate/Boat House, Above right, Rec. District Board (l. to r., Deborah Brown, A.J. Johnson, John "Rash" Hendryx, Peter Eggers, Hank Alderfer, Dick Wulf. Not pictured, Dan Lincoln).

GIFTS OF NATURE (p. 33-45)

The wet springs of the early '90s produced wonderful crops of wildflowers in the Evergreen area. We call 1993 the Year of the Iris because of the lush vistas of lavender-blue in the Alderfer and Indian Hills meadows.

The most dramatic wildlife event in the past 6 years was the appearance on Bear Creek of a Baikal teal duck, usually found in Siberia. Discoverer was our local champion birder, Bill Brockner, who found himself playing host to many of the more than 500 enthusiastic birders flying and driving in from all over the nation. This was only the 19th sighting of a Baikal teal in the wild in the whole of North America.

Canyon Courier Editor, Tony Messenger, observed in a 1992 column that Evergreen seems at times a "wondrous town ruled by wildlife." Few issues rouse such interest, emotion and controversy as the hunting or trapping of wildlife, the killing of a bear or mountain lion which has become dangerous to humans or pets, or the reduction of habitat for water fowl, elk or deer.

Werner, who writes regularly in the *Courier* on wildlife issues, urges residents to remember that they moved to this area in order to live close to nature and its creatures. She says that the foothills area provides excellent bear habitat: biologists estimate there is an average of 1 bear to every 7 square miles along the Front Range. Typically, bears are secretive and sightings are rare. But ongoing subdivision and development of land keeps reducing the habitat of wildlife. "In my role as a wildlife manager, I do everything I can to influence zoning decisions so all wildlife, including bear, have a place to live. I try to recommend that drainages and meadows remain free from development to allow free movement of wildlife, and to protect cover and feeding areas."

A rare event in Idaho Springs in January of 1991 alerted us to the presence in our midst of that beautiful predator, the mountain lion or cougar. These are normally elusive creatures, keeping out of the way of human beings. In the last 100 years only 10 people have been killed by mountain lions in the entire

Apparently there are not enough lion or bear to keep the numbers of elk and deer in balance with their food supply. So the battle between hunters (who pay most of the expenses of the DOW through license fees) and animal lovers (who abhor seeing animals shot, especially on private lands where the animals have safely grazed until hunting season) goes on.

Scott MacKenzie.

For most Evergreen residents, the question as to how many elk and deer are too many comes in the gardening season, when flowers, shrubs and vegetables can be swiftly browsed or grazed into oblivion. Many give up gardening, letting their yards revert to the natural and opting to enjoy the rare privilege of wild animal watching. Others struggle on, alert to every new idea or gadget that may discourage the wild things from eating their flowers and vegetables.

Beavers also pose a dilemma. Hunted nearly to extinction in the nineteenth century for their pelts, beavers have made a stunning comeback. In the wild, their life-style creates dams and meadows. The disappearance of aspen and willow from certain stretches of a stream creates no great hardship. When the aspen are all gone, the beavers move on and the trees replenish themselves in time. But we, like most people who live on the stream, found no way to compromise with our industrious beaver. We cherish every aspen in our yard, since we planted each one of them, and we cannot realistically permit a dam across Bear Creek to flood our yard. After losing some 60 aspen trees, as well as most of our willow screen along the stream, we called upon DOW to come and trap the critter. Live-trapping is not an option, apparently, because there is nowhere to relocate beavers.

The EMD took a lot of criticism for trapping the beavers that took up residence on Evergreen Lake: they feared the animals might spread the disease Giardia into the water supply. We would question, even if the disease problem could be resolved, whether the District could afford to go on planting enough new trees to keep a growing beaver family supplied with food!

Bird-watching has an enthusiastic following in Evergreen, and TENAS continues to conduct its annual Christmas Bird Count here as part of the national effort. In 1991, the 22nd annual count numbered 47 different species and 5,427 individual birds. Highest numbers of individual species were Crows, Steller's Jays, Black-billed Magpies and Pygmy Nuthatches. In all, since the local bird count started, 83 species have been sighted.

THE EVANS-EVERGREEN CONNECTION (p. 60-72)

In March of 1993, at the age of 77, death claimed John Evans Jr., great-grandson of Governor John Evans. We interviewed him in 1984 at his home on the Evans ranch. He served as a paratrooper in

World War II. Like his father, John Sr., his grandfather William, and his great-grandfather, John, he divided his life between the family's many business and real estate interests and public service. From 1959-69, he presided over the Board of Trustees of Denver University, which Governor Evans founded, and in 1963 raised $10 million for the University. For his civic services he received many honors. He was married three times. By his first wife, Lucille Humphreys, he had two daughters and one son. His third wife, Martha McLendon, died one month before he did. He was survived by his sister, Ann Evans Freyer Sweeney of Englewood, his three children, none of whom live in Colorado, and three grandchildren.

We described the unique subdividing of the 3,200 acre historic Evans Ranch at the end of Upper Bear Creek Road (p. 71) under the auspices of the organization Colorado Open Lands. The plan had two aims: to maintain the character of the ranch by preserving the existing ranch operations and headquarters, and to protect the status of the area as a wildlife sanctuary, by subdividing most of the ranch acreage into five parcels of around 600 acres each and requiring, through covenants, that only one home could be built on each parcel. The last of the five ranches was sold in 1990.

The legal protection from development that this arrangement provided was by means of covenants on the land. This was fine as a way of getting the land platted into large parcels and preventing development in the short term. But for long-term protection, there was a need for some agency other than the landowners themselves to permanently enforce the covenant. So a unique national organization called the American Farmland Trust was granted a permanent conservation easement on the land.

We learned from Peg Hayden (p. 68) that she and the other children of Margaret Evans Davis are working hard to secure a similar protection for the some 2,000 acres that her mother owned. The land is in a trust. An attempt is underway to provide for some income for trust beneficiaries by creating a few specific home sites on a small part of the land, putting the rest under a permanent conservation easement to preserve its scenic values and its character as a resource for many types of wildlife and vegetation.

John Evans Jr.'s own home on the Evans Ranch was the Anne Evans house,

designed by Burnham Hoyt (p. 66–8). Evans sold the home to longtime Denver art connoisseur and patron, Frederick Mayer, and his wife Jan. Before they sensitively restored and updated the house, they commissioned the Denver architectural firm of Long Hoeft to prepare a Historic Structure Report. This formed the basis for having the home placed on the National Register of Historic Places on January 28, 1992. There are plans to secure a similar designation for the home of Margaret Evans Davis.

A new addition to Denver's historic treasures is the Byers-Evans House, adjacent to the Denver Art Museum. It was opened to the public in January of 1992 and doubles as the Denver History Museum. This somewhat gloomy mansion was both the childhood home of Peg Hayden's wonderful mother, Margaret Evans Davis (whom we had the joy of interviewing in 1981), and her last Denver residence. She returned to it late in life, after the death of her husband, to help care for her unmarried sisters.

New Evergreen Parkway sign (Exit 252 from I-70 to State Highway 74).

TRANSPORTATION

Evergreen Parkway, the new sign for exit 252 from I-70, looks bold and promising. The name was recommended to the Highway Department by a group of Evergreen citizens. So far, it is only a name. Let's hope that the right-of-way on both sides, and the median strip, will be landscaped to help it live up to its name. The Evergreen Beautification Council, sponsored by the Kiwanis Foundation, stands ready to assist with appropriate landscaping.

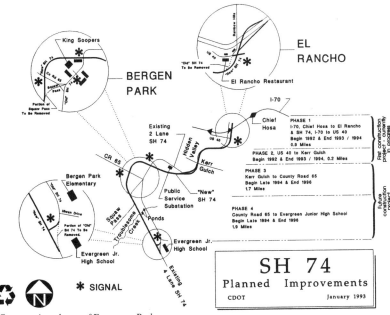

Construction phases of Evergreen Parkway.

King Soopers

BERGEN PARK

EL RANCHO

El Rancho Restaurant

Existing 2 Lane SH 74

I-70

Chief Hosa

Hidden Valley

Kerr Gulch

CR 65

Bergen Park Elementary

Public Service Substation

"New" SH 74

Squaw Pass

Troublesome Creek

Ponds

Evergreen Jr. High School

Existing 4 Lane SH 74

Portion of "Old" SH 74 To Be Removed

Hiwan Drive

PHASE 1
I-70, Chief Hosa to El Rancho
& SH 74, I-70 to US 40
Begin 1992 & End 1993 / 1994
0.9 Miles

PHASE 2, US 40 to Kerr Gulch
Begin 1992 & End 1993 / 1994, 0.2 Miles

PHASE 3
Kerr Gulch to County Road 65
Begin Late 1994 & End 1996
1.7 Miles

PHASE 4
County Road 65 to Evergreen Junior High School
Begin Late 1994 & End 1996
1.9 Miles

First construction project - currently in progress

Future construction project

SH 74
Planned Improvements
CDOT   January 1993

✳ SIGNAL

One still-unresolved traffic problem, which has been the subject of joint discussions between citizens and local and state highway departments ever since we came to Evergreen, is the congestion at the junction of Highways 73 and 74 in downtown Evergreen. Many solutions have been recommended. A 1970's State Highway Department proposal to construct a bypass around the west end of the Lake, to connect Highway 74 to Buffalo Park Road, was shot down by the public. Four-laning of the roadways leading to the intersection is difficult because business properties line both highways. In 1992 a Jeffco traffic count showed 19,000 cars daily passing through the intersection from Highway 73 onto 74: "that's a very, very large number for a two-lane highway," said a State traffic engineer. Some suggestions for minor improvements are floating around and the State Department is doing a Highway 74 Safety Study from Evergreen Lake to Morrison, which may come up with further ideas. In the meantime we should remember, according to a transportation official quoted by the Courier, that it could be worse. "At least it isn't Manhattan, where they'd kill each other at an intersection like this. It's amazing it works as well as it does. That's because people are so polite in Evergreen."

The main efforts of the Jefferson County Highway Department have been maintaining the local road system and upgrading as many roads as possible to become good all-weather surface facilities. Since many of the subdivision roads started as narrow summer service roads, such improvements have often been limited by rough terrain and lack of right-of-way. State and federal funds have contributed to these efforts. Many guardrail and traffic control improvements have been constructed with state and federal funds.

Four structurally-deficient bridges were replaced along Upper Bear Creek at a cost of $800,000, with 80% of the funds provided by the State Bridge Replacement Program. Citizens of Upper Bear Creek tried very hard to persuade the Highway Department to design these bridges with sensitivity to the beautiful canyon environment, with its many walls and roadside structures of native stone. At that time, the budget for the bridges was around $400,000. The citizens were told that improving the design as they suggested would cost a few thousand dollars: there was no room in the budget for such an increase. Somehow, it later became possible to *double* the budget for construction of the bridges, yet still no effort was made to meet the modest requests of the residents and taxpayers, who travel over the bridges daily, for finish treatment that would harmonize with the environment.

While Evergreen offers its residents a considerable variety of goods and services, most residents work in Denver and the suburbs. The main commuter route serving the Evergreen area is Colorado Highway 74, connecting Evergreen to Denver via I-70 at El Rancho. Much planning, design, and discussion has been focused on the issue of Highway 74, questioning whether improvements should be made and how extensive they should be. According to the Highway Department, a 1972 transportation corridor study of Highway 74, from El Rancho to Evergreen, rather accurately predicted the future traffic volumes which developed in the 1990s.

Environmental studies and a design report by the Colorado Department of Transportation in 1984 established the alignment for the four-lane arterial roadway now being constructed. Phase I and II of the development consist of a new interchange of Highway 74 and I-70 at El Rancho and the first segment of Evergreen Parkway, a four-lane highway, to Kerr Gulch Road. This project was started in April 1992 and will be completed in October 1993 at a cost of $10.4 million. Phases 3 and 4, which will include the Bergen by-pass and complete the connection to the existing four-lane segment running past Elk Meadow Park, is expected to be completed in late 1995. The cost of the remaining work is estimated at $12 million. Part of the expense will be the provision of an elk bridge which will take traffic across Troublesome Gulch, west of the current Highway 74. The Parkway will intersect with Highway 103 just north of the bridge, which will be approximately 400 feet in length and rise 40 feet from the Gulch. There seemed to be a community consensus that $1 million for this bridge, to protect the elk herd, was money well spent.

A primary trail corridor connecting El Rancho to Evergreen is being developed by the Jefferson County Open Space Department. It will use the state-owned right-of-way in some places. The cost of the trail is likely to exceed $1 million.

While private auto is the primary travel mode for Evergreen people, express RTD transit service to Denver does exist. Hopefully it will be more used in the future and additional Park 'N Ride facilities provided.

Another major traffic project, which affects those who drive to work via Highway 285, is the four-laning of that highway for the ten miles from Parmalee Gulch Road to Foxton Road, and the construction of a flyover ramp to take traffic from Parmalee Gulch Road onto Denver-bound 285. Work on this major project, which involves literally moving mountains, is expected to take until 1999 to complete, at a cost of approximately $50 million.

Stone pumphouse on Upper Bear Creek.

251

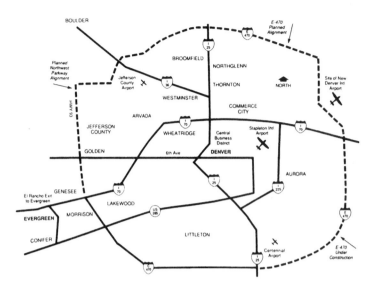

Travel time from Evergreen to:
Downtown Denver   35 minutes
Stapleton Airport   45 minutes
Interntnl Airport   ?
Federal Center   25 minutes
Denver Tech Center   45 minutes

RESORTS (p. 86-97)

There is still no hotel here in Evergreen. A small conference hotel and restaurant was included in the latest of many plans for development on the site of the old Troutdale Hotel (p. 88-90; yes, the old hotel is doomed as soon as some viable project jells) but was dropped in favor of an all-residential proposal.

We do now have a bed and breakfast in our town. The Marshdale Lodge and cabins (p. 96) were purchased in April 1991 by Joe and Carol Lundock, who opened the Lodge as a bed and breakfast in June. After the National Repertory Orchestra left Evergreen in 1987, the property was purchased by Jim and Mary Gordan, who did a good deal of necessary refurbishing at the Lodge before the sale to the Lundocks.

Additional accommodations are available at El Rancho. The upstairs rooms (p. 144), which were used as a hotel briefly in the early 50's, have been renovated.

Gail Riley and Tom Statzell work continually on upgrading and remodeling their charming cottages, suites and sleeping rooms at Highland Haven (p. 97-8). Their cottages now offer fireplaces, VCRs and Jacuzzi tubs.

Maurice and Mildred Bauer, former Evergreen residents who developed the Bauer Spruce Island Chalets on Brook Forest Road, celebrated their 60th wedding anniversary with a family reunion at the chalets in June of 1989. The complex is now owned and operated by the Bauer's daughter, Maureen, and her husband Paul Harrison. The chalets, varying in size from 1 to 4 bedrooms, are rented by the day or the week.

These facilities, together with Davidson's Lodge on Lower Bear Creek, comprise the sum total of Evergreen's accommodations for visitors. Paul is the 1992-93 President of the Evergreen Kiwanis Club.

Maureen and Paul Harrison.

OPEN SPACE (p. 100-119)

The Mount Evans Wilderness Area (p. 117-9) is Evergreen's spectacular backdrop. Proximity to such a national treasure is one of our community's greatest assets. The controversy over whether or not to rebuild Gus Roehling's Crest House (p. 118-9) was debated and argued through the courts and in the metro newspapers. The Forest Service's decision to build a simple unmanned viewing platform with interpretative signs, incorporating the Crest House ruins, was upheld.

Mountain Area Land Trust. Twenty mountain area citizens met on April 4, 1992 at the Hiwan Homestead for a workshop organized by Linda Williams. The purpose was to explore the possibility of forming a Land Trust with a focus on our local community. These were citizens dedicated to preserving important local open space, who realized that taxpayer-financed agencies like the Jefferson County Open Space cannot

Bauer's Spruce Island Chalets.

possibly do the entire job. A Steering Committee developed land protection criteria and contacted landowners to discuss preservation alternatives. Gerry Dahl wrote by-laws and articles of incorporation and applied for 501(C)3 status. Incorporating officers were Dan Pike, President, Sylvia Brockner, Vice-President, Linda Dahl, Secretary and Dave Scruby, Treasurer. At the April 26, 1993 meeting the Trust was officially formed and a Board of Directors elected.

The Trust believes that the future of much of our remaining open lands will be determined in the next decade. Its purpose is "to assist landowners and neighborhoods in the mountain areas west of Denver in preserving open lands and natural areas. Lands to be sought for protection include properties valuable for scenic buffers and open space, greenbelts and trail corridors, wildlife habitat, and the safekeeping of our natural heritage."

In its efforts to preserve significant open lands in the mountain area, the Mountain Area Land Trust joins the **Clear Creek Land Conservancy**, which now has approximately 500 acres of Clear Creek Canyon under its protection.

What happens to the **Denver Mountain Parks** (p. 100–108) is of vital significance to the Evergreen area, interwoven as they are throughout the Genesee, Bergen Park, Evergreen and Kittredge landscape. There was a flurry of planning activity during the tenure of Mayor Federico Peña and his husband-and-wife team of Carolyn and Don Etter, who headed the Denver Parks Department. A joint assessment of the 150,000 acres in Jefferson County owned by 20 different agencies (local, county, State, federal, private non-profit groups) was undertaken in 1988–9. So far, there do not seem to have been many concrete results of the planning.

In 1988, Denver applied to have 11 of its mountain parks properties included on the National Register of Historic Places, including 9 parks (Bergen, Colorow Point, deDisse, Genesee, Red Rocks, Lookout Mountain, Corwina/O'Fallon/Pence), the Lariat Trail Scenic Trail out of Golden and the Bear Creek Canyon Scenic Drive. The applications contain much interesting history about the original ownership of the parks, how they were acquired, and who designed their facilities: the documents can be examined in the Colorado Historical Society's files at 13th and Bannock in Denver.

Lease of the Chief Hosa campground near Genesee, owned by Denver as part of its mountain parks system, was taken over by Conifer resident David Christie

on May 1, 1988. Christie was formerly employed by Denver Mountain Parks. On the site is a 70-year-old lodge, now camp headquarters, which has had a number of uses in the past, including service as a World War I museum and as a restaurant. Christie is working hard to make both the campsite and the Lodge an asset to the Denver metro area.

In 1992, the **Jefferson County Open Space** agency (p. 108–115). celebrated its 20th anniversary. Since 1972, more than 22,000 acres of parks, recreational areas and trails have been purchased, of which 15,560 are located in the foothills and mountain areas of the county. An agency which administers a multi-million budget annually, and is virtually the only one now able to purchase public open space in the Evergreen area, is obviously a Very Important Entity on our local scene. JCOS has to perform a number of simultaneous balancing acts. It must acquire land accessible to "flatlanders", the majority of the County population, and at the same time not lose opportunities to acquire less expensive foothills and mountain properties which the entire county enjoys. It must acquire land now, while it is available, but yet spend enough money and time on development to make the properties it has acquired accessible to the public. It must also spend enough on maintenance to keep its parks attractive and prevent deterioration. Where it has acquired historical sites, especially buildings, it must make them available for public use. But it must be careful not to spend too much on operating functions and so limit its funds for acquisitions.

Developments in the mountain area since 1987 include: The lovely **Alderfer/ Three Sisters Park** property on Buffalo Park Road, already acquired by 1987, has seen several significant additions and improvements. Because the JCOS did not want to get into the business of preserving the ranch buildings or opening them to the public, it negotiated in November 1990 a $1.00 per year lease for 25 years with the EPRD. The Rec District took over management and development of 5.5 acres, which includes the ranch house, barn and four sheds. Its first step has been to construct on the west end of the site a parking lot, restrooms, picnic tables, and facilities for an outdoor classroom. The District is eligible to apply for, and did receive, matching funds for this development from JCOS. Meantime, JCOS added 440 acres of Colorado State land to the park, by means of a lease, bringing the total acreage accessible to the public to 770. It designed and built wider trails to accommodate a variety of trail users, creating an attractive new network of trails on the park property south of

Buffalo Park Road and bringing the total of multi-use trails throughout the park to 15 miles.

The 319-acre **Lair of the Bear**, acquired in 1986 after a long campaign, spearheaded by Sylvia and Bill Brockner and TENAS, was opened for public use on June 8, 1991. Located in Bear Creek Canyon between Kittredge and Idledale, the park has 1.5 miles of stream frontage, 3 miles of trails, picnic tables, barbecue facilities and parking for 100 cars. Initially, OSAC voted to ban bikes, horses and dogs from this park because of the delicate nature of its environment. The ban was overturned by the County Commissioners, who said it was too arbitrary. They did however indicate that some restrictions on types of use allowed in different parks may be acceptable, provided all interested parties have input and different needs are balanced.

An additional 1400 acres stretching across both sides of Bear Creek Canyon, between Idledale and Morrison, was purchased by JCOS in 1992. Difficulties arose between the seller, Bear Creek Development Corporation headed by Leo Bradley, and open space officials, so the sale was brokered by a national organization, the Trust for Public Land. The purchase preserves the entryway to Bear Creek Canyon.

Pine Valley Ranch, purchased in 1986, is expected to be open to the public in spring 1994. The North Fork of the South Platte, which runs through the park, will provide excellent fishing. 5 miles of trails are being developed. Picnic facilities for large groups are in the plans, which will be available on a reservation basis. A paved road into the park will provide access from County Road 126.

Hiwan Homestead Museum sustained some real "people" losses in the past 6 years. Mary Helen Crain (p. 159–60), whom the Courier described as "Evergreen's Historian Emeritus", died of a massive stroke in 1988. Connie Fahnestock, Director of the Museum since its inception in 1975, resigned to move to Fort Collins with her husband and do the things which have taken priority in her life: flying, golfing, spending time with children and grandchildren. Then in February 1992, Sandy Crain, Connie's long-time collaborator and replacement as Director, resigned. The original trio of strong and dedicated women, who founded the Jefferson County Historical Society and spearheaded the drive to save the Hiwan Homestead by persuading the newly-formed Jefferson County Open Space to secure it as its first purchase, was gone. Crain was first a volunteer at the

253

Museum, then its second paid staff member. A native of Indiana, she came with her husband, Evergreen native Dick Crain, to live here in 1970. She helped to found the Jefferson County Historical Commission, was one of its original members and chairman in 1982. She built up the artifacts collection at the Museum and had a particular interest in Native American art. She also had a knack for attracting enthusiastic volunteers. When she retired, the Museum had a paid staff of 5 and 80 volunteers. Already ill at the time of her retirement, Sandy Crain died on June 12, 1992.

In March 1992, Jennifer Karber was appointed to succeed Crain. She came to Evergreen from Lakewood's Belmar Village Museum where she was Collections Curator. Her prior experience included a stint as curatorial assistant at the Colorado Historical Society. She is a graduate of Colorado College and currently pursuing an M.A. in American History from CU Boulder.

The Homestead is getting a facelift. Its 100-year-old log façade has suffered from water damage and insect infestation. Using an exterior study by Long-Hoeft Architects, Open Space's Park Services Section will perform the necessary repairs. There are also plans to restore two bathrooms inside the Museum, one to a 1918 time period and the other to a time around the 1930's.

The Jefferson County Historical Society also suffered some setbacks and personnel losses but entered a new phase of energetic activity with the election of Jo Ann Dunn to the presidency in the spring of 1993.

Jo Ann Dunn.

It is clear to most Evergreen residents, to the Rec District Board and management, to the District Wildlife Manager, and everyone else knowledgeable about wildlife habitat in this area, that the beautiful **Noble Meadow** along Highway 103 should be bought and preserved as open space by JCOS. Not only is the meadow a visual treasure, it is adjacent to Elk Meadow Park, Bergen Peak and the Mount Evans Elk Management Area and, with these properties, forms an essential part of elk habitat. Both calving grounds and winter feeding grounds are found on the property. Purchase of the land by Open Space has been discussed for many years. In the latest go-round, the Hiwan Ridge Corporation offered to sell 405 acres of the property to Open Space as part of an offer they were making to the land's owner, Gayno Inc of Colorado Springs, for its remaining 508-acre holding. The Open Space Advisory Committee, after authorizing the staff to enter into negotiations with the sellers, voted against the purchase in March of 1993. This was in spite of support from realtors, builders, and 3,026 individuals who signed a petition urging the purchase. The prime consideration appeared to be a preference for purchasing land in the flatlands or hogback area rather than in the mountains. A final decision will be made by the Board of Commissioners.

A **Trails 2000 Action Plan** was launched in 1992 by Jefferson County Open Space. At a cost of $12 million, this is a network of 8 trails covering 82 miles. Three of the trails pass through Evergreen, with the Lake as the hub. One trail will go from El Rancho to the Lake, parallel to Highway 74, one from the Lake to Conifer and the third from the Lake along Bear Creek to Morrison and Kipling, eventually joining Evergreen to the South Platte River Greenway Trail. The trails will be developed with 8–10 foot concrete surfaces for walking and bicycle riding, with a 3–5 foot natural surface alongside for equestrian use and jogging. JCOS will fund the trail corridor acquisitions and development. Funds raised by the Evergreen Kiwanis Foundation for the People Path will fund shelters, rest stops and landscaping along the Evergreen area trails.

Ken Foelske.

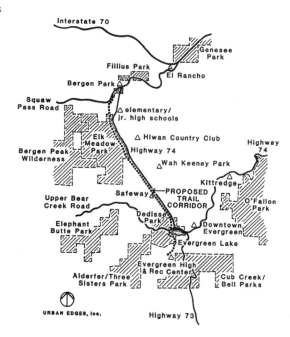

Proposed trail between Bergen Park and Evergreen.

Jennifer M. Karber.

Too many agencies are involved in the trails for the progress to be rapid. For the El Rancho to the Lake segment, for example, there is the City and County of Denver, the State and Jefferson County Highway Departments, JCOS and EMPRD. Negotiations have been underway for years already. But the trails will eventually become reality and will be an enormous addition to the amenities of life in this hiking, jogging, biking, nature-loving community. The plan's timetable is: acquisition within 5 years, full development within 8 years, by the year 2000. The 82 miles of trails will link users with existing trails in Open Space and other parks. When completed, this will be one of America's most extensive multiple-use trail systems. A persistent and imaginative Open Space staffer behind the trails plan is Ken Foelske. Foelske has a degree in landscape architecture and a master's in public administration and had experience in both private practice and municipal and state parks agencies before coming to JCOS 18 years ago. He is now Manager of Planning and Development, a position which involves advance planning, before lands are acquired, and the planning and design of lands after acquisition. He was the JCOS staff representative on the OSAC committee which came up with the current master plan guiding JCOS.

The Colorado Trail is a magnificent accomplishment of 469 miles of hiking trails through some of Colorado's most spectacular scenery, running from Denver to Durango. Its realization is largely the result of 20 years of unstinting devotion on the part of a remarkable Lookout Mountain resident,

Gudy Gaskill. She has raised money, coordinated the efforts of hundreds of volunteers who have worked on the trail, and overcome the divisions among the different agencies owning the land. The trail began as a concept in 1973, was dedicated in 1987, and was substantially completed in 1992. Among many honors for her work, Gudy Gaskill was named one of President Bush's 1000 Volunteer Points of Light in 1990.

Evergreen had a ceremony in Elk Meadow Park to mark its inclusion as a trailhead along the **American Discovery Trail**. This is planned as a 4,920 mile route across the entire country, incorporating such historic trails as the Pony Express route. In Colorado the trail will wind 750 miles, from Grand Junction through Evergreen and east to Lamar.

MOUNTAIN SCHOOLING
(p. 120–134)

Two physical pieces of Evergreen school history disappeared: the red brick building dating back to 1922 and the adjacent 1948 white concrete structure, originally the Evergreen High School and most recently used to house the Open High School. They were demolished to make way for the new Evergreen Library.

"Turbulent" is one word that comes to mind in reviewing the history of the **Jefferson County R-1 School District** since 1987. Money was a problem for the entire period in the state's largest school district, which had more than 81,000 students in 1993. Many of the problems were created by the financially beleaguered State of Colorado, which limited the amount of tax increases local school districts could levy in exchange for a commitment to supply a substantial part of school funding. This was to equalize educational opportunities throughout the state. Increasingly, the State has failed to meet its commitment. In response to a variety of public pressures, the Legislature has also continued to mandate expensive new programs in public schools, while failing to fully fund them.

There were also major problems within the School District. Dissatisfaction with the performance of

Senator Hank Brown visits Evergreen for dedication of American Discovery Trail (Bill Bennett, Arden Larsen, Gene Sternberg, Sen. Brown).

Superintendent John Peper was widespread, along with a conviction that the school administration had become too expensive, too removed from the action in the classroom and too arrogant. A lightning rod for this public anger was the purchase in 1986 of a plush new high-rise building to house the administration. This was presented as an economy measure. The public vented its dissatisfaction by defeating a $16.5 million mill-levy increase in December, 1987. Peper was criticized for the bitter and adversarial character of the 1989 teacher contract negotiations, though there were members both of the Board and the public who, like Peper, wanted changes in the traditional contract (e.g. to increase the District's ability to weed out poor teachers and to find a way to pay more for excellence in teaching.) But the majority's perception was that Dr. Peper's administration, supported by the existing School Board, was a big part of the District's problems. The issue dominated the May, 1989, School Board election campaign. Three Evergreen residents vied for the District 2 mountain area seat: incumbent Liz Baum and challengers David D'Evelyn and Jon DeStefano. After what the Canyon Courier called "a muddy fray", DeStefano won easily. So did two other challengers to the status quo, Jan Urschel and Nancy McNally. DeStefano is a publisher (p. 161–2) and amateur soccer enthusiast: at the time of his election, he was president of the Evergreen Junior Soccer Association.

In September 1989, Peper announced his decision to step down as Superintendent the following January. In spite of this, and of strenuous efforts on the part of the largely-new Board to convince voters of the urgent need for more money, a $180 million capital bond issue, paired with a proposed $14.1 million mill-levy increase for operating funds, was defeated in November 1989. A majority in the mountain area voted for the bond issue, which would have provided a

Alderfer/Three Sisters Park: trail system.

255

new high school somewhere between Evergreen and Conifer and eliminated the existing high school. Budget cuts had been made after the 1987 defeat. The 1989 failure necessitated more drastic measures. In all, some 355 staff positions were cut, including most in-school nurses and nearly half of school aide time.

In seeking a new superintendent, the School Board charged a head-hunting team to "find someone to boost our sagging morale; a communicator; a person who will reunite our people and refocus our energies." Lewis Finch took over the position July 1, 1990. The 52-year-old Finch, who was an assistant principal at Evergreen Junior High in the mid-60's, came back to Jeffco from a superintendency in Minnesota. In September 1990, the R-1 School District celebrated the 40th year of its existence.

For all Finch's efforts to communicate the District's desperate need for increased operating funds, voters turned down a November 1990 proposal for a $27.7 million mill-levy increase. Once more, the proposal passed in the mountain area.

Frustrated by the unwillingness of voters in other parts of the district to vote more money for schools, two responses surfaced in the mountain area. A number of parents organized a private fund-raising drive to provide money for specific needs (e.g. library books, computer software, band instruments, maps) in area schools. **The Mountain Schools Fund** launched its first "Phone-A-Thon" in May of 1991. Some $36,000 was raised in that first year, $46,000 in 1992 and $50,000 in 1993. The Fund serves the nine schools in the Evergreen High School attendance area. Money is distributed by a Board which includes representatives from each of the schools: half of the funds go on a per-student basis directly to the schools, and half are distributed on the basis of needs, from priority lists submitted by each school.

A prime mover in the Fund drive was a lively Evergreen newcomer, Greg Dobbs. Dobbs worked for ABC for 23 years, most of those as a news correspondent. He was posted to London in 1977, Paris in 1982, and Denver in 1986, covering many memorable stories, domestic (Exxon Valdez oil spill, San Francisco earthquake, Watergate hearings, execution of Gary Gilmore, etc.) and foreign (revolution in Iran, Soviet invasion of Afghanistan, the agony of Beirut, Solidarity struggles in Poland, the treaty between Israel and Egypt, etc.) When asked, early in 1992, to transfer

Greg Dobbs.

from Colorado, he opted to retire from the network. He is now writing a book about his experiences as a war correspondent, hosting a 4-hour nightly radio talk show on KOA and writing a bi-weekly column for the Canyon Courier. His civic contributions include serving on the board of the National Repertory Orchestra, helping to raise money for Bootstraps, Newborn Hope, Channel 6 and Children's Hospital, and managing his two sons' soccer teams. The object of the Mountain Schools Fund, according to Dobbs, is "to provide technology to promote every type of literacy in our schools. Not just computer literacy . . . but mathematic literacy, scientific literacy, geographic literacy, cultural literacy and . . . literacy with books."

A second response was to advocate the breaking-up of the huge R-1 School District into smaller units. We had already heard about this idea from former School Board member Paul McEncroe. It was articulated by Canyon Courier Editor Tony Messenger in a September 23, 1992 column. When the District was formed, it had a total of 11,117 students: now it has 81,370. The different areas of the county have different populations and different interests. The mountain area would benefit from a locally-based School Board and administration, he argued, one more responsive to mountain area needs.

Financial pressures for the R-1 District continued to build. Additional operating funds were sorely needed, and also money for new schools and for extensive additions and repairs to existing ones.

The mountain area's last new school was the charming Elk Creek Elementary, located in Conifer at 13304 Highway 285 in Pine. It opened its doors in 1988

and was designed by the architectural firm of NBBB.

As the region's economy improved, student enrollment in the mountain area started to climb. Nine schools comprise the Evergreen High School attendance area. In the 1992–3 school year, total enrollment in the elementary schools was 3254 (Bergen 743, Elk Creek 489, Marshdale 603, Parmalee 241, West Jefferson 497, Wilmot 681), compared with 2755 in 1987. For the Junior Highs, Evergreen (787) and West Jefferson (583), 1992–3 enrollment was 1370 compared with 1264 for 1987. Only the Evergreen High School's enrollment was lower, (1082 compared with 1987's 1372) and this was largely for general demographic reasons reflecting the period of "baby bust."

Temporary buildings began to multiply again on school grounds. Yet another bond issue for capital construction was put before the voters in October 1992. Voters finally said yes, choosing the smaller ($325 million) of two packages presented to them. Funds designated for the mountain area are as follows. **High School Facilities:** A joint citizen-District task force worked for six months, with input from consultants, on the best program for the Conifer area: in May, 1993 it recommended to the School Board that a new 1000-student high school be built for Conifer, most likely on the 45-acre Rancho Lobo site off Highway 73 near Shadow Mountain Road, with a target completion date of Fall, 1995. Much of Evergreen High School to be razed and replaced by more up-to-date facilities for a student body of 1200, to be completed by Fall of 1996. Both schools to become four-year high schools.

Junior High. After the high schools are completed, the two junior highs become middle schools with students in grades 6, 7 and 8. Evergreen Junior High will have a $3 million addition and remodel job to convert it into a middle school. What funds will be available for West Jeff Middle School will depend on the cost of the proposed high school. The most urgent problem in the West Jeff schools complex is, in a word, sewage! At present, sewage is stored and pumped daily: a treatment plant that could serve all three schools (including the new high school) might be economically feasible, in which case the funds for wastewater improvement listed under West Jeff Elementary School below would be used for this purpose.

Elementary Schools. By 1997, the Evergreen area will have one new

650-student school in North Evergreen, to relieve overcrowding at Bergen and Wilmot schools. The School District has an option on a site in the Ridge development, but is also looking at other sites. Wilmot will have some asbestos abatement and mechanical systems improvements. Bergen, which had a major addition in the 1980's, will just get some mechanical system improvements from the current bond issue. West Jeff is slated for roof replacement, improvements in its mechanical systems and replacement of its wastewater holding facility. Elk Creek will have a 7-classroom addition. For Parmalee, a four-classroom addition, partial roof replacement and plumbing and mechanical systems improvements. Marshdale gets minor improvements in its lighting and mechanical systems.

An ugly series of racist incidents at **Evergreen High School** in 1989 made headlines in both local and metro Denver newspapers. An incident of expensive ($10,000) vandalism, in which a construction adhesive was used to cover walls with anti-Black, anti-Semitic and pro-white-supremacy slogans and symbols, was hushed up by the school and no students were punished. In September, three popular black students requested a transfer from Evergreen to Green Mountain High, citing the continuing racial hostility of a group of white students towards them, which they felt would ultimately lead to physical violence. Their parents were active participants in the school community, but they, like the students, felt that the administration at EHS had been unresponsive to complaints of racial harassment. In October Joe Knight, the only black teacher at EHS and a popular and respected faculty member who had been at the school since 1980, requested a transfer after receiving a threatening racist note.

While firmly maintaining that a very small group of students were causing all the trouble, the school administration finally assembled a representative group from the community to form a task force, along with some school personnel, to get to the root of the problems and recommend solutions. The **Evergreen Task Force on Racism** worked diligently with antidiscrimination groups, minority members of the community and students to develop specific recommendations for new activities in the Evergreen schools and in the R-1 District as a whole, to promote awareness and appreciation of cultural differences and to develop a policy on harassment and discrimination. Among the tireless members of the Task Force were Jim Smith, Judy Albers, Ken

Dailey and Hispanic teacher (and popular wrestling coach) Miguel Elias. The policy was adopted by the R-1 School Board in May, 1990. In December a district-wide Cultural Diversity Council was established. A much more active curriculum relating to racial differences was adopted and District policy on the celebration of the Martin Luther King holiday was changed. Its short-term goals accomplished, the Evergreen Task Force changed its name to the **Citizens Equity Awareness Committee** and goes on working on "the continual problem."

After two years of negative publicity, not only in connection with the racism incidents but also over a string of tragic student deaths in traffic accidents, many of which involved drinking, Evergreen High School was ready for a new principal and some fresh educational approaches. The winds of change were starting to blow throughout the R–1 system. John Vidal, an Evergreen resident, came to head EHS in July 1991 from a 7-year stint as assistant principal at Golden High. Vidal's plans for Evergreen High School: restore public confidence in the institution, vigorously support the District's restructuring efforts and "put everybody, from administrators to teachers to custodians, on an improvement plan. If we want kids to learn self-improvement, we have to model it. I'm not an exceptional principal, but I will be." Vidal believes that the block schedule introduced into the high school, which gives longer class periods, will be better academically and also allow students time to volunteer their services in the community.

Vidal, born in Cuba, was one of a plane-load of 200 children flown out just after the Bay of Pigs invasion. He spent three years in a Pueblo orphanage before his parents arrived in the U.S. He graduated from a Catholic High School in Denver and has a bachelor's degree from CU, a Master's from UNC and his principal's certification from CSU. At Golden High, he met the challenge of a nationally-touted series of 7 student suicides in a 21-month period by helping to create a suicide prevention organization, and writing a nationally-used book about schools and suicide.

Vidal's first major public test at Evergreen High was a "senior prank" that included vandalizing school property and scrawling graffiti with sexual and racial obscenities on school walls. Vidal ruled that the students involved could graduate, if they completed all assignments satisfactorily, but barred them from participation in graduation activities. He stood firm against parental

protests that this was too harsh a punishment for a "boys will be boys" episode and garnered a lot of public support.

Jon Vidal.

One enthusiastic supporter of Vidal's ambitions for the high school is Allyson Gottsman. She has given uncountable hours of service to the Evergreen schools and was the regional winner in the 1993 National Outstanding School Volunteer Awards Program. Cited among her accomplishments were initiating the EHS Community Service Recruitment program, which matches students with community service projects, and the apprenticeship/internship program, which places students in appropriate short-term jobs. She was also a prime mover in preparing the Evergreen AAUW's handbook to help students and parents with successful college planning. She is the 1993 co-chair of the EHS PTA, and has co-chaired the lively community-sponsored All Night Party, which provides a safe, fun alternative to drinking and driving after the prom. This Party is the main legacy of one of Evergreen's more imaginative volunteer groups, the MAFIA (p. 176), co-founded in 1983 by Marilyn Sandifer, Carol Merkel and Vicky Haluza, to promote alcohol- and drug-free alternatives for local teenagers. The group disbanded in the spring of 1991, donating its remaining funds to the All Night Party and two other programs serving teens.

In 1991, the R-1 School Board adopted a series of proposals designed to re-structure education, R-1's version of the new buzzword in educational circles, "site-based management." All schools were to have much more control of their programs and budgets with input from students and community. Joint Cooperative Decision Making Committees were to be formed in each school, with representation from staff, students, parents and citizens. The Board deliberately left their functions and powers somewhat vague in hopes of encouraging diverse proposals for improvement from individual schools. High schools, with EHS the first guinea pig, were to convert to longer blocks of learning. All eventually would become four-year institutions. Junior highs were to become middle schools, in the hope of better meeting the needs of students making the transition from childhood to the uncertain world of the teen-ager.

It would have been pleasant if these ideas could have had a peaceful trial time, to find out if they led to real improvement or were only the latest in a series of educational reforms by image and jargon. But in the fall of 1992, all school districts in Colorado were hit hard in the pocketbook by the passage of tax-limitation Amendment 1. A budget shortfall of massive proportions loomed. Discussions as to how to trim expenses engaged the administration, School Board, teachers, citizens and individual schools. Superintendent Finch wisely decided to get rid of the image of a cushy administration shielded from budget cuts, by announcing that the administrative highrise would be sold or leased and administration personnel trimmed by 100 positions. This would reduce costs by some $3 million annually. Next came serious discussions on cuts throughout the system.

Eventually, the cuts were not quite as drastic as feared at the beginning of the 1992–3 school year ($24.5 rather than $34 million) but they were severe enough. Especially for a growing district. The State Legislature's funding formula is based on enrollment for the previous year and allows no money for increased enrollment in the year in which the increases take place. The R-1 District expects 2,000 more students in the 1993–4 year: at a cost of $4,000 per student this puts the District another $8 million behind. The cuts are a combination of staff reductions (more students per teacher), cuts in programs offered, and increased fees for certain school services.

One of the ways the R-1 District tried to reduce expenditures in 1993 was to offer attractive early retirement "packages" to senior teachers and replace them with new, less costly ones. This, together with normal retirements, has meant the loss of a great many familiar faces in our Evergreen schools. One dynamic teaching couple were Marcia Younger, who retired from Wilmot School after 30 years of teaching, and her husband Gene, who left EHS in 1992. This ended his career as building trades teacher, head

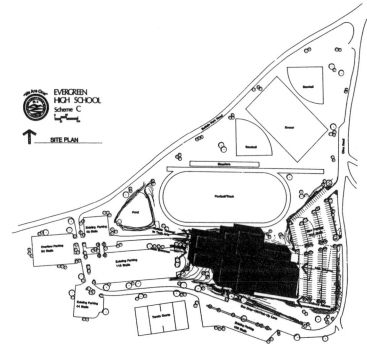

Evergreen High School Master Plan.

of a unique program that taught kids a lot about construction and work habits while producing one house a year for sale since 1974. Kathie Kuehn, who had been at EHS since 1969, first as an English teacher then as library media specialist, also retired in 1992, as did Dick Reed, who taught "special ed" EHS kids for 25 years and Alan Carlson who decided, after teaching for 25 years, to work in the private sector as a chemist. Marshdale lost Jerry Mallow, who had been a 5th grade teacher since the school opened in 1981, Wilmot students said goodbye to a loved music teacher, Mike Smith, and West Jeff Junior High lost William Lambert, who devoted 30 years of his life to being a track coach and technical arts teacher. Sondra Jackson (p. 134), longtime Principal of Bergen Elementary, retired at the end of the 1992-3 school year after 33 years with the school district.

Clear Creek County School District, which includes part of the Evergreen area, has had its own history of successes and reversals, financial problems, and the need to provide for growth as the economy of the mountain area picks up. A $10 million bond issue proposal in the fall of 1990, which included funds for construction of a new middle school to be built on school-owned property on Floyd Hill, failed decisively. A more conservative $5.5 million version passed comfortably a year later. For the King-Murphy School, this provided something over a quarter of a million dollars for two new classrooms, carpeting and roof repairs.

Education for the Youngest. **The Children's World Learning Center** on Highway 73 was closed in February of 1989. According to corporation spokesmen, this was because of the inadequacy of the facility. At the time of closure, 37 children were enrolled, down from a one-time high of over 50. Children's World does however offer after-school programs at Wilmot and Bergen Schools. The non-profit **Children's Center of Evergreen**, the first private preschool in Evergreen which started with 26 children at the Church of the Cross in 1972, expanded. It moved from its location in a house across from the High School into new quarters in Bergen Village. There it has 4640 square feet of carpeted floors, gaily decorated walls, tricycle paths and a tri-level playground. **Our House Children's Learning Center** in Marshdale, located in a house on the grounds of the Newkirks' Evergreen Professional and Technological Center, is operated by the Newkirk's daughter Victoria and her husband Christopher Lierheimer. The facility contains a pre-school, kindergarten and after-school care center. The **Mountain Open Preschool**, which had operated out of the white concrete school on Highway 73 since 1971, had to close its doors in May 1989 when the Jefferson County Open High moved to Lakewood. Part of the District's preschool program, it served 32 children and always had a waiting list. There were some changes in the area **Montessori School** picture: the center in Kittredge closed, the new Treeview facility at the corner of Highway 74 and

Troutdale Scenic Drive came under the aegis of Betsy Hoke, who now directs both the Marshdale and Troutdale branches of **Montessori Children's House of Evergreen**. Instruction for children in 1st through 3rd grades is now available, in addition to pre-school classes. **Montessori Preschool Child Care** continues to operate in Conifer.

Adult Education. Mountain area adults are quite richly served with educational opportunities. **Red Rocks Community College** offers a variety of credit and non-credit courses at different locations in Conifer and Evergreen. The **Evergreen Metropolitan Parks and Recreation District** puts out a lively catalog of available courses twice a year. The offerings of the **Jefferson County School District Adult Education** program are available to mountain residents, but almost all classes are now in the District's Manning Adult Education Center at 32nd and Youngfield.

Singin' River Ranch (p. 91), a non-profit, non-denominational conference center located in a secluded valley on Upper Bear Creek Road, started its participation in the world-wide **Elderhostel** program in January of 1992. Elderhostel programs offer to seniors the opportunity to take college-level courses on a huge variety of topics in residential settings. Many programs use college facilities in vacation time. Singin' River's programs are all related to Colorado (pioneer history, prehistoric cultures, water conservation, profiles of early Colorado women, trout-fishing, etc.) and can accommodate up to 50 people in one session. The Ranch offers economical opportunities for people living in the area to take part in Elderhostel programs on a non-residential basis.

A Potpourri of Educational Developments. Hoping to raise "more money for more students", Evergreen's two unique scholarship organizations, the Evergreen Scholarship Association and Bootstraps (p. 128-130), merged in March 1992 to become **Evergreen Scholarship/Bootstraps Inc.** with Dick Scheurer as its first president. The new group continues the fund-raising efforts of both organizations, including an annual mail appeal, the sale of grocery coupons, sponsoring of special events and the Ride the Pines family bicycle tour, co-sponsored by Paragon Sports and various other area businesses. It raises between $15,000 and $20,000 a year. The new group also administers a number of other community scholarships (Schutt, Rotary Club, Elks, etc.) as well as the **Mountain Protective Association** scholarship. For one large donation, the fund can indirectly thank Walmart! The

successful community effort to defeat the plan to locate a Wal-Mart store in Bergen Park, headed by Tandy Jones and Sheila Clarke, ended up with a surplus of $6,262 in its treasury, which was donated to the scholarship fund. . . . **The Jefferson County Open High School** (p.126-7) closed its doors in Evergreen at the end of the 1989 school year and was united with the Tanglewood Open Elementary school into a K-through-12 program, housed in the former Lakewood Junior High facilities. The move was largely dictated by the District's financial difficulties and the fact that 75% of the students came from the flatlands. **Forest Heights Lodge** (p. 130–2) continues its unique services to emotionally disturbed boys in its Evergreen facility. Its 75-year-old Lodge was expanded and extensively renovated in 1988–9, and a more spacious playfield added. Significant and ongoing relations with Russian professionals in the field of treatment of emotionally troubled boys were established by Executive Director Russ Colburn and his staff, offering to the Russians the benefit of the Lodge's 40-year experience. Assistant Director Glen Lein retired in 1991 after 27 years of service. Director Russ Colburn said of him, "Glen played a major role in the growth of the Lodge. His sensitivity, insightfulness, dedication and caring to both kids and staff and the philosophy of the Lodge was unmatched." The Forest Heights staff and boys said goodbye in an emotional ceremony. In his honor, Evergreen Sculptor Tom Ware was commissioned to create a bronze bust.

Bust of Glen Lein, sculpture by Tom Ware.

MAKING A LIVING (p. 135-152)

An eventful six years. Evergreen did not get a Wal-Mart, thanks to intensive community opposition to the prospect of a colossal building, out-of-scale with the mountain community, in the middle of a waste of asphalt. We did get a MacDonald's. Some local businesses flourished, despite the hard times. Some went under. Bergen Village, a bulldozed vacant space in 1987, was built up in stages. Ambitious plans are afoot for commercial development on part of the Means land on Highway 74 at Stage Coach Boulevard.

Were 1987-93 "Years of the Woman" in Evergreen? The town got its first woman bank president, first woman head of Public Service Co. Of the first four recipients of the Chamber of Commerce's "Small Business of the Year" award, one was owned by a woman, two were co-owned by husband and wife teams. Women were among the top real estate salespeople in the area and figured prominently among those setting up new businesses. Women physicians and attorneys are now practicing here.

In **banking**, our town is losing the man we called Evergreen's banker (p.139-40). Dave and Jean Scruby, who have been involved in almost every good cause in the community since they came here in 1959, are moving to the more temperate climate of Greeley where they will be able to golf several more months of the year than in Evergreen. They will be missed.

Banking in Evergreen has not been immune from the industry's serious ups and downs. The Jefferson Industrial Bank, which became Presidents' Mortgage Industrial Bank-Evergreen, affiliated with one in Golden, was seized in September 1987 by the State of Colorado, which alleged unsafe business practices. It was one of 14 closed down throughout the State. The depositors' funds were frozen. A tragi-comedy of outrageous attorneys' fees, lawsuits and delays ensued. After 6 years, depositors had received 50–70% of their original principal (no interest) from various sources, including some state unclaimed funds, and anticipated further small annual payments.

The Bergen Park branch of World Savings and Loan closed in March 1989, not out of insolvency but because, according to a spokesman from its California headquarters, our area's growth had not come up to expectations, "We wanted it to grow a little faster and be a little bigger." The Capitol Federal Savings branch in the Safeway center was affected by the insolvency of its

259

parent company in 1990: it became an affiliate of Central Bank. In June 1993, First Bank Systems of Minneapolis, which owns the Central Bank network, also acquired the holdings of Colorado National Bank. The Evergreen CNB will absorb the operations of the small Central Bank outlet, which will be closed.

The Bergen Park Bank was declared insolvent in April of 1990, a situation partly caused by embezzlement of $261,000 of its funds by a former vice-president, Mark Lamphier. The assets of the bank were acquired by Nederland National and the institution renamed Peak National. It moved into its new premises in the Bergen Village shopping center in June of 1991.

There was a local flurry of anxiety in mid-1991 when two Evergreen banks—Evergreen National downtown, and Colorado National—were rated by the Massachusetts firm, Veribanc, as being in potential trouble. Through dealing with problem loans, reducing staff through attrition and, in the case of ENB, getting an infusion of capital, both banks survived the lean years. Colorado National of Evergreen appointed Penny Hawkins as its new President in January of 1992. Penny, who graduated from Sweet Briar College in Virginia and CU's Graduate School of Banking, has lived in Evergreen since 1969. She has been an active participant in school affairs and such community organizations as the CPO, Bootstraps, Rotary. Before coming to work at CNB, she had worked at the Evergreen National Bank and as a French teacher. As noted above, Evergreen's Colorado National Bank was sold, along with its parent company in Denver, to First Bank Systems of Minneapolis.

The Bank of Evergreen also changed its ownership and its name. In 1989, it was bought by Mountain Parks Financial Corporation, which also owned the Mountain Valley National Bank in Conifer. The two banks were combined in 1993 under the name of The Bank.

Mary M. (Micki) McMillan was appointed Manager of Public Service Company's Front Range Division, following the transfer of her predecessor Byron Hansford. Micki is the first woman to be appointed as a Division Manager at Public Service Co. She started with the company in 1979 as an information specialist and most recently was the director for service excellence. McMillan will oversee a workforce of 65 employees who operate the gas and electric distribution system, which extends from Genesee on the East to the Eisenhower Tunnel on the West.

Penny Hawkins.

Evergreenites like to eat out. The area has a somewhat larger array of fast food eateries than six years ago: the Village Inn (which became totally non-smoking in mid-1992) and Pizza Hut, off Lewis Ridge Road, seem to fill a need for reliable food available at all hours, with the welcome mat out for children. . . . McDonald's opened with considerable fanfare on New Year's Eve 1991 in the Bergen Village shopping center, after clearing a series of what the *Courier* couldn't help calling McHurdles. . . . In March 1992, Harv Teitelbaum celebrated 10 years in his popular downtown Baskin Robbins ice-cream store on the banks of Bear Creek. Harv is an environmentalist and community activist, founder of the local Mountain Greens group. Like many others, he says that if he could change one thing about Evergreen, it would be "to give the community a say about how Evergreen develops." He does not want to close the door to development, but would like to see the community determine its own future.

As for individual restaurants, there are some new entries on the scene and some good older ones that have survived and flourished. One of the area's oldest and its largest, El Rancho, (p. 144) was sold in 1988 to a group of Colorado investors headed by R. D. Roush. Sellers were Paul and Donna McEncroe and other minority family shareholders. Paul and Donna had operated the restaurant for 31 years. Other "oldies and goodies" are the Whipple Tree in Bergen Park, the Tivoli Deer and Dick's Hickory Dock (dubbed the best outdoor rib eatery in the nation in the August 1989 *People Magazine*) in Kittredge, and, in Evergreen, Key's on the Green, the River Sage and Jonathan Wolf's (formerly the Wolf House). Owner Hans Wolf (p. 144) received the Chamber of Commerce's first "Small Business of the Year Award" in 1989. New and popular are the New Shanghai in the North Evergreen

Shopping Center (which started small on Main Street and has expanded greatly in its new location), J. Williams in the King Soopers shopping center in Bergen Park (which also offers a large catering service), Lizbeth's Restaurant in downtown Evergreen and the Columbine Restaurant located in the old Colorado Philharmonic quarters in Marshdale.

On the retail scene, Evergreen's smallest (physically) and one of its oldest stores went out of business. The Evergreen Taffy Shop was a local landmark and a favorite of tourists browsing on Main Street. Started in the 1930's by Jeanne Morrison and Rusty Clough, it had been owned and run for 22 years by longtime Evergreen residents, Jim and Sydney Henley. They used the same taffy recipe as the original owners and added only one flavor, grape, to the original ten. The store was next to Jonathan Wolf's Restaurant in a tiny log building, which was demolished to make way for the restaurant's summer dining patio.

The second recipients of the Evergreen Chamber's "Small Business of the Year" award were an old-time Evergreen couple, Walt and Doris Anderson (p. 83–4), who with their son Jodey own and operate a busy gas station and the Anderson Mountain Market convenience store on Highway 73, just beyond Buffalo Park Road. Walt opened a towing and fuel delivery business in 1960, sold it in 1975 and opened up a small self-service gas station in 1976. His wife Doris has always been his business partner. They added a small store which flourished, and eventually invested over $1 million in the present facility, offering gas, deli sandwiches, groceries, newspapers. The Andersons were described by the presenter of the Award as "a couple who have always been there when the community needed them." The last addition to the Anderson Market was a wing they expected to lease as a liquor store, but the license was denied by the County Commissioners on the grounds the location was too near the Open High School (which has of course since moved). They rented the space instead to the Evergreen Music Center, which had been located across the street but needed more space. George Taylor tunes pianos, repairs instruments, rents band instruments and has rooms where a variety of lessons, voice and instrumental, are taught.

The 1991 Small Business award went to one of the hardest-working and most imaginative retailers Evergreen has seen in some time. Lynne Bright operated Whitney's, a furniture store in downtown Evergreen. She was a dynamo, active in community affairs as well as the promotion of her business. Her drive was partly fueled by grief that she could no longer care at home for her severely handicapped daughter, Whitney, after whom she named her store. Whitney's later moved from Evergreen to become Whitney's of Cherry Hills.

Paragon Sports, founded by Casey and Jennifer Boone, arrived on the scene in downtown Evergreen in May of 1985. When the Boones met Phil Downing, a bike enthusiast with experience in the sales, repair and riding of bicycles, they combined their talents and hit on a winning winter/summer combination: "Performance Ski and Bicycle Shop plus Spirited Sportswear." Paragon expanded several times in its downtown quarters. In 1990, it moved to premises in the Mine Shops complex after the former occupant, the Sports Mine, went out of business. The cheerful atmosphere of the store, the steady emphasis on customer service constantly stressed by Casey and Jennifer and store manager Becky Cook, and Paragon's many contributions to the community earned the store the 1992 designation as Evergreen's Small Business of the Year. Among its community services Paragon co-sponsors the annual Ride the Pines family biking affair benefiting ESA/Bootstraps, donates mountain bikes to the annual Kiwanis Benefits Breakfast, Children's Hospital Bargains Unlimited and the All-Night Party. For several years Paragon put on a lively fashion show, along with the latest Warren Miller Ski movie, as a benefit for various community causes.

The Evergreen Drug Store (p. 212), an important continuing institution in the history of our town, was bought by Ed Skaff in 1962 when it was still in its Main Street location. From 1963–74 the store was located in the then-new Hiwan Village shopping center, next to Safeway and the Post Office. The drug store moved along with Safeway to its present location. Its size was expanded in 1978 to 29,000 square feet. Evergreen Drug is one of the last successful independent drug stores left in the state. Skaff, who graduated from CU Boulder with a degree in pharmacy, strives constantly to make it "the best store of its kind in Colorado." He wants it to be competitive in price, fun to shop in, stocked with every kind of merchandise the customers desire. The staff numbers 60 employees, whose interest in the business is enhanced by their participation in a profit-sharing plan. Skaff, who is married and has four children, is now helped in his enterprises by his son, Ed II. He has expanded his ownership from a single store in Evergreen to drug stores in Idaho Springs, Aspen Park, Fraser Valley and Buffalo Park Medical Center. He has been a consistent supporter of

Mary McMillan.

community causes in Evergreen and the other towns where he does business.

Small enterprises run by hard-working individuals are what lend vitality and color to the economic scene, and Evergreen fortunately has its share of these. Alas we cannot pay tribute to them all by name, only update and add to our earlier sampler (p. 135–152). Roger Dougherty's Evergreen Pastry Shop continues to satisfy the community's sweet tooth and appetite for good fresh breads. Olde's Texaco has now been in business in Evergreen for 72 years (p. 142) and is still run by the descendants of Herman Olde. Buddy Richardson, the Mobile Mechanic, still makes house calls on your Subaru. Children are better served since the arrival in Bergen Park of two imaginative retailers, the Colorado Kid Company, which carries a fine variety of children's clothing, and Little Rascals, which offers toys of every imaginable kind from all over the world, conveniently separated

into age groups. John's Barber Shop is located in the row of former cabins between the Bank of Evergreen and the Safeway shopping center. It was opened in 1980 by John Golba, who came here with his parents and sister from Kansas in 1976. The business did so well that John found himself working 12–14 hour days, so he asked sister Carolyn to join him. They inherited the habit of hard work from their father, John, who retired many years ago from a physically demanding job at the General Motors plant in Kansas City, but still fills his days with hard work, caring for people's homes and gardens. The family finds time to fish, hunt and ski. Evergreenites sure do love to travel. We conclude this from the astonishing fact that there are 8 travel agencies in our town, with an additional one in Genesee and one in Conifer. Some have been here along time, like Bon Voyage and Jane O'Reilly's Around the Globe Travel. New kid on the block is Breezy Travel on Main Street, which gets its name from owner Diane Brisse who purchased the agency from former partner Bonnie Stanbro, after the Stanbros left Evergreen for Florida. Brisse has a staff of six and cheerfully contributes her volunteer time through membership in Evergreen Kiwanis and the Evergreen Chamber of Commerce. Two businesses which are helping to create a lively atmosphere in Kittredge are Ted Mann's Mountain Ranch Supply, which caters for all the needs of horse-owners in this horse-loving community, and Steve and Robin Cohen's Evergreen Nursery. This has grown from small beginnings to a year-round garden center offering landscape design and installation services as well as every kind of material imaginable— plants, trees, shrubs, soils, mulches, stone products. For its consistently high level of service to customers, the Evergreen Nursery was the first monthly

Paragon Sports: owners and staff.

winner of the SOS (Service is our Specialty) award sponsored by the Evergreen Area Chamber of Commerce. Colorado's One-Stop Bunny Shop (Rocky Mountain Rabbits) is an enterprise in Kittredge operated by Dan and Beth Lincoln's daughter, Liz, and her husband Dave Stieren. Opened in 1987, the operation now sells 18 varieties of purebred rabbits as well as a special formula of feed, shavings, water bottles and a converted indoor/outdoor hutch invented by Stieren. Fly fishermen have a unique resource in the Blue Quill Angler, owned by Mark Harrington and Jim Cannon and housed since 1988 in half of the octagonal barn on Highway 74 near Bergen Park. Blue Quill caters exclusively to fly fishermen, offering not only bamboo and graphite rods, but flies, float tubes, kits, classes and guided expeditions "for companies looking for an out-of-the-ordinary corporate getaway." The other half of the barn is occupied by the Snow Leopard ski rental store, owned by the energetic Buzz and Laura Sampson. For Jeanine Casaday and her husband, Bob, the opportunity to purchase the Yankee Doodler Book Shop in the North Evergreen Shopping Center was the opportunity they were looking for to return to live in Colorado, where they had both been to college. Jeanine has always been a book lover and avid reader. She found that Evergreen has a lot of book lovers and book buyers. There have been a number of attempts to establish a successful taxi service in Evergreen but none have lasted very long. You must have noticed the white cars with green lettering, successively parked in different locations to advertise the EVERGREEN 674-TAXI. Diane Lezark, who moved to Evergreen with her husband from Florida in 1989, got a PUC license and opened up her taxi service in 1991. She had one used police car, painted white with green lettering. By 1993, there were 6 vehicles: 3 taxis, 2 airport shuttle vans and a stretch limousine. Evergreen Taxi, the Evergreen Airport Shuttle and Evergreen Limo, the special province of Diane's husband, are all at your service. Diane has found that 85% of her business is travel to the airport and anticipates that this will only increase when the new airport opens. She has now been granted an ICC license, which will enable her to transport passengers anywhere in the state, unlike the PUC license, which limits her to a 20-mile radius from Evergreen.

We reported on two unusual and successful "cottage industries" in Evergreen, the Newkirks' Denver Biomaterials and the Moores' Snugli (p. 147–8). In December, 1986 the Newkirks sold Denver Biomaterials Inc. to Codman and Shurtleff Inc., a subsidiary of Johnson and Johnson. The

Ed Skaff.

Carolyn S. Golba.

John R. Golba.

Newkirks retained ownership of the building and the new company continued to manufacture the patented shunt products there. In late 1988 the company announced they were moving the plant operations to the East coast. Doug and Shirley Freeman (she had been production manager for over 8 years) bought rights to two of the products, though not to the original hydrocephalic shunt, leased the premises from the Newkirks, and continue to manufacture in Marshdale. In the meantime, inventive Jack Newkirk developed another patented product, a tiny micro-dissecting needle used in many types of micro-surgery. The product was developed to

serve a few specific surgeons but is developing a national and international market. There are other family enterprises on the Newkirks' "campus." Daughter Victoria and her husband have a preschool and daycare center. Son John has inherited some inventive genes: he is a pilot and his Personal Cockpit Recorder is having considerable success. Youngest daughter Christina is also a pilot and co-producer of an English-language version of a high-quality Italian aviation magazine.

After the sale of "Snugli" in 1985, Ann and Mike Moore, together with Leslie Beauparlant, formed a new Evergreen-based company, Air Lift Unlimited Inc. The company designs and produces soft-sewn cases in which to carry portable medical products and laptop computers. For her design of a line of carriers for portable oxygen, Ann was granted her second U.S. patent. Her work was featured in a Smithsonian Institution exhibit in Washington titled "A Woman's Place is in the Patent Office." Only 3% of U.S. patents are registered to women. Mike is also involved in the management of Camp Kazoo, another Evergreen-based company founded by Susan Matthews, which markets a growing line of fashion accessories for juveniles.

Ann and Mike continue their dedicated involvement in causes which tug at their heartstrings. They perform in the Evergreen Chorale and the Baroque Folke. They serve on the Rocky Mountain Regional Advisory Board of the Environmental Defense Fund. Mike was a leader in the campaign to get voters to approve the Metropolitan Scientific and Cultural Facilities District, and serves on the Cultural Council in Jefferson County which distributes funds from the District to arts organizations throughout the county.

The Australian Outback Collection is a unique enterprise headquartered in Evergreen. It was founded by Australian Chris Blundell in a small corner of the Showbarn Plaza in 1985. The firm manufactures clothing, based on traditionally rugged, durable Australian staples, and markets it around the world. Manufacturing is in the U.S., Australia and Canada. Eight years after its founding, the company occupies most of the Showbarn Plaza building and sells its products to thousands of retailers across the United States and in an increasing number of foreign countries.

Real Estate Blooms Again (p.152)
When some of our most able and creative women friends in Evergreen start studying for licenses to sell real estate, we know that the slump is over. The ranks of realtors affiliated with the

Evergreen-Conifer Board of Realtors have risen again to 235 working in more than a dozen different real estate firms. We were wrong in 1987 when we predicted that the slowdown in land development and real estate would be permanent. Evergreen and the surrounding mountain area is once again booming. "Buildout" looms on the horizon: there a number of predictions from respectable sources that virtually all land zoned for development will be built on by the year 2000.

In 1989, the Van Schaack office in Evergreen—the first branch of a major real estate company to be established here—closed after more than 20 years. The company filed for bankruptcy in Denver. Gary Jarrett acquired Don Stanbro's Main Street real estate company, when Stanbro left for Florida, then formed a partnership with Bill Moore, owner of Moore and Company Real Estate. Moore Realty is the major sponsor of a yearly competition to select 12 monthly mountain area photographs for a calendar. Proceeds benefit Mount Evans Home Health Care/Hospice. In 1993, the Evergreen-Conifer Board of Realtors started a new tradition, awarding $5,500 in scholarships to 7 local high school graduates.

In 1988, 111 single-family homes were sold in the Evergreen-Conifer area, compared with 1954 in 1992. One of the hottest sales areas throughout the 1987–1993 period was the Ridge at Hiwan.

The **Evergreen Chamber of Commerce** has moved a couple of times since 1987, but has been established in the Lakepoint Center for the past two years. Executive Secretary for the past two years has been Andrew Petrick, an Evergreen native. The Chamber's membership is around 290. It's prime job is to promote local businesses, which is done through breakfast programs with speakers on topics of concern to members, an informational newsletter, member services such as a health insurance plan and discount long-distance telephone rates and special promotional projects. It also seeks to contribute to the well-being of the community: two of its latest efforts are the sister-city liaison with the Russian town of Tver and a recycling program whose profits will be used to help insulate seniors' homes.

SPREADING THE WORD
(p. 153-162)

New on the Evergreen media scene is a unique monthly newspaper, **Upbeat**, which first appeared in January 1991. This is a free publication promoting volunteerism and community involvement. According to Linda Kirkpatrick, its originator, owner and publisher, the paper is mailed to all residents of the 80439 zip code area, which gives it a circulation of some 10,000. It carries only good news and factual information about the more than 150 nonprofit organizations, churches, schools and homeowner associations in the area. Evergreen is a unique community, according to Kirkpatrick, because of its abundance of volunteer opportunities and its ready acceptance of new people. She decided that one way she could help was by offering free, regular publicity to non-profit organizations to increase awareness, membership, donations and attendance at events. Of course, someone has to pay for the costs of printing and distributing the paper, so a part of Kirkpatrick's' work is securing ads from local business owners.

Kirkpatrick herself is a longtime and dedicated community volunteer. For her many contributions, including the raising of $150,000 in cash and in-kind donations for the construction of Evergreen's ambulance barn in 1983–5, and coordinating its successful "barn-raising", she was selected to receive the 1991 Evergreen Community Service Award.

An imaginative new magazine, the **Grapevine**, came out with its first issue August 1, 1990. It was edited and published by Hannah Hayes of Evergreen and Susan Schoch of Idledale. Hayes is a former teacher at the Open Living School and also ran a Health Food Store in Evergreen. Schoch is a free-lance photographer, writer and poet. Grapevine aimed at being an outlet for creative talent in the mountain area, weaving together interests in "the arts, environment and well-being." The magazine was printed locally on recyclable paper by PDQ Printing. Unfortunately, the tough problems of financing the enterprise through advertising proved intractable and the magazine ceased publication in 1991.

The **Canyon Courier** continues to serve Evergreen well as a lively, readable local newspaper, a fact which is underscored by its many awards from the Colorado Press Association. In annual competition with all other weeklies of its circulation in the state, it consistently places in the winners' circle in many categories (best special section, best news story, best sports story, advertising excellence, etc.). In 1988, it was the No.1 weekly (for general excellence) in Colorado in its category of 4,000–10,000 circulation, and again in 1992 placed second only to the *Aspen Times*. It manages to maintain

Linda Kirkpatrick.

its high standard of journalism despite many changes in personnel.

Debbie Marshall retired after seven years as Editor in January of 1989 and was succeeded by Mark Ohrenschall, who remained at the helm until June of 1991. Mark was young, cheerful and courageous (as was evident from his lonely stand against the U.S military involvement in the Gulf, "Patriotism is more than just flag-waving"). Before leaving Evergreen for Seattle, Mark and his new wife garnered pledges for their hike along the Colorado Trail to support the Evergreen People Path campaign.

In June, 1991, Tony Messenger was named editor of the *Canyon Courier* to succeed Ohrenschall. Just over a year later, publisher Kamal Eways promoted him to the position of Executive Editor of the *Courier*, the *High Timber Times* and the *Columbine Community Courier*. Messenger's background in journalism included work as copy editor, reporter, sports writer in Nebraska and S. Dakota. He lives in Evergreen with his wife and four children, and is active in the Blue Spruce Kiwanis, Evergreen Junior Soccer Association, the Mountain Family Project and the Evergreen Players.

Popular columnist and former *Courier* editor John Fellows had to decide between his job as manager of community affairs for Coors and his outspoken opinions in the *Courier*. He wrote a piece in 1990 commending the Denver International Film Festival for severing relations with Denver's weekly newspaper, *Westword*. He castigated the newspaper for its "muddy path of the low road" and described it as "arrogant, insensitive, journalistically unethical,

263

Tony Messenger.

smug and filled with self-importance." Editor Patricia Calhoun retaliated with a column denouncing Coors for its "odious corporate problems" including water quality and hazardous waste violations. She pointed out that Coors had refused a request to help sponsor the festival. We miss Fellows' column.

Fine young reporters came and went during the last six years. Gone, among others, are Jill Jamieson-Nichols (to a stint with the *Golden Transcript*), Valerie Ann Brown, Lee Hart, Tracy Salcedo. Current Associate Editor of the three newspapers is Ann Morris, who joined the staff in 1991. She grew up in Kansas, did a stint in Washington D.C. as legislative correspondent for a senator, got a master's in journalism from the University of Iowa and moved with her husband to Colorado in 1991. The main thing she likes about Evergreen is the great variety of interesting people who live here. Ann Addison knew from her junior year in high school in Boulder that she wanted to be a writer or photographer, but first enjoyed life as a ski bum. She settled in the 285 corridor in 1990, did some freelance photography

for the *Courier* and joined the staff of the *Courier* and *High Timber Times* in 1991. Curt Olson came to Colorado 17 years ago as a hitch hiker from Northern Illinois. He was to stay with friends for a few days but never left. Instead he got a degree in journalism from Metro State, married, had a family, and tried his luck in the theater before becoming sports editor for Evergreen Newspapers in 1992. Robert Mook's family lived in a number of states before coming to Lakewood in 1970. Mook got his degree in journalism from Metro State and married in 1987. He worked for a cable news service, as a video store clerk and freelance reporter before being hired as a reporter for the Evergreen Newspapers in 1992. A departing staffer, Valerie Anne Brown, noted in her traditional "farewell to Evergreen" column that "the field of journalism . . . is underappreciated and underpaid. . . . It's certainly not a 40-hour-a-week job you can put away when you go home at 5 P.M.—or at 1:30 A.M. after a school board meeting." When you look at the sheer volume of articles (schools, county government, land use issues, general news, special features, community organizations, detailed coverage of all local sporting events) these young reporters have to prepare each week, and think of all the meetings, interviews, telephone calls that each article involves, you develop a lot of respect for their energy and ability.

The mountain area now has its own TV program, a "not-for-profit public cable casting service". The **Mountain Channel** received its non-profit status in September, 1991. This is a community-oriented channel, so far operating totally on volunteer time. It offers a community bulletin board and video programming on the Intermountain Cable Service and shares a community channel with Jones Intercable for the areas which Jones services. It offers at present 4 hours of video coverage of local news and cultural

events. Its longer term aims, according to tireless volunteer Debbie Jalanovich, is to increase its coverage of school affairs, cultural activities and local news, to create some good jobs in the mountain area and to offer in the local schools education in video production and an opportunity for the students to see their work aired. In the meantime, the volunteer team (Dick Dedrick, an experienced independent video producer, Ed Aleski, the channel's engineer, Roxanne Turnbull, camera and PR person and Ron Saunders, the channel's newscaster) keep up their "day jobs."

The long-running charade of the **Evergreen Radio Station** goes on. If ever there was an argument for streamlining of bureaucratic red tape, this story is it. The process of selecting a licensee for the new frequency started with FCC hearings in Washington D.C. in 1982. Eleven years, two awards of the license to different companies, and multitudes of legal and organizational dollars later, there is still no radio station in operation. Delays are caused by lengthy appeal processes built into the licensing procedure.

In 1987, we left the story of the **Evergreen Library** (p. 154-8) at the point at which funds were secured to provide more library space in the mountain area, but with no decisions about how much, or where, or when. In 1989, the Library Board decided that the existing site was the best one overall, but that a new building would be a better solution to library space needs than an addition. At the time, there were three existing buildings on the approximately 6.5-acre site: the old red brick Evergreen School, the lower level of which was being used as local county offices, the existing Evergreen Library and the white concrete building, built in 1948 as the Evergreen High School and occupied until May of 1989 by the Open Living High School.

Robert Mook.

Ann Morris.

Ann Addison.

Curt Olson.

Negotiations between the Library Board, the County Commissioners and the R-1 School Board resulted in the County's acquiring the existing library building and 2 acres of land for use as county offices, and the Library Board acquiring the remaining land and buildings. We must confess to having a dream that one day the attractive former library building will become the Evergreen Town Hall!

With some local nostalgia but no real opposition, the red brick building was demolished in September 1990. The demise of the old Open Living High School was noisier. For at least twenty years, the need for more community space in Evergreen has been widely discussed. There was a lot of momentum behind a drive to convert the old school building into a community center. A **Coalition for the Evergreen Community Center** was formed, co-chaired by B. J. Schaugaard and Kathie Davis. The only practical method to accomplish this, since Evergreen is not a municipality, was to have the Recreation District be the lessee or buyer of the building, with a volunteer board raising the necessary capital to remodel it and fees for use providing the majority of operating expenses.

Perhaps, with the best will in the world, the project could not have flown. But the Library Board disappointed the Coalition and the community by what was perceived as its uncooperative attitude and inflexibility during the brief few months of intensive negotiations from October 1991 to March 1992. This was regrettable since the services and staff of the local library are held in high esteem in the Evergreen community. Among the difficulties were: the Library Board's insistence on a sale of the building for $100,000 (the Coalition thought it should be either leased to the Rec District for a nominal sum, or sold for $1.00, since Evergreen taxes had paid for the building in the first place); the Library Board's conviction that it would cost $1 million to renovate the building and bring it up to code, while community representatives felt it could be made adequate and usable for $50,000; the question of parking. The Board believed that all existing parking space, plus that occupied by the school building, was needed for library parking. The Coalition felt that there would be enough parking for both institutions. If not, they could explore acquiring more land for parking behind the school building.

The mountain area Library Board member, Howard Smith, was an enthusiastic supporter of the community center project, but was unable to persuade his fellow board members of its desirability. Smith, a 30-year Evergreen

resident and, until his recent retirement, a teacher at Parmalee School, has been on the Library Board since 1973: his current term expires in January of 1996.

There were other problems. The Rec District was in process of building its new warming house on Evergreen Lake and could not offer much financial support for the Community Center project. Because the Library Board would not agree to discuss the project until fall of 1991 (although it had owned the site since 1989) there was too little time to get realistic operating figures and firm financial commitments from community organizations, to know whether the project was financially feasible. Also, to be fair to the Library Board, the Evergreen community had missed it's chance to lobby the Rec District to directly acquire the Open Living building from the School District, when it became vacant in May of 1989.

At the end of May 1992, the building was demolished. Construction of the new library was delayed by the finding of soil pollution. This was due to a leaking heating oil tank believed to have been buried in the 1920's or 30's. The soil had to be hauled out. The firm of Childress Manning Knapp, selected in September of 1991, proceeded with its design for the new library. Ground was broken in August, 1992, and construction went on throughout the cold, snowy winter with completion scheduled for Christmas, 1993. There was one clear advantage of eliminating the old Open Living High School building. For the first time ever, it was possible to design a total landscaping plan for the entire site, from the unsightly gash that always existed behind the old red brick building to the banks of Cub Creek. The new library

will be the site of a commissioned piece of outdoor sculpture. The initiative came from the Board of the Friends of the Evergreen Library, inactive since 1987, which voted to donate its remaining funds to the Library Foundation as seed money for this purpose.

The construction cost of the new library is projected to be around $4.5 million dollars. The building has 18,000 sq. ft. on the main floor, with an additional 15,000 sq. ft. in the basement. It will have a capacity of 62,000 books, a 32-seat meeting room and seats for 100 readers.

MEETING SOCIAL NEEDS (p. 163-76)

Two new and creative responses to social needs in the mountain area are the **Evergreen Christian Outreach** and the **Mountain Family Project Inc.** with its **Conifer Resource Center**.

The seeds of **Christian Outreach** were planted in 1985, when Father Bob Bryan of the Episcopalian Church of the Transfiguration (p. 54–9), realizing there was a need for ongoing short-term assistance to local people who found themselves in difficult circumstances, got a small committee together to plan a relief program. Robert Bunch DDS chaired the group, which provided practical items such as food and clothing with an attitude of love, concern and respect. As more people in need appeared, other area churches were drawn into the program. First was the Evergreen Fellowship, especially members Paul and Barbie McCollister, then the Presbyterian and Lutheran congregations and, by 1988, a total of 21 area churches.

New Evergreen Public Library: perspective sketch by Carol and Paul Clayton.

In 1987, the program outgrew the Transfiguration Church's kitchen and moved into Whitney house on the Church grounds. Barbie McCollister became Executive Director, her salary paid by the Evergreen Fellowship. In 1990 Bancroft House and The Long Barn on the old Evergreen Conference grounds were added to Outreach's facilities, so that it could better serve its now steady client base of around 110 families a month. Bunch retired as President in 1990, succeeded by Paul McCollister. By 1993 the original 6 volunteers of Christian Outreach had expanded to over 100 and its budget from $10,000 to $110,000 annually. It has become a solid institution in the community and a worthy place for individuals to donate material items (food, clean seasonal clothing and household items in good condition), services, and money with a feeling of assurance that they everything will be put to good use. The Outreach program does operate from a forthrightly Christian viewpoint, offering spiritual guidance along with its tangible items. But there is no discrimination in clients: they help anyone in need.

A similar service program, St. Lawrence Outreach, operating out of the St. Lawrence Episcopal Church, serves families in the Conifer area.

Forums exploring community needs of various kinds are not uncommon. But tangible results are. **Mountain Family Project Inc.** (MFP) was formed after a 1990 gathering in the Conifer/Evergreen area, sponsored by Governor Romer's Early Childhood Initiative office and attended by first lady Bea Romer. The meeting uncovered significant unmet needs of children and families in the mountain area. A dedicated volunteer task force, chaired successively by Linda Carter and Carol Carper, worked on identifying needs and resources and creating MFP as a 501(c)(3) organization able to receive tax-deductible contributions. The task force found that, along the 285 corridor from Indian Hills to Kenosha Pass, almost 25% of families could be classified as "working poor". The mountain area lacked: a trauma center for emergency medical care, providers of routine care for Medicaid patients, accessible social services, family planning or reproductive health services, teen pregnancy programs, and alcohol and drug abuse services. Many programs theoretically available to these families were not in fact available because of transportation difficulties.

With the aid of grants, donations, help from county social services and other departments, MFP opened the **Conifer Resource Center** in the Conifer Safeway

Maryellen Jagel.

Vista Exline.

Shopping Center in July 1992. It offers an expanding range of direct services from a variety of public and private organizations. Eventually, MFP hopes to sponsor similar "single entry" points for health and social services in the Bailey area of Park County and the Evergreen area of Jefferson County. In June, 1992, Mountain Family Project received the Volunteer Group of the Year Award from the Colorado Child Health Council for outstanding service to women and children.

Another imaginative service agency, founded by Evergreen resident Maryellen Jagel, is **Victim Outreach Information**, a non-profit organization which helps victims of crime get their lives back on track. Herself a former victim of assault and burglary, Maryellen realized that everything in the criminal justice system was geared to the rights of the defendant not to those of victims. Since she started the agency in 1986, there has been an increase in the awareness of the public and law enforcement personnel of the plight of victims, but much remains to be done. The Jefferson County Sheriff's Department now works directly with most victims in the mountain area while VOI has a contract to serve Golden, Wheatridge and Edgewater. Jagel says that victims of crime suffer financially, physically if they have been assaulted, beaten or raped, and also emotionally. VOI provides emotional support as well as information about services and financial help available to victims. Whether its a Kleenex or a cup of coffee or an experienced companion to help guide a victim through often lengthy and complicated court procedures, VOI personnel is "just there to take care of them, whatever that may include." The VOI staff consists of Jagel, Vista Exline, another longtime Evergeen resident who is full-time case manager, a volunteer co-ordinator and 20 trained volunteers. In 1992, the agency assisted about 1000 victims of crime.

Clubs and Voluntary Organizations (p. 163–70) continue to multiply in the mountain area and volunteerism flourishes. Here we can give only a sampling. Our town's oldest service club, the **Evergreen Woman's Club**, celebrated its 50th anniversary in 1988 with four of its charter members present. The **Evergreen Branch of the American Association of University Women**, under the 1992-94 Presidency of Anita Mahoney, is a growing organization catering to a wide variety of interests. The AAUW is the largest women's professional group in the U.S. and also has international affiliations. The Evergreen group started in 1988 and now has around 130 members. It offers programs and projects to fulfill the organization's goals of promoting "equity for women, education and self-development over the life span and positive societal change." It also has specialty groups for gourmet cooks, book lovers, hikers, bridge players, culture enthusiasts and those concerned with international relations. The **Evergreen Elks Lodge** celebrated its 25th anniversary in April 1992 with a mortgage burning party. With more than 400 members, it is the largest service club in the area. Among their many community projects, they have been particularly generous to senior organizations: they re-roofed the Resource Center's "Yellow House", and provide major funding for the purchase of "Senior Wheels" vans. In 1987, the **Blue Spruce Kiwanis** first broke the "gender barrier" in local male service clubs by inviting three women to join. This Kiwanis group coordinates a grand clean-up of the Evergeen community every year, and raises funds for community organizations serving all ages, from tots to seniors. Later that same year, three women joined the **Evergreen Kiwanis Club** which, in 1993, had 70 members including 15 women. This group's primary fund-raising project, a pancake breakfast, was transformed into the Community

Benefits Breakfast in 1990. The new title emphasized that the event is not to raise money for the Kiwanis but for worthy community organizations and projects. The **Evergreen Rotary Club**, chartered April 15, 1985, inducted R-1 Area Superintendent Ann Brady as its first female member in February 1988. It now has 40 members. Among its main activities are working with high school students (vocational mentoring, leadership training) and working for the establishment of an after-hours medical emergency facility for Evergreen. It raises money to support community organizations such as Christian Outreach, Mount Evans Home Health/Hospice and the Senior Resource Center, and has an international outreach, sponsoring international student exchanges and providing equipment to Moscow's Open University. Gary Matson is the 1993–4 President.

Health services. Evergreen got its own nursing home in April 1990. **Life Care Center of Evergreen**'s 120-bed facility, located on Highway 74 just south of Elk Meadow Park, offers skilled and intermediate medical care, respite care, a senior day-care center and occupational, speech and physical therapies. The 43,000 sq. ft. building includes a chapel, ice cream parlor, day/activities room, physical therapy room, physician's examination room, two dining rooms and a third one for small groups. The Center employs around 100 full and part-time people, as well as an enthusiastic corps of volunteers, with the goal of "preserving the dignity, health, and happiness of each and every individual we are privileged to serve."

Mount Evans Home Health/Hospice Care (p. 173) celebrated the tenth anniversary of its beginnings in 1990. Carol Linke, founder and first Director of the agency resigned and was succeeded by Louisa Walthers. The organization still serves a huge mountain area between I-70 and Highway 285, from Silver Plume to Lookout Mountain and Indian Hills to Shawnee. It offers a licensed hospice program and care of those who are homebound due to illness, disability or injury. Total support in 1992 for this agency, which started as a compassionate volunteer service in 1980, was $975,700, of which approximately three-quarters came from fees for patient services (private insurance, Medicare and Medicaid) and 18% from donations, grants and fundraising projects such as the annual July 4th Freedom Run and Evergreen Calendar sales. United Way supplied 6% of the budget in 1992. More than three-quarters of all expenditures are for patient services, with fund-raising taking 7% and general management

Life Care Center of Evergreen.

about 13%. Volunteer services are an indispensable part of this agency's program. In 1992 they had 65 active volunteers, bereavement counselors, respite workers (who offer relief to families taking 24-hour care of disabled or terminally ill members), drivers and office help. In addition, 150 volunteers help out with special projects.

There is a varied and growing roster of conventional medical services (physicians, dentists, psychiatrists and psychologists, ophthalmologists, optometrists, occupational and physical therapists etc.) available to people in the mountain area. But there is also a fascinating array of alternative therapies, from acupuncture to chiropractic to many kinds of body work and massage, stress management, etc. One of the most respected "alternate therapists" in Evergreen is Donn Hayes, a practitioner of Chinese acupuncture and herbal medicine. Hayes was brought up in what he calls the "Football Coach Philosophy of Life," the conviction that only women cry and that masculine strength comes from being controlled, hard and protected. While serving in Vietnam he came into contact with Chinese medicine and "felt that he had come home." He learned that strength comes from softness, healing from restoration of the flow of life's movement (Ch'i) in a healthy flow through the body. In a *Courier* interview, Hayes said that Chinese medicine makes no separation between the physical, emotional and spiritual aspects of a person. Western medicine views disease as a mistake that the doctor, with intervention through surgery or drugs, will fix for you. The Chinese view is that "the disease is not a mistake . . . the universe is in harmony if you get out of the way and don't fight it. . . . Because we were given free will . . . we can, so to speak, step on the garden hose and stop the flow of C'hi."

Meeting the *social needs of teens* in the mountain area is difficult. **The Link**, a

brave attempt to provide a resource center where kids could hang out, study in the evenings, do projects or go on group outings to metro places of interest in summertime, operated in quarters on Meadow Drive for almost 2 years. The Link opened on March 1, 1990 and faltered when its major benefactor died and no other adequate funding could be found.

Unlike teens, *seniors* are quite well-served in the mountain area. Having completed the remodeling of the carriage house at the old Pearl Jarvis home on Highway 73 in 1986, the **Senior Resource Center/Mountain Services** appealed to the community to raise funds to remodel the main house and pay off the $135,000 remaining on the original $220,000 mortgage. The actual remodeling of the **Evergreen Senior/ Community Center** (p.170-1) was completed in October 1988 and celebrated with a well-attended dedication. But the fund-raising went on until September of 1990, when the total cost of $250,000 was raised. This included contributions of all sizes, from small personal donations to Little Bear benefits, "Fiddle, Frolic and Food Fests" and a $30,000 donation from the Adolph Coors Foundation. In addition to the cash raised, almost $100,000 was given in in-kind donations of goods and services. SRC estimates that at least 1400 mountain area seniors use the Center, as well as many other groups who enjoy the Center's 50–75 capacity community room.

The Center has a staff of 6, headed by Bob Macdonald. The face you are most likely to see when you visit is that of Bernadette Giampapa, who is the Center's cheerful receptionist and assistant program coordinator. She started as a volunteer senior aide at SRC in Evergreen in 1983, one year after moving to Conifer from Florida.

Evergreen resident John Zabawa, who preceded Macdonald as director of

SRC's Mountain Services Program, is the Executive Director of the entire Jefferson County SRC, now headquartered in the new Human Services Building. Zabawa maintains his active commitment to the Evergreen community, being the immediate past-president of the Evergreen Rotary Club and a member of the Chamber of Commerce as well as serving on a variety of Jefferson County and metro groups devoted to serving seniors.

The number of active environmental groups has increased, reflecting this area's strong concern with environmental issues. The longest-running one is the lively, well-respected The **Evergreen Naturalists Audubon Society (TENAS)** founded by Sylvia and Bill Brockner in 1968 (p.34). This group runs an excellent yearly nature education course, conducts field trips, publishes a newsletter, *The Dipper*, hosts an increasingly prestigious annual juried art show and sale, and takes stands on important local environmental issues as well as statewide ones. The **Mount Evans Sierra Club** has had a bit more checkered history, but continues its efforts to safeguard the area's natural heritage. A 1993 newcomer on the scene is the **Evergreen Beautification Council** headed by Gisela Davis. This is a not-for-profit offshoot of the Evergreen Kiwanis Foundation "dedicated to ensuring that Evergreen remains a beautiful place to live and work." The Council will work with county authorities, local business, developers and individuals "to retain, enhance or regenerate natural mountain landscapes within Evergreen and its surrounding areas, particularly along its highways."

Evergreen's highly-regarded **Alpine Rescue Team** (p. 205) celebrated its 30th year of existence in 1989. In December of the same year, ground was broken for it's new building at El Rancho near Highway 70. The $170,000 facility, paid for by donations, was completed in November of 1990. Since ART draws its volunteers from all over the Denver metro area, the new facility is much more accessible than the old site on Independence Mountain, and also makes possible a quicker response time to most emergencies.

Evergreen is a modern community which acknowledges the needs of people at different times in their lives for help, support and sharing. Support groups abound for people coping with addictions (alcoholism, drugs, overeating) and for their family members (ACOA, Al-Anon), for sufferers from specific diseases (cancer, diabetes, lupus, multiple sclerosis) and for those caring

Gisela Davis.

for them (families of Alzheimer's sufferers, caregivers), for the bereaved, the co-dependent, the parents who have lost children. A special group in Evergreen is **People Comforters**, whose members believe that the "warmth of a lovingly crafted quilt can help comfort victims of crime and other trauma." The group was founded in 1990 by a group of six women, spearheaded by a true Evergreen old-timer, Minnie Schneider. It fashions quilts and quilt kits, to be made up by other volunteers, which are donated to the Jefferson County Sheriff's Department's victim advocate program.

Entertainment, Social Life, Celebrations (p. 164) All the seasons of the years are celebrated by some event or festival in Evergreen, though there have been a few changes since 1987.

Once a year, the **Bear Creek Rodeo Association** still puts on its wonderfully nostalgic parade through downtown Evergreen and two rodeo performances at the El Pinal Arena. The dates have been changed to the end of June. The 1989 Rodeo had two unlikely but thoroughly appropriate Rodeo Queens: the former Stransky sisters, Lucille Counselman and Louise Hendryx. Their father, Josef, staged the first Evergreen Rodeo in 1935. He came with his wife Carrie and three children to the Evergreen area in 1918, homesteaded land in the Brook Forest area and eventually had a ranch of 900 acres on which the family raised cattle and horses and cultivated mountain peas and lettuce. The girls started school in a one-room schoolhouse called Sprucedale on Highway 73 (now, according to the sisters, part of the Conference Baptist Church's buildings), went through 8th grade in the then-new red brick school, and attended high school in Denver. They had a fine entree to the grand summer social life at the old Troutdale Hotel (p. 88-90) when their father purchased a nearby saddle livery. The family made the horses available to Troutdale guests, and in 1935 the manager of Troutdale asked Stransky to put on a small rodeo for hotel guests. It took place on pasture land that is now occupied by the Safeway shopping center, with wranglers and local cowboys from surrounding cattle ranches as

participants. There were "on" years and "off" years for the rodeo, which was moved in 1947 to the present Public Service Co. site. Whenever there was a rodeo, the Stranskys were part of it. The rodeo went professional, but was still intermittent until the Bear Creek Rodeo Association was organized in 1966. From then on, there has been a Rodeo every year. The two sisters got degrees from Denver University, Louise was a counselor in the Aurora Schools for 29 years, Lucille taught for a few years, worked in a department store, then settled on waitressing and bartending. They both married and had children: Lucille Counselman's son is Rodney, Louise has a daughter Adajane Knoll and a son, John "Rash", a well-known Evergreen personality who is a member of the EPRD board. All the children have been active in rodeo festivities.

John Zabawa.

Bernadette Giampapa.

Bob Macdonald

The spectacular traditional July 4th fireworks display at Evergreen Lake has had to be canceled since 1992, due to regulations of the National Fire Protection Association about how far spectators must be set back from a display. The Fourth of July weekend still has plenty of activities, including the **Summerfest Evergreen** 2-day celebration at Heritage Grove, with continuous entertainment and a wide variety of craft and food booths, and the **Mt. Evans Home Health/Hospice Freedom Run**.

In early August **The Mountain Rendezvous** still lures people from all over the metro area to enjoy the entertainment, the food, games and products sold at booths manned by volunteers from community organizations, and to learn about the lives of mountain men. Evergreen's most famous "mountain man" is Al Huffman, who has been impersonating the legendary Buffalo Bill Cody for over 20 years. He looks impressively like Colonel William with his flowing white hair and authentic costumes.

One entertainer who captivates both the Summerfest and the Rendezvous crowds is Patty Murphy. The daughter of Jim and Ellece Murphy, Patty spent many years away from Evergreen in professional show business. She came back to become, in the family tradition, a realtor and developer. Also in the family tradition, she acts, sings, choreographs and directs in productions of the Chorale and the Players. Her favorite roles so far have been Aldonza in *Man of La Mancha* and Sister Hubert in *Nunsense*. As vocalist for the Sterling Ensemble, she performs in schools throughout the county and at the Central City Jazz Festival.

Also in the first week of August, the annual 10K and 5K **Town Race** fills Upper Bear Creek Road with thousands of runners. In the last weekend of August, the **Evergreen Artists Association** holds its annual **Fine Arts Fair** at Heritage Grove.

A new addition to the celebration scene is the **Evergreen Music Festival** which offers summer concerts in a tent in the park by the Lake. At least one of these is usually by the National Repertory Orchestra (p. 225–6).

Evergreen honors its volunteers on many occasions: most nonprofit organizations have ceremonies annually to recognize the simple fact that they could not function without the hundreds and thousands of hours donated to helping them do their work. From 1973 to 1988, the Chamber of Commerce selected the Person of the Year in Evergreen. The

last, and richly-deserving, recipient of this award was Marilyn Sandifer (p. 93).

After the Chamber decided to switch its recognition to the Small Business of the Year, the *Canyon Courier* in 1989 decided to sponsor an annual **Evergreen Community Service Award** for a person or persons who have contributed significantly to "making Evergreen a better place to live." Nominations are solicited each year and selection is made by a community committee. The 1989 recipient was Bill Marshall, whom the *Canyon Courier* described as a "low-profile man who made a visible impact." In addition to the careful craftsmanship of his Woodpecker homes (p.195), Marshall has been a quiet contributor to many of Evergreen's finest institutions: he helped start the Volunteer Fire Dept., was one of the first members of Evergreen Kiwanis, a charter member of TENAS, a board member of Bootstraps and Forest Heights Lodge, was involved with the Evergreen Design Council and a member of the Community Advisory Group which helped develop the Evergreen Area Community Plan.

The 1990 recipient was Hank Alderfer, "whose resume of community service is as deep as his roots in the Evergreen soil." Hank's parents (p. 84-5) owned the handsome ranch on Buffalo Park Road that is now part of the Alderfer/Three Sisters Jefferson County Open Space Park. Hank graduated from Evergreen High School and Claremont Men's College in California. He is married to Barbara and they have two young sons. Hank is in the construction business. The list of his community service contributions is voluminous But, as one nomination letter suggested, "the delightful part of it is that he always performs his self-obligated duties in an amiable, gentle fashion." Hank is currently chairman of the Board of the EPRD.

For 1991, the community honored Linda Kirkpatrick, a remarkable embodiment of the power of volunteerism in a community. We describe Linda above in connection with her unique newspaper, Upbeat. One speaker at the award lunch for Linda said, "one of her greatest strengths is her persistence in solving seemingly unsolvable problems. No project is too big and no task beneath her."

It would be immodest for one-half of this writing team to say anything about the 1992 recipient, Gene Sternberg. But the other half can say something about him. He is not really a good organization man, since he thinks no meeting should last longer than 10 minutes, but he is willing to put a lot of energy and time into

projects he believes will benefit the community. He has an infectious enthusiasm and an unending fund of creative ideas about what needs to be done and how it might be done, especially in matters relating to the physical beauty and harmony of Evergreen. At the award lunch, *Courier* Editor Tony Messenger commented that Gene was a quiet person. A number of those present obviously did not agree. Tony gracefully admitted that it is easy to make a mistake. "After all," he said, "Gene has described me as a nice young man!"

Losses. Many people dear to Evergreen have left us in the last six years, some by moving elsewhere and some by a more final farewell. We have mentioned some of these already. Lively, attractive arts activist Jenise Harper (p. 231) went to join her husband in Seattle. . . . In June of 1993, Evergreen loses one of its most valuable "people" assets: softspoken but outspoken Sheila Clarke (p. 111), has decided to move into a completely different life. She has been studying Spanish intensively for the past 4 years, is building a home in a small Mexican seaside village, and wants to find out if she can actually become an integral part of a totally different culture. She will teach English to people who want to learn it. "What about your urge to improve things?" we asked. Well, she does have in mind a low-key effort to involve kids in recycling, something apparently unheard of right now in Puerto Escondido! . . . Our community will miss the innovative genius of psychiatrist Foster Cline (p. 172-3) when he and his wife, Hermie, leave our community later this year to take on new challenges. . . . Architect Chuck Younkman (p. 192) died November 16, 1990. . . . The "best friend" of many Evergreen residents, Joe Cook, was killed early in 1993 in a helicopter accident in Alaska. A memorial service for Joe, held in Heritage Grove, was at the same time a heart-warming and heart-breaking occasion. Hundreds of people came together to celebrate his life and give support to his wife, Becky, and their three children. . . . Pioneer Lillian Ralph Hicks (p. 81-83) died September 26 1988 at the age of 93. . . . Melvin A. "Swede" Crosson, member of a pioneer Evergreen family, died in August, 1987. A longtime employee of ESCO Construction Co., he spent most of his life in the Evergreen area . . . George Walpole (p. 145) died in March, 1989 at the age of 85. . . . James Murphy died June 24, 1990 at the age of 72 at his home in the Circle K Ranch. Murphy was born and educated in Pennsylvania. He married Ellece King (p.145) in what was then the Church of the Transfiguration and later became the

269

Little Log Theater. For many years, this was the home of the Evergreen Players, of which Jim and Ellece were founding members. Gifted head of a talented family, Murphy had a distinguished career in law in Colorado and served the Evergreen community in many capacities . . . Pat Sayward (p. 141) died in California in June, 1990, at the age of 87. . . . Paul Hammond (p. 146) passed away September 19, 1991. . . . Josephine Berrian Fleming, born in 1916, grew up on the pioneer Berrian Ranch located between Conifer and Evergreen. She received her teaching certificate from Colorado Woman's College and taught for 20 years at Kittredge, Parmalee and Bergen schools. She married Jack Fleming in 1936. They lived in a number of different communities but returned to the Berrian Ranch in 1946 to live and raise their 4 children. She died in December 1992. . . . Jay Bright, a career employee of the U.S. National Park Service and a landscape architect, died August 30, 1992 at the age of 59. Bright was in Taiwan doing consulting work and was killed with his whole team in a freak accident caused by Typhoon Polly. Bright made many contributions to the life of our community. . . . Dr. Joseph Gardner passed away January 19, 1993 at the age of 69. "Dr. Jo" was a longtime resident of Evergreen. Before coming here, he taught in several medical schools and was a beloved general practitioner in Nebraska. He came to Colorado to head several departments at the Denver Clinic . . . J. F. "Brud" deDisse, 48, passed away February 11, 1993. An Evergreen native, deDisse was the great-grandson of Julius Caesar deDisse who homesteaded in Evergreen in the 1860's (p. 105-8). At the time of his death he owned the Old Mine Mini Storage on Highway 73, the site of the old Augusta Mine, which was worked by his great-uncle Charles deDisse in the late 1800's. From 1970 until his death, deDisse lived on, and managed, the Indian Creek Ranch. . . . The Evergreen Players lost a beloved and talented member in Rick Deutsch, who died unexpectedly of heart failure at the Little Log Theater on Dec. 20, 1991. He was 41. . . . Father Charles H. Blakeslee, Rector Emeritus of the Evergreen Church of the Transfiguration, died at home on Nov. 13, 1991. Father B., as he was affectionately known, grew up in Oak Park, Ill., served in the infantry in World War II and served 34 years in the ministry, coming to the Episcopal Church in Evergreen in 1964.

Because of its long history as a summer colony for all ranks of society, including the well-traveled rich, Evergreen has always had connections with other parts of the world. This is no less true today.

Perhaps the oldest organized link is the variety of international student exchange programs at Evergreen High School. The school may have as many as a dozen foreign students a year, from Asia, S. America, Europe. They live with local host families and spend one academic year learning about American life and also sharing their own culture and customs with their host families and school classmates. They come through a number of different sponsors, the two largest being the **American Institute for Foreign Study Foundation** (AIFS) and the **Educational Foundation for Foreign Study** (EF). Both organizations have local coordinators who help match up students with willing homes and act as a resource for the families. Coordinator for the Greenwich, Connecticut-based AIFS is Venessa Simone and for EF, the husband and wife team of Andrea and Phillip Dodge, who have lived and worked in Europe.

Over the past 6 years, articles on visits by groups or individuals from foreign countries have been frequent: 22 Japanese students visited families in the Lookout/Genesee area in 1990, two separate groups of Russians visited Conifer and Evergreen, the Friendship Force organized homestays by groups from Germany and Japan.

Pat Stephenson.

Our across-the-stream neighbor, Pat Stephenson, is largely responsible for bringing the **Friendship Force** organization to Colorado. This organization, founded by Wayne Smith and President Jimmy and Rosalynn Carter, fosters exchanges of groups of 20-80 Goodwill Ambassadors for a one-week intercultural learning experience. Members of the groups stay in homes. The network of Friendship Force now extends to more than 40 countries. Pat Stephenson is herself a one-woman international goodwill ambassador. A

native Kansan, she says has been coming to Evergreen "ever since I was born." Her father, Harold Rolley (p. 90) and mother Marion drove the family to summer lodgings either in Evergreen or in Manitou Springs for years before they bought their first cabin on Upper Bear Creek Road. After Pat married, she lived with her husband and six children outside Washington, D.C. Visits to Evergreen then were few. But after the children were grown and Pat was alone, she came back and bought herself a "home base". Almost by accident in 1978 (except Pat doesn't believe much in accidents) she then started what has become a unique lifestyle: taking advantage of opportunities that come into her life to live abroad for varying lengths of time. She has lived in London, in a village in southern France, on the Greek Island of Naxos, in Capetown, South Africa. She managed to get into Saigon before it was legal for American civilians to do so and journeyed by train across the huge expanse of Russia. She finds new projects wherever she goes. A visit to Bangkok somehow resulted in Pat organizing homestays in Evergreen for a group of Thai teen-agers. She came back from Capetown fired up with the need to gather science textbooks for black schools in Ciskei. In Finland she met the young Bulgarian painter, Nikolo Balkanski, who came to visit her in Evergreen and decided to make Colorado his home.

Another resident who connects Evergreen with exotic parts of the world is author-photographer Boyd Norton (p. 241-2), whose most recent book is **The Art of Outdoor Photography** (Voyageur, 1993). In 1990, Norton was in Siberia working on his recently published book, **Baikal: Sacred Sea of Siberia** (Sierra Books.) Baikal is the world's oldest lake at 25 million years, the deepest at 5750 feet, and the largest by volume, holding 20% of the world's liquid fresh water. Norton met an attractive young Siberian native, Leonid Yevseyev, who served as his translator, guide and researcher for the project as he did for other environmental groups. In 1991, after selling some personal possessions and saving his money, Yevseyev came on a visit to the U.S. Barbara and Boyd Norton's invitation to visit them in Evergreen began what Leonid calls his "love affair" with our town: he loves the people, the beauty of the mountains and forests and the warmth of our winters! In Siberia, he says, 30 degrees below zero is considered a heat wave. Leonid decided to take classes at Red Rocks Community College to help prepare him for a career in the new, market-oriented Russian economy. Leonid also teaches a course in

Russian Culture which is proving useful to tourists and to people interested in business relationships with Russia. He plans to become a consultant to facilitate joint business ventures in Russia, and also to be involved in the developing tourism industry, especially in his beloved Lake Baikal area.

Leonid Yevseyev.

The Evergreen-based **Friendship Bridge** is "a non-profit, all-volunteer organization to heal the wounds of war between our people and Viet Nam through the vehicle of medical care." It was founded in 1988 by Evergreen residents Ted and Connie Ning, after they visited Viet Nam in 1988 and saw first hand how much the country lacked in medical supplies and training. Since its start, the group has sent 31 delegations of medical professionals and others to Vietnam to help in training personnel there in the latest medical technologies, shipped 120 tons of medical supplies, hosted 13 Vietnamese physicians and nurses to Denver for further training and been involved in a variety of other humanitarian projects. One of the biggest needs was training and supplies for treating burn victims: children playing peacefully in the countryside still activate 20-year old land mines. A January 1993, delegation to Viet Nam consisted of 15 nurses, doctors, an ultrasound technician and others all wanting to "do work of the heart", according to organizer Connie Ning.

SENSE OF PLACE (p. 178-199)

People have come to live in Evergreen for its special sense of place, a small-town lifestyle focused on the natural beauty of the area. The future of Evergreen can be what the individuals who live here today want it to be, provided they are willing to work and fight for it.

Evergreen will change, must adapt to change, if it is to have a sustainable future. There will be new structures built, but the terrain presents rare creative opportunities for architects, developers

and builders. Sadly, the houses built here recently could have been built anywhere in the country. They have no relevance to this place, to this mountain environment. The challenge is to design human spaces respecting the small-town character and irreplaceable beauty that are the essence of Evergreen. Planning and zoning alone cannot do it: they cannot produce character or beauty.

Perhaps it would help to have a design review committee made up of experienced, committed, creative citizens. They would have to be appointed by the Commissioners, and their recommendations would have to be given some real weight. Such a committee must be able to come up with actual design alternatives, not just with rules from the book and words which cannot be translated into architecture. They must be able to show alternative siting of buildings on the land for best orientation, maximum privacy, minimum disturbance of the natural environment. They must be able to suggest convincing alternative architectural solutions to proposals that are too complicated and wasteful, have too many different roof lines, require too many different sizes and shapes of window and door openings, use too many materials, or create too many useless chopped-up spaces in the interior on too many levels. Some of these new houses, because of their scale and lack of charm, make us fearful for the future: they remind us of Victorian mansions that have become white elephants, burdens to the communities in which they are situated.

A new member of the Planning Commission, Eric Maule, will be a plus for our community. His background and experience as an architect will enable him to evaluate proposals according to whether they respect the site and achieve a high quality of design.

in 1989, Christian Outreach planted the first seeds from which grew the **Blue Spruce Habitat for Humanity** organization, affiliated with the Georgia-based Habitat for Humanity International. Founded in 1976, this organization seeks to "break the cycle of poverty by working in partnership with needy families to construct new homes." The families must invest at least 500 hours in Habitat construction work. When they move into a house, they pay no-interest housing payments averaging $200 a month over 15–10 years. Housing costs are kept low because many of the building materials and most of the labor is donated. Some 40 Blue Spruce Habitat members have worked on Habitat houses in Denver and other locations to gain experience in construction. With donations so far, the chapter has bought one lot in Brook Forest (another was

donated) and broke ground for its first home in May 1993. The first homeowner-partner selected is a single mother with three children. Preliminary studies indicate that 3–400 families in the mountain area are potential Habitat clients—i.e., they are working, low-income families who could assume regular house payments but, without Habitat, could not afford to own a home. Tom Ramsey has been a pillar of the Blue Spruce Habitat since its inception and currently functions as both PR person and office coordinator. Judy O'Brien is the enthusiastic president who says, "Our objective is to work hard, build homes and communities and have fun along the way." There is also a severe shortage of housing that middle-income people, the backbone of our community, can afford. Teachers, policemen, construction workers, bank and retail employees. Evergreen could benefit from the example of other mountain towns like Aspen, Steamboat Springs and Vail, who have found ways to provide people of modest incomes with simple, attractive and affordable accommodations.

From time to time a development issue arises that galvanizes the community into intense activity. This can be positive, as with the fund-raising for the Senior Center or, a few years earlier, for the construction of the ambulance barn. Sometimes, in order to preserve something seen as essential, the uproar is about saying "no". Such was the case with the proposal to build a **Wal-Mart** store in Bergen Park. There were some supporters. But opponents, ably organized by ENABLE leaders Sheila Clarke and Tandy Jones, were much more numerous. Their reasoning was that the sheer size and standardized design of the building was incompatible with the community, that the range of products sold would hurt almost every local retail business, that the economic benefits would be slim since the store pays most of its employees minimum wages. Overall, the project would contribute greatly to the conversion of a unique community into a homogenized suburban duplicate. The proposal was eventually defeated by the County Commissioners.

On the same piece of land today, 13.9 acres behind King Soopers, the $25 million, multi-phase Rocky Mountain Baptist Village is under construction.

Bergen Creek at Hiwan is the official name of the development on Lewis Ridge Road that is located on the 16.3 acres purchased by the Genesee Company from the Evergreen Council on the Arts. The land was subdivided and approved for 28 single homes. It is being constructed in two phases, with some of the land in open space. Genesee has also agreed to provide a trail easement through the property for Jefferson County Open Space.

Evergreen lost one of its more famous citizens when Willie Nelson had to sell his beautiful property on Upper Bear Creek to meet his other financial obligations. The property is being marketed this spring by Rita Hansen. Forty-six acres of the total property were sold with the old house and other buildings. Seventy-two acres were subdivided to nine single-home sites varying from 3-1/4 to 8-3/4 acres in size. Sixteen acres of land on both sides of the creek bordering Upper Bear Creek Road are designated as open space. Objections were raised by neighbors about the proposed use of this open space for horse grazing and for barns and corrals. Like the Noble Meadow and the beautiful meadow on Bear Mountain Vista, this project raises questions about just what constitutes open space in the mountains and how it can be permanently preserved. To attempt to deal with this vital matter, the County Commissioners in May, 1993, instructed the Planning Department to come up with recommendations as to how the zoning of areas of open space in subdivisions could be made more permanent and more specific as to permitted uses.

One of the largest construction projects pending as we go to press has been in the making for many years—the Means Meadow Development. This is a 160-acre commercial and residential development on both sides of Stage Coach Boulevard at Highway 74. Newcomers may have been shocked to see what they thought was part of Elk Meadow Park sprouting "Sold" signs. When the Means family sold its land to Jefferson County Open Space in 1977 to create the park, the land next to the highway was reserved by the family. Developer is Chris Elliott and the owner is Tradition Concepts. The development will be known as Tanoa.

In downtown Evergreen few changes have occurred, except for a second-floor addition to Byron Angevine's building, now called Evergreen Plaza, on the bridge on the east corner of Highway 74-73 intersection.

THE SPORTING LIFE (p. 200-207)

Evergreen lost one of its major annual sports events, the **Colorado Open**, and gained another, the **Evergreen High Country Triathlon**. Hiwan Golf Course had been the site of the Colorado Open since 1964 (p.200). But in 1991 the

University of Colorado Foundation Inc. became the new owner of the event and decided that it would be able to generate more money for the new beneficiary of the tournament, the CU Cancer Center, by moving the Open. The 1991 Open, the last held at Hiwan, was a cliff hanger right down to the rare sudden death playoff that merited the *Courier*'s headline, "Hiwan Era Ends in Style."

1990 was the first year for the **Evergreen Triathlon**, which attracted 168 participants. The second year, the swim section moved out of the swimming pool and into the cold waters of Lake Evergreen for a mile-long swim, which was followed by a 50-mile bike ride over Squaw Pass and a 10-mile run on a hilly trail through Elk Meadow Park. In 1991, there were 278 individual competitors and 60 team entries.

Biking continued to be a prime sporting and recreational activity in Evergreen. **Team Evergreen** was described in the *Courier* as "a club just waiting to happen." It was started in 1989 by bike enthusiasts Bob and Carol Middleburg. In a few months it grew from an idea to a membership of 200 cyclists of all ages and levels. The club offers camaraderie through regular meetings, scheduled training rides and organized rides offering challenges to all levels of expertise. Its toughest ride is the annual Triple Bypass, a grueling 108-mile ride crossing Squaw, Loveland and Vail passes.

Ride the Pines, a family bicycle event along Upper Bear Creek Road (which is closed to traffic for the ride) provides three routes of varying difficulty, all beginning and ending at Evergreen Lake. The event started in 1987 and is an annual benefit for the Evergreen Scholarship Association/Bootstraps.

Another favorite sport here is jogging and running, and the two annual events for these sports are the **Freedom Run** and the **Evergreen Town Race** (p.202). The Freedom Run attracts about 1500 joggers, runners, race walkers and walkers and takes place on July 4th. The Run, which is a benefit for Mount Evans Home Health Care/Hospice, raised $20,000 in 1992. The Town Race offers a 5-kilometer and 10-kilometer race down Upper Bear Creek Road, on what is usually a fine early morning in August. It attracts about 2500 runners of all levels of ability from pros to almost-

strollers, with a good representation of wheel-chair contestants.

The Evergreen Junior Soccer Association (EJSA) which started around 1977 is part of a nationwide phenomenon. On every level from Junior High to the professional, all the hoopla, glitz and publicity goes to teams playing American-style football. But young kids are spending their time and energy learning to play the worldwide game of soccer in little league organizations. And the years of training and playing experience are paying off. In May 1990 the EHS girls' soccer team won their first state championship, followed in November by the boys' team, under the coaching of Emilio Romero, who also had been the EJSA's Director of coaching since 1986. About 1350 kids from 7 to 18 years old play soccer with the EJSA, coached by somewhere around 100 coaches. All are volunteers except the Club Coach who is responsible for coaching standards and training in the League. Finding enough soccer fields to play on is a perennial problem for the EJSA leaders, and they cooperate with the Rec District and the R-1 Schools to find the best solutions.

Tennis bubble.

The **Evergreen Athletic Club** was sold in December of 1989 to Sunset Beach Properties Inc., which renamed it the **Evergreen Fitness and Racquet Club** and affiliated it with its other similar club in Golden. Many Evergreenites were appalled to see a huge white plastic bubble appear behind the Village Inn and Colorado National Bank in early May of 1993, especially those who remembered that the County Commissioners had turned down a proposal for such a facility in August of 1992. Apparently, the original proposal was on a different piece of land which required re-zoning. The bubble, covering indoor tennis courts, was eventually built on land already zoned in such a way that no planning approval was required. We sympathized with feelings expressed by our representative of community conscience, Sheila Clarke, "It looks like a huge white slug. I hope they will find a way to landscape it."

Ray Kachel.

HIWAN DEVELOPMENTS
(p. 208-219)

The era of the Buchanan family's association with the Hiwan Ranch (p. 208–13) is now showcased in a permanent exhibit on the second floor of the Hiwan Homestead Museum.

At the end of the Hiwan chapter, we noted that the development of the former Hiwan Ranch lands, so influential in determining the pattern of growth for Evergreen, was drawing to a close. Bill Bennett reports that, by the end of 1993, the Hiwan Golf Club area will be substantially built out, with approximately 870 families living in 770 single-family homes and 110 in multi-family condominiums, townhouses and duplex units. The Ridge at Hiwan (p. 217) will be built out by 1995, housing 520 families in single homes.

At the Hiwan Golf Club itself, David Fowler has continued to improve and update clubhouse facilities. The Club is unusual in being owned, not by its members, but by an independent corporation. Club Manager Ray Kachel, who came to Hiwan in 1986 after managing clubs in California and Texas, has a simple goal: to make the Hiwan Golf Club the finest club in Colorado. In summertime, the Hiwan Club employs over 100 people.

At the golf course, a new computerized irrigation system was installed in 1990–1 which has greatly improved playing conditions. A new 196-car landscaped parking lot was added in 1990 and an additional 100-car lot is planned for 1993. Plans for the near future are to replace the existing tennis courts with 6 or 7 new ones, and to provide larger pool facilities.

A somewhat sad commentary on our times: in 1993, due to increasing vandalism and trespassing, the Club had to increase its security measures and planned to install a guardhouse at the entrance to the clubhouse area.

ARTS IN THE MOUNTAINS
(p. 220-242)

The Evergreen Center for the Arts (p. 229) evolved into **The Evergreen Area Council for the Arts** (EACA), with a restated purpose and a different focus for its activities.

Several different developments made the ECA Board realize that their longtime goal of building one expensive facility for use by all of the arts groups in Evergreen was not realistic. Their new mission statement is "to provide support for existing and future arts organizations which will stimulate, promote and nurture all aspects of the arts for the mutual benefit of artists, their audiences and the mountain community." The organization sold its Lewis Ridge site, which it had acquired for $25,000 (essentially a gift) from Jefferson Land Associates, to the Genesee Company for $275,000 for a residential development called Bergen Creek.

One of the factors involved in this shift of purpose was the acquisition by the Evergreen Chorale of the facility in which it had been performing for many seasons, the Evergreen Conference Meeting House. Another was the building of the new Lake Boathouse/ Skatehouse at Evergreen Lake, with the accompanying landscaping and parking facilities. These create attractive summer performing possibilities, using a tent. The National Repertory Orchestra has already returned to Evergreen for two seasons to perform here.

The Chorale renamed its facility Center/Stage and has had an infusion of significant funds from the EACA ($45,000) and the Scientific and Cultural Facilities District ($45,000), which was voted into existence in 1988 by metro area voters. In addition to supporting Denver's major cultural organizations, the tax provides significant financial assistance to small local arts and scientific organizations. Through 1992, the District has made grants totaling $86,000 to EACA (in addition to the $45,000 for Center/Stage) for the Evergreen Children's Chorale, Evergreen Children's Theater/Kamikaze Kids, Artists in the Schools, the Evergreen Handbell Coalition, the Evergreen Music Festival, the Shadow Mountain Arts Council, Fourth of July Concerts at Evergreen Lake, and the canopy over the stage at Summerfest. The EACA continues to sponsor Summerfest and Winterfest.

Most of the artists described in our book are still active and creative. William

Laura Mehmert.

Matthews (p. 238) is becoming nationally-known as a Western artist, which is now his full-time occupation. He has opened his own gallery in lower downtown Denver and his work is exhibited in prestigious galleries throughout the country. The studio of Tom Ware (p. 236) overlooking Evergreen Lake is as busy as ever, with talented artists and friends sketching and sculpting from live models. Tom's reputation as a sculptor is growing: he was commissioned to do a bronze bust of Glen Lein for Forest Heights Lodge and a bas-relief of Ross Grimes for the park below the dam for the Evergreen Metro Water District. He has won four awards in the North American Sculpture Exhibition and his largest piece to date, Mujer Del Lago, is in Loveland's Benson Park Sculpture Garden. In June, 1993, Ware was commissioned to create a bronze sculpture for the new Evergreen Library. Nikolo Balkanski (p. 239) had three one-man shows in 1990, one in Arizona and two in Dallas, Texas, sponsored by the American Heritage Institute. In 1991 he was a featured artist in the Colorado Springs Rotary Club's Artists of the West Show and in 1992 had a one-man show at the Broadmoor's Hayden-Hays Gallery. In 1993 Balkanski demonstrates portrait painting during the Denver Rotary Club's annual invitational fall group show, Artists of America. The paintings on the cover are by Balkanski, "Summer on Evergreen Lake" (Owners Nancy and Ken Knudsen) and "Iceskating on Evergreen Lake" (Owner Mrs. Marion Rolley.)

Photographer Ron Brown came to Evergreen by choice, and continues to choose to make his living here. Brown moved here with his family from Southern California when he was 40. He brings a practiced artistry to his work, whether it is photographing individuals, scenes from local theater productions, weddings or portraits of high school seniors. One of our favorites is his portrait of Philip, the Library Cat, which he donated to the Evergreen Library.

Another multi-faceted artist is Laura Mehmert, whose work is inspired by the natural environment surrounding her in Evergreen. Her favorite subjects are horses, clouds, landscapes and people. An award-winning watercolorist, she recently started to work in sculpture. Mehmert also teaches classes in her studio.

Kathi Burns, a newcomer to the Evergreen scene since 1989, is a talented sculptress from California. She spent three summers working in Marble with other sculptors from around the world. Her work is in stone, contemporary in shape and form. Her work has been seen recently in the Loveland Museum and, in Evergreen, at the Hiwan Gallery in Lakepoint Center.

A new element in the Conifer arts scene is the **Shadow Mountain Center for the Arts and Humanities**, which "provides a vehicle for artists and people interested in the arts to perform and produce art, provides access to the performing and visual arts to area schools and businesses, and works through the arts for the benefit of the entire community." Founded in 1990 by a group of local artists, including Gail Widmer, Michael Fulks and Fran Arniotes, the Center has helped more than 100 local artists through sale of their work in the Shadow Mountain Gallery, a cooperative art and craft center located in the house by the Yellow Barn on Highway 73 at Barkley Road. The Shadow Mountain Theatre Company was formed in 1991 through the efforts of Michael and Johanna Rowan: its premises are in Aspen Park, behind Superfoods, and its season runs from September to July. It has also performed at the DCPA. Its children's shows play in area schools and at public libraries in Denver. The Center also sponsors many types of performances (musicians, writers, poets, storytellers) and offers classes year-round in art, craft and drama. The Center's dream is to purchase the property at Highway 73 and Barkley Road, including the historic Yellow Barn, converting it into theater, art studios and community meeting place.

The **Evergreen Players** (p. 226-7) lost their home at the Little Log Theater at the end of 1991. They have continued to present productions but are actively seeking a home they can afford. Kathie Davis, the Players' President, together with B.J. Schaugaard, was one of the prime movers in the campaign to secure the Open Living building as a community performing and arts space. When that fell through, the search went on. The latest, we hear, is a multi-faceted plan to convert the original Olde Texaco station on Main Steet, which has most recently been used for a complex of small antique stores, into a Cultural Center for our town. If the complicated sale goes though, we can expect to hear about plans for remodeling the existing main floor area into a theater/auditorium space and two small stores, and for adding on an upper floor for artists' space and some small community meeting rooms. Generous plans also include meeting the crying need for public restrooms downtown. We wish this project well. Along with Center/Stage, the new Lake Building, the Rec. Center and possibly some additional meeting rooms in the old warming house building, we will be on our way to meeting our community's needs for space for the arts, for celebrations, for meetings and for performances.

A children's theatrical group for Evergreen sounds like a respectable idea, but when it has a name like **The Kamikazi Kids**, you suspect that the irrepressible Jimy Murphy has something to do with it. Jimy was one of the members of the gone but not forgotten Kamikazi Klones that entertained Evergreen in its "hippie" years. Jimy went off to Los Angeles with his wife and two children to be part of the entertainment industry, but came back to Evergreen after a few years to find a way to make a living without so much hassle. Children's theater is an avocation for him, a labor of love. Jenise Harper's departure left the job of theater director at the high school vacant, and Jimy stepped right in. Besides being in their own productions, he gives high school students the opportunity to gain valuable experience by helping with the Children's Theater plays.

Evergreen now has its own mystery writer. Diane Mott Davidson made her authorial debut in 1990 with **Catering to Nobody**. To get authentic background, Davidson volunteered for a week's full-time work with J. William's catering and set the action in a mountain community remarkably like Evergreen. Her book was selected as a featured alternate of the Mystery Guild, rare for a first-time author. Davidson's second book, **Dying for Chocolate**, was the means of

renewing a college friendship with one Hillary Rodham, now Clinton. When the campaign fuss about cookie-baking arose, Diane sent Hillary a copy with a note that she could solve her problems by baking the delectable chocolate cookies from the recipe in the book. They have been corresponding since. **The Cereal Murders** will be published in November 1993 and then Diane starts on **The Last Suppers** for a new 2-book contract with Bantam Books: the topic will use her extensive background in Episcopal Church affairs. Davidson is an ordained preacher and has sat for ten years on the Diocesan Examining Board for Chaplains.

Patty Murphy in **Nunsense.**

There are two new sources of enjoyment for our community on the music scene, the **Evergreen Music Festival** and the **Evergreen Children's Chorale**. The **Music Festival** organizes delightful summer concerts in a tent in Evergreen Lake Park, at least one of which is by the National Repertory Orchestra (p. 225-6). The **Children's Chorale** was started in the spring of 1991 by Linda Biery and Peggy Fetchenhier with a $2,500 grant from the Scientific and Cultural Facilities District. Biery had a wealth of experience: she was a music teacher and accompanist at area elementary schools and ran her own Music Studio for preschoolers, based on Orff's philosophy that "when you're singing, you need to move." Fetchenmeir's experience was in choreographing for children's shows and for the Evergreen Chorale. The couple held auditions and set out to fulfill the grant's requirements for two productions within a year. Marcia Henderson became the volunteer business manager. Each parent is expected to help with some aspect of the production: promotion, making costumes, fund-raising, etc. The first production, Broadway Kids, was at Center/Stage and filled the place to capacity. Then came an adaptation of Pirates of Penzance, fast-paced, funny, and musically impressive. The group's grant from SCFD increased to $4500 a year. This, together with modest fees from Chorale participants, ticket sales, and donations, pays small salaries to Musical Director Biery, Choreographer Fetchenmeir, an accompanist and new Business Manager Joanne Miller.

If people, especially young people, in the Denver area know only one thing about Evergreen, it is likely to be the weekend goings-on at the **Little Bear** on Main Street. This institution not only consistently books great talent that draws Friday and Saturday night crowds, but also shares its profits with the community in the form of benefits for a variety of causes, from ongoing ones like the Senior Center and the Alpine Rescue Team, to one-time needs such as a teenager needing funds for cancer treatment.

Alan Frederickson (p. 195) is still active on the jazz scene. Born in Iowa "the year Lindbergh flew the Atlantic", he and Central City piano player Bill Murray formed the **Queen City Jazz Band** in 1957. Frederickson guided this band for 22 years and still plays with them occasionally. But he also has a new 7-member group, the **Alan Frederickson Jazz Ensemble**. He co-produces each year an annual jazz party in Denver, Summit Jazz, which is in its 14th year.

The **Evergreen Chorale** (p. 227-8) celebrated its 20th anniversary in March 1993. Since its inception, it has given us 54 wonderful concerts and 39 musical theater productions. In all, over 400 people have been members of the Chorale since 1972: 80 currently participate.

Alan Frederickson Jazz Ensemble.

Cowboy art by William Matthews.

Evergreen Lake, painting by Nancy Hendryx, in collection of Evergreen Library.

A FINAL NOTE

Whoever takes up the unfolding story of this mountain community in the future will have a chance to fill in many gaps. We have had to leave out so much. For every fine individual we have named, there are a hundred we could not. But it is the caliber of people here that make Evergreen a privilege to live in. We have watched new challenges being met as they arise, because there are always enough concerned and active individuals who will join together to get the job done. Fortunately, Evergreen's growth is limited, by water supply, terrain and by the volume of publicly-held lands. As our community moves towards "build-out", we face some of the greatest challenges in its short but vivid history. Will we find ways to ensure that new homes are better sited on our hilly terrain, so that they fit into the incomparable landscape rather than dominating it? Will we be vigilant and imaginative enough to preserve enough open space for wildlife to thrive and our souls to be refreshed? Will we continue to find ways to bring the community together to provide a good environment for kids and parents and seniors, for artists and performers, for eccentrics and conformists?

We've been associated with Evergreen for almost 50 years and we've seen it adapt rather well to great changes. We are confident it will meet the challenges that the end of the twentieth century has in store.

275

AND 11 YEARS LATER!

Our Evergreen community, and the county of which we are a part, were impacted by the major economic trends and dramatic events of the last eleven years: the high-flying nineties, followed by the economic collapse of 2000; the searing Columbine school shootings; the tragedy of 9/11, which brought new demands on our county's "first responders"; the drought and fires of 2002, and the blizzard of 2003. These years also brought growth — in population, new parks, trails, and recreation opportunities; new civic and cultural buildings; and in offices and retail structures. With growth slowing down, and important choices looming ahead for our country, 2004 is not a bad year to pause and take stock.

WHO'S IN CHARGE IN A CITY THAT ISN'T A CITY?

Still no City of Evergreen. There were a couple of flurries of interest in incorporation in the last 11 years, but trial balloons sank with hardly a trace. Evergreen residents still seem pretty well-satisfied with the tapestry of official and volunteer organizations that meet its community needs. Jefferson County provides police protection through its Sheriff's Department. Local government comes in the form of special districts with taxing powers (water and sanitation, parks and recreation, fire protection and emergency medical needs), which are under the direction of elected boards. Then there are a number of indispensable multi-purpose agencies, meeting needs with a combination of volunteer fund-raising and channeling of resources from state and county departments. Outstanding among these are Mount Evans Hospice and Home Health Services, Christian Outreach (EChO), and the Mountain Resource Center (MRC). Supplementing the work of these agencies, and providing for the fulfillment of an exotic variety of interests and needs, is a huge array of organizations, events, clubs and classes. Some idea of the extent of this network can be gleaned from the weekly listings in the *Canyon Courier* in segments labeled *Clubs and Organizations, Happenings, Calendar* and *What's Up: Cultural Events in the Mountains and Beyond.*

The Jefferson Board of County Commissioners (BCC) is still the overall governing body for Evergreen, which is one of a large number of unincorporated communities in the county. The 1992 Democratic takeover of the 3–member Board of County Commissioners (p. 244) did not last. After the 1996 election, Republicans Pat Holloway and Michelle Lawrence joined incumbent John Stone to form an all-Republican Board. The voter anger faded over how the Taj Mahal, the derogatory nickname applied to the County Administration Building completed in 1993, was financed. Indeed, the Taj, which will be paid off two years ahead of schedule in 2008, has become an accepted part of the county landscape and its 10th anniversary was modestly celebrated in September, 2003.

One of the commissioners responsible for getting the Taj built, Marjorie "Bunny" Clement, died of complications from a heart attack in February, 2004, at the age of 81. She was eulogized in a memorial gathering at the Jefferson County Fairground which noted her many services to the County. She was remembered as a politician in the best sense of the word, a public servant who relished the political process as a way of accomplishing good things for her beloved Jefferson County, the Denver metro region, and Colorado. Bunny Clement's husband, Robert, was a builder and a Jefferson County Commissioner who spearheaded the county's acquisition of the Hiwan Homestead Museum and promoted the preservation of Jefferson County history. Bunny was appointed to replace him on the Board of Commissioners when he died in 1981. She served until 1993 (p. 29, 158, 244) and in that time was instrumental in developing the Jefferson County Open Space Program, a greatly expanded library system, and the new county government campus in Golden.

In spite of the economic downturn of the early 2000's, and consequent rise in the unemployment rate, the overall challenge facing Jefferson County in the nineties and the first years of the 21st century is population growth and its accompanying traffic woes, though paradoxically, the County School District is coping with a decline in school enrollment. Population, estimated at 535,000 residents in 2003, is projected conservatively to reach 680,000 by 2025. The BCC in the summer of 2003 debated its planning approach to the growth and traffic problems. Frankly in favor of commercial and residential growth for Jefferson County, the Commissioners

Marjorie (Bunny) Clement.

said their concern was that such growth be properly channeled and that new economic enterprises be of the right kind. In 2003, more than 50% of residents commuted daily to work outside the county. The Commissioners, working largely through the Jefferson Economic Council (JEC), would like to attract a number of large new corporate enterprises to the County, targeting especially renewable energy, biotech, medical devices, aeronautics, aerospace, and nanotechnology. But, recognizing that most employees work for small businesses employing 5–10 people, the JEC hopes also to be of service to them, particularly in areas like transportation. Although the BCC's primary approach to solving traffic problems is "to ensure that roadways can handle traffic as it comes" they are also interested in promoting more mass transportation, including the 2004 RTD FasTracks proposals. In November, 2004, Holloway and Lawrence will be forcibly retired by term limit restrictions and voters will decide who will join Rick Sheehan on the BCC.

Of special interest to the horse lovers' population in Evergreen is the County's approval of a Master Plan for the **Jefferson County Fairgrounds**, preserving them as an equestrian and agricultural facility in metro Denver. Improvements include the construction of a new maintenance building, additions to an existing barn for 55 more horse stalls, a multi-purpose indoor arena, traffic upgrades, additional picnic facilities and additional outdoor arenas. Completion of the $8.2 million improvements was celebrated by a rededication ceremony in late July, 2004.

Updating the 1987 **Evergreen Community Plan**, a process which started in April 2002 and took more than two years, was approached somewhat differently than in the original model. Instead of an ongoing Task Force, selected to be representative of the community, meetings were open to anyone who desired to participate. Though totally democratic, this process had its drawbacks, chiefly a slowing up of progress because at each meeting those who had not attended before had to be oriented to what was being discussed, and also because there was a tendency for citizens interested in a specific area to flock to the meeting devoted to that topic, and perhaps never appear again. There was a core group of some thirty citizens who came regularly. After a draft plan was developed, there were opportunities for public comment. The Plan then wound its way through hearings before the Planning Commission and was expected to be adopted by the County Commissioners in late 2004.

The area covered by the Plan is bounded by the Jefferson County line on the west, with its farthest northern line being along part of Highway 6 and the farthest southern line along part of Highway 285 and between these, an irregularly shaped area that includes part of Genesee Park, Kittredge, Bergen Park, Brook Forest and all of what is usually considered Evergreen. It seems difficult to get accurate estimates of population in the Plan area: figures in both in the original plan of 1985 (18,120) and for 2000 in the new plan (21,048), do not seem quite credible The Evergreen Area Chamber of Commerce has an estimate of 39,720 within an 8–mile radius of downtown Evergreen for the year 2000. The new Plan estimates that if all areas were to be built-out according to existing zoning regulations, the population would approach 60,000, and if built-out according to recommendations in the Plan, which would limit density according to considerations of slope, animal habitat etc. would be about 46,000.

The Plan contains a great deal of information about the community and aspirations to maintain its character as a mountain environment with a variety of unique natural assets. It comes with valuable visual supplements and is well worth reading by anyone interested in the Evergreen community. Just how far its recommendations will actually shape the future of Evergreen remains to be seen. There are many pages of what different agencies "should" do, recommendations about conditions to be met by developers before building permits should be issued, about desirable changes in State legislation that would facilitate better development in the area, and some modifications to the boundaries and permitted uses within designated "Activity Centers." An Activity Center is defined as "an area of the community where a mix of more intense land use occurs, including residential, retail, office, mountain light industrial, community uses and public and private open space." Six such centers are defined: El Rancho, Bergen Park, North Evergreen, Downtown Evergreen, Kittredge and Marshdale.

New design guidelines were developed in conjunction with the Plan. The first section covers site design, including recommendations to ensure air quality, odor control, minimum nuisance from lighting fixtures, noise abatement, traffic circulation, pedestrian access and trails, landscaping, respect for vistas, view corridors and scenic areas, wildlife conservation, and considerations promoting "the development of a clearly defined and well-coordinated built environment." The introduction to the Design Guidelines section recognizes that ultimately good design is an art. These guidelines are formulated with the best of intentions and with the idea of encouraging high quality developments in the community: only time will tell whether they are administered in the spirit of positive encouragement and actually produce well-designed developments.

The major concerns of participants, generating the most heated debates, were two related issues — **growth and water supply**. At one end of the water debate spectrum were those who felt there should be no more growth in the Evergreen area because population probably already exceeds its reliable water resources. If many drought years lie ahead, they insisted, more and more wells would run dry and the ability of Bear Creek to sustain even the existing number of water taps would be problematic. At the other end were many developers and water optimists who pointed out that very little about what water resources actually exist in the mountain area is scientifically established. Fairly accurate records of precipitation and stream flows exist, though not for geologically significant time periods, but the subsurface water contained in different hydrological formations — how much there is, how long it takes to recharge, etc. — is virtually unknown and probably highly variable. The conflicts came to a head in the decision about minimum lot sizes to be permitted in newly developed residential areas, outside the boundaries of a water and sanitation district. The final decision of the planning group was that such lots should be a minimum of 12 acres, unless the developer or individual builder could prove there was an adequate water supply to justify a smaller size. One drawback to the effect of any such regulations is that the County accepts existing lot sizes where lots are already platted, and so new restrictions apply mainly to new subdivisions. However, there is a recommendation that the Commissioners be urged to pursue legislation permitting them to vacate or consolidate old plats containing virtually unbuildable lots.

Many articles have been written in the *Canyon Courier*, by Peter Link and others, about the need for a great deal more research about mountain subsurface water supply. The 2003 report of the *Mountain Ground water Resource Study of the Turkey Creek Basin*, conducted by the U.S.G.S. and Jefferson County, was something of a landmark in this area. It determined that the basin averages between 17 and 20 inches of precipitation per year, of which more than 80% either evaporates or is consumed by vegetation. So the scientists warned that already, in the Turkey Creek Basin, more water is being taken out via underground wells than is going in. Population there has more than doubled in the last 25 years, and unless something is done to curb population growth, water shortages will be inevitable. Many mountain homeowners across the county have already seen their wells go dry, and no accurate count exists of how many people are already regularly hauling water.

Federal cutbacks in grants to states since 2000, and Colorado's fiscal woes, both stemming in large part from a combination of tax cuts and economic recession, have had their impact on Jefferson County. Budget cuts at the state level have forced counties to take on an increasing number of "unfunded mandates" — services the State requires counties to provide, but which it cannot find the money to pay for. County revenues also dropped because of lower sales tax collections and reduced revenues from fees such as the auto ownership tax. The 2004 budget was reduced by 12% from that of the previous year, with reductions in funds for health care, social services and libraries. Increased funds had to be allocated for hiring 17 new deputy sheriffs, and for the Clerk and Recorder's office, which must comply with federal voting requirements following the 2002 Florida election debacle.

The Jefferson County Sheriff's Department had its ordeal by fire during the Columbine High School shootings in 1999. It came in for much national, state and local criticism for the manner in which it conducted itself during the tragic episode, for its lack of serious investigation into some complaints against the young perpetrators filed before the shootings, and for its reluctance to share its findings after the event. John Stone, the Sheriff at the time, survived a recall effort but decided against running for a new term. After the completion of the new Evergreen Library in 1993 the old building was taken over by Jefferson County, centralizing its services in Evergreen and including a branch of the Sheriff's Department and the Motor Vehicle Department. In November of 2003, Sheriff Ted Mink put forward plans for the Department, which called for new premises for the Evergreen substation, saying that the old library building was too small and did not have enough parking. Which raises the interesting question of what use would then be made of the charming former library building?

For mountain area residents, one of the most important roles of the Sheriff's Department is as a provider of **emergency services**. All 911 calls go initially to Jefferson County's dispatchers, who route them appropriately to law enforcement, fire or emergency medical services. The Evergreen Fire Protection District gets both the fire calls for the area and the emergency medical calls. They have trained their dispatchers in giving medical instructions, in addition to reassurance to those on the scene, until medical help arrives. The Sheriff's Department deputies are involved in many kinds of emergencies in the Evergreen area, including traffic accidents, wildfire emergencies, reports of domestic abuse and crime. *The Sheriff's Calls* section of the weekly *Canyon Courier* is still well-read, describing as it does, without name identification, the routine and sometimes bizarre harassments for which help is sought.

Since the 9/11 tragedy, the Sheriff's Department has been the coordinator of response to potential terrorist attacks. They have organized training exercises in dealing with possible mass casualties and have ongoing "terrorist patrols" at sites deemed to be vulnerable. Federal funds have helped to buy new

equipment, such as a new bomb squad truck and communications equipment for the county and its special districts, but cannot be used to fund the more than $19,000 a month in deputy overtime hours spent on terrorist patrols.

The last decade saw its share of traffic accidents and deaths in our community, the most tragic being those of teenagers. Too often alcohol is involved. The sad little roadside crosses, adorned with plastic flowers and teddy bears, attest to the needless loss of young lives.

On controversial issues of **development** in the mountain area of Jefferson County, the BCC is the final arbiter. Though it holds public hearings, and listens respectfully to the views of citizen groups like ENABLE (p. 245, 271), its decisions are made in the general context of a pro-development philosophy. The defeat of the proposal to build a **Wal-mart** store, in Bergen Park, was only temporary — Wal-mart appeared in 1996 on the old Tepees site at El Rancho, adjacent to the I–70 highway, soon followed by a flowering of commercial development, including automobile-related businesses, a Sears store and a Home Depot. In April of 2004, Wal-mart filed a preapplication with the County for expanding the present 98,350 square ft. store into a 157,715 sq. ft. Super Center: no rezoning or replatting is required, so the process of approving the building plans will not involve public input. The new commercial center, part of the Tanoa project on State Coach Boulevard, has brought Albertsons, a third major grocery chain store, to Evergreen as the anchor tenant.

New housing construction, mostly catering to upper income brackets, has continued at a fast pace since 1993. The Tanoa subdivision between Stage Coach Boulevard and Highway 74, is virtually built-out. In February of 1994, the venerable Troutdale Hotel was finally torn down to make way for a new subdivision of high-end homes. Most of the new housing is of a design that has little to do with its mountain setting — the homes could have been built anywhere, on the plains, on the east or west coast. One clustered development in Bergen Park, the Lodges, fits more comfortably into its setting, with a dark green monotone theme that mirrors its evergreen backdrop.

The **Jefferson County Department of Health and Environment** has faced a number of challenges in the last decade, including the new threat of West Nile virus, a 30–year high in flu cases in 2003, with school children especially

hard hit, and attempts to deal with health consequences of smoking in the county. The Commissioners have the legal ability to enact tough **smoking restrictions** in public facilities in unincorporated areas of the county including Evergreen, but not in the county's municipalities. Restrictions are already in place: restaurants for more than 30 people must provided designated smoking areas, though in bars and taverns whose primary sources of revenue are sales of beer, wine and liquor, smoking is permitted. Citing the hazards of secondhand smoke and the ineffectiveness of present regulations, Dr. Mark Johnson, Director of the Department, colorfully likened them to "having a peeing section in a pool. It just doesn't work." The BCC had reservations about the proposed ordinance, based primarily on concern for the property rights of those who would be impacted by it. Their preference was to wait for significant input from citizens and eventually put the matter to the voters.

One public service provided by the Health Department is that of **restaurant inspection**. Site inspections take place unannounced, and occur about every six months. In November of 2003, the Jefferson County Food Service Establishment Inspection website was launched so that prospective diners can check whether a particular restaurant has incurred any "critical" violations. The most common critical violations are related to rules about scrupulous adherence to hand washing regulations, and maintenance of temperature cold enough to keep food safe. Over half of the 42 food establishments in the mountain area (Evergreen, Kittredge, Morrison, Genesee) had no violations in 2003 inspections.

Two health statistics in a report presented to county child advocates by the Colorado Children's Campaign in April 2004 brought expressions of surprise and disbelief. The county's **infant mortality and child immunization rates** were below Colorado averages — and Colorado's immunization rate was itself the lowest of all the states. The Children's Campaign representative recommended that child advocates in Jeffco need to come together and focus on one or two issues at a time. One issue that finally did get enough focus to make a difference was the passage of Referendum 1A in November of 2003 (it failed in 1994) which raised the level of funding for the developmentally disabled from .48 mills to 1.0, the full amount permitted by Colorado law. The estimated additional revenue of $3.4–6 million will make a significant difference to hundreds of families. At the time, it was estimated that there were 8,373 people with mental retardation living in Jefferson County . 1,633 families were receiving services such as early intervention, skills training, residential supervision or respite care for care givers, while 1,597 were on waiting lists, some for as long as 15 years. The widely-respected Director of the Developmental Disabilities Resource Center in Lakewood is Evergreen resident Art Hogling.

Building Codes are administered by the Jefferson County Planning and Zoning Department, which has a difficult role to play, often caught between conflicting forces. For example, an attempt was initiated in November, 2003 to reconcile county fire regulations with the often stricter requirements of local fire districts' codes. The Evergreen Community Plan Update strongly recommends that "If development applications do not meet fire protection district standards, they should be denied."

Under a new regulation in force as of January, 2004, **septic systems** must be inspected by the Jefferson County Department of Health and Environment before a property can be sold or remodeled. The Department finds that most of the County's 20,000 individual sewage disposal systems are in the Evergreen-Conifer area, and calculates that the new system will result in about 1,000 inspections a year. The primary purposes of the new inspection program are to prevent the pollution of ground water and to protect home buyers from unanticipated and costly repairs.

State Government. In 1998, being term-limited,7–term Republican State Representative Tony Grampsas ran successfully for the District 13 State Senate seat, representing most of the Evergreen area. Open-minded, and particularly interested in issues affecting the health and well-being of children, Evergreen resident Grampsas quickly made his mark in the Senate as he had in the House. Sadly, he died in February, 1999. He was valued by a wide spectrum of Evergreen citizens and is memorialized in two lovely places here. At the Evergreen Library, an evergreen tree was planted outside the main entrance in his name, and a popular piece of sculpture from the first Sculpture Walk was bought and permanently placed outside the building in his memory. "Check it Out" by Jerry Boyle is a bronze of a small girl with a pile of library books up to her chin,

"Check it Out" by Jerry Boyle.

appropriately remembering Grampsas's support for children, public art, and education. Beside one of the ponds in the new Buchanan Park, an evergreen tree and a bench are dedicated, in gratitude for services to the children of Colorado rendered by both Grampsas and State Senator Sally Hopper.

Elected to fill Grampsas's seat in the House of Representatives was Evergreen resident John Witwer, a retired doctor and a Republican. He was reelected in an uncontested race in 2002 and appointed to the powerful Joint Budget Committee, an assignment which Grampsas had also held. Because the Colorado budget must by law be balanced, this has always been a demanding assignment. But after the economic crash of the late nineties, a number of circumstances combined to make it a heart-breaking and destructive task. The problem was largely due to the crushing effect of two voter-passed amendments to the State Constitution — the 1992 TABOR amendment and Amendment 23 — which together

*Spruce Tree and Bench
dedicated to Senators Grampsas and Hopper.*

EMD Administration Building, Eric Maule Architect.

drastically limited the amount of money the state could spend without appealing to the voters for a tax increase, and, in the case of Amendment 23, required a certain level of expenditure on K–12 education. Together with the large and growing bite that the state's matching funds for Medicaid takes out of state revenues, it meant that the mandatory large cuts must be made from a relatively small area of the budget. Headlines in the *Canyon Courier* throughout the 2003/4 legislative session described some of the pending cuts — services for youthful violent offenders, colleges, libraries and state parks.

In the 1998 election, Lookout Mountain resident and Democrat Joan Fitzgerald was elected to Grampsas's Senate seat in a hard-fought campaign, and reelected in 2002. Fitzgerald, who had previously served as Jefferson County Clerk and Recorder, had the rare distinction of serving for a very brief period as Senate Majority Leader, when Democrats briefly controlled the Senate by a majority of one vote. In 2002 however, the Republicans regained control, and Joan endured what she termed "brutal" years as the underdog in more than usually bitter partisan political struggles.

SPECIAL DISTRICTS
Not all of the Evergreen area has access to water and sanitation services. Those parts which do are served by five districts — Evergreen Metro, West Jefferson County Metro, Kittredge Water and Sanitation, Upper Bear Creek Water and sanitation and El Rancho — reduced by mergers or consolidations

from the nine which existed ten years ago. The **Evergreen Metropolitan District** is the central coordinating agency and supplies water to all of the districts. Its water source is Bear Creek, with storage in Evergreen Lake.

New Buildings, New Technology, New Challenges. Growth of population and the building of new homes and commercial buildings in its area of service, as well as improvement in technologies of waste water treatment and water purification, have stimulated many improvements and additions to the District's facilities. In 1994 came the first of two major water treatment plant expansions (in the buildings visible from Highway 73 just below the dam). The second came in 2002–3, incorporating some of the most advanced water treatment technology available at the time. Called membrane filtration, this technology will filter out particles down to .01 microns in size, actually filtering out viruses. The District believes that this plant, under the management of Dave Lightheart, puts it "far ahead of the water regulations curve" for current and future regulations of both the State Health Department and the EPA. This latest technical improvement is for the removal of ammonia nitrogen, a need arising out of the 2002 drought when the flow in Bear Creek was at an all-time low. The existing treatment plant had trouble removing ammonia and this was fingered as a possible source of a fish kill down stream. There are three waste water treatment plants in the Evergreen Metro area: the main one, concealed beneath tennis courts, just off Highway 73 near its junction with Meadow Drive; the Kittredge plant, adjacent to the "green pond" visible

from Highway 73; the West Jefferson District plant at the end of Lewis Ridge Road. All three plants are maintained and operated, with contracts as needed with other Districts, by the Evergreen Metro District.

The District is proud of its attractive new **Administration Building**, designed by Evergreen architect Eric Maule, which fits effortlessly into its site on Stage Coach Boulevard and is designed to meet the District's space needs for many years to come.

The 2002 **drought** which challenged the Fire District with an unprecedented outbreak of serious wildfires, also severely tested the emergency preparations of the mountain area water districts. The Evergreen Metro District had developed a drought response plan in 2001, using the recommendations of a Water Conservation Committee representing all five water and sanitation districts. However, it was difficult to be totally prepared for what was later characterized as a "500–year drought episode", with both Bear Creek and Cub Creek drying up, and the strange sight of a dam with absolutely no water going over it. The District banned all outdoor watering and appealed to the Evergreen community to drastically conserve water as long as the emergency lasted. The appeal was successful, and the appearance of the **Great Blizzard** of March, 2003, which dumped seven to ten feet of heavy wet snow on the area, saved the District from putting draconian measures into effect in that year. In April of 2004, the District announced that it did not yet see a need to impose restrictions on the use of water for the coming summer. EMD believes it can operate without undue restrictions with 60% of average stream flow in Bear Creek. If a drought situation should develop, the first steps would be to appeal for a voluntary cutback of water use, especially outdoor use, and to impose a ban on outdoor watering between 9 a.m. and 6 p.m. Later steps would include strict limits on outdoor watering, then an absolute ban. Next time, the District would not wait until zero water was flowing over the dam before imposing stringent measures. This policy was blamed indirectly for considerable fish kill in 2002, but the District's opinion is that the small amount of water that would have been saved by banning outdoor watering earlier in the drought cycle would not have been enough to save the fish.

The blizzard had an undesirable side effect for many Evergreen residents. As power was knocked out, their water stopped flowing — a condition they shared with well-users. The District was without power from March 18 to 22, an outage which included all water and waste water plants, water pump stations and waste water lift stations, as well as the office on Stagecoach Boulevard. Generators kept the plants going, and neither water nor waste water quality was compromised, but the 15 pump and lift stations that get water to customers and take waste water away were immobilized. The District only had one working portable generator which was used mostly at the Troutdale lift station so it would not overflow onto the ground. The District has since acquired 7 generators of which most are on lift and pump stations which have automatic switches if power is knocked out. The blizzard strained EMD's waste water resources almost to their limits. The plant was built to handle up to 1 million gallons per day and usually processes 600,000 gallons. At the height of the runoff from the blizzard, it was dealing with 2,400,000. It was determined that part of this load was due to the existence of so many old clay pipes which become permeable in very wet conditions and allow additional water to enter the system. In the fall of 2003 the District began a program of slip-lining the clay pipes, threading inside them new impermeable PVC lines.

The ironic effect of the success of conservation measures was a substantial drop in District revenues from the sale of water. When EMD bought the water distribution service from Public Service in 1979 (p. 22) the base rate for water service was $17.50 per month, with additional cost per thousand gallons of $1.60. In 1983, EMD lowered the base rate to $12, with the cost per thousand remaining the same. As millions of dollars were invested in updating facilities, rates were slowly increased. In 2004 the base rate was raised to $17.50 and the cost per thousand to $2.50. Between 9,000 and 14,000 cost is $3 per 1000 gallons, and above 14,000 it more than doubles to $7 per 1,000. 91% of users never exceed 9,000 gallons so the Board was considering lowering the high use rate. Because Evergreen water rates are already at the high end for the Denver metro area, most of the money for improvements must come from tap fees, which in 2004 were raised to $17,000. For waste water (sewer) service, the charges vary somewhat from District to District. The Evergreen Metro District itself charges a flat monthly fee of $30, with a tap fee of $12,500.

Using a conservative estimate of water availability, i.e. reckoning only on the

Evergreen Metro District: Jack Christenson, Treasurer; Tom Ware, President; Gerry Schulte, Manager. Photo courtesy of EMD.

years of lowest stream flow since 1920, the District determined that it could service no more than 6,500 water taps. In 2004, there were 5,500 taps in use. An additional 250 taps were already owned by developers in the El Rancho area, leaving only 750 taps for the District to sell. Their rationale for the price of water taps is that the new users should carry the cost of system expansion needed to serve them. The District hopes to build up a considerable reserve fund by the time all taps are sold.

Water Pay Station: An intergovernmental agreement between the Evergreen Fire Protection District and EMD provided for the EFPD to build a fire substation on the almost one-acre lot owned by EMD in Kittredge. No lease charge was made, but the Fire District agreed to install a new water pay station to replace the existing one, and to landscape and maintain the site. The water pay station in Kittredge is intended for temporary use by people filling hot tubs or having well problems or during construction, but in the Fall of 2003 there were complaints that in some cases water from this station was being consistently trucked out of the Bear Creek basin, and in other cases was being used regularly as a substitute for wells. New

regulations provided that water hauling was to be only for temporary uses, and that if the water was to be taken outside the Bear Creek or Turkey Creek basins, the water hauler must apply for a temporary permit.

District Leadership and Personnel. The district has been fortunate to have had the quiet and steady services of General Manager Gerry Schulte (p. 24) through all the ups and downs of the last ten years. Schulte has been with the District since 1977 and has seen it grow from a sanitation service only to a water and sanitation district serving 5,500 customers with water. By approval of measures put before District voters in 1998, EMD has both exempted its Board members from the application of term limits and "deBruced." This is an exemption from one clause of the so-called TABOR amendment, passed by the voters in 1992 and authored by Douglas Bruce, which requires that any tax collections exceeding a specific formulaic amount be returned to the taxpayers. In 2004 no election was held, the only challengers having withdrawn, thus retaining in office the existing Board of Tom Ware, President; Jack Christenson, Treasurer; Jim Villenave, Secretary; and Directors Mark Davidson and Scott Smith.

Evergreen Fire Rescue — 2003 EMS Staff. Photos courtesy of EFPD.

Board of Evergreen Fire Protection District:
left to right, Janie Hamilton, Lloyd See, Phil Shanley, Bob Wallace, David Klaus.

Evergreen Volunteer Fire Department.

282

How Much Water Is There? This vital and controversial question is an underlying theme to much discussion of the future of our community and the wisest use of its resources. EMD has decided, in the area of this question that they control, to limit the number of water taps they will sell, based on the lowest Bear Creek stream flows in the years since 1920. They feel confident they will be able to service that number of water customers. The issue of limiting the number of water wells is one of the most contentious topics discussed by participants in the Evergreen Area Community Plan.

Evergreen Volunteer Fire Department (EVFD) & Evergreen Fire Protection District (EFPD)
The network of volunteer fire districts serving the mountain area was tested beyond its normal limits by forest fires caused by the drought conditions of the late nineties and first years of the 21st century. The year 2002 was a disastrous year for Colorado, with the red-orange glow and smoky smell of fires penetrating much of the state for days and sometimes weeks on end. Evergreen was most affected by the Snaking Fire, which threatened the Black Mountain area and caused the evacuation of many houses off Brook Forest Road.

To get a clear picture of how the Evergreen community's needs are met in the event of fire, traffic or other serious accidents, or medical emergencies, it is helpful to understand what exactly are the functions of the **EVFD** and the **EFPD**. Though they are two aspects of one operation, and indeed are combined for the sake of quick public access into one telephone listing as the **Evergreen Fire Department**, they are, and need to be, organizationally separate.

The **EFPD** is the Special District authorized to levy taxes, within legal parameters, which are collected by Jefferson County. The district is administered by an elected Board of five members who serve without pay. The five in 2004 are Janie Hamilton, Lloyd See, Bob Wallace, David Klaus and Phil Shanley, who has been on the Board since 1974 and President for the last 15 years. Voters have consented to exempt the District Board members from term limitations, and also to what is commonly in Colorado termed "de-Brucing." The Board of EFPD is very clear that its reason for being is to support the volunteer fire fighters and the medical personnel who do the arduous and sometimes dangerous work of fighting fires and caring for people in

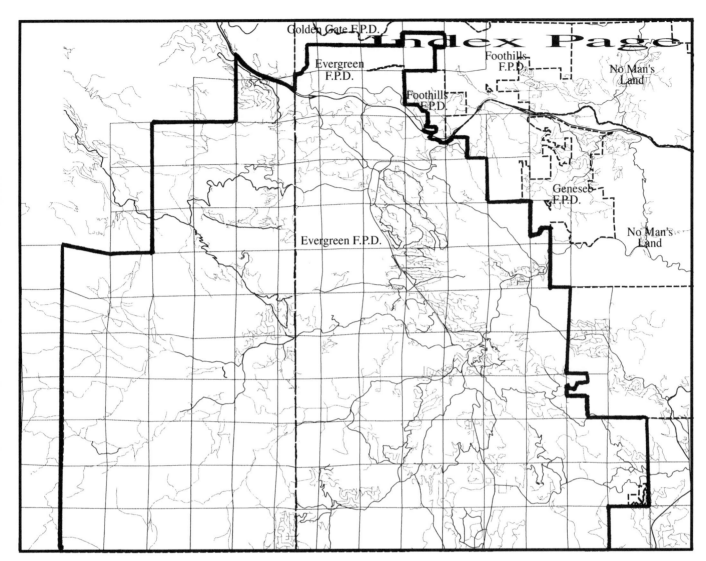

Map of Evergreen Fire Protection District: dotted vertical line is boundary with Clear Creek County.

accidents or medical emergencies. The EFPD has just under 30 paid employees. The current District Administrator is Tom Hayden, a great-great-grandson of Governor John Evans and lifetime resident of the Evergreen area Tom closed his sawmill operation (p. 76) down and was appointed Administrator in 2002. Assisting the Administrator are an office manager and 2 clerical assistants. The Fire Marshal is Frank Dearborn, whose job includes checking buildings and building plans for compliance with fire regulations, checking driveways as to grade and turn radius, etc. The Marshal has one paid assistant, and some of the ambulance crew are also trained as inspectors. Three supervisors oversee the main aspects of the District's operations: Shaina Lee is responsible for the staff of paid and well-trained dispatchers in the communications center, the folks you talk to when you call 911 for a fire or medical emergency. Avan Fosler is the Fleet Maintenance Supervisor, and the Department in the summer of 2004 was looking to hire a new Supervisor for the staff of Emergency Medical Technicians

(EMT's) and paramedics who man the ambulance services round the clock.

The **EVFD** is the organization of the volunteer fire fighters. Its bylaws allow for up to 100 fire fighters, but they normally find that somewhere between 80–90 is a manageable and adequate size. This is the largest volunteer fire department in Colorado and has a fine reputation. The volunteers elect a president and officers to administer their corporate activities and a fire chief and other officers to conduct operations. There was a concern that recruitment of volunteers may prove difficult as Evergreen changed in character, since they originally came from the ranks of those who worked in Evergreen on a more leisurely schedule than today — Public Service and telephone employees, for example, who were free to drop what they were doing and dash off to a fire with their Companies' approval. But new types of volunteers have come forward and the Department continues to be fully-staffed, well-trained and capable of meeting the challenges it confronts. Volunteer fire

fighters serve without pay, go through a rigorous training for a probationary period, and must undergo periodic additional training and respond to a certain minimum number of calls to remain on the roster. These days, their training and equipment is largely paid for by the EFPD. From time to time, the Volunteer Department solicits funds, either for a particular cause (like the appeal for help for the families of the firefighters killed in the 9/11 bombings) or for providing certain morale-boosting "perks" (a picnic, an awards dinner, an occasion honoring long-suffering spouses).

New Facilities. As housing developments in the Evergreen area during the past ten years spread over more and more valleys and hillsides, it became clear that the existing facilities could not meet the needs for quick access to fire equipment from all parts of the extensive Fire District. Furthermore, **Station One**, the native

283

stone building on Highway 73 designed by Evergreen architect Alan Fredericksen and built in 1966, is now severely handicapped by its location on the narrow, heavily-trafficked two-lane highway, which makes access for both firefighters and fire vehicles difficult and inefficient. The Board of the Evergreen Fire Protection District, in consultation with its paid staff and the personnel of the Volunteer Fire Department, put together a comprehensive plan which included proposals for new buildings of various sizes, some remodeling and additions to existing buildings — ultimately eliminating Station One as a working fire station — and buying additional equipment. In 2002, many of these proposals were packaged into a bond issue of $9.75 million and presented to the voters. The bond issue passed comfortably, and implementation of the plan is proceeding. To keep good control over the construction process, the Board decided to hire one architect for all the new building and remodeling. They selected Evergreen resident Eric Maule, who designed the headquarters building for the Evergreen Metro Water and Sanitation District on Stagecoach Boulevard. They also elected to hire their own project manager/general contractor and have been satisfied with their choice of Greg Mickevich who, according to Board President Phil Shanley, "watches every dollar."

It was decided to name all the new and existing buildings except **Station One**, since that name has accumulated many memories over the years and is destined eventually to be phased out as a working fire station. There are various proposals for the destiny of this station, such as becoming a back-up facility housing older equipment, or it could eventually be sold. **Bergen Park**: The EFPD purchased additional land at this site from the Jefferson County R1 School District to create a campus of three free-standing buildings. The original building was expanded in 2002 with the addition of a state-of-the-art communications center, part of the overall Evergreen 911 system. A new, free-standing maintenance building moves the maintenance facilities from the existing fire house, which has a large bay added to accommodate the new aerial (ladder) fire truck. Administrative functions of the District are moved to the second floor of a second new free-standing building, which has training facilities for the entire District on the ground level. The space vacated in the original building is turned into decent living space for the ambulance crews, which have long made do with makeshift quarters. The site plan for the Bergen Park facilities includes a split block wall buffer to

screen District facilities from most of the residential area, and grants the Recreation District an easement for a trail from the Buchanan Recreation Center into the Hiwan subdivision.

Upper Bear Creek is one of a number of unmanned two-bay substations that house fire equipment and have a small office and bathrooms for the use of firefighters. Initially, these stations have a quick-response truck, fast and well-equipped, fabricated in the District's own shops by Evan Fast. Eventually each substation will also have a tanker truck. The Upper Bear Creek Station was completed in 2004. It is located at Echo Lake Road and Upper Bear Creek Road in Clear Creek County. **Brook Forest**: a proposed two-bay substation to be located near the Brook Forest Inn. **Skyline** is the name given to the site at Highway 73 and Skyline Drive, where the original Evergreen Ambulance Service, with much community help, erected a building to house its personnel and equipment (P. 19). Since the integration of the Ambulance Services into the Fire District in 1985, the site has belonged to the District. Plans call for the remodeling of the original building to improve living quarters for the ambulance crews since the building was originally designed for volunteer emergency medical personnel and not for its present complement of paid 24–hour staff. A new 3– or 4–bay building will house front line fire apparatus. **Kittredge** is a new 2–bay station constructed on property belonging to the Evergreen Metro Water and Sanitation District. **Troutdale**, to be located on land next to the Montessori School, is planned as an important station which will eventually house some of the the apparatus from Station 1 and take over some of its responsibilities. **Marshdale**, located on the east side of Highway 73, is built on land formerly belonging to Ron Lewis. It is an unmanned 3–bay station, and like the other unmanned stations in the District has a small office and bathroom facilities for the use of firefighters. **Floyd Hill/1–70**. Many in Evergreen are surprised to learn that the Fire District boundaries extend as far as Floyd Hill and include the new Clear Creek High School. This substation is at County Road 65 and I–70.

New Equipment. The District's Master Plan called for seven new fire trucks. Two new wildland fire engines, which are already in use, were assembled by the District maintenance staff at an estimated savings to taxpayers of $40,000. They will be garaged at the Skyline and Brook Forest Stations. The maintenance crew has also assembled a wildland/structural water tender, which will be housed at the Upper Bear Creek

Station. Three multi-purpose engines for structural or wildland fires, which can travel off-road and are equipped with a compressed air foam system for use when water is critically short, will be housed at Floyd Hill/I–70,Kittredge and Marshdale. The seventh purchase is an 80 foot ladder truck, a first for the EFVD, housed at Bergen Park.

Return of the Red Fire Engine. The new equipment was ordered in red. A switch back from lime green to red was felt to be desirable by both by the firefighters and the EFPD. Some small public controversy erupted when this became public, mainly on the grounds that the change would involve extra expense. Officials of the District explained that the changeover, which will take time to complete, will involve no additional charge to taxpayers. As equipment becomes obsolete, replacements will be ordered in red. The older lime green stock will only be repainted in red when such maintenance is required by the deteriorating condition of existing paint jobs.

Emergency Medical Services are provided by paid professional staff. Two full-time crews are on duty at all times. The ambulance service is provided by the EFPD because no private ambulance service is available in this area. It is a necessary and expensive item for taxpayers, costing more than $400,000 a year over and above reimbursements received for services.

Drought and consequent fires drive changes. A new stress on measures to be taken by homeowners to minimize the possible damages from fire is being stressed by the fire department. Cutting down of trees within 30 feet of homes is a major one, heart-breaking to some homeowners who cherish their forest hideaways. Jefferson County cooperates with local fire districts to sponsor low-cost slash collections at convenient mountain sites each year so that homeowners can drop off tree limbs, and other combustible fuels. In cooperation with other local fire departments, Jefferson County Open Space now conducts "prescribed burns" in the spring as a preventive measure in many of its parks. The Evergreen population is most likely to see the burns in Elk Meadow, where they can safely experience the vicarious excitement of watching stalwart firefighters, in their yellow and black protective clothing, first torch and then monitor rapidly advancing lines of fire as they consume dead grass and small shrubs over carefully limited areas.

Evergreen Park and Recreation District (EPRD) Originally called the

Evergreen Metropolitan Recreation and Park District and renamed in 1992, this District has also experienced a great increase in its facilities and programs over the past ten years. When we left its story in 1993, the District had just resolved the long-lasting controversies over the uses of Evergreen Lake, the fate of its small but vital wetlands, and the functions and size of the new boat rental, skate rental and winter warming house.

Since its opening in 1993, the **Lake House** has become an indispensable asset to community life here. The attractive log building enhances the extraordinary beauty of its environ-ment — the surrounding evergreen-covered hills, the well-maintained greens of the golf course, the adjacent landscaped park and parking areas and the reflective waters of the small Lake. The Lake House is the prime Evergreen locale for events ranging from private celebrations (weddings, graduation parties, family reunions, memorial gatherings) to public service meetings (candidate forums, Earth Day exhibits, planning information sessions) and lively fund-raising galas for a wide spectrum of Evergreen's non-profit organizations (Art for the Mountain Community's "Starry Western Night", Friendship Bridge's "Evening in Evergreen", the "Big Chili Cook-Off and Music and Arts Festival" benefiting local fire departments, and many others.) The area adjacent to the Lake House is perhaps the most attractive community park in Evergreen, and is much-used both for individual picnics and for outdoor summer events such as the rousing July Fourth celebrations and the Evergreen Jazz Festival.

The old **Boat and Warming House** is being painstakingly repaired and restored with the aid of funds from the Colorado Historical Society. The structure is owned by Denver, operated by EPRD. To tear down the remains of the old structure and replace it with a new one would have been much cheaper, especially since the interior of the deteriorated building was gutted by fire, but the building has long-ago affectionate memories for generations of skaters and boaters on Evergreen Lake and besides, is listed on the State Register of Historic Buildings. Designed by Denver architect Burnham Hoyt, it originally had an earth-covered log roof. But eventually it leaked, and the logs began rotting away. A grant from the Colorado Historical Society funded a structural assessment in 1999, and the reconstruction work was scheduled in two phases. Phase One, which includes replacement of the roof logs with a modern roofing system that

resembles the original but prevents the accumulation of moisture, is costing $158,000, of which $118,500 is a grant from CHS. It will be completed in 2004. The original sod roof will be restored. Phase Two will cover non-structural log work, utilities and flooring and will be undertaken when funding help can be secured from the Historical Society. A final Phase Three will complete the interior finishing. As of the time of writing, the functions of the building when completed have not been determined. Possibly it may once again be a skate rental and warming house in the winter, a boat rental facility in the summer, and community meeting space in between.

The big new element in EPRD's facilities is in the Bergen Park area. It is a large and growing complex of ball fields, park land and buildings which has been named **Buchanan Park**, after one of Evergreen's pioneer families (pp. 208–13). In its ownership and administration pattern, Buchanan Park is typical of EPRD's facilities. The entire complex is being treated, from a planning standpoint, as one entity. But the 25–acre Bergen Park is a Denver Mountain Park and remains under the control of the City and County of Denver Parks and Recreation Department. On May 3, 1994, voters in the District passed a $700,000 bond issue to buy 17 acres which formed the nucleus of Buchanan Park, and also to help preserve Noble Meadow as open space (see later under M.A.L.T. and Jeffco Open Space). The ponds, which add such a delightful dimension to the complex, were purchased by the District from the same bond issue funds. As privately-owned lands in the area became available, the District made additional purchases, and plans to go on doing so until it can hopefully own, or control by cooperative agreements, all the land between County Road 65 and the ball fields and ponds, and between Bergen Parkway and Highway 74.

The acquisition of the so-called **Lutheran Land** involved many delays and protracted negotiations. This 11 acres, lying between Bergen Park and Bergen Parkway, was acquired by the Lutheran Medical Center Community Foundation with the intention of placing medical facilities on it. This never happened, and the community became aware in the mid-nineties that a developer had the land under contract. As has happened a number of times in Evergreen when a cherished piece of vacant land was slated for development, a community committee materialized and put a great deal of energy and time into having the land acquired for public use. **ELCC** (the Evergreen Land

EPRD Board 2004; Mike Jacoby, Dan Lincoln, Linda Dahl, Peter Eggers, Peter Jacobsen. Photo courtesy of EPRD.

Community Coalition) was formed in August, 1999, and incorporated as a 501(c) 3 non-profit charitable organization, with the primary objective of securing the 11–acre parcel as part of a 40 to 60 acre preserve including park, recreation and open space areas, along Evergreen Parkway. The ELCC sponsored occasions for citizen input on the best uses for the integrated lands, including the Denver Mountain Park land, and came up with a plan to present to the Board of the Recreation District. But when crunch time came in May of 2000 and the Board was ready to go for a bond issue to finance the proposed new recreation center for Buchanan Park, as well as money to acquire more of the individual homes adjacent to the land owned by the District, prospects for acquiring the Lutheran land were still uncertain. The District went ahead with the $6.7 million bond issue, passed on May 2, 2000, with no funds in it for the Lutheran land. With the invaluable aid of the **Trust for Public Lands**, a national organization that facilitates the acquisition of lands for public use, often by supplying funding that bridges the time period between a sale to a public agency and the actual availability of public money, the problem was solved. After a second bond issue of $3,500,000 was approved by the voters on November 7, 2000, the sale to the Recreation District was finally concluded.

In 2003, the District opened the handsome new **Buchanan Recreation Center**, designed by the Denver firm of Barker Rinker Seacat. Original plans had to be scaled down to bring the total cost within the District's budget. The Center has an attractive leisure pool, with many facilities for young children, two lap lanes, and a vortex for walking against the current. The 41–foot climbing pinnacle, housed in the entrance rotunda, is a dramatic

introduction to the facility. A weight room, with a variety of exercise machines, a multipurpose room, that can be divided into two sections, provides for classes for pilates, yoga, Tai Chi and many other uses. There is also a party room adjacent to the pool, a nursery, and what was to have been an amenity for seniors has turned into a "multi-generational room." Inevitably, there has been criticism about what is not yet provided — a gymnasium, indoor ball-playing space, an ice rink, a pool for serious lap swimmers and swim teams, to supplement the overcrowded facilities at the older Evergreen Recreation Center behind the high school. Exploration of how to provide these facilities, as well as extensive upgrading of the Evergreen Recreation Center, are items included in the Recreation District's Plan for 2004–9, which was adopted by the Board on April 20, 2004.

In a brief section of this Plan devoted to the history of the District, there is the following statement, "From the beginning, the aims of the District have included environmental protection, scenic conservation, and intergovernmental cooperation. The district maintains a wide network of relationships with organizations whose recreational resources contribute to the quality of life of District residents. Through purchase and cooperative agreements, the District has acquired an array of recreational assets, including parks, playing fields, and facilities that benefit the entire community." Every Evergreen resident familiar with the wonderful patchwork of open space ownerships here — Denver Mountain Parks, State of Colorado, Federal Government, Jefferson County Open Space, Jefferson County R1 School District — and with the variety of private organizations providing recreational opportunities for children

and adults, realizes that the ability of the Recreation District to work cooperatively with public and private agencies is essential to secure the best possible array of recreational resources and programs for the Evergreen community.

One new element in the Buchanan Park complex is the **Evergreen Arts Center**, opened in the Spring of 2004 and located just behind the new Recreation Center. This lively new center for the visual arts is covered later in the arts section.

The diversity of recreational interests in the Evergreen area poses a challenge to the District. The difficulty of obtaining enough playing fields, especially **soccer fields**, is a perennial one and apparently influenced the outcome of the May, 2004 elections. Six candidates, all well-qualified, ran for two Board positions to replace long-time, term-limited members Peter Eggers and Dan Lincoln who had both contributed so much to the healthy development of the District. The *Canyon Courier*, commenting on the victory of Jeff Knetsch and Jeff Wormer, noted, "The wins made a statement about the importance of athletic fields to Evergreen voters, as both men were viewed as very pro-sports and interested in finding ways to acquire or have access to more playing fields." The two candidates seemed to feel that sharing fields with the School District was not working so well, and that more fields under the direct ownership of the district would guarantee better practice and game schedules for groups like the Stingers, which annually enrolls some 1300 players in its different teams.

Evergreen "**horse people**" have also felt strongly about the lack of facilities, other than trails to ride on. A promising collaboration with the Evergreen Rodeo Association, whereby the District might acquire the right to open up the arena for horse training and exercise, and also develop the adjacent Association-owned acreage for one small playing field and a small practice field, has run into some legal difficulties. But meeting the needs of Evergreen's sizable equestrian community remains one of the District's goals.

"Doggie" interests have fared somewhat better. Like many other parks departments, EPRD has become sensitized to the needs of dog owners for some open spaces where dogs can — legally — run off leash. One off-leash park opened in part of Jefferson County Open Space's Elk Meadow Park, on the west side of Stage Coach

Buchanan Recreation Center.

Boulevard. The District's 5–year plan anticipates the addition of more such parks, possibly on what are known as "SB 35" lands, areas donated by developers in accordance with legal requirements of Senate Bill 35.

Another "specialty park" that has gained increasing popularity around the country is the **skateboard park**. One of these has appeared in the District, on a site behind the Evergreen Recreation Center. This is well-used but there have been some complaints from parents (incidents of noise, rudeness, smoking, drinking, foul language). It has not proved feasible for the District to close the park or to monitor it constantly. The best they have been able to do so far is to post the times when it will be monitored by District personnel so that parents who are concerned can choose to have their kids there at those times.

Over 9500 acres of park lands lie within the boundaries of the District, which is one of the largest in the state — covering 50,000 acres, or 78 square miles. Aside from the 32.6 acres of Buchanan Park, only a few small parks are actually owned by the District. The vast majority of public park lands are owned by other governmental entities: the U. S. Government (1,040 acres of the Arapahoe National Forest are in the District), the State of Colorado (790 acres of the State Wildlife Area), Denver Mountain Parks (some 4,785 acres) and Jefferson County Open Space (3,212 acres in the EPRD.)

The District operates six of what it classifies as **community parks**: a few acres of land improved with some or all of the following amenities: parking, playground and picnic equipment, ball fields, bicycle paths, and where feasible, grass. They are: Buchanan Park, Indian Hills, Kittredge, Marshdale, at the Evergreen Lake House and the Evergreen Recreation Center. In the District's 5–year Plan, the most extensive development is scheduled for the Buchanan Park Area where portions of the Buchanan Park Master Plan, developed by ELCC and adopted by the Board of the EPRD, will be implemented. These will include locating mowed pathways over the 11 "Lutheran" acres, with benches and sculpture along the paths, constructing a small open air amphitheater, defining a site for a community center building for cultural and general community activities, providing infrastructure such as restrooms, lighting, parking, and constructing a system of paved and unpaved trails over the entire area, by agreement with Denver Mountain Parks for its part of the overall property.

Goodbye to part of old Main Street!

The District also hopes to develop additional community parks in the vicinity of Bergen Valley, the landfill transfer facility near Bell and Cub Creek Parks, and **El Pinal**. The El Pinal possibility has been the subject of much lobbying by El Pinal residents, both of the District Board and at meetings to update the Evergreen Area Community Plan. They were pretty unanimous in wanting to see the area remain as open space. 11 acres lying along Highway 74, between El Pinal Drive and Stagecoach Boulevard, was offered by its owners in 2003 to the District — or to Jefferson County Open Space — for $1.5 million. JCOS, having just spent $4.25 million on the Blair Ranch and preparing to bid on the State land Board's 440 acres on Evergreen Mountain, was not interested in the acquisition. As of this writing, the Rec Board was inclined to include purchase of the El Pinal property in a proposed bond election, perhaps in 2005.

Trails. How the meaning of "trail" has changed! Once routes like the Santa Fe Trail and the Oregon Trail were the major transportation highways in the west. Now "trail" denotes recreation routes, free from motorized traffic, catering especially for hikers, bikers and horseback riders. There is a growing network of trails throughout the Evergreen area. Though most of these so far are the responsibility of Jefferson County Open Space, the EPRD has an important role in suggesting new trail locations and taking on some maintenance responsibilities. In 2004, the latter included managing the Evergreen Lake Trail, Dedisse Park Trail and the 73/4 underpass. **Unmet trail needs** that the District sees within its boundaries, as described in the

2004–9 Plan, include: providing public access to all the usable public lands, and providing linkages between public parks where these do not now exist; remedying as far as possible the deficiencies of past development in the Evergreen area, which has not included establishment of local urban trails within and between residential areas and business centers, with the result that, with few exceptions, "foot, bicycle, and equestrian traffic must share the roadways with automobiles. More trails linking the various regional and community parks, residential and business centers, and other public lands would spread the impact of growing numbers of trail users, provide for a greater variety of trail types, and offer alternatives for resolving trail user conflicts."

Personnel. The EPRD has been fortunate in having the continuing services of Dick Wulf, who was the first director and the first full-time employee, hired when the Evergreen Recreation Center was still under construction. Wulf celebrated 25 years with the District in 1997, and was still enjoying his expanding job when we went to him for information in 2004. He said he will miss the reliable help of Jay Goldie, the District's first Deputy Director, hired six months after the Lake House opened in 1993. Goldie resigned in 2004 to take a job as the first administrator of the City of Cherry Hills Parks and Trails. He was replaced as director of Buchanan Park Recreation Center by Pat Callahan. The District has approximately 60 full-time employees, including four Supervisors — Facility, Robbie Furler; Aquatics, Becky Browne; Recreation, Sharon Martin; and Gymnastics, Nancy Whisman. Depending on the season, there are around 290 part-timers. Policy decisions

287

Pedestrian Walkway at new 73/74 intersection. Photo courtesy of Jefferson County Highways and Transportation Department.

about the operation and development of the EPRD are made by an elected 5–person Board of Directors. Members are elected for four years, and are limited to three consecutive terms. As of May, 2004, the Board consists of Peter Jacobson, President, Michael Jacoby, Linda Dahl, Jeff Knetsch, Geoffrey Wormer.

Programs. An idea of the astonishing range of activities offered by the EPRD can be gleaned by looking at the seasonal "Activities Guide" distributed free by the District. Programs are developed and managed in four categories: recreation, athletics, gymnastics and aquatics. In addition to programs offered directly by the District, space and assistance are provided to organizations such as the Evergreen Swim Team, Evergreen Arts Council, Jazzercize and a number of lively athletic associations, which provide their own programs and registration arrangements. Day care is available for preschool children whose parents are using District facilities, as well as a Before and After School recreation program during the school year for children 5 to 13 years old. So whether you are looking for an opportunity to ice skate, paint or pot, learn Tae kwon do or ballet dancing, hike or back pack or go cross-county skiing, join a class in sailing or archery or yoga, look first to the Rec District!

TRANSPORTATION.
Nothing in the past eleven years occupied so much time, caused so much discussion, received so much community input, or took so long to execute as the **new 73/74 intersection**. Alternative solutions to the bottleneck problems of this crossroads had been debated at least since the early 1970's. Though the congestion at the intersection during rush hours had reached a point where plainly something had to be done, there were those who believed that, because all the traffic would feed into three two-lane highways, no real improvement was possible. However, after three years of meetings with the Evergreen Task Force appointed by the County Commissioners, the County Highway and Transportation Department finally had a plan. It involved acquiring and tearing down the venerable Davidson and Shephard buildings, as well as part of the Bear Creek Mall, and providing an underpass planned to become part of the Bergen Park to Main Street trail. Construction started on this major project on July 30, 2001 and was completed June 21, 2003. To the surprise of many of us, the new traffic pattern is working surprisingly well, as drivers get used to the continuous traffic lane coming down the hill from 74 to 73, and develop the courtesy needed to merge two lanes of traffic rather swiftly into one.

Undaunted by all the skepticism attending this project, and concerned about the rapidly increasing traffic and high accident rate on Highway 73, the Jefferson County Highways and Transportation Department in 2003 started developing plans, and soliciting public input, on improving safety along this busy road. Wider shoulders and left turn lanes for major intersections along the entire stretch of the road were popular suggestions at the first public meeting. Putting a roundabout near the Conifer Safeway generated a lot of interest. Creating more lanes on the Buffalo Park Road to downtown segment drew more mixed reviews. The second meeting seemed to draw out the "aginners," who believed people should accept a slower pace in a small town in the mountains and wrote comments like, "Please go and improve something else." Greg Dobbs greeted the proposals with triple "Ohmigods" and insinuated that Jeffco's road engineers were simply "fishing for a new project." There were also letters of support for the proposals with such sentiments as "This small, out-of-date connector with no shoulders, few guard rails, no turn lanes and ever increasing volumes of traffic, is totally inadequate." As of this writing, widening of shoulders and creation of turn lanes was to start in the fall of 2004 with the Shadow Mountain/Barkley Road segment, and to be continued in sections over several years. No decisions about the Buffalo Park Road to downtown segment, or the Conifer Safeway area, had yet been made.

In 1988, something new in Jefferson County appeared in Bergen Park — a traffic roundabout. Though at first it was criticized as being too small for trucks and school buses, people are getting used to it, and it seems to achieve the Highway Department's goals to "improve safety, provide traffic calming, ease the congestion at this intersection. Art for the Mountain Community has placed a pleasant abstract sculpture in the middle of the central circle and the Garden Club has taken over the planting and maintenance of what was formerly a rather unsightly weed patch.

No unfavorable comments were elicited from the proposal by Jefferson County Road and Bridge to improve its **Fleet Maintenance Facility on Lewis Ridge** Road so that it becomes "a more pleasant neighbor." The 5–acre site once sat in mostly vacant surroundings but is now in the middle of a residential neighborhood. Replacement of the 40–year old shop building will locate the facility as far away from homes as possible, and vehicles will park near electric pedestals which allow operators to warm up equipment without turning over the engine, so as to decrease noise and exhaust fumes. The salt and sand storage will be protected so that it does not "sandblast neighboring houses", in the words of Wiley Timbrook, Director of the Road and Bridge Department. These measures will go far to meet complaints of neighboring homes.

Mass Transit. To use this term in connection with Evergreen, with its huge inventory of personal cars, vans and trucks, and the small presence of buses, may seem laughable. Nevertheless, some progress has been made since 1993. There are now three RTD Park 'N Rides (p. 251), all well-designed, well landscaped and well-maintained, at Aspen Park in Conifer, on the frontage road across from Christ the King Church in Evergreen and in Bergen Park at Highway 74 and County Road 65. Express bus service to Denver tends to be heavy in the morning and evening for working commuters, and light the rest of the day, but this is no doubt governed largely by demand. The **Evergreen Call 'n Ride** is a welcome innovation that started service in March 2002 with a lot of lobbying and negotiation by the Seniors' Resource Center and the Curmudgeons group. A clearly defined Evergreen area is served by small green buses, which respond to calls, preferably at least one hour in advance. They make door to door pick-ups and deliveries anywhere within the service area, and service is available to everyone, though understandably most of the riders are those who cannot drive. Fares started in 2002 at $1.10 and 55 cents for elderly, disabled and students, and were raised to $1.25 and 60 cents in 2004. Buses are provided by RTD, which subsidizes 75% of the cost, but the service is actually operated under

contract by the Seniors Resource Center. All that RTD requires is that a certain level of ridership be maintained and so far that has not been a problem. A major boost to the mass transit alternatives available in the Denver metro area will be generated if the **FasTracks** $4.7 billion plan, which RTD is putting before the voters in November 2004, passes. The plan calls for an expansion of mass transit with 137 miles of additional light-rail and commuter-rail lines in six corridors, including one called the west corridor line which would connect the Jefferson County Government Center in Golden with downtown Denver. Construction would be partly financed by a .4 percent sales tax. The rationale for mass transit was put succinctly by Lakewood Mayor Steve Burkholder at meeting at the Jeffco County Government Center, "transportation funding cannot all be earmarked for highways...we can't pave our way out of congestion."
Debate is ongoing, as we write this, about whether or not we can pave our way out of the scarcely believable congestion that has developed on **I–70**. The morning and evening commute from the Evergreen area is 'slow and go' too much of the time. And who would have believed that by 2002, this relatively new, six-lane, scenic interstate would see bumper-to-bumper traffic from Denver to the mountain resorts in winter as well as summer? A 2003 CDOT study predicted that by 2025, without major improvements, a trip on I–70 from C–470 to Silverthorne would average three and a half hours. Many ideas have surfaced to solve this problem. A high-speed monorail. More traffic lanes. Rail lines. Guided bus lanes. Some combination of these. Since 2002 CDOT has been working with the

Federal Highway Administration on an environmental impact statement for improvements on the whole 150 miles of I–70 from C–470 to Glenwood Springs, and discussing transportation alternatives. **CARE (Canyon Area Residents for the Environment)**, the Mount Vernon Canyon organization, has a clear position against the proposal to expand I–70 from 6 to 8 lanes from Morrison Road to El Rancho, on the grounds of increased noise and air pollution from nitrous oxide, hydrocarbons, benzene and other toxic emissions. According to Carole Lomond's *city and mountain Views*, CARE prefers "the high efficiency and low environmental impact of fixed guideway transit for the I–70 corridor from DIA to Glenwood Canyon." Jefferson County Commissioners have made it clear that they can see no solution to the problem without substantial help from the federal government. County and state funds are inadequate for the job.

RESORTS (p. 86–97 & 252)
Yes, there is now a hotel in the Evergreen area! It does not have a ballroom or conference facilities or a fancy restaurant open to the public. But it does have comfortable suites, an indoor pool, fitness room, spa, sauna, a sun deck with outdoor hot tubs and wonderful views over the Continental Divide. It is the **Quality Suites at Evergreen**, next door to El Rancho Restaurant...Gail Riley and Tom Statzell continually improve their lovely and historic **Highland Haven Creekside Inn**, tucked away on Bear Creek a short walk away from Main Street. They celebrated their 25th year of ownership in 2004, and have won many awards for their distinctive establishment, including being cited as a Best Bed and Breakfast in North America by the national magazine *Mt. Living* and "Best Place to Pop the Question" by Denver's *5280*...The sturdy 1930's stone house and adjacent buildings on Highway 73 on the banks of Little Cub Creek, which was for a while the Evergreen location of Children's World preschool, has been completely restored and updated, and is now the **Abundant Way Chalet**...**Bauer's Spruce Island Chalets**, 8 units, varying in size from 1–4 bedrooms, are housed in five buildings "on 20 peaceful acres of meadows and mountains" on Brook Forest Road...Davidson's Lodge on Bear Creek, a mile from Main Street, has become **Bear Creek Cabins**. Each cabin has full kitchen facilities and fireplace...The former Marshdale Lodge (p. 96 & 252) already a Bed and Breakfast in 1993, continues now as the Bears Inn Bed and Breakfast, with 11 guest rooms...**Mountain View Bed and**

Call-n-Ride Bus and some of the Curmudgeons: Sterling Nelson, Rocky Graziano, Bill Mounsey, Carl Keiser, Gene Sternberg.

289

Dos Chappell Nature Center.

Breakfast, located in Indian Hills, was built in the 1920's as a writer's retreat. It offers a choice of accommodations: 2 rooms, a suite and a cottage, and, in addition to a gourmet breakfast, English tea in the afternoon...**Brook Forest Inn** (p. 96–7) has been through a number of ownerships and uses since 1992, none of which lasted very long. In 2003, new owners opened Isabella's Restaurant at the old Inn, and in May of 2004, announced that the rooms at the Inn had been refurbished and were opening once more to visitors. "16 rooms and suites ranging from basic to luxurious" are offered for overnight travelers...**The Evergreen Conference Center**, now owned and operated by The Attachment Center at Evergreen, Inc., has a six bedroom guest house that sleeps twelve. Built in 1923 and on The National Register of Historic Places, its parlor can be rented as an informal meeting site for up to twelve people.

OPEN SPACE (p. 100–119, 252–55) One of the glories of life in Evergreen is the access to an incredible variety of open space. There have been some significant additions, some changes in personnel and significant increases in the number of trails, so here we "update the update" of 1993.

Mount Evans Wilderness Area is described by photographer Bob Smith in an article in *Evergreen Living Magazine* as the "jewel in our own back yard." Sylvia Brockner, in her Canyon Courier article of July 14, 2004, says, "I have had a love affair with Mount Evans

ever since I first laid eyes on him in 1957...There are, of course, many other mountains in Colorado, but Mr. Evans is the patriarch, the grand old gentleman in a white hat. We are so fortunate to have this magnificent mountain in our backyard and that there is a highway which runs nearly to the summit." The easy access to this wilderness area, via Highway 103 and the Mount Evans Road from Echo Lake (still the highest paved automobile road in North America), is indeed a gift. Named a Colorado State Scenic and Historic Byway in 1991, the road was designated also as a National Forest Scenic Byway in 1993. New since 1993 i s the million dollar Dos Chappell Nature Center on Mount Goliath, staffed by a U. S. Forest Ranger from June to September. The Walter Pesman Trail (p. 118) had deteriorated with over-use and lack of maintenance so the Garden Club of Denver, the Denver Botanic Gardens, the Forest Service and 230 volunteers from Volunteers for Outdoor Colorado cooperated in the effort to rehabilitate the site. The trail was redesigned, incorporating a 400–foot loop to accommodate wheel chairs and walkers, and a renowned Czech rock garden designer was commissioned to designed the highest man-made rock garden in the world. The Nature Center and trails have ample interpretive markers and brochures available, besides the knowledge of Rangers and volunteer docents, to help visitors distinguish the 120 species of wildflowers and the adaptive genius of 2000–year-old bristlecone pine, as they ascend from the 11,500 ft. subalpine terrain through the krumholtz to the tundra at

over12,000 ft. The U. S. Forest Service's major concern in the Evergreen area since the disastrous wildfire year of 2002 has been the careful planning of fuel reduction operations on 500 to 1000 acres of forest lands adjacent to urban areas. Colorado's thinning plans are solely aimed at reducing fuel loads by thinning trees and cleaning up scrub, and do not have to generate profits for lumber companies doing the work. Public input has been solicited. Thinning in the predominantly lodge pole forest will be done by a mix of patch cuts and clear cuts since stands of lodge pole pine do not respond well to actual thinning. Cuts can be visually jarring, and the services of a landscape architect will be used to mitigate the effects by "feathering" the cuts round the edges. Research is being done, especially in the west, to find economic uses for the thinned material (as biomass for heating purposes, as particle board, animal bedding, etc.) Interior Secretary Gail Norton signed an agreement in July, 2004 to begin a feasibility study looking into creating a biomass energy demonstration facility in Jefferson County which would use forest debris to create electricity. In the meantime, thinned material from the Arapaho Forest areas adjacent to inhabited areas near Evergreen will be either hauled out or burned in piles on site.

Mountain Area land Trust (MALT). One of the most active and effective organizations in our community, MALT has accomplished a great deal of what it set out to do at its founding in 1993 (p. 252–3). The first major success was its role in the acquisition and conveyance of the 402–acre Noble Meadow to the county and Evergreen Park and Recreation District. For the last 7 years, MALT, which celebrated its tenth birthday in 2003, has worked unceasingly toward the incremental purchase of the 6,000 acre **Beaver Brook Watershed** by the U. S. Forest Service from the City of Golden. This important land is the missing link in creating a 17–mile long corridor of preserved land for wildlife habitat from the Mt. Evans Wildlife Area to Noble and Elk Meadows. The small reservoir on the property supplies water for 500 Jefferson County families and Clear Creek High School. The Watershed is also highly valued as a hiking area and, if added to the Arapahoe National Forest as planned, can potentially provide recreation for millions of Front Range residents. The City of Golden needed the money from selling the land to purchase additional water rights. An installment purchase deal was worked out between Golden, MALT and the U.S. Forest Service under which the

USFS would purchase the land, using money appropriated by Congress, in five phases over five years. But under the proposed federal budget for 2005, the last year under the contract to complete the purchase, only a token payment is proposed. Securing the appropriation has required generating public pressure on the White House and Congress each year, an increasingly difficult task as budget surpluses disappeared and budget cutting for domestic programs became the order of the day. By 2004, about 3,800 acres of the watershed had become part of Arapahoe National Forest, but about 1800 of the most valuable acres remained. If the $7.6 million balance is not appropriated in 2005, the contract would expire and Golden could sell all or part of the remaining land for development. MALT is exploring all possible other options for the purchase and preservation of the land. MALT's fundraisers are imaginative and usually related directly to its mission: "A Night in the Park" celebrating the acquisition of Blair Ranch by JCOS, when participants ate dinner under a huge tent and walked over parts of the new property; a bike swap, started in 2003 and becoming an annual event; holiday sales at local stores and craft fairs of mixes for Beaver Brook Dam Good Brownies, Preservation Pancakes and Save-a-Trail Mix. In its work to secure **conservation easements**, MALT has had many quiet successes. For owners of ranches and large acreages, property and estate tax policies often force the sale or development of land to pay the taxes on it. Conservation easements are an alternative for landowners who wish to keep their land open or in agricultural or ranching use. Such easements can reduce taxes: property taxes, because the development rights have been reduced, estate taxes, because the property's potential use has been limited. The property can still remain in private ownership, be farmed, wildlife habitat can be protected and desirable scenic features preserved. To qualify for such benefits, the conservation easement must be made in perpetuity to a public agency or public charity, and must meet other important criteria. Easements are held in the mountain area by MALT, the American Farmland Trust, Jefferson County, the Clear Creek Conservancy, Colorado Open Lands (p. 71, 250). In July of 2003, Jefferson County Commissioners decided that the County would no longer accept conservation easements because of maintenance and supervision problems and potential litigation, and would try to transfer the five it had accepted to a land trust. In 2003, MALT began to focus more attention on preserving open lands along the 285 corridor. With the help of

a GOCO (Great Outdoors Colorado, which receives money from Colorado lotteries) grant, they sent out informational letters to some 60 owners of 40 acres or more, and discussions are underway with a number of these. In November of 2003, capping almost 6 years of negotiations between the heirs of Margaret Evans Davis and MALT, a conservation easement on 1700 acres of the **Davis Ranch, adjacent to the Evans Ranch**, was donated to MALT. The first steps towards this donation were taken by Peg Hayden (p. 68, 250) before she died in 1999. The Ranch is in a Trust set up by Margaret Evans Davis (p. 64) to run until 5 years after the death of the last of her children, when the Trust will end and the property will pass into the ownership of the 8 grandchildren. All of these have agreed to the terms of the easement. To date, this 1700-acre easement is the largest private conservation effort in the Evergreen area. Most of MALT's activities are undertaken by volunteers, but they do have two part-time paid staff members, an office manager and and executive director. They are fortunate indeed in having the services of Tandy Jones in the former capacity and, until mid 2004, of Ginny Ades in the latter. Mel Andrew is the patient negotiator. There are costs associated with the process of investigating the feasibility of conservation easements and also with effectively monitoring them after they are donated. One of MALT's objectives is building up an endowment fund to assure that it will be able to meet those costs.

Jefferson County Open Space (JCOS) (p. 108–115 & 253–55) Developments in the Evergreen/Conifer area since 1993 are adding greatly to our visual delight, securing treasured vistas we enjoy daily as well as increasing the recreational possibilities for hiking, biking, horseback riding, and preserving habitat for wildlife. In our last update, the fate of **Noble Meadow** was unknown. JCOS had voted against acquisition, on the grounds that they had been spending too much money on mountain area land and needed to concentrate on the flatlands. In effect, JCOS gave out the message that if mountain area citizens were so sold on the vital importance of preserving the meadow as open space, they had better give some tangible proof of their interest. So, organized by MALT, the citizens rose to the occasion and raised some $100,000 towards the property's cost...Acquisition of the 316-acre **Blair Ranch**, which adjoins the Alderfer Three Sisters Park and the Elephant Butte property of Denver Mountain Parks, followed somewhat the same pattern. The Ranch was acquired in

January of 2002 for $4.5 million. But first, money was raised and the acquisition lobbied for vigorously by TENAS (The Evergreen Naturalists Audubon Society), MALT, Upper Bear Creek citizens and groups interested in less building development and more trails. JCOS is the major planner of trails and other amenities in the expanded park, with the cooperation of Denver Mountain Parks on its properties — the previously virtually inaccessible Elephant Butte area, and Dedisse Park, which abuts Alderfer Three Sisters. According to Ken Foelske, Supervisor of Planning for JCOS, construction of trails on the Blair Ranch property was underway in 2004. In the meantime, people do have access to the property as long as they follow Open Space rules of use...Everyone who traveled Highway 73 valued the serene vista of the Schoonhovens' **Flying J Ranch**, and the DeLaCastro land which adjoined it, and hoped that when the owners decided to sell, it could be preserved unspoilt. 360 acres of the Schoonhoven property was acquired in stages between December 1997 and May 2000, with 42 of those acres being a donation from the Schoonhoven family. The 38-acre DeLaCastro acres were bought for $275,000. In 2004, trails were opened on the Flying J property, with log shelters handcrafted by Open Space staff...JCOS acquired the 445 acre **Beaver Ranch** in Conifer between May, 2001 and December 2002 for $1,285,000, as a passive and active community park. Under the conditions of acquisition, a community organization was to manage the facility and pay for operating costs with revenue raised from renting out the two lodges and 8 cabins on the property, fees charged for events, services in-kind, and donations. The Ranch has become a lively hub for many social and arts activities in Conifer, but making ends meet is a struggle. In the fall of 2004, Conifer area residents — who have twice voted down the opportunity to form a Recreation District of their own — will have a chance to vote for inclusion in the Foothills Recreation District, which could help to stabilize the future of Beaver Ranch...A particularly challenging problem was presented by the possibility of preserving intact a large part of the beautiful **Elmgreen** property, visible from I–70 and located partly in Clear Creek and partly in Jefferson Counties. The eventual solution was complex but achieved the objectives of both the family and the preservationists. Linda Williams of the MALT Board wrote that the easiest way to explain the deal was to imagine the land as a square parcel consisting of four quadrants, bisected north to south by the county line. The

291

northeast quadrant was bought by JCOS. The family donated a conservation easement on the northwest quadrant to MALT, and then sold it to Clear Creek County Open Space, which used a grant from GOCO for half the purchase price. The two southern quadrants were not sold, but instead the United States Forest Service purchased a conservation easement on them with funds from its Forest Legacy Program. The family retained ownership of the 67–acre meadow running along the south side of I–70. Mel Andrew, MALT's vice-president for land conservation, represented MALT in structuring this deal, and credit for the overall coordination of public and private entities to accomplish the successful outcome goes to Katie Paris of the **Trust for Public Lands**...The **Clear Creek Open Space Program** came into being in 1999 when voters approved a 1 mill property tax levy which raises approximately $160,000 a year. Augmented with grants and donations, this enabled the county to begin a program of acquiring and thus preserving desirable tracts of land.

A lot of work has been done on **Trails** in our community, following the JCOS's Trails 2000 Plan (p. 254). Of

Conceptual Plan for Bear Creek Trail. Photo courtesy of Jefferson County Open Space.

the three segments planned which will pass through Evergreen, most progress has been made on the one from El Rancho to the Lake. The **Pioneer Trail** from Bergen Park to the Lake was completed in 2004. This trail passes through Elk Meadow Park and is essentially the **People Path** for which the Evergreen Kiwanis raised money and enthusiasm in the 1990's. The Kiwanis built a sturdy and attractive shelter along the trail in Elk Meadow, which was dedicated in a ceremony in the fall of 1999. Whether a Bergen Park to El Rancho segment will be built is under discussion, but in any case it will not be considered until work on the remaining trails is completed. Work on the first segment of the **Bear Creek Trail**, from the Lake to Morrison, was to start in 2004 with the construction of a pedestrian bridge from the top of the dam to the new intersection underpass. But when the huge and unsightly $662,000 structure appeared, public protests erupted. Respectable movers and shakers linked arms in front of what a correspondent in the *Courier* characterized as "one ugly dam girder," to prevent the pouring of any more concrete. Ralph Schell, head of Jefferson County Open Space, admitted in a *Denver Post* interview "we fell short on working with the community." In addition to its obtrusive size and its

marring of the view of the Dam and Lake from the road, protesters objected to its industrial aesthetic (rusting metal) and its potential hazards. Its grade — over 11% with no intermittent flat landings — would make it unsafe for wheel chair visitors, and its surface was likely to be perilous in snow and ice for anyone walking the trail. It is in the nature of bringing the story of a community up to date that some issues are unresolved at the time of "going to press." And the resolution of this one, involving as it does many leaders of the Evergreen community, the County Commissioners, and the normally respected officials of the Jefferson County Open Space, will be worth watching. The next segment, through downtown Evergreen to the Church of the Transfiguration, is in the planning and design phase in 2004. As for the third trail, from the Lake to Conifer, negotiations for rights of way are ongoing but there are many hurdles still to overcome, and the plans will need to be synchronized with the Transportation Department's decisions about widening of Highway 73.

Hiwan Homestead Museum (p. 110–1, 253–4) and the **Jefferson County Historical Society** (JCHS) (p. 254). The JCHS celebrated its 30th birthday in the spring of 2003. Thirty

years earlier at the urging of Mary Helen Crain, the society was formed. 27 members, interested in exploring and preserving local history, began meeting regularly. It was already established as a 501 (c) 3 charitable organization under the chairmanship of Connie Fahnestock when the buildings that now comprise the Hiwan Homestead Museum came up for sale. By a fortunate synchronicity, this was the time when the measure to establish and fund Jefferson County Open Space was passed. The buildings were purchased by Open Space in September 1974. The county still owns and maintains the buildings and pays the Museum staff, which consists of: Administrator, Curator, Educational Coordinator, Museum Programs Coordinator, and Custodian. In addition, there are two part-time people, an administrative assistant and an interior custodian. Since 1994, the Administrator has been John Steinle who succeeded Jennifer Karber in that position. Originally, the Historical Society took on the responsibility for programming and acquisition of collections, but over the years these have become shared responsibilities. The Society still owns most of the acquisitions, funds the exhibits and educational programs, and supplies most of the volunteers necessary to the museum's operation. It also owns Heritage Grove (p.111, 182), which is one of Evergreen's prime venues for outdoor celebrations, arts and craft shows and popular music concerts. One of our favorite events, the Mountain Rendezvous (p. 269), came to an end, mainly we gather because the pool of volunteers willing and able to take on the huge commitment of organizing and running it ran dry. Thanks especially to the ongoing efforts of Joanne Dunn, the small historic Medlen School was restored, acquired by JCHS, and is used as a demonstration to school children of what schooling was like in an earlier age. The Hiwan Museum building itself received a lot of attention in recent years: logs were repainted and rotten ones repaired, the heating, ventilating and air conditioning system was completely replaced, the old footbridge between the Museum and Eric's house was rebuilt. An exhilarating example of "what goes around comes around" is the return to the Hiwan Homestead of some 39 pieces of Indian pottery that were part of the collection donated to the Denver Art Museum by the Douglas family (p. 51–3 & 55). The D.A.M was de-accessioning them, and through the efforts of Angela Rayne, Hiwan's curator, the JCHS was able to buy them. They raised most of the money for this through an imaginative "Adopt-A-Pot" campaign.

Douglas Pottery Adoption Certificate

Congratulations! As an adoptive guardian you now have the responsibility and right of regular visitation of your pottery at the Hiwan Homestead Museum in Evergreen, Colorado. Your generous contribution ensures the continuation of collection additions efforts by the Jefferson County Historical Society.

"Adopt-A-Pot" Certificate, Hiwan Homestead Museum.

Evergreen, do we want to keep this gift? Evergreen's second museum, the **Humphrey Museum**, opened its doors to tours by appointment in 1997. The bequest of Hazel Humphrey, the property consists of the ranch house and other buildings, gardens, and 43 acres of the original 350–acre ranch. 78–year-old Hazel Humphrey (p.164) died in 1995, bequeathing the home in which she had lived since she was two to Evergreen as the Humphrey Museum. Hazel was a beloved figure in many Evergreen organizations, including the D.A.R., Eastern Star and the Jefferson County Historical Society. She often said that her father, who worked for the Rocky Mountain News, was the original commuter. The house was filled with treasures and trinkets collected from travels all over the world by Hazel, her parents and grandmother. It is a monumental task to keep a private museum going without a large, steady source on income. Although Hazel Humphrey left a Trust Fund which she thought would be adequate to fund museum operations, board members found that the buildings were in need of a lot of expensive maintenance, from new roofs to new septic tank and leaching field to new plumbing pipes and electrical wiring. Grants from sources like the SCFD and the Colorado Historical Society required matching funds, and with only one paid employee, the ability to put on fund-raising events was limited. Much of the trust fund has had to be used to make the property safe for public use. Without a significant infusion of energy and money, the future of the Museum is in doubt. The Museum Director, Peggy Shaw, is the third person to hold that office, having served on the board for almost 5 years before being appointed. She is contemplating nominating the Museum for placement on the national list of Endangered Historic Places, which would be accomplished through Colorado Preservation Inc., so as to bring attention to the seriousness of the situation. If the Museum cannot make it, the property, according to Humphrey's will, goes to the National Humane Society, which would probably liquidate the building's contents and sell the property to the highest bidder.

The Denver Mountain Parks
(p. 100–108 & 253) punctuate our landscape in Evergreen and their fate is integral to our well-being. A *Denver Post* article on March 22, 2002, announced that Denver parks, including the 14,000 acres of mountain parks, needed $100 million in funds to catch up with delayed maintenance projects. Because of the slow economy and necessity for budget cuts, park officials expected that it would be a number of years before a bond issue could be put to the voters to take care of all the problems. Jefferson County Open Space

293

has worked closely with Denver to create trails in parks, such as Elk Meadow and Bergen Peak, where the two have adjoining properties. Since the late 1980's, Denver Mountain Parks has been carrying out a welcome program of rehabilitating the park shelters and restoring their historic character. Many were built between 1915 and 1919, and designed by Denver architect Jacques Benedict. Denver did make a $16 million investment in remodeling and updating Red Rocks Theater. Denver's leasing activities affect Evergreen, especially in two locations: the Golf Course and Keys on the Green, and Chief Hosa Lodge and Campground. Many in our community were unhappy with the outcome of a conflict over the Key's on the Green lease. It was necessary for Denver to get a new lessee for the Golf Course who claimed that the Golf Course lease included the right to operate the restaurant. When he won the legal battle over this, he ousted long-time restaurateur Dave Rodriguez, who was widely known and respected in the Evergreen community. At Chief

Hosa, a similar situation arose when the lease for this popular lodge and camp ground came up for bidding. A new lessee, David Peri, was chosen in January, 2000 over the incumbents, Dave Christie and his wife. Homeowners surrounding the site felt that the Christies had worked hard to improve the Lodge and campground and to be good neighbors. However, Peri found the premises quite run down and the camp ground little-used, and has invested a quarter of a million dollars into the Lodge and the utilities for the campground. Use of the Lodge for weddings and other celebrations is up, and the campgrounds are kept clean and attractive with the work of 10 "work campers" living on site in the RV park. The designations of the Lariat Loop and the Bear Creek Canyon Drive as Scenic and Historic Byways is a source of pride to Denver and its mountain parks administrators, and is in keeping with their present policy of emphasizing and preserving the historic values of these properties.

MOUNTAIN SCHOOLING
(p. 120–34 & 255–9)

Of Bond Issues, Mill Levy Raises and Rising Enrollments. Jefferson County R-1 School District, when we left its story in 1993, was dealing with increased numbers of students every year and the stimulating task of building new facilities and updating older ones with the proceeds of a $325 million bond issue which finally passed in 1992. From this bond issue, the Mountain area got the new Conifer High School, the new Bergen Meadow Elementary School, some major improvements and additions to Evergreen High School, and modest improvements in other schools. A second bond issue for $265 million passed in 1997, from which the mountain area received more major improvements to Evergreen High School and a complete "makeover," with additions, to Wilmot School. During this period, the Evergreen schools, along with the rest of the District, changed the distribution of grade levels: Junior High Schools, serving 7th, 8th, and 9th grades, disappeared. Middle Schools appeared, taking in sixth, seventh and eighth grades. High Schools, with ninth through twelfth grades, became four-year schools. Passing bond issues and mill levy increases for operating expenses has never easy task in Jefferson County. But a mill levy increase for operating was finally passed in 1999, albeit a convoluted one with annual increases tied to results in the CSAP (Colorado Student Assessment Program) tests. These were a new element on the state educational scene in the 90's, Colorado's version of the passion for standardized testing sweeping the nation.

Superintendents, School Boards, Columbine, and Public Trust. Superintendent Lew Finch (p. 256) was succeeded by Wayne Carle, whose relatively peaceful tenure ended with his retirement. Jane Hammond, Jeffco's first woman Superintendent, took over after a nationwide search. The Columbine shootings, which profoundly shook the entire school system, took place on her watch. Enough has been written and analyzed about this event for there to be any need for us to add our opinions, except to say that the only substantive changes seem to have been in increased school security measures and some pro forma anti-bullying policies. No fundamental enquiry has been undertaken into the nature of the culture in our huge high schools, or the root causes of the extreme alienation of some students. Hammond served until she left to take a position in California in the summer of 2002. At that time, the

Keys on the Green Restaurant, with sculpture "Posse" by George Manus.

Board decided to forego another nationwide search and quickly appointed Deputy Superintendent Cindy Stevenson to the position. Stevenson is described as the District's first "homegrown" leader, having risen through the ranks of the system and being herself a K–12 graduate of Jeffco schools. She inherited huge financial problems and widespread public ambivalence about the goals and operations of District leadership. She has stated that her long-term goal is that 100% of Jeffco students graduate from high school, knowing that this means constant attention to every student's progress from kindergarten on. During these years, the School Board went through some controversial episodes. The five-person School Board's members are term-limited, serving a maximum of three continuous 4–year terms. Each of them represents a specific area in the school district, but all voters vote on each vacancy. Elections take place every two years and participation is usually quite low, although the introduction of all-mail balloting has apparently increased the percentage voting. Normally, this system assures continuity of board experience, but a peculiar constellation of circumstances resulted in new board member Jane Barnes, who was only elected in November 2003, being elected President on March 10, 2004 because of the prospect of four out of five seats being up for election in November of 2005. This unusual situation arose because one incumbent, Karen Litz, was reelected in 2003, but suffered two brain aneurysms and a stroke and could not take up her seat. Next, Evergreen's representative and Board President Jon DeStefano, who had served altogether 13 years, resigned in February of 2004 because he was moving out of the district. The Board appointed Hereford Percy and Steve Dixon, neither from the mountain area. There was some frustration and disappointment in Evergreen from those who believe the area has specific characteristics and conditions that warrant representation on the Board.

Vanishing Students, Budget Cuts and More Cuts. Starting in 2000 overall student enrollment stopped growing, and then began to fall. While still the largest district in the state, it was the only metro area school district where this was happening. Why? A number of factors were cited. The economic recession, which meant that young families were leaving the area for jobs elsewhere. Increased numbers of retired people moving in, with demographic studies showing that Jefferson County's median population age was almost 37, compared to 33.1 in Denver and 33.7 in

New Entrance, Evergreen High School.

Douglas County. Housing values in the county had increased rapidly, and there was anecdotal evidence that young families were preferring to locate in Douglas County which had good schools and better buys in newer housing. Population projections by Colorado's Department of Local Affairs showed that, while the county's total population was expected to continue rising, its school-age population would continue to decline until 2010, when the trend was expected to reverse. The downward trend could not have come at a worse time. State funding is based on the number of students enrolled, so declining enrollment automatically meant less money. The District, which had met the performance goals in the first two years of the 1999 mill levy raise, failed to do so in the third year and so forfeited the $9.2 million that success would have brought in. The budget situation became more and more stringent from 2001 on. Committees were set up by the Board, representing teachers, parents and staff, to seek out every possible area where cuts could be made, and the budget was cut by millions in each school year from 2001/2002 on.

2003: How to Handle the Continuing Budget Crunch? The School administration and the Board, as well as the committees working wearily on budget cuts, were convinced that the District needed more money if its educational quality was not to suffer.

But a poll commissioned by the Board in 2003 showed that voters were clearly not yet sold on the need for an increase either in operating funds to offset decreasing revenues or in bond money for upgrading aging schools. The predominance of older, conservative voters with no children in school (75%) was a major hurdle, the pollsters said, and advised waiting until 2004 when the presidential election would bring more younger voters to the polls. So the Board settled for raising a variety of school fees (student parking, athletic fees, game admissions, etc.), yet more budget cuts, and a major commitment to communicate to the public by the Fall of 2004 just why the District needed more money, both for a capital bond issue and a mill levy increase for operational expenses, and how it would be spent. They subsequently spelled out for each school in the District how much money would be spent and for what. While overall enrollment is declining, the school population in the northern end of the county is still increasing. Two new grade schools are needed there. For the mountain area the largest expenditure would be at Evergreen Middle School, $10.5 million for an addition and renovations to bring it up to 700–student capacity. $2.2 million would go to Evergreen High School for a new gym floor, roofing, and mechanical systems upgrading. West Jeff Middle School would be in line for $1.3 million for electrical, plumbing and roof improvements. Grade schools, with the exception of Parmalee, Wilmot and West Jeff, would get small investments in mechanical systems and security improvements.

2004: Just what do the public need to know in order to pass both a mill levy increase and a capital funds bond issue? First, they need a context: Colorado as a state is doing a fairly miserable job of its commitment to adequately fund public education. In the ranking of state levels of support, Colorado comes in near the bottom. This puts a major burden on local tax payers. Second, they need to be aware that, in spite of many years of financial belt tightening, the R–1 School District is doing a pretty good job, according to the Colorado Schools Accountability Reports (all the mountain area schools received one of the two top grades — High or Excellent). Then they need a sense of just how large Jefferson County R–1 District is, and how varied are its offerings. There are 93 regular elementary schools, 19 middle schools and 17 high schools. In addition to these, the District offers many choices to students with different needs and interests through 12 charter schools and 7 what are called option schools.
Option schools include the paired original alternative schools: the **Jefferson County Open Schools**, preschool through 12th grade, which started in Evergreen but were relocated to Lakewood, and what was originally known as the Dennison fundamentals school, now known as a **Core Curriculum School**, with its own highly successful college prep high school component, **D'Evelyn**, in a new building. Both of these option schools have long waiting lists. Also classified as option schools are the **Mount Evans and Windy Peak Outdoor Lab Schools**. All sixth grade students have the opportunity to attend one of these mountain schools for a week and evaluations of graduating students consistently describe this week of outdoor learning and living together as a highlight of their school years. Other fine option schools include **Warren Tech**, a Technical and Vocational School, **Fletcher Miller**, which caters to students with special needs, the **Rocky Mountain Deaf School**, and the **Johnson Program**, which serves students who have been expelled and those "at risk" kids who would probably not be staying to graduate from the regular high schools. A high school option for gifted kids is the prestigious **International Baccalaureate Program** at Lakewood High School. Because of the stringent financial situation, the School Board reluctantly postponed its 2003 decision to build an eighth option school in the north end of the District, a counterpart of D'Evelyn High School. An increasing number of students from the Evergreen/Conifer area with talents in the arts are auditioning for the **Denver School of the Arts**: if they are successful. Jefferson County pays the fees to the Denver Public Schools. There is a movement in Jefferson County to submit a charter application for a Colorado School for Arts and Scholarship. As of mid-2004, the District had fourteen **charter schools**, which made their debut in Jeffco in the early 1990's after the 1993 passage of the act authorizing the establishment of charter schools in Colorado. These are public schools usually formed by an enthusiastic group of parents, students and potential teachers who are focused on a specific philosophy of education. They must be approved by the School Board and receive a proportion of the District's per pupil money. In the 2003/4 school year, per pupil spending for the District averaged $5,788. Charter schools received $5,526 for each student enrolled. One charter school is located in Evergreen, the **Rocky Mountain Academy of Evergreen**, on Bryant Drive. This is a Core Curriculum school with a strong emphasis also on music and the arts, which opened its doors in 2001. The sponsors had a difficult time finding a site. They regard the present one as temporary, and hope ultimately to build on land overlooking Elk Meadow. In March of 2004, the school received permission from the School Board to expand their numbers cap from 191 to 374, preschool through 8th, grade. Their preschool opened in the fall of 2003 in the lower level of the new Beth Evergreen Synagogue. How successful are charter schools so far? The District Administrator for Charter Schools, John Peery, says that results are mixed — some are doing very well, others have run into difficulties. It will probably take a few more years of experimentation to make any definitive evaluation of this new venture in pubic education, but it certainly does offer a genuine opportunity for energetic and innovative parents to create more educational choices within the public school system.

The Mountain Schools Fund (p. 256), started in 1991 to raise money for the nine schools in the Evergreen High School attendance area through an annual Phone-a-Thon, operated successfully until December of 2001. At that point, the energy of the volunteers who had spearheaded the effort for 10 years ran out, and no replacements for them could be found.

Clear Creek County School District (p. 258) finally passed in 1999 a bond issue large enough to tackle the major need of the district for a new high school. It was decided to build this on the Floyd Hill property owned by the district, and to convert the Idaho Springs building, which had served as both high school and junior high into a middle school. Controversy over the location of the high school — so close to the county's boundary and so far from its traditional home in Idaho Springs — was prolonged and serious, provoking an attempt to recall members of the School Board. But the recall failed and Superintendent Don Middleton and the Board stuck to their decision. The new high school opened in the fall of 2002 with an enrollment of 230 students. The building in Idaho Springs was renovated and converted, with funds from the same bond issue, in the summer and fall of 2003. A decision about whether to move sixth graders from the District's elementary schools, including King-Murphy, is being considered for the 2006–7 school year.

Private Schools are an option in the Evergreen area for those who can afford them, or who are fortunate enough to qualify for financial aid offered by the individual schools. The **Montessori School** e.g. has a foundation set up by parents in 1995 for this purpose. The school on its Troutdale site has expanded its grade level offerings, now goes through 8th grade and enrolls around 300 students, preschool through 8th, grade. It makes a large contribution each year, through the combined efforts of parents and students, to benefit a good cause in the community. In 1995, through an entertaining hop-a-thon and trike-a-thon, they raised $8,000 towards the cost of Art for the Mountain Community's first sculpture at the Lake House. In 2004, joining with 18 Montessori Schools in a number of other states attempting to raise enough money in pennies to build a school in Pakistan, they collected 1,400 pounds of pennies worth almost $3,000. ..."Why send your child down the mountain?" asks a lively ad for the **Evergreen Mountain School**, claiming that its students perform as well or better than the best private schools in Denver. Formerly the Children's Center of Evergreen (p. 258) it is now a preschool, starting at 2 years and 9 months, through 5th grade institution, using the Core Knowledge curriculum and operating in expanded facilities in Bergen Park...**Grace Christian School** located on Floyd Hill celebrated its tenth anniversary in 2002. They have a maximum of 18 students per class and make transportation available throughout the Evergreen/Conifer area...The **Evergreen Academy**, also a Christian School, evolved from Our House Children's Learning Center in Marshdale. It offers a core knowledge curriculum from kindergarten through 7th grade as well as extended day care and after school enrichment classes.

Home Schooling in the mountain area, as in the entire United States, has become more of a mainstream option. A *Denver Post* article in 2003 reported that up to 2 million children in the nation were being educated at home. In our area, home schooling is well-established with a number of organized groups that provide regular meetings for parents, field trips, enrichment classes and workshops in particular study areas. Children here have access to sports opportunities through the many privately organized leagues like the Stingers Soccer and Little League Baseball. They are also eligible to participate in the athletic programs of the public schools.

Evergreen Scholarship/Bootstraps, Inc. (p. 259), incorporating the oldest continuous charitable organization in Evergreen, goes from strength to strength. It has two components: the one that awards outright scholarships, and the Bootstraps segment which offers non-interest-bearing loans to students who may not be of conventional scholarship material but who show promise. Some scholarships are named funds honoring or memorializing a particular individual, some organizations donate to endow a student with a specific interest or talent, fund-raisers such as the "Jazz it Up" bash at the Lake House and general donations increase the total scholarship money available. Income from Bootstraps loan repayments is also a significant revenue source. Selection from all the worthy and talented students who apply is extremely difficult and time-consuming, but immensely rewarding, according to Barbara Hadley, current president of the organization. The organization disbursed some $160,000 in scholarships and loans in 2003.

MAKING A LIVING
(p. 135–52 & 259–63)
We left the economic fortunes of Evergreen in 1993 with congratulations to the community for beating back the efforts of Wal-mart to place a big box store where Rocky Mountain Village Estates now stands, with residential real estate on a huge roll, and with construction about to start on the Tanoa housing subdivision and the new Stage Coach shopping center, anchored by Albertsons. The rest of the 90's saw the mountain area of Jefferson County participating in the almost delirious national economic expansion. High-end housing developments appeared everywhere, in North Evergreen and Bergen Park, but also in unexpected

places — on the steep hills overlooking Kittredge and on both sides of the 285 corridor. The gentrification of old cabins proceeded apace with buildings, even on odd-shaped sites up impossible roads, getting upgraded and expanded and fetching eye-opening prices. Five new buildings housing offices and retail space appeared almost overnight in Bergen Park, adjacent to the new Buchanan fields and Rec Center. Three new office buildings materialized on the ridge above the Wilco gas station, and one across the highway near the Life Care Center. The El Rancho area and the site of the old Tepees tourist attraction were totally transformed: Wal-mart got its big box site (and in 2004 announced that the box will become even bigger.) A large MacDonalds accompanied it. Home Depot debuted in 2003, joining a Sears' Appliance Store and a number of auto-related enterprises. There is room for more stores, and possibly some affordable housing. Next to the old and reinvigorated El Rancho Restaurant appeared Evergreen's first hotel — a useful Quality Suites, offering comfortable rooms for business travelers and visitors to the area.

The recession of 2000 saw rough times for many of our town's new elite, those in computer-related professions and enterprises. Evergreen felt the effects of the recession, with more houses for sale and fewer selling, heavier case loads for Christian Outreach and the Mountain Resource Center, and some businesses closing down. The almost 2–year construction at the 73/74 intersection was an exceedingly difficult time for **Main Street** businesses. When it was finished, the survivors put out the message loud and clear that Main Street was more accessible because of the new traffic pattern, and fully open for business. Helping it to thrive are sturdy long-established businesses like Meryl Sabeff's Evergreen Gallery, the Evergreen Crafters, the Silver Arrow gallery of Indian arts and crafts, the Holly Berry, Breezy Travel (sold by Diane Brisse to genial Jerry Mallory) and the Little Bear, as well as flourishing newcomers (since our last check-up) like the sophisticated Soho Restaurant, the laid-back, folksy Wildflower cafe, and Beau Jo's Pizza. The revitalized Evergreen Hotel is a triumph of determination over adversity on the part of owners Judy and Ken Jeronimus, who contribute so much to the economic vitality of Main Street. When the restoration and remodeling of the decrepit old hotel was well on its way to completion, a fire gutted the building. It would have been easy to give up, raze the remains of the building and put up something new. But they

Evergreen Conference Center

carried on with the original plans, and the result, with its downstairs coffee shop and bar and upstairs mix of retail and offices, is working well and making a real contribution to maintaining some of the original flavor of Main Street. Another creative and flourishing remodel is the Creekside Cellars in the former Olde's Texaco building, where our first Evergreen winery is busy producing palatable table wines to serve with its delectable Italian sandwiches. The old Trail movie theater (p. 170) which at our last go-round was being occupied by the Coal Mine Dragon Chinese restaurant (now located in the Lakepoint Center) was another restoration and upgrade effort of the Jeronimus's — to accommodate the popular Thuy Hoa Vietnamese restaurant.

The **Evergreen Chamber of Commerce** was in the Lakepoint Center and under the direction of Andrew Petrick when we left its story in 1993. It has been headed since by Nancy Brown and Terry Hoffman and, since early in 2004, the President is Gary Matson. It is now located on the second floor of the old Evergreen Hotel building on Main Street. Membership is up sharply in the last 10 years, now standing at around 750 representing some 240 businesses. Matson has a vision for the organization, with a major emphasis on reaching out to the segmented and isolated elements of the community and getting them to work together "to protect what we all cherish about living here." He perceives that the long phase of land development that has helped Evergreen flourish for the past 40 years (even while arousing some resentment at the pace of growth) is drawing to a close. He thinks community leaders need to be considering what economic activities could, and should, replace it? Matson has lived in Evergreen since 1972, working for many of those years for Public Service Co., and has served on the boards of more than 20 non-profit organizations here.

The Hardware.

The Survivors, the Vanished and the New. Making a living in retail is tough in Evergreen, as is evidenced by the number that do not survive. Looking over our brief survey of this segment in 1993, we find the Evergreen Drug still provides a huge variety of goods in its relatively small premises, a reliable pharmacy and a popular liquor store. The Hardware in its historic building, though undoubtedly affected by the coming of Home Depot, is still a place where you can find many of the things you need and cannot find elsewhere. Paragon Sports goes on meeting the needs of sports lovers, from skiers to Stingers, but the lively Snow Leopard, operated by Buzz and Laura Sampson in the octagonal barn building and later moved to Bergen Park, closed after the two decided to retire, and their son elected to carry on with an Internet version of the business. Olde's Texaco has a handsome new gas station and a separate service station on the frontage road next to the Post Office. The venerable Whipple Tree Mexican Restaurant in Bergen Park still greets you with a bar full of cowboys, a pool table, and great margaritas. Independent book stores struggle everywhere to survive against the overwhelming competitive advantages of the big chains. But they are so vital to the healthy balance of a community. We lost the Yankee Doodler. Next the community thoroughly enjoyed Linda and Jim Lovin's Book Store and Coffee Shop next to Paragon Sports, which was sold in March 2001 and became Hearthfire Books. After going through a couple of ownerships, the store passed in to the welcoming arms of Lori Underwood, who came with her husband to live in Hiwan after spending 14 years in London. Underwood began

immediately to implement her plans to increase the stock of books, especially children's books, expand the used book section, schedule author appearances and book signings, and continue serving a variety of high quality coffees and teas. In Kittredge, Ted Mann retired and closed his Mountain Ranch Supply. Steve and Robin Cohen sold their Evergreen Nursery, which is still very much alive. The Tivoli Deer remains one of our area's premier restaurants. There are also more casual eating opportunities in Kittredge, from breakfast at the Country Road to lunch at one of two new delis, Cee Gee's and A Taste of New York, to the hearty fare of Dick's Hickory Dock. A new and different eating experience was at the British Invasion on Meadow Drive, but it closed abruptly in August 2004. Across the road is the reliable Rib Crib and Sports Bar. Off Highway 74, strange changes: the still-missed Village Pancake House became Old Chicago restaurant became the Lotus Chinese buffet became Wendy's. The Pizza Hut, which was certainly a prime venue for eating out with children, quietly closed its doors. The building, long empty, suddenly blossomed into a dental clinic in the summer of 2004. The ambiguous delights of fast food chain franchises have arrived in Evergreen: in addition to already-mentioned MacDonalds and Wendy's, we have Taco Bell, Quizno's Subs, Subway Sandwiches, Domino's Pizza. On the Health Food side of the scale, we lost two small operations but acquired a Vitamin Cottage. We seem to have had an explosion of frame shops and art galleries, some of the latter are mentioned in the Arts section below. Julie Jones' Frames for All Reasons has won several awards as an innovative business, which gives back in many ways to the community. From 1977–81, Julie had the Daylight Donuts store on Main Street before opening her frame shop in August of 1981.

Banks. In 1992, it was clear that Evergreen had been greatly affected by the upheaval in banking, mostly caused by the savings and loan deregulation debacle. Things have stabilized markedly. In 2004, there are six banks represented in Evergreen. Evergreen National, with its main office on Main Street and a branch in Bergen Park; Community First, formerly The Bank and soon to change its name again celebrated its expanded and updated building in August, 2004; First Bank, in a new building in the Stage Coach Boulevard shopping center; Peak National Bank in Bergen Park; U.S. Bank on the frontage road off Highway 74; Commercial Federal Bank on Swede Gulch Road in the Wal-mart shopping area.

SPREADING THE WORD
(p. 153–62 & 263–5)
Evergreen is quite well-served by a variety of publications. Stalwarts like the *Canyon Courier* and the *High Timber Times* continue to inform and document the happenings in this mountain area. Some ventures active ten years ago have disappeared, several new publications have been launched. There is probably a finite number of publications that can be financed out of subscriptions and the sale of advertising from such a relatively small base, but that does not seem to discourage new journalistic entrepreneurs from trying their luck.

The *Canyon Courier*, our little hometown newspaper, is now owned by Landmark Community Newspapers, Inc. of Shelbyville, Kentucky, which in turn is a division of Landmark Communications, Inc., a privately held media company based in Norfolk, Va. with coast-to-coast interests in newspapers, specialty publications, TV broadcasting, cable programming and outdoor advertising. Evergreen Newspapers is a subdivision of Landmark Community Newspapers whose Publisher, Brad Bradberry, oversees three papers (Canyon Courier, *High Timber Times* and one covering the Columbine area) as well as the Idaho Springs *Clear Creek Courant*, acquired in February 2003, and two "shoppers" — the Evergreen and 285 *Hustlers*. The *Courier*, with a paid circulation of approximately 8500, strives diligently to cover local and county events and developments in depth. The paper continues to deal with a rapid turnover of reporters who, as is usual on a small weekly paper, work too many hours for too little money and are expected to move on and up as soon as they can. One who has stayed longer than most is Bonnie Benjamin Skopinski, whose byline has appeared on an astonishing number of articles. Her husband's job brought them from New Mexico, where Bonnie worked as a public health nurse, to Denver, where she decided to follow her long-time dream of becoming a journalist. There has been a pretty frequent turnover of editors also, and great hopes are invested in Steve Jackson, who took over the job in July, 2004. A Colorado native and Evergreen resident for more than 10 years, Jackson graduated in 1979 from the Colorado State University School of Journalism and has worked as a reporter and editor in many different states, and most recently as a staff reporter for *Westword* from 1993–2001. He has written seven non-fiction books, several of which have won awards. Among his goals for the newspaper are more local stories "about things that matter" with writing that "is tight and bright." The national scene gets a workout from columnist Greg Dobbs (p. 256) whose forthright opinions generate lively pro and con letters to the Editor. Greg started hosting a Friday evening talk show, Colorado State of Mind, on Channel 6 in January of 2003 which, within its first year, won a regional Emmy for best discussion program. Sylvia Brockner's unique column on the state of the natural world (p. 34) around us continues to delight and inform.

The Mountain Connection, a monthly newspaper, now has a circulation of 22,000, of which over 19,000 are mailed to homes and businesses in the Evergreen, Conifer, Bailey, Pine and Morrison area and the rest distributed through 125 business locations. It was launched in 1993 with a novel intent: to donate money from each issue to a worthy non-profit community organization, and of course to spotlight the organization's purposes and needs, thus hopefully increasing its support base. The money for publication and the monthly donation was raised from advertising revenue. The paper's founder and first publisher and editor was Margaret Hennessy. It was originally based in Conifer and covered most intensely the cultural events and business activities of the 285 corridor (Hennessy noted that for the first time in her life, her community was "a corridor") but its area of interest extended to the Evergreen area. In January of 2003, the paper was sold and Jacque Scott became the new Owner, Publisher and Editor. She is a Colorado native, with a long history of newspaper work in Jefferson County. Scott graduated from the University of Hawaii with a degree in journalism then became one of the early TV reporters and anchors who helped break the barriers for women in this area. She returned to Evergreen in 1978, becoming publisher of the *High Timber Times* and Associate Editor of the *Canyon Courier* and then moved on to become publisher of a group of newspapers including the *Golden Transcript, Wheatridge Transcript* and the Arvada and Lakewood *Sentinels*. Scott has instituted some changes in the *Mountain Connection*. In order to help defray the cost of the monthly donation to a beneficiary, she secures a "beneficiary sponsor", frequently an area business, and spotlights both organizations. While covering all aspects of community life and business, Scott has made art one of the primary interests of the paper, organizing an annual issue featuring area art and artists, and running a competition for a piece of art by a Colorado artist to be

featured as the cover for that issue. The large, vivid sunflower painting by Indian Hills artist Denise Bellon West graced the 2003 cover, and "Colorado Lynx", a painting on a turkey feather by Peg Fennimore appeared in June, 2004. As of mid–2004, the paper had donated almost $70,000 to mountain area non-profits.

The quarterly ***city and mountain Views*** describes itself as "a community news-magazine created by and for residents of the I–70 Corridor, Mt. Vernon Canyon — from Lookout and Lininger Mountains west through Riva Chase, Genesee, Mt. Vernon and Spring Ranch to El Rancho and Rainbow Hills since 1993." The publication is free, although subscriptions of $15 a year are welcomed. It is largely financed by advertising, and has a print run of 7,000 copies — 3,000 mailed directly to Mt. Vernon residents and an additional 4,000 distributed through area real estate offices, public libraries and Chamber of Commerce offices. Publisher and Editor is Carole Lomond, and the paper is largely the product of this one energetic and hard-working writer. She writes profiles on interesting area residents and businesses, highlights the ongoing work of worthwhile local organizations and institutions, and delves into area history. She has consistently fought for the rights of Lookout Mountain residents to have their concerns about the health effects of TV Towers heard by the Jefferson County Commissioners. She campaigns for old towers to be removed from their present sites as non-conforming uses, and for new ones to be located to available alternate sites where they would not affect the health of some 30,000 nearby residents. Carole wrote, and through her Views Publishing Company published, an attractive and informative booklet, ***Lariat Loop: Scenic and Historic Byway***, about the things to do and see along the newly-designated Lariat Loop Mountain Gateway Heritage Area.

Colorado Serenity, which describes itself as "Colorado's Premier Lifestyle Magazine" has a circulation of 24,400, of which 22,400 are sent by direct mail to homes and businesses in Evergreen, Genesee/Lookout Mountain, Kittredge, Morrison, Indian Hills, Conifer, Pine and Bailey and 2,000 distributed through area businesses. The magazine's contents include original feature stories covering art, outdoor activities, social service activities, regular department articles, including one spotlighting a "business of the month" selection, and what are billed as "Community Advertorials." These are short articles by business and

professional people living in the community which simultaneously give information about their fields of expertise and advertise their services. Founder and Publisher of Colorado Serenity is Doug Kinzy, who started the magazine in November of 1992. Kinzy, who has a master of science degree in electronics, worked for the defense industry in California and then in the space industry in satellite communications. He came to Colorado to be interviewed for a job with Martin Marietta. The day before the interview, he drove up to the mountains, discovered Evergreen, and promptly decided that he was going to move here whether or not he got the job. He did work for Martin Marietta until 1981, then spent 10 years as a realtor. Serenity started as a real estate newsletter. But having discovered the delights of publishing, he wound up his real estate business and turned *Serenity* into a "lifestyles magazine." One thing he learned while in real estate is that most people who live in Evergreen do so, not because they have to, but because, like him, they choose to — and he believes this makes a big difference in the character of the community. The magazine has grown from 12 to 60 pages, and the staff from its one-man start-up to a complement of 4 full-timers: in addition to Kinzy, there is a Graphic Designer and Business Coordinator, and a Managing Editor. Since 2000, this position has been filled by Linda Azzi, who started in 1997 as copy editor. The magazine uses free lance writers. It regularly includes articles with a spiritual theme, and also covers alternative medical therapies.

Evergreen Living Magazine made quite a spectacular debut on the local scene with its first issue for July/August 2003. This is a high quality, glossy magazine published bimonthly by owner, Publisher, and Editor-in-Chief Cat Stone. She writes that the magazine is "committed to providing you, the reader, with rich editorial content and photographs highlighting people, lifestyles, and events of Evergreen and the surrounding mountain communities." An enthusiastic profile of Stone in the Canyon Courier describes her as a 'fiery redhead' raised in Allentown, Pa. with a degree in Radio and T.V. from Penn State. Before her husband's job brought them to Colorado and they selected Evergreen as the place they wanted to live, she had been a disk jockey, a steel worker, an advertising executive, a Mom and a producer of children's books and musical CD's. She is a lifelong community activist and participant, and hopes through her magazine to contribute to something she calls "multi-directional community communication." The first two issues of the magazine were mailed free to 20,000 households in the mountain area, with additional copies available in selected outlets, after which subscriptions were solicited. The magazine is packed with articles on a wide range of topics: local authors and artists, fascinating historic incidents, information about local happenings, leisure interests of all kinds. It also provides a rare showcase for the work of Evergreen poets selected by poet Murray Moulding, who is responsible for getting local poets together in an informal setting to share meditations on poetry.

One of the casualties of the decade was Linda Kirkpatrick's *Upbeat* (p. 263). Linda sold the paper in 1996 to Tim Burland but without Linda's energy and total dedication, it folded in less than a year.

The new **Evergreen Library** (p. 264–4) opened on December 18, 1993. Designed by architect Cabell Childress, the building provides well-designed space to house a welcome expansion of the Library's long services to Evergreen. All the public spaces of the Library are on one floor, covering 17,367 square feet, with an additional 15,000 square feet in the basement. This houses the Jefferson County Library's "support collection", consisting of books which have been withdrawn from library shelves but are deemed to be worthy of saving for the relatively few readers who may still wish to consult them. The collection is accessible to the public via the Library catalog. The entire site, which includes the old library building now used for County Services, is attractively landscaped. Parking for the Library is plentiful and well-designed, set among trees and garden areas. The building opened with a collection of 59,000 books, which had grown by mid–2004 to 90,000. But this figure is a little misleading, because the entire Jefferson Library book holdings are in a very real sense one collection, available to readers throughout the County. Unless they are checked out, books from any of the Library's eleven branches can be delivered to the Evergreen Library in two days. The Library has a Community Room, seating up to 45 people, a useful addition to the all-too-few public meeting spaces in Evergreen. There are however significant limitations on its use. In addition to the Community Room, there are two study rooms available for individuals or small groups. Use of these can be reserved at the Library and there is no charge.

There is some welcome exhibit space in the building. A large glass case is available to non-profit groups for a display about their activities. Each exhibit lasts for one month, and the same group may not exhibit again for 18 months. A wall exhibit is available for local artists on the same conditions. Small table exhibits are presented from time to time, as well as space for distribution of seasonally useful items like tax forms, political campaign literature, etc. The Children's Library also has space for exhibits of work by local school children.

Change is a constant in the life of libraries these days, and the Jefferson County Library staff tries to work with the evolving situations and public demands created by technological innovations. 19 computer terminals are available to the public in the general

Evergreen Library area, 3 of which are limited to catalog searches and the remainder accessible to the internet and for searching online data bases. In 2004, wireless internet capability was added to the Library's resources so that library patrons can hook up their own laptops from anywhere in the Library building. 5 computer terminals are in the Children's section, of which two have CD ROM capabilities. In general, the library finds that books are still the preferred mode for reading fiction and entire non-fiction works. But reference materials are increasingly more efficiently used on line. The Library conducts free computer classes and one-on-one sessions to help people develop their computer skills. The Jefferson Library web site makes possible the searching of catalogs and data bases from home computers, as well as the ordering of books to be held at or

Evergreen Library, Children's section.

delivered to the Evergreen Library, and the renewal of books.

Evergreen Branch Manager Gail Alden was succeeded by some temporary appointees, then by Ann Cress. Since November, 1999 Priscilla Winter has held this position. As of mid–2004, there were 17 salaried staff members at work in the Library, 17 pagers (shelvers) and 9 volunteers. The rather startling number of active Evergreen Library card holders in 2004 was 26,000. The Library keeps track of "foot traffic" and estimates that 14,552 people came into the building in May of 2004, up from 12,552 a year before. And so one must conclude that the new Library is a resounding success and and a great addition to the resources of our community.

MEETING SOCIAL NEEDS
(p. 163–177 & 265–271)
The demographics of the mountain community are changing. Although this community still has a pretty good balance between children, young adults and seniors, we are getting older. According to Jane Weinberger, Director of Evergreen's Senior Center, the average age of Evergreen residents is now 42.5 years.

The **Seniors' Resource Center** (SRC), is happily settled into its comfortable Yellow House quarters on Highway 73, which have undergone several additions, improvements and renovations in the past ten years. The most recent addition to its amenities is the creation of a community garden, designed by long-time master gardener, Mary Gauden Beardslee, with the goals of: showcasing xeriscape landscaping, serving as an educational resource for the whole Evergreen community, and making possible a program of horticulture therapy for seniors. SRC has expanded its services since 1993 partly in response to the increasing case load, which adds about 200 seniors each year. In its Yellow House cafe, it offers inexpensive nutritious and appetizing lunches on Tuesdays and Fridays to community members over 55. It also manages the area Meals on Wheels program and offers assistance with small home repairs through its volunteer Minor Home Repair program. Transportation is a difficult problem for seniors in the mountain area, especially when they have to limit or stop their driving. SRC offers transportation for a fee in its own vans and also operates the RTD's Call 'N Ride green buses which, partly through the efforts of the Curmudgeons, provide customized wheel chair accessible, door-to-door rides to community members, including seniors, within their operating zones for

a small fare. SRC offers in-home personal care services (light housekeeping, laundry, meal preparation, errands, shopping), adult day and respite programs, job training services and care management in Jefferson, Park, Clear Creek, Gilpin and a small part of Boulder Counties. SRC's two major fundraisers traditionally have been rousing and enjoyable events. In the spring, the Little Bear Benefit is a community celebration. The 2004 version, "Murder At the Evergreen Hotel, An Interactive Murder Mystery Dinner by the Morrison Theatre Company" was especially imaginative. In summer, the Mountain Music Festival at the Evergreen Lake Park for many years attracted over 1,000 participants. However, revenues and attendance have fallen due to increasing competition, so SRC decided that 2004 would be the last of this event. They will transfer their energies to another annual fundraiser, Art from the Heart, an art auction held for the first time in 2004 in a prestigious Denver location benefiting the Wheatridge and Evergreen SRCs and their clients throughout an 11–county area. Jane Weinberger came to be Director of Mountain Services in 2001. Under her management, the SRC does an excellent job of getting its services and its achievements widely known in the community.

Congratulations are due to the **Mountain Resource Center** (MRC) and its hard-working Executive Director Bob Over on being the first of the 24 Resource Centers in Colorado to build its own facility. $1.25 million in cash and pledges was raised to construct this 9000 square foot building on a site behind the Conifer Safeway. Ground-breaking ceremonies took place on July 26, 2003. MRC's purpose is "to identify and advocate for needed services for mountain area residents and to bring institutions and individuals together to provide services through a local, single point of entry." The organization has come a long way from its beginnings (p. 266). With the help of some 500 volunteers, MRC in 2002 served over 6,500 children, youth and family members. Services ranged from meeting crisis needs for food, rent, shelter from abusive situations, to locating job training opportunities, supplying back-to-school supplies for needy kids, programs for teens and disaster relief. While located in Conifer, MRC offers services to the whole mountain area: 35% of its cases are from Evergreen, 35% from Conifer, 20% from Bailey and 10% from other areas including Clear Creek County. Some services are offered in Evergreen at 28268 Buffalo Park Road, on the

SRC's Yellow House.

grounds of Church of the Hills. MRC's fundraisers include a sparkling "All that Glitters" event at the Mount Vernon Country Club and a Fall "Run for the Resource" 5K race.

Evergreen Christian Outreach
(p. 265) had a major increase in its fund-raising capabilities when Liz Begalla and Dorinne Reid established the EChO Resale shop in the North Evergreen shopping center in 2000. Indeed, the store quickly became the primary source of funds for EChO, and was so successful that it expanded in 2003 into the 2000 square feet space formerly occupied by Stefanzo's Ristorante, enabling the store to carry many more items. Nina Sampsell and Donna Christianson took over the management of the store in 2004. The purpose of Christian Outreach is "to reach out to anyone in need and provide relief of the crisis at hand", in the words of Sandy Madigan, EChO Director from 1997–2003. The organization's most important services are emergency provision of food, clothing, and a listening ear when loss of work, medical problems, divorce, abandonment or abusive situations create a crisis. They provide short-term assistance, supplementary to the provisions of social service agencies, along with a respectful and caring concern for the people who come to them. They help clients to develop a plan for themselves to attain independence and prevent homelessness and hunger. They cover an area of some 250 square miles with their services, reaching as far as Golden, and from Morrison and Bailey on the 285 corridor. With a paid staff of seven, all part-time except for Director Lesley Jackson, and some 120–30 volunteers, they draw support from their 19 sponsoring churches and from local businesses and individuals. In the fall of 2004 they will have their first fund-raising event at the Lake House, a relatively low-key dinner with a motivational speaker.

Mount Evans Hospice and Home Health Care (p. 173 and 267) is an indispensable part of the medical/social network of the mountain area. The organization offers a variety of community programs such as bereavement counseling, support groups, transportation services and respite care for families, staffing clinics and the Channel 9 Health Fair, and Camp Comfort, the unique summer program for kids 6–12 who have sustained a significant loss in their lives. Some of the children's stories are chilling, where a parent has been murdered, most are heart-breaking. The weekend summer camps pair each child with a volunteer buddy of the same sex and the program, which has received much recognition, is conducted by experienced professionals. Mt. Evans' services enable many elderly people to remain in their own homes much longer than they could without the loving and regular attentions of Mount Evans nurses and volunteers. The home health aspect of the organization's services provides care to patients who are either recuperating from illness or injury, or who have chronic ailments and need medical assistance to stay in their homes. The hospice aspect serves patients diagnosed as having terminal illnesses, with nursing care, support and counseling for them and for the family members or other care givers who are committed to seeing the patient through the last months of their lives. There is no residential hospice facility as such in the mountain area, but Mt. Evans staff do now work successfully in partnership with Evergreen's nursing home, the Life Care Center. Mt. Evans uses a team approach to hospice patients and their families, involving some combination of nurse, social worker, personal care provider, physical and other therapists, dietitian and chaplain. The organization relies heavily on volunteers in many aspects of its work, and provides training. In 2004, the organization had a paid staff of 50, of which 37 work directly with patients and 13 staff the office doing billing, training of volunteers, keeping medical records, scheduling of services, organization of fundraising etc. There are also some 80 volunteers doing on-going work for Mt. Evans, and a further 200 or so helping with special projects. Financial support comes from a combination of fees, insurance and Medicare payments, grants from foundations, donations, and income from a variety of fund-raisers. These run from the lovely tradition of selling Christmas angel decorations made by volunteers, to the sale of the unique limited edition silver angel designed and sold by Evergreen Fine Art as a benefit for Mt. Evans, to the popular 5K July 4th Freedom Run — a course running through residential neighborhoods from the Evergreen Middle School to the Evergreen Fitness Center — and the sale of the annual "Seasons of Our Mountains" calendar. Realtors Moore and Co. started this tradition, which was carried on by Coldwell Banker when they bought out Moore. Submissions are invited from photographers (around 200 are received each year), the field is then narrowed to 24 semi-finalists with the public choosing the final 13, one for each month and one for the cover.

Sickness and Health (p.171–4, 267) No hospital for Evergreen. The 11 so-called "Lutheran" acres in Bergen Park, originally intended for some kind of large-scale medical facility, were sold to the Evergreen Park and Rec District, and with all the changes in medical technology and rapid transportation, it seems unlikely that a hospital will ever be a practical proposition for the mountain area. There is a small urgent care facility in Bergen Park operated by Dr. Kit Brekhus. The explosive growth of health care providers of all types and specialties, noted in our earlier brief surveys, continues, and we are indeed a far cry from the small one-doctor town that was Evergreen until the 1960's. The offices of doctors and other medical professionals are located in many different office buildings around town, and there two new all-medical buildings on Stagecoach Boulevard. Alternative therapists have also multiplied: for example, there are more than 20 listings in the 2004 Evergreen telephone directory for massages services. The success of Evergreen's first day spa, **Tall Grass Aveda Spa and Salon** on Upper Bear Creek Road, seems to have encouraged the opening of four or five more in the Evergreen/Conifer area. The Life Care Center of Evergreen (p. 267) has become an essential component of our health facilities, and it now has a neighbor, **Elk Run Assisted Living**, which provides much-needed residential/medical services for those whose needs fall between independent senior housing and nursing homes. One problem area in medical services here is the dwindling number of physicians who will accept new Medicare patients. Many will accept senior patients affiliated with an HMO, but problems with the amount and timeliness of Medicare payments to physicians, which have made this is a national concern, affect services here. At the other end of the life spectrum from seniors, **child birth classes** once taught by Peggy Eggers are now taught by certified childbirth educators Jennifer Boone and Gina DeRosa, both also trained as "doulas." A doula (from the Greek) supports a woman going through the entire process of labor and delivery. She does not take the place of the medical staff, nor of the husband or other supportive friends or relatives the woman may want at her side. But the doula maintains a constant, knowledgeable, helpful attention to the woman and her needs, and acts as her advocate — often through a number of nursing shifts and other personnel rotations.

Some lively new organizations have made their appearance on the Evergreen scene. Others which had somehow run their course, disappeared. **PFLAG Evergreen** (Parents and Friends of Lesbians and Gays) came into being after the passage of Amendment 2 to the State Constitution in 1992. While sold by its Colorado Springs proponents as a measure to prevent gays receiving "special rights" it was in truth designed to make illegal any ordinances protecting gays and lesbians from discrimination and was eventually struck down by the U.S. Supreme Court. With help and information from the well-established Denver chapter, the new organization was established in April,1993. Along with a sea change in general social attitudes regarding sexual orientation, the chapter is quietly helping to further the acceptance of lesbians and gays as an integral part of the social fabric of our community. **Leadership Evergreen** is an interesting newcomer. Started in 1996, this organization puts on a year long program "designed to identify and develop the leadership potential of community-minded citizens in the Evergreen area." Each class brings together a mix of emerging and existing leaders. It meets once or twice monthly and covers such topics as community infrastructure, services, and governance. By 1904, five classes had been graduated,varying from 5 to 15 members each, with another class to be enrolled in 2005. The first graduating class is responsible for the distinctive "cornerstone" signs signifying an entrance to "Evergreen, Our Mountain Community" and, at the boundaries of downtown, "Welcome to the Heart of Evergreen, Estd. 1875." At a Leadership of Evergreen Alumni Reunion in May, 2004, an award was given to 1996 graduate Peter Eggers as "Leader of the Year" in recognition of his many contributions, including 10 years on the Rec Board, during which time the Lake House and the new Buchanan Rec Center were built and many ball fields added to the District's roster, and 8 years and counting on the board of Art for the Mountain Community, including a term as President. A Canyon Courier profile lauded Eggers as a skillful consensus builder. In private life,

Peter Eggers.

Eggers is the owner of a high-end, high quality woodworking shop in Denver. Special recognition at the Reunion was also given to Bruce Brown, a 2003 graduate running for District Attorney of the 5th Judicial District, and Gary Matson, class of 1996, who is President of the Evergreen Area Chamber of Commerce. The **Curmudgeons**, "Grouchy old men with hearts of gold" as the *Mountain Connection* described them, are an informal group of retired men who get together every Thursday morning from 9–11 a.m. to chat socially, and to make a contribution when they can to the betterment of our community. They had a hand in the establishment of the Call-n-Ride service and are generally interested in issues such as water resources in the mountain area, transportation and housing, including affordable housing. The **Evergreen Branch of A.A.U.W.**, which was for 25 years a major channel for the energy and community service drive of women in the mountain area, foundered in 2003. Exactly why is still somewhat of an enigma, but the overt cause was that the organization had worn out its willing leaders, and no new volunteers were stepping into the breach.

Most mountain area clubs and service organizations (p. 163–70 and 166–7) have flourished in the last ten years. **Evergreen Kiwanis** is the oldest service club in Evergreen, having started in 1951, and is proud that three of its charter members, Hal Davidson, Gerry Olde and Walt Anderson, are still active. The club has lunchtime meetings and continues its long tradition of helping the community in many different ways, from picking up trash along a section of Highway 74 to putting on its traditional yearly Pancake

Breakfast and Raffle fundraiser in the Fall to making grants to worthy community non-profits and programs, distributing $30,000 to $40,000 each year. In 1995, the Club elected a woman president for the first time in its history. **Blue Spruce Kiwanis** was founded in 1969 and, with early morning breakfast meetings, was designed to cater to members who work in the Denver area. Their major fundraiser is a Chili Supper at the Evergreen Elks Lodge, which has been a staple on the Evergreen calendar for 30 years. They also carry out a busy schedule of grants and activities designed to improve our community. The energetic **Evergreen Rotary Club** meets at 7 a.m. at El Rancho. It had 40 members when we last looked at it, now has around 130 members and a full array of services it performs in the community, including its 2003/4 project of helping to make the Center/Stage's dream of an adequate lobby into a reality. It has been joined by two more clubs, the **Conifer Rotary Club** and the **Mountain Foothills Rotary Club of Evergreen**, the newest addition, which had 40 members in 2004, and was engaged in a current project of tree-planting in our community. It meets weekly at the Mount Vernon Country Club from 6-7 p.m.

Blue Spruce Habitat for Humanity (p. 271) has built 14 homes in the Evergreen area since its founding in 1976, and in 2004 is working on its 15th and 16th. A great boost to its fundraising capacity was the establishment of its "Resale Emporium" (Upscale Resale), which in April, 2003 moved into larger quarters on Bryant Drive. Habitat is in the business of building affordable housing for working people with families in our community. The adult or adults in the family must be able to contribute their own labor.

Habitat builds the homes largely with volunteer labor and raises funds to buy land and materials. The biggest hurdle in the mountain area is getting hold of land. They are very pleased to have lots in Kittredge, a combination of purchase and donation, which will, in the words of affordable housing advocate Jim Shelton, "keep us busy for years to come." Admirable as is the effort of Habitat, it cannot be the entire solution to the lack of affordable housing, which is an ongoing challenge in the Evergreen area. The price of housing continues to rise while wages for the lower-paid occupations (retail clerks, secretaries, nurses and health paraprofessionals, police, teachers, etc.) make owning or renting here impossible. An **Affordable Housing Task Force**, which grew out of the effort to update the Evergreen Community Plan, was formed in February, 2003 at the initiative of Jim Shelton, to work on this problem. A year was spent in learning about resources and looking for land. Two possibilities presented themselves — one in Wah Keeney, with an owner interested in developing affordable housing, possibly rental, on his property, and one at El Rancho, which may be suitable for owner-occupied housing. The Task Force is working with Mercy Housing, a nonprofit affordable rental and home ownership developer, to see if this is feasible, targeting families with incomes below $55,000.

Drive Smart and **Skate the Lake**. In the aftermath of traffic accidents in the early 1990's that killed six teenagers, **Cheryl Ladd** became, in the words of an *Upbeat* article, a driven person. Particularly since one of those accidents took the life of a neighborhood teenager only moments after she left the Ladd home with a group of other teenagers. Ladd spearheaded the formation of DRIVE SMART Evergreen/Conifer, affiliated with DRIVE SMART Colorado. Her organization sponsored innumerable and imaginative programs targeting safety concerns in the mountains, focusing especially on children. Although Ladd trained as an emergency room nurse she found her real vocation as a community volunteer. Initially her efforts were at Evergreen Middle School and Bergen elementary. She was a member of the first Leadership Evergreen class and believes that "We don't value volunteerism enough, If we want to keep Evergreen a nice place to life, we all need to give something back to the community." On New Year's Eve, 1996, she helped to launch Skate the Lake, an alcohol-free family event at the Lake and the Lake House. The event, which benefits

303

DRIVE SMART, was an overwhelming success the first year, and has continued to be one of the best-attended and most enjoyed festivals of the Evergreen year. But there have had to be adjustments. Thomas Carby, who has coordinated the event for the last four years, says that they learned the hard way that 2,500 tickets is the maximum they can sell and have a safe celebration. Preparing for the event is a year-round task for a dedicated committee, but the pay-off is "seeing all the families having a great time."

The **Salvation Army** presents a public face to the community only during the Christmas season, when as many as 650 bell-ringers — from all the major services clubs, social service organizations, high school clubs, churches, as well as some individuals — staff the familiar red kettles at public locations in the mountain area. This is their major fundraiser, bringing in over $30,000 for needy families in the Evergreen area. The rest of the year, the Salvation Army in Evergreen quietly meets family needs, either from direct appeals or through the requests of organizations like the Mountain Resource Center, Christian Outreach and Mount Evans Hospice.

One of the most energetic and popular clubs in the mountain area is the **Evergreen Newcomers Club**, which describes itself as "a non-profit club with membership open to everyone" providing opportunities for "new, and not so new, residents to meet new friends and to help make Evergreen feel like home." With a membership of 275 in all age groups, the club schedules activities for weekdays and week nights as well as weekends. It offers many activities and interest groups, luncheons with a variety of programs, and special events.

There are problems that tug at the heart, and for which sympathy and funds are easily raised once the public becomes aware of them. And then there are the hidden sufferings which bear a social stigma and to which we tend to react with denial. **Domestic violence** is one of these. Knowing some of the statistics, as well as some poignant individual stories, a small group of courageous individuals have banded together as the **Mountain Domestic Violence Coalition**. What they know is that in wealthy, middle class and poor neighborhoods alike, one in three women encounter some form of domestic violence in their lifetimes. The only shelter in the mountain area is in Park County, and 22% of its case load comes from Jefferson County. And a significant percentage also at the

Women in Crisis shelter in Jefferson County, under the umbrella of Family Tree, come from the mountain area of the county. Some help is available to victims of domestic abuse here in the Evergreen area in the form of a part-time counselor from Family Tree. Coalition members found out that, on the national level, there is some new thinking about domestic violence: even in areas with quite extensive resources available, including safe houses, the rate of domestic violence does not seem to go down. A new component is needed, that of education, to lift the level of public awareness about domestic violence, about healthy and unhealthy relationships, about the extent of the problem, and how it affects business efficiency, performance of children in school, health costs etc. Coalition members are speaking to service clubs, women's groups, churches, both to educate and to seek more information about conditions in our community, so that its next steps can be based securely on community concerns.

When it comes to updating organizations that connect Evergreen with the world, we find the **Friendship Bridge** (p. 217) has significantly shifted its focus. While it still does some medical work in Viet Nam, a decision was made to broaden its Mission Statement and start working in a more accessible country, where help could be offered with less bureaucratic red tape to cope with. The country chosen was Guatemala and the primary mode of helping was offering well-structured micro-credit opportunities to women. A major fundraiser for the organization is "Evening in Evergreen," an event at the Lake House in May featuring a silent and live auction, with a great variety of goods and services from local merchants, mini-vacations, and colorful hand-crafted items from Guatemala. In 2004, the Eleventh Annual "Evening" raised some $60,000. In 2003, Friendship Bridge's co-founder, Dr. Ted Ning, was one of three Coloradans given the prestigious Jefferson Award by the American Institute for Public Service. The award recognizes individuals who better their communities through public service. Like all the organizations in this section, Friendship Bridge can only succeed with devoted help from many volunteers.

The Evergreen Naturalists Audubon Society (TENAS) (p. 34 & 268) celebrated its 35th Anniversary at its annual banquet at Mount Vernon Country Club in January of 2004. It continues to be a vital contributor to our awareness of the natural environment in which we are fortunate enough to live,

and a leader in community efforts to preserve that environment. The Society maintains a lively program of meetings with interesting speakers and of trips to see birds and wildflowers, and continues its lobbying efforts on environmental issues. TENAS still participates in the annual Christmas Bird Count, which locally is showing a small annual decline in species and numbers counted, but nationally is showing a greater and disturbing decrease. The organization has taken on a demanding and important project which they call Birds in the Balance. In its 10th year in 2004, it involves year-round monitoring of the birds in the Bear Creek Basin. So far the findings are that while the more hardy species are holding their own, there are verifiable declines in numbers of the more delicate species. For a donation of $5, TENAS provides a Backyard Habitat Enhancement Packet, containing current information on creating more natural backyard environments attractive to Colorado's native songbirds as well as booklets about bird houses and feeders, a bird checklist for the Evergreen area, and information about noxious weed control. This latter is another new activity for TENAS. Its members are taking a very active role in the battle against noxious weeds, in cooperation with other concerned organizations. What the attractive weeds have in common with unlovable thistles and spotted knapweed is that they are not native to our area, and if given a chance will multiply rapidly and drive out our lovely natives. "We were known all over the world for our beautiful wildflowers," says Sylvia Brockner, "but if we cannot keep these strangers in check, we will lose an irreplaceable part of our heritage." TENAS, the Mt. Evans Group of the Sierra Club and The Evergreen Garden Club co-sponsor the **Community Weed Awareness Campaign** (CWAC) chaired by Cathy Shelton, which conducts various educational efforts to alert people to what are noxious weeds in our area and how to tackle them with the least environmental damage. Under legislation which went into effect in 2003, property owners have certain legal obligations with respect to specific weed species. Community Weed Day at Evergreen Lake, an annual event, is a combination of weed-pulling, weed identification and enrolling people in the "Adopt a Plot" campaign, in which they undertake to keep a specific plot at the Lake weeded. Winner of a competition held in 2004 for a slogan for CWAC was Stacy Smith with "Killer Weeds: New Outlaws of the Wild West" which was incorporated into a logo by artist Mildred Keiser, with a cartoon of a vicious thistle choking to death a virtuous Columbine maiden.

For newcomers to Evergreen, especially those coming from parts of the country with plentiful rainfall, decent soil, and a less than mile high altitude, attempts to establish a garden here can be discouraging. Add the voracious appetites of elk, deer, ground squirrels and chipmunks, and prospects can get downright depressing. And then you drive past the dam and see that lovely mass of flowers, shrubs and grasses and wonder, "Who plants and takes care of that, and how on earth do they do it?" Well, it is the **Evergreen Garden Club**, that's who, and these wizards are also responsible for the cheerful display outside the Post Office, the orderly succession of blooms surrounding the abstract sculpture in the center of the Bergen Park traffic circle, the garden at Evergreen Metro's office building on Stagecoach Boulevard, the little xeriscape demonstration garden outside the Library and the two unusual gardens at the Hiwan Homestead Museum. One is a piece of nostalgia — a Victorian era garden displaying flowering plants that settlers might have planted in the late 1800's — and the other a demonstration of the herbs that can flourish in Evergreen. The seventh garden that is planted and maintained by the Garden Club is at the northwest corner of the Church of the Hills, honoring Mrs. Mary Johnston, a former Garden Club president. The Club has a commitment to community education about gardening, and to that end maintain a "horticultural hotline" where master gardeners answer questions about gardening problems. They have monthly meetings featuring speakers on topics from Roses to Xeriscaping, how to foil deer and elk and the art of "amending" a bed of rocks and sand on your mountain site into soil that will grow almost anything. Every other year, the Garden Club sponsors a Garden Tour, a demonstration of just what can be accomplished by skillful gardeners in the Evergreen area in spite of all the handicaps. Proceeds from the event benefit their scholarship at Evergreen Scholarship/Bootstraps Inc. On alternate years, the Club features a Plant Sale offering us all the chance to buy plants raised by local gardeners. The Club conducts field trips to places like specialty gardens and greenhouses and the Denver Botanic Gardens and, like an increasing number of well-established non-profits in Evergreen, maintains a useful web site. The Garden Club was started in 1967, the result of a chance encounter between Louise Mounsey and Gretchen Stoeppelwerth who agreed that they both missed the garden clubs

they had enjoyed in the towns from which they came. Since gardening in the mountains is so challenging, they decided it was time to start a garden club in Evergreen, especially to help the many newcomers beginning to settle here.

The **Mount Evans Group Sierra Club** meets monthly at the Evergreen Rec Center. The Club keeps its members informed on local and regional environmental issues and participates in such activities as the Sept. 2004 Walk for Wilderness, commemorating the 40th Anniversary of the Wilderness Act.

The **Recycling Story** is another triumph of volunteer effort. King Soopers had a statewide recycling program, housed here in facilities behind the Bergen Park store, which was closed in February of 2000 because the King Soopers recycling contractor could no longer make a profit on selling the recyclables. Evergreen recyclers turned to the Clear Creek County Transfer Station in Idaho Springs, but within a month that station was overwhelmed and its use was restricted to Clear Creek residents. A wonderful and indomitable 80+ lady named **Martha Mott** gathered together the leadership of Evergreen's environmental groups, forming **Mountain Recyclers**, and approached Tri-R Recycling of Denver about taking over the recycling operation. After a summer of negotiations and with the cooperation of King Soopers, the center reopened on October 1. It is open Friday through Monday, for a total of 40 hours per week. Almost immediately, a major problem arose when people began dumping trash, along with recyclables, at times when the center was not open. Volunteers again to the rescue. A group of "Happy Helpers" was formed to clean up the site on Thursday afternoons, allowing Tri-R to continue to serve the center without cost to the mountain community. A second challenge ingeniously met was when it became clear that people wanted to recycle all glass containers, and not just the brown ones that Coors would buy — but Tri-R could not afford to recycle the others for free. Mountain Recyclers got to work again, persuading five Evergreen banks to subsidize the effort. A year later, the program was paying for itself. The *Canyon Courier* has been most cooperative in running articles about the recycling effort, so that the community is kept continuously informed about recycling opportunities and the benefits of recycling. When Martha Mott became too ill to continue, Mereth Meade assumed the leadership of Mountain Recyclers. Bruce Glenn, always active in the recycling

movement, took the initiative in tackling a specific unmet recycling need, that of electronic waste. Because of the harmful components contained in such items as computers, monitors, VCR's. DVD's cell phones, these should not end up in our landfills. A special e-waste recycling day, sponsored by Wild Rose Congregational Church, the Evergreen Rotary Club and the Mountain Recyclers, was held on May 1, 2004 at the Xcel Energy parking lot. The day was a resounding success. Tri-R Recycling hauled away three large truckloads of electronic devices for reprocessing, reconditioning or recycling. As at all locations where e-waste is collected, a modest fee was charged, except for printer cartridges. These were donated to Mt. Evans Hospice, which has an ongoing program of collecting them as a fundraiser.

Evergreen Disposal Service offers curbside recycling of plastic, aluminum, glass, and all paper to its customers for an additional $8 a month. They also offer recycling at their transfer and recycling station at the dump on highway 73. Several times during the summer, Jefferson County sets up stations in the mountain area where residents can dispose of slash, leaves, pine needles, etc. for a small fee. The County Recycling Center at Rooney Road accepts slash during the wildfire season, and is also the year-round place to dispose of harmful chemicals and other waste that should not be put into landfills.

Garden by the Dam, planted and maintained by the Evergreen Garden Club.

The abundant **wildlife** that live among and around us here in Evergreen is a never ending source of wonder and delight. Sometimes they are also a source of exasperation, and occasionally of tragedy. As the Department of Wildlife likes to remind us, it is we human beings who moved in on the territory of **deer, elk, mountain lion, bear, coyote, and fox**. Unless we want to follow man's ancient recipe for dealing with animal/human conflicts — extermination — we must mitigate undesirable outcomes by some adaptations in our life styles. Rule number one is "do not feed wild animals!" Our food on the whole is not good for wildlife and it upsets natural balances. (Thank goodness we are still encouraged to feed the birds — with the right stuff.) The fear of mountain lions, or cougars, whose numbers are on the increase, is not substantiated by the facts. Since 1900, according to the Colorado Division of Wildlife (DOW) only two people have been killed by mountain lions in Colorado, far less than are killed by domestic dogs or by lightning. Mountain lions tend to live in remote, primitive country, but as numbers of deer and elk in suburban areas increase, so does the presence of the cats that hunt them. Another predator, but one with fewer friends than the cougar, is the coyote. After centuries of being classified as a "bad" animal, recognition is increasing that this animal is a valuable part of the

ecosystem. A speaker for Sinapu, an organization devoted to the restoration and protection of native carnivores and their habitats in the Southern Rockies, gave a talk at the Evergreen Rec Center and pointed out that, when coyotes are removed from the environment, populations of what she called "mesopredators" — raccoons, foxes and house cats — explode, causing the numbers of songbirds, food for these predators, to decline rapidly.

The Colorado Division of Wildlife has the awesome responsibility of redressing the imbalance between predators and prey in order to keep numbers within the capacity of the food supply. In our area, this mainly means balancing hunting permits with the numbers of deer and elk. In 2004, DOW increased to 147,000 the number of "antlerless and either sex rifle permits" for elk hunters in Colorado: their long-term goal is to reduce the elk population from 270,000 to 190,000. In 2003, hunters took 64,787 elk. Deer licenses were also increased from 95,000 in 2003 to 103,000 in 2004.

A harbinger of Spring, and the first public event after the ice-skating season is over, is the **Mountain Area Earth Day Fair**. The 15th annual celebration of Earth Day in Evergreen took place in April, 2004 at the Lake House. The origins of Earth Day go back to the 1970's, but the Evergreen event started in 1989 at the old brick school which was demolished to make room for the new Library. The event is sponsored by TENAS, Mt. Evans Group Sierra Club, Evergreen Park and Rec District, Evergreen Newspapers, and by Earth Day and Beyond, a dedicated group of environmentally concerned citizens including Mary Dickhoff, Carl Keiser, Anne Harding, Bruce Glenn, Christie Green, Cathy Shelton and Etta Debenham. The occasion is fun, educational, and nourishing with some 50 exhibitors/participants, including raptor displays about living with wild animals, informational tables manned by many governmental and non-profit groups, environmental games for children, sales of art work benefiting environmental cause, and plenty of food.

Unless you are yourself a horse-lover or have friends who are, it is easy to overlook the fact that, in spite of the increasing number of suburban developments here, Evergreen is still **horse country**. The Jefferson County Horse Council has an Intermountain Branch which meets monthly at the Evergreen Rec Center to hear guest speakers on horse-related topics, and to share information on local and

statewide horse issues. The Council also represents the interests of horse owners in matters such as trail usage and County horse regulations. In 2004, the County has under consideration changes in zoning regulations as they relate to the keeping of large animals in unincorporated areas, the areas which are under the direct jurisdiction of the County Commissioners. On the other hand, keeping horses is part of the traditional western lifestyle, and some estimates indicate that Jefferson County has the biggest horse population in the state. One the other hand, the reality is that the county is becoming more urban, with housing subdivisions eating up rural enclaves. At present, large animals are permitted in 83% of the county, with 47% of lands east of the foothills and 87% of the land west being zoned for large animals. We were surprised to learn that on properties over one acre, there are no limitations on the number of large animals that can be kept, and even on an acre or less, up to four animals are permitted. Don MacDougall, president of the Horse Council, was quoted in the *Courier* as believing that the real key to horse ownership that does not raise conflicts with neighbors is good management (disposal of waste, adequate food supply, rotation of pasture etc.) and that this is difficult to achieve through regulations.

How sincere is the concern of horse lovers for the welfare of all horses is evidenced by the mission of two organizations. **Harmony Horseworks**, formerly Conifer Horse Rescue, was formed to prevent horses from being sent to slaughter auctions. They aim to rescue, rehabilitate, and retrain abused, neglected, and unwanted horses in Colorado, primarily in the I–70 and 285 Front Range corridors, although they will pick up horses anywhere in the state. They also provide temporary foster care for horses with special needs until they become adoptable. The 2002 wildfire season brought out a distressing reality: state and local governments have extensive plans for evacuating people when disasters strike, but not for animals. So a volunteer team of foothills horse owners, the **Jeffco Horse Evacuation Assistance Team**, was formed in 2004 to work in cooperation with local disaster authorities to help rescue large animals in the event of fires, flooding or other disasters. Organizers note that one important preparation large animal owners can make in advance is to accustom their animals to being loaded onto a trailer.

Of course, the big event for Evergreen area horse owners and lovers is the annual **Rodeo and Rodeo Parade**

MOUNTAIN AREA EARTH DAY FAIR

Celebrate the Earth

Saturday, April 24
10 a.m. - 4 p.m.
Evergreen Lake & Lake House

☆**FREE ADMISSION**☆

HawkQuest   Family Fun
Children's Activities   Refreshments
Environmental Exhibits   Community Information

Earth Day Fair Poster.
Illustration by Mildred Keiser.

(p. 205–6, 268). 2004 saw the 38th annual Evergreen Rodeo on June 19 and 20. The town is transformed on rodeo weekend, with the parade on Main Street on Saturday morning when floats of all kinds, from the comical to the spectacular, marchers with banners for good causes, and hopeful political candidates wave at the watching crowds. The rodeo experimented with one evening show and one daytime in 2004, both offering activities for kids and booths of craft items and food. Popular bands played at a number of venues on Saturday night and for yet another year the town celebrated its western and cowboy roots.

For **birders**, the past 11 years were quite fruitful. The well-designed lake improvements and its wetlands attract an amazing variety of water birds each year. Cormorants, pelicans, many varieties of duck, and not-so-welcome Canada geese draw bird-watchers to this attractive site. Birding has been described as the simple joy of observing a living thing going about its daily activities. And thereby, becoming engaged in the natural world in which we live. One recent Evergreen bird story, that could not help drawing out the comedian in readers, was about a carefully planned operation to capture 15 local turkeys and relocate them to Buena Vista. Who did not respond mentally with some variation of, "I could name a few other local turkeys I'd like to see shipped off to Buena Vista!"

Fish Stories. The drought year of 2002 was hard on fish throughout the state, and hard on those who make a living from supplying fishing tackle and guide services. Among these was Jim Cannon, owner of Blue Quill Angler in the old octagonal Hiwan barn. Blue Quill employs experienced guides who take clients to prime fishing locations within two and a half hours of Evergreen. Cannon says that hiring a guide is more than a day on the water — it is a learning experience. "It would take you years of fishing to learn what a guide can teach you in one day." Improvement of fish habitat in our cherished Bear Creek is one of the major objectives of **Evergreen Trout Unlimited**. In 2004, after years of planning, getting grants and fund-raising, the organization launched a major project in cooperation with Friends of Bear Creek, TENAS and Denver Mountain Parks. This is the improvement of stream habitat along a quarter-mile section of the creek at O'Fallon Park. Improvements include the planting of 10 trees and 50 shrubs, the addition of rock and soil to stabilize the bank, and the creation of five bend pools, eight "riffle pool sequences" and four cover logs to provide little niches,

deeper water and more oxygen for fish. Trout Unlimited, along with the Department of Wildlife, has long advocated that Bear Creek be put on the list of "impaired streams" under the Clean Air Act, and in August of 2004 the EPA decided to overrule a state decision and initiate the process of public hearings to take this step. The prime reason is to improve water quality and cold water fishery.

As for our own animals, it is important to remember that Jefferson County has a **Dog Leash Ordinance** which requires that dogs be confined to their own premises or on a leash at all times. This goes against the grain for some old timers, who remember that one reason people moved up to the mountain areas was so their dogs could run free. But wandering dogs are a menace to wildlife, sometimes chase cars and bicycles, and can frighten children. Jefferson County Animal Control Manager Carla Zinanti said in a 2003 *Courier* interview that, although the mountain areas of the County have far less that 25% of the total population, they constitute 25% of all complaints. And the great majority of complaints are about loose and nuisance dogs. A secure kennel and high fence are the best control methods, she said. Invisible fences are inadequate: Animal Control picks up a lot of dogswearing electric fence collars, and the fences do not keep other dogs out. The leash law applies even on private roads: neighbors and mailmen have the right to come and go on these, the same as on public roads, without interference from dogs. The Animal Control Department has guidelines for people to follow in making complaints about loose dogs, but sometimes recommends that the best solutions come from mediation between neighbors, where there is a

willingness to sit down and listen to each other's point of view.

RELIGIOUS AND SPIRITUAL LIFE

There are more than 20 Christian churches and fellowships holding services in the Evergreen-Kittredge-Indian Hills area; Catholic, Baptist, Lutheran,Presbyterian, Methodist, Episcopalian, Christian Scientist, Evangelical Free, Congregational (UCC) and Community. There are also two more broadly spiritual groups meeting regularly, Mountain Light Unity and the Evergreen Spiritual Center. Most of these congregations meet in their own church buildings but some assemble in premises belonging to other churches or in places like El Rancho or Center/Stage. A heart-warming story of inter-faith sharing is that of the Beth Evergreen Jewish Congregation, which started in 1974 as a small group meeting in homes, and then as it grew was welcomed to worship in the United Methodist Church for almost 20 years. Beth Evergreen, with a congregation of 197 families, opened the doors of its new $1.8 million synagogue in September, 2003. They decided to continue the tradition of one denomination opening its home to another by taking in the Evergreen Fellowship Church. In 1997, the Church of the Transfiguration (p. 54–9) celebrated its 100th anniversary, and in 2003, the 371 members of the Presbyterian Church of the Hills celebrated its 50th, remembering that in 1953, 17 people attended the first meeting of the group that developed into the church. Rockland Community Church also had a ceremony in 2003 to mark the completion of the expansion of its sanctuary, from a capacity of 300 to 450, needed because membership was then 1,100 and climbing. The

Congregation Beth Evergreen Synagogue, Laura Greenfield Architects Inc.

307

religious institutions in our community contribute greatly to its depth and richness. In addition to their religious services and music, they provide some of the only available meeting places for social and service organizations, and quietly fill many social needs. A safe but lively place for teens to hang out has been difficult to sustain in Evergreen, and much appreciation is due to Linda Juntunen who, along with her husband, is the moving spirit behind the Higher Ground Youth Coffee House held every Saturday night at the Lutheran Church of the Cross. Since March of 2000, an average of 50–60 young people come to drink gourmet coffees, listen to live music, usually of a Christian nature, and spend time with friends.

LOSSES. Many Evergreen old timers passed on in the last 11 years. Jack Rouse (p. 17,18, 20–21, 216) died in October of 1995 at the age of 75. He and his wife, Collette, an Evergreen native, lived in Evergreen from 1946 to 1972, when his job as an executive with Public Service took him to Boulder. He was the first president of the Evergreen Kiwanis Club and a founding member of many Evergreen institutions including the Evergreen Volunteer Fire Department, Evergreen Sanitation District, Evergreen State Bank, the Evergreen Boy Scout Troop, Chamber of Commerce, and the Hiwan Golf Club...Paul McEncroe (p. 133, 144, 260) died on November 23, 2002. Known best for owning and operating El Rancho Restaurant for 31 years with his wife Donna, Paul was also active in education, having served on the Jefferson County School Board, and in the promotion of tourism in Colorado...Several people whose lives were part of the history of the Evans Ranch (p. 60–72, 250) passed away in this period. Peg Hayden (p. 68), who was so wonderfully helpful to us when we wrote our original book, passed away in March of 1999... Holcombe McCulloch Austin, who spent 40 summers on the Elbert-Austin Ranch, died in 2003 at the age of 96. He married Ethelind Elbert, the grand niece of Samuel Elbert, sixth Territorial Governor of Colorado. Elbert's niece, Louise, bought the property, which was part of the Evans-Elbert Ranch, and built the home (p. 65) the Austins acquired in 1964, which is listed on the National Register of Historic Places. Holcombe Austin had a distinguished career as professor of philosophy at Wheaton College in Massachussetts and was influential in drafting the legislation that established the National Endowments for the Arts and Humanities...Former Evans Ranch foreman Bryan Schwartz died in 2000 at the age of 103...Margaret (Marge) T.

Brasel, the wife of George Brasel, who succeeded Schwartz in the foreman's job, passed away in 2002 at the age of 86. The Brasels lived for 40 years in Evergreen, where Marge was a founding member of the Church of the Hills...Some of our former Upper Bear Creek neighbors are among the losses of these 11 years. Thomas Glenn Peters, 87, passed away in 1997, preceded by his wife Velma in 1996. Peters was a member of the Evergreen Kiwanis for more than 25 years, and owned the T Bar S Guest Ranch on Upper Bear Creek Road from 1956–1969...Lewis Everett Ault, who worked on the Hiwan Ranch in his earlier years and later became a finish carpenter, died in 1995...Owen Strand (p. 233), son of Norwegian immigrants, who was active in many civic endeavors in Evergreen along with his artist wife, Harriet, died in 2003. They had moved for health reasons from Evergreen to Sedona, Arizona...Two deaths of people connected with the Blue Creek area brought back memories of our early years here, when we were building our cabin on that lovely road. Bruce Livonius (p. 75, 79, 80, 81) died in Delta at the age of 68. Until he moved with his wife to Delta in 1994, he had spent his entire life in Evergreen...In 1998, James Carl (Jim) Schneider died, having lived his whole life on the family homestead in Blue Creek Valley. Because 200 acres is not enough to support a family, Jim Schneider always worked other jobs (carpentry, shoeing horses, selling wood, and 16 years as a Jeffco schools custodian) to supplement his ranching income... Jim's wife, Minnie (p.268) survived him by a year, continuing her work with People Comforters, crafting quilts, caps, booties and toiletry bags for people needing assistance as well as quilts to be used in Jefferson County patrol cars for victims of domestic violence and accidents... Ann Austin Clark, the wife of Bud Clark (p. 149), died in March 2004. She was born in Pennsylvania, trained as a nurse and joined the U. S. Air Force during the Korean War, where she met Bud and married him in 1953, living the rest of her life in Evergreen...Abel Manzanares was an Evergreen institution, who graduated from the old red brick high school here in 1920, and married one of his classmates, Dixie Jane. He joined the U. S. Navy in 1944 and served for 20 years. After retiring in 1969, he returned to Evergreen, set tile and quietly helped a succession of young people get a decent start in life. Abel was an active member of the Elks Club, where a memorial service was held for him when he died at 86 in 2003...Helen Nelson Brush, who was a leader in community activities in Indian Hills as

well as in Denver, died in 2003 at the age of 94. Helen was a Denver native. She and her husband, Francis Brush, went in 1941 to the Philippines with their two children to serve at the university church there, and were interned by the Japanese during World War II. They returned to Denver where Francis became a professor of philosophy and Helen pursued her graduate studies, receiving a doctorate in psychology, a subject she taught at D.U. before moving to Colorado Woman's College and establishing the counseling center there. The Brushes built a home in Indian Hills where Helen helped to develop the Environmental Inventory and co-authored with Catherine Dittman a definitive book on the history of that community. From 1980–4, Helen chaired the Board of Directors of Swedish Corona Cooperative, creating a retirement center which has since become the Englewood Meridian. The Brushes' daughter, Maryanne, who lives in Indian Hills, is still remembered fondly for her term as Evergreen Branch Librarian...Evergreen's Recycling Heroine, Martha Mott, also died in 2003, just before her 88th birthday. A lifelong activist, Martha took on her husband's Quaker faith when she married. In Evergreen, she lived in the Greenridge senior apartments and was involved in many community activities, including ENABLE. Rounding up the troops and getting them down on a bus to a county commissioners' meeting, when the organization was pressing for a change in developers' plans, was one of her strong points...Walter Bryant Wilkinson, lawyer, businessman and realtor, was 93 when he died in 2000, having lived in Evergreen for 53 of those years. Born in Michigan, he was in business there until 1949 when he moved to Colorado to become controller of an oil well survey company, and later of Jolly Rancher Candies. In 1963 he and his wife came to Evergreen and opened up Wilkinson and Co., a real estate agency for Hiwan Development Co. properties. He was one of the founders of the Church of the Hills, the Evergreen Elks Lodge and the Evergreen Board of Realtors. Wilkinson was the father of Mimi Nelson, one of Evergreen's most productive volunteers...One of Evergreen's best and most widely-known musicians passed away in 2003 at the age of 76. Doris Bohling accompanied and performed with the Evergreen Chorale for 20 years, was organist and composer-in-residence at Evergreen Lutheran Church, and had her oratorio performed at an Easter sunrise service at Red Rocks...Leo Bradley, a major player in the development of Evergreen's Main Street, died unexpectedly in the spring of 2004 at the age of 78. Born in Des Moines to a father who owned coal mines, Bradley at first followed a mining career, getting a degree from the Colorado School of Mines and buying a coal mine near Rifle. Later, he got a law degree from D. U. and set up in practice in Golden, becoming general counsel to Coors Brewing Co. We described earlier (p.136–9) how his marriage to Pat Quaintance eventually put him in control of the extensive properties and lands owned by the Quaintance family, including the Ross-Lewis Trust which controls a large part of Main Street. Bradley sold some 2,300 acres of family land to Jefferson County Open Space. He was interested in historic preservation and restored a number of buildings in Morrison, Idaho Springs and Georgetown. Along with Jack Rouse and some other business men, Bradley established the first bank in Evergreen. "Leo Bradley often riled residents," according to the *Denver Post*, "but the lawyer left his mark with some of Jefferson County's most notable projects."...Two warm and interesting people, whom we knew originally from their connections with the Open Living School when it was located in Evergreen, also passed away unexpectedly — and too soon — in 2004. Mark Harrington was 56 when he died suddenly at his Evergreen home of heart failure. He came here in the late '60's, "the ultimate hippie" as one friend remembered him. He worked closely with students at the Open Living School, obtaining ski equipment for those who could not afford it and accompanying them to ski areas for instruction. When the Open High School was established in 1975, he helped establish apprenticeships and "shadowing" opportunities to students. He bought the historic octagonal barn and opened a ski rental and repair business, the Snow Leopard, in half of it in 1982. In the other half he and partners opened The Blue Quill Angler. Mark later sold the Snow Leopard to Buzz Sampson and the Angler to his partners, having bought a small spread outside Sterling where he was enjoying learning how to raise cattle and sheep...Dagnija (Dag) Langberg came to Evergreen in 1975, when her husband Arnie became the first principal of the Open High School and she one of the founding faculty members. Born in Latvia, Dag came to the U.S. in 1950 and to Denver in 1952. After graduating from CU Boulder, she got a job at New York's Lynbrook High School where she met her husband. As her three children were growing up, Dag became involved in the Evergreen community, principally as a board member, then president, of the Evergreen Center for the Arts. She left the Open School in

1979 and held various community and teaching jobs in the metro area. Dag spoke four languages fluently, was a skilled potter and a devoted mother and grandmother to six grandchildren. Her *Canyon Courier* obituary noted her "boundless energy and optimistic view of life."...Gene Younger (p. 258), mentor to generations of high school students through his innovative Building Trades Program, died suddenly and too soon in 2002. The Blue Spruce Kiwanis Club is raising funds for a memorial to take the form of a covered area for group picnics and celebrations...Evergreen has a large number of horse-lovers. A brave and lovely member of that community died in 2003 at the age of 57, after a long struggle with Parkinson's disease. Carol Klug was born and raised in England. She and her husband had a ranch, Foxholes, in the Hangen Ranch area where Carol raised horses and other animals, which she loved to share with school children. She was an accomplished horsewoman and for many years a 4–H leader. She also owned a gift shop in downtown Evergreen for a number of years. In the later years when she could not do much physical activity, Carol turned her talents and emotions into poetry... In 2004, Eugene (Gene) H. Lowrance also succumbed to complications of Parkinson's disease. He came to Evergreen in his retirement years with his wife Evelyn (Nicki) Rigoni who died in 1994. In 1997 he married Norma Sallee. Gene had a long and distinguished career as a naval pilot and then a pilot for the FAA. In Evergreen, he was a defoted participant in Evergreen Kiwanis, a volunteer for Salvation Army, Meals on Wheels, Health Fair and an usher at Christ the King Church...Too many teenagers have died on the roads in our community in the last decade. Their deaths, cutting short the promise of precious young lives, sadden us all. In 2004, 16–year-old Collin Fisher's car was hit broadside at the intersection of Highway 74 and Lewis Ridge Road, by a car that crossed over into the wrong traffic lane. He was a young man, beloved by his Evergreen High School classmates, who said that he brought teens of all social circles together. His funeral at Christ the King Church was the largest ever held there.

THE SPORTING LIFE
(p. 200–207 & 272)

Cougars and Lobos. The advent of a high school in Conifer introduced a spicy new element into the sporting life of our community — hot competition between the Evergreen Cougars and Conifer's chosen totem Lobos. EHS has had some outstanding teams and individual competitors in recent years.

Coach Anthony Boettcher's Swim team in 2003 won the Jeffco League championship. Successively, Asher Werthan and Nate Rothman powered the team. Rothman, who broke two state records, achieved All-American status. Boettcher also coaches the Evergreen Swim Team, formerly known as the Evergreen Hurricanes. The Evergreen Pom Squad captured their third straight State dance championship in 2003 and came in 12th out of 200 schools at the nationals in Florida in 2004. Nathan Dern, characterized as a "student-scholar" by the *Courier*, graduated in 2003 with a perfect 4.0 GPA and a perfect 1600 on his SAT's, and won a scholarship to Harvard University. On the sports scene he played soccer, wrestled and ran cross-country. The EHS Ski Team is rather unique in that it draws members from high schools all over Jeffco. In 2003, only 9 of its 23 members were from Evergreen, the rest coming from Conifer, Golden, D'Evelyn, Bear Creek, Lakewood and Columbine High Schools. New to EHS in 2004 was the game of lacrosse. Like its ski teams, the new EHS lacrosse teams are designated as magnet programs, open to students in any school in the area that does not have a lacrosse program of its own. Both the ski and the lacrosse programs are entirely "self-funded", with quite a hefty cost per student. Fund-raisers are held to offset some of these costs. Also overcoming the customary rivalry between Evergreen and Conifer, which one coach described as "huge," is the new Evergreen-Conifer high school varsity ice hockey team, Mountain ICE, which practices at The Edge, ice arena of the Foothills Park and Recreation District.

Hockey, Ice and Inline: There are others in the mountain area besides Mountain ICE who would love to see an ice rink here, perhaps combined with an inline skate arena. Some 100 players in the Mountain Hockey Club play inline games on smooth blacktop at West Jefferson Elementary School in Conifer, where they have put up wooden walls and for which they pay a monthly fee to the school district. The Club is officially sanctioned by U.S.A. Hockey Inline. During the last part of January, the club runs ice hockey drills and scrimmages on Evergreen Lake, depending on ice conditions. The Evergreen Ice Skating Association floated plans in 2003 to build a 27,000 square ft. building, containing ice rink, lobby, offices and storage, on an 11.8–acre property on Soda Creek Road owned by their president, Larry Gomba. The rink would be used for public skating, hockey league games and practices, and figure skating. The neighbors did not

309

react kindly to the idea but the association planned to go ahead with a formal application to the county, since the proposal involved obtaining a setback variance. While there have been no apparent developments on this plan, and the Rec District has not shown any willingness to invest money in such a proposal, it seems as if demand in this area is growing, and it will only be a matter of time before a determined group of ice enthusiasts manages to materialize an ice rink somewhere in the mountain area.

In the bicycling arena, **Team Evergreen** rides on. It sponsors several road bike and mountain bike rides every week for different skill and fitness levels, and also supports causes in the Evergreen community through donations of time, talents and funding, often cooperating with other organizations. Team Evergreen sponsors the aptly named annual **Triple Bypass**. This is a one-day bicycle ride from Evergreen to Avon over three mountain passes, covering 120 miles and 10,300 feet of climbing. It started as a club event in 1989 and has grown steadily since, with 2,600 participating in 2002.

Runners and walkers look forward to the annual **Freedom Run** and the **Evergreen Town Race** (p. 272). The July 4 Freedom Run, starting at the Evergreen Middle School and ending a winding course through Hiwan at the Evergreen Fitness Center, celebrated its 23rd anniversary in 2004. It continues to draw on the efforts of some 200 volunteers and is a major fund raiser for Mt. Evans Hospice and Home Health Care. The Town Race down Upper Bear Creek is run on a Sunday early in August, and benefits the Alpine Rescue Team.

Soccer is very big in Evergreen. The former Evergreen Junior Soccer Association has become the **Stingers** and they are over 1300 players strong. The need for more and better soccer fields has preoccupied the Rec Board and been an issue in its elections throughout the 90's, including the one in 2004.

Et Cetera ...After Harv Teitelbaum retired as the first proprietor of Baskin Robbins Ice Cream Emporium on Main Street,he went to Naropa Institute in Boulder to study Ecopsychology and Environmental Leadership. He worked for years in a number of environmental positions, then developed a new passion — Tree Climbing. Believing that "People Need More Tree Time," he is starting a new "Grove" of Tree Climbers International in Evergreen...Jake Fleshman of Denver caught a 37–inch tiger muskie at Evergreen Lake in June, 2004. The big fish made a fight of it and, although Fleshman said he is normally a catch-and-release fisherman, he felt he had to take home his "once-in-a-lifetime" fish...Paragon Sports continues to sponsor Warren Miller's annual ski film as a benefit for a variety of school causes. Their popular annual Fashion Show, preceding the movie, moved in 2003 from Evergreen High School to the new Clear Creek High School...Tanya Haave (p. 203), a former stand-out EHS athlete, was inducted March 4, 2004, into the Colorado Sports Hall of Fame, a rare honor. After graduation from the University of Tennessee, she played professional basketball in Europe for more than ten years, then returned to Colorado to coach first at Regis College and then at CU-Boulder...Yoga's popularity increased steadily throughout the 90's and early 2000's. By 2004 it was being taught in at least 12 locations in the Evergreen area, and its value as a complement to traditional western medical therapies was being widely acknowledged. Many in our community have been introduced to yoga by petite Tysu Jung, who teaches at both Rec Centers and at the Kinetic Arts Center.

ARTS IN THE MOUNTAINS
(p. 220–42 & 273–5)
At last — an Evergreen Arts Center!
It isn't the grand, multi-million dollar combination of art galleries, classrooms and performing arts facilities that the Evergreen Area Arts Council had in mind when we first came to live full-time in Evergreen in the 70's. The performing arts groups have continued to add amenities to their historic Center/Stage facility, which left the visual arts as the primary art area without a home. As part of the long-term planning for the Buchanan Park/Lutheran land/Bergen Park complex the question of incorporating a new community/art center building came to the fore. But that was still a relatively distant dream. The Miller house, which had been acquired by the Rec District and used as construction headquarters while the new Buchanan Rec Center was being built, was scheduled to be demolished. Thanks to the vision of Evergreen Arts Council Director Lorene Joos and board members of the ECA, and the support of the Rec District Board (especially from Peter Eggers, whose term expired in 2004, and Mike Jacoby, elected in 2002) the 3,600 square foot house was leased to the ECA for $1.00 a year for at least five years for an Art Center. Extensive remodeling and updating was required. The cost of $85,000 was met by a combination of dipping into ECA reserves, suspending their grants program for one year, an $8,000 contribution from the Evergreen Artists' Association, and an imaginative "Build Me, Buy Me" campaign held at the house, with vivid hanging signs indicating what part of the remodeling specific donations would purchase, which brought in $30,000. Remodeling design was a pro bono contribution by architect Judy O'Brien. Hank Alderfer was the general contractor. There were many in-kind donations of materials and labor. The Center's facilities include on the main floor, a large open gallery space and three classrooms, with a pottery and sculpture studio downstairs. Outside is a sculpture garden of which Tom Ware is the volunteer curator.

Joos and the EAC Board regard this Art Center as a "starter home." An opportunity to demonstrate just how interested the Evergreen community is in supporting a space for a great variety of art exhibits, art classes of many kinds, a sculpture garden and art events. The house as remodeled is pleasant, functional and quite spacious. It may be adequate for many years to come, it may be possible to add on to it, or indeed the grand vision of a new, expensive Art Center located

Lorene Joos at Clay Exhibit.

somewhere in the Buchanan/Bergen Park complex may one day materialize. But this facility is in operation now, and is bursting with activity.

The Center opened in December, 2003 and in its first seven months of operation hosted seven exhibits: Holiday Art, a juried Clay Show, the Evergreen Invitational, show casing twenty seven artists, the Evergreen Artists' Association Spring Show, a two person show featuring work of susiehyer and Andi Mascarenas, the Colorado Pastel Society Show and a Contemporary Art Exhibition juried by Patty Ortiz from Denver's Museum of Contemporary Art, open to any Colorado artist over 18. Exhibits of student artists also took place in this time period, as well as many classes and workshops in different art areas and classes offering opportunities for anyone in the community to explore creating art. Children's art classes and summer art camps proved popular. The Center has made an impressive start to carrying out its mission: "To provide a showcase for artistic excellence and opportunities for art exploration, experiences, education and appreciation."

The **Evergreen Arts Council** (EAC), its name changed from the Evergreen Area Council for the Arts, now has offices at the Art Center and continues to sponsor Summerfest, a juried show of some 115 artists and crafts people at Heritage Grove, and Winterfest at Evergreen High School as its primary fund raisers. As befits its changing role in a changing community, it is modifying some of its emphases. In discussion with its constituent organizations in the visual and performing arts, it was determined that some of these non-profits needed help in marketing themselves and their events to the community more even than monetary grants. Efforts to meet those needs were underway in 2004, starting with a community arts calendar monthly in *Serenity Magazine* and an attractive tri-fold brochure, listing all arts organizations and events for a four-month period, to be mailed three times a year to 17,000 community addresses. Art in the Schools is a major project of the EAC, created to help local schools fund art projects, purchase materials and promote art education. Lorene Joos is nursing an ambitious new role for Evergreen — to become a metro magnet as an arts community. She knows that there are problems to be tackled, parking and transportation among them. But she finds that there is so much talent here that should be shared with the wider metro community. And seeing what Lorene

Evergreen Art Center and Sculpture Garden.

has already accomplished, it would be a little foolish to bet against her!

The Art Center is a participant, along with Apostrophe Arts and Design, Evergreen Fine Art, the Evergreen Gallery, Millsap-Moore Gallery, Shadow Mountain Gallery (newly moved from Kittredge to Evergreen Main Street), Silver Arrow, and Timberline Gallery, in **First Thursday Gallery Nights** — a venture launched on April 1, 2004. The galleries publish a guide to the shows and locations, serve refreshments and create a festive and welcoming atmosphere for visitors, some first timers, exploring local art galleries.

In September, people interested in seeing where and how art is produced in Evergreen can take part in a self-guided tour of artists' studios. The annual event, **Open Door Studios — Artists of Evergreen**, was started in 2002. A free guide booklet is available in many locations in the community giving location directions and maps, artists' biographies, and brief descriptions of their works. Studios — there were 21 of them in 2003 — are open for three weekend days from 10 a.m. to 4 p.m. The goals of the tour are to acquaint the public with the amount of work that goes into the creation of an art work, to invite people to ask questions of the artists, and of course to allow visitors to purchase or commission art works.

Trudy Chiddix and her work at Clay Exhibit.

Sculpture by Maureen Scott at Clay Exhibit.

311

Center/Stage: new staircases and patio.

Also in September, the two-day **CARE Artist Studio Tour** invites the public to tour studios in the Mount Vernon Canyon area. This event is a fund-raiser for Canyon Area Residents for the Environment (CARE), so there is a $15 charge for tickets, and artists donate 10% of the two days' sales to the organization dedicated to preserving and enhancing community and environment.

The Evergreen Artists' Association (EAA) is of course delighted to have the new Art Center as a regular venue for its indoor exhibitions. Its annual summer Evergreen Arts Festival reached its 38th year in 2004. This is a Fine Arts and Fine Crafts show, rated among the top five shows of its kind in Colorado according to a Harris Poll, which takes place at the end of August in Heritage Grove. Artists from all over the country display and sell their works and there is always good food and lively entertainment. The event is a fundraiser for the EAA, supporting its art education grants to schools and other community arts-related activities.

Center/Stage (p. 273), the primary performing venue for the **Evergreen Chorale**, the **Evergreen Players**, the **Evergreen Children's Chorale** and the **Baroque Folke**, has undergone many improvements in the last decade. Originally a summer meeting house for the Episcopal Church's Evergreen Church Music Conference, it became the venue for the Chorale's twice-yearly musical productions in the mid 70's. Conditions were primitive — no indoor plumbing, no heat, no insulation. The County's 1989 red-tagging of the

building proved to be a blessing. The Chorale negotiated a long-term lease with the Episcopal Diocese which allowed them to start a methodical series of modernizations and expansions of the building: in 1992, lobby and restrooms;1993, patios; 1994, orchestra pit and costume storage; 1995, green room and dressing rooms; 1997, theater seating and a new lighting system; 1998, gardens; 2004, a $250,000, 1200 sq. ft. spacious new lobby designed by the Denver architectural firm of Semple Brown Design, with room for people to gather and talk and gallery space on the walls which will be planned, mounted and managed by the **EAA**. Center/Stage is available for rental for meetings, weddings, social gatherings. The cost of

all these remodelings and additions has been greatly helped by grants from the Scientific and Cultural Facilities District or SCFD (p. 273), that unique source of funding for metro area cultural institutions which, hopefully, will be reauthorized by the voters in November 2004. Veteran Chorale star and Board member Mike Moore (P. 148, 228–9) co-chaired the Lobby Expansion Project Committee with John Davis, president of the Players. New Chorale stars Gail and Bruce Montgomery spearheaded two lively fund—raisers that netted $15,000. Other sources of funding have been the Evergreen Arts Council, foundations, individual donors and, in the case of the lobby project, the Evergreen Rotary Club.

The Evergreen Players (p. 226–7), having been without a satisfactory home since they lost the use of their Little Log Theater in 1992, signed an agreement in 2000 with the Chorale to jointly use and manage the Center/Stage building. According to John Davis, the collaboration has been a fruitful one, allowing the two organizations to "pool our resources, share everything from equipment to expertise and even create a *Center/Stage Magazine*. There are many things we could not do separately but now can do together." The Players, still an all-volunteer enterprise with just two paid part-time paid staff members, typically stage four or five productions a year, including several straight plays and one musical. They host a Youth Drama Camp for children 5–15 each summer. The group has won many honors for its dramatic productions at the annual Colorado Community Theatre Coalition festivals. Its 2003

Evergreen Chorale: "Kiss Me Kate: Spank": Petruchio (Bruce Montgomery teaches Kate (Gail Montgomery) a lesson while Baptista (Bud Holp), Lucentio (Randy Hise), Gremio (Eddie Perez), and Hortensio (Ron Welch) enjoy the show. Ellen Nelson, Photographer.

Children's Chorale: "Annie", with Daddy Warbucks (Matt Adrian), Annie (Katrina Atkinson) and Grace (Amy Lovin). Photo by Ellen Nelson.

production of *The Trip to Bountiful* won virtually every major award, including First Place, People's Choice, Best Director, Best Set Design, Best Actress and Best Costume Design. In the spring of 2004, they staged the world premiere of *Hallelujah House: A Musical Ballad of the Gold Rush West* by Carolyn Evans Campbell.

The Chorale, under the skillful musical direction of **Michael Weiker**, continues to offer superb musical theater and concerts to the Evergreen community. A new venture started in 2002, the **Dandy Lion Theatre Company**, is a company of adults performing for children.

Another permanent venue for stage productions opened in Conifer. This is a 100–seat theater with a three-quarter round plan, the **StageDoor Theatre**, located in the Aspen Park Village Shopping Center. It is the culmination of a long-time dream for Conifer thespians, though they regard it as an interim home. A lively and popular branch of StageDoor activities is the Conifer StageDoor Theatrical School for kids who love to perform. By Spring of 2004, the School had 110 students, divided into three classes: the Junior Company for 6–11–year-olds, the Broadway Company for 10–18–year-olds and the Marquee Company, selected 13–18–year-olds who have the desire and talent to perform the more intense and challenging Broadway shows. There is a waiting list for each group.

The **Evergreen Children's Chorale** (p. 274) had its 10th anniversary in 2001. The Chorale started a new venture, the Prelude to the Chorale, giving younger children in grades two to four a chance to develop their voices and performing skills to prepare them for the more demanding regular Chorale schedule.

Art for the Mountain Community (AMC) evolved out of the efforts of the Library Art Committee to select and fund a suitable piece of sculpture to celebrate the new Evergreen Library building (p. 265). The Committee was appointed by the Jefferson Library Foundation, after the defunct Friends of Evergreen Library organization voted to donate its remaining funds to the Foundation as seed money for such a sculpture. The large bronze piece, *Planting Evergreen* by Evergreen sculptor Tom Ware was ceremonially unveiled in the fall of 1994. The Evergreen members of the Art Committee found great satisfaction in this new venture and, augmenting their numbers by inviting other community members interested in the arts, they started meeting and planning. Fortunate in securing the pro bono services of attorney Paul Cockrel and CPA Bill Valentine, Art for the Mountain Community (AMC) was incorporated in November 1994, and certified as a 501(c) 3 charitable organization. For the first few years the focus was on commissioning one large piece of sculpture at a time for a public place

Evergreen Players: "Hallelujah House". Old West Prostitutes (Michelle A. Grimes and Emily Faith Smith) dream of a better life in Carolyn Evan Campbell's original musical ballad. Ellen Nelson, Photographer.

313

"Planting Evergreen", by Tom Ware at Evergreen Library.

"Spirit of the Rockies" with sculptor Ivan Kosta.

"Spirits of the Land", by Madeline Wiener. Photograph by Phil Shanley.

"The Foreman", by Laura Mehmert, at Hiwan Homestead Museum.

whose owner was interested in cooperating with the project. The first piece was Denver sculptor Madeline Wiener's large limestone *Spirits of the Land* outside the Lake House, with ownership vested in the Evergreen Parks and Recreation District. The second was Evergreen artist Laura Mehmert's *The Foreman*, a large bronze piece outside the Hiwan Homestead Museum. Before the installation of the third commissioned piece, Colorado Springs' sculptor Ivan Kosta's metal *Spirit of the Rockies* placed in 2001 at the Tanoa Center adjacent to the new Pioneer Trail, AMC had embarked on an additional venture. This was aimed at bringing a changing annual selection of sculptures to venues on Main Street and beyond. Christened "The Heart of Evergreen Sculpture Walk," this is a show of works chosen by a selection committee from slides submitted by artists, which are placed for one year each June. The selection is described in an article in *Serenity's* September, 2003 issue as "deliberately diverse in theme, medium, color, and size, the artwork evokes a range of sentiments, including likes, perhaps dislikes, and often humor." All those whose works are chosen receive a $500 honorarium and a chance at the $500 People's Choice and $500 Best of Show awards. All works are for sale, and AMC cooperates financially with individuals or organizations interested in purchasing works from the Sculpture Walks for permanent public display. As of the summer of 2004, there were altogether 16 permanent sculptures on display in public places by AMC, the most recent acquisition being the bronze *Free Wheeling* outside the Buchanan Rec Center which was part of the 2003 Sculpture Walk. The first Sculpture Walk placed eight pieces, by 2004 the number had risen to fourteen. The next major commission offered by AMC will be for a piece, selected by competition, which will honor Evergreen's volunteer firefighters and be placed outside the Bergen Park Fire Station.

People who invest time, energy and money in getting sculpture into public places hope that each piece will resonate deeply with someone and make the effort worthwhile, as the sculpture *Ann Louise* did with Peggy Eggers. This is a bronze figure by David Wright of a tall slender woman holding a bunch of beets.

She never moves. She never speaks. She never even opens her eyes. Time leaves its mark on the rest of us, but she never ages — in fact, never changes. And yet, she is one of my best friends. Depending on the weather, this friend towards whom I feel so warm can be cold to the touch. Sometimes she even wears a thin sheet of ice over her short-sleeved dress — without a shiver. But that's understandable. My friend Ann Louise is made of bronze. As one of the pieces chosen for display in Art for the Mountain Community's second Heart of Evergreen Sculpture Walk, she stood for a year outside the bank on Main Street. Art for the Mountain Community and the Evergreen Arts Council presented Ann Louise as a gift to the citizens of Evergreen in 2001. Today she stands on the front lawn of the Evergreen Lakehouse, where I always know I can find her. There, though her eyes are shut, she oversees the coming and going of every skater, voter, runner, wedding guest, fisher,canoer, and person like myself come to shake off the week's corporate commuting dust and reconnect with what makes us whole. There she stands in skirted solidity — feminine, strong, serene — eternally available to anyone who cares to pause and partake.

She may be young, but my statuesque friend posses the mighty wisdom of the ages. She doesn't speak words but her strong, graceful image speaks volumes. On my slouchy days Anne Louise — so poised and proud and alert — invites me to align my spine and re-right myself. At other times she squares her diminutive shoulders wide like angel wings and advises me to carry my burdens lightly. Her graceful neck rising out of those shoulders like Nefertiti of the Nile reminds me that despite what my teenage son might think, I too have reasons to hold my head high. I have come to her raw, out of synch with the world. Ann Louise stands tall and singular like a lighthouse, lit by something lovely from within, and shows me peace.

AMC raises funds from individual donors, from the SCFD and EAC and other grant sources, and from "Starry Western Night," an annual dinner event at the Lake House, featuring a live art auction, a silent auction of art and other goodies, music and entertainment. The successful fundraising activities owe much to the creative efforts of Mimi Nelson who, not content with working full-time in the development area for organizations like the Catholic Charities, Habitat for Humanity and Trust for Public Lands, volunteers her time and talents to a variety of community non-profits.

Evergreen **sculptors** are making their mark outside of their own community. Tom Ware (236, 246, 259, 273) continues to be a moving force in the art life of Evergreen. His own sculpture appears at the annual Loveland Show, and at the North American Sculpture Exhibition at Foothills Art Center. Two of the "Ware House Gang" of aspiring sculptors, who attend a sculpting group in his studio, are receiving recognition and commissions. Maureen Scott in 2003 had two of her works selected for inclusion in the Colorado Art Open at Foothills Art Center in Golden, in 2004 was among 68 sculptors from the U. S. and Canada with work accepted for the annual North American Sculpture Exhibition. Evergreen sculptor Nancy Golden, whose work "The Athlete" is on permanent display outside the Post Office, has completed a group of life size bronze golfers (Babe Didrikson Zaharias, Ben Hogan, Tom Morris and Bobby Jones) for the Murphey Creek Gold Course. Former civil engineer Harold Linke started sculpting in 1990. He has sold some 280 bronze pieces to people around the world.

Art opportunities in the Evergreen area are no longer confined to showing in galleries or submitting pieces to juried shows. Several venues, like the Evergreen Library, the Evergreen Metro offices on Stage Coach Boulevard, and Frames for All Reasons, host art exhibits throughout the year. There is an annual competition for the Evergreen Christmas Greeting Card sponsored by Julie Jones, owner of Frames for All Reasons,open to artists in all media except photography and juried by a panel of judges from the EAA. Proceeds from sales benefit "Memories in the Making", an art program for Alzheimer patients. The Evergreen

"Ann Louise" by David Wright, at Lake House Park.

"The Athlete" by Nancy Golden, at Evergreen Post Office.

"Voices" by Tom Newport, at Center/Stage.

Animal Protection League holds an annual competition for a holiday card design with an animal theme.

The **Evergreen Chamber Orchestra** (p. 228) pioneered a new annual venture in the spring of 2002 — putting on the free Mountain Area Orchestra Festival Concert at Evergreen High School, with student musicians from Evergreen and Conifer High Schools and Evergreen and West Jeff Middle Schools sitting and playing alongside Chamber Orchestra members. The Chamber Orchestra, still under the masterful baton of Dr. William Morse, celebrated its 10th anniversary in 2003. It offers four concerts a year, usually at Rockland Community Church, and three delightful chamber music concerts in area homes. Joint concerts with the Evergreen Chorale are frequently on its annual performing schedule. The orchestra also plays a Young Persons' Concert each year at the Lake House, designed for both young people and adults, to stimulate interest in classical orchestral music. It features demonstrations of different instruments and classical music with a narrator to guide the audience through the pieces. The summer Evergreen Music Festival brings back to our community the spirited and wonderfully talented musicians of the **National Repertory Orchestra** (p. 225–6 & 273) conducted by Carl Topilow, a genius of sorts in working with eager young musicians,

whose dry sense of humor engages players and audiences alike. They play in a new venue — an attractive tent set up in Alderfer/Three Sisters Park, with ample parking. There are usually two concerts each summer, plus a rousing patriotic performance by the Lake on the Fourth of July.

And All That Jazz! The Evergreen Jazz Festival is the brainchild of Sterling Nelson, longtime resident of Evergreen and an aficionado of traditional jazz, i.e. jazz up through World War II. The first effort was in 2001. Sterling lined up major talent and the Festival garnered enthusiastic reviews but financially, it was somewhat disastrous. The following year, a power-packed board of directors headed by Ted Mann, with wife Jeanne Mann as Treasurer and Sterling still very much involved, especially where the booking of talent was concerned, put on just one concert at Heritage Grove, with the Queen City Jazz Band, and spent their time in planning for the staging, publicizing and funding of a second three-day Jazz Festival in 2003. Venues included the Lake House and Elks Club, and the occasion was a success both artistically and financially. Determined to make this a major jazz event for the entire state, the board went on to plan enthusiastically for the 2004 version. Vice-President and marketing expert Jim Reiners said in a *Courier* interview that he sees the Evergreen Jazz Festival one day becoming as significant and recognized as the Evergreen Rodeo, but hopes that it will be able to sustain its unique combination of Big Talent, Small Venues, Great Setting.

Festivals and Celebrations, involving a number of the arts and frequently benefiting a good cause, punctuate the Evergreen community calendar throughout the year. **The Annual Big Chili Cook-off Music and Arts Festival** at the Lake House benefits the mountain area volunteer fire departments. It started in 2002, the Year of Wildfires, and features local bands, visual artists and great chili. The annual **Mountain Music Festival**, started in 1988, raises money for the Mountain Services program of the Senior Resource Center. Sponsored by the Little Bear, it takes place at the Lake House Park in August and features live bands, food from local vendors, retail booths and a Kiddie Korner. A free **Summer Lake Concert Series** has been delighting families and groups of friends since 1998. It takes place on the first and third Wednesdays of June, July and August. Each concert features an opening band, paid for by Evergreen Signs, and a headliner, sponsored by Beau Jo's and Evergreen Rotary Club.

316

The concerts move inside the Lake House in case of rain. Even without the fireworks show that once delighted lakeside audiences (the Fire Department ruled it too dangerous) **July Fourth** celebration beside the Lake is a wonderfully varied and good hearted affair, running from 10.30 in the morning to 5 p.m. In addition to the NRO's afternoon concert, the Denver Brass plays, often with the Colorado Isle of Mull and Drum Corps and the Rocky Mountain Highland Dancers. There is a puppet show and face painting for kids and booths vending soft drinks and a variety of foods. Conifer acquired a much-needed venue for community celebrations when the 450–acre Beaver Ranch Open Space Park was acquired by Open Space in December, 2002. **Arts Alive!**, Conifer's umbrella arts organization, along with local businesses, sponsors the **Mountain Arts Open House and Festival** in May, featuring local artists and artifacts for sale at moderate prices— along with a pancake breakfast to benefit the Elk Creek Fire Department, entertainment and children's activities. In June, Arts Alive! sponsors an annual **Conifer Arts Festival** with 100 artist booths, performances and children's art activities. In July and August, Arts Alive! presents a series of six Saturday evening concerts in the open air, when "Nashville favorites, local artists and other musicians and singers perform from 4 p.m. until dark."

Children and the Arts in the Mountain Area. We are fortunate that the Jefferson County Schools have not abandoned the arts, though there have been serious funding cuts. The Middle and High Schools offer performing opportunities for talented youngsters. **Evergreen and Conifer High Schools** both have creative drama and music departments and stage competent and entertaining plays, concerts and musicals. Attendance is well worth the modest ticket price: if nothing else, take in the lovely EHS Madrigal dinner to start off your winter holiday season. For children seriously interested in vocal music and performance, the **Children's Chorale** and the **Pre-quel to the Chorale** for younger kids are unmatched. The EAC's summer **Art at the Lake** features three occasions "for the young and the young at heart (because an adult must accompany children who enroll) to paint, sculpt, dance, sing." Both the **Evergreen Players** and **Conifer's StageDoor Theatre** offer acting and learning opportunities for young people. A new private organization, the **Center for Performing Arts Studies** (CPAS), offers voice, piano, guitar and strings

Rita Kiefer. Photograph by Ellen Nelson.

instruction for all ages, along with a popular Broadway dance class and college prep music theory. Since 1995, the **Monart School** in Evergreen has offered a year-round fine arts program for students of all ages, with a variety of art camps during the summer. The School is licensed by the Monart International Institute founded by Mona Brookes, an internationally known art educator. For children with a yen to dance, there are classes at Elaine Folkesson's **Evergreen Dance Center** located at the Evergreen Recreation Center, at the **Kinetic Arts Studio** in North Evergreen, which was established in 1973 and is headed by Merle Wurth, and at the **High Pointe Dance Academy**, founded in 2001 by Liz McAdams Graham.

As for **Literary Evergreen**, the roster of local authors, writing on an amazing variety of topics, is expanding. Mystery writer **Diane Mott Davidson** (p. 274) continues to produce intriguing cliff hangers with a culinary theme, about a mythic community that sounds suspiciously like Evergreen. By contrast, **Francine Matthews** — whose mysteries divide into three categories, the wonderfully imaginative series casting Jane Austen as a sleuth, a New England series featuring a hard bitten female detective, and spy stories reflecting her own time working in intelligence — says she would never dream of locating her mysteries in the community in which she lives. Poet **Rita Brady Kiefer** first enchanted an Evergreen audience with a talk and poetry reading at an AAUW "College for a Day" program. At the time, she was Professor of English Literature at the University of Northern Colorado,

EVERGREEN

A town of shy trails where
    we wander at sundown as
velvet antlers wave their honeyed seduction.
And under the porch a red fox with
more than prayer in its eye. We always knew
we would one day live in such a place
        late winter when muted
falls, perhaps fearing their own excess,
    insinuate
what is about to be.

A town permanent residents have seen change
shape like some giant amoeba. Still the faithful
red-wing and finch, blue-spruce and penstemon
argue no pattern, as if like us they have learned
to live with just the omniscient stars as 4 a.m.
companions, the same stars that taught ranchers,
settlers, an architect/Brit-author team from Europe,
lovers of history whose hands made water at ease
for children and boats to skate on and trout to feed.

But beauty is complex the poet has warned us:
weeds pose as flowers, and this human town
can claim no utopia, no Camelot, no promise
a child will be safe or a woman will escape scars
of a man's desperation. Houses may collapse,
hunger go unattended and the dry kiss of the sun
jealous of rain might sometimes lie with this
beauty too long. Still true to its name
it will endure.

rita brady kiefer

317

Madame Mattie Silkes, No Sure Shot

Caroline Evans Campbell.

*Mattie Silks was perhaps Denver's leading Madam.
She and Jenny Rogers were competitors and friends.
Jenny sold Mattie The House Of Mirrors in 1880 in
Denver. Both ran "first class" establishments.*

Good morning, Your Honor.
Last time I seen you, the morning sun
was glinting off the rim of your gold
spectacles, reflecting in every mirror
of my parlor—ceilings, walls, side boards,
the belladonna eyes of your last lady.
We served raspberry tarts for breakfast
that morning, I recall.

Yes, Your Honor, I dueled Kate Fulton
last night over Cort Thomson, my man.
I shot at her. She shot at me.
We both missed, but one of us
shot Cort in the neck!
She's cross-eyed, Your Honor, and mean
as a chained bear. I'm a gentle soul,
and respectable, Your Honor.

My boarders have the softest bosoms,
smoothest thighs, most aristocratic toes,
dainty enough to pull a silver dollar
out of your pocket or tickle you
under the chin or behind the ears.
Of course, you know that, Your Honor.

You say I owe fifteen dollars for disturbing
the peace and breaking Kate's nose—which
happens to always be in my business,
and which was in the way of my parasol—

Fair enough. She said my ample ears
looked like oyster shells,
said they grew eavesdropping on clients.
Shows she don't know about oysters.

Come by and see me sometime.
Here's my business card—*Mattie Silks.*
You like cigars, Your Honor?
Have a Havana—one for you
and one for your missis.
Tell her, regards from Mattie Silks.
She knows who I am. All the wives do.

318

Carolyn E. Campbell

where she received every major award for teaching and scholarship offered by the university. When both she and husband Jerry retired, they chose Evergreen as the place they wanted to live. Rita is an accomplished poet with three published books of poetry to her credit — *Nesting Doll, Trying on Faces,* and *Unveiling* — as well as having had nearly 100 poems published in journals, magazines, and anthologies. Her passion for empowering all potential writers, especially survivors of domestic violence, has taken her to safehouses. She was honored in 2003 as the Volunteer off the Year for her weekly writing sessions with residents of Gateway Shelter for Battered Women in Denver. Rita gallantly responded to Eugene's request to write a poem about Evergreen for inclusion in this Chapter. Outdoors enthusiast **Martin Tessmer** departed from his academic writing in the field of instructional technology to write a series of trail guides to "pocket" wildernesses in the U. S., areas that can be explored in three days or less. Animal rights is the passion of local author **Brian Barger** and is the theme of his first published novel, *Fontana.* Barger moved to Evergreen in 2002. He writes short stories, works in sales for a medical magazine and writes stock forecasts for a business website. Sports, or more precisely sports refereeing, is the major subject matter of the many books and articles written by **Jerry Grunska**, although his first book was a biography of Hawk Wilson, a home run leader of the National League who died in 1948 without having made it into the Baseball Hall of Fame. He was inducted after the book was published. Grunska was for many years a referee and a high school English teacher. *Guide to Search and Rescue Dogs* is the title of **Angela Snovak**'s book published in the spring of 2004. Angela trains her own dogs and works with both the Alpine Search and Rescue Team and with Search and Rescue Dogs of Colorado. **David Wann**, who used to live in Indian Hills but now is part of the interesting co-housing project, Harmony Village, in Golden, co-wrote *Affluenza*, a stimulating critique of our contemporary consumer society, and in 2003 *The Zen of Gardening*, a loving and humorous how-to book on the techniques and mental attitudes necessary to enjoy foothills gardening in spite of the challenges of hail, drought, hungry animals and a short growing season. If there were an award for all-around, Renaissance-style, Arts Person of Evergreen, it would have to go to **Carolyn Evans Campbell**. Poet, novelist, artist, playwright, and superb teacher of poetry, she is a valuable community asset. Campbell, a native of Denver and graduate of CU, lived and traveled in a number of different parts of the world with her husband, Russ, before settling in Evergreen in 1990. She has had five books of poetry published, one of which, *Tattoed Woman*, won the Colorado Book Award in 1998. Her first published novel, *Fireweed*, which brings alive the hardships and adventures of the women who came west on the Oregon Trail, debuted in 2003. And in 2004, in addition to exhibiting her spritely art work in local galleries, Carolyn had the rare experience of seeing her musical play, *Hallelujah House* produced by the Evergreen Players. The play, which she called "A Musical Ballad of the Gold Rush West" was based on her book of poetry, *Soiled Doves of Colorado and the Old West*. And — to crown her efforts — Campbell also wrote the music for the production. In spite of all this productivity, she finds time and great joy in sharing with classes her passion for poetry. She has a gift for eliciting an authentic poetic voice from people who never imagined they had any talent in this area.

A LOOK AHEAD

Evergreen is maturing. The 2004 Evergreen Plan Update anticipates a population growth of about 1% a year. The Chamber of Commerce President believes that, in a very few years, the Evergreen area will approach build-out of reasonably accessible large development sites and continuing building will be in fill. Certainly, there is a lot of residential building underway in the summer of 2004. But perhaps, instead of growth spurts that have periodically changed the very nature of our community, we can look forward to a measure of stability. This will give us time to deal with some as yet unsolved problems: how to integrate into the fabric of Evergreen life the large numbers of people who work "down the hill" and are not involved up here; how to find a meaningful place for *all* our young people in the social, economic and cultural life of our community; how to create affordable homes for those who do our town's work; how to preserve our magnificent natural environment, keeping those noxious weeds at bay and conserving its precious water supply. We are still confident that Evergreen, having met its challenges so well so far, will continue to do so with originality and flair.

319

REFERENCES AND RESOURCES TO FIND OUT MORE

Our major sources for this book have been:
— Interviews with longtime residents. Our own are listed in the acknowledgements. We also used some of those conducted by the Jefferson County Historical Society, which are listed below.
— The contacts and conversations we have had as participants in the community, as well as more formal information which many people supplied to us on request.
— The Canyon Courier, which we have read and clipped for almost 10 years.
— The treasures of the Western History Department of the Denver Public Library, especially its clippings files.
— A relatively small number of published books, articles and pamphlets, listed below.
— Some unpublished materials which have come to us by various routes, also listed below.

Our tapes and photographs have been donated to the Hiwan Homestead Museum, and our clippings, copies of unpublished papers, etc. can be found in the Evergreen Library.

To keep this list as brief as possible, references which are clear in the text are not repeated here.

Published Books and Booklets
— Bird, Isabella. **A Lady's Life in the Rocky Mountains.** Oklahoma, University of Oklahoma Press, 1960. (Originally published in 1875.)
— Bowles, Samuel. **A Summer Vacation in the Parks and Mountains of Colorado.** Springfield, Mass., Samuel Bowles and Co., 1869.
— Brigham, Lillian Rice. **Travelore: A Pocket Guide.** Peerless Printing, 1938.
— Brown, Georgina. **The Shining Mountains.** Self-published, 1976.
— Brush, Helen N., and Dittman, Catherine P. **Indian Hills: The Place, The Times, The People.** Denver, Graphic Impressions Inc., 1976.
— **Colorado Prospector.** Vol. 6, No. 1. Historical Highlights From Early Day Newspapers. Issue on Evergreen, January 1975.
— **Colorado State Business Directories,** 1880 to 1956.
— Colorado Writers' Project, WPA. **Colorado: A Guide to the Highest State.** New York, Hastings House, 1941.

— Crain, Mary Helen. **Evergreen, Colorado.** Boulder, Pruett Publishing Co., 1969.
— **A Circle of Pioneers.** (Reprinted from articles in Canyon Courier.) Colorado, Tri-Canyon Publishing Co., undated.
— **Ever-Exciting Evergreen.** Booklet published in Evergreen for the Evergreen Area Chamber of Commerce in by Dick Gero, Head 'Em Off at the Pass Publishing Co., 1973.
— Evergreen Chambr of Commerce. **Evergreen, The Paradise of Bear Creek Canyon.** Undated booklet, c. 1925.
— Fahenstock, Connie. **From Camp Neosho to the Hiwan Homestead.** Jefferson County Historical Society, 1985.
— Hamilton, C.M. **Our Memories of Bergen Park.** (Booklet published c. 1950.)
— Hayden, F.V. **Geological and Geographical Atlas of Colorado and Portions of the Adjacent Territory.** New York, J. Bien Lithographer, 1877.
— **From Scratch: A History of Jefferson County.** Jefferson County Hisotrical Commission, Colorado, Astor House, 1985.
— Moynihan, Betty and Waters, Helen E. **Mountain Memories. From Coffee Pot Hill to Medlen Town. A History of the Intercanyon Area of Southwest Jefferson County.** Lakewood, Limited Publications, 1981.
— Ringrose, Linda Wells and Rathbun, Linda McComb. **Foothills to Mount Evans: A Trail Guide.** Evergreen, Wordsmiths, 1980.
— Roehling, Justus. **My Castle in the Sky.** 1976.
— Sprague, marshall. **Colorado: A History.** New York, W.W. Norton and Co., 1984.
— Whitney, Gleaves. **Colorado Front Range: A Landscape Divided.** Boulder, Johnson Books, 1983.

Articles
— **Denver Muncipal Facts** (1909 to 1931), numerous articles on the Denver Mountain Parks.
— Dittman, Catherine. "Bergen Laid Foundation for County." **Canyon Courier,** 12 January 1977, p. 25. Also, "The Story of a Pioneer Family: The Thomas Bergens of Bergen Park." Two-part article in **Evergreen Magazine,** Fall/Winter, 1977 and Spring/Summer, 1978.

— **Evergreen Magazine.** In addition to the above, many well-written articles on historical and contemporary themes were published during this magazine's 6 years of existence, including: "Rec District," Spring/Summer 1977; Brockner's nature articles in Summer 1981, Summer 1983 and Winter 1983; "Mount Evans Elk Herd" by Jacque Scott, Spring/Summer 1979; "They Remember When," Spring/Summer 1977; "EST Served up with Kilgore Cuisine," by Sally Bassett in Fall/Winter, 1979; "John Brisben Walker," two-part article by Catherine Dittman in Fall/Winter 1978 and Spring/Summer 1979; "He Gave Evergreen a Voice" (Willard Crain), by Catherine Dittman, Winter, 1981/2; "Walking a Thin Line to Victory" (on Coach Hunter) by Ron Peck (Winter 1981/2; "The Smell of the Greasepaint" (Players), Fall/Winter, 1977; "These Hills are Alive," (Chorale), Spring/Summer 1977; "The Writer as Doer" (Joanne Greenberg) by Dyan Zaslowsky, Spring/Summer 1980; "First by the Lake" (Eddie Ott's) by Betty Moynihan, Winter 1983; "Boyd Norton: A Reformed Physicist, Now Conservationist," Sally Bassett in Spring/Summer 1979.

Interviews by the Jefferson County Historical Society
— Bancroft, Caroline, 24 June 1977.
— Bromfield, Helen, 28 March 1977.
— Douglas, Anne Woodward, 28 March 1977.
— Hicks, Lillian Ralph, 1 April 1977.
— Quaintance, Mary, 19 June 1979.

Unpublished Materials.
— Bergen, William Henry. "Niwot and Spruce Park Counties." Interview with Mr. Thomas F. Dawson, Curator, State Historical Society, July 1921.
— Dark, Ethel. "History of Jefferson County, Colorado." Unpublished M. A. Thesis, Colorado State College of Education, Greeley, 1939.
— Klepetko, Kay. **Tales of the Bar PD.** A History of the Jefferson County Outdoor Education Laboratory School, Mt. Evans, Evergreen, Colorado. Jefferson County Public Schools R-1, Lakewood, Colorado, 1978.

—Record (Land) Books in County Assessor's Office, Jefferson County Courthouse, esp. Books A and B.

Following are resources for some individual segments.

Who's in Charge
— DeBoer, S.R. **Green Thumb Magazine,** December 1972. (Entire issue is a tribute.)
— "Denver Park, Recreation and Open Space Plan." Draft. Royston Hanamoto Alley and Abey. October 1986.
— "Fact Sheet. Proposed Evergreen Recreation and Park District." 1968-9. Mimeo.
— "The Feasibility of Becoming a City: A Cost and Revenue Analysis for Evergreen, Colorado." A study performed for the community of Evergreen and the Jefferson County Planning Department by Dames and Moore, principal authors. Two volumes, report and supporting documentation. Fall 1982.
— "The History of the Denver Mountain Parks System." Edmund Wallace. **Green Thumb Magazine.** June/July, 1964.

Gifts of Nature
— Bailey, Alfred M., and Niedrach, Robert J. Pictorial **Checklist of Colorado Birds.** Denver Museum of Natural History, 1967.
— Brockner, Sylvia Booth. **Birds in Our Evergreen World: a Layman's Guide to the Birds of the Mountain Area.** (Complied from Brockner's columns in the Canyon Courier.) 1974.
— Craighead, John J., Craighead, Frank C. Jr., and Davis, Ray J. **A Field Guide to Rocky Mountain Wildflowers.** Peterson Field Guide Series. Boston, Houghton Mifflin, 1963.
— Humphrey, Harry Baker. **Makers of North American Botany.** New York, Ronald Press Co., 1961. (Information about Parry.)
— **LaRousse Encyclopedia of Animal Life.** London, Hamlyn Pub. Co., 1967.
— Pesman, M. Walter. **Meet the Natives.** Published by author, 1952.
— Pearl, Richard M. **Exploring Rocks, Minerals, Fossils in Colorado.** Denver, Swallow, 1969.
— Peterson, Roger Tory. **A Field Guide to Western Birds.** Boston, Houghton Mifflin, 1961.
— Weber, Wm. A. **Rocky Mountain Flora.** Boulder, Associated University Press, 1972.

Williams-Douglas Legacy
These books and booklets:
— Breck, Allen Dupont. **The Episcopal Church in Colorado 1890-1963.** Denver, Big Mountain Press, 1963.
— Dalglish, Garven. **From These Hills: A History of the Church of the Transfiguration in Evergreen, Colorado.** Boulder, Johnson Publishing, 1971.
— Ellinwood, Leonard and Douglas, Anne Woodward. **To Praise God: The Life and Work of Charles Winfred Douglas.** New York, Hymn Society of America, 1958.
— **Mission of the Transfiguration, Evergreen, Colorado. Golden Jubilee Year 1948.** Prepared by the Bishop's Committee.
and these, among many, articles:
— Bancroft, Caroline. "George A. Jarvis of Jarvis Hall." **Colorado Magazine,** October 1949.
— **Colorado Episcopalian.** "Evergreen Honors Archdeacon Marsh," April, 1971.
— Dallas, Sandra. "Let's Remember the Real Caroline Bancroft." **Denver Post,** 20 October 1985.

Evans-Evergreen Connection
The following books:
— Bluemel, Elinor. **One Hundred Years of Colorado Women.** Denver, self-publ., 1973.
— Breck, Allen duPont. **John Evans of Denver: Portrait of a Twentieth Century Banker.** Boulder, Pruett Publ. Co., 1972.
— **William Gray Evans: Portrait of a Western Executive.** Denver, Alan Swallow publ., 1964.
— Kelsey Jr., Harry E. **Frontier Capitalist: The Life of John Evans.** Denver, State Historical Society and Boulder, Pruett Publ. Co., 1969.
— McMechen, Edgar Carlisle. **Life of Governor Evans, Second Territorial Governor.** Denver, the Wahlgreen Press, 1924.
and, among many articles and unpublished papers:
— **Anne Evans.** Unpublished paper by great-great-granddaughter of Governor Evans. (Loaned by Peg Hayden.)
— **Denver Post** (Empire Section. **"The Evans Dynasty, a Century of Power."** 23 February 1969, 2 and 9 March 1969.

— "Evans Ranch Master Plan." Prepared for Colorado Open Lands by Design Studios West, Inc, assisted by Bowes and Co., Ian L. McHarg and Ed Holmberg. 1984.
— Lunt, Horace. Leter to Phelps Dodge, 29 July 1955. (Loaned by Peg Hayden.)

Mining, Logging, Ranching:
— Anderson, Pearl. Handwritten autobiography, written when she was 79. (Copy supplied by Anderson family.)
— **Canyon Courier.** Articles on pioneers, including: 4 November 1981 (Fleming family), 10 and 17 June 1981 (Maggie Schneider), 6 January 1982 and 6 June 1982 (Pearl Jarvis, 27 February 1985 and 14 August 1985 (Pearl Anderson), 10 July 1985 (Marie Hendrickson), 7 August 1985 (Lillian Ralph Hicks), 22 January 1986 (Elin Herzman Lewis).
— **Mountain Commuter.** "Sawmills," August 1981.
— Means Meadow. Map showing history of land ownerships prepard by Arleta Alderfer for Jefferson County Open Space.
— Moore, Paula C. "Settlement Pattern of a Specific Colorado Foothills Community, 1859-79." Typewritten, 13 December 1979.

Resorts and Dude Ranches:
— Brochures of Troutdale, Greystone, Marshdale Lodge, Bendemeer, etc. in the DPL's Western History Department.
— **Denver Post.** "Greystone Manor," Empire section, 3 April 1977; "Troutdale-in the Pines: Elegant Past, Uncertain Future," Empire section 31 May 1981.
— Greystone. Large notebook with original photographs apparently prepared by Mrs. Genevieve Phipps.
— **Rocky Mountain News.** Articles on Greystone 22 June 1947, 3 September 1947; on Troutdale, 7 July 1979.

An Abundance of Open Space:
— Annual Report of Denver Board of Park Commissioners, 1918.
— Ball, George, (engineer and designer of Evergreen Dam.) Abstract of testimony v.13, 16 February 1927.
— **Denver Municipal Facts.** Articles on acquisition of mountain parks, building of roads and dam are found throughout the volumes, 1909, 1931.

— **Denver Post.** "Colo. Wilderness Act Protects Select Sites," 9 August 1981, "Rebuild the Crest House on Scenic Mount Evans," 19 December 1983.

— Ditmer, Joanne. "Jeffco Rumbling: Building on Open Space?" in "Raising the Roof" column in **Denver Post,** 19 January 1986.
— Jefferson County Open Space publications.
— League of Women Voters of jefferson County. "Jeffco Open Space 1973-1984." December 1984.
— **Golden Transcript.** 25 April 1957 and 28 July, 1976 (Walker)
— **Rocky Mountain News.** Articles about Mountain Parks, 29 September 1964, 30 September 1964, 24 July 74.

Mountain Schooling:
— Articles of Incorporation of Evergreen Scholarship Association, 1945. Amendments through May, 1961.
— **Ballots for Bear Creek.** CBS Documentary on the controversy over the consolidation of Jefferson County Schools.
— Coleman, Alice. "Early Days Preserved," **Jefferson County Sentinel,** 30 November 1967.
— **Denver Post.** "The Lodge Where Boys come to Find Themselves," 14 March 1971; "Dreams Flourish in Open School", 16 March 1984.
— Jefferson County School District, R-1. Materials supplied by Robert P. Eckhardt.
— Stalder, Dorothy E. "Forest Heights Lodge." Handwritten, 11 May 1976.

Spreading the Word: —On 19 October 1983, the **Courier** republished much of its inital issue of 23 October 1958, together with a summary of the later history of the newspaper.
— **Colorado Editor.** "It's a Living, and It's Fun," (Gilfillans) April 1956; "Ball of Evergreen," November 1965.
— **Denver Post.** "The 'Story book' Library," 25 November 1952.
— Douglas, Julia B. "A Small Library in Colorado," **Library Journal** 15 May 1932.
— **Evergreen Library Scrapbooks.** Ongoing history of Library from its earliest days. Can be seen in Evergreen Library.

— "History of Evergreen Library: Slide Show, with Commentary". Prepared for Jefferson County Historical Society by Josie Hoover, 1986.
— Kemble, Jane. ' 'History of the Evergreen Public Library." Unpublished paper, mid-50's. Also "History of the Evergreen Public Library: An Oral Interview with Mrs. Jane Kemble," conducted by Barbara A. Braswell, JCPL Oral History Project, 1973.

Meeting Social Needs:
— Arnold, Marian and John. History of Evergreen Cemetery. Handwritten report prepared for Foothills Genealogical Socy.
— Burdick, Liz, of Foothills Genealogical Society. Information and historical clippings.
— Mayo, Peg and Ralph. Clippings and letters about Paul T. Mayo. Poems of Margery Reed Mayo.
— Smith, Maude. "History of Evergreen Woman's Club."

Architecture and Nature:
— Brochures on early subdivisions in the DPL's Western History Department.
— Brochures, subdivision plats and photographs of land and housing from developers of Hiwan and Genesee.
— Early subdivision plats from Jefferson County Planning Department.

Arts in the Mountains
Two books:
— Douglas, Frederic H. and d'Haroncourt, Rene. **Indian Art of the United States.** Museum of Modern Art, Plantin, 1941.
— Trenton, Patricia and Hassrick, Peter. **The Rocky Mountains: A Vision for Artists in the Nineteenth Century.** Norman, University of Oklahoma Press, 1983.
and the following, among many, articles:
—Crain, Mary Helen. "The Bentons, Ruth and Cliff." **Canyon Courier** 27 June 1963.
— **Rocky Mountain News.** Articles on Eric Douglas 9 July 1938, 12 June 1949, 24 April 1856 (obit.)
— **Spree Magazine**, published and edited by Peg and Jon DeStefano, is devoted to the Evergreen arts scene.

325

The infamous bridge.

ERRATA. P. 20, 4th para: continued (not contined). P. 32, 2nd para: Too rapid (not two). P. 36, we should have included the violet-green swallow as a common summer resident along our stream. P. 37, we omitted the serious flooding of 1965. P. 42, 3rd para: Bowles (not Bowls). P. 43, 2nd para: bearberry is a common name for kinninnik; the plant referred to here is a bush or swamp honeysuckle and the creeper is fiery (nor firery) red. P. 45, 1st para, last column: significant event (not even). P. 82, on photo credit: Davis (not Dvais). P. 83, end of 4th para, 1st column: enough (not enoguh). P. 84, 1st line, 3rd para: should read, Frank's father Gustav. P. 84, 3rd column, 4th para: Elmgreen (not Elmgren). P. 98, last line of 6th para: should read "it's" (not is). P. 167, middle of 1st para: "later she was an instructor in the" should not be repeated. P. 172, 1st para: should read portable building (not portable time building). P. 175, 2nd col., 4th para: should read Chivington's army (not arm). P. 216, end of 2nd para: Scheduled (not scehduled). P. 224, 1st para: Denver (not Denvar). P. 243, middle column, 5th entry: Fahnestock (not Fahenstock).